The Political Role of the Military

THE POLITICAL ROLE OF THE MILITARY

An International Handbook

Edited by
**Constantine P. Danopoulos
and Cynthia Watson**

Greenwood Press
Westport, Connecticut • London

Library of Congress Cataloging-in-Publication Data

The political role of the military : an international handbook /
  edited by Constantine P. Danopoulos and Cynthia Watson.
     p. cm.
  Includes bibliographical references and index.
  ISBN 0–313–28837–2 (alk. paper)
   1. Civil-military relations—Handbooks, manuals, etc.
  2. Comparative government—Handbooks, manuals, etc. I. Danopoulos,
  Constantine P. (Constantine Panos) II. Watson, Cynthia Ann.
  JF195.C5P67   1996
  322'.5'09045—dc20   95–46134

British Library Cataloguing in Publication Data is available.

Library of Congress Catalog Card Number: 95–46134
ISBN: 0–313–28837–2

First published in 1996

Greenwood Press, 88 Post Road West, Westport, CT 06881
An imprint of Greenwood Publishing Group, Inc.

Printed in the United States of America

The paper used in this book complies with the
Permanent Paper Standard issued by the National
Information Standards Organization (Z39.48-1984).

10 9 8 7 6 5 4 3 2 1

To Sam Sarkesian and Tim and Nitsa Mellos,
and to the memory of Thanasi Paraskevopolous (1922–1996)

CONTENTS

PREFACE

This volume has offered more challenges to the editors than the usual manuscript. Not only was it a task to bring more than two dozen chapters together from authors spread across the country, but it was also a challenge to ask authors from the wide-ranging world to produce a cohesive and interesting book. We have seen how dramatically the world can change in the post–Cold War era; we saw changes in the Peruvian and Mexican militaries after the book was begun, as well as the perpetual reevaluation of the Russian military. Time does not stand still for anyone.

Although we recognize that each and every detail cannot remain current in any published volume, we believe that we have captured a range of militaries around the world, illustrating their varying political roles. Though never intended to be comprehensive, for a variety of reasons, this volume is, however, intended to create a body of literature that shows how complicated military-civilian "relationships" are around the world. We are pleased with the range of our information and the light it sheds on the military in societies that too often have been seen as monolithic (Western European or former Soviet-bloc armed forces, for example).

We hope that we have already conveyed our thanks to most of the many people whom we want to acknowledge. We will cite here, however, a few for their patience, persistence, and humor through it all. Mildred Vasan, at Greenwood Publishing, was a patient but guiding voice through a long evolution. Dan Zirker has been particularly helpful in suggesting contributors and being generally supportive. Sam Sarkesian, in some ways "dean" of this field in political science in the United States, was also most helpful. Support from the National War College was important.

Finally, we want to thank our families and spouses for their support. Without them—and a phone/fax line with which to communicate—we would not have survived, or still be speaking with one another.

Cynthia Watson
Constantine Danopoulos

INTRODUCTION

Cynthia Watson and Constantine Danopoulos

Standing armies are one of the most visible and powerful forms of social organization associated in the West with the evolution and consolidation of the modern nation-state. In eastern-bloc countries, the armed forces helped to keep Communist parties in power and played a role in the downfall of Marxist-Leninist regimes and the democratization of these societies. In the 1960s, 1970s, and 1980s, the armed forces intervened, directly or indirectly, in the political affairs of many developing or changing communities of the Third World; this was followed by a wave of withdrawal and disengagement from the levers of political power.

The end of the Cold War has often been described in terms of its effects on nation-states or on governments within nation-states. Far too little emphasis has been placed on the impact that this sea change in world affairs has had on militaries around the world. Although many armed forces see their roles as precisely the same today as in 1975 or 1980, for a significant number of militaries the change has been as fundamental as for the world at large. Indeed, military changes have led to dramatic modifications in society at large. Similarly, societal transformations have resulted in a reconsideration of the armed services as members of societies across the world.

Yet this commonsense perception of the changing world since 1989 ignores the important role of the military in society regardless of the Cold War. For many societies, the Cold War enhanced the role of the military, but did not create a radically different one. In a number of countries, the military has historically been a path for advancement into different social strata. In others, the military has channelled men who were not going to become landholders into a more productive enterprise. In still others, the military has been a key political and social player as a corporation, acting as a single body with a collective interest. In sum, armed forces across the world have played various roles in societies, fulfilling multifaceted interpretations of "defense" requirements.

The role of the military in the Third World has received considerable scholarly attention. Experts on different areas have sought to understand and analyze the causes of praetorianism, to evaluate the performance of soldiers as political governors, and, more recently, to comprehend the reasons that have prompted the military to return to the barracks and to allow civilian rule. Some scholarly attention has also been devoted to understanding the role of the military and the party-military relationship in Marxist-Leninist states. The role of the armed forces in the West has received only sporadic attention. Yet, there are strong indications that the armed forces of western, developing, and totalitarian countries alike are powerful social and political organizations willing and able to play key political roles in the domestic politics of all societies. In spite of this, little in the literature of civilian-military relations examines the political role of the military in various countries from a comparative perspective.

PURPOSE

We define a political role to mean substantial and purposeful involvement in the making and allocating of wealth and of social and political values. On the basis of this definition, each chapter traces the historical background of civil-military relations in the country, identifies and analyzes the processes used by the armed services to exert political influence, evaluates the success and results of the political role of the military, and projects future developments.

The purpose of this volume is to look at the varying positions that militaries hold around the world as the twentieth century draws to a close. As with any dynamic, organic body, the armed services in various countries change quickly and sometimes unpredictably. Although we have been striving to keep the volume current, the pace of political, social, and defense developments will always outpace publishing deadlines.

The purpose of the handbook, however, goes beyond merely reporting on whether a particular military is in the barracks at any certain date. Instead, we are offering analyses of the roles that militaries have played in their societies, the historical forces that have shaped those roles, the socioeconomic constraints upon them in the past and present and as far as we can see into the future, and the "current" positions that armed forces occupy in the last decade of the century.

THE CHANGING SOCIETAL CONTEXTS

Although civilian governments are the goal of many states in the 1990s, military regimes seem unlikely to disappear from the political scene. In many states, the military has a significant interest in the economy, for example, in maintaining control over segments of the production and sales of arms. The armed forces in Brazil and Argentina have historically played a role in weapons production and spin-off activities for civilian purposes. In the United States,

arms industries have close links to the various services, facilitated by the re-
volving door between serving and retired officers.

In states where regimes pursued Marxist policies, such as the former Soviet
Union, Eastern Europe, the People's Republic of China, and Cuba, the issues
facing civilians and military alike are a far cry from the relatively easily articulated ideology of the Marxist period. In Marxist states, the military was an
instrument of the people, forwarding their goals of promoting revolutions abroad
and keeping down suspect intransigent bourgeois elements at home. That the
military had to be called out in the Eastern Europe of the 1950s and 1960s to
protect the "revolution" was a measure of the lack of political legitimacy of
the regimes involved. The armed forces were the proletariat's weapon to continue the revolution, as crucial to the system as the apparatchik or ideologue.

Since the Berlin Wall came down in November 1989, the military has become
a separate actor with considerable freedom to affect the nature of the postcommunist system. The Russian military continues to waver between serving as a
potent political actor and acting as a disengaged, disorganized observer. The
armed forces in Poland have remained passive, as the political system has
evolved into a far more decentralized, volatile setup.

The armed services in the remaining declared-Marxist states—Cuba, the People's Republic of China, and North Korea—are still working through many of
the issues that Russia has already tackled. In these states, the militaries have
been dominant economic players, as in some non-Marxist regimes, and it remains a question how these transformations will affect both the armed services
and the economies. In none of these cases is the future outcome of political
change obvious. The militaries must consider generational shifts, political roles,
and many other variables.

Armed services around the world have been involved in government and
politics in ways besides the economic. In a number of states, the military has
its own political party or is the power behind a particular party. Some of the
militaries of the world have always held themselves to be above politics, as a
professional standard; but a great number have seen their role as the protection
of society from various threats—all too often threats signified to them by politicians. In Latin America, for example, the military has defined its mission as
one of protecting the *patriae*. Encompassing a broader idea than the northern
European "patriotism," the *patriae* is the fundamental living being of the nation. The need to defend it against all threats, foreign and national, economic,
political, and social, is instilled in the soul of Latin American officers. Altering
that basic mission to allow civilians to govern who may have advocated policies
and positions the military feels have threatened the *patriae* is a transformation
difficult for many proud professional soldiers, sailors, and airmen to accept. The
necessary social metamorphosis is going to be a long one in some of these
societies, despite the superficial appearance of elections. The Argentine and Brazilian chapters point to the pitfalls that the component parts of society, military
as well as civilian, face as they try to build a new civic contract.

The position of the military in societies where they have recently been apolitical may be a fascinating study as the devolution of the world political system continues. The armed forces in northern European states such as Britain, Denmark, and the Netherlands appear likely to continue their positions as defenders of national security. In eras of decreasing budgets and diminishing traditional threats, however, these militaries may undergo turbulence as they seek to clarify their national missions. The militaries are relevant protagonists in the political debate about the expansion of NATO, international exchanges with former Warsaw Pact enemies, and other broad questions. The connections between the European states, through various political and economic organizations such as the Western European Union, NATO, the European Union, and the United Nations, still need sorting out as the complex relationships of nation-states around the world evolve. A key underlying question is the role that the United States will choose to take in the post–Cold War era.

Similarly, Japan struggles with the major question of its military. Japanese society, while ambivalent about certain aspects of the debate, continues to oppose nuclear weapons for defense. In addition, Japanese society has no clear answers about the character of defense spending. The United States faces tensions over trade policies and about footing the bill for Japan's defense at a cost to U.S. needs. Should isolationist factions succeed in diminishing the U.S. commitment to the area, Japan would need to confront its options more directly. The role of Japanese military forces in this political question could be problematic.

Societies with a powerful religious faction face an interesting evolution if the rise of a militant religious movement challenges the propensity toward modernization that characterizes most militaries. In Indonesia, which houses the world's largest Islamic population, religion does not appear to play a significant role in the society or in the armed forces. In an era of increased tension, as the prospect of a political succession struggle looms, one faction or another could trot out the religious militancy card. While Indonesia would appear more likely to focus on the succession itself, it offers an interesting case that includes a growing economy, a heavily vested military, and various religious and ethnic differences that could escalate into tensions. In Iran, the role of the Islamic state in promoting its revolution affects the military and its relationship to the rest of society in an unpredictable manner. In Nigeria, where religions cut across society, the military retains its insistence on controlling the political process; yet there are few indicators that it will in the end produce a more equitable society, as the religious and ethnic minorities demand.

Perhaps the most fundamental evolution faced by any military is that of the Republic of South Africa. While other states have been wrestling with threats anticipated or expected according to beliefs, the South African regime that surrendered power in 1994 had determined its enemies by an immutable fact: skin color. Retraining that military to consider everyone a member of society regardless of skin color is a most difficult challenge, particularly when the economic, social, and political stakes are so high. Other African states, such as Nigeria, face comparable socioeconomic distribution questions, but the reversal of apartheid based on race is a reorientation of truly epic proportions.

THE HANDBOOK: ORGANIZATION AND VARIABLES

This handbook was designed to identify and explain the factors responsible for the political role of military organizations in different societies. The political role here means the substantial and purposeful involvement of the armed forces in the making and allocation of wealth and of social and political values, including national security. The relevant variables involve class, the size of the military organizations, recruitment patterns, the social background of the officer corps, professionalism, and geopolitical factors. In addition, economic factors such as trade, budgetary concerns, dependency, and the level of economic development are issues for consideration. Each contributor has chosen the relevant weighing of variables for the particular national context.

Not every country's military is examined. Instead, larger, more representative states have been selected to describe the regions of the world—Africa, Europe, Asia, the Middle East, and Latin America. The volume contains cases that are interesting in and of themselves as well as in their regional context.

Militaries can be studied from a variety of approaches. This volume offers twenty-five studies of the political role of the military in society. The armed forces of any particular state can be examined in depth, and one can look at the militaries from a regional perspective. One may see the armed services of the nations in a region as a body within that region. Unfortunately, that typology assumes that all states in a region have a common experience. Additionally, it assumes that the armed forces have engaged in similar behaviors across the region and that all factors are relatively equal for the region.

A difficult way to consider militaries is to compare them across the types of political systems in which they operate. Will a state that has had an authoritarian system with a single strong political party, as in Mexico, produce a different role for the armed services than a state with a multiparty system, as in Argentina? One might learn more by comparing the Mexican case with a comparable political system such as South Korea, rather than with another Latin American state. The reader will find among these country studies a variety of comparative analyses and different perspectives on armed forces around the world.

The Political Role of the Military

ARGENTINA

Rut Clara Diamint and Cynthia Watson

The armed forces in Argentina have had a significant role in the political system for much of the twentieth century. Between 1930 and 1989, no elected government completed its term without some sort of intervention, many of these incidents caused by the armed forces seizing power to protect Argentina from enemies. Civilian control over the military was, for much of this time, problematic because of weakness on the part of civilians and distrust by military that the needs of the country were being met.

The last prolonged period of military governance was between 1976 and 1983. During that time, Argentina suffered through a *guerra sucia* (dirty war), a traumatic military defeat in the South Atlantic, and a period of economic crisis caused by mismanagement and massive external debt. When civilians assumed office on 10 December 1983, the Argentine armed forces were humbled but angered that their role in saving the nation had been misunderstood by the people they sought to protect. Within a decade, however, the military had taken what appears to be a position which will make it permanently subservient to civilian control. Rather than looking at national security as solely based on the need to protect the *patria*, it has become one of the most frequently used armed forces for international peacekeeping operations. It is one of the most dramatic transformations of a civil-military relationship anywhere in the world.

This chapter will examine the position that the Argentine military has occupied in society since 1930 and explore the changes that have transformed it from a force to intervene frequently into one which has an increasingly external outlook for national security.

ROLE OF THE ARMED FORCES WITHIN ITS SOCIETY: THE MILITARY'S PERSPECTIVE

One of the fundamental issues which must be understood about the armed forces in Argentina is the perception that they have about their role in society.

The Spanish term *patria* is more than the view of protecting the country because the view of the nation or the country is a more encompassing one than true in the United States or Anglo-European context. *Patria* is the blood, the soil, the value, the history, and the all integrating view of the subject to be protected. The Argentine military, as true with most armed forces in the Latin American region, believes that it alone understands the nature of threats against the nation and it has often been the only reliable institution in society to protect Argentina from various threats to its survival.

A brief historical reminder here will give some indication of the nature of the Argentine system. Argentina achieved independence in the early nineteenth century as Spaniards born in the colonies, known as *criollos,* threw off peninsular controls during the Napoleanic Wars.[1] The Spanish had occupied Argentina by coming from the northwest into the rest of the country. Buenos Aires soon became the primary city for the country but vast areas of Argentina were empty of Europeans in the middle of the nineteenth century, inhabited only by native Americans who were not integrated into the Argentine state. From the middle of the 1800s until the World War I, Argentina opened its door to millions of European immigrants *after* the army had cleared out the non-European population from the interior. While many of the immigrants eventually populated Buenos Aires, the point for the army was that it had secured Argentina for its destiny. The ruling class in the Republic was almost entirely Spanish (*criollos,* a few generations removed), Catholic, land-owning, and conservative in nature.

By the second decade of the twentieth century, the heirs of independent Argentina were forced to open the political process to growing numbers of immigrants, illustrated by the Saenz Pena Law of 1912 which opened the political system to universal male suffrage and the military was given a statutory role in cases of electoral mischief.[2] This meant that politics were no longer the purview of upper class but, instead, a much more open, diverse, and torn system. With the military composed of many leaders who came from the decreasingly powerful upper class, the changes that the new political dynamic brought were bound to raise eyebrows. The result of the changes that occurred during this period was that the homogeneity of Argentina's political system prior to 1912 was significantly diminished by many people with different economic goals (often a European socialist vision), different religions (particularly Jewish and Islamic), and a different history for Argentina was on the horizon.

The major political force which initially challenged the status quo was the Unión Cívica Radical (UCR), or the Radicals. Long-term UCR leader Hipólito Yrigoyen, who had been president in the early 1920s, was reelected President of the Nation in 1928 but the military engaged in its first presidential ouster in September 1930. At that time, reports indicated that Yrigoyen was too senile to govern during a period when Argentina was suffering the initial pain of the global Great Depression. The military moved to calm the situation when Yrigoyen was unable to tame factions in his cabinet in dealing with the economic

and social crisis developing. "After 1930 the country was increasingly compelled to search for substitutes" for the way it had been progressing.[3]

In the first decade of its independence, Argentina evolved tremendously from
a small, Spanish, Catholic society based on agricultural exports into a much
more heavily populated state with religious, ethnic, and value heterogeneity with
a burgeoning middle class and a dominant city that only seemed destined to
grow larger. The political process had been opened and the society was wrestling
with how to change to take advantage of the new international context which
was not one centered around traditional economic ally Britain but one of much
uncertainty. By going to the military as an option to the civilian leadership,
Argentina was setting a precedent it was to repeat several times over the following six decades.

THE PERONIST PERIOD

Argentina faced the Great Depression as a state needing to redefine its relationship with the international community because the north star for Argentina,
Great Britain, was going into what became a permanent decline as a political
and economic actor. Some of those who instigated the coup in September 1930
were nationalists, a coalition of economic interests from the export sector as
well as many in the armed forces, believed that Argentina was being short-
changed by sectors of society putting outside interests above some assuredly
well understood "national" interests for the country. Most frequently cited examples of groups who would injure the nation included Liberals, Communists,
and non-Catholics; this doctrine embraced the idea of a superiority based on
hispanidad (roughly, being Hispanic). The nationalism of the 1930s penetrated
society through several propaganda instruments, seeking to remind Argentines
of the need to support the values of patriotism, faith, family, blood, tradition,
and race. The Great Depression was the manifestation of this externally created
control over national sovereignty. The other major faction that cooperated in
ousting Yrigoyen were the conservatives who wanted to return to an Argentina
that was no longer attacking the landed oligarchy. The military, most particularly
the army, was an assembly where these nationalist and conservative factions of
society came together because of concern about the "unnatural" attacks on the
nation.

Argentina was in the midst of trying to create a new working relationship
between upper, middle, and lower class interests while protecting the nation
against threats internal and external. The landowning oligarchy in Argentina,
working in coalition with the nationalists, sought to protect its role in society
in the face of increasing numbers and political power from the middle and lower
classes. The middle class was working to create a more equitable distribution
of economic and political power which would further the effects of the political
reforms of the 1910s. The military took control over the government in the
1930s as a partial attempt to return to a nation with the land-owning oligarchy

at the top of the political system and other groups left to remain inconsequential actors. Much of the decade of the 1930s was spent on trying to come to grips with the economic dislocation caused by the Great Depression but not seeing any amelioration of Argentine standards of living or clear growth to create a more viable Argentina which was charting its own course rather than relying on the guidance (or interference) of other states. The legacy of the 1930s was that the military coups indicated that armed men would disobey the Constitution and civilian government with the understanding that "the government itself becomes a faction rebelling against the *patria*."[4] Democracy was sacrificed for the protection of the *patria*: the sectors of the society which had the ability threw aside political participation to protect their particular vision of the nation.

By the 1940s, Juan Domingo Perón sought to take control over Argentina by putting political classes into a corporatist model. Corporatism is a vision which organizes a society around group relationships which serve as the links both horizontally and vertically. Rather than the government responding to individual needs, a corporatist system constructs groups with which the government can interact for greater efficiency and control. The colonial experience in Latin America had been somewhat corporatist, with the roles for the Church, the political establishment, traders, and the military, during the colonial period so this was not an entirely new vision for any state in the region. In the 1930s, however, corporatism was taking on a prominence in Mussolini's Fascist and Hitler's Nazi states. The armed forces took a noteworthy position with the objective of defending the national spirit, the *patria,* itself. The military wanted to claim that *patria* belonged to a particular group and that corporation, the armed forces, saw defending the *patria* as more important than any other function that any group had in society.

Defending the *patria* became more urgent after the historic events in Europe, where the conflict was between the freedom of historic national traditions and the international threat of communism. Believing that a crisis was at hand, the GOU, a clique of younger officers seeking to prevent the expansion of communism and threats to Argentine economic sovereignty, decided on a strategy beginning with the army, intending "to extend our doctrine until we succeed in permeating it throughout the army,"[5] to create a political perspective that was nationalist, industrialist, and neutral in the context of World War II. A prominent member of this officer corps was Perón.

Perón was a mid-level officer who was a power behind the throne in the military governments of the early 1940s, each seeking to set Argentina on a more independent ("sovereign") course in its development, access to resources, and foreign trade. The military in this period continued to oppose liberalism, seeing it as linked to British interests. Perón led the 1943 revolt in Argentina which promoted self-sufficiency, known as *Justicialismo,* that would no longer put Argentina in the hands of groups seeking to undermine it. This view was a variation on the "Third World" orientation advocated by Nehru's India, Nasser's Egypt, and Sukarno's Indonesia in the late 1940s and 1950s. Perón, through the 1940s, appeared populist and industrial nationalist, meaning that he was putting Argentine workers into the dominant position in society and seeking to improve their lot in life. This was an evolution in society which further organized society into blocks for a corporatist model, leading to a reliance on more recent, poorer workers than many in the military were comfortable with. While the Catholic church initially distanced itself from *Justicialismo,* Perón was eventually able to pull Catholic nationalism into the movement. In sum, the Peronist movement took on a mass movement in Argentine society but one which put pressure on the military to take sides between the traditional, conservative oligarchy and the growing power of the organized labor unions and new social groups.

Perón adapted military concepts to his political movement: verticalism, organization, separation of branches, and command authority. This model was eventually extended throughout the state and society. The monopoly on mass media, through the controlled conglomerate of radio and almost all written press, allowed the silencing of opposition voices and maintained a permanent propaganda offensive. This hammering propaganda succeeded in confusing national interest with that of the *justicialista* movement. The society was divided between those *peronistas* who were captivated by a regime that cultivated the favors and prerogatives of its followers and the anti-*peronistas,* who shared only their rivalry with the powerful and authoritarian Perón.

The chosen economic model was conducive to the strengthening of the state, which led to control of the union as well as the oligarchy. The new element in this policy was that unions were granted rights they had never had while the oligarchy saw its power reduced. As Alain Rouquié indicates, this policy was the crystallization of a new set of power relations.[6] The economic policy was based on national independence and industrial development, and its goal was to become self-sufficient. This was also related to the satisfaction of defense needs. A structure of military industry was organized to include a wide range of activities, including metallurgy, chemistry, and construction. However, the same state protectionism was the cause of its failure when several groups whose interests were affected withdrew their support.

By 1953, there was an attempt to change the economic model through attracting foreign capital and also by approaching the United States for the acquisition of military equipment. This demonstrates the predominance of the economic rather than the ideological project in the government's selection of allies. The desire to achieve self-sufficiency in all affairs was less enduring than the desire for economic growth through outside assistance.

While concentrating power, the government was distancing itself from its initial partners. It directly confronted the Catholic church, an institution around which all of the opponents of the government gathered. The offensive against the Church was epitomized in the 1954 law which granted divorce.[7] When the church had to face government attacks or the *Peronistas'* public demonstrations, two contingents were formed: the pro- and anti-*Peronistas*. Within the second group, a new coup d'etat was planned.

Days after the revolution in September 1955, during which a new military government replaced a free elected regime, General Benjamín Rattenbach (ret.) explained what happens to the armed forces when a revolt in which they participate takes place. He noted that

No state institution suffers an internal commotion more deep than the one suffered by the armed forces. This is primarily due to the extreme imbalance produced between doctrine and reality, theory and practice. Contrary to what happens in other institutions and in the population, there is no place other than the armed forces where there is a more constant preaching against military participation in politics, and against all subversive movements. And now, all that preaching falls down, to be replaced by disarray, confusion, and perplexity.[8]

The new government under General Eduardo Lonardi attempted to establish a government under the slogan "God Is Fair" but confronting the deep divisions in society which nine years of *peronization* had created. It became obvious that the army had too many wounds itself and the "fair" government policy of political equilibrium did not satisfy nationalists. Soon factionalism within the groups which had united to defeat Perón became evident and Lonardi was ousted in the name of "the maintenance of democracy."

New president General Pedro Aramburu proposed to come back to morals, justice, and liberty as a way to eliminate remnants of *peronismo* which had been identified as against the *patria* and, by extension, became the fundamental schism between the military and those segments of society it saw as antithetical to the needs of the nation. This meant banning the *Justicialista* party and the power of the *Confederación General de Trabajadores* (CGT, the General Confederation of Workers) while creating new authorities, messages, and texts. Additionally, military links to the United States were renewed with expectations that the fight against communism pervading U.S. security doctrine at the time could be applied to eradicating *peronismo* at home since both movements were seen as subversive. In the economy, Argentina was reopened to international markets, incorporated into the Bretton Woods economic system, and generally renouncing the self-sufficiency of Perón.

DEVELOPMENT OF THE NATIONAL SECURITY REGIME

The military promised to "clean" society before returning it to democracy but both the military and the society at large were split on *peronismo*. In the 1958 election, the winner was Dr. Arturo Frondizi, who had Peronist support. Frondizi campaigned that the country's industrialization would resolve all economic problems and would produce the social harmony that the nationalists had failed to achieve. In sum, development and social peace would repair society's fissures. The military still believed, however, it had the right to control the president's action, as did the progressive industrialists who supported him. All actions favoring an internal recomposition and stability and providing benefits to the more unprotected sectors had repercussions.

The nationalist model, the love for *argentinidad* (roughly, being Argentine), promoted by both nationalists and the military, represented different things depending on who claimed it. An overwhelming understanding of *argentinidad* was absent. Concern mounted that some clearly articulated and accepted view of being Argentine in some mystical way would be an answer to growing fears that communism, once an ideological fear in the 1920s, would spread from Cuba south to Argentina. Consequently, there was objective support to promote the primary need of *argentinizar* (roughly, "to Argentinize"); after 1960, this concept became synonymous with anti-communist campaigns. Anything not Argentine was subversive. This formed the basis for the national security doctrine, which motivated the training and action of the armed forces from the 1960s until the 1980s.

The army began considering counterinsurgency as a priority, relying heavily on learning from the French experience in Algeria and southeast Asia.[9] Counterinsurgency training was extended to include the formulation of a doctrine supporting the new action, by using elements of French psychological warfare doctrine.

The armed forces' position as society arbitrator was tested in the environment created between the communist danger and Frondizi's benevolence towards *peronistas.* A series of military demands and uprisings led to Frondizi being forced to resign under fanciful accusations of his being head of a procommunist dictatorship in 1962. Senator Dr. José María Guido, a puppet of the military, assumed the presidency.

The next elections occurred in the middle of a deep societal confrontation. The winner, Dr. Arturo Illia, was a simple and honest man who only proposed peace and tranquillity but was inefficient.[10] Illia warned the military about the consequences of frequent coups:

What violence are you talking about? The only violence in the Republic is the one you occasioned. You provoke violence. Throughout the country, I have preached peace and concordance among the Argentines, I have protected freedom, and you did not want to become the echo of my preaching. You did not have anything to do with the Army of General San Martín and General Belgrano. You have caused many calamities to the *patria,* and you will keep doing so. The country will incriminate you because of this usurpation, and I doubt your own consciences will be able to explain what you have done.[11]

The military again seized the opportunity to build a new society, the definitive modernization, the true Argentina.

In 1966 the Argentina military sought to "repair" the country by achieving perfect order, inspired by the "Directivas para el planeamiento y desarrollo de la acción de gobierno" (Directives for the planning and development of the government's action), strictly delimiting three time periods. The first was the economic period, and it stated that Argentina had achieved industrialization without modernization. Therefore, it was necessary to favor the concentration of capital, even though this orthodox liberalism occasionally went against the limits that the military nationalism designed for the military industrial complex. The second was the social period, during which a redistribution of benefits obtained through correct management of the economy was to occur. The third was the political epoch, once the destroyed political parties and unions learned the new rules. Failure could not be avoided even through the change of military leadership on two occasions by Generals Roberto Levingston and Alejandro Lanusse.

History repeated itself once again. In 1973, a civilian government was elected by more than half the electorate. The nation went back to its constitution and to its history: "The *patria* has acquired a solemn compromise with our heroes and with our martyrs. Nothing and nobody will separate us from the path that they drew with Spartan stoicism."[12]

The same sentiment was found in the army, now supposedly committed to civil society. Army chief General Jorge Raúl Calcagno, and leader of a democratic army close to the position of the *peronista* left, stated in 1973, "In this way, we will be dignified by those who preceded us after May 29, 1810. We will have interpreted with clarity our heroes' legacy. A legacy of virtues, in which nobility, courage, respect for the human being, and personal detachment, are foremost incarnated in General San Martín, who we invoke for his example to guide us."[13]

This new approach was countered, however, with the militarism of another sector: the guerrilla, particularly the armed Peronist youth known as *Montoneros*. Military language took a more hostile tone to the provocations: *Peronistas'* houses were *Montoneros* forts or the idea of "Perón or death, *Viva la Patria.*"[14] The *Montoneros* responded with similarly militarist content in statements such as this by leader Mario Firmenich:

"The guerrilla is only one way to developed armed confrontation; it is without a doubt the highest level of political confrontation. . . . We define ourselves by this way of fighting, as politico-military organizations. Our fundamental goal always was, and still is, a political one. . . . In the current circumstances in which we are moving from 'Perón is back' to 'Perón to power', we find a change of phase that forces a change of methods."

"This means you are abandoning arms?", asked a journalist.

"No way: the political power emerges from the barrel of a rifle."[15]

As the nationalist right had always done, now the militarized left was using history to explain a path that was conducive to them. The argument was the same, but the holders of that heritage had changed.

The military staged another coup in March 1976, with more violence and extermination. As ideas could not be eliminated, the military annihilated men. Paradoxically, the discourse of nationality appeared, with references to General San Martín, while at the same time, the country was being devastated, economically as well as in lives. The military dictatorship called itself "Proceso de Reorganización Nacional" (Process of National Reorganization) and ostensibly sought to restore order. Later, it bypassed government after failing at the political, military, and economic levels. This coup attempted to redefine the economic bases of Argentina, obliterating the import substitution, self-sufficiency model. It was replaced by a political-economic system based on long-term military control and the welcoming of foreign capital for technology and economic growth. The military sought to "cleanse" society of subversives and to transform society by the military maintaining control over all resources of power. Any use of violence would be by the armed forces rather than by those opposing the *Proceso.* The monopoly of violence on the part of the military during the 1976–1983 period led to the disappearance (and presumed death) of at least 9,000 Argentines who were, for various reasons, considered subversive threats to the *patria.* The military clung to the belief, however, that it was the only actor in society which had the moral, political, and ideological integrity to save the *patria* from the threats that had put it under siege.

The principal political mistake of the *Proceso* was to get involved in a short, disastrous war with Great Britain, demonstrating erroneous military grasp of the external and domestic political contexts. The 1982 conflict also indicated the absence of mediating institutions that could articulate the different interests and priorities found among societal groups and sectors.[16] The rigidity and impertinence of the Argentine military increased the weight of their defeat.

The errors made by the administration, the moral rupture, the external debt that increased from seven billion dollars in 1976 to forty-four billion dollars in 1984, the human rights violations, and the lack of legitimacy made too heavy a load for society not to question it, particularly after the defeat in the South Atlantic War. The only positive consequence of that sad adventure was the fall of the military regime and the end of the *Proceso Nacional.*

The armed forces that emerged after the *Proceso* were affected by corruption, bureaucratization, inefficiency, lack of discipline, illegality in the high ranks, and rejection by the population.[17] The armed forces had one year to organize their retreat but did not see themselves as destroyed.[18] Because of this, the armed forces made corporative demands during the government of *radicalismo* (1983–89). After seven years of military rule, multiple patterns had been weakened from those of political parties, student and professional organizations to everyday practices.[19] The new government had a devastated country to administer, economically, politically, and socially.

1983 TRANSITION

The government of Dr. Raúl Alfonsín did not know how to handle the military problem. Civil society had neither the strength nor the resources necessary to reconsider the military issue because the military believed it had acted properly in intervening to reorganize society while civilians frequently disagreed. Alfonsín was unable to resolve the conflict with the armed forces or establish a defense policy with approval from both the services and civilians. Alfonsín initiated his mandate with two decrees while nullifying the amnesty the military granted itself in September 1983.[20]

The new design for the armed forces included strengthening the Ministry of Defense with the Minister managing military directives as well as controlling the budget, salaries, and defense production. In an attempt to create a new legitimacy for the armed services, military reform was proposed to ''procure a new moral tone within the framework of absolute respect for the institutional order.''[21] Unfortunately, this military reform required a clarity of purpose in society that did not exist. Because the new president had to spend so much time and political capital on economic and debt reduction schemes, Alfonsín did not manage to satisfy either the civilians seeking to curtail radically military prerogatives or the armed forces still seeking a preferential position in the distribution of national assets. The reform proposals collided with economic difficulties, the lack of human resources to confront changes, inefficiency and lack of experience in privatizing the economy, and, mostly, demands from the armed forces.

The military did not accept the legitimacy of civilian power, particularly after many years of taking decisions without consulting with others. Since 1943, the Argentine military had been both partners with economic groups (hence seeing their role as a legitimate actor in politics) and arbitrators in society to defend the *patria*. The armed forces were also a powerful educational mechanism structured by the dominant classes in the 1920s to make up for power lost in the electoral reforms, such as Saeñz Peña, and the legalization of a preferential position for the military in society. To subordinate the armed forces as a military arm of the political power was a difficult task that required the creation of a political system dominated by civilians and based upon trust in democratic mechanisms as a way to resolve confrontations.

Presidential decree # 187/83 created CONADEP, an investigative commission on people who disappeared during the Process. Its members were distinguished personalities of different political affiliations, because the issue of human rights was beyond the government realm, moving into the civil society and international community. Alfonsín intended CONADEP to prevent anything that could be construed as political and could detract from the goal of reconstructing society. The armed forces responded that they were being attacked by the government, which they saw as the enemy, harshly criticizing the civilian government. The dangers of an unplanned transition, as Henri J. Barkey explains, is that the diminished prestige of the military institution could weaken its ability to undertake its primary mission. They did not accept changes within the institution, and they reinforced their esprit de corps.[22]

The military's feeling of being under attack grew worse with the beginning of trials against the former uniformed leadership of the *Proceso* in April 1985. Tensions between civilians and the military deepened and the Alfonsín government tried to dilute a separate judicial process for the military. The latter demonstrated the government was acting unilaterally, upsetting even civilian political opposition. For the armed forces, however, the effect was clear: it was no benefit from constitutional democracy. The armed services did not believe they could have a professional role in society if not engaged in various political activities.

Not surprisingly, military crises characterized the democratic transition under Alfonsín. A group of officers led by Lieutenant Colonel Aldo Rico initiated the first uprising during *Semana Santa* (Easter) of 1987. This revolt was part of a bigger movement, the "dignity operation," which was intended to recover honor and establish discipline. These officers considered themselves heroes of the Malvinas war and martyrs in the fight against subversion. They functioned against the civilian, democratic system, with a clear nationalist tendency.

In April 1988 Defense Law was sanctioned, defining the armed forces in external defense while limiting their participation in domestic affairs.

As a paradox of the confrontation between the government and the armed forces, the development of strategic weapons began during this period. The Condor II project, developed with secret funds, German technology, and Arab financing, indicated that the uniformed services had specific goals. The navy had long had control over the nuclear program. Now, the air force became privileged for economic reasons (development of the "Pampa" plane was expected to lead to profits from exports) but also because the government sought an alliance with some sector of the armed forces. The air force was the branch least sullied by the *guerra sucia* and the most successful during the Malvinas. Therefore, it could separate itself from the negative acts of the other services and use the opportunity to transcend its third ranking within the force.

The balance that Rouquié described in 1988 demonstrates another of the truths emerging from the transition:

I have the feeling, according to what you have lived during Easter, in Monte Caseros, etc., that, although there are some nostalgic remembrances of a strong power (and this is true for all societies, no matter how stable and democratic they are) the military does not attract important civilian sectors as happened before 1976. It is possible to observe a more conscious understanding of the need to defend institutions. From all political parties, from all sectors of society, from all ideologies, everybody realized that there are no good dictatorships. I believe that this is a cultural change.[23]

ARGENTINA'S MILITARY IN THE 1990s

The transition from authoritarianism to democracy did not contemplate a "pact" with the military. The transitions initiated in the 1980s showed the difficulty of demilitarizing society. Many misunderstandings occurred between the first democratic government and the armed forces, resulting in four military revolts. Consequently, a deeper and broader fragmentation between civilians and the military followed, with the same thing happening within the services themselves. When *peronista* Dr. Carlos Saúl Menem took office in July 1989, nothing foretold the changes in direction that would ensue.

A struggle took place between Menem's government and the military with Menem emerging victorious. When confronted with the narrow space for maneuver that the high concentration of capital and the internationalization of trade left the "national enterprises," the armed forces had to accept the risk of military reform.

Another element of change under Menem was redefinition of the government's strategic alliance. Two major characteristics of this process were the restoration of relations with Great Britain, followed by a series of confidence-building measures between both states, and abandonment of the Non-Aligned Movement, showing a more defined commitment toward western policies. As a result, Menem's administration favored nonproliferation policies supported by the United States, while introducing changes in security policy consistent with the new international context.[24]

Another element that contributed to the shaping of Argentina's external profile was the role of international organizations and security alliances, including Argentina's participation in the Gulf War with two ships and supporting army transportation operations. Additionally, Menem has made Argentina a key contributor to United Nations peacekeeping operations, such as Croatia, where the military has assumed high visibility. This series of actions has given the military a new raison d'être as a substitute for domestic governing. In a completely unexpected turn of events on the part of a president from the *peronista* movement, Menem attempted to send Argentine troops to assist U.N. forces in the restoration of Jean Bertrand Aristide to power in Haiti in October 1994 but was thwarted by the Congress in Buenos Aires.

These changes deeply redefined the main pillars of the traditional relations with the military. Political participation affected the professionalization of the army, which resulted in that service's loss of its capability to act autonomously, creating yet another bureaucratic institution. Consequently, internal fissures occurred, there was a breakdown in the chain of command, hierarchies became vulnerable, and the institution lost prestige. The confrontation with the government, together with the residual effects of poor administration of public resources, resulted in a significant budgetary and salary delay. Following this, officers and subordinates frequently "moonlighted" to supplement their incomes, the identity of the military deteriorated, and its specific role became diffuse. Other ingredients that added to the conflictive situation of the armed forces included the sentences against leaders of the *Proceso* as well as the various post-1983 uprisings, the loss of military control over various portions of the economy as a result of privatization, and a significant decrease in the armed forces' budget. The exercise of democratic control over the armed services stripped them of their arbiter's role in the Republic.

The last military insurrection occurred two days before President Bush visited Argentina late in 1990, and it embodied a benchmark in civilian and political control of the institution. For the first time, the rebellion was strongly resisted by the armed forces themselves; and the rebels found a firm determination on the part of the government not to negotiate with illegitimate groups and not to establish any type of pact that guaranteed the insurgents an escape. The army commander resigned as a result of disagreements with the minister of defense. The subsequent election of a new commander in chief was followed by the retirement of ten generals and many more colonels. This last transformation of the army, which earlier could have resulted in another military coup, went practically unnoticed.

Menem's government instituted a defense policy that limited the autonomy exerted by the armed forces in areas of national strategy. This allowed effective civilian control of the military structure. One could characterize this as a new process of strong civilian influence over the armed services and a new professionalization of the institution within the challenges of the post–Cold War era. No one predicts a new confrontation over constitutional powers.

Menem's military is a downside one but better trained and better paid. In 1994 Menem declared that the Argentine military would end conscription. The state could not financially support a military structure as it had been designed throughout the century. Cutting down state expenditures also required a cutback in military costs.

The then army commander, General Martín Balza, took on the task of restructuring the military, defining himself not as a liquidator of the army but rather as credible with defensive capabilities.[25] Additionally, the armed services were to prepare for participation in peacekeeping operations at the international level.[26] The need for participation in joint operations with other states, which was evidenced in the Malvinas, was confirmed after the Persian Gulf experience, in which Argentina played a small part. In Washington, D.C., Balza announced that the principal concerns of his armed forces were to be the defense of democracy, the fight against narcoterrorism, the disparities between the rich and the poor, systematic corruption, and the destruction of the environment and natural resources. Communism disappeared as a threat.[27] Furthermore, there was an emphasis on the priority of defensive doctrine in the Argentine military that, as with any other modern military force, is concerned with the international community's well-being.

THE FUTURE FOR THE ARGENTINE MILITARY

One issue present, current and future, in the hemispheric definition of security is the fight against drugs. Despite some bureaucratic resistance, drugs are now considered of central importance as a convergence point between the armed forces and the police forces. The role of internal versus external defense is regulated by the defense laws, which prohibit the armed forces from carrying out internal intelligence tasks that they performed during the *Proceso*. Only their logistic support and provision of "lateral information" are allowed, but they cannot be independently responsible for any mission. The differences among gendarmerie, aviation, and army, and between navy and coast guard are still topics for discussion in terms of allotment of funds, infrastructure modernization, and assistance from the United States.

Throughout the early 1990s, training programs and conferences with the support of the United States were developed, in which the idea of strategy stemming from the post–Cold War world was incorporated. Specialists of the U.S. armed forces discussed the new challenges on several occasions, such as things taught through the International Military Educational Training (IMET) program from the United States. Similarly, the organization of symposia on strategy have been held between the joint staffs of Brazil, Uruguay, Paraguay and Argentina. This gradual extension of exchange with the other states of the Mercosur economic market shows how that economic strategy is increasingly important in the Argentine view of national security. In the past, Argentina would have been hesitant to participate in such a symposium with these states. The inclusion of traditional enemy Chile is likely in the future.

All of these changes indicate that the era of military intervention in government has come to an end in Argentina. The success of military coups was explained by the intimate relationship between the interests of the big economic groups and their institutional loss of political control. The electoral victory of Carlos Menem in 1989 allowed for the power of big business and lessened the power of the church and the military to supplant the military as a key protector in the Republic. The close connection between the military and the church, which some believe has had sinister consequences in Argentina, may be accounted for by Perón's words, "Before the eyes of many appeared an identification between the Army, present wielder of power, and the Church, since both institutions firmly hold such values as order, discipline, verticality, and obedience."[28]

This connection reappeared and was expressed in the "carapintadas," a nationalist, Catholic, and anti-democratic group that forged fissures within the army: "We fight for the values of the old Army. We fight for honor, value, and loyalty."[29] It was also present in the opposition to Aldo Rico's discourse. General Caridi proposed to "revitalize the strength out of those principles originating from independence leader San Martín's military ethic: honor, loyalty, respect, austerity, spirit of sacrifice, modesty and love of service." He later added:

I remind my fellow citizens that it is their Army, everybody's Army, the same that fought in fields all throughout America to contribute to the freedom of their fellow peoples; the same one that gloriously fought in Chacabuco and Maipú, and managed to endure with firmness and spirit of sacrifice the hardships of Vilcapugio and Cancha Rayada; the same one that, with the rest of Argentine society, shared success and mistakes, triumph and defeat.[30]

This is the message that has always been underlying the control exerted by the armed forces and that, although it has not been made explicit, has been the basis for its power. There has been only one glorious army, that of the independence. On the basis of their former honors, the army survived all its defeats and errors. Now, it seems to be overwhelmed by that image of medieval heroism. The new international challenges can no longer be defined at the margins of the nation-state or by a national army centered in territorial sovereignty.

The armed forces felt that during their experience with political power they accumulated a loss of operational capability; they became bureaucratic state institutions, and internal breakdowns affected their hierarchies. The risk of loss of professionalization and the lack of institutional prestige that resulted from the *Proceso* are now associated with a different problem: the financial support of military organizations in societies that lack resources.

Democracy has been shown to have a powerful vitality when it comes to the mediation of political conflict. It could face the consequences of a military defeat in which young Argentines died. It was able to channel the role of the armed forces in society by assigning them a more appropriate position for a military institution of a non threatened country. It also accepted the need for a change in the relationship with the United States. The mediation that a democratic system can exert in societal conflicts is of extraordinary relevance. The armed forces also processed their defeat, but were less successful in attempting to define their role in the new order.

Future potential conflicts seem to be associated with economic situations: market competition, traffic control, border disputes, territorial usurpation, and exploitation of nonrenewable resources or resources renewable in exclusive areas. Moreover, it seems that the strength of the state in negotiating depends on other elements like natural resources and the size of the internal market, rather than on technological development. This brings along problems in the definition of a technical concept of defense when facing so many diverse and confusing threats.

Latin American societies organized themselves under the legitimacy conferred by a republican system, maintaining, despite their fragility, an autonomous division of powers. The same architecture supports space for political freedom, one that needs to be guaranteed. The preeminence of political institutions developing their functions with autonomy and responsibility, the existence of armed forces responsive as a whole to directives of the political system, the maintenance of an educational system that is among the best in Latin America, the continued support for technological development and research, and the reality of an open and pluralist debate strengthening democratic values could be the elements allowing the development of a society operating as a full member of the world community.

NOTES

The views in this chapter are those of the authors alone and do not represent the views of their governments or any agencies of their governments.

1. For histories of Argentina, there are many to consult. During this time period, see David Rock, *Argentina 1516–1987: From Spanish Colonization to Alfonsin* (Berkeley: University of California Press, 1987), or James R. Scobie, *Argentina: A City and a Nation,* 2nd ed. (Oxford: Oxford University Press, 1971).

2. See Rock, *Argentina,* pp. 189–90.

3. See Rock, *Argentina,* p. 213.

4. Cristian Buckrucker, *Nacionalismo y Peronismo* (Buenos Aires: Editorial Sudamericana, 1987), p. 125.

5. Robert Potash, "International regulations of the G.O.U.," in *Perón y el G.O.U.: Los documentos de una logia secreta* (Buenos Aires: Editorial Sudamericana, 1984), p. 78.

6. Alain Rouquié, *Poder Militar y Sociedad Política en la Argentina,* 2 vol. (Buenos Aires: Editores Emece, 1982).

7. This law was later dismissed in 1955, when *justicialismo* fell, and reinstated with difficulty only during the liberal government of Raúl Alfonsín (1983–1989). The 1954 law was followed by one that allowed the installation of brothels. On 20 March 1955, the government ordered a decrease in the number of national holidays. Several traditional religious holidays became workdays. In a society constitutionally Catholic, with the Church taking a considerable role in politics, the situation led to Perón's fall. On May 11, the Senate revoked religious education and canceled tax exemption for religious institutions and their dependencies. The last was a blow to church finances. To augment this legislation, the government approved a request for constitutional reform aimed at the separation of church and state. Unification of the two was supported economically and mandated in the 1953 constitution. Finally, more than fifty priests were incarcerated under the accusation of threatening the government, and two priests were expelled from the country.

8. Benjamín Rattenbach, "El Telon," *Revista Militar,* 633 (September–October 1955): 6.

9. "Between January 1958 and December 1962, of 60 articles published by the Escuela Superior de Guerra's magazine, 16 refer to the subversive war, and 7 of those were written by French authors. Be it translations from specialized French magazines or essays written purposely by French military advisors, the Indochina and Algeria experiences, and the techniques of psychological war, are found frequently in the table of contents of the *Revista Militar,* or in the more austere *Revista de la Escuela Superior de Guerra.*" (Rouquié, *Poder Militar,* vol. 2, p. 158).

10. Rouquié, *Poder Militar,* vol. 2, p. 230.

11. "Act of destitution of President Arturo Illia," in Marcelo Cavarrozi, *Autoritarismo y Democracia (1955–1983)* (Buenos Aires: CEAL, 1983), p. 107.

12. Héctor Campora before the Legislative Assembly on 25 May 1973. See Victoria

Itacovitz, *Estilos de Gobierno y Crisis Política (1973–76)* (Buenos Aires: CEAL, 1985), p. 116.

13. General Jorge Raúl Calcagno, "Discourse on occasion of the Day of the Army," 29 May 1973, presented in Itacovitz, *Estilos*, p. 124.

14. See *El Peronista,* year 1, vol. 3 (4 May 1974), pp. 29–30.

15. *El Descamisado,* vol. 17, (11 September 1973), p. 3.

16. Joseph Tulchin, *La Argentina y los Estados Unidos: Historia de una desconfianza* (Buenos Aires: Editorial Planeta, 1990), p. 270.

17. Augusto Varas, "La relaciones civico-militares en un marco democratico," in Louis W. Goodman, Johanna Mendelson, and Juan Rial, eds., *Los militares y la democracia* (Montevideo: PEITHO, 1990).

18. Atilio Boron put this idea forward in "Crisis militar y transicíon democrática en Argentina," *Cuadernos de Marcha,* vol. 19, (Montevideo), 1987.

19. Alain Rouquié, "La demilitarización y la institucionalización de los sistemas políticos dominados por los militares en América Latina," in Guillermo O'Donnell, Philippe Schmitter, and Lawrence Whitehead, eds., *Transiciones desde un gobierno autoritario* (Buenos Aires: Paidos, 1988).

20. Alfonsín signed decree #157 on 12 December 1983, which ordered a judgment on guerrilla leaders who had acted during the 1970s, and #158, which affected the *juntas* between 1976 and 1983. The canceled amnesty was decree #22.924 (22 September 1983), "la Ley de pacificación Nacional," the final attempt by the military to configure the future constitutional government.

21. Alfonsín remarks at an armed forces' friendship dinner, reported in *Clarín,* 6 July 1985, p. 3.

22. Henri J. Barkey, "Why Military Regimes Fail: The Perils of Transition," *Armed Forces and Society,* (Winter 1990).

23. Interview with Alain Rouquié, *Página 12* (1 November 1988), p. 10.

24. See Rut Diamint, "Cambios en la Política de Seguridad. Argentina en busca de un perfil no conflictivo," *Fuerzas Armadas y Sociedad,* (January–March 1992), Santiago.

25. See interview in *Clarín* (17 November 1992), p. 2.

26. See *La Nación* (9 October 1991), p. 5.

27. See *Página 12* (9 November 1991), p. 9.

28. Letter from Juan Domingo Perón to the EAP, 12 February 1970, in *Cristianismo y Revolucion,* Year 4, 25 (September 1970): 67.

29. Colonel Aldo Rico, *La Nación* (20 January 1988).

30. *La Nación* (30 May 1987), p. 4.

REFERENCES

Buchrucker, Cristian. *Nacionalismo y Peronismo.* Buenos Aires: Editorial Sudamericana, 1987.

Cavorrozi, Marcelo. *Autoritarismo y Democracia 1955–1983.* Buenos Aires: CEAL, 1983.

Potash, Robert. *The Army and Politics in Argentina,* vol. 1. Stanford, Calif.: Stanford University Press, 1969.

———. *The Army and Politics in Argentina,* vol. 2. Stanford, Calif.: Stanford University Press, 1980.

Rock, David. *Argentina, 1516–1982: From Spanish Colonization to the Falklands War.*
    Berkeley: University of California Press, 1985.
Rouquié, Alain. *Poder Militar y Sociedad Politica en la Argentina,* 2 vols. Buenos Aires:
    Editores Emece, 1982.

BRAZIL

Daniel Zirker

Are military organizations immortal?[1] Such immortality tends to be an unchallenged assumption in the political life of Latin America, and civil-military relations are deeply conditioned by it. Indeed, the rare occasions of mortality of military organizations in the region have by themselves defined some of its most profound political moments. Four events in Latin American political history—the Mexican revolution, the Bolivian revolution of 1952, the Cuban revolution, and the Nicaraguan revolution—are referred to as *revolutions* in large measure because of the destruction in each case of the previously existing military organization. Only Costa Rica, with its qualified success in constitutionally abolishing its armed forces, was able to unravel the complex web of civil-military relations with limited social and political trauma. As articulate, focused, trained, and powerful institutions, military establishments tend to survive and prosper even when their missions are most tenuous; they aggressively seek out—and find—ways to support their expensive existence.

The Brazilian military has long struggled to balance its self-defined and often contradictory domestic political missions of fostering national development and guaranteeing national political stability, while suffering institutionally from what might be termed a conventional-mission deficiency: the traditionally faint need to defend the nation against enemies, "foreign or domestic."

Ever since a military coup toppled the Brazilian Empire in 1889, domestic politics have preoccupied the military officer corps. Bluntly put, military involvement in domestic politics has been the most likely forum for revealing the "emperor's new clothes," that is, the transparency of the Brazilian military mission. Hence, the numerous military interventions have always involved the frustration of military elites with specific policies of civilian governments. A political coup engineered by rebellious junior officers (*tenentes*) in 1930 brought an end to the "Old Republic" after a right-wing populist politician was denied electoral victory; that same politician was removed from office in 1945 after snubbing Brazil's returning war heroes and showing signs of continuing his dictatorship; the military removed him yet another time when his left-wing populism threatened to begin transforming the social system; and an antipopulist military intervention in 1964 removed his protégé, a leftist populist, from the presidency after he began tampering with military discipline. This last intervention led to the twenty-one-year military dictatorship. After retiring from power in 1985, the military manipulated a fragile civilian presidency, exercising a powerful influence on the drafting of the 1988 constitution.

During virtually all of this century, the relative absence of foreign threats compelled the Brazilian military to turn inward in an almost unique process of self-justification for its institutional survival. Although it has continued into the present with over three hundred thousand military personnel and an immense share of scarce national resources, the establishment of a new mission is vital.

Today, Amazonian development and urban social stability have become perhaps the last best hopes of the institutional well-being of the military establishment. Claims of meaningful threats from foreign enemies or internal communist subversion, never before compelling in the Brazilian case, ring ever more hollow. In a bureaucratic context, this mission deficiency means that the Brazilian armed forces are losing their rational claims upon the national budget.

As one of the Brazilian military's key remaining policy prerogatives, a particularly intrusive form of developmentalism is envisaged in Amazônia; civilian allies linked to slash-and-burn cattle ranching, large- and small-scale mining, and massive forestry and agricultural enterprises have come to see themselves, along with the military, as the nationalistic heroes of a nation threatened by international ecological imperialism. "National security," a term that has been repeatedly defined and redefined by military ideologues over the past three decades, has recently come to mean the colonization of the region: populating, but not democratizing, what is regarded by them as a zone of "future" national security.

Rallying to the slogan "*A Amazônia é nossa*" ("Amazônia is ours"), reminiscent of the nationalism of the 1950s,[2] a civil-military political pact emerged in the early 1990s, albeit with decidedly mixed results by the end of the presidency of Fernando Collor de Mello. An alternative, or perhaps addition, to the military's institutional survival strategy posited "social war" resulting from chronic inflation and economic recession as a new "enemy,"[3] although officers continued to reject antidrugs police work as an acceptable institutional role.[4] With chronic inflation and growing national dissatisfaction with the political and economic processes in Brazil, such concerns took on increasing significance. There is little doubt that the future structure of civil-military relations in Brazil will be vitally affected by the chronic and acute mission deficiencies of the armed forces.

BACKGROUND TO 1985: PODER MODERADOR, INCREASING POLITICAL INTERVENTION, AND CRISES OF LEGITIMACY

The origins of the Brazilian military are to be found in the Portuguese colonial army, one that evinced a parasitic and politically domineering character that underscored a decided lack of a popularly acceptable raison d'être. The colonial organization of military institutions in Brazil reinforced regional and local loyalties in a bid to build local support. Nevertheless, conscription frequently had to be carried out in the form of impressment and caused considerable fear of, and outrage against, the military in the colony, as it would continue to do after independence.[5]

The peaceful declaration of Brazilian independence in 1822 led to the creation of the empire by an heir of the Portuguese royal house of Braganza. This non-violent transition is generally cited as the primary factor behind Brazil's relative freedom from military intervention prior to 1889,[6] although broadscale popular resistance to the military was evident at the time. Shortly after independence this popular discontent materialized in public reaction to an incident involving the use of Portuguese troops to control legislative deputies; a series of incidents that followed pointed to growing tensions between creole and Portuguese officers.

The Constitution of 1824 provided for the role of a *poder moderador,* or moderating power, for the emperor, which ostensibly established his primacy and placed him above partisan politics.[7] After deposing Pedro II in 1889, the military adopted this role as a bridge between the elites and the masses, a raison d'être that would continue at least into the 1970s.[8]

Emperor Pedro I had become thoroughly unpopular with the Brazilian political and economic elites by 1830. The military intervention in the Plata region, a war that many Brazilians felt was being fought to support Portugal's (rather than Brazil's) interests in the region, cost eight thousand lives and created yet another situation in which young Brazilians fled in fear of military conscription. The government was forced at one point to resort to the use of Irish and German mercenaries.[9] The loss of the war (and of political control of Uruguay) led to widespread discontent that found expression in military mutinies, the abdication of the emperor in favor of his young son, and the "virtual dismissal" of the imperial army for "military indiscipline."[10] The army did not recover in numbers from this drastic action, except during the brief period of the Paraguayan War, until after their coup of 1889. Violent revolt, often the product of troops who deserted to regional rebellions, continued, moreover, at a "peak intensity" in Brazilian history until Pedro II was crowned in 1840.[11]

The Paraguayan War (1865–70), during the generally peaceful forty-nine-year reign of Dom Pedro II, marked an important turning point in the politics of the empire. It was from this conflict that the army can be said to have emerged as a major political actor in Brazil.[12] The new awareness on the part of the officers of the serious lag in military technological development in Brazil was driven home by the costs of the war, which were largely borne by Brazil.[13] The popularity of the returned military heroes and the attempts by civilian political groups to coopt them, moreover, created a military consensus that a threat to the "corporate self-interest" of the officer corps existed[14] and that civilians were conducting themselves unpatriotically.[15]

Seizure of political power by the military in 1889 came during a period in which the mission of the military was especially amorphous and followed solicitations for support from the military by civilian politicians in what were described as "cynical bids for power."[16] The situation closely parallelled the 1964 military golpe seventy-five years later.[17] Creation of the "Military Club," which followed civilian calls for the political participation of military officers, led almost immediately to the public rejection by senior officers of the demeaning military mission that had been assigned to them by civilians: the capture of runaway slaves.[18] The subsequent abolition of slavery initiated a chain of events that likewise revolved around the fragility of the military mission. The military moved to oust the emperor with a sudden burst of (apparently shallow) unanimity, despite the deep cleavages between the officers who were moving to uphold the honor of the military and those (mainly positivists) who used the "military question" as a mere pretext to overthrow the government.[19]

The "Old Republic," 1889 to 1930, began with the early military dictatorships of marshals Manoel Deodoro da Fonseca and Floriano Peixoto, both of which were frankly corrupt and militarist,[20] behavior that directly antagonized many of the younger officers, who were imbued with the ideals of Comptean positivism. Hence the major impact of this period on the military institution was a widening of the rift between junior and senior army officers. Senior officers consistently supported the oligarchy,[21] while civilian governments—direct expressions of that system—made little effort to confront the rapidly changing social and economic conditions in the country.[22] Furthermore, the suppression in 1896–97 of Antônio "Conselheiro," a messianic figure who had attracted an army of devout followers in the Northeastern backlands—at great cost to, and humiliation of, the federal army—marked a "new stage" in military anxiety regarding its role in the political system and is thought to have led to the evolution of a "Brazilian Bushido" among junior and middle-level officers.[23]

The issue that increasingly became central to the growing distance between junior and senior officers was that of *national development,* with the junior officers searching for opportunities to lead the way to this new and exciting mission, one that would ostensibly begin with the professionalization of the officer corps.

In the 1920s, junior officers discontented with the slow pace of national development, the *tenentes,* became proponents of institutional and systemic reform and insisted upon the withdrawal of military support from various parts of the power structure.[24] They are thought by some observers to have represented a "bourgeois impulse,"[25] and their economic program was excessively vague and "simplistic."[26] Their outbreaks of rebellion in 1922 and 1924 led to a gradual acceptance of the fostering of national development as a key political raison d'être of the military organization, however.

The São Paulo uprising of 1924, in particular, represented the kind of ultra-nationalistic and loyalty-building event that is often associated with bureaucratic organizations struggling to survive.[27] Beginning on the second anniversary of the 1922 uprising, it pitched five thousand rebels under the leadership of General Isidro Dias Lopez against a federal force of over twenty thousand men.[28] This time the *tenentes* enjoyed enough popular support in São Paulo to resist the vastly superior federal force for several weeks. When they finally did retreat, it was to the interior, where they met with rebel forces from Rio Grande do Sul, forming a joint force that subsequently made a quixotic fourteen-thousand-mile trek through the Brazilian *sertão*, or savannah backlands, ending with the survivors' exile in Bolivia. This adventure deeply influenced a generation of junior army officers; their perceptions of the underdevelopment of the backlands, in particular, graphically reinforced the appropriateness of the role of the military as that of a political proponent of national development.[29]

The dictatorship of Getúlio Vargas, which lasted from 1930 to 1945, and particularly its most authoritarian expression (the Estado Nôvo, or "New State," from 1937 to 1945), is most plausibly regarded as a "military regime in its essence,"[30] despite the civilian status of the president and many of his ministers. Launched by a civil-military coalition that centered on the *tenentes,* the "Revolution of 1930" formally installed a "civilian dictatorship" with extensive military support.[31] The Vargas dictatorship lasted until 1945.

Two events, both tied directly to the Vargas dictatorship, served as necessary "stages" in the maintenance of the long-term political role (and hence the comfortable survival) of the Brazilian armed forces after 1930: the 1932 São Paulo revolt and the communist "*Intentona*" of 1935.

The São Paulo revolt represented the inevitable challenge of regional interests to the moves by Vargas to centralize and nationalize the process of formulating public policy. The immediate causes of the revolt appear to have included the active presence of federal military officials in key administrative positions in the state, particularly that of *tenente* João Alberto Lins de Barros as the state's federal "interventor."[32] The conflict that began in July 1932 was the largest internal conflict in the history of Brazil, with three hundred thousand combatants, of which nearly one hundred thousand were volunteers from São Paulo. With the surrender of São Paulo in early October of the same year,[33] Vargas became more dependent than ever on the support of the army[34] for his increasingly centralist and authoritarian policies.

The communist uprising, or *Intentona,* of 1935 likewise centralized and unified both the national political milieu and the command structure of the army, so that military involvement in politics became the norm and the cooperation of the general staff of the armed forces became a vital prerequisite for any political involvement of military units.[35] Although completely unsuccessful in stimulating broad-based resistance,[36] the "threat" of the communist revolt was quickly extended to include all people thought to be associated with "subversive activity." Thus, although there was some (very limited—albeit bloody) street fighting in the Northeast and though several officers were killed,[37] the primary effect of the revolt was the widespread government suppression and censorship of all opposition.[38] The armed forces created a special decoration for loyal officers who had served in the suppression of the revolt and established an annual celebration with parades and ceremonies to mark the date of the suppression.[39] The "communist threat" became a powerful tool of the military leaders in the forging of internal cohesion within the officer corps,[40] while providing a shadowy "internal enemy" for a military whose national borders were not threatened.

This enhanced concern with internal national security subsequently would cause the military to support a high degree of state involvement in key sectors over the next four decades, particularly regarding petroleum supplies[41] and—in the 1960s and 1970s—arms production. When the break with the Axis powers finally came in 1942, the rationale for the military resistance to the move included the fear of Brazil's own military unpreparedness, especially in strategic petroleum supplies.[42]

The Brazilian Expeditionary Force (FEB), which fought in Italy during 1944–45 with the U.S. Fifth Army, exposed a generation of officers to military action and to the worst aspects of personalistic dictatorship (by 1944 Italy lay in ruins) and created close brother-officer ties with a number of Americans. The most noteworthy of their American colleagues was Vernon Walters, liaison officer between the FEB and General Mark Clark's Fifth Army, who maintained longtime friendships with key Brazilian officers such as General Castelo Branco.[43] After their return to Brazil in 1945, Vargas made several political appointments that appeared to military leaders to be preparations for the suspension of the 1945 presidential elections.[44] The FEB officers promptly removed him from office and allowed him to "retire" to his ranch in Rio Grande do Sul. The Vargas dictatorship's economic and developmental priorities remained, however, as did the profound changes that it had brought to the military institution.[45]

The period between 1945 and 1964 represented a serious attempt by the military to legitimize its political role by associating itself with democratic practices: the election of General Eurico Gaspar Dutra (Vargas's former minister of war) to the presidency was engineered to remove the stain of its long and close relationship with the Vargas dictatorship.[46] Moreover, Vargas' election back into the presidency in 1950, this time as a left-wing populist, threatened elites and officers alike. The army's removal of Vargas in 1954, resulting in his suicide, plunged the country into instability. During the next two years, several "stabilizing" interventions were carried out; constitutionalist officers finally supported the election of a developmentalist civilian, Juscelino Kubitschek, to the presidency in 1956.

During this period, Argentina was increasingly regarded by Brazilian officers as a rival regional military power. The "rivalry," in fact, appears to have been mutually beneficial to the two nations' defense budgets. During the next three decades, a rough parity in major weapons systems, such as aircraft carriers and advanced jet fighters, was maintained by reference to the possibility of eventual conflict. Kubitschek's building of Brasília in Brazil's interior was even justified in part on national security grounds.

Kubitschek's successor, Jânio Quadros, directly challenged the new internal military mission by awarding Che Guevara Brazil's highest decoration. His unexpected resignation after only several months in office left the military establishment in a quandry. On the one hand, they were visibly glad to see him leave. On the other, his vice-president, João Goulart, was a leftist populist who had been a protégé of Vargas. Despite pressures from constitutionalist officers for a peaceful succession, the military cabinet demanded and received a compromise in which the constitution was modified to include a prime minister; the powers of the presidency were greatly reduced. Although a referendum restored the full powers of the presidency in 1963, allegations of communism and overt threats to military discipline ultimately pushed the armed forces into a full-scale military intervention.[47] On 31 March 1964, officers seized the federal government, overthrowing Goulart and initiating a twenty-one-year military dictatorship.

The dictatorship arguably represented the apotheosis of mission-seeking behavior in a mission-deficient environment. Robert Hayes refers to this "military project" as unique in its "setting of psychological goals such as transfering military notions of nation-building, public service, discipline, a sense of global mission, and even such matters as physical fitness to society at large."[48] Some observers have attempted to attribute banal objectives, such as the protection of the military budget, to the persistence of the dictatorship far beyond the limited interventions sanctioned by the "moderating power" doctrine. Its strident and persisting ideological emphases on national security and national development, however, underscored its fundamental character as a pervasive and ideological military *mission*. In fact, as the dictators struggled to maintain a modicum of legitimacy, military budgets were continuously sacrificed.[49]

The self-appointed tasks of the dictatorship, social order and national development, were ultimately eclipsed by spreading economic dysfunction after 1973. Civil-military relations deteriorated as the middle class became increasingly concerned with declining prosperity and susceptible to international concerns regarding human rights violations; growing nationalism within the officer corps also undermined the dictatorship.[50]

DEMOCRATIZATION AND MILITARY PREROGATIVES AFTER 1985

It is important to note that the dictatorship initiated its own demise with a process of "decompression," a significant reduction in human rights violations concurrent with a decline in the regime's legitimacy[51] after 1974, and then a political "opening" (*abertura*) beginning in 1979. Alfred Stepan argues that the Brazilian military establishment initially liberalized the political system for its own reasons, thereby imbuing the subsequent process with a "voluntaristic fragility."[52] The military handover of formal power in 1985 was notably incomplete. Ronald M. Schneider observed that "the Brazilian armed forces have not 'gone back to the barracks,' because they have never been apolitical and fully subject to civilian control as that term implies."[53]

The first civilian presidency following the dictatorship, that of José Sarney (1985–90), arguably retained much of the character of the "*ditamole*" (in Portuguese, a pun meaning "soft dictatorship") that preceded it, particularly as regarded the central political role of the active military officers in the presidential cabinet. Military influence in the civilian policymaking process, and even in the drafting of the Constitution of 1988, went largely uncontested. The subsequent presidency of Fernando Collor de Mello, on the other hand, the first directly elected presidency in three decades, initially resisted, albeit unevenly and ambivalently, military participation in the policymaking process.

The military "mission" was, by 1990, severely threatened in several regards. The decline of communism and the Cold War as credible "threats" to Brazilian national security robbed it of its postwar internal mission; the further stabilization of international relations in Latin America, the decline of Argentina as a credible rival, and the continuing economic dysfunction in Brazil further weakened the rationale for continued military budgets. The role of the 317,000-strong armed forces was directly questioned after the 1990 transfer of power, and the military response became correspondingly strident and defensive. A deficiency of an orthodox military mission was increasingly felt by the military organization.

Stepan has argued regarding the political involvement of the military that a critical dimension of the complex civilian-military relationship in bureaucratic-authoritarian regimes is useful in evaluating such a situation. He emphasizes the identification and tracing of *military prerogatives,* including the "constitutionally-sanctioned independent role of the military in the political system," the "military relationship to the chief executive," the "coordination of the defense sector," "active-duty military participation in the cabinet," the "role of the legislature," the "role of senior career civil servants or civilian political appointees," and the military role in intelligence, in the police, in military promotions, in state enterprises, and in the legal system. These prerogatives are said to represent revealing indicators of military involvement in the national political processes. They are areas in which, "whether challenged or not, the military as an institution assumes they have an acquired right or privilege, formal or informal, to exercise effective control over its internal governance, to play a role within extramilitary areas within the state apparatus, or even to structure relationships between the state and political or civil society."[54] Military prerogatives are counterpoised in Stepan's analysis to *open civil-military contestation,* the contrasting and complementary dimension of civil-military relations. Obviously, as Stepan notes, any given prerogative could become the object of open contestation and thus complement that dimension. Nevertheless, prerogatives also contrast with contestation, as "the military could go from a position of high prerogatives to relatively low prerogatives without contestation."[55]

The first civilian presidency of José Sarney was described by Stepan as representing a situation of "unequal civilian accommodation," in which a high level of military prerogatives contrasted with a low level of open military contestation. Stepan concluded that, because of this, "Brazil is therefore on the margin of not being a democracy,"[56] a situation that was graphically illustrated by the patently political behavior of the military ministers in Sarney's cabinet,[57] essentially allowing the military to "retain significant control over much of the political space they had occupied during the twenty-one years of military rule."[58] Stepan noted in a 1989 interview with the Brazilian newspaper *Jornal do Brasil* that Brazil had the highest level of formal military prerogatives in the world and that direct military participation in the Sarney government represented "the consolidation of prerogatives, not of democracy."[59]

Three general areas outline the military's political priorities during this period: national security, military funding, and the maintenance of unrestricted property rights in Brazil. The three categories overlapped in a variety of issue-areas in which the military insisted upon its predominance over the civilian state. These appear to have stemmed primarily from the need of the military organization to establish and defend a diversified and convincing raison d'être.

One of these was clearly illustrated in the military's unqualified opposition to agrarian reform, which was paralyzed and defeated despite the launching of a historic federal program during Sarney's first weeks in office. Moreover, military influence in all three of these policy areas was reinforced by the Constitution of 1988, the passage of which included the extensive and intensive political involvement of the military ministers. As Schneider put it in 1991, the military remained "much more than just a potent veto group, if . . . less than an active tutor or intrusive arbiter."[60]

At least two other military concerns besides the veto of agrarian reform emerged during the Sarney presidency (1985–1990). These persisted through the Collor presidency (1990–1992) and into the presidency of Itamar Franco (1992–1995). They were the inflation readjustment policy for military salaries and national/military sovereignty over Amazônia and its development.

The salary question triggered incidents of military insubordination during the Sarney presidency, although the military ministers were successful for the most part in maintaining salary and budget readjustments—important in a highly inflationary system—at least on a par with those of other sectors, despite the fact that any budgetary favoritism seemed unjustified by the continued diminishing of international and internal "threats" to Brazil during the period. Rather, the 1980s witnessed the establishment of harmonious ties with potential rival powers, particularly Argentina, and the decline of international communism, which was further vitiated by the growing (moderating) influence of Eurocommunism on Brazilian communist parties.

Brazil's national sovereignty and military hegemony in Amazônia went further in its potential as a unique and acceptable alternative mission for the military. It likewise involved a complex of political priorities, including national security, property rights, and military budgets and salaries. The initial autonomy of the military ministers in this policy area was striking. Although apparently perpetuating the tradition of an "excessive concentration of power in the executive branch" in Brazil,[61] the Sarney administration deferred completely to the military ministers on matters relating to Amazônia. In March of 1989, for example, Sarney abruptly cancelled his scheduled appearance at an international environmental conference in The Hague after meeting with the military ministers. Shortly thereafter, in an embarrassing *volte-face,* Sarney publicly lamented the "intolerable" interference of international ecologists in Brazilian domestic politics.[62] National policies relating to Amazônia had, by 1989, come to be seen by the military as within its necessary and legal jurisdiction, as outlined in a 1985 secret plan for the region, the *Projeto Calha Norte* (PCN), or "Northern Trench (or 'Northern Banks') Project."

The military, acting through the Sarney government, created an influential set of allies through a series of fiscal incentives that encouraged large-scale economic investment, particularly in ventures such as cattle ranching, in the region.[63] The cattle ranchers, in turn, had undertaken the removal—often through violent means—of Indians and other forest dwellers, thereby polarizing domestic and international sentiment.[64]

Maria do Carmo Campello de Souza observed in 1989, in commenting upon Stepan's work, that the Brazilian "military's increasingly explicit power does not come from their political and social characteristics alone, but is related also to the existence of institutional prerogatives in effect since the end of the Brazilian Empire."[65] The progressive erosion of the traditional raisons d'être of the Brazilian military, external and internal national security, had increasingly underscored the need for effective surrogates. Amazônia, as a military policy prerogative, had come to be used as such a surrogate,[66] although with mixed results.

THE COLLOR GOVERNMENT: FURTHER EROSION OF THE MISSION?

The 1989 campaign for direct election to the presidency presented a series of threats, in varying degrees, to military prerogatives. Of the three candidates who proved to be most popular, two of them, Luís Ignácio (Lula) da Silva and Leonel Brizola, had both been leftist critics of military prerogatives. The third, Fernando Collor de Mello, while a rightist and former political appointee of the dictatorship, likewise preoccupied key military officers with some of his campaign promises and his apparent emotional instability, although ultimately they quietly backed him.[67]

Rumors of a possible coup should his eventual runoff opponent (Lula) win the presidency, while formally denied by the military ministers, circulated throughout the last weeks of the campaign and were reportedly mentioned by President Sarney.[68] Collor's willingness to engage in character assassination just prior to the final election probably assured victory, although the vote margin, thirty-five million for Collor and thirty-one million for Lula, might have suggested the wisdom to Collor of establishing a more centrist administration.

Collor initially disbanded the National Intelligence Service (the SNI), the directorship of which had been a key military post since the 1970s. Stepan describes the SNI as having been one of the "two most powerful administrative clusters attached to the office of the presidency,"[69] adding that "the Brazilian SNI had an extraordinary degree of legally sanctioned prerogatives and bureaucratic autonomy found neither in other democracies nor in other bureaucratic-authoritarian regimes."[70] It is arguable that Brazilian military prerogatives were significantly narrowed by Collor's action. However, his disbanding of the SNI may have been more idiosyncratic and emotional than tactical, based as it was on a direct interpersonal conflict with the chief of the SNI when Collor was governor of Alagoas.[71]

Although Collor attempted to limit the most obvious aspects of the military cabinet ministers' political influence, beginning with the announcement of his new cabinet in mid-January 1990, his moves initially appeared to be symbolic.[72] While the subsequent occupation of military ministers with petty tasks and their drift into relative anonymity[73] represented a considerably more significant trend, their vital support for Itamar Franco during Collor's impeachment may have reversed this policy direction.

Aside from political scandal, salary and budgetary crises of the Collor administration undermined its political support and polarized contending interests, leading to episodic political confrontations with the military. Although salary and budgetary increases are of critical concern to the corporate military, the generals have never been particularly effective in pursuing them directly.[74]

While Collor initially kept military pay raises well below the rate of inflation despite mounting military opposition, including the election to Congress of a former army officer who had been arrested for threatening to set off a series of bombs in protest over the Sarny government's military budget,[75] the proliferation of threats of violence in 1991 by local military officers may have persuaded him to introduce a "Provisory Measure" in early June raising military salaries by 25% while providing far lower raises for civilian public employees.[76] The timing of the measure was likely significant: Its drafting followed closely an Amazonian border incident in which Colombian "guerrillas" allegedly attacked Brazilian troops, provoking bloody reprisals and military warnings of a growing "threat" to national security. The defeat of the measure in Congress that July persuaded the military ministers to release a note, apparently approved by Collor, that declared the military to be preoccupied with the "national development and modernization of the country and the social well being of its people" and that the executive and legislative branches "are not able to implement, harmoniously, adequate measures" to overcome the country's problems. The reason for this, they said, was often based upon "the satisfaction of minor interests" and resulted in the "immobilization" of executive power.[77]

Following their defeat over the salary increase, military opinion hardened, with incidents of military indiscipline involving junior officers.[78] By 1 October a 45% pay increase was approved by the Congress,[79] although inflation of over 20% during some of the intervening months had seriously weakened its effect. An embarrassing series of scandals that same month, moreover, undercut the military activists.[80]

The chronic and acute political needs to reinforce budget and salary concerns with legitimate military "mission" activities inevitably suggests border questions—and hence Amazonian policy. The presidency of Itamar Franco, which had not yet revealed a clear pattern of civil-military relations by mid-1993, seemed likewise to be vulnerable to these tensions.

AMAZONIA, CALHA NORTE, AND THE MILITARY: A LONG-TERM MISSION?

The current ideological bases of military hegemony in Amazonian policy-making dates at least back to the 1950s, when the geopolitics associated with such military ideologues as General Golbery do Couto e Silva began to be shaped in military institutions such as the Superior War College (ESG). The "natural permeability" of Amazônia figured prominently in Golbery's conclusion that the region would have to be penetrated, integrated, and "valorized" as national territory.[81] A series of development plans for Amazônia were launched by the military dictatorship in the 1960s and 1970s, most of which related to a master program, the National Integration Plan (PIN). This called for the building of a road network, the TransAmazônica, a related colonization scheme, and the intensification of large-scale mining and forestry projects, ostensibly to be based upon foreign investment and geared toward export.

The overriding question of land ownership had come to be a central concern in this and subsequent regional development programs. Conflicts, particularly between peasants and major landowners, long a problem in the Northeast,[82] had gradually increased in Amazônia; and by 1980 "land conflicts [began] to be regarded as a question of national security."[83] Military encouragement of large mining and agricultural investments in Amazônia, reinforced with fiscal incentives, increasingly became the primary stimuli of violent conflicts over land[84] because of the consequent displacement of Indians, peasants, and forest workers (such as the rubber tappers). Furthermore, the military itself was Brazil's largest landowner, with the army directly controlling five million hectares in Amazônia, and the General Staff of the Armed Forces another four million there.[85]

The military and the National Security Council (CSN) drafted the Calha Norte Project shortly after the transfer of power to Sarney in 1985 "to promote the occupation of the frontier strip along Brazil's northern borders."[86] The proximity of the traditional lands of the Yanomami Indians to the Venezuelan border, the growth of drug smuggling in the region, and the fear of a recurrence of guerrilla activity similar to that experienced in Araguaia (in the Amazon region) in the 1970s—or even alleged international attacks from Colombian guerrillas—served as formal, although decidedly unconvincing, justifications for the project, which was launched as a "confidential" document and whose very existence remained unknown to the Brazilian Congress for two years after its creation.[87]

While some observers suspected that the CSN had posited the unlikely scenario of a future war in a relatively narrow 150-kilometer frontier strip,[88] this "Northern Trench" is far larger, encompassing as much as 14% of the territory of Brazil and 24% of Amazônia,[89] and hence its implications for military autonomy in defining national security "threats" are much broader. It was tied, moreover, to nationalistic xenophobia, and its ramifications for the military budget were significant. Of the approximately US$80 million initially allocated for the project, the military ministries were scheduled to absorb about 78.2%.[90]

Collor was said to have "deactivated" Calha Norte in 1991, according to the governor of the state of Amazônas, at the insistence of José Lutzenberger, Collor's Secretary of the Environment, although there is persistent evidence, including the firing of Lutzenberger and the substantial reshuffling of the cabinet in March 1992, that at least some elements of PCN had been allowed to remain intact.

Indian policy, and particularly the fear—ultimately realized in 1991—that the Yanomamis would eventually be granted a national reserve, also figured prominently, relating to the "threat" to national sovereignty posed by the "possibility" of Indian communities becoming independent states.[91] Despite the establishment in 1989 of a nominally environmental program, *Nossa Natureza,* which had created several national forests and parks, independent prospectors continued to enter the region, apparently with the military's blessing. The region had essentially been colonized,[92] rather than being included in a national integration envisaged by PIN.[93]

Tension between the military and environmentalists had grown markedly after 1985, and continued apace into the Collor presidency. Although the military reluctantly became involved in Collor's later attempts to limit the annual burning of forests and even trained special environmental agents to carry out the task,[94] strong criticism of international efforts to save the rain forest figured prominently in statements by the Superior War College (ESG); the implication was that there was an international plot to take the region.[95] Extreme hostility toward José Lutzenberger, the first environmentalist to occupy a Brazilian cabinet position, became the norm prior to his firing as Minister of the Environment in March 1992 and was tinged—significantly—with the language of anticommunism.[96] If anticommunism had become an obsolete buttress of military prerogatives, antienvironmentalism, as outlined in Calha Norte, seemed poised to replace it.

João Pacheco de Oliveira Filho emphasized that Calha Norte was "not circumscribed by defined spatial limits," but rather widened and narrowed to cover a range of activities. It was, in his view, "a window through which we may observe certain adjustments which have taken place at the central nucleus of power."

"Calha Norte was a rehearsal for the gradual restrengthening of the CSN's influence upon the Presidency of the Republic, utilizing a subject that appeared to be within military competence and which dispensed with the need to consult or mobilize political forces."[97] It was a military mission drill, as it were, a complex range of policy options, unified around a single spatial theme, in which the military might soon exercise autonomous control and thereby exert itself as an independent and influential political actor. A renewed civil-military pact seems to have been emerging prior to President Collor's impeachment and removal from office, moreover. The verbal attacks by senior military officers upon environmentalists such as Lutzenberger and the apparently contrived periodic border incidents all had an artificial and stagemanaged character and seemed to relate directly to the "need" for military autonomy in Amazonian policy. A Colombian border incident, in particular, clarifies this point.

On 26 February 1991, forty Colombians, described as guerrillas associated with the Armed Revolutionary Forces of Colombia (FARC), attacked a Brazilian military outpost on the Rio Traíra, killing three soldiers and wounding others, after dozens of Colombian miners had been arrested for straying into Brazilian territory. Brazilian news media accounts stressed that the conflict had occurred within the territory of "two Latin American countries, with governments [that are] broke and with poorly equipped armies, incapable of guaranteeing anything more of their borders than a chalk line lost in the forest."[98]

The Brazilian military response on 5 March, which was witnessed by an invited press corps, backfired when it became apparent that the seven Colombians killed in reprisal were not guerrillas, as the army had claimed, but humble prospectors.[99] Press photographs of the incident were immediately impounded by the authorities,[100] and Colombians detained during the operation claimed to have been tortured by the soldiers.[101] The "counterinsurgency" action, the first by the military in Amazônia since the Araguaia action in the 1970s, encouraged General Antenor de Santa Cruz, Amazonian army commander, formally to request weapons and supplies to deal with the problem, a request that in turn was translated into a moderately successful petition to Collor for increased military funding.[102]

Venezuelan border incidents were also reported and may have been somewhat more significant because of their proximity to Yanomami lands; also important were the alleged incursions into Brazilian territory by Venezuelan troops attempting to arrest Brazilian prospectors accused of border violations.[103] Increasing antagonism in the Venezuelan press regarding "Brazilian expansionism"[104] were attenuated to some extent, however, by a border revision in 1992 granting Venezuela as much as five thousand square kilometers previously claimed by

Brazil. Nevertheless, encouragement of the prospectors in the Yanomami region appears to have been central to Calha Norte.

Collor's growing insistence upon the removal of these prospectors from Yanomami lands,[105] culminating in the creation of a joint Brazilian-Venezuelan reserve for the tribe in November, drew the public ire of senior military officers, some of whom made a last-ditch effort to retain a corridor between the Brazilian reserve and the Venezuelan border,[106] referring to the joint reserve as a "danger to national defense."[107] Army Minister General Carlos Tinoco, present at the signing ceremony, refused to applaud at the signing,[108] a most unusual public display of politics for an officer who was widely regarded as an "RDE" (acronym for the Disciplinary Regulation of the Army, which prohibits political demonstrations) because of his rigorous avoidance of political positions.[109]

The creation of the Yanomami Park is the most significant indication to date that Projeto Calha Norte has been "deactivated," although by no means a conclusive one. The United Nations conference on world ecology, held in Rio de Janeiro in June 1992, had spurred Collor to begin preparing a public defense of Brazil's dismal environmental record. This may have explained his actions far better than did arguments to the effect that he had turned against Calha Norte.

When Collor's impeachment by the Brazilian Congress seemed imminent two months later, the military high command exercised its political power passively: It merely endorsed the democratic process. Collor's subsequent impeachment and resignation, however, have merely reopened the military's search for an organizational mission; and the new presidency of Itamar Franco, threatened immediately with the political instability that has always accompanied high inflation in Brazil, is in no position to threaten the organizational survival of the Brazilian military.

Despite subsequent explorations of alternative military missions in urban development, it is reasonable to assume that the military will return to national politics. In most scenarios of such military reentry, the orthodox military missions of protecting national borders and guarding the national patrimony from "external threats" would likely be cultivated if only for legitimation. In April of 1993, for example, an organization of retired senior military officers, the "Grupo Guararapes" (named after the seventeenth-century battle that expelled the Dutch from Northeast Brazil), declared in a manifesto to the nation the need for the "restoration of morality" to the Brazilian Congress.[110]

CONCLUSIONS

The search for a politically efficacious mission has historically challenged the Brazilian military organization while encouraging it to intervene in national politics. The current struggle to identify a new and acceptable mission, given the recent collapse of the amorphous ideological mission of anticommunism, continues. Although some role in the development of urban society may yet prove to be acceptable to senior military officers, the most likely mission short of another major political intervention—or, perhaps, in conjunction with it—appears to be "protection" of the development of the national patrimony. Hence, the formal maintenance of the unrestricted development pattern that has persisted in the Amazon region promises to continue to be dominated by "the military bureaucracy and its special cadres,"[111] and key aspects of the military dictatorship may continue to persist there. Moreover, these nationalistic and authoritarian activities will likely be used to reinforce wider claims of a broad-based military mission.[112]

If the democratization process in Brazil is unable to challenge the size and assumed missions of the Brazilian military, if it remains unable to deal rationally and effectively with a huge, expensive, and politically interventionist organization, then this failure will represent a severe blow to the future economic and political well-being of the country. An observer in the early part of this century noted, "The army has its vast and elevated field of action and, if it is kept there independent, surrounded by great respect and prestige, it will be a guarantee of peace and order; if it camps, however, on the ground of negotiations and civil posts, we will have in it the ferment of disorder, the dangerous element of reaction, and of revolt."[113]

Are military organizations immortal? In a situation in which there is little objective rationale for a massive military organization, relatively low popular support, and virtually no resources to support it, its organizational future ultimately becomes a measure of democracy.

NOTES

1. Herbert Kaufman provided the stimulus for this question with his classic study of American bureaucracy, *Are Government Organizations Immortal?* (Washington, D.C.: Brookings Institution, 1976).

2. The cry at the time was "o petróleo é nosso" ("the oil is ours").

3. *Latin American Weekly Report,* 10 December 1992, pp. 6–7.

4. *Latin American Regional Reports—Brazil,* 9 July 1992, p. 8.

5. Caio Prado, Jr., *The Colonial Background of Modern Brazil,* trans. Suzette Macedo (Berkeley: University of California Press, 1967), pp. 361–62.

6. June Hahner argues this point, while setting the date of military interference in government in the 1860s. Hahner, *Civil-Military Relations in Brazil, 1889–1898* (Columbia: University of South Carolina Press, 1969), p. 1. There was at least some intensification of military tensions after the declaration of independence by Pedro I; and, according to Barroso, for about three years afterward the Brazilian military uniforms bore a green-and-yellow emblem that read, "Independence or Death." Gustavo Barroso, *História Militar do Brazil* (São Paulo: Companhia Editôra Nacional, 1935), p. 37.

7. Jordan M. Young, *The Brazilian Revolution of 1930 and the Aftermath* (New Brunswick, N.J.: Rutgers University Press, 1967), p. 10. Young contends that the role of *poder moderador* "is key to the whole structure of Brazilian political life from 1824 to 1889."

8. Robert A. Hayes describes *moderating power* in the following terms: "the elite,

who preferred 'yielding a little to risking too much,' tended to make concessions to the demands of the masses as registered by military leaders.'' *The Armed Nation: The Brazilian Corporate Mystique* (Tempe: Center for Latin American Studies, Arizona State University, 1989), p. 7.

9. John J. Johnson, *The Military and Society in Latin America* (Stanford, Calif.: Stanford University Press, 1964), p. 182.

10. Edmundo Campos Coelho, *Em Busca de Indentidade: o Exército e a Política na Sociedade Brasileira* (Rio de Janeiro: Forense-Universitátia, 1976), p. 39. This led to the establishment of the National Guard, according to Coelho.

11. Johnson, *Military,* pp. 183–84. The creation of the National Guard in 1831 represented an unsuccessful move by the *latifundariarios,* the large landowners, to break the power of both the regular army and the central government. Johnson, *Military,* p. 184. Nelson Werneck Sodré, *Historia Militar do Brasil* (Rio de Janeiro: Editora Civilizacao Brasileira, 1968), p. 117.

12. This point has been widely accepted. One source that makes it persuasively is Rollie E. Poppino, *Brazil: The Land and the People* (New York: Oxford University Press, 1968), p. 207.

13. The country lost between thirty-three thousand and fifty thousand men and spent over US $300 million in the quixotic campaign, which caused a consequent weakening of the national currency. E. Bradford Burns, *A History of Brazil* (New York: Columbia University Press, 1970), p. 165.

14. Frederick M. Nunn, ''Military Professionalism and Professional Militarism in Brazil, 1870–1970: Historical Perspectives and Political Implications,'' *Journal of Latin American Studies* 4, part 1 (1972): 31–32.

15. Hayes, *Armed Nation,* p. 62.

16. Johnson, *Military,* p. 191.

17. Lewis A. Tambs, ''Five Times against the System: Brazilian Foreign Military Expeditions and Their Effect on National Politics,'' *Perspectives on Armed Politics in Brazil* (Tempe: Center for Latin American Studies, Arizona State University, 1976), p. 183.

18. Hayes, *Armed Nation,* p. 69.

19. Coelho, *Em Busca de Indentidade,* p. 56.

20. Burns notes the common practice of conferring military rank upon sympathetic civilian politicians as an example. Burns, *History,* p. 205.

21. Johnson, *Military,* p. 197.

22. Johnson notes that ''oligarchical government left economic and social matters largely to take care of themselves. It showed a general lack of imagination in molding opinion and policy relating to commerce, industry, transportation, and power. It deprived the nation of effective leadership in the field of education. It did little or nothing to incorporate over a million immigrants into the body politic. It permitted provincialism to flourish; Brazil remained split into a half dozen regions.'' Johnson, *Military,* p. 197.

23. Nunn, ''Military Professionalism,'' pp. 33–34.

24. Sodré, *História Militar,* p. 214.

25. Sodré, *História Militar,* p. 214. Octávio Malta regards *tenentismo* as a manifestation of bourgeois revolution in Brazil. Malta, *Os Tenentes na Revolução Brasileira* (Rio de Janeiro: Civilizção Brasileira, 1969), p. 2.

26. Poppino notes that ''they tended to regard economic problems largely as problems of fiscal policy or law enforcement. They denounced profiteering and tax evasion

by merchants and industrialists as violations of existing laws. They seemed to agree on the desirability of industrial development, but implied that this would come when state and local governments provided suitable incentives. In this vein, their only specific recommendation for economic reform was a tax measure to give municipal governments larger revenues and greater autonomy in fiscal matters." Poppino, *Brazil,* p. 255.

27. In his work on American bureaucracy, Herbert Kaufman mentions both nationalism and institutional loyalty in precisely these terms, concluding that "when the agency's existence is threatened, its people rally around it in ways sometimes surprising even to themselves." *Are Government Organizations Immortal?,* pp. 9–10.

28. The five thousand included the very competent Força Pública of São Paulo and a number of European immigrants with extensive military experience. Peter Flynn, *Brazil: A Political Analysis* (Boulder, Colo.: Westview Press, 1979), p. 45.

29. Burns refers to the march as an "odyssey" (Burns, *History,* p. 283), and Macaulay likens it to Aeneas and the Trojans. Neill Macaulay, *The Prestes Column: Revolution in Brazil* (New York: New Viewpoints, 1974), p. x.

30. Coelho, *Em Busca de Indentidade,* p. 97.

31. E.g., Johnson, *Military,* p. 194. Johnson added that "the revolution of 1930 propelled the armed forces into the center of Brazilian politics." Johnson, *Military,* p. 206. He concludes that Vargas remained under the control of the military and that politicians after 1945 likewise depended upon their "*dispositivo militar.*"

32. The "interventor" was the president's personal political representative to the state, in effect an appointed governor. Young describes the reaction in São Paulo to João Alberto's appointment as "stunned." Young, *Brazilian Revolution,* p. 84. It was a direct curtailment of the prior political autonomy enjoyed by state elites. Karl Loewenstein, *Brazil under Vargas* (New York: Macmillan, 1944), pp. 19–20. Young, *Brazilian Revolution,* pp. 85–86.

33. Loewenstein refers to the "complete defeat" of São Paulo (*Brazil under Vargas,* p. 20), although Young and Dulles prefer to stress the relative lack of advantage of the *paulistas.* Young, *Brazilian Revolution,* pp. 86–87. John W. F. Dulles, *Vargas of Brazil: A Political Biography* (Austin: University of Texas Press, 1967), pp. 113–16. Flynn concludes that the failure of the revolt pointed to the decisive role of the army in determining the outcome of coups in Brazil. Flynn, *Brazil,* p. 64.

34. Flynn, *Brazil,* p. 61, 69.

35. Coelho, *Em Busca de Indentidade,* pp. 111–12.

36. Sodré cites Prestes's testimony, given nearly twenty-eight years later, to the effect that although the communists constituted the vanguard of the National Liberation Alliance (ANL), "the insurrection of 1935 was not, however, an exclusively communist movement, nor did the insurrectionists of '35 intend to install in our country a dictatorship of the proletariat, much less a communist government." Cited in Sodré, *Historia Militar,* p. 255.

37. Dulles, *Vargas of Brazil,* p. 149.

38. E.g., Sodré mentions the massive book-burnings that followed the Intentona. Sodré, *Historia Militar,* p. 259.

39. Flynn, *Brazil,* pp. 83–84.

40. Coelho, *Em Busca de Indentidade,* p. 109.

41. Peter Evans, *Dependent Development: The Alliance of Multinational, State, and Local Capital in Brazil* (Princeton: Princeton University Press, 1979), p. 90.

42. Coelho, *Em Busca de Indentidade,* pp. 107–8.

43. Out of fifteen thousand combatants, roughly two thousand were wounded and 450 killed. The FEB received the first surrender of a German division in Italy. Richard Bourne, *Getúlio Vargas of Brazil, 1883–1954: Sphinx of the Pampas* (London: Charles Knight & Co., 1974), p. 112. Dulles, *Vargas of Brazil,* p. 244. A number of observers point to the importance of this influence, both in its application to the further professionalization of the Brazilian officer corps and in its resultant enthusiasm among the returning officers for Western liberal democracy, a feeling that found expression in the military overthrow of Vargas in 1945. Georges Andre Fiechter, *Brazil since 1964: Modernization under a Military Regime,* trans. Alan Bradley (London: Macmillan, 1972), p. 27. Alfred Stepan, ''The New Professionalism of Internal Warfare and Military Role of Expansion,'' in Alfred Stepan, ed., *Authoritarian Brazil: Origins, Policies, and Future* (New Haven: Yale University Press, 1973), p. 63. Johnson, *Military,* pp. 207–8. Bourne, *Getúlio Vargas of Brazil,* p. 112. Tambs, *Getúlio Vargas of Brazil,* p. 199. Tambs, moreover, stresses the importance of Vargas's intentional slighting of the homecoming commanders by the last-minute diverting of their plane away from the welcoming parade to a deserted airfield.

44. The critical appointment was that of Vargas's brother Benjamin as chief of police in Rio de Janeiro (the federal capital at that time). This provoked General Góes Monteiro to set the intervention in motion. Dulles, *Vargas,* pp. 272–74.

45. Skidmore notes that ''in the area of economic policy, as in the sphere of political institutions, it was to prove far easier to overthrow the dictator than to repudiate his legacy.'' Thomas Skidmore, *Politics in Brazil, 1930–64: An Experiment in Democracy* (London: Oxford University Press, 1967), p. 47.

46. Hayes, *Armed Nation,* p. 195.

47. Ibid., p. 212.

48. Ibid., p. 224.

49. Alfred Stepan notes that, though military budgets grew dramatically during military dictatorship in Argentina, Uruguay, and Chile, in Brazil the drastic decline in the military budget may explain the military's ultimate willingness to end the dictatorship. Stepan, *Rethinking Military Politics: Brazil and the Southern Cone* (Princeton: Princeton University Press, 1988), pp. 57–58.

50. Daniel Zirker, ''Civilianization and Authoritarian Nationalism in Brazil: Ideological Opposition within a Military Dictatorship,'' *Journal of Political and Military Sociology* 14, no. 2 (Fall 1986): 263–76.

51. Bolivar Lamounier argues, however, that the decline of authoritarian legitimacy after 1974 ''amounted to a revitalization of governmental authority—since such authority was thus invested in the role of conductor of the decompression (later baptized normalization and eventually redemocratization).'' Lamounier, ''Brazil: Inequality against Democracy,'' in Larry Diamond, Juan J. Linz, and Seymour Martin Lipset, eds., *Democracy in Developing Countries: Latin America* (Boulder: Lynne Reinner, 1989), p. 113.

52. Alfred Stepan, ''Paths toward Redemocratization: Theoretical and Comparative Considerations,'' in Guillermo O'Donnell, Philippe C. Schmitter, and Laurence Whitehead, eds., *Transitions from Authoritarian Rule: Comparative Perspectives* (Baltimore: Johns Hopkins University Press, 1986), p. 75.

53. Stepan, *Rethinking Military Politics,* pp. 94–97.

54. Ibid., p. 93.

55. Ibid., p. 98.

56. Ibid., p. 123.

57. Ronald M. Schneider, *"Order and Progress"*: *A Political History of Brazil* (Boulder: Westview Press, 1991), p. 310.

58. Stepan, *Rethinking Military Politics,* p. 104.

59. Emir Sader and Ken Silverstein, *Without Fear of Being Happy: Lula, the Workers Party and Brazil* (London: Verso, 1991), p. 133.

60. Schneider, *Order and Progress,* p. 377.

61. Maria do Carmo Campello de Souza, "The Brazilian 'New Republic': Under the 'Sword of Damocles,' " in Alfred Stepan, ed., *Democratizing Brazil: Problems of Transition and Consolidation* (New York: Oxford University Press, 1989), p. 382.

62. Observers noted the relation of Sarney's comments to the public pronouncements of the Minister of the Army, General Leônidas Pires Gonçalves, that "false ecologists" were attempting to "internationalize" the Amazon. Richard House, "Brazil Declines Invitation to Conference on Ecology," *Washington Post,* 4 March 1989, p. 3.

63. Sader and Silverstein, *Without Fear of Being Happy,* pp. 130–131.

64. In December 1988, a leader of the rubber tappers' union in the Amazonian state of Acre, Chico Mendes, was gunned down by a local cattle rancher. Although hundreds of similar murders had been ignored by the authorities during the previous decade, international pressure for an investigation and trial of Mendes's murderers was immediately brought to bear on the Brazilian authorities. The subsequent conviction of a local cattle rancher and his son further publicized the destructive development process subsidized by the government and hence suggested impending challenges to the military's autonomy in its Amazonian policy prerogatives. The pair's escape from prison in 1993 is significant in this regard.

65. Campello de Souza, "Brazilian 'New Republic,' " p. 381.

66. This theme appears frequently in the analyses of Brazilian intellectuals. As J. O. de Meira Penna, an ambassador, writer, and professor, put it in an editorial in 1991, "every armed force needs a potential enemy over which to exercise its latent combative ardor and thanks to which it can carry out its training and its plans. The two principal 'enemies' of the [Brazilian] Forces have, miraculously or diabolically, disappeared: Argentina, as an external adversary, and communism, as an internal threat. The 'Evil Empire' evaporated and Argentina, companion in disgrace, became a partner in the Common Market. There is no more reason [for the military] to arm, to mobilize to act. It lost its reason for being, its moral justification of a civic-patriotic mission. It was necessary to invent substitutes for [its] strategic adversaries, even if phantasmagoric ones. One did not take long to appear: 'The foreign threats against Amazônia.' " Penna, "Angústia nas Forças Armadas," *Jornal da Tarde* (28 October 1991), p. 4.

67. Ostensibly as the "lesser of two evils." Sader and Silverstein, *Without Fear of Being Happy,* p. 133.

68. Ibid.

69. Stepan, *Rethinking Military Politics,* pp. 139–40.

70. Ibid., p. 25.

71. *Veja* (24 February 1988), p. 25. The rapid emergence of a similar organization, the Secretariat of Strategic Subjects (SAE), which has apparently replaced the SNI in its intelligence and policy functions and even employs many of the same personnel, suggests that the change was primarily cosmetic. Military pressure in 1991 in support of the SAE's special role in the Brazilian nuclear program and information suggesting that the SAE receives 90% of its budget from secret government funds reinforce reports that the agency enjoys the "absolute confidence" of the military establishment and was essentially "Col-

lor's SNI." *Latin American Regional Reports—Brazil* (19 September 1991), p. 4; *Latin American Weekly Report* (22 August 1991), p. 4. The organization is said to be directed by the son of a general.

72. When he presented the ministers of the army (Carlos Tinoco Ribeiro Gomes), the air force (Sócrates da Costa Monteiro), and the navy (Mário César Flores) in civilian clothes, it prompted *Veja*, a national news magazine, to comment that "In a country that passed the last twenty years accustomed to seeing military commanders dressed in uniform even in bleachers at sporting events, a unique situation was witnessed—by the decision of Collor himself, they were all dressed in coat and tie like civil public functionaries, a category in which all of the ministers have been placed, even those with military portfolios." *Veja* (24 January 1990), p. 26.

73. After one year in office, a public opinion poll showed the military ministers to be "among the least known members of President Collor's cabinet." *Latin American Weekly Report* (25 April 1991), p. 7.

74. Stepan argued, in fact, that the inability of the military dictatorship to raise the military salaries and budget (because of the low legitimacy accorded to such policies) explains in part their willingness to relinquish power in 1985. Stepan, *Rethinking Military Politics*, pp. 57–58.

75. *Latin American Regional Reports—Brazil* (10 January 1991), p. 3.

76. *Veja* (5 June 1991), p. 16.

77. *Veja* (10 July 1991), pp. 16–17. Reports of this confrontation in the national media, such as *Veja*, evinced unprecedented sarcasm vis-à-vis the military ministers. One report concluded with the reminder to Collor of the words of the nineteenth-century Spanish politician Emílio Castelar, who cautioned that "bayonets can serve for everything except to sit upon." *Veja* (10 July 1991), p. 22. *Veja* asked why, given the reduction in force of two hundred thousand civil servants, the military was unwilling to reduce its own numbers from 317,000 and even raised Robert F. McNamara's argument for the elimination of the armed forces in Third World countries.

78. *Latin American Weekly Report* (12 September 1991), p. 3.

79. *Latin American Index* (11 October 1991), p. 72.

80. A newspaper, *O Globo,* had uncovered a purchase order of 130 billion cruzeiros for military uniforms that, it argued, could be bought retail for 50 billion. *O Estado de São Paulo* (22 October 1991), p. 4. Continual national coverage of the unfolding scandal (e.g., *O Estado de São Paulo,* 23 October, p. 4; 30 October, p. 6; 31 October, p. 5; etc.), as well as a second scandal involving the forging of business documents by three officers (*O Estado de São Paulo,* 6 November 1991, p. 6; 7 November, p. 6), effectively deprived the military of any political momentum that it might have gained from its belated salary victory.

81. General Golbery do Couto e Silva, *Geopolítica do Brasil* (Rio de Janeiro: José Olympio, 1967), p. 47.

82. One of the primary rationalizations of military intervention in 1964 had been the alleged threat to national security posed by the Peasant Leagues (*ligas camponêsas*) in the Northeast region.

83. Alfredo Wagner Berno de Almeida, "The State and Land Conflicts in Amazônia, 1964–1988," in David E. Goodman and Anthony Hall, eds., *The Future of Amazônia: Destruction or Sustainable Development?* (New York: St. Martin's Press, 1990), p. 233. Questions relating to land ownership and Indian affairs were increasingly "militarized," and "the closer the military rulers came to the date set for the 'change of regime,' and

the 'beginning of the democratic transtion under civilian government,' the more they applied authoritarian mechanisms in the countryside, and particularly in Amazônia. These new measures, together with those related to the earlier creation of [regional programs], made it clear that democracy would not be allowed to prevail in the countryside, and especially not on the frontier." Ibid., pp. 233–34.

84. Keith Bakx, "The Shanty Town, Final Stage of Rural Development?", in Goodman and Hall, eds., *Future*, p. 67.

85. *Veja*, 8 June 1988, p. 49.

86. Márcio Santilli, "The Calha Norte Project: Military Guardianship and Frontier Policy," *Cultural Survival Quarterly* 13 (1989): p. 42.

87. João Pacheco de Oliveira Filho, "Frontier Security and the New Indigenism: Nature and Origins of the Calha Norte Project," in Goodman and Hall, eds., *Future*, p. 156.

88. Santilli, "Calha Norte Project," p. 43.

89. Suzana Hecht and Alexander Cockburn, *The Fate of the Forest: Developers, Destroyers and Defenders of the Amazon* (New York: Harper Perennial, 1990), p. 136.

90. Oliveira Filho, "Frontier Security and the New Indigenism," pp. 160–61.

91. Ibid., p. 170. One observer noted that "The area along the northern border contains almost 25% of Brazil's Indian population. Here, the military authorities have full control over regional decisions, including land use and Indian policy. The concurrence of military bases and Indian lands in the area appears far from random. In fact, where perhaps half the land of this Calha Norte region is Indian territory, 13 out of 18 military bases have been established in or adjacent to Indian areas, and only 1 in 13 airstrips lies outside Indian land." Barbara J. Cummings, *Dam the Rivers, Damn the People* (London: Earthscan Publications, 1990), p. 92.

92. Ibid., p. 102.

93. Philip Fearnside concludes that "one of the principal impacts of the [PCN] is that it is impeding the demarcation of Amerindian reserves." Fearnside, "Environmental Destruction in the Brazilian Amazon," in Goodman and Hall, eds., *Future*, p. 208.

94. *New York Times*, 26 March 1991, p. C17.

95. *Latin American Weekly Report*, 10 October 1991, p. 8.

96. The ex-Minister of the Army under Sarney, General Leônidas Pires Goncalves, proclaimed in late 1991, in significant language, that Lutzenberger was guilty of "selling out" (*entreguismo*) and that he inspired in Goncalves "the same hatred that I felt for the communist leader, Luiz Carlos Prestes." *O Estado de São Paulo*, 11 October 1991, p. 5.

97. Oliveira Filho, "Frontier Security," pp. 173–74.

98. *Veja*, 13 March 1991, p. 41.

99. *Latin American Weekly Report*, 28 March 1991, p. 3.

100. *Veja*, 13 March 1991, p. 41.

101. *Latin American Weekly Report*, 28 March 1991, p. 3.

102. *Latin American Weekly Report*, 21 March 1991, p. 12; 2 May 1991, p. 6.

103. Foreign Broadcast Information Service (U.S. Department of State), *FBIS-LAT-91-192*, 3 October 1991, p. 30. EFE (Madrid), 2141 GMT, October 1, 1991.

104. *Latin American Regional Reports—Brazil*, 14 February 1991, p. 7.

105. *New York Times*, 26 June 1991, p. A9.

106. *Washington Post*, 16 November 1992, p. A24.

107. *O Estado de São Paulo*, 27 October 1991, p. 5.

108. *New York Times,* 19 November 1991, p. A3.
109. *O Estado de São Paulo,* 27 October 1991, p. 5.
110. *Latin American Weekly Report,* 13 May 1993, p. 214. *LAWR* notes in the report that retired officers are often used to express the political views of active-duty officers, who are prohibited from commenting publicly on political matters.
111. Berno de Almeida, "The State and Land Conflicts," p. 242.
112. The supreme irony of the military's call to arms against the "internationalization" of Amazônia and the devastation that large-scale development would do to the region was perhaps best expressed by Tuca Angerami, a deputy in the Brazilian Congress, who noted that "the object of this polemic is to sensitize Congress to the necessity of reequipping the Armed Forces. Amazônia has already been internationalized for a long time, and this denationalization occurred precisely in the time of the military dictatorship." *Istoé/Senhor,* 16 October 1991, p. 23.
113. Dunshee de Abranches, *Atos e atas do governo provisório,* 2d ed. (Rio de Janeiro: Dunshee de Abranches, 1930), p. 140, as cited in Raymundo Faoro, *Os Donos do Poder; Formaão do Patronato Político Brasileiro,* vol. 2, 2d ed. (São Paulo: Editora Globo/Editora da Universidade de São Paulo, 1975), p. 539.

REFERENCES

Campos Coelho, Edmundo, *Em Busca de Identidade o Exército e a Política na Soceidade Brasileira.* Rio de Janeiro: Forense-Universitátia, 1976.
Faoro, Raymundo. *Os Donos do Poder: Fomacão do Patronato Político Brasileiro,* 2d ed. São Paulo: Editora Globo/Editora da Universidade de São Paulo, 1975.
Hayes, Robert A. *The Armed Nation: The Brazilian Corporate Mystique.* Tempe: Center for Latin American Studies, Arizona State University, 1989.
Stepan, Alfred. *Rethinking Military Politics: Brazil and the Southern Cone.* Princeton: Princeton University Press, 1988.
Werneck Sodré, Nelson. *Historia Militar do Brasil.* Rio de Janeiro: Editora Civilizaçado Brasileira, 1968.

CANADA

Douglas Bland

Most Canadians, if asked to describe the influence of the Canadian Armed Forces on politics in Canada, would say that there is none at all. The armed forces is a small, professional organization widely dispersed across the country. Few politicians are interested in military affairs, mainly because they assume that there are no votes in defense issues and because defense policy has been directed for so long by the politics of alliances. The media have an amateur approach to foreign and defence policy, and the "defense community" is small and often more concerned with the high politics of international security relations than with Canadian defense affairs.

Yet this disinterest—and some say neglect—in one of the basic policy responsibilities of a sovereign state masks a nice paradox in Canadian politics. Soldiers at times have taken advantage of the situation to fashion an armed forces structure and a national strategy that they prefer, and at times these professional choices have surprised and caused difficulties for politicians. In these circumstances, defense policy has figured prominently in several federal elections and in the agenda of governments. On those few occasions when the armed forces were of interest to politicians, they found that the armed forces had more influence than many had expected.

Defense policy and the relationship between politicians and the senior members of the Canadian Armed Forces (CF) is shaped by Canada's customs, traditions, and its unique strategic situation. The armed forces of Canada are situated in a Westminster tradition. Officers' assumption of the supremacy of Parliament is so strongly embedded in the traditions of the profession that it is not even a subject of staff-college lectures. Rather, civil-military relations in Canada circle about politicians' concerns about auditing the "expert" advice they receive from the military and soldiers' frustrations with politicians who seem content to ignore that advice. According to General Guy Simonds, an influential postwar officer who was never a raging democrat, the defense problem in Canada "is not one of attempting to devise ways and means of enabling the military to encroach upon political prerogatives but of getting politicians to face the unpleasant duty of making realistic decisions."[1] The devil, however, lies in the definition of reality.

THE ABSENCE OF STRATEGIC VISION

Canadian citizens, soldiers, and politicians rarely consider the defense of Canada outside the context of the country's relationships with major powers or international organizations. Canada is simply too large and has too many miles of seacoast to be defended by its scattered population. On the other hand, the country's invulnerability to military attack is usually so absolute that building a military force is not often a central concern of governments. There were notable exceptions to this assumption in the nineteenth century, when the United States was a serious menace, but Canadians looked to Britain for its defense during most of this period.[2] While the United States was the main threat, British policy toward America was good enough for Canada. After all, everyone understood that it was British arms and military leadership that had secured the British colonies from the Americans in the past, and Canadians expected them to do so in the future.

Generally, diplomats and soldiers tended to think of Canadian strategy only as part of some grander international strategy. This expectation and the continuing influence of British professional officers on Canadian military affairs after confederation prompted a close association between national defense policy and imperial defense policy, at least in the minds of many Canadian officers. It was only realistic, so they thought, for Canada to play its part in the grander schemes of the empire, but Canadian politicians were not so sure.

Defense planning during the early years after Confederation, therefore, was characterized by political neglect acting against an intense military effort to bring the Canadian armed services into war on the side of the British Empire if war should break out. Although politicians were reluctant to act, Canada followed the British lead into the South African War in 1900 and into the Great War in 1914. It was the effort military officers in Canada had taken to build and maintain a close association with British commanders and imperial war plans that facilitated and, some would contend, promoted this response.

When war was declared by Britain in September 1939, Canada followed suit, but this time at a discreet distance of several days. Prime Minister Mackenzie King, always suspicious that officers were making secret plans with the British General Staff to involve Canada in a continental war, tried to avoid any army commitment in Europe, but the enthusiasm for empire in the population was too strong. King was right to be suspicious of the military, for it did have an independent view. When participation in a wider war could no longer be avoided, the military activated its preferred war plans and set about integrating Canada's wartime policies within first the British and then the allied policies.

In all these cases, politicians reaped the fruits of neglect, for they had no national strategy built on national interests to direct the armed forces nor a military profession conditioned to think in national terms outside alliances.

After the war, Canadians fell easily and logically into the developing western security community centered on the United States and NATO. Canadian politicians and diplomats were active participants in the formation of the North Atlantic alliance. Their efforts were snagged, however, by the competition between the need to play a role in the direction of alliance policy, to protect Canada's interests, and their desire to avoid any military commitments, especially in Europe. In the end, Canada accepted substantial military commitments to NATO, which became the armed forces' principal source of influence on national policies.

During the Cold War, Canada was never threatened directly except by nuclear weapons, and defense against the nuclear threat was not a military problem per se. It was (and remains) a problem for diplomacy and deterrence, and in North America that was a responsibility of the United States. Thus, the impossibility of the defense task and the lack of credible threats spawned a laissez-faire attitude toward national defense among politicians and the population and a tradition of alliance building in the foreign and defense community.[3]

Canadian politicians and soldiers have long accepted a subordinate role for Canada in international security affairs and national defense policy. The easy acceptance of major powers' and NATO's strategies as Canadian strategy reflects this attitude. Soldiers generally value of this outlook, not only because it seems a sensible course for a small nation to follow but also because being linked to a major power's strategy can serve the special interests of the military services in a small country.

"Playing a part" in a grand strategy allowed soldiers, and sailors too, to make demands on governments to support "commitments" and to live up to allied obligations that would never have been tolerated otherwise. When governments were not careful and allowed the military to define commitments in terms of expenditures and operational missions, national defense policy became entangled in the assumptions and priorities of allied planning in ways that dislocated other national interests and even the national defense.

In 1949, Brooke Claxton, who was an alert and diligent defense minister, warned against "the great danger" of military planning conducted by "very bright officers . . . [who] live and work without due regard for the facts of national life." The control of officers who naturally work for what Claxton called "ideal solutions" must come from politicians who work to balance the ideal solution with these national facts of life.[4] Unfortunately for civil-military relations in Canada, bright officers have tended to their business full time, and politicians have not.

Politicians have always struggled under Canada's military commitments. They believe intuitively, if not on much reflection, that Canada's military contributions have been tokens paid for a "seat at the table" in international fora. They know, although they would never declare it, that in extremis the Americans will safe-guard Canada, if only in their own interest. NATO commitments aimed at de-fending Europe, therefore, have always been bothersome; they have become even more so as domestic demands multiplied and the relative power of Europe increased after 1955. Europeans, the politicians contend, can look after them-selves. Meeting defense commitments, especially commitments defined by allied generals, seemed a frightful waste; but most politicians acknowledged that they could not be avoided entirely for fear that Canada would lose what influence such commitments bought in international associations.

Defense policy is a frustrating irrelevance in the minds of most Canadian politicians and has little bearing on the everyday world of Canadian politics. Lacking any real ability to control strategic direction or to escape from com-mitments, defense policy in Canada has become centered on domestic issues and policies and especially on the ''benefits'' that can be transferred to local communities from the defense budget. This ''national fact of life'' in turn frus-trates military planners, who strive for the elusive efficient military force free from the interference of politicians.[5]

Defense relations between the military and the civil authority, therefore, are focused on questions about the domestic distribution of defense resources and not on questions of strategic purpose. General Gerald Theriault (chief of the Defence Staff, 1983–86) once remarked that defense policy ''has probably never represented a deliberately chosen course of strategic direction, or a thoughtfully integrated element of national purpose and objectives.''[6] In the absence of stra-tegic purpose defined by political leaders, that purpose and the defense structure to support it has been decided largely by choices made by soldiers when poli-ticians were busy with other responsibilities. In crisis and when politicians have attempted to radically change defense policy, they have discovered that their abilities to direct defense policy and the range of responses open to governments have been foreclosed by the tyranny of past military choices.

THE CLOSED SHOP

Between 1950 and 1963 the military profession in Canada shaped the armed forces and reinforced the missions it preferred. Cabinets and defense ministers imposed only a few rules on the service chiefs and were content with the military direction of the military as long as the CF met the minimum needs of the alliances, was largely invisible to the population, did not stimulate any national debate on defense policy, and accepted domestic realities, which meant no open contests with the government over the defense budget. Within these strictures the CF, stimulated by its special commitments in NATO and NORAD, became a highly professional and technically competent force that increasingly saw itself as inseparable from its alliance missions. Within a few years after entering NA-TO's ranks, the services had developed strong institutional norms tied directly to their self-image as "professionals" and to their separate allied operational commitments.

The continued expansion of the armed forces in the 1950s and the concentration on separate missions encouraged the separate evolution of the armed services and competitiveness among them for funds and attention. This development was accompanied by a curious, but typically Canadian, acceptance of foreign command and direction of the armed services. Politicians, and most generals and admirals, assumed that Canada did not need a central command function.[7] It followed, therefore, that there was no need for a national war plan, and none was developed. Instead, each service developed its own set of plans and war books. Few politicians seemed concerned with the prospect that in a crisis the government would be confronted with three separate military timetables and command arrangements and that it would not have any central headquarters staff to direct the armed forces in the national interest. In the absence of crisis and political interest in the details of national defense, no one seemed at all worried about this latent challenge to Parliament's ability to control the armed forces in wartime.

When the Progressive Conservative government was elected in 1957, there were signs that the civil-military understanding that had guided defense planning in Canada since 1947 was eroding. In the very first days of Diefenbaker's government, the defense staff presented the prime minister with the complex NORAD agreement that had been negotiated by the previous Liberal government. The prime minister accepted the documents, but he was subsequently criticized for acting too hastily. The chairman of the Chiefs of Staff Committee, General Foulkes, has since been chastised for hoodwinking the government into accepting a major defense agreement simply to serve military interests, without due consideration of all its other national implications.[8]

Diefenbaker, a suspicious politician at best, immediately drew away from the military, but he took no action to reform the defense policy process. Even worse, in some estimations, he appointed defense ministers who were friendly toward the generals and sympathetic to their interests. It was business as usual in the defense headquarters, where decisions about national defense planning and obligations to NATO and NORAD were left in the hands of the service chiefs. The weak central planning staff, moreover, only reinforced bottom-up, service-directed planning, which left the service chiefs with the final say in force development and command relationships. Thus it was usual for the services "to carry out their planning and operational functions in semi-isolation [from each other and the government] where lack of criticism was assumed to indicate approval."[9]

When the Cuban missile crisis broke into the open in October 1962, the Canadian forces predictably reacted in different ways. The army began to mobilize individuals and units for dispatch to Europe, and the air force brought its squadrons to high alert. It was the navy, however, that caused the most obvious difficulties for the government, when it began to load war stores and unexpectedly sent several ships to sea. The commotion in Halifax harbor could not be concealed, and the government was soon asked to explain these warlike preparations.

Unfortunately the Diefenbaker government, which was undecided about what course Canada should follow in the crisis, found that its position had been preempted by the services' reaction to allied alerts. When the prime minister attempted to regain control of the situation, he discovered that there was no national plan to substitute for allied plans and that his recall notices simply threw the defense establishment into confusion. The defense minister sided with the services and resigned. In the aftermath of the crisis the media and the public blamed the government for the uncoordinated and unauthorized responses of the armed forces. The incident shattered Diefenbaker's cabinet and was a primary factor in his defeat a year later.[10]

These two episodes have been interpreted from different points of view, but most analysts agree that governments had not paid sufficient attention to defense policy. Inattention left the military to act in the government's place and to define national interests and to respond to them in ways that supported the military's own views and preferences. No one should be surprised that strong institutions have their own interests and tend to interpret issues in ways that sustain those interests.

In 1963 the Liberals returned to power. The new defense minister, Paul Hellyer, acted immediately to impose the government's will on the armed forces. In his view the problem was caused by the commitments strategy that had encouraged the separate development of the armed forces. He recognized also that interservice competitions aggravated policy difficulties and placed the minister in the position of a referee. The service chiefs, he said, "try to get you alone so they can force their own views on you without any coordination with anyone else."[11] Hellyer soon decided that he would be the team manager and not the referee and that service-directed, bottom-up planning would be replaced by policy-directed, top-down planning.[12]

The minister cancelled or placed in abeyance all major defense procurement projects. He dismissed the navy's just-completed and comprehensive future's plan (comprehensive in naval terms) and began a defense review aimed at finding a national strategy and a structure that would fit it. The details of this review and the strategy that resulted are not important here, but Hellyer's assault on the assumptions of postwar defense planning and the services' reaction to it are critical to understanding civil-military relations in Canada over the last thirty years.

Hellyer outlined two major concepts in his White Paper on defense in 1964. First, defense plans would be redrawn around a single national strategy aimed at defending Canada and providing forces for international missions with NATO and the UN. These international commitments, however, would be adjusted so that they could all be met by a single, mobile, and harmonious national force. The armed forces, therefore, would be unified into one structure, with one planning and command staff responsible for the preparation and supervision of a coordinated defense plan and one scheme for force development.

The service chiefs and their supporters immediately realized that Hellyer's policy would strip them of the power to decide what was best for their own services. Changing the commitments would remove the mainstay of traditional force-development planning. Strengthening the central direction of defense policy would also remove the services' ability to control the defense budget. Finally, Hellyer's radical notion to replace the service chiefs with a single chief of defense staff would leave the services exposed to the dictates of an individual who could not be counted upon to defend each service's interests with equal vigor.

The greatest shock was felt from Hellyer's rejection of the first and immutable assumption that had always guided service planning, namely, that the maintenance of three strong services was good for Canada. The service chiefs saw this objective as their primary purpose, and each officer accepted that it justified every effort to strengthen his own service's interests. Each service chief expected his colleagues to do the same. Together, a strong army, navy, and air force would assure the defense of Canada; but if there were insufficient funds for all, then that was the government's problem.

Hellyer stood this assumption on its head. He believed that a unified national defense was good for Canada and that the allocation of resources to that defense depended on a strategic threat assessment made from Canada's perspective and on the choices the government made from that assessment. He argued, for instance, that it was not obvious how spending money on the air force's plan for a new fleet of aircraft to deliver nuclear weapons in Europe would serve the national interest.

Under Hellyer's assumptions, the service chiefs lost their raison d'être. They became policy takers and not policy makers. In a sense, Hellyer created a competing power center, the national defense, and placed it over the service centers. This new competitor arrived with assumptions, ideas, and objectives different from those of the services and demanded control of the budget allocation process. The service chiefs naturally attacked this new rival in what came to be called, if only in comic opera terms, "the admirals' revolt."[13]

The admirals, and a few generals, never stood any chance once Hellyer convinced the media and most of the public that his contest with the military was about civil control of the military. Broadsides fired at the minister by the admirals proved ineffective, partly because they were loaded with obviously self-servicing arguments and unconvincing statements. Once the prime minister assessed that there was little political danger for the government if it went on with Hellyer's reforms, the admirals were sunk.

Ironically, the very political indifference military leaders counted on to give them a large measure of policy freedom undercut their positions when they tried to rouse political support for their services. Furthermore, the service chiefs' inability to present a united front against Hellyer weakened their arguments and proved the unreasonableness of the defense establishment in ways that worked in the minister's favor. He merely seized the weapons the military leaders provided and used them before parliamentary committees to adroitly disarm his military critics.

Hellyer clearly won the battle to unify the armed forces, but it is problematic that Parliament won any long-term victory over the administration of defense policy. Unification as an organizing concept was dependant on Hellyer's notion of a national strategy free from the dictates of allied commitments. Unfortunately, the prime minister was not much concerned with military efficiency, and he certainly was not prepared to revamp Canada's foreign policy in Europe and NATO to get it.[14] Thus the necessary link between strategy and structure never matured; once Hellyer's strong hand was lifted from the defense department, the CF began a slow return to the status quo ante.

Other governments and ministers tried to reorient and reorganize the armed forces, but their power in cabinet and their attention was never sufficiently concentrated for the task. In 1968 Pierre Trudeau complained that Canada had no defense policy except NATO policy; he set out to change that situation. He reduced the forces in Europe and, with his anti-NATO defense minister, Donald Macdonald, directed the armed forces toward national development and "sovereignty" operations. The armed forces were ordered to give up their nuclear roles, their mechanized forces, including tanks, and their high-seas fleet requirements. Not surprisingly, the military balked. In less than three years Trudeau's government, under pressure from foreign governments, domestic interest groups, and a foot-dragging defense staff, reversed itself and authorized the forces to purchase long-range patrol aircraft for antisubmarine warfare roles and new tanks for Europe. The CF reaffirmed their overseas priorities and their related equipment requirements.

This change in direction occurred partly because the prime minister simply did not maintain enough control over the defense establishment to discipline its internal policy process. Macdonald was minister for less than two years; and he was followed by several weak "caretaker ministers," politicians who were not equipped politically or intellectually to enforce the prime minister's ideas on a stubborn department. Before he left the defense portfolio, Macdonald attempted to redress the government's lack of attention to defense policy by amalgamating the civil service bureaucracy of the department of defense with the military staff of the CF headquarters. His idea was that civil service control of the military could make up for the lack of parliamentary control of the military. Unfortunately for Parliament, the idea may have only exaggerated the problem of control.

After the amalgamation of CF headquarters and the civil service departmental staff in 1972, the chief of the defense staff (CDS) created by Hellyer became a coequal with the deputy minister, the senior civil servant in the department. Together they held all legal powers over the CF and the department under the minister. Whereas previously they had acted separately to advise the minister, they now acted in concert. Naturally, the individuals who have held these offices have attempted to "get along before ministers"; as a result, the CDS and the deputy minister have tended to reach consensus on important issues before they meet with the minister. Defense decision making, therefore, has been pushed down inside the system and not liberated from the military as Macdonald intended.[15] Canadian politicians, by attempting to control the military by passing that responsibility to the civil service, created a new political problem for government, for now Parliament needs to control a unified civil service–military defense establishment—and that is a much more difficult challenge.[16]

The armed forces, unified in law since 1967, never really accepted the concept of unification or the subordination of service interests to national defense. Slowly at first, then with growing confidence, the traditional services rebuilt their position as controlling centers in the defense policy process. The continuation of the three service-oriented alliance commitments provided the base from which the navy, army, and air force built their new organizations. By 1975 three service headquarters had been reestablished, and in 1984 the government reintroduced three new old-pattern uniforms that gave the appearance, at least, that unification was dead.

Unification, however, remains the law, and the reborn so-called service chiefs are a shadow of the former service leaders. They have no right of access to the minister and need not be consulted on every defense policy decision. Nevertheless, the service commands are competing power centers with the national headquarters that try to influence defense policy in their own interests.

The effect of this campaign has been uneven. On the one hand, the notion that strong services provide for a strong national defense has regained credibility, at least in the defense establishment. This view is reflected by the inclusion of the service commanders in Defence Council meetings with the minister and their routine attendance at senior defense-management committees in National Defence Headquarters. The commands are routinely involved in major internal policy decisions, even when the need for triservice participation is not obvious. The CDS in 1993 directed that a "joint staff" be established in Ottawa. How one might join together a unified organization is a puzzle that exemplifies the conceptual confusion that infects the defense establishment.

This realignment of powers away from the unified direction of the CF by a central staff in Ottawa presents an outward impression of power in the commands. The reality regarding issues that are of political interest to the government, however, may be different. When, for instance, the government decided to sharply reduce the defense budget in 1989, the commanders were not consulted and only the CDS was asked for military advice. The CDS is the chief military officer in Canada, and protocol and tradition reinforce his position as unquestioned leader of the officer corps. It is impossible to think of a situation in which a commander would openly contradict the CDS and remain in his position. Therefore, from the point of view of hierarchy the CF is unified, but the reappearance of the services as semi-independent entities has distorted defense relations with the government in subtle ways that may become apparent only as the country moves away from NATO strategy to a more independent national strategy.

Few fundamental decisions about defense organization and the distribution of funds were required when defense policy was directed at meeting commitments to NATO and to NORAD. The collapse of the Soviet Union, and with it the main threat to the western world, ended for all practical purposes the rationale for the composition of Canada's defense budget. By 1989 it was obvious that the changed strategic situation demanded a review of policy that would carry with it an assumption that defense spending patterns and the structure of the CF would change.

The change, however, has not occurred. In the ten-year period between 1984 and 1994 the distribution of defense spending among the services has been constant. Generally, the navy receives 17% of the defense services program, while the army gets 19% and the air force 24%, with the remainder going to "common support" services. Similarly, personnel are consistently divided at a ratio of 15%, 20%, 26%, and 39% respectively.[17]

This division of defense funds represents more than a strategic response to Cold War commitments; It represents a hard-won internal consensus of the defense establishment about what is required to keep each service functioning at its preferred status. Any CDS or service chief who attempted to change this arrangement would face a serious confrontation with his peers. More important to the theme of civil-military relations in Canada, any government that attempted to upset this consensus would face a service revolt as troublesome as the one Hellyer faced when he assaulted fundamental service interests in 1964. Yet the changed strategic environment requires a fundamental reassessment of the defense program, and the Liberal government elected in 1993 has begun that process. The resistance to change is already evident.

A NEW REALITY?

Canada's secure geopolitical situation has allowed politicians to worry about things other than defense policy. When they did consider the defense of the dominion, they tried to minimize the effort and expense while maximizing the return. Canadian soldiers and sailors understandably spend their careers considering ways to meet defense problems and commitments efficiently and effectively in military terms. Perhaps more than with any other problem, however, Canadian military leaders have struggled against the indifference of politicians in an effort to build and maintain a credible military force against the uncertainties of a violent world. Their efforts usually have brought them small returns and little attention, but neglect has its own rewards.

The Canadian officer corps has always been led by a small group of dedicated professionals who have assumed a personnel responsibility for the state of the armed forces in Canada. Left to their own assessments, these officers have taken what governments have given them and fastened onto missions that seemed to aid in the defense of Canada and to provide room and reason for the forces to prosper as professional services. When budgets are tight, and they usually are, officers in the three services compete with each other for missions, money, and attention. When funds are lavish, cooperation is easier. As long as ministers bought into this scheme or stayed out of the way, relations with defense ministers were cordial at least. When, however, ministers arrived with some personal agenda (or government policy) that went outside the extant military-political consensus and the military's own view of its roles and needs, then ministers invariably met stiff resistance from the service chiefs.

Civil-military relations in Canada resemble a dynamic process searching for a consensus between officers and politicians about what objectives, expenses, processes, and organizations will most effectively meet Canada's defense situation. It is generally agreed that Canada has two defense imperatives, the defense of Canada and the defense of North America in cooperation with the United States, after which the country is free to undertake voluntary security acts with other nations and organizations. Disagreements between the military and political leadership are usually concerned with the nature and extent of "voluntary" acts. From 1950 until the end of the Cold War, the voluntary act has been NATO and, to a lesser extent, NORAD and UN peacekeeping commitments. Politicians, generally, have been content to allow the CF to build on these missions until they step beyond political tolerance, at which point a conflict erupts, leading to a new consensus. That is the history of unification, the Trudeau era, and the ill-fated (but uncharacteristically bold) defense policy devised by the defense department in 1987.

The end of the Cold War, serious problems with CF operations in Somalia and in the former Republic of Yugoslavia and a continuing debt crisis at home have broken the postwar consensus again. Politicians are actively reviewing policy, and soldiers are actively scrabbling to defend their present positions. Past reviews of "Canadian options" seemed incredible and unsatisfying because the strategic objectives and means for national defense were held by the superpowers and the alliances. Like the participants at the Mad Hatter's tea party, politicians, soldiers, academics, and critics involved in such reviews circled the same table and the same menus, ending in essentially the same place as they began.

In these circumstances, military officers and politicians argued about crumbs and spilt tea, but in the mid-1990s the situation is different and may be changed absolutely. Canada has a real opportunity to embark on a defense policy largely independent of any other states' policies. Finding and implementing a new strategy may challenge assumptions and policy preferences that have guided the CF for years and could consequently present a political challenge to the CF that might strike deeply into the military realm. If the government is genuinely intent on redirecting defense policy, then civil-military relations in Canada are headed for a rough ride. If, however, one can trust history, then the CF and the government will be content to find some new consensus (but at a lower level of expenditures); and defense policy will return to its natural state of neglect, and the soldiers will be happy for it.

NOTES

1. Douglas Bland, *The Administration of Defence Policy in Canada, 1945–85* (Kingston: R. P. Frye, 1987), p. 1.

2. R. A. Preston, *The Defence of the Undefended Border: Planning for War in North America, 1867–1939* (Toronto: University of Toronto Press, 1977); Desmond Morton, *Ministers and Generals: Politics and the Canadian Militia, 1868–1904* (Toronto: University of Toronto Press, 1970).

3. Bland, *Defence Policy;* and D. W. Middlemiss and J. J. Sokolsky, *Canadian Defence: Decisions and Determinants* (Toronto: Harcourt Brace, 1989).

4. James Eayrs, *In Defence of Canada: Growing Up Allied* (Toronto: University of Toronto Press, 1980), p. 132.

5. Douglas Bland, ''Controlling the Defence Policy Process in Canada: White Papers on Defence and Bureaucratic Politics in the Department of National Defence,'' *Defence Analysis* 5, no. 1 (1989): 3–16.

6. G. C. E. Theriault, ''Reflections on Canadian Defence Policy and Its Underlying Structural Problems,'' *Canadian Defence Quarterly* (July 1993), p. 3.

7. See for example the influential *Royal Commission on Government Organization* (Ottawa: Queen's Printers, 1962), pp. 65–66.

8. Joseph Jockel, *No Boundaries Upstairs: Canada, the United States and the Origins of North American Air Defence, 1945–1958* (Vancouver: University of British Columbia, 1987).

9. Peter Haydon, *The Cuban Missile Crisis: Canadian Involvement Reconsidered* (Toronto: CISS, 1993), p. 90.

10. Basil Robinson, *Diefenbaker's World: A Populist in Foreign Affairs* (Toronto: University of Toronto Press, 1989), pp. 283–96.

11. Interview, Hellyer, 1993.

12. J. L. Granastein, *Canada 1957–1967: Years of Uncertainty and Innovation* (Toronto: McClelland and Stewart, 1988), pp. 218–42. See also Paul Hellyer, *Damn the Torpedoes: My Fight to Unify Canada's Armed Forces* (Toronto: McClelland and Stewart, 1990).

13. Jeffry Brock, *Memoirs of a Sailor: The Thunder and the Sunshine,* vol. 2 (Toronto: McClelland and Stewart, 1989), pp. 141–326. See also Hellyer, *Torpedoes,* pp. 170–91.

14. Hellyer, *Torpedoes,* p. 46.

15. J. L. Granastein and Robert Bothwell, *Pirouette: Pierre Trudeau and Canadian Foreign Policy* (Toronto: University of Toronto Press, 1990), pp. 253–56.

16. For example, in 1987 the defense establishment presented to the cabinet a defense program that would have required almost doubling defense expenditures and would have given the CF a fleet of nuclear submarines and other capabilities far outstripping any they had held since World War II. The civilian deputy minister and the chief of the defense staff worked together to push this program through the government, whereas one might have expected the deputy minister to act as a brake on plans that were obviously overly ambitious.

17. Canada, Department of National Defence, *Defence Estimates, Part III, 1984–1994* (Ottawa: Department of National Defence, n.d.).

REFERENCES

Bland, Douglas. *The Administration of Defence Policy in Canada, 1947–85.* Kingston: R. P. Frye, 1987.

Eayrs, James. *In Defence of Canada,* 5 vols. Toronto: University of Toronto Press, 1964–1985.

Granastein, J. L. *Pirouette: Pierre Trudeau and Canadian Foreign Policy.* Toronto: University of Toronto Press, 1990.

Harris, Stephen. *Canadian Brass: The Making of a Professional Army, 1860–1939.* Toronto: University of Toronto Press, 1988.

Haydon, Peter. *The 1962 Cuban Missile Crisis: Canadian Involvement Reconsidered.* Toronto: Canadian Institute for Strategic Studies, 1993.

Hellyer, Paul. *Damn the Torpedoes: My Fight to Unify the Canadian Armed Forces.* Toronto: McClelland and Stewart, 1992.

Jockel, Joseph. *No Boundaries Upstairs: Canada, the United States and the Origins of North American Air Defence, 1945–1958.* Vancouver: University of British Columbia Press, 1987.

Morton, Desmond. *Ministers and Generals: Politics and the Canadian Militia, 1968–1904.* Toronto: University of Toronto Press, 1970.

Pope, Maurice. *Soldiers and Politicians.* Toronto: University of Toronto Press, 1962.

Stacey, C. P. *Arms, Men, and Government: The War Policies of Canada, 1939–1945.* Ottawa: Queen's Printers, 1970.

CHINA

Zhiyong Lan

No other Chinese words were made so well known to the world in a single day as the words "Tiananmen Square." No other country's symbol of pride was so well known to the world in association with the word "massacre." Indeed, the Tiananmen military action not only shocked the people outside of China but also surprised many Chinese, including a good number of high-ranking government and military officers. The armed confrontation between the People's Liberation Army (PLA) and the unarmed civilians over political issues raised a serious concern about the army's future role in the country's political life. This chapter, by reviewing the history of the Chinese civil-military relationship and the means and processes through which the PLA interacts with civilian life, tries to identify the major factors leading to the PLA's political role and their continuing effect on its future.

HISTORY OF THE PLA AND ITS POLITICAL ROLE

The PLA is an army of more than three million men and women, consisting of a navy, air force, artillery, field armies, local garrisons, and military regions and equipped with massive conventional as well as nuclear weapons. Over the years, the PLA has consistently played an active role in the country's political life. To understand why, its history best tells the story.

Before 1911, China suffered chronic war and poverty. In its four-thousand-year civilization, every change of dynasty (about two to three hundred years a cycle) was accompanied by massive wars, deaths, and destruction. Every period of glory and prosperity was also associated with war and conquest.[1] To many Chinese, military power is the synonym of political power. Whoever has military power is bound to have political power. Unfortunately, China's modern history has reinforced this traditional wisdom.

Toward the end of the nineteenth century, Sun Yatsen, a Hawaiian-born, overseas Chinese, returned to China with western ideas of freedom and democracy. His ideas drew a large group of followers whose efforts, coupled with a series of western intrusions after the Opium War, led to the downfall of China's last feudal society in 1912.[2] However, the revolutionaries failed to gain rule over the country. Yuan Shikai, a more powerful military man who had no sympathy for Sun Yatsen's revolution and ideology, became the president of the new republic.[3] As Sun Yatsen's ideas were not being carried out, he sought Soviet aid to establish his own military academy in Canton, the Huangpu Military Academy, to train a military officer corps for the Nationalist government that he established.[4] After he died of illness on 12 March 1925, warfare broke out among warlords everywhere. Chiang Kaishek, one of Sun Yatsen's followers and president of the Huangpu Military Academy, launched his war against the military warlords in central and north China in 1927 with his Huangpu army. Chiang quickly gained control of the vast territory of China proper. The Chinese communists also took an active part in Chiang's expedition. The Communist party was also formed in this time period, with its first national conference held on 1 July 1921. Though small in number, communists were an active influential group within the Nationalist government and army, because of Sun Yatsen's policy of "Uniting the Russians, the Communists and Assisting the Workers and Peasants." In fact, the vanguard Chiang Kaishek's North Expedition Army was led by Ye Ting, a communist, and many soldiers and officers in his regiment were communists. Once Chiang Kaishek had defeated the other warlords, he launched a military coup d'etat, gained control of the government, and began an anti-communist purge. He believed that the communists were so dangerous that he later issued an order to his troops to "rather kill 3000 by mistake than to let go of a single one of them."[5] As a result, the Chinese communists started to build their own military.

In August 1, 1927, Zhou Enlai (the premier of the People's Republic of China from 1949 to 1976), Zhu De, Ye Ting, Ho Long, and Xiao Ke, all communists, led a military insurrection in Nanchang, Jiangxi Province. Four thousand of Ye Ting's troops and a few companies under Zhu De's local police participated. One month later, Mao Tsetung (later chairman of the People's Republic of China until 1976) and others organized a series of Autumn Harvest peasant uprisings in Hunan Province. In November, Mao set up the first permanent communist regime, "the Chinese Soviet" at Chalin, Hunan. Both Zhu De and Mao Tsetung's uprisings were defeated quickly. Mao withdrew his troops into the Jingang Mountains at the border area of Jiangxi and Hunan provinces. In a small village named San Wan in the Jingang Mountain area, Mao reformed his peasant army by establishing communist party systems within the army. Down to the company level, there was a political commissar. At the squad and platoon level, there were formal party groups. In May 1928, the troops from the Nanchang Insurrection and the Autumn Harvest Uprising joined together in the Jingang Mountains, forming the earliest Chinese national military—the Fourth Army of the Red Army of the Chinese Workers and Peasants, commanded by Zhu De with Mao Tsetung as the political commissar.

Because the new army consisted of soldiers from old armies, war captives, and peasants from various uprisings, discipline was of foremost importance. In the spring of 1928, Mao set down three disciplinary rules. Later in the summer, he added other points for attention. These rules and points were reissued in 1947 with some language modifications when the communists' military forces were about to stage a massive offensive against all the Nationalist-ruled areas and take over all of China. The three disciplinary rules read: "1). Obey orders in all your actions; 2). Don't take a single needle or piece of thread from the masses; 3). Turn in everything captured." The points for attention read: "1). speak politely; 2). pay fairly for what you buy; 3). return everything you borrow; 4). pay for anything you damage; 5). don't hit or swear at people; 6). don't damage crops; 7). don't take liberties with women; 8). do not ill-treat captives."[6] These rules and points for attention were Mao's earliest attempt to define a civil-military relationship between his army and the people. They made a major difference in the people's view of Mao's army. This tradition is one of the two claimed treasures that led the communists to win all of China.

The other "treasure" is the "party leadership." It should be noted that both nationalists and communists emphasized the role of the party. Chiang Kaishek and his men called his regime the Party's State (Dangguo). Mao and his men emphasized the central leadership of the party and made no apology for listing the party before the country and the people in their formal documents. The western world has always wondered how the Communist leadership had effectively and efficiently used its armed forces for a wide variety of extramilitary purposes while averting the crisis of military domination or takeover.[7] One important reason is its emphasis on the supremacy of the party. The military is only a tool of the party, having as its mission to accomplish what the party directs (see, for example, Yang, 1959). This point is succinctly expressed by Mao in the resolution of the 1929 historic Gutian Conference. "The Red Army is an armed group whose responsibility is executing class-oriented political tasks. In addition to fighting battles, it must also carry out the tasks of conducting propaganda among the masses, organizing the arming of the masses, and creating organizations of political power. Otherwise fighting would lose its significance and the existence of the Red Army would lose all meaning."[8]

The Gutian Conference was a party congress in the Fourth Army of the Red Army, the central military forces of the Chinese communists. The conference was meant to correct the nonproletariat tendencies of the army.[9] In the resolution, later entitled "On Correcting Mistaken Ideas in the Party" in Mao's selected works,[10] Mao systematically criticized "the pure military viewpoint," "ultra-democracy tendencies which disregard central party decisions and organizational principles," "roving-rebel ideology," and formally crystallized the methods of political penetration of the party into the military to guarantee political control. The resolution specified the rules of the game for a "two-line-

command'' system in the Chinese military (the military officer command line
and the political commissar command line)[11] and institutionalized the idea that
at every level of the military, starting from the company and up, there should
be a political commissar in charge of education, ideology indoctrination, mobilization, mass work, and party system maintenance within the unit. The political system headed by the political commissar at each military unit also served
as a balance check on the behavior and decisions of the military commanders
(captain, colonel, general, etc.). This conference was a landmark in the building
of the Chinese army and laid the foundations for the long-lasting principles of
the Chinese military. The missions, the organizational methods, and the role of
the Chinese military in China's politics were explicitly defined then by Mao
Tsetung. The conference also served as the first of a series of rectification campaigns within the army to build a new type of military force governed by the
high type of ideological leadership.[12]

The appropriate political role of the military was later reemphasized in another
article titled with Mao's well-known dictum that ''political power grows out of
the barrel of a gun.'' In this article, Mao wrote:

Our principle is that the Party commands the gun, and the gun will never be allowed to
command the Party. But it is also true that with guns at our disposal we can really build
up the Party organizations, and the Eighth Route Army has built up a powerful Party
organization in North China. We can also rear cadres, create schools, culture and mass
movements. Everything in Yanan has been built up by means of the gun. Anything can
grow out the barrel of a gun. According to the Marxist theory of the state, the army is
the chief component of the political power of the state. Whoever wants to seize the
political power of the state and to maintain it must have a strong army.[13]

The identification with and concern for the people and an adherence to party
leadership became two major principles of the Chinese communist military. The
first principle entails the military's mission to serve the masses, to protect them,
and to be concerned with their welfare. The second principle establishes the
absolute authority of the party over the ''military,'' defining the military as a
multifunction tool of the party. This principle requires the military to serve both
as a fighting force engaging in battles to protect the party's leadership and as a
working force that educates, organizes, and mobilizes people for the party's
cause, which in theory is also the cause of the people.

In the years between the formation of the Red Army and the founding of the
Chinese People's Republic, the names and the professed tasks of the Chinese
communist military altered several times,[14] but these two basic principles remained unchanged. Mao and his central government had always sustained a
strong grip over the military establishment,[15] and that military had always kept
a ''fish-and-water relationship'' with the people. Wherever the People's Liberation Army (PLA) went, it helped to create or strengthen the local communist
regime and helped with the creation of schools and with the allocation of land

and food for the peasants. The peasants likewise showed their enthusiastic support for the PLA. They sent their children to join the army. The people would rather have been killed themselves than give up the communist soldiers they hid during the waves of massive encirclements by Chiang Kaishek's troops (1928–34). The soldiers would rather have died of hunger than to touch the food left behind by the civilians during the Long March (1934–35). The army and the people fought a guerrilla war side by side against the Japanese during the anti-Japanese war (1937–45). Thousands of peasants and militia travelled hundreds of miles with their single-wheel carts[16] or with cattle on their shoulders to transport military supplies for the millions of soldiers in the People's Liberation Army in their offensive to take over southern China. All these were outcomes of the exemplary "mass line" of the Chinese military. Without the people's support, the PLA's victory over the Chiang Kaishek troops, which were several times more numerous than the PLA at the beginning of the Third Civil War,[17] would not have been possible. Few military forces in Chinese history, including that of Chiang Kaishek's, have enjoyed such enthusiastic and massive support from the people. The communist victory in China came as a surprise to many western politicians as well as to western China watchers. Some to this day are still trying to look for other reasons that can account for these happenings. To the Chinese communists themselves, their victory was a result of their insistence that the military is an inseparable part of the masses and that the military is a multifunctional tool subject to control by the political leadership of the party.

From the very beginning the Chinese military was an integral part of Chinese politics. The PLA not only "fought and won one of the greatest revolutionary wars in human history, played an active role in the creation of Communist power in China, it also participated extensively and effectively in economic and social transformation." This later role is even more evident in the years of the post-liberation socialist nation-building.

PROCESSES AND MEANS THROUGH WHICH THE MILITARY INTERACTS WITH DOMESTIC POLITICS

As in many developing countries, the Chinese military (the PLA) played a vital role in the creation and protection of a civilian regime, both internationally and domestically. However, unlike the military in other developing countries, the PLA also played an extensive role in civilian politics and social transformation.

Important military functions of the PLA after 1949 included campaigns launched to wipe out the remnants of Nationalist troops, warlords, and bandits in order to stabilize the social order (1948–55); the Korean War to fight against international threats to the existence of the communist regime (1950–53); the "peaceful liberation of Tibet" (1950); the military oppression of the insurrection of the Dalai Lama's local forces (1959); the China-Indian border war (1962);

the China-Soviet border war (1969–73); the China-Vietnam skirmishes in the South China Sea (1974); and the China-Vietnam border war (1979).[18] In the 1990s, the PLA continues to threaten to solve the mainland China and Taiwan problem by force. In a way, each of these events reasserted the importance of the PLA and gave it more weight in domestic politics. However, what really gives the PLA the power of influence over domestic politics is its performance of its designated extramilitary duties.

One of the most important ways that the PLA exercises its influence over civilian politics has been the massive transfer of military personnel to the leading posts at various levels of civilian government.[19] The tradition started in the late 1940s and early 1950s, when the Communists envisioned their full-scale victory over the nationalist government. In a telegram sent to the field armies fighting the final battles in February 1949, Mao wrote:

The army is not only a fighting force. It is mainly a working force. All army cadres should learn how to take over and administer cities. . . . The occupation of eight or nine provinces and scores of big cities will require a high number of working cadres, and to solve this problem the army must rely chiefly on itself. The army is a school. Our field armies of 2,100,000 are equivalent to several thousand universities and secondary schools. We have to rely chiefly on the army to supply our working cadres.[20]

This method was used well into the 1970s. The military officers retired from the military not as average civilians, but as leading cadres. Often, they were assigned to work as party secretaries, mayors, department heads, and factory managers. There were established protocols that certain levels of military officers should be given a job of equivalent rank and importance in civilian government, thus taking to civilian life the ideology, skills, methods, and, most important, loyalty to the party that they had acquired from their military life. They also held a loyalty to the military leaders in charge of the branch of military that they came from; not infrequently, returned military cadres go to their old leaders, now also civilian cadres at a higher level of government, for help in solving local problems. With retired military officers stationed in all walks of life and at every level of government carrying out the ''Party line,'' the communist social and cultural transformation was extremely successful.

However, the effectiveness of this method has been on the decline since the early 1980s for a number of reasons. First, Deng Xiaoping started his economic reform, which called for a respect for knowledge, specialization, and local initiatives. As most of the former military men have a rural background and no college degree, their previous military experiences were inadequate in competing with college graduates in terms of their management capabilities.[21] Second, the increased sense of pragmatism and the downgrading of political studies accompanied by economic reform reduced the importance of the role of political leaders at all workplaces. Many cadres in charge of political inculcation (most of them retired military cadres) have actually little to do. Third, the bloated bureaucracy at all government levels, plus the massive military personnel reduction implemented since 1978, created too many middle-level bureaucrats; and the retired military officers after 1978 had little real responsibility. Fourth, the retired military men are less highly regarded, as they were the results of the military's efforts to downsize.[22] If Deng's reform deepens and his emphasis on the professionalization of the military prevails, this method of military influence over civilian life is likely to decline further in prominence.

A second means the military employs in influencing civilian politics is model building. The Chinese military men have always been praised as the most altruistic and disciplined men who understand the difficulties and problems of others and are always willing to help. Starting in the 1960s, with Lin Biao as the chief military man,[23] the PLA initiated a series of mass campaigns with a strong political-ideological reorientation. After the failure of the "Big Leap Forward,"[24] Mao's authority was seriously challenged.[25] Liu Shaoqi, the vice chairman at that time, and his followers (including Deng Xiaoping) had long argued for another approach to socialist nation-building. The failure of the "Big Leap Forward" was proof that Mao's way did not work. Mao felt threatened. Lin Biao, seizing this opportunity to win Mao's favor, headed campaigns such as the "Four First," the "Three-eight Work Styles," "Four Good Company," and "Five Good Soldiers."[26] These campaigns were first carried out within the army and then in the entire nation. A few soldiers[27] who died during incidents in saving civilian lives during this period of time were idolized as the heros for the whole nation to admire and emulate. Slogans appeared everywhere that the whole nation must learn from the PLA.[28] In 1964–65, the political work structure within the military was copied extensively by civilian bureaucracies, school systems, and economic enterprises. One example was the extensive establishment of political departments, which took charge of cadre personnel systems, propaganda, and education in areas of finance, trade, industry, and communications.[29] Examples of PLA soldiers helping civilian organizations to study Mao's works and handling political work were countless in the newspapers of those days. These movements attempted to induce political loyalty and ideological commitment to Mao himself. This work overshadowed the attempt to criticize Mao's "Big Leap Forward" movement and reasserted Mao's role as the sole and great leader of the Chinese revolution. This method of "Learning from the PLA" is still used; sending college students to the military for training after the June 4th Tiananmen crackdown of 1989 is a perfect example of this approach.

The "Learning from the PLA" movement protected Mao's image and position but did not totally solve his problems. People high in civilian positions pursued their own agendas. Feeling that he was surrounded by a large and disloyal bureaucracy, Mao started the Cultural Revolution.[30] But when the turmoil of the revolution began to threaten the stability of the basic social order,[31] the military intervened. This is a type of intervention perhaps no other military in the world has ever used.

At the start of the Cultural Revolution, the military was ordered specifically not to participate, but a time came when Mao felt the military had to step in. A directive coissued by the Chinese Communist Party Central Committee, the State Council, the Military Affairs Commission of the Central Committee, and the Cultural Revolutionary Group of the Central Committee on 23 January 1967 indicated:

All of our army's commanders and fighters must resolutely carry out Chairman Mao's directive. 1). The previous directives concerning the army's noninvolvement in the Cultural Revolution on the local level and other directives that violate the spirit of the above are all nullified. 2). Actively support the broad revolutionary masses' struggle to seize power. Whenever the genuine proletarian leftists ask the army to come to their aid, the army should dispatch a unit to actively support them.[32]

This is the well-known "Support the Left" movement. In essence, the military intervened to control all levels of government by participating in the revolutionary activities. Prior to this, the governing bodies of many state and local governments were essentially destroyed. In other places, where the forces supporting the older establishments were still strong, Mao's intention to do away with the old system was not realized. Mao ordered the military to send working units to each level of government to establish a revolutionary committee consisting of revolutionary leaders, some previous officials who agreed to be on the revolutionary side, and the head of the military working unit. The military person normally served as the first party secretary or executive committee, with absolute power over resource allocation, production direction, and determination of the political destiny of the individuals working in that organization.

The "Support the Left"[33] movement quickly stabilized the situation, however, at the expense of labeling many loyal communists as counterrevolutionaries, as Mao wanted because he intended to do away with the old administrative system and start over afresh. In many cases, the military supported those who were the most revolutionary, most destructive, and more often than not the most unpopular groups. Without the support of the military, many "new revolutionaries" would never have gained any legitimacy.

While the military was effective in achieving Mao's political purpose, the Chinese people, the military, and Mao himself all paid a heavy price. Mao won a personal victory over his political foes, such as Liu Shaoqi and Deng Xiaoping. However, his image as the savior of the Chinese people and the nation was heavily damaged by the "Support the Left" movement. Many military working units, through their ignorance of the local situation or in carrying out orders from above, supported ruthless, politically ambitious, and unpopular people who had no sense of conscience. The general public became disillusioned with the military and with Mao himself. Lin Biao, a military marshal and the minister of defense before the Cultural Revolution, became a new rival. In 1969, after the Ninth Congress, Lin Biao became the second most powerful man in the country and a constitutionally recognized successor to Mao. Later, as party vice chairman, he schemed to assassinate Mao, but the plan failed; Lin Biao died in a plane crash when fleeing to the Soviet Union in 1971.

The Cultural Revolution increased military representation at all levels of government,[34] and the whole country was virtually under military control. The military cared more about directives from above than about economic growth, people's livelihood, welfare, and citizen rights. The military's image as the army of the people was seriously shaken and created serious problems for the military for many years after the Cultural Revolution.

The fourth method the Chinese military used to intervene in civilian politics is reflected in the Hua Guofeng incident. Immediately after Mao's death in 1976, Mao's widow Jiang Qing and her supporters were planning to seize power. They were in control of the central media, and they had had a close relationship to Mao, China's god. They had the leverage to oppose Mao's supposedly appointed successor, Hua Guofeng. However, Ye Jianying, a military-power man and then vice chairman of the Chinese Military Commission,[35] organized a military coup using the Beijing Garrison troops. They arrested Mao's widow and her aide Wang Hongweng, Zhang Chunqiang, and Yao Wengyuan. This intervention guaranteed Hua's temporary position and the future rise of Deng Xiaoping to power.

The fifth way that the Chinese military has intervened in civilian politics is what the western world called the exercise of "martial law." This approach had rarely been used since 1949, until it resurfaced in 1988 in Lasa, Tibet. Reportedly, when demonstrations facilitated by the Dalai Lama and his men in the Lasa streets to oust communist rule in Tibet turned into riots, Yang Shankun, the chairman of the Chinese Military Commission called for martial law in Tibet. Although the uprising was quickly controlled, a precedent was set for armed military confrontation with unarmed civilians. When massive student demonstrations in 1989 were out of control, some central leaders in Beijing summoned the military, resulting in the world-shocking people-military confrontation. Martial law stabilized the political disputes between the party hardliners and the reformers and the people through the use of force to suppress the disagreement. It also sent out a strong signal that the water-fish relationship between the military and the people was no longer treasured. The Tiananmen crackdown again increased the importance of the military role in civilian government. In the party's Fourteenth Congress, held in October 1992, twenty-two military officers were elected into the party's Central Committee; and one career military man, Liu Huaqing, entered the highest, seven-member civilian governing body, the Standing Committee of the Political Bureau of the Communist Party. The increased awareness of military importance in domestic politics serves as a coercive power to check challenges against the Central Committee's governing authority.

Since liberation, the Chinese military has continued its traditional active role in China's politics. However, at no time has it gained complete control of the civilian government. The Lin Biao case came closest to complete military control, but his legitimacy to rule did not emanate from his military power but from his endorsement by Mao as the recognized civilian leader. By emphasizing that the military is the tool of the party and by establishing powerful controlling mechanisms within the military, Mao's military system has made it extremely hard for any single military commander to gain full control of the military power or to achieve legitimacy for the governance of civilian affairs through the use of coercive military power. Yet the party supremacy system gives the party leaders a chance to migrate between the military and civilian systems. For example, Deng Xiaoping, the political commissar of the second field army during the liberation war period (1946–49), was a typical military officer. In the 1960s, he served as secretary of the Central Committee's Secretariat, a civilian party job. After his downfall during the Cultural Revolution, he rose again as the vice chairman of the Central Military Commission and chief of staff of the Chinese military (1975), a typical military position; later he was vice premier of the State Council. As the party is above both the army and the civilian government, many military officers can legitimately become civilian officials and participate in the governance of civilian affairs. Liu Huaqing, a career military man and former commander of the navy, now serves as a member of the Standing Committee of the Central Party Political Bureau. The party-military two-in-one system defines an intensive and unconventional political role for the military. It has also defined the approach for a military man to step into civilian affairs, by working through the party system.

FUTURE PROSPECTS OF THE CHINESE MILITARY'S POLITICAL ROLE

Since 1975, when Deng Xiaoping became the vice chairman of the Central Military Commission and concurrently the chief of staff, he has brought about military reform. He began an endeavor to reduce the size of the bloated army and to solve the problem of factionalism carried over from the cultural revolution.[36] In 1981, he proposed the idea of "establishing a powerful, modernized, and professional revolutionary army.[37] This new direction is in tension with the Maoist tradition that the military should be a multifaceted team that can both fight and carry out tasks of mass mobilization. In his study of the military as a profession, Huntington argues that "the distinguishing characteristics of a profession as a special type of vocation are its expertise, responsibility, and corporateness."[38] If this is indeed the case, Kau argues,

The professional is marked by his specialized knowledge and skills in a vocation, which are acquired only through prolonged training and experience. As a result of this process, he internalized a code of professional ethics and a sense of social responsibility through the process of socialization into the profession. . . . Once the military becomes highly professionalized . . . the military man is likely to be proud of his special training and competence in military affairs and to guard jealously his professional autonomy, prerogatives, and authority against outside interference. Any external attempt to impose control over what professionals, in this case the military, define as their legitimate activities is bound to be resented and resisted.[39]

In fact, the military's professional orientation and resentment of party control was strong in the early 1950s, when Peng Dehuai, then minister of defense, advocated a military professional orientation by arguing that "we must intensify our study of modern military science and technique, the art of commanding a modernized army in battle and new military system."[40] Peng's idea was later criticized as revisionist by Mao and his successor Lin Biao; and Mao's model of political work supremacy was reasserted, illustrating the tension between professionalization and party control. Before 1989, many argued that the military should be a professional, modernized army independent of politics, but they were hushed. The Fourteenth Congress of the Communist Party in 1992 urged the need to build a modern and professional army, but one under the strict leadership of the party. Liu Huaqing called for a powerful, modernized, and professionalized army.[41] However, Zhang Zhen, a new vice chairman of the Central Military Commission, led a group of military officers to visit the Jingang Mountains after the Fourteenth Congress in order to reassert Mao's tradition that the party commands the gun. A recent *PLA Daily* (official newspaper of the PLA) commentary was titled, "The Army Should Obey the Party: Second Discussion on Carrying Forward the Traditions and Retaining the True Qualities of the Old Red Army."[42] This unique combination contains within it a tension between the traditional role of jack-of-all-trades and the modern role of a professional army. Though the tension may be suppressed by force at the initial stages, inevitably it will resurge as the professional level of the army increases and the absolute power of the party leaders diminishes.

Another issue related to army modernization is to what extent a changed military organization strategy would affect the political role of the army. Currently, the PLA is organized in such a way that its navy, air force, artillery troops, military academy system, military industry system, and seven major military regions and garrison troops are relatively independent army units. Each unit is capable of massive striking capabilities and is able to conduct independent battles. Units are also geographically and strategically dispersed and are powerful intermediate checks against each other and against any individual military man trying to gain power in the central government. No single military commander is powerful enough to control the political situation by force. This organizational strategy, however, has its shortcomings. It is not flexible enough for coordinated modern battles, and it can easily be manipulated by powerful field military leaders to resist the orders of the central government. Both Mao and Deng worked hard to control the military field commanders, even though both of them had indisputable political and military charisma. Military modernization calls for more integrated military command within the military system.

Military professionalization demands the downplay of charisma. If reorganization is conducted so that the commanding power of all the military regions, navy, airforce, and artillery are in the hands of a few career military men, the chances of coercive military power being used to interfere with politics will be much higher.

A third antithesis is that between economic reform and the military's political role. The economic reform movement is drastically changing the way people think and behave. An army career, which was viewed as glorious, is now viewed by many as a waste of time. Today's soldiers are mostly conscripted from young people who failed to get into universities, foreign-venture businesses, or other skilled professions. Unlike in the early 1960s and the 1970s, when many aspiring young men sought military careers, the best opportunities for young people in the 1990s seem to lie in business, entrepreneurship, or higher education. An old Chinese saying, "Good men don't make soldiers," seems to be in fashion again. Recruiting high-quality soldiers has already become a problem. Economic reform has also been creating and will continue to create a large middle class, who will eventually demand political democratization and participation. The newly risen middle class will be a powerful force in the governing of the nation, resisting military attempts to interfere with domestic politics. The chances for retired military men to control leading positions will diminish; they will need to start afresh and work their way up again in civilian careers like many retired military officers in the West. If the economic reform can continue peacefully for another five to ten years, the chances for an active political role by the military will be drastically reduced.

History has illustrated a successful political role for the Chinese military, but with heavy costs. The "Support the Left" movement during the Cultural Revolution and the Tiananmen Square military action exemplified such costs at the extreme. The involvement of the military in civilian politics and the use of the military as a tool to suppress differences between the people and the government threatens the legitimacy of the government and undermines popular support. Now that the "mass line" is heavily devastated, will "party leadership" alone solve the governing crisis of the party? Chiang Kaishek's loss of China provided a forceful answer.

Nevertheless, different Chinese leaders may have learned different lessons from the previous incident. Ambitious military men may view the Lin Biao and Tiananmen incidents as positive examples of asserting the rule of the communist regime. Reformists worry that the military presence in civilian affairs will hold back the country's reform endeavor. Deng Xiaoping, trapped in his desire for modernization and his nostalgia for "the glorious revolutionary past and unified totalitarian control," is constantly fighting the dilemma of introducing more economic vitality while trying to subdue ideological diversity. The antithesis he created made it hard for even his closest aides to launch any initiatives, either moving forward toward more reform or surrendering to the conservative party elders. This is exactly why Hu Yaoban, Zhao Ziyang, and even Jiang Zeming, his handpicked men, can hardly understand what he really wants.

Deng is reportedly trying to shuffle the military again in order to ensure that there is no trouble for the new generation of party leaders, none of whom has had a strong military background. The current campaign that the military should obey the party can be seen as Deng's effort to get the military back to barracks, a strategy he enticed Mao to use in 1975 to control the military after the chaotic Cultural Revolution. Deng could succeed again, on condition that further economic reform continues without a serious threat to the communist regime. Deng's mode of thinking is becoming more discernible. He has considered the party and the central leader to be the elite representatives of the people. When people were against the party and the leader, the people were just not smart enough to understand the good intentions of the party leadership. The precedent has been established that they have gone as far as to use the military to suppress any threats to their regime. The question is, if new military actions occur after Deng's death, can the new generation of party leaders, many of whom had no military background, get the military back to the barracks? The answer can hardly be positive.

NOTES

1. Qing Shi Huang, Han Wu Di, Tang Tai Zong, Song Tai Zu, Qing Shi Zu, etc.

2. Sun Yat-sen's Xin Hai Revolution happened in 1911. On 12 February 1912, the Empress Dowager Lung Yu renounced in the name of the Child Emperor Xuan Tong the Mandate of Heaven his imperial ancestor Shun Zhi had acquired in 1644. See Samuel B. Griffith II, *The Chinese People's Liberation Army* (New York: McGraw-Hill, 1967), p. 1.

3. Yuan proclaimed himself the new emperor in December 1915, the fifth year after the 1911 revolution. He died on 6 June 1916. His position and power disappeared with his death.

4. At the Huang Pu's (Whampoa) opening address, Sun Yat-sen stated: "We have established this academy in the hope that the revolutionary movement may be revitalized. Therefore you, the cadets of this academy, must dedicate yourselves to forming the backbone of the revolutionary army. Otherwise, failing to achieve this armed might, the Chinese revolution will be foredoomed from its beginning. This academy, therefore, has the sole purpose of creating a new revolutionary army for the salvation of China." See F. F. Liu, *A Military History of Modern China* (Princeton: Princeton University Press, 1956), p. 8.

5. He was sent as a representative of Sun Yat-sen to visit the Soviet Union in 1925, but the destructive behavior in the Soviet Union changed his attitudes towards communism. He said on a number of occasions later that China should not go the Russian way.

6. Mao Tse-tung, *Selected Military Writings* (Peking: Peking Foreign Language Press, 1961), p. 155. The last two points for attention were added after 1929.

7. Kau, Ying-Mao, *The People's Liberation Army and China's Nation Building* (White Plains, N.Y.: International Arts and Sciences Press, 1973), p. 106.

8. Mao Tse-tung, *Selected Military Writings* (Peking: Peking Foreign Language Press, 1929), p. 106.

9. See *Selected Works of Mao Tsetung* (Peking: Foreign Languages Press, 1966), p. 80.

10. See ibid., pp. 105–116.

11. For example, in the section on the "Question of the Relations between the Military and Political Systems of the Red Army" in Mao's presentation at the Gutian Conference, Part C reads: "In all matters of provisions, health, the march, combat, pitching camp, etc., the political system should accept the direction of the military system. In all matters of political training and mass work, the military systems should accept the direction of political system." See Kau, *The People's Liberation Army*, p. 50.

12. Kau, *The People's Liberation Army*.

13. Mao Tsetung, *Selected Works of Mao Tsetung*, 1954, p. 272.

14. In 1937, the Red Army changed its name to the Eighth Route Army, its major task to anti-Japanese invasion. In 1946, the Red Army changed its name to the People's Liberation Army, with its major task as "down with Jiang Kai-shek and liberate the whole China."

15. Except for a short period of time between 1932 and 1934, when Mao was deprived of his military command by the Communist International.

16. A typical transportation tool of the Chinese peasants. It can carry from two hundred to three hundred pounds of goods, depending on the strength of the operator.

17. Mainland Chinese historians divide their military history into four periods: the First Civil War Period (1925–27, the North Expedition War), the Second Civil War Period (1927–36, the five anti-Nationalist encirclements and the Long March), the Anti-Japanese War Period (1937–45), and the Third Civil War Period (1946–49). In July 1946, the Nationalist Party headed by Jiang Kai-shek had 4,300,000 men; the Communist party had 1,200,000 men (see Mao, *Selected Works of Mao Tse-Tung*, 1961, p. 287).

18. The war against Vietnam is publicized in China as the Chinese Self-defense Attack against Vietnam. In Deng Xiaoping's words, it is meant to teach Vietnam a lesson so that it would stop making trouble along the border.

19. Kau, *The People's Liberation Army*, p. xiv.

20. Mao Tsetung, *Selected Works of Mao Tsetung*, 1962, pp. 337–338.

21. Intellectuals had never been duly respected since the liberation. Mao treated them as hairs attached to the skin (the masses). When there is a problem, it is the skin that should be protected first. Further, intellectuals were not considered to be part of the proletariat, the leading force of the society. They should be led instead of leading. During the Cultural Revolution, the social status of intellectuals sunk to a new low, worse than even the enemy. Deng's call for respect for knowledge is the first time in the forty years since liberation that the party has consciously promoted intellectuals to leading posts.

22. One million men were cut in the first few years of the 1980s.

23. Lin Biao was appointed the Minister of Defense in 1959. He started to use his military power to catch the attention of Mao and succeeded very well.

24. In 1958, Mao initiated an economic movement named "Big Leap Forward," owing to pressure coming from the western world as well as the Soviet. He vowed to catch up with the western industrialized world within a fixed number of years (e.g., in fifteen years surpassing Great Britain). He forcefully demanded a high yield in industrial and agricultural products, a high level of communitarian life symbolizing the level of com-

munist society, and so on. These campaigns led to high consumption and nonproduction, with time and energy spent in making up false reports. Together with natural disasters and the repayment of the Soviet debt, these results meant that thousands died of hunger and disease.

25. Mao reluctantly admitted his faults in 1962, during a national conference chaired by his rival Liu Shaoqi and attended by seven thousand senior and mid-level civilian officials.

26. The "Four First" stresses "the human factor first with regard to the relationship between men and weapons, political work first with regard to the relationship between political work and various other work, ideological work first within political work, and living ideology first within ideological work." The "Three-eight Style" refers to three phrases and four characteristics (eight Chinese words) enumerated by Mao: a firm and correct political direction, a preserving and simple style of work, and flexible strategy and tactics and "unity, intensity, solemnity, and liveliness." The "Four Good Company" requires the military companies to compete for "goodness in political and ideological work, goodness in the three-eight work style, goodness in military training, and goodness in management of army livelihood." The "Five Good Soldier" movement encourages soldiers to be "good in political ideology, good in military techniques, good in the three-eight work style, good in carrying out assigned tasks, and good in physical training."

27. Lei Geng, Wang Jie, Ouyan Hai, Mai Xiande.

28. See "The Whole Country Must Learn from the PLA," *People's Daily,* 1 February 1964.

29. See, for example, *People's Daily,* 7 June and 30 September 1964.

30. The Cultural Revolution was started in 1966 with the intention to criticize the "Capitalist Roaders with the Communist Party." It is essentially a political movement by which Mao was to get rid of his rivals. He planned it to be one or two years long. However, once things were stirred up, it rolled on for ten years, and its aftermath is still strongly felt today.

31. The basic political order was tumbled over. Party organs, public security, and governmental organizations were paralyzed because their leaders were criticized by the masses as capitalist roaders. Everyone who could assemble a team of supporters could easily claim himself as the representative of Mao's correct political line, thus gaining the power to imprison and even kill people he did not like.

32. Also known as "Three Support and Two Militarization": support agriculture and support the left; militarize governing control and militarize people training.

33. Kao, *The People's Liberation Army,* p. 316.

34. See, for example, Kao, *The People's Liberation Army,* p. xvii. Out of the twenty-five political bureau members between 1969 and 1971, thirteen were military men; 70% of the provincial revolutionary committee chairmen were military men; and so on.

35. Mao was the Chairman.

36. See Deng's speech "The Military Needs to be Consolidated and Rectified," made on 25 January 1975, from *Selected Works of Den Xiaoping* (Beijing: People's Press, 1983).

37. See Deng Xiaoping, *Selected Works of Deng Xiaoping,* p. 349.

38. See, for example, Samuel P. Huntington, *The Soldier and the State* (Cambridge: Harvard University Press, 1957), p. 8.

39. Kau, *The People's Liberation Army,* p. xxxix.

40. Kau, *The People's Liberation Army,* p. xli.
41. *People's Daily,* 16 October 1992.
42. *Foreign Broadcast Information Service,* 13 November 1993, p. 42.

REFERENCES

Deng Xiaoping, *Selected Works of Deng Xiaoping.* Beijing: People's Press, 1983.

Gittings, John. *The Role of the Chinese Army.* London: Oxford University Press, 1967.

Jane's Information Group Limited. *China in Crisis: The Role of the Military.* Surrey: Jane's Information Group Limited, 1989.

Joffe, Ellis. *The Chinese Army after Mao.* London: Weidenfeld and Nicolson, 1987.

Kau, Ying-Mao. *The People's Liberation Army and China's Nation Building.* White Plains: International Arts and Sciences Press, 1973.

Lin, Changsheng, "A Model of the Chinese Party-Military Relations," *Journal of Exploration* (Hong Kong. September 1992), pp. 31–37.

Liu, Bih-rong. "Communist China's Civil-Military Relations in the Mid-1980s: The Implications of Modernization," in Yu-ming Shaw, ed., *Continuities in Chinese Communism,* 211–29. Boulder: Westview Press, 1988.

Mao Tse-tung, *Selected Military Writings.* Beijing: Foreign Language Press, 1966.

CUBA

Sharyl Cross

While a democratization wave has swept away military regimes throughout Latin America during the last decade and the communist totalitarian edifice in the former Soviet Union and Eastern Europe has crumbled, there has been no accompanying fundamental alteration in the militaristic and authoritarian traditions of Fidel Castro's Cuba. The Cuban leader was intransigent in responding to the political and economic reforms transforming the societies of his neighbors and former allies by vowing *"socialismo o muerte"* (socialism or death).

The Cuban revolutionary state has survived as the sole Marxist-Leninist regime in the Western Hemisphere almost exclusively on the basis of the overwhelming charismatic appeal of Fidel Castro, support from the former Soviet Union and Eastern bloc nations, and the allegiance of Cuba's Revolutionary Armed Forces (FAR) and other defense and security institutions. The collapse of the Soviet Union has meant the severing of Cuba's material lifeline. The military and the military-directed security apparatus will be critical in determining whether the Castro regime survives in the short term and in influencing future political outcomes. This chapter discusses the historical foundations of the contemporary militarized Cuban state, the evolution of civil-military relations, and the missions of Cuba's armed forces. The chapter also examines the impact of the collapse of the Soviet Union on Cuba's military and its future prospects.

HISTORICAL TRADITIONS

The military has assumed a role of disproportionate significance in the development of most nations in Latin America. In a region that has experienced a colonial heritage, stifling the development of viable political institutions, military force has often served as the only source of stability and functional government. *Caudillismo,* or the supreme reign of the military strong man, has colored Latin America's political mosaic. Beset by political turbulence and violence, many countries of the region have been prone to resort to military intervention. Cuba is no exception to this pattern.

Several historical tendencies provided the impetus for the emergence of the contemporary militarized Cuban state and society. Indeed, the military has been the predominant force in Cuba for centuries. Many of the first governors of the island were military officials sent from Spain. Because of Cuba's location in the Caribbean, it has always held significant strategic value; and the clash of foreign powers for influence in Cuba has contributed to militarization of the island.

Cuba's history is replete with instances of U.S. intervention prompted by the desire to protect its security and economic interests on the island. In an effort to establish hegemony in the Western Hemisphere, U.S. forces assisted Cuba in achieving liberation from Spain in 1898. Following independence, a U.S. military government remained in Cuba until 1902; under the auspices of the Platt Amendment, legitimizing the U.S. right to intervene in Cuba, Washington sent forces to maintain order on the island in the early post-independence period in 1906–1909, 1912, and 1917.

Prompted by an uprising in 1906 against the government of Tomas Estrada Palma, who served as the first president of the new republic following U.S. occupation, the United States assisted in creating Cuba's first professional military force. American forces promoted the conversion of the Cuban Rural Guard into the professional permanent army. The collaboration of Washington with Cuban military officials in pursuit of their respective interests would prove decisive in subsequent political developments.

As might have been anticipated, the military assumed a paramount role in Cuba's post-independence politics. Although the military intervened to oust elected leaders only twice, in 1933 and 1952, Cuban presidential figures relied on the military as the key source of power, to the exclusion of other governmental institutions. This was most evident during the rule of Gerardo Machado (1924–33) and Fulgencio Batista (1940–44 and 1952–59). Both leaders had been serving in the army at the time when they made successful bids for power.

Cuban political life during the Machado and Batista eras was characterized by electoral fraudulence, periodic suspensions of legislative and judicial power, restrictions on civil liberties and the press, and sometimes outright terror and violence against the population. The military was coopted with resources and promotions. Ultimately, the failure to maintain military allegiance in face of increasing domestic unrest and the decline of U.S. confidence in the capacity of the Cuban leadership to maintain stability brought about the collapse of both the Machado and the Batista regimes.

The armed forces also frequently performed duties outside the typical professional domain. During the Machado and Batista periods, military officers occupied key governmental administrative positions and sometimes assumed the responsibility for providing social services.

The national heroes and myths of the Cuban state were military, rather than civilian, figures and concepts. Jose Marti's death in the struggle for independence from Spain contributed to making him a revered historical figure. Fidel Castro resurrected Marti's image in achieving what appeared to be an impossible victory against a force of overwhelming advantage. Self-sacrifice and willingness to confront the superior enemy were the essential elements of the myth that gave impetus to the revolution.

Fidel Castro's guerrilla offensive found its antecedents in the struggle of the Cuban *mambises,* the independence fighters, in the Ten Years War (1868–78) and the War of Independence (1895–98). Cuban forces resorted to guerrilla warfare in carrying out skirmishes against the superior Spanish forces.

In 1953, Fidel Castro orchestrated an armed attack on the Moncada Barracks in Santiago de Cuba, hoping that, by issuing an impassioned appeal, he could incite a mass insurrection to topple the Batista dictatorship. Although the Moncada assault failed, it was the first military offensive by those who constituted the nucleus of Fidel Castro's Rebel Army, and it served as a precursor to the 1959 triumph.

Following their release from prison on the Isle of Pines in 1955, participants in the Moncada escapade joined Castro to form the Movement of July 26 (M-26-7). The M-26-7 carried out armed insurrection from the Sierra Maestra mountains, employing guerrilla tactics tailored to the Cuban context with the assistance of the Argentine Ernesto "Che" Guevara. Disloyalty and desertion from the ranks of Batista's military force, the U.S. arms embargo imposed on Cuba in 1958, and growing disaffection in society with the corrupt dictatorship all worked to Castro's advantage.

Unlike the Soviet armed forces, which emerged in the postrevolutionary civil war, Castro's guerrilla fighters executed the revolution in Cuba. The Bolsheviks carried out revolutionary victory primarily by political rather than by military means. Whereas the Communist Party had served as the major institution in the Soviet Union, the single leader who defeated the "oppressive" dictator and his Revolutionary Armed Forces (FAR) became the major sources for governing the new regime. Cuba's historical traditions set the stage for propelling the guerrillas to power.

THE MILITARY IN CASTRO'S CUBA

Fidel Castro triumphed with a moderate platform, *nuestra razon* (our purpose), calling for an end to corruption, democracy, and a relationship of "constructive justice" with the United States. He waged the revolution on the basis of patriotism, sacrifice, and *Cubanidad* (the essence of being Cuban). However, shortly after taking power, Castro moved to radicalize the revolution as he confronted suspicion, which rapidly evolved to outright hostility, on the part of the United States. Domestic and foreign enterprises were nationalized, and an Agrarian Reform Law was implemented. In 1961, the Cuban leader pronounced his commitment to Marxism-Leninism and thereby succeeded in binding the Soviet Union to support his project.

Castro did not initially attempt to institutionalize the Cuban state in the image of the USSR. Castro ruled in the tradition of *personalismo,* with ultimate power resting in the single charismatic authority. The *líder máximo* viewed himself as the modern-day Simón Bolívar, devoted to the cause of liberating Cuba and ultimately the entire Latin American continent from its subordinate relationship to the "North American oppressor."

In the immediate postrevolutionary period, there was no vanguard party. The successor to Castro's Rebel Army, the Revolutionary Armed Forces (FAR), was used to consolidate the revolution and to take control of the state apparatus and the economy. Themes of the revolution such as *la lucha* and *el cumplir de su deber* called for struggle against "counterrevolutionaries" and "imperialists" and justified the need for constant defense preparedness and for a permanent preeminent role for the military. The Bay of Pigs invasion and subsequent U.S. aggression gave credence to the argument that the beleaguered island must remain in a constant state of defense preparedness.

The National Revolutionary Militia (MNR) was created in 1959 to serve as a check against any potential opposition within the armed forces that might consider a plot against Castro and established a foundation for the militarization of nearly the entire society.[1] In 1963, a policy of three-year compulsory service for all young Cuban males was instituted.[2] By 1967, Cuba was maintaining the largest military force per capita in all of Latin America, with only Brazil exceeding percentages for Cuba since the late 1980s.[3] Cuba's defense expenditures ranged from 8% to 11% of GDP throughout the 1980s, compared with those of Brazil and other military regimes in Central America, which never exceeded 1% to 2% per year.[4] This figure is even more dramatic in that it did not include Soviet weaponry and other military aid provided annually to Cuba nearly gratis.[5]

Cuba's military arsenal includes hundreds of T-34 and T-54/-55 tanks, a wide array of missiles and rocket launchers, foxtrot submarines, koni-class frigates, and fast-attack and missile boats. The Cuban Air Force has acquired long-range transport planes, a number of Mi-8, Mi-17, and Mi-25 attack helicopters, and sophisticated MIG fighter aircraft capable of targeting neighboring states in Central America and the Caribbean and the southern United States. With Soviet equipment and training, Cuba developed the most modern and effective combat force in Latin America, enabling Castro to command attention on the world stage.

CIVIL-MILITARY RELATIONS

Relations among Castro, his Fidelista followers, and the predecessor of the Cuban Communist Party (PCC), the orthodox Popular Socialist Party (PSP) had been strained during the prerevolutionary period.[6] The PSP criticized Castro's Moncada assault as putschist adventurism and rendered no assistance in the M-

26-7 guerrilla offensive against Batista. Recognizing the PSP's value in solic-
iting Soviet assistance and in strengthening the domestic base of the revolution,
Castro moved to enlist the backing of the PSP in the aftermath of the guerrilla
victory. At the end of 1961, Castro promoted the establishment of the Integrated
Revolutionary Organization (ORI), merging the M-26-7, the PSP, and his revolutionary directorate. PSP member Anibal Escalante was assigned to administer
the organization of the ORI. Castro later dismissed Escalante, charging that he
was attempting to staff the ORI with PSP members, resulting in additional delay
in party formation.

Finally, in 1965, Fidel Castro announced that the new Communist Party of
Cuba (PCC) would be instituted to promote the transformation to socialism.
PCC membership increased from approximately sixty thousand in the late 1960s
to two hundred thousand in 1973, five hundred thousand in 1986, and six hundred thousand in 1992.[7]

From the inception of the PCC, there was a high degree of overlap between
the party and the military. Corresponding with the creation of the party in the
civilian sector, a party apparatus was created within the armed forces; and membership in the Communist Party became increasingly important for advancement
within the armed forces. The selection of the "exemplary combatant" was based
on "conduct," "discipline," "technical competence," and "political preparation."[8] Leadership posts in the party were traditionally occupied by active-duty
military men or veterans of the guerrilla war. More than two thirds of the
original Central Committee was composed of military and former military officials.[9]

The interlocking relationship between the party and the military helped to
diffuse institutional conflict more so than in other communist regimes where
such arrangements did not exist. For example, in the Soviet case, civil-military
strains have been explained as a by-product of the facts that military officers
did not monopolize leadership posts in the party and that the lines of demarcation between party and military were clearly defined. This is not to suggest
that there has never been tension between the PCC and FAR.[10] Military officials
have complained about issues such as party political indoctrination of the armed
forces and the meddling of political commissars in military affairs. In turn, party
members resented the military's failure consistently to take political training
seriously and have shown some resentment of the expenditure of resources on
military pursuits.

Some observers argued that the expansion of the Cuban Communist Party
(PCC), corresponding with the fashioning of the Cuban system in accordance
with the Soviet model in the 1970s, translated into diminished influence for the
armed forces.[11] William M. LeoGrande contended that the increased influence
of civilian institutions and differentiation of civil and military roles reduced the
influence of the military, while others argued that the expansion of the party
was not synonomous with demilitarization of Cuba.

Several factors are cited as evidence of the demilitarization of the Cuban state.

First, the Cuban Constitution of 1975 designated the party as the "highest lead-ing force of the state and society." The increased number of party members and the expanded influence of civilian, as opposed to military, officials in key governmental posts were offered as additional evidence. Finally, scholars argued that institutionalization of the revolution was accompanied by professionaliza-tion of the armed forces and that the FAR surrendered many of its nondefense functions to the civilian sector.

However, the first point that should be made is that changes undertaken in Cuba in the 1970s were prompted by Soviet urging. Moscow had always ex-pressed concern about Cuba's viability, given that the revolution rested on Fidel Castro's personal authority. As Edward Gonzalez and Irving Horowitz persua-sively argued, Castro, while succumbing to pressure to restructure Cuba in ac-cordance with the Soviet system, was careful not to relinquish his control.[12] For example, in conjunction with the expansion of the PCC, Castro placed loyal members of the FAR in key party and government leadership positions.

Furthermore, the deepening of Soviet-Cuban relations in the 1970s not only entailed expansion of the PCC but also involved increased military assistance from Moscow, enhancing the capacity of the FAR. In addition, military officers continue to constitute a sizeable portion of the Central Committee, 25 of 220 members in 1992.[13] Active-duty military officers continue to staff government ministries, presently including interior, communication, transportation, and fish-ing.[14] Also, despite growth in party membership, the PCC still includes only six of every one hundred Cuban citizens. Finally, although the military did begin to retreat from performing central economic tasks in the 1970s, instead focusing on international missions in Africa and elsewhere, it is now clear that this was only a temporary retreat. More recently, as the subsequent section will illustrate, the military has again been called to provide the manpower for production tasks.

MISSIONS OF THE CUBAN MILITARY FORCES

Though in many societies there are clearly identifiable distinctions between military and civilian officials and their respective duties, this is not so in Cuba. Jorge I. Dominguez has coined the term "civic soldier" to characterize the military officer in Cuba. Dominguez describes the "civic soldier" concept:

Cuba has been ruled in large part by military men who govern large segments of both military and civilian life, who are held up as paragons to both soldiers and civilians, . . . who have politicized themselves by absorbing the norms and organization of the Com-munist party, and who have educated themselves to become professional in political, economic, managerial, engineering, and educational as well as military affairs.[15]

Cuba's military personnel have performed military and security functions as well as production functions, depending on circumstances and priorities of the re-gime.

The Cuban military includes an army, navy and air force, with a combined active-duty enlistment of 175,000.[16] The Army of the Working Youth (UJT) and other paramilitary reserves provide thousands of additional personnel. The Territorial Troop Militia (MTT), including over one million people, was formed in 1981, and combined with the Committees for the Defense of the Revolution (CDRs), including 5.2 million people, create a militarized society that can be readily mobilized to meet the security and economic needs of the regime.[17]

Castro has frequently emphasized that Cuban society possesses the capacity to wage a "War of All the People," a protracted struggle that would enlist virtually the entire population in defense against an external aggressor. The government periodically stages civil emergency and defense exercises involving the armed forces and millions of Cuban citizens. For example, in May 1990, *Granma* reported that "Cuban Shield Maneuvers" were conducted involving "approximately one million militiamen, thousands of pieces of combat equipment, fighter planes and naval vessels."[18] The *Granma* report stated that these maneuvers, "prepared by the Cuban people," organized into the "regular FAR troops, the Territorial Troop Militia and societal Defense Brigades," had "increased preparedness" to "confront U.S. aggressors." A 1992 report stated that "millions of people" underwent training to "repel foreign attack" and that a program coined "Guerrillas 92" was initiated to enhance "guerrilla warfare preparation" and increase "revolutionary vigilance in neighborhoods, communities, student and work centers."[19]

The Cuban military and intelligence organizations are under the jurisdiction of two organizations, the MINFAR (Ministry of the Revolutionary Armed Forces) and the MININT (Ministry of Interior). MINFAR assumes responsibility for directing Cuba's army, navy, air force, and territorial troop militia; and MININT administers the national police and security and intelligence forces.[20] Cuba's intelligence organizations had closely coordinated their activities with the Soviet KGB. Although there had been some rivalry between FAR and MININT, recent staff changes have resulted in FAR predominance over MININT.[21]

In the early postrevolutionary period, the FAR created opportunities for guerrilla officers to assume important military and civilian posts. The military institution has identified closely with the working class and continues to offer a means of upward mobility for economically and socially disadvantaged groups.[22] One report indicates that blacks have advanced in the military under Castro, despite evidence of continued racial prejudice in the military.[23]

Several military academies were instituted in Cuba for training officers and rank-and-file members of the military.[24] Almost immediately after assuming power, the new leadership took on the task of educating what they described as "mostly illiterate" and "technically incompetent" guerrilla fighters. MINFAR's senior school for training middle- and upper-level officers, the General Maximo Gomez Revolutionary Armed Forces Academy, was established in 1963. The curriculum included courses in national security issues, military strategy, and leadership. Several other training academies offer courses paralleling civilian schools along with training in the use of various types of military equipment. Select Cuban military officers received instruction in the Soviet Union or pursued postgraduate study in the F. V. Frunze Military Academy in Moscow, and Soviet instructors taught in the Cuban military institutions.

Political training is also included in the military education programs. Curricula include courses in Marxism-Leninism, the history of the international revolutionary movement, and current political and economic issues. The FAR's weekly official publication, *Verde Olivo,* was also a vehicle for ongoing political education. *Verde Olivo* consistently offered Marxist interpretations of political, social, and economic phenomena, extolled Cuba's leaders, and promoted the siege mentality, calling for constant defense preparedness against internal and external threats to the regime. In addition, the training and education programs in the Cuban armed forces include engineering, agriculture, and other technical skills, thus equipping military personnel to assume many civilian duties.

Military training has also been promoted among Cuba's youth. The Camilo Cienfuegos schools for secondary education were established in the early postrevolutionary period. In 1980, the Society for Patriotic-Military Education (SEMPI) was created with the stated objective of inculcating Cuba's youth with the "spirit of socialist patriotism and internationalism."[25] SEMPI has provided both political and military training to thousands of children and young adults and serves as a screening function for higher-level military education. Such training has been increasingly promoted to help offset the declining faith among Cuba's youth in the aspirations of the revolutionary regime.

The military missions of the Cuban armed forces have included national defense, countering domestic and foreign subversion, the export of revolution, and participation in overseas combat. In the early postrevolutionary period, Cuba's armed forces struggled against "counterrevolutionaries" in the Escambray mountains and defended the Cuban state against the CIA-supported Bay of Pigs invasion. In the early 1960s, the armed forces were used to suppress attempted assaults against the Castro regime thoughout the island.

The military in Cuba, as in many Latin American countries, also carries out police functions. Cuba's pervasive military force is a powerful deterrent for subduing potential opposition. MININT's Department of State Security (DSE) is charged with the tasks of identification and apprehension of individuals posing potential political or security threats.

Despite Soviet designation of Cuba as a "socialist state," Cuba was never included in the Warsaw Pact as were the nations of Eastern Europe. Accordingly, it was always understood that the Cuban armed forces were responsible for securing the nation's own defense. Since the collapse of the Soviet Union, Cuba's military officials have reaffirmed that the FAR must assume responsibility for defending the revolution.

Although the realities of U.S. domestic politics render the feasibility of U.S. military invasion of Cuba highly unlikely except in the most extreme circumstances, Cuban leaders have consistently echoed the theme of the threat of U.S.

attack. Furthermore, such statements are not exclusively intended for propaganda purposes or to justify the shortcomings of the revolution, but reflect a genuine perception that the United States might in fact undertake such action. Evidently, such concerns have been expressed to Soviet officials and scholars over the years; and reports indicate that elaborate underground tunnel fortifications, referred to as the "civil defense tunnels," have been constructed to place Cuba's citizens underground in the event of U.S. attack.[26] Official statements published in *Granma* indicated that fear of U.S. attack heightened after the U.S. invasion of Grenada, leading to intensification of the "War of All the People."

Cuba's armed forces and intelligence organizations have been called to perform a range of international missions. During the 1960s, Cuban military and intelligence forces were utilized to assist in promoting armed insurrection in several Latin American countries. During the first decade of the revolution, Cuban forces fought alongside communist guerrillas in the Congo, assisted Algerian forces against Morocco, and provided training and logistical assistance to the North Vietnamese.

In more recent years, the Cuban armed forces have acquired substantial combat experience and shown the capacity to project thousands of forces outside their own theater, as displayed in the African campaigns orchestrated in concert with the Soviet Union. In 1975, several thousand Cuban troops were airlifted to Angola to assist the MPLA (Popular Movement for the Liberation of Angola). Between 1975 and 1989, four hundred thousand Cuban troops were rotated through Angola.[27] Beginning in 1977, several thousand additional troops were dispatched to the Horn of Africa to assist in the Ethiopian War against Somalia.

In the early 1980s, Cuban military and intelligence forces played an active role in exporting revolution in Central America and the Caribbean.[28] Cuba supplied military aid to the FSLN (Sandinista National Liberation Front) for the final offensive against the dictatorship of Anastasio Somoza in Nicaragua. One estimate indicates that more than 50% of the *Terceristas,* the dominant faction in the FSLN, had received military training in Cuba. In the postrevolutionary period, thousands of Cuban military personnel were stationed in Nicaragua to train the Sandinista military and to assist with other security matters. Cubans fought against U.S. forces during the invasion of Grenada in 1983. The Cubans also supplied military aid to the FMLN (Farabundo Marti National Liberation Front) and other Central American revolutionary groups in the 1980s.

Although the Soviet military occasionally assisted with nonmilitary tasks such as food production and construction, it was inclined to restrict its activities nearly exclusively to professional military tasks. In contrast, the Cuban military forces have performed many production functions. This tendency was displayed most dramatically when Castro mobilized some seventy thousand military troops to assist with the effort to attain the ten-million-ton sugar harvest in 1970. The FAR has consistently proved to be the best organized and disciplined institution for serving the needs of the regime. Cuba's officers have assumed responsible civilian posts; and the armed forces have performed production tasks in industry, transportation, construction, and agriculture. Military personnel displayed versatility in performing construction, medical, and educational tasks in Central America and the Caribbean, Africa, and elsewhere.

Since the collapse of the Soviet Union, at a time when financial and technical resources in Cuba are increasingly scarce, the regime is again relying on the armed forces to provide the resources and manpower for many civilian functions. In a recent interview, Brigadier General Leonardo Andollo and Colonel Reynaldo Munoz emphasized that the "strategic objective" of "our main enemy today [the United States] is to strangle the revolution economically."[29] They stated that the military forces must be "put at the service of the nation's economy." They noted that military manpower was being used in the sugar cane, coffee, and tobacco industries and that military hospitals and medical personnel were providing services to the Cuban population. Recent *Granma* reports indicate that the FAR and the Army of the Working Youth have assisted with sugar cane harvests and other agricultural tasks and that military vehicles have been used with increasing frequency to transport produce and equipment needed for various industrial and agricultural tasks.[30]

THE END OF THE COLD WAR: DIFFICULTIES FOR CUBA

The recent transformations in the former communist bloc have created tremendous difficulties for Cuba.[31] The Castro regime owed its capacity to survive to the socialist bloc lifeline. Prior to the collapse of the Soviet Union, Moscow was providing three billion dollars or five to six billion dollars (depending on Soviet or U.S. estimates) in aid annually to Cuba, supplying nearly all the island's petroleum, and purchasing Cuba's sugar, nickel, and other commodities at above-market prices.

Fidel Castro rejected Mikhail Gorbachev's *glasnost* and *perestroika.* Rather than pursuing liberalizing reforms, the Cuban leadership responded to the changes in the communist world by adhering to a policy of *rectification,* which featured increased party control, centralization of the economy, and a return to moral, rather than material, incentives in production.

During Gorbachev's tenure, the Soviets began to reduce oil supplies to Cuba, a major source of hard currency for the island. Beginning in 1991, the Soviets would agree to pay only twenty-five cents per pound for Cuba's sugar, whereas they had paid approximately forty-two cents per pound from 1979 to 1987. One of Gorbachev's last foreign policy initiatives, the proposal to remove the brigade (1,500 soldiers) that was stationed in Cuba since 1963, demonstrated just how far Moscow had come in reversing its longstanding commitment to Cuba.[32]

Cuba's relations with the new Russia and other Soviet successor states have become even more precarious. Russia's president, Boris Yeltsin, has been openly sympathetic to Castro's opposition and has stated that Russia will no longer render economic support to Cuba or permit the Cuban issue to undermine relations with the United States.[33] Yeltsin has indicated that Russia will no longer purchase Cuba's exports at preferential prices or render credits for trade and development. The Castro regime has responded by rationing food and other basic commodities and sounding the familiar themes of austerity and self-sacrifice.

The collapse of Cuba's former patron is directly impacting the Cuban military. Russia still maintains the Lourdes listening post in Cuba; but with increased U.S. pressure, Moscow could agree to close the facility.[34] The new Russian leadership has stated that it would no longer supply military aid to the island without payment.[35]

In a recent interview, Fidel Castro admitted that the Cuban air force and navy "had been hardest hit by the drying up of former Soviet arms and aid."[36] Under military agreements signed with Cuba during the Gorbachev era, Moscow was to provide a squadron of forty MIG-29 aircraft to Cuba, but only ten have been delivered. Various reports indicate that Cuba received some spare parts from Moscow in 1991, but no additional military supplies have been provided. Soviet oil-supply cutbacks have also led to rationing in the armed forces.

Given these constraints, the Cuban leadership has started to downsize the military, eliminating nonessential personnel.[37] In a recent speech, Raul Castro stated that Cuba's armed forces were "too big and too costly" given the resource constraints brought on by the collapse of the Soviet Union, suggesting that additional cutbacks may be forthcoming.[38]

DISSENSION

Because the armed forces served as the central institution in revolutionary Cuba, they will surely be a significant factor in determining whether the Castro regime survives and play an important role in the next leadership transition. Does Fidel Castro retain firm control of the military? This is a difficult question to answer in dealing with a closed society such as Cuba. Nonetheless, recent developments in Cuba and statements of defectors provide some clues concerning the issue of support for Castro within the military.

Beginning in the mid-1980s, the *rectification* campaign increasingly targeted the FAR, suggesting that the Castro leadership was concerned about officer loyalty.[39] In accordance with the effort to secure unwavering support within the ranks of the FAR, a 1987 statement published in *Verde Olivo* emphasized that the FAR must demonstrate "absolute loyalty to the party and its leaders, unlimited fidelity to the working class and Marxism-Leninism . . . and participate directly in political and ideological orientation activities."[40] The offensive, aimed at enhancing political commitment in the armed forces, appears to have been prompted by evidence that several military officers objected to the manner in which the African campaigns were conducted, viewing these involvements as "Cuba's Vietnam." According to General Rafael del Pino, who defected from the island in 1987, there were fifty-six thousand desertions from the military ranks during the three-year period of the Angolan war.[41]

The regime has also been concerned about lack of commitment among younger officers who did not share the same revolutionary experience as their Fidelista and Raulista superiors. General del Pino claims that the Castro brothers actually feared that younger officers could organize a conspiracy against the regime.

The most significant development pertaining to the issue of dissension in the military was the 1989 scandal involving one of Cuba's top military figures, General Arnaldo T. Ochoa. Ochoa, recipient of Cuba's most prestigious military honor, "Hero of the Republic of Cuba," was arrested on charges of corruption and drug trafficking. In a trial reminiscent of Stalin's "show trials," Ochoa was convicted and executed. Some have speculated that the Castro brothers feared that Ochoa's popularity would provide a base for a successful plot against the regime. This argument gains even more credence given that there were previous charges of narcotics trafficking against Cuban officials that were never prosecuted.

Although there is some evidence of unrest within the military in Cuba and although the recent high-risk defections of General Rafael del Pino, Air Force Major Orestes Lorenzo, and others are evidence of dissatisfaction, the Castro brothers appear to be responding vigilantly to retain their trusted associates in leading posts. For example, corresponding with the Ochoa trial, the Minister of the Interior, General Jose Abrantes, was charged with participation in illegal narcotics trade. He was replaced by Army Corps General Abelardo "Furry" Colome Ibarra, a hardline Castro loyalist.[42] In addition, General Ochoa's execution was followed by the arrest of several other officers who might have been feared as potential conspirators, including General Patricio de la Guardia and Colonel Antonio de la Guardia, twin brothers who were both employed by MININT. Finally, unlike leaders in the former Soviet Union, who were not simultaneously designated general secretary and commander in chief of the armed forces, Fidel Castro retains the titles of president and commander in chief, another factor securing his hold on the armed forces. His brother, Raul Castro, is general of the armed forces, and all FAR generals are Castro loyalists.

The party and intelligence forces have deeply penetrated the military in Cuba, making it difficult for any group of officers to carry out a coup attempt. Even General del Pino concluded his discussion of dissension within the Cuban military by stating, "It is truly difficult to become organized for concrete action inside the armed forces, because Castro dedicates many resources, immense resources to the military counterintelligence." The public trial and execution of General Ochoa sent a clear message regarding the grave consequences that may befall potential challengers of Fidelista command.

FUTURE SCENARIOS

The collapse of the Soviet Union has led many to believe that Castro's days are numbered. What significance will the military play in the survival of the

Castro regime and in Cuba's future? No one can answer this question with certainty, but there are a number of possibilities.

Global democratization, sweeping the former communist bloc and many of Castro's Latin American neighbors, could ultimately overtake Cuba. The Clinton administration has called for democratization of Cuba as a condition for normalizing relations with the United States. The prospects of acquiring U.S. aid and an end to the economic embargo may provide powerful incentives for change. Further cutbacks during the Yeltsin era may in the long term diminish the capacity of the armed forces to perform various missions and reduce the likelihood that the military could serve as an impediment to democratic transition. Another important consideration is that Fidel Castro's designated successor, Raul Castro, lacks the imposing presence of his brother and may not be able to resist the pressures for regime transformation. The establishment of a democratic regime in Cuba does not necessarily require that the military leave the scene. Russia and Nicaragua illustrate cases in which the armed forces remained intact as the regimes moved to democratize under civilian rule.

Another possibility is that dissension within the military will escalate as economic conditions become increasingly austere and dissatisfied officers will manage to capture control and serve to reform society as the progressive military reformers that appeared in Peru and other Latin American countries in the late 1960s and early 1970s period. In fact, the PCC may suffer declining legitimacy as a result of the discrediting of communist parties in the political systems of Cuba's former allies, rendering the military the only institution capable of leading a regime transformation.

Conversely, Cuba's political cultural tendencies of authoritarian/military rule and corruption may be perpetuated by Castro's successors. The island's future may represent a continuation of the past, a repressive state apparatus relying on military force as the base for governing.

The military is still recognized as the most capable institution in Cuba, and it will remain so at least in the short term. One of the impulses leading the armed forces to retreat from politics in Latin America is the perception that the military institution is no longer an effective governing agent. Though the Cuban military has suffered budget cuts, perhaps diminishing the capacity of the institution, all institutions in Cuba will suffer during this difficult period; and there is no evidence that the military is assuming a role of lesser significance than in the past. All indicators signal that the Castro regime will continue to rely on the military to maintain political control and to perform the necessary tasks to sustain the regime during this crisis period.

Furthermore, as conditions inevitably continue to worsen in Cuba, other grim realities may develop. Escalating dissatisfaction in society, aggravated by U.S. pressure, could plunge this militarized nation into bloody civil war. In such a scenario, the military may be pitted against various groups in society, or the military itself may be split into warring factions, perhaps divided among older and younger officers.

Finally, should Fidel Castro be cornered by his colossal enemy, the United States, perceiving himself to be in a position of strategic inferiority, he could utilize the military and its resources to resort to extreme measures. Castro tried to persuade the Soviets to launch a preemptive nuclear strike against the United States during the Cuban missile crisis, and testimony by Rafael del Pino indicates that the Cubans considered bombing a U.S. nuclear power plant during the Grenada crisis. Such suicidal measures would be consistent with Cuba's tradition of martyrdom; given Castro's propensity for extremism, such a final military showdown should not be ruled out.

NOTES

The author would like to express appreciation to the School of Social Sciences at San José State University for providing research grant support for this chapter.

1. See reference to Hugh Thomas, *The Cuban Revolution* (New York: Harper and Row, 1977), in Damian J. Fernande, "Historical Background, Achievements, Failures and Prospects," in Jaime Suchlicki, ed., *The Cuban Military under Castro* (Miami: North-South Center University of Miami Press, 1989), pp. 6–7.

2. Marta San Martin and Ramon L. Bonachea, "The Military Dimension of the Cuban Revolution," in Irving Louis Horowitz, ed., *Cuban Communism* (New Brunswick, N.J.: Transaction Books, 1982), p. 539.

3. *Statistical Abstract of Latin America* (Los Angeles: University of California at Los Angeles, 1992); *The Military Balance* (London: International Institute of Strategic Studies, 1992); *The World Fact Book* (Washington: Central Intelligence Agency, 1992).

4. *Statistical Abstract of Latin America, Stockholm International Peace Research Institute Annual Summary* (London: Oxford University Press); *World Military Expenditures and Arms Transfer* (Washington: U.S. Arms Control and Disarmament Agency).

5. Ibid.

6. For discussion of the formation of the Communist Party in Cuba (PCC), see Edward Gonzalez, *Cuba under Castro: The Limits of Charisma* (Boston: Houghton Mifflin, 1974), pp. 102–4.

7. Richard F. Staar, ed., *Yearbook on International Communist Affairs* (Stanford, Calif.: Hoover Institution Press) and *The World Fact Book.*

8. Louis A. Perez, Jr., *Army Politics in Cuba 1898–1958* (Pittsburgh: University of Pittsburgh Press, 1976), p. 266.

9. Seventy-two members of the one-hundred-man Central Committee of the PCC held military titles. See Gonzalez, *Cuba Under Castro,* p. 104.

10. For discussion of several specific instances of civil-military conflict in Cuba, see Jorge I. Dominguez, *Cuba, Order and Revolution* (Boston: Harvard University Press, 1978) and "The Cuban Army," in Johnathan R. Adelman, ed., *Communist Armies in Politics* (Boulder: Westview Press, 1982).

11. See William M. Leogrande, "A Bureaucratic Approach to Civil-Military Relations in Communist Political Systems: The Case of Cuba," and Irving Louis Horowitz, "Military Outcomes of the Cuban Revolution," in Horowitz, ed., *Cuban Communism.*

12. Horowitz, "Military Outcomes," in Horowitz, ed., *Cuban Communism,* p. 592;

and Edward Gonzalez, "Castro and Cuba's New Orthodoxy," *Problems of Communism* (January–February 1976), pp. 1–19.

13. Edward Gonzalez and David Ronfeldt, *Cuba Adrift in a Post Communist World,* R-4231-USPD (Santa Monica: Rand Corporation, 1992), p. 40.

14. Frank E. Blair, ed., *Countries of the World* (Detroit: Gale Research, 1993).

15. Dominguez, "Cuban Army," p. 45.

16. *Military Balance* and *Stockholm International Peace Research Institute Annual Summary.*

17. Gonzalez and Ronfeldt, *Cuba Adrift,* p. 18.

18. "The Best Protection against Surprise," *Granma Weekly Review,* 13 May 1990, and "Cuban Shield Maneuvers Are Over," *Granma Weekly Review,* 27 May 1990.

19. *Mexico City NOTIMEX,* 17 December, 1992, in *FBIS-LAT,* 18 December 1992, and "Defense Capacity Increases," *Granma Weekly Review,* 14 February 1993.

20. Rafael Fermoselle, *Cuban Leadership after Castro: Biographies of Cuba's Top Generals* (Miami: North-South Center University of Miami Press, 1992), p. 4.

21. Gonzalez, *Cuba Adrift,* p. 40.

22. M. L. Vellinga, "The Military Dynamics of the Cuban Revolutionary Process," *Comparative Politics* (January 1976), pp. 250–51; and Phyllis Greene Walker, "The Cuban Military Service System: Organization, Obligations and Pressures," in Suchlicki, ed., *Cuban Military* pp. 112–14.

23. Clifford Krause, "Blacks Praise Cuban Revolution," *Wall Street Journal,* 9 July 1986, p. 26, cited in Greene Walker, "The Cuban Military Service System," in Suchlicki, ed., *Cuban Military* pp. 113–14.

24. For information on education programs in the Cuban armed forces, see Vellinga, "Military Dynamics," pp. 252–53; and Juan M. del Aguila, "The Changing Character of Cuba's Armed Forces," in Suchlicki, ed., *Cuban Military* pp. 30–31.

25. William Ratliff, *Military Affairs in Cuba, January 1985–June 1988,* Working Paper in International Studies I-89-28 (Stanford, Calif.: Hoover Institution, 1989), p. 19.

26. Sergo A. Mikoyan, seminar held at the Hoover Institution, Stanford University, 18 April 1993.

27. Fermoselle, *Cuban Leadership after Castro,* p. 8.

28. For documentation of Cuba's response to the Nicaraguan revolution comparing U.S., European, and Latin American sources, see Sharyl Cross, "The Soviet Union and the Nicaraguan Revolution," Ph.D. diss., University of California at Los Angeles, 1990.

29. *Havana Vision Network,* 2 December 1992, in *FBIS-LAT,* 4 December 1992.

30. "Food Program's First Harvest, Government Priority to Transportation," *Granma Weekly Review,* 31 March 1991.

31. For analysis of Cuba's relations with the Soviet Union under Gorbachev and with Russia and the other Soviet successor states, see Sharyl Cross, *Gorbachev's Policy in Latin America: Origins, Impact and the Future,* Working Paper in International Studies, I-93-6 (Stanford, Calif.: Hoover Institution, 1993).

32. The last brigade of Russian troops left Cuba in June 1993; see "Last Russian Combat Troops Leave Cuba," *San Francisco Chronicle,* 16 June 1993.

33. According to the vice-director of the Latin American Department of the Russian Foreign Ministry, Alexei A. Ermakov, the Yeltsin government presently maintains ties with Castro's opposition in Miami and Cuba and seeks to promote democratization in the island. Author's interview with Alexei A. Ermakov, Vice-Director, Latin American Department, Foreign Ministry of Russia, 20 July 1993, Moscow, Russia.

34. When questioned concerning the Lourdes facility, the Latin American specialist of the Institute of Peace in the Russian Academy of Sciences, Sergo A. Mikoyan, stated that President Yeltsin probably would not object to closing the listening post, but might confront opposition to such a move from military officials, in a seminar held at the Hoover Institution at Stanford University on 18 April 1993. According to Ermakov, this issue might be dealt with on the basis of "reciprocity," in that if the United States removed intelligence facilities from the borders of the former Soviet Union, Russia could respond with the closure of the Lourdes facility. Author's interview with Ermakov, 20 July 1993.

35. For discussion of the anticipated impact of cutbacks from the socialist bloc on Cuba's weapons supplies, see Fidel Castro's speech at the Bay of Pigs anniversary, *Granma Weekly Review,* 5 May 1991. Author's interview with Dr. Leve Klochkovsky, Director of the Department of Economics, Institute of Latin America, Russian Academy of Sciences, Moscow, Russia, August 1992.

36. "Cuba Reducing Its Armed Forces," *Reuter Library Report,* 22 April 1993; and "Cuban Navy to Test Fuel Saving Methods," *Reuter Library Report,* 20 January 1993.

37. Ibid.

38. Raul Castro, interview with *El Sol de Mexico,* in *Granma Weekly Review,* 5 May 1993.

39. Ratliff, *Military Affairs in Cuba,* p. 13.

40. Ibid., p. 14.

41. *General Rafael del Pino Speaks: An Insight into Elite Corruption and Military Dissension in Castro's Cuba* (Miami: Cuban-American National Foundation, 1987).

42. Gonzalez and Ronfeldt, *Cuba Adrift,* p. 40.

REFERENCES

del Pino, Rafael. *General del Pino Speaks: An Insight into Elite Corruption and Military Dissention in Castro's Cuba.* Miami: Cuban American National Foundation, 1987.

Dominguez, Jorge I. "The Cuban Army." In Johnathan R. Adelman ed., *Communist Armies in Politics.* Boulder, Colo.: Westview Press, 1982.

Fermoselle, Fafael. *Cuban Leadership after Castro: Biographies of Cuba's Top Generals.* Miami: North South Center University of Miami Press, 1992.

Gonzalez, Edward. *Cuba under Castro: The Limits of Charisma.* Boston: Houghton Mifflin, 1974.

Gonzalez, Edward, and David Ronfeldt. *Cuba Adrift in a Post-Communist World.* Santa Monica: Rand Corporation, 1992.

Horowitz, Irving Louis, ed. *Cuban Communism.* New Brunswick, N.J.: Transaction Books, 1982.

Judson, C. Fred. *Cuba and the Revolutionary Myth: The Political Education of the Cuban Rebel Army 1953–63.* Boulder, Colo.: Westview Press, 1984.

Perez, Louis A., Jr. *Army Politics in Cuba 1898–1958.* Pittsburgh: University of Pittsburgh Press, 1976.

———. "Army Politics in Socialist Cuba." *Journal of Latin American Studies* 8, no. 2 (November 1976).

Ratliff, William E. *Castroism and Communism in Latin America.* Washington, D.C.:
    American Enterprise Institute, 1976.
Suchlicki, Jaime, ed., *The Cuban Military under Castro.* Miami: North-South Center
    University of Miami Press, 1989.

DENMARK

Henning Sørensen

Danish civilian-military relations can be traced back twelve hundred years in writings. Consequently, any short historical description of civil-military relations in Denmark will have to be painted with a broad brush and therefore be personally biased.

In this chapter five civil-military topics will be touched upon: Denmark's security policy, defense policy, the organization of the armed forces, public opinion on defense matters, and finally a profile of the officer corps and its political opinion compared to that of the Danish population.

SECURITY POLICY

Any historical presentation of a country's security policy can be divided into different periods depending on the criterion used.

Two different criteria will be used for the description of Denmark's security policy over the last twelve hundred years. First is the official belief in and use of military power abroad, and second is the presence and/or absence of enemies and allies. In the first case three and in the second six different periods can be identified.

From 800 to 1810, Denmark believed in military power. However, from the beginning of the 1800s, this conviction shifted toward peaceful settlement of conflicts even in matters such as territorial disputes, independence, and ethnic upheavals, in which cases wars were normally to be waged.[1] This peaceful security approach continued in the Cold War period[2] as we pursued our security policy goals of stopping aggressions, defending democracies, and protecting human beings only verbally, never forcefully. A new and third phase, rather unnoticed, has been introduced. Since 1990, Denmark is prepared to apply military power to realize our security goals, that is, to die for these goals, to phrase it lyrically.

The second criterion for the description of Denmark's security policy is its enemy identification and membership in alliances.

In the first period, the Viking era, from 700 to 1050, Denmark had neither specific allies nor enemies. Nevertheless, attacks were expected from all directions. Also Danish Vikings initiated what can be seen as preemptive expeditions to France and, in particular, to England while other Nordic Viking expeditions reached Europe, Russia, and even America.[3] The Scandinavian Viking nations thus pursued an "all-around-the-compass" foreign policy.

After this *universalistic* period in the Viking era, Danish security policy confined itself to a *North-European* orientation because of the aggression of the Hanseatic League and the Wenders in the period from 1100 to the mid-1300s. As a result of these southern attacks, Denmark, Sweden, and Norway decided to unite their defense efforts and established the Kalmar Union in 1387, heavily persuaded by the Danish queen, Margrethe I, who made nobles from all three countries elect and crown her son Erik as their common king.

A third period emerged from around the mid-1400s to 1814. In this period Denmark's security position was mostly *Nordic*-oriented, characterized by hostilities between Denmark and Norway on the one hand and Sweden on the other and without persistent allies for either of the combatants.[4] This struggle ended with Swedish victory in 1658,[5] followed by several Danish attempts at revenge over the next 150 years; however, all were unsuccessful.

The fourth period runs from the beginning of 1800 to 1945. It is *German*-dominated, in particular because of the contending positions of the duchies of Slesvig and Holstein. On the one hand, both Denmark and the German nations had confirmed the right of the two duchies to remain undivided. On the other, Slesvig had strong connections to the Danish monarchy, Holstein to other German nations.

This question was solved by a public referendum in 1920, when the northern part of Slesvig came to Denmark, the rest to Germany. And from 1920 to 1945, German expansionism made this country the single state most dangerous to Danish security.

In 1949, a fifth period began, with the Warsaw Pact countries as enemies and NATO countries as allies. In this period, an *American* orientation is decisive.

But since 1990, a new and *universalistic* era has emerged, because of the absence of enemies and the continued presence of allies. Denmark and other NATO countries are experiencing an international situation in which each country is *selecting* its individual security problems. Security policies of Western countries are now less influenced by our allies and more by national preferences. Denmark chose to deploy Danish soldiers in the UN mission in the former Yugoslavia for the protection of its population, but declined to do so in Somalia. Germany did the opposite. Today, we have more room for security policy maneuvering than before.[6] But at the same time, we can expect more debate in each country on what goals to pursue and how to do it.

Denmark's six different security policy situations, according to the presence

Figure 1
Four Types of Security Positions

                                            Enemies
                                    −   +

		INDEPENDENT SECURITY 1) 700–1050	ISOLATED SECURITY 2) 1050–1300 4) 1450–1949
Allies	−		
	+	SELECTIVE SECURITY 6) 1990	COLLECTIVE SECURITY 3) 1300–1450 5) 1949–1990

Figure 1 shows the four different types of security policy pursued by Denmark based upon the presence of enemies and allies. In the first period of the Viking era, Denmark was placed in an INDEPENDENT security position without either enemies or allies. In the Middle Ages and again from the Renaissance period and onwards, Denmark stood ISOLATED, confronted with German and Swedish and again German enemies, but had no allies. Only in two periods, around the Kalmar Union of 1387 and again in the Cold War period, 1949–1990, Denmark did rely on COLLECTIVE security, because of the combination of enemies and allies at the same time. Today, Denmark experiences SELECTIVE security, having no enemy, several allies, and many security issues to select among.

and/or absence of enemies and allies, are shown in Figure 1. To what extent has Danish security policy in the six different periods been influenced by the military, that is, the king?

In the Viking era, the king had the monopoly to decide when, how, and where "leding" should take place.[7] Besides this fleet, the king was in control of a personal and professional army, the "hird,"[8] organized and paid for by himself. Therefore, the king/the military no doubt dominated society at that time.[9]

But even then and throughout the Middle Ages and onwards, disputes between king and people occurred. They are, for instance, documented in the coronation charters issued by the Thing in 1320 and in 1326, by the Assembly of the Estates in 1648,[10] and finally and most decisively by Parliament and the government based upon the first Danish constitution of 1849.

Two concluding observations can be made. First, over the last thirteen hundred years, Denmark has had different security positions. Today, Denmark experiences selective security, accepting military power even "out-of-area" and in all directions, a universalistic orientation, and preemptive "expeditions"[11] together with the absence of enemies and presence of allies. This new policy has been established almost without public debate and with no public protest.

Second, the making of decisions about Danish security policy has been democ-
ratized.

DEFENSE POLICY

Defense policy is the regulation of the military establishment in accordance
with national security goals. In this section, two main aspects of Danish defense
policy shall be touched upon: the deployment of Danish armed forces within
and outside national borders and the relationship between the armed forces and
politicians in Denmark during the last century.

Deployment of Danish armed forces outside Denmark is recorded as early as
793.[12] In the Viking era, this expansionism took place almost every year. The
Vikings set sail in the spring and returned, if possible, in the autumn of the
same year.

Since then, the deployment and use of Danish military power abroad did
occur, but on a lesser scale and in a less regular manner. From 1660 and onwards
it seldom happened; and after 1810, Danish armed forces as combat units normally stayed at home.[13]

It was the case in the period of the Cold War, too. The Danish army division,
Jyske Division, was meant for use only in Denmark or in Northern Germany.
Apart from NATO exercises abroad and participations in peaceful UN missions,
Denmark's armed forces were kept within its borders.[14] But since 1990, the
country has tripled the number of soldiers for UN missions to fifteen hundred,[15]
established a new Danish International Brigade of forty-five hundred soldiers
for such UN missions, and for the first time in centuries deployed soldiers "out-
of-area."

The deployment of armed forces within Denmark goes back to the Viking
era as well. Most spectacular are the four famous Viking castles from around
1000.[16] They probably served as tax-collecting and conscriptive strongholds for
the king.

Military installations have often been established or closed for national or
even local reasons.[17] Which part of Denmark was the most vital to defend varied
over the years. In 1832, it was the capital of Copenhagen[18]; in 1840 Fredericia
in Jutland[19]; in 1870–1905 Copenhagen[20]; in 1909 Jutland[21]; and from 1949 to
1990, it was Jutland and Bornholm, judged by the number of military personnel
per capita.[22]

The debate about the relationship between politicians and military in Denmark
over the last century can be summarized in two words, *disintegration,* that is,
the military expertise has failed to influence Danish political parties,[23] and *politicization,* that is, the Danish defense issues are political conflict areas.[24]

Apart from a short period from the beginning of the 1960s to the mid-1960s,
the relationship between the armed forces and politicians has been disinte-
grated.[25] Officers, in particular, are to be blamed for this.[26] Their expertise is no
excuse for a lack of political "touch" towards the political system. Officers are,

as any other interest group of professional practitioners, obliged to communicate in a way understood by decision makers and citizens and to do so as successfully as do physicians, accountants, or lawyers.[27]

The degree of politicization of defense issues is more disputed and complicated.[28] However, the lack of political conflict and minor initiatives concerning the armed forces cannot be seen as a lack of political interest or a low degree of politicization. On the contrary, political silence on the armed forces may be a result of heavy politicization.

Two conclusions on Danish defense policy can be made. First, today Denmark is deploying armed forces "out-of-area." Second, as military installations in Denmark are more often established and shut down for national than for international reasons, local politics far better explain Danish defense policy than does Denmark's international security position,[29] which again indicates inefficient defense policy planning because of the democratization[30] and politicization of the military.[31]

ORGANIZATION OF THE ARMED FORCES

Four aspects of the Danish military organization will be focused upon: management, structure, recruitment, and military expenditures.

In the Viking era, management of the armed forces was in the hands of the king alone, and only he decided leding. But apart from his military leadership, the king's civil position vis-à-vis other nobles was "primus inter pares."

In the Middle Ages, the king combined the civil and military leadership. With the introduction of the absolute monarchy in 1660, his influence reached its peak as he at the same time was head of the legislative, the executive, and the judicial powers. However, by the new constitution of 1849,[32] Parliament, government, and courts took over even if the monarch formally continued as General/First Sea Lord.

The central civil-military issue here is neither the "old" struggle between people and king on the latter's right to command troops in battle nor the fundamental right of the king to define and decide Denmark's security policy. What was at stake, throughout many centuries, was the establishment of civilization. In a civilized society, people abstain from personal punishment of a criminal offender, leaving it to the authorities. The condition for this is the dual monopoly of a nation to collect taxes and to be in control of violent organizations such as prisons, policy, and the armed forces.[33] In Denmark, as in other civilized countries, each citizen has individually and voluntarily given up the right of personal defense and instead legitimized authorities to do so. In return, citizens have democratic rights. Democracy and conscription are thus closely related. In Denmark, in fact, conscription was introduced in 1848 and democracy by the new constitution in 1849.

The struggle for a civilized Denmark thus goes back at least to the Viking period and remained an area of conflict up till 1849. However, one problem remained unsolved.

Parliament may be unable to mobilize after occupation of the country. This happened on 9 April 1940, when Hitler's Germany occupied Denmark and made the Danish government tell the Danes not to resist. Therefore, after World War II, in 1953, the Danish Parliament passed a bill, the "Forholdsordre" ("Standing Operational Procedure") demanding every soldier to join his unit to meet external attack without being formally asked to do so by legal authorities such as Parliament, government, and the military. A main goal of the "Forholdsordre" is to deter an aggressor from a surprise attack it hopes will paralyze the Danish armed forces from being mobilized. Therefore, the phrase "Never another April 9" is a central one in the Danish defense debate.

The discussion of the structure of the Danish armed forces will touch upon five aspects: the establishment of the two services, the size of the armed forces from 1700 and onwards, the appropriateness of the army organization, the army personnel rate, and the officer rate.

Ever since the Viking era, Danish armed forces have included both an army and a navy. Both services of today thus go back to the Viking era, with the king's professional army, the Hird, and the conscription-based leding fleet. For centuries, this division has resulted in a different recruitment pattern, organization, and expenditure level, types of leadership, bureaucracies, garrison facilities, and cultures for the two services of the Danish armed forces.[34]

The exact size of the Danish army/navy has remained uncertain from the Viking era onwards, almost up to the first Danish constitution of 1849.[35] However, for the last three centuries, data on the strength of the Danish armed forces have been compiled and calculated.[36] In 1700, Danish armed forces numbered twenty-five thousand soldiers per million inhabitants. In 1705, the same figure reached forty-five thousand soldiers with the introduction of conscription, but it has decreased ever since. Between 1775 and 1860, it was around thirty thousand soldiers; in 1970, eleven thousand, and in 1993, only seventy-one hundred soldiers.

These figures illustrate that Denmark had a strong army in the rather peaceful period of 1700–1790, but a small one in the mid-1800s, when Denmark was at war with Prussia (in 1848–50 and again in 1864). The same situation with a small Danish army is found in the mid-1930s, when Germany rearmed while Denmark almost disarmed.

For many years, the Danish army has been criticized for its inappropriate organization[37] without effective political initiatives to meet the criticism. At first glance, the political acceptance of a less efficient military could be interpreted as an insufficient political control of the armed forces. It may be the case. But, politicians may be unwilling to take initiatives to avoid running into problems[38] as the "Minister of Defense . . . and (his) Department are weak in contrast to a resourceful Defense Command."[39] Moreover, it is argued that Danish politicians lack military insight and that "they should be forced to take a more qualified position to . . . (military) subjects.''[40] Finally, promilitary politicians who do know the military system are silent, as they do not want to squeeze the armed forces.

Two manpower figures shall be introduced to demonstrate the importance of new technology. The first is the army rate, that is, the number of army personnel compared to the total number of navy and air force personnel. It has dropped over the last thirty years from 67% in 1965 to 52% in 1985 and to 55% in 1993.[41] It illustrates the shift from man to technology, a change also reflected in the increasing percentage of military investments out of all military expenditures. The second figure is the officer rate, that is, the ratio of officers to all other military personnel. It has increased, too, because new and expensive technology demands professional officers to handle it.

These two rates have never been disputed. They are taken for granted by politicians when presented by the Defense Command. Therefore, they confirm a lack of political influence and interest, compared to the interest taken in the sex-role debate. In general, the organization of the armed forces is seldom a topic for political discussion. In the last half century, the only personnel group politically debated has been the conscripts.

The description of the *recruitment* system of the Danish armed forces shall focus on three themes: Conscription vs enlistment, professionalism, and conscientious objection.

The recruitment of soldiers is typically based upon either conscription or enlistment.[42] As mentioned above, Denmark has from the Viking period and onwards almost always had both recruitment systems. The Hird was the professional force, while the leding fleet was based on geographical conscription, that is, each region/town was obliged to ''go to the wars'' by deploying a specific number of ships and men at the king's request for the defense of the country. This combined system of conscription and enlistment existed throughout the Middle Ages[43] and up until 1803,[44] when only conscription was accepted.[45]

Geographical conscription in the Middle Ages could be replaced by money given to the king by those landowners who were unable to find conscripts from their county for the army.[46] Geographical conscription lasted to 1788, when it was replaced by personal conscription, but only for the rural population. The urban population paid either in cash or by lodging soldiers in their homes. This system ended in 1803, when personal conscription was applied to all adult males.

From 1803 to 1951, only conscription prevailed, and the mercenary army was brought to an end. In 1951, enlistment was reintroduced; and in 1970, conscripts were given the right to choose between compulsory military and civil service. These developments, together with the establishment of a National Home Guard, mean that all three types of recruitment—conscription, enlistment, and militia (for the Home Guard)—exist in Denmark today.

The rate of enlisted men compared to conscripts has changed significantly since 1803, but it is now at the level it was two hundred years ago.[47] In 1764, the professionalization rate was 56%[48]; from 1803 to 1951 it was zero; in 1965, 12%; and in 1993, 59%. The professionalization of the armed forces over the last forty years is obvious and shows clearly the increased importance of technology.

In 1917, Denmark was one of the first countries in the world to recognize conscientious objection (CO) and to provide civil public service instead.[49] In 1968, further liberalization followed so that CO status was automatically granted to everyone who asked for it, with no investigations or sanctions. This liberal policy did not increase the CO rate dramatically. From 1917 to 1943 we have no precise figures; but in the period 1943–67, the CO rate at its highest reached 2%, from 1968 to 1970 it was between 4% and 9%, in 1971–74 (in the aftermath of the Vietnam war) it was over 10%, in 1982–87 it was only 1%, and for the six years 1988–93 it was 4%. The low CO rate is even more surprising when the far better service conditions for the COs compared to those of the military conscripts are considered. COs don't do unpleasant military exercises, they don't have to stay in the barracks after working hours, they work indoors in nice civilian buildings, and on top of that they are paid the same salary as military conscripts.[50]

One explanation of the low CO rate is that around 80% of all the military conscripts are volunteers, that is, they have declared themselves willing to serve. Another is the liberal treatment of gay military conscripts. They only need to declare themselves homosexuals and unable to serve; the Danish military organization then will administratively reject them without further investigations or notes in their personal files.

Three themes related to military expenditures will be mentioned: the expenditures of the Danish armed forces compared to all government expenditures, the proportion of hardware investment related to all defense expenditures, and the army's share of the defense budget.

Military expenditures over a span of years are difficult to compare. However, it is possible to get an impression of the importance of the armed forces by comparing military expenditures to all government expenditures.[51] In 1820, 42% of all government expenditures was used for defense purposes; in 1866–67, 33%; in 1925–26, 18%; in 1949–50, 10%; in 1970–71, 4.5%; and finally, in 1991, 3.4%. These figures clearly show the reduced importance of Danish armed forces, compared to all other governmental institutions.

However, it does not mean that less money goes to the military, partly because the proportion of the defense expenditures to the Danish gross national product has remained stable at around 2.4% from the fiscal year 1960/61 to 1992 and in 1993 is 2.0% and partly because the gross national product has grown.

Because of expensive weapon systems, an increased share of the defense budget for hardware investment is to be expected, and this is the case. In 1949/50, equipment investment came to only 2.7% of all military expenditures; in 1951/52, it was 14.1% due to the Marshall aid; in 1980, it rose to 22%; and in 1993, it dropped to 16%.[52]

These figures show unstable investment expenditures but stable defense expenditures because Danish politicians since the mid-1950s have decided on a nil growth for military expenditures. It may be interpreted as reduced political interest and control of military expenditures. At least, financial control is reduced to this nil-growth defense budget and a post-audit of the defense account. There is no ongoing control of military financial decisions or discussion of the security aim of, for instance, a newly bought weapon or frigate, or an "information and account system which can document . . . that sound economic consideration . . . has been taken."[53]

This presentation of the organization of the Danish armed forces can be summarized into three conclusions. First, recruitment for the military organization has turned into a "supermarket" with all products offered (conscription, militia, enlistment, soft service for the COs, and liberal procedures against homosexuals), leaving the consumer/citizen a free choice. The basic reason for this military "supermarket" model is the increased importance of technology. The military organization cannot function in a professional way with reluctant conscripts and poorly motivated officers. Besides, the professionalization and democratization of the armed forces have narrowed the gap between civil and military organizations.

Second, the size of the Danish armed forces has not reflected our different historical security positions, cfr. the Danish armed forces' inappropriate size compared to that of our enemies, and the stable military expenditures to gross national product. In short, the size of the armed forces is regulated for national not international reasons.

A third conclusion is that many present organizational features can be traced back to the Viking era: First, the monarch is still (however, only symbolically) in command of the Danish armed forces. This is another way of saying that the Danish military has always been a national force. Second, the two services, the army hird and the leding navy, were created at that time. Third, the dual recruitment system of conscription (the leding fleet) and enlistment (the hird) goes back to this period, as well. Fourth, today conscription comprises all Danes, as it did in the Viking era; while in the Middle Ages and up till 1803, it applied only to the rural population. Fifth, debate on military expenditures has existed ever since the Viking era.

PUBLIC OPINION ON DEFENSE ISSUES

Discussion of the Danes' attitude to the armed forces will concentrate on two themes: public opinion about military expenditures and "the Defense Will of the Population."

Danish public opinion about military expenditures has been surveyed for almost fifty years and is, next to "support of Danish membership of NATO," the most-asked question[54] in twenty national surveys conducted from 1950 to 1990. Even if different formulations have been used, it is possible to summarize the results: that around 40% of the Danes are for maintaining the current expenditure level, another 40% want reduced military budgets, and 20% prefer more military expenditures or "don't know." These attitudes are neither influenced by a decrease/an increase in international tension nor by the actual level of military expenditures. Thus, as "the public is less willing to pay for the military than are the politicians,"[55] Denmark may spend more money on defense than the public wants.

"The Defense Will of the Population" has been tested nine times from 1975 to 1994.[56] In 1975, the average score on a scale of zero to ten was 3.9. Until 1984, "the Defense Will" increased to 5.6; it decreased to 4.8 in 1990; and it reached 5.7 in 1994.

One of the questions asked in this survey was, "Do you think the armed forces contribute to peace in Denmark?"[57] In 1975, 53% agreed; in 1994, 75% did. This means that the armed forces are believed to play an increased role for peace in Denmark in spite of the absence of enemies. The military's role as peace-contributor seems not to be thought connected to the presence of enemies or the presumed effectiveness of our armed forces. Most probably, the armed forces are credited for the lack of enemies. Thus the Danish population has become more positive about the military as an institution than before[58] not for its own sake but for that of absent enemies. Nevertheless, the more positive attitude towards our armed forces is a fact.

Two conclusions can be made. First, divided public acceptance of defense expenditures is no new phenomenon and is not related to the level of international tension or the defense budget or the "Defense Will." "Defense Will," therefore, seems to be more a personal than a financial issue. With reference to the voluntary and unpaid Home Guard system, this may be a reasonable conclusion.[59]

Second, the Danes are today more positive toward the armed forces than they were in 1975, but for less obvious reasons, such as the absence of enemies.

THE DANISH OFFICER CORPS

Six themes regarding the Danish officer shall be touched upon: recruitment, education, occupation, esprit de corps, career pattern, and political orientation.[60]

In contrast to other Western countries, the recruitment background of the Danish officer is very like that of our population, socially and geographically. In 1983, 30% of Danish officers have a working-class background, as in the whole population, but in most other countries less than 10% of the officers come from working-class families. Of the Danish officers, 70% come from urban areas, which hold 67% of all Danes. In most Western countries officers from rural areas are overrepresented, but not in Denmark.

Today, the education of officers is more civilian-dominated than before. For instance, the civilian contents of the curricula of the military academies have increased. Measured by the number of lectures, officers are now taught more civil technical and political subjects than before, compared to military training and tactics. However, in one respect, Danish officers contradict the overall pattern of increased civilization. Only 4% of Danish officers have studied at and graduated from civilian colleges and universities. In other Western countries this figure is much higher.

The occupation pattern, however, confirms the increased civilization. In 1983, 37% of Danish officers described their job as administrative, 16% see themselves as technicians, 14% as teachers, 7% as having other functions, and only 27% as warriors. There are no significant differences in the warrior rate for the three services. In the army 24% of the officers describe themselves as warriors; in the navy, 30%; and in the air force, 31%. But age and rank are essential: 61% of all younger officers have operative functions, while for majors and captains the figure is only 30%–35%.

Most literature on esprit de corps accepts the thesis that officers share the same attitudes towards their profession. But the thesis has never been empirically tested. However, in a study Danish officers were asked the same questions about their military profession[61] twice, that is, as their personal opinion and as that of the officer corps. The officers should choose from a variety of answers given in the survey and select the same combination of answers if esprit de corps could be said to exist. However, no common answers were given and therefore no esprit de corps found, for several reasons. First, every fifth Danish officer believed his/her personal opinion to deviate from the presumed opinion of the officer corps. Second, age, rank, service, and function played a decisive role for the answers; more precisely, all four indicators deviated more than 100% from that of the average officer. Especially, younger officers rarely agreed with their elder colleagues. Third, the hypothesis of esprit de corps has to be abandoned because many officers gave mutually contrasting answers. Instead, six different roles or officer types were deduced. Danish officers identify themselves as civil managers, technicians, or professional warriors and, to a lesser degree, as citizens, union members, or fellow human beings. This disagreement within the officer corps on aspects of their profession is reflected in their different cultures[62] and in their confused approach to politicians[63] as well.

The career pattern for Danish officers shows that 30% of all officers are promoted to lt. colonel/commander or higher echelons. However, as many as 70% of all potential career officers, nevertheless, expect to reach a higher rank. This has to do with the fact that more officers receive the theoretical qualifications necessary for promotion. In 1834–68, only seven army officers passed the decisive tactical course at the Defence College; in 1950–80, 117 army officers did.

These figures showing an overproduction of promotable officers may be one example of the reduced political control of the Danish military profession. Another is the circulation of the position of Joint Chief of Staff among the three services without political interference by the secretary of defense. In contrast, any other secretary in the government will normally appoint his or her permanent undersecretary. But this right has been passed over to the armed forces. A third example is the lack of a young general. Politicians will often want "new and young blood" with whom to cooperate. But it has almost never happened in Denmark. Seniority is a stronger career catalyst than is efficiency. All in all, the three examples indicate essential signs of reduced political control. On the other hand, if the secretary really wanted a specific person for the top job, he or she could easily be appointed.

In 1983, the same population of officers was asked to indicate their political orientation on a scale from one to ten, where one is the most left-wing point of view, ten the most right-wing view. Only 16% of the officers placed themselves within the categories one through five (from left to center), while 48% of the electorate did so. In categories six through eight, 78% of the officers placed themselves, but only 45% of the people do so. In the most right-wing categories, 9 and 10, the officer corps and the people had almost the same proportion: 7% of the officers and 6% of the people. Danish officers thus are not radically rightist, but they express a center-right opinion compared to the Danish population. However, it is noted that other civil servants, like police officers, will probably have a center-right orientation, as well.

The overall conclusion is that the Danish officer corps has become more civil oriented, considering its social and geographical recruitment background, the increase of civilian subjects and number of lectures at the military academies, the reduced number of officers in military jobs, and the different views among Danish officers of their function as we find it among other professional practitioners such as physicians, teachers, and lawyers. Only with respect to career pattern does the general thesis of an increased civilization have to be abandoned, as Danish officers with combat functions are relatively more often promoted than officers without them.

Another conclusion is that no esprit de corps as a common attitude among all officers was found. One reason for the esprit de corps thesis may be a confusion of attitudes with behavior. The uniform behavior of officers has wrongly been interpreted as reflecting a common opinion among them. Moreover, not even lack of opinions can be seen as shared opinions.

A third conclusion is the lack of political influence on the officer corps. In particular, it is seen in the career pattern where the three services in turn deliver the Joint Chief of Staff without political interference.

CONCLUSION

Three main tendencies in the Danish civil-military relations over the centuries can be traced.

The first tendency is *democratization.* Today, democratic institutions such as Parliament and the government make decisions on Denmark's foreign policy within the new selective security position. The same process of democratization has happened to defense policy matters. In both fields the old struggle between king/military and people, fought for more than a thousand years, was stopped in 1849 with the introduction of the first Danish constitution. Since then, the armed forces have been regarded as just another interest group. The third area of democratization is the recruitment system of the defense organization, as in the "supermarket model," where conscription, militia, and enlistment are offered at the same time and where conscripts are treated very liberally. However, within most areas of the military profession such as function and career pattern, politicians do not exercise any significant influence. In short, from security policy through defense policy and military organization and to the officer corps, a declining degree of political influence is found. But, as the new selective security policy will make politicians responsible for the death of Danish soldiers in the "out-of-area" UN/NATO/CSCE missions, an increased democratic influence on the armed forces is likely. On the other hand, with more masters to serve (such as the Danish Parliament, the government, the UN, NATO, and CSCE), all military establishments will gain more room for political maneuvering by playing both ends against the middle. Actually, this has happened lately, when the Danish armed forces in UN units in the former Yugoslavia criticized the civil UN authorities for prohibiting Danish tanks there from operating and made members of the Danish Parliament question this UN policy.

The second tendency is *civilization*, that is, the armed forces have introduced into its organization several civil aspects from the other governmental agencies. Here, civilization is most clearly found at the lowest levels. Education, lack of esprit de corps, and increased career competition exemplify these trends. With the new policy of selective security demanding Danish armed forces for the battlefield, the civilization process is expected to stop.

The third tendency is *professionalization*. Evidence of this development is fewer conscripts per professional soldiers, fewer soldiers per capita, more enlisted men and officers, and more need for different types of professional practitioners due to the many new technological weapon systems implemented within the Danish armed forces. This process of professionalization with increased need for expertise will continue in the era of selective security. But at the same time, the professional influence will be challenged by the politicians. In the future, officers and politicians will meet in more open confrontations discussing the conditions, aims, and methods for Danish military contribution to UN, CSCE, and other international operations. The outcome is determined already. In a democratic society, where politization and professionalization meet, the latter is bound to lose because of the democratic legitimacy of the former.

In short, selective security will increase politization and limit civilization and professionalization.

NOTES

1. Denmark accepts the independence declaration of Norway in 1814, of the island of Iceland in 1944, and the Home Rule of the Faroe Islands in 1946 and of Greenland

in 1979. Moreover, Denmark and Norway accepted the International Court's rule in the case of East Greenland in 1937. Finally, Denmark did sell the Caribbean Islands to the United States and accepted the border with Germany in 1920 after a referendum. This border was actually the only border Hitler respected.

2. For instance, Denmark kept a low profile in NATO by abandoning deployment of nuclear weapons on its territory and concurrently denying allied submarine vessels armed with nuclear weapons access to Danish harbors. For the sake of the USSR, Denmark never accepted deployment of allied troops to the Island of Bornholm situated in the Baltic Sea. Moreover, Denmark spoke strongly for improved relations with the Warsaw Pact countries. Finally, Denmark argued more often for peaceful cooperation with the Warsaw Pact countries than did many other NATO countries and took a specific interest in human rights.

3. Russia is the Slavic word for Viking. "Russia" actually means "Viking-land."

4. In the period from 1430 to 1520, Denmark and Sweden were in conflict over how to cooperate (cf. the Kalmar union). From 1520 to 1658, they fought six major wars on which country should dominate the Nordic region.

5. Denmark lost one third of its area by the capitulative peace agreement in Roskilde in 1658 with Sweden by ceding territories in Norway, in the present southern Sweden and northern Germany.

6. Here, I disagree with Nikolaj Petersen, "Denmark's Foreign Relations in the 1990s," in *Annals* 512 (1990): 97. "Somewhat ironically, the relaxation of European tensions may give Denmark less scope for independent action than the Cold War did." On the other hand, in the last part of his article, Petersen argues and exemplifies the new possibilities of action for Denmark after the Cold War period in the Balkan area and with respect to social and human values, but is in agreement with Michael H. Clemmesen, "Efterkoldkrigstidens danske forsvarspolitik" (Danish Defense Policy after the Cold War Period), in DUPI, *Dansk Udenrigspolitisk Årbog 1994* (Danish Foreign Policy Yearbook 1994) (København: Dansk Udenrigspolitisk Institut, 1994), pp. 41–55. On page 44, "Det ... giver landet en betydelig udenrigspolitisk handlefrihed" (It ... gives the country room for significant foreign-policy maneuvering).

7. "Leding" means "got to the wars." The king had the right to demand the Viking fleet be manned and equipped with contributions from each local community.

8. A runic inscription says, "King Svend gave this stone to his hirdman Skarde, who went west but now died in Hedeby."

9. The remains of four big, identically constructed Viking castles of Aggersborg, Fyrkat, Nonnebakken, and Trelleborg give evidence of the central position of the king in Denmark at that time.

10. In 1648, after the death of the famous Danish king, Christian IV, the Assembly of the Estates of the Realm forced the new king to accept a coronation charter depriving him of the right to declare wars and collect taxes without the approval of the Assembly.

11. After World War II, Danish foreign policy has had at least four projects. The first is the universalistic project on human rights, taken care of through membership in the United Nations. The second is the Atlantic project on security, solved by membership in NATO. The third is the European project on economic growth and wealth, signified by membership in the European Union. The fourth is the Nordic project on social and cultural values, realized through membership in the Nordic Council.

12. July 8, 793 is the date of probably the most famous Viking attack on the monastery of the island of Lindisfarne.

13. The last time an organized Danish military unit waged war was in Denmark and more than 125 years ago, in the Danish-German war ending in 1864 with the Danish defeat.

14. Since 1948, Denmark has participated in twenty-two of the thirty-one UN missions with more than forty thousand soldiers, mostly serving as observers.

15. Of fifteen hundred Danish army soldiers deployed in UN missions, twelve hundred are in the former Yugoslavia, which makes Denmark one of the relatively biggest contributors to the UN-mission countries.

16. One argument for the four Viking castles has been as a place of disembarkation for England; see note 9. A more convincing use is, in my opinion, at the Viking king's fortress for recruitment and control of Danish squires.

17. See Hans Christian Bjerg, "Hvorfor byer bliber garnisons-byer: Samspillet mellem staten og lokalsamfundet" (Why towns become garrison cities: The correlation between government and local communities), in *Historiallinen Arkisto* 104 (1994): 49–59, saying that local political and economic forces did influence the establishment and maintenance of garrisons; and Keld Jensen, *Den militære beskæftigelse i Danmark: Indledende undersøgelse* (The military occupation in Denmark: Initial research) (Roskilde: Roskilde Universitetscenter, 1991), working paper 111, p. 63: "Garnisoneringerne ligger oftest i byer med over 10.000 indbyggere" (The garrisons are often situated in towns with more than 10,000 inhabitants).

18. See Just Rahbek, *Danish militærpolitik fra tronskiftet i 1839 til krigens udbrud i 1848* (Danish military policy from the accession of a new king in 1839 to the outbreak of the war in 1848) (København: Universitetsforlaget, 1973), p. 19.

19. Ibid., p. 40.

20. See Kristian Hvidt, *Venstre og Forsvarssagen* (The Liberal Party and the defense option) (Århus: Jysk Selskab for Historie 1960).

21. Michael H. Clemmesen, *Jyllands Landforsvar 1901–1940* (Jutlands ground defense 1901–1940) (København: Forsvarskommandoen, 1982), p. 2.

22. In 1989, the Ministry of Defense engaged one seventh of all public employees. In Jutland, 2.4% of all working places in Viborg county belong to the Ministry of Defense; at Bornholm county the same figure is 3%. In 1960, the occupational center of the Ministry of Defense was the town of Roskilde, close to Copenhagen; in 1988, it moved to Juelsminde. See Jensen, *Den militære,* pp. 58 and 61.

23. Michael H. Clemmesen, *Jyllands,* gives examples of how military expertise was ignored (p. 2).

24. Compare Petersen, "Denmark's Foreign Relations": "Compared to nuclear issues, defense policy has largely retained a consensus" (p. 431); or Bertel Heurlin, "Seks forsvarskommissioner: En vurdering" ("Six defense commission: An evaluation"), in Henning Sørensen, ed., *Forsvar i Forandring* (Defense in transition) (København: Samfundlitteratur, 1991): "den bevidste afpolitisering af forsvarspolitikken. . . . Alt i alt kan det konstateres, at forsvarspolitikken har . . . en tung ballst af konsensus" (the conscious depoliticization of the defense policy. . . . All in all, it can be said that the defense policy has a heavy ballast of consensus); and Nikolaj Petersen, "Forsvaret i den danske opinion" (Defense in Danish public opinion), in *Fremtiden* (*Future*) 172, 2 (1976): 43, "fra (i 1960) at være et indenrigspolitisk konfliktområde blev forsvarspolitikken til et konsensusområde i hvert fald for en tid" (from being a conflict area, the defense policy became a consensus area, at least for some time).

25. See Michael H. Clemmesen, *Værnskulturerne og forsvarspoltikken* (The culture

of the armed forces and the defense policy) (Århus: Politica, 1986) p. 75, especially the enclosed section, "Dansk forsvarspolitik i den eksisterende litteratur" (Danish defense policy in existing literature).

26. See Knud Larsen, *Forsvar og Folkeforbund* (Defense and the League of Nations) (Århus: Politica, 1976): "Venstre tabte troen på den militære sagkunskab" (the Liberal Party lost faith in the military expertise), p. 421, and "hæren svigtede sin opgave at forsyne konservative med grundlaget for et forsvarsstandpunkt" (the army failed to produce a basis for defense policy for the Conservative party), p. 420; or Clemmesen, *Jyllands,* who concludes for the period 1901–40 on the grounds of defense of Jutland, "sjælden overensstemmelse mellem den politiske hensigt og forsvarets forberedelser" (seldom compatibility between the political aim and the initiatives of the military), pp. 10–14.

27. See Michael H. Clemmesen, "Opponering til Nikolaj Petersen: Den forsvarspolitiske proces i Danmark" (Critic of Nikolaj Petersen: The political defense process in Denmark"), in Henning Sørensen, ed., *Sådan skal Danmark forsvares* (In this way Denmark should be defended) (København: Nyt fra Samsfundsvidenskaberne, 1987), p. 158.

28. Compare Petersen, "by 1960 a broad consensus had [been] formed . . . [even though] . . . consensus was never perfect" ("Denmark's Foreign Relations," p. 90) with "Den forsvarspolitiske proces i Danmark" (The political defense process in Denmark), in Henning Sørensen, ed., *Sådan skal Danmark forsvares,* pp. 137–155. "The political system's affairs with the armed forces is still influenced by the profound politicization that happened a hundred years ago. . . . But at the same time, the (situation) is paradoxically influenced by a limited interest and insight in defense issues among politicians" (author translation), p. 142 f.

29. See Larsen, *Defense and the League of Nations,* "Langt mere frugtbart vist det sig at være, når udgangspunktet tages i partimæssig og parlamentarisk problemstilling" (It is far more fruitful [for the understanding of Danish foreign policy] to look for party and parliamentary factors), p. 421.

30. See Heurlin, "Six defense commission," p. 21.

31. Clemmesen, in Sørensen, *Sådan skal Danmark,* 1987, "Det er længe siden, at en dansk regering sidst satte sin vilje igennem og sikrede at forsvaret blev opbygget og virkede på et også militært holdbart grundlag. Sidst det skete var . . . i perioden 1905–1908" ("It has been a long time since a Danish government willingly guaranteed the establishment and function of the armed forces on a sound military basis. The last time it happened was . . . in the period from 1905 to 1908"), p. 30.

32. See Rahbek, *Danish military policy,* "Øverstkommanderende var kongen . . . han forbeholdt sig ret til at placere sit militær hvor han ville" (Commander in chief was the king . . . he decided where to allocate his troops), p. 17.

33. See Norbert Elias, *Über den Prozess der Zivilsation* (Munich: 1969).

34. See Clemmesen, "Opponering til Petersen," in Sørensen, *Sådan Skal Danmark.*

35. See, for instance, Rahbek, *Danish military policy,* p. 17.

36. This calculation is based upon Jensen, *Military Occupation;* Hans Christian Johansen, *Danish Historical Statistics 1814–1980: Finansstatisktik* (Financial Statistics). (København: Gyldena, 1984), p. 304ff; Gunner Lind, "Det danske forsvar idallangsigtet historisk perspektiv: Optimal ressourceudnyttelse og militær struktur" (The Danish armed forces in a historical long-term perspective: Optimum use of resources and military structure), in Sørensen, *Sådan skal Danmark,* pp. 13–22; Rahbek, *Danish military policy; Samfundsstatistik 1993,* p. 80; Forsvarskommandoen, *Forsvarets rolle* (The role of the

armed forces) (København: Forsvarskommandoen, 1987), p. 74ff and 90; and Rigsrevisionen, *Beretning til statsrevisorerne om en undersøgelse af hærens opgavevaretagelse og økonomistyring, RB 1901/94* (København: 1994), pp. 9 and 40.

37. See Rahbek, *Danish military policy,* p. 28ff; or Clemmesen, *Jyllands,* "det militære bureaukrati . . . er sammensat af interessegrupper, der ikke nødvendigvis beslutter ideelt, rationelt eller frit" (the military bureaucracy consists of interest groups who do not act appropriately and freely), pp. 14–15; or Henning Sørensen, *Den danske officer: Fra kriger til administrator* (The Danish officer: From warrior to bureaucrat) (København: Nyt fra Samfundsvidenskaberne, 1988), pp. 144–146ff; or Rigsrevisionen, "Hærens organisatorske struktur bygger på en videreudvikling af de principper, der introduceredes umiddelbart efter 2. Vk. . . . Efter rigsrevisionens opfattelse stiller den sikkerhedspolitiske situation i dag helt andre og ændrede krav til hæren" (The organizational structure of the Army is built on principles developed right after World War II. . . . It is the opinion of the National Accountant that the security situation of today demands changes in the Army), p. 25.

38. See Petersen, in Sørensen, *Sådan skal Danmark,* "Det politiske systems manglende interesse" ("The political system's lack of interest"), p. 149.

39. See ibid.

40. See Clemmesen, *Jyllands,* p. 14.

41. Calculated from the figures in Forsvarskommandoen, *Role of the Armed Forces,* p. 74ff, for 1965; and Rigsrevisionen, for 1985 and 1993.

42. This section is based upon Hans Christian Bjerg, *Til fædrelandets forsvar: Værnepligten i Danmark gennem tiderne* (For the national defense: Conscription in Denmark throughout history) (København: Værnepligtsstyrelsen, 1991).

43. See Lene Rold, *13-tallets stridsdragt set på baggrund af den militære organisation* (14th century battle dress observed on the basis of the military organization) (Unpublished Ph.D. dissertation, København, 1980?), p. 92.

44. See Lind, in Sørensen, *Sådan skal Danmark,* "Ved periodens begyndelse [1660] fandtes det stort set to militære systemer: Lansknægte og landeværnet" (At the beginning of the period two military systems existed: lansquenets [a professional army in Denmark to match the professional German soldiers] and militia [conscripted army to match the Swedish conscripted solders]), p. 14.

45. Ibid., p. 18.

46. See Rold, "I stedet for alment opbud til leding kunne dette allerede på Jyske Lovs tid (1241) konverteres til skatteleding. . . . Militære præstationer fra befolkningens side var fastlagt efter indviklede regler om personlige arbejdsydelser og konvertering af disse til skatter" (Instead of leding . . . it could already in 1241 be converted to taxation leding. . . . Military performances depended on complicated rules on personal output and their conversion to taxes), p. 87.

47. See Lind, in Sørensen, *Sådan skal Danmark,* for the period 1700–1803 (p. 18); and Forsvarskommandoen, *Role of the Armed Forces,* p. 74ff, for 1965 and 1973 figures; and Rigsrevisionen, *Beretning,* p. 9, for the 1993 data.

48. See Lind, in Sørensen, *Sådan skal Danmark.* The figures relate to drawn conscripts of the total number of soldiers in the infantry, p. 14 f. Conscripts did serve in the navy and the artillery, as well, but they served for eighteen months, followed by eight years in the reserve unit, p. 16.

49. This section is based on Henning Sørensen, "Denmark: The Vanguard of Conscientious Objection," in Charles C. Moskos and John Whiteclay Chambers II, eds., *The*

New Conscientious Objection: From Sacred to Secular Resistance (New York: Oxford University Press, 1993), pp. 106–113.

50. Ibid., p. 110.

51. Compiled and calculated from Johansen, *Danish Historical Statistics,* pp. 336, 356, and 362ff, for the period 1820–1955/56; and *Samfundsstatistik 1993,* p. 80, for 1970–91.

52. The figures show investment expenditures compared to all defense working expenses. See Johansen, *Danish Historical Statistics,* pp. 336, 358, 362; Forsvarskommandoen, *Role of the Armed Forces,* p. 90; *Samfundsstatistik 1993,* p. 80; Rigsrevisionen, *Beretning;* Forsvarsministerens Rådgivnings-og Analyse Gruppe, *Fremtidige konflikttyper og konsekvenser for forsvaret* (Future types of conflicts and their consequences for the armed forces) (København: n.p., 1994), p. 87.

53. See Rigsrevisionen, *Beretning,* p. 25, for the army.

54. After World War II, the first Gallup survey on defense issues was on military expenditures held in 1950, Gallup survey no. 1950. 23.

55. See Nikolaj Petersen, "Sikkerhedspolitik og indenrigspolitik folhekingsralges den 10 Maj 1988" (Security policy and domestic policy: The parliamentary election of May 10, 1988), *Dansk indenrigspolitik Årbog 1988* (Danish foreign policy yearbook 1988), p. 48.

56. See Forsvarets Center for Lederskab, *Befolkningens forsvarsvilje maj 75–apr 94* (The defense will of the population May 1975–Oct 1990) (København: n.p., 1994), p. 2. In fact, eight different questions are asked in each survey. The answers are then combined and calculated so that the most defense-negative person scores zero and the most defense-positive person scores ten.

57. See Forsvarets Center for Lederskab, publications 1979, no. 80; 1983, no. 99; 1985, no. 108; 1987, no. 113; 1989, no. 122; and *Befolkningens forsvarsvilje,* 1994. The "do not knows" are excluded in surveys from 1980 to 1992.

58. See Petersen, "Defense in Danish Public Opinion," 1976, p. 25, who found the opposite to be true some years ago: "The Danish population is not very positive against the military as a population."

59. The Danish Home Guard consists of seventy thousand volunteer male and female soldiers, only lightly armed and unpaid but nevertheless ready to defend their community and showing it by participating in military exercises, current assistance to the armed forces, and the like.

60. The following data on the Danish officer corps are based on Sørensen, *Sådan skal Danmark;* see "English summary," pp. 349–57, in particular.

61. See Henning Sørensen, "New Perspectives on the Military Profession: The I/O Model and Esprit de Corps Reevaluated," in *Armed Forces and Society* 20, no. 4 (1994).

62. See Clemmesen, *Værnskulturerne og forsvarspolitikken.*

63. See, among others, Larsen, *Defense and the League of Nations,* p. 447; or Clemmesen; or Rahbek, "Danish military policy."

REFERENCES

Bjerg, Hans Christian. "Forsvarskommissioner i Danmark gennem 125 år" (Defense committees in Denmark in 125 years). In Henning Sørensen, ed., *Forsvar under forandring,* 7–17. København: Samfundslitterartur, 1991.

————. *Til fædrelandets forsvar: Værnepligten i Danmark gennem tiderne* (In defense of your country: Conscription in Denmark throughout the ages). København: Værnspligtsstyrelsen, 1991.

Clemmesen, Michael H. *Vænskulturerne og forsvarspolitikken* (The cultures of the services and defense policy). Århus: Politica, 1986.

————. "Eferkoldkrigstidens danske forsvarspolitik" (Danish defense after the Cold War). *Dansk Udenrigspolitisk Årbog 1994*. København: DUPI, 1994, pp. 41–55.

Lind, Gunner. "Det danske forsvar i langsigtet historisk perspektiv" ("The Danish defense in broad historical perspective"). In Henning Sørensen, ed., *Sådan skal Danmark forsvares*. København: Nyt fra Samfundsvidenskaberne, 1987. An English version is "Military Absolutism: The Army Officers of Denmark-Norway as Social Group and Political, 1660–1848." *Scandinavian Journal of History* 12 (1987).

Petersen, Nikolaj. "International Power and Foreign Policy Behavior: The Formulation of Danish Security Policy in the 1870–1914 Period." In K. Goldmann and G. Sjøstedt, eds., *Power, Capabilities, Interdependence: Problems in the Study of International Influence*, 235–69. London: 1979.

————. "Denmark's Foreign Relations in the 1990s." *Annals* 512 (November 1990): 88–100.

Sørensen, Henning. *Den danske officer: Fra kriger til administrator* (The Danish officer: From warrior to administrator). København: Nyt fra Samfundsvidenskaberne, 1988, with an English summary.

————. "Danish Public Opinion of Foreign Policy Issues after World War II: A Stable Distribution?" In Philippe Manigart, ed., *The Future of Security in Europe: A Comparative Analysis of European Public Opinion.* Brussels: Royal Military School, 1992.

EGYPT

Ibrahim A. Karawan

Since 1952, Egypt's domestic politics and foreign policy have undergone a fundamental restructuring or radical alteration in orientation and defining characteristics. The one-party system of the Arab Socialist Union was replaced by a managed political pluralism, an Egyptian version of a controlled glasnost. The state-centered economy based on central planning shifted to an open-door economic system, or *infitah iqtisadi*. The external alliance with "the mother country of socialism," the Soviet Union, was scrapped in favor of a close alignment with the United States. And the "conflict of destinies" with Israel that had started with Egypt's involvement in the Palestine War in 1948 was brought to a dramatic end three decades later at Camp David. Despite the far-reaching and multidimensional nature of these changes, one political fact has never changed in Egypt since Nasser's "Free Officers" seized power: Egypt has been ruled by presidents who had a military background and who relied on the army as their main power base.

This chapter examines the political role of the Egyptian military against the backdrop of these changes. It places the evolving role of the military establishment, within the context of societal and political transformation, as they have challenged state managers at critical junctures. In 1965, 1967, 1977, and 1986, the authoritative control or the political management of the military became crucial for the regime's survival and political viability. The current political decompression or relaxation of restrictions on freedom of expression has made it possible for researchers to have access to the views of former military and political leaders as well as the critics of the special role of the military institution. The conclusion identifies the main trends concerning the political role of the Egyptian military to date and speculates about future directions.

THE MILITARY SEIZURE OF POWER

With the collapse of the monarchical regime, the Free Officers Organization became the real power in the country. Egypt's short-lived "liberal experiment" came to an end, and an era of military dominance of Egyptian politics was clearly set in motion. Whereas the monarchy had represented a system of civilian rule and military influence, the new regime exemplified a strong military rule or full-blown praetorianism with a technocratic civilian influence, particularly during the first half of the 1960s. Different from other cases in which the military officers coordinated their moves with oppositional political parties, Nasser's seizure of power was purely a military operation without any civilian participation.[1] Once the Free Officers gained control, all political parties were suspended and then banned and replaced by political organizations (the Liberation Rally, the National Union, and the Arab Socialist Union), all under the control of the military officers. During the first years after *al-harakah al-mubarakah,* or the "blessed movement," all major decisions were made by the Revolutionary Command Council (RCC), composed exclusively of the leadership of the Free Officers, using the all-civilian cabinet as an instrument to carry out its own policies.[2]

Military dominance was soon manifested in the ranks of the core elite, the cabinet, political organizations, the diplomatic corps, the public sector, and the state bureaucracy. Subsequently, the military leaders managed to assert their hegemony over political power and the state machinery for policy making. Officers and former officers controlled strategic posts as presidents, vice-presidents, prime ministers, and important ministeries (e.g., defense, interior, and foreign affairs). Often the president assumed as well the posts of prime minister, supreme commander of the armed forces, head of the national security council, and party chief.

Civilians lacked any independent power base after political parties were banned. They were first and foremost technocratic cadres who owed their roles to one group of the military. Moreover, they competed with military officers who had acquired graduate degrees in management, physics, and engineering. The rise of those "officer-technocrats," as Richard Dekmejian called them, "was the military's answer to its civilian critics, since it now has its own trained experts to cope with the new and diverse complexities of an industrializing society."[3] Between September 1952 and June 1967, the military accounted for an increasing share of the composition of the cabinet, reaching 66% in 1967. In general, the officers enhanced their share of leadership positions; 56% of the Higher Executive Committee of the Arab Socialist Union, more than 80% of the governors, and a high representation among Egypt's ambassadors to the outside world.[4]

The core elite of the new regime had a similar mindset about the basic issues of the political and social system. The eleven officers who engineered the seizure of state power were all born between 1917 and 1922. The few schools they attended during the 1930s were major centers of the nationalist movement that witnessed frequent anti-British demonstrations. Nine of these officers graduated from the military academy in the same year (the 1938 *duf'a,* or graduating class). Most went to Palestine in 1948 to fight as part of a military force hurriedly deployed, inadequately trained, and badly equipped, and experience that nourished feelings of betrayal and embitterment toward the monarchy, which they saw as responsible for the defeat. Not surprisingly, it was in Palestine that the first plans to seize power were discussed by the Free Officers.[5] They were all Muslims. Most were recent lower-middle-class migrants to the cities who resented the privileges enjoyed by the upper landowning classes. For example, candidates to the military academy had to come from families that owned land or had at least a mid-level status in the bureaucracy. When the Wafd party changed that policy in the mid-1930s, some people like Nasser and Sadat were able to join the military. Most of the Free Officers had similar experiences in a societal setting that influenced their political attitudes.[6]

The most important component of such political attitudes on the part of the new military rulers was a vehement hostility toward liberal democracy in general and multiparty systems in particular. After all, it was such a system that had failed to put an end to the prolonged British occupation of the country, and its main political parties had competed with each other to gain favors with the British ambassador. Moreover, the young military officers found the "liberal system" guilty of neglecting the popular demands for socioeconomic reform that led to an escalation of protest, riots, assassinations, and acts of violence during the last five years prior to the collapse of the old regime.

The political predispositions of the military officers were in essence opposed to liberal democracy. If one starts with what Morris Janowitz has called "professional self-images,"[7] the army officers perceived themselves as efficient nation-builders, as members of a meritorious and not-ascriptive institution, as possessing highly needed organizational and administrative skills such as discipline, planning, and familiarity with modern technology. They compared these self-images with their images of the politicians of the old order: social decadence, endemic corruption, privileges for the few, and lack of effectiveness in meeting the national challenges. These challenges, the leaders of the new order argued, could be met only by getting rid of the divisive features of competitive systems and building one organization to mobilize the public in pursuit of superior objectives for the nation.

Equally significant in shaping the political attitudes of the Free Officers who seized power in July 1952 was the influence of a set of ideas associated with two radical nationalist and Islamist movements that became more appealing during their formative period in the late 1930s and during the 1940s: the Young Egypt Society (YES) and the Society of Muslim Brethren (SMB). Nasser was a member of YES, while other military officers such as Abdel Moneim Abdel Ra'uf, Kamal Eddin Hussein, and Anwar al-Sadat were either members or sympathizers with the SMB. YES was interested in social reform and had been influenced by the model provided by fascist Italy in search of lost national glory. SMB focused on cultural autonomy from the West and the urgent need for Islamic populism. Despite differences between the two movements, they shared a certain hostility and contempt toward liberal democracy and competitive politics. Their core objectives of attaining political independence, safeguarding the "national honor," and restructuring cultural and social life could not be attained without a strong state with power concentrated at the top.[8] Individual liberties, the autonomy of intermediate groups, and political pluralism were not regarded as positive notions.

The Free Officers proved to be rather good students, who learned quite well from the doctrines of these two nationalist and Islamist movements. They soon banned political organizations and put under house arrest, imprisoned, or executed leaders of both movements and deprived former politicians in general from the right to assume public office or even to vote. An element of political engineering enhanced state capacity under a "presidential monarchy," described by some as the Egyptian version of Bonapartism. Major political issues remained the monopoly of the presidential center, and all presidential policy undertakings were above discussion by Parliament or other institutions. The president could submit policy initiatives directly to the people, a mechanism borrowed from Gaullist France to legitimize his broad political powers on plebiscitarian grounds.

The new constitution was fundamentally a document more concerned with enhancing than with limiting vast state power.[9] The regime's socioeconomic reforms and anti-imperialist policies were used as part of a trade-off for mass support or political consent.[10] In this relentless pursuit of hegemony or, rather, strict avoidance of competitive politics, the military leaders liquidated all alternatives to their rule, whether coming from the parties of the old elite with whom they clashed ideologically and politically or from the populist parties and movements that inspired them ideologically but could have become serious political rivals.

The regime that emerged was more interested in mobilizing support than in promoting political participation among popular classes or *al-Jamahir* (the masses). Through populist policies in areas such as education, health, and employment, it presented its own credentials as biased toward the socially underprivileged majority. A political cult of personality around the leader of the Free Officers, Nasser, developed via the state's total control over the mass media and educational system. All open critics of the regime were deemed "enemies of the people," and they could be found under house arrest, in prison, or in exile. The state developed a multitude of security agencies to monitor dissent and to maintain law and order by crushing opposition, whether from the right or the left.[11]

The predominance of military officers over security agencies was unleashed against leftists during the late 1950s and early 1960s, ironically, when the regime was implementing socioeconomic measures that the Egyptian left had been advocating for years and developing its ties with the Soviet Union. Security agencies tortured and violated the most fundamental human rights of many leftists, leading to the death of some of them in prison.[12] The regime agreed to allow many leftists to join the secret organization it formed, the "vanguard of socialists," provided they agreed to disband their parties and stop advocating any radical ideology of class struggle. Such "licensed infiltration"[13] was conducted under the watchful eyes of security agencies.

In 1965, the regime was confronted with a major challenge when a resurrected radical wing of the Muslim Brethren under the doctrinal guidance of Sayyid Qutb tried to bring it down. To the leaders of that wing, Nasser was a communist agent bent on using the secular state to de-Islamize society. Concentrated in the urban centers, the organization attempted to extend its activities to the army. At that time, the leadership of the regime was concerned about political stability after the toppling of its populist counterparts in Algeria and Ghana. Its response to the Islamist threat was true to its military bureaucratic nature. It was the office of the strong military man, Field Marshal 'Amir, and more particularly the Military Criminal Investigations under his close collaborator Brigadier Shams Badran, that took charge of the situation. This included thousands of arrests, interrogation of those arrested under highly abusive conditions, a persistent pattern of torture, and military tribunals leading to death sentences for some and to long prison terms for others. The state stipulated that the thousands found innocent after months of imprisonment could not take their grievances to the courts, because the actions of the security agencies were conducted under a state of emergency.[14]

During the same year the regime identified another threat to its policies from rich families in the countryside. In one of his secret meetings with the "vanguard of socialists," Nasser warned that the rural bourgeoisie opposed to the regime was still controlling the villages and intimidating "revolutionary elements."[15] When a peasant activist was killed, a prominent local family was accused of involvement in his murder; the issue became nationally known as the *Kamshish* affair. Leftists within the Arab Socialist Union and the Socialist Youth Organization favored launching a protracted political-ideological confrontation against "forces of reaction opposed to the socialist transformation" in the agricultural sector.[16] Instead of such confrontation, the regime formed the Higher Committee for the Liquidation of Feudalism, also under 'Amir, who was never considered sympathetic to leftist causes. The committee subjected a sample of wealthy landowners to administrative penalties, but refrained from the sociopolitical restructuring advocated by the political left. In the words of Leonard Binder, it did not "open thousands of Egyptian villages to the ministrations of militant leftist cadres."[17]

Clearly, the period 1952–67 was characterized by military dominance. The Free Officers who toppled the monarchy dominated important aspects of the state machinery and sought to eliminate all political alternatives to their rule. The military role expansion extended to the public sector, the governmental bureaucracy, and the diplomatic corps. In what amounted to a peaceful coup, the military under 'Amir enjoyed during the period 1962–67 considerable autonomy from Nasser himself, as evidenced by the fact that it was able to prevent the president from exercising his constitutional powers in appointing and promoting high-ranking officers. It also rejected any political or ideological role for the Arab Socialist Union in the affairs of the military. The military relied on Soviet weapons but did not import with them the political indoctrination known in the Soviet system.

Moreover, the military establishment assumed additional responsibilities while involved in a protracted warfare in Yemen after 1962. The army and its security and intelligence agencies flexed their muscles against suspected political opponents of the regime in urban centers. The leadership of the regime throughout that period belonged to the top echelons of the Free Officers, a leadership that adopted hostile attitudes toward political pluralism and competitive politics. The mobilization of mass support, not genuine political participation, was its main objective.

GRADUAL MILITARY DISENGAGEMENT FROM POLITICS

A main turning point in the contemporary history of civil-military relations in Egypt was its humiliating and shocking defeat at the hands of Israel in June 1967. The defeat had multifaceted effects on the role of the military. A good case for comparison is that of the Argentinean military after its defeat in the Falkland/Malvinas war in June 1982, which undermined in a dramatic way the credibility of the military establishment.[18] A crushing defeat is effective in discrediting a dominant military regime claiming to be able to solve a political and economic crisis. Such regimes often assert their legitimacy based on certain unambiguous statements of core objectives as maximizing military strength and safeguarding national integrity. A sudden and massive defeat can demolish the credibility of those leaders. Those segments in society most afflicted by the costs of defeat may question the leaders' credentials for managing the polity and the economy, in light of their failure to perform the professional military tasks they were trained to perform.

The Egyptian leaders in the aftermath of the 1967 defeat were confronted with such a situation. The society that for years was led to believe that its state had built the strongest army in the Middle East realized abruptly that it had been blatantly deceived, that Egypt was beaten and had lost Sinai to Israeli control. When the "revolutionary" regime was confronted with its moment of truth, it did not fare better than the "reactionary" monarchy it had overthrown. Despite state attempts to downplay the political significance of the outcome in 1967 by calling it a "setback," wide segments of society were convinced that the gross negligence and incompetence of Egypt's "new pashas" had led to the major and costly defeat.

As in Argentina after June 1982, an outraged public in Egypt after June 1967 was made more bitter and restless by proliferating accounts of recriminations within the top leadership over the conduct of the war and blame for an embarrassing defeat. On the one hand, Field Marshal 'Amir and the top officers in charge of the main military branches stressed that the blunder was basically a political one, for which Nasser himself was responsible: Because he was engaged in a political bluff, he had refused to take offensive military action, hoped for a last-minute diplomatic solution, and left the Egyptian forces vulnerable to crushing Israeli strikes.[19]

Nasser and his supporters in the Arab Socialist Union and the state bureaucracy, on the other hand, argued that the defeat resulted from incompetence at the highest levels of the Egyptian military establishment. However, that argument did not absolve Nasser from responsibility for placing incompetent military leaders in positions of great authority and for embarking on a serious confrontation with Israel under such conditions. That military group supporting 'Amir attempted to regain its influence by challenging Nasser's authority, but they failed and were put on public trial.[20] The most significant aspect of that trial was that it revealed to the attentive public, as a result of the divisions among the Free Officers, the extent of corruption and incompetence in the inner circles of the junta; in the process it contributed further to the erosion of the credibility of the entire defeated regime.

As a sign of that erosion, large demonstrations by workers and students erupted in Cairo and Alexandria during 1968. These demonstrators, enraged by the massive defeat and the light sentences received by military officers presumably responsible for it, demanded a change in the costly business-as-usual attitude. They stated loudly and clearly that the system of domination by the "praetorian stratum" and *dawlat al-mukhabarat* (state run by intelligence agencies) had to be brought to an end; they insisted that to regain legitimacy the political leadership would have to rein in the security apparatus, allow a legislative assembly with real power, and remove restrictions imposed on the press. The linkages between the military defeat and these political demands were clear in their minds; the closed polity had enabled a privileged but grossly incompetent elite to persist and thrive in the absence of any accountability.[21]

Some critics on the left thought that the post-defeat era warranted a restructuring of civil-military relations by undoing the "exclusiveness" of the ruling military class and politicizing the army to make it a revolutionary force ready for launching a "protracted people's war," similar to the struggle in Vietnam. The demoralized regime that at first tolerated such calls put an abrupt end to them by stipulating at the highest level that the only solution was to maintain the corporate or professional identity of the regular army and to enhance the skill structure of the armed forces, after purging incompetent military leaders.[22]

That Nasser had prevailed in the power struggle against 'Amir at the top of the regime and vigorous popular pressures for reform a few months later produced a decline in the political influence of the military establishment. For example, the military represented 66% of the cabinet in 1967, a percentage that dropped to 41% in 1968, and to 22% by 1972.[23] After getting rid of 'Amir's group, Nasser could promote younger meritorious commanders to leading military positions and gradually professionalize the army by making it accountable to his leadership, one that had originated in the military ranks.[24]

The main task of the new military leaders during Nasser's last three years and Sadat's first three years in office focused on preparing the army for action on the Sinai front. While a showdown with Israel was perceived before 1967 as a long-term objective, after 1967 imperatives of regime survival, improving the army's institutional image in society and enhancing Egypt's international bargaining position, required such emphasis on the war effort, which culminated in October 1973 with the crossing of the Suez Canal. Although the military had lost much of its autonomy and influence, its claims on the budget and the allocation of resources were stronger than ever before, as expressed in Nasser's slogans, "the battle first and last" and "no sound is louder than the sound of the battle." In fact, military expenditures increased from 7.4% of the GNP during the first half of the 1960s to 13% in 1969–70 and to over 21% by the mid-1970s.[25]

THE MILITARY AND THE CHALLENGES OF LIBERALIZATION

The 1973 war was widely perceived in Egypt and in the Arab world as a victory of sorts that rectified the damage done to the image of the military by the 1967 defeat. At a minimum, they were able to take the initiative in a large-scale confrontation and use the element of surprise effectively against the Israeli forces in Sinai. The army leadership was by then quite professionalized and was committed to abide by the constitutional authority of the political leadership. All army promotions to the rank of colonel or above required presidential endorsement. To use Amos Perlmutter's terms, we are dealing here with "professional soldiers" who act on the basis of corporate professionalism and conceive their role as guided by the supremacy of political authority.[26]

Despite some radical shifts in Egypt's regional and global alignment following 1973–74, the military leadership as a whole abided by the decisions made by political leaders, even when not adequately consulted or not consulted at all.[27] The case with which Sadat shifted Egypt's foreign policy toward peace with its main enemy for three decades (i.e., Israel) and toward rupture with its sole arms supplier for two decades (i.e., the Soviet Union) illustrates how the political leadership has subordinated the military officers and succeeded in purging military leaders like General Sadiq and General Shazli, who possessed the ambition and following necessary to potential rivals for power.[28] Moreover, the decline of the military's share in the cabinet continued after the 1973 war: In the cabinet formed a year later it dropped to 15% under a civilian prime minister, Abd al-Aziz Hijazi.[29]

The postwar restructuring was not confined to foreign relations but included the domestic economic and political arenas in ways that impacted the role of the military. If one starts with the economic front, Egypt witnessed its own version of *perestroika* through an Economic Open Door Policy (ODEP) that activated market forces. One by-product of that policy and of a greater exposure to the international economic system was an inflationary wave that swept the national economy and reduced the purchasing power of fixed-income strata in society. Low- and mid-level officers in the army were among those adversely affected by these economic trends and resented the fact that ODEP led to the enrichment of import-export businessmen and currency dealers. The salary of a secretary working in a branch of a foreign bank or oil company could easily exceed that of an army brigadier. Cases of resignation on economic grounds by military officers were reported during the 1970s.[30] Rather than expressions of ideological opposition to the ODEP, these were attempts to follow the economic avenues that had become more rewarding under the ODEP.

The ODEP has influenced the political role of the military on the domestic front in another way. It became clear by the mid-1970s that the public's expectations of a *'ubur iqtisadi* (economic crossing) paralleling in its success the military crossing of 6 October 1973 were not going to be fulfilled. The inflation rate was between 25% and 30%. Under pressures from the International Monetary Fund (IMF), in 1974 the government raised the prices of many basic commodities and services, which threatened a steeply rising cost of living, beyond the modest means of many city dwellers in particular. These decisions were met in January 1977 by an explosion of protest and riots by public sector workers, government employees, pension recipients, and an urban lumpen-proletariat of unemployed and semiemployed groups. These riots are considered the worst in Egypt's contemporary history, often compared with the January riots of 1952 that signalled the looming disintegration of the monarchy. Faced with the threat of a total loss of control, the regime ordered a fourteen-hour curfew and deployed the army into the restless urban centers to restore its control over society.[31]

This was not a role that the military leadership was eager to assume. Many officers may have felt a degree of sympathy with the demonstrators against soaring inflation, increasing corruption, and provocative consumerism. They may have felt reluctant to be used by the rulers in crushing their own people. This may explain why the army's leadership asked the president to cancel the price increases before sending the troops to the streets.[32] However, this was not the last time the military was deployed to the streets to help restore law and order. Under President Hosni Mubarak, the army played a major role in 1986 in crushing violent riots by the paramilitary forces known as the Central Security Forces, whose task, ironically, is to quell riots.[33] It is important to note that in 1977 and 1986, the armed forces withdrew to their barracks after performing the tasks assigned by the political leadership, which attests to their professionalism.

Along with ODEP, the state relaxed its exclusive control over political life. In other words, the regime's strategy was one of liberalization of the economy and of the polity as well. By the mid-1970s, some political parties emerged on the scene, the capricious use of power was curtailed, opposition groups had their own publications, the spectrum of political opinions in the "national" press was broadened, and the corporatist structures became more pluralistic.[34] This climate made it possible for political activists to discuss, though within certain limits, the role of the military in Egyptian society, a topic previously beyond discussion. Since 1952, matters related to the military had not been subject to civilian scrutiny, and information about such matters had not been found in the public domain. In the 1970s, the opposition pressed increasingly for an open discussion of civil-military relations.[35]

The first contentious issue in that discourse centered around the need to make the military budget subject to supervision by civilian agencies, particularly Parliament. Even among those who did not advocate cutting the military budget after the end of the state of war because of economic hardships,[36] some argued that the military should be held responsible to the political institutions for its expenditures. The management of the large resources involved should not be left to the military to perform and monitor, particularly under a system that claims to be based on political pluralism and the rule of law. The persistence of such practices means in effect that the countries that supply Egypt with military assistance and technical training know more than Egyptian civilian institutions about Egypt's military budget.[37]

The second issue in the discourse about the political role of the military establishment concerns its ability to translate its crucial role in regime stability into socioeconomic privileges. The leftist critics in particular have warned against military privileges as violations of equal citizenship that increase social tensions and resentment.[38] On the other hand, the military has felt the adverse effects of ODEP translated into a downward mobility compared to the new fat cats in society. In response, the military leadership has engaged in economic projects and cooperatives in housing, transportation, and agriculture to insulate the army (and particularly its officers) against soaring costs of living and to maintain their support for the regime. One general, responding to critics of such projects, described them as avoiding a situation in which the armed forces are left vulnerable to market forces.[39]

The third issue concerns the political relationship between the military establishment and the ruling party led by the president. The constitution prohibits political activities by the professional military. It was in violation of this rule that Minister of Defense Abu-Ghazallah became a member in the politbureau of the ruling National Democratic Party (NDP). Though this violation was brought to an end in October 1984, Abu-Ghazalah continued to address only the NDP's conventions, a behavior criticized by opposition parties as putting the country's army squarely on the side of one party against all others. Stated differently, such military bias on behalf of the ruling party may substitute the old direct political role of the military with an indirect one,[40] but still at the expense of democracy.[41]

FUTURE PROSPECTS

Predicting the future political role of the Egyptian military can be a hazardous exercise in crystal-ball gazing. A few years ago a keen observer of Egyptian politics, Robert Springborg, concluded that defense minister Abu-Ghazallah had become the functional equivalent of Field Marshal 'Amir. Because of his support in the army (through providing subsidized goods and services), and his role in arms sales, manufacturing, agriculture and construction, and his linkages with private sector interests, his removal would have required a real "rectification revolution." Shortly after the publication of that assessment, Abu-Ghazallah was removed from his position, in April 1989, without any revolution, to be replaced by the governor of Cairo, a former army general.[42]

One can safely argue that the main challenge faced by the Egyptian regime in the 1990s comes from the militant Islamist groups that have mounted a relentless campaign of violence. This campaign has proved to be costly in human life, for state revenues, and in weakening the regime's credibility by demonstrating its inability to protect its officials or to end protracted acts of defiance. Over the years, radical Islamist groups have attempted to penetrate the armed forces to recruit followers among the lower and middle ranks of the officer corps. The Islamic Liberation Party's members in the Technical Military Academy attempted to bring Sadat's regime down, and it was the military wing of the Jihad group, led by Colonel 'Abbud al-Zumur, that ultimately assassinated him. The group that killed President Sadat included three officers who served in various capacities in the army.[43] Though the attempt to eliminate Sadat succeeded, the subsequent effort to mount a military uprising has failed drastically. Quite recently, the press spokesman of another militant group, the Islamic Group, warned that its military wing, formed largely of young officers and soldiers, has been preparing for assassinations of state officials to be followed by a seizure of power.[44]

The question of the role of the military in this confrontation between the regime and militant Islamist groups continues to intrigue the students of Egypt.[45] One component of the militants' strategy in the 1990s, which they emphasize in their writings and trials, is a strong interest in recruiting "Islamically minded" low- and middle-level military officers, most of whom have socioeconomic and generational characteristics similar to those of the Islamist militants. The militants also hope to use such recruits in assassinations and in creating divisions within the army, making decisive action against the militants more difficult for the regime.

There are some signs, however, that the military institution seems to be getting involved in the state confrontation against the militants, although not to the degree of its counterpart in Algeria 1991–94. The army has been training the paramilitary antiterrorist squads of the Interior Ministery since finding out that radical groups include cadres trained in advanced military techniques in Afghanistan.[46] Militants stand trial in military tribunals, not in civilian courts, and

membership in violent groups is punishable by death. Army generals who served
in these tribunals have been targeted for assassination by the militants.[47] Moreover, the media gave wide coverage to Mubarak's visits to the military in 1994
and his denunciation of terrorism in his address to the officers; the latter responded that state power has "sharp teeth" to be used against the "terrorists
who aim at destabilizing Egypt."[48] The military's role during this critical juncture may prove to be a major determinant of the direction of Egyptian politics
in the next decade.

NOTES

1. On comparing the cases of Egypt and Turkey see Mostafa Kamel El-Sayyid, "The
Role of Leadership in the Civilianization Process of Reform Oriented Military Regimes,"
(master's thesis, University of California, 1971); and Richard H. Dekmejian, "Egypt and
Turkey: The Military in the Background," in Roman Kolkowicz and A. Korbonski, eds.,
Soldiers, Peasants and Bureaucrats (London, Allen and Unwin, 1982), 28–51.

2. Ibrahim A. Karawan, "Egypt's Defense Policy," in Stephanie Neumann, ed., *Defense Planning in Less-Industrialized States* (Lexington: D. C. Heath and Co., 1984), p.
150.

3. Dekmejian, "Egypt and Turkey," p. 33.

4. Aliezer Beeri, *Army Officers in Arab Society and Politics* (New York: Praeger,
1970), pp. 28–29; Shahrough Akhavi, "Egypt's Neo-Patrimonial Elite," in Frank Ta-
chau, ed., *Political Elites and Political Development in the Middle East* (Cambridge:
Schenkman, 1975), pp. 85–89; Richard H. Dekmejian, *Egypt under Nasir* (Albany: State
University of New York, 1971), pp. 172–74; and Anwar Abd al-Malik, *Misr Mujtama'
Jadid Yabnih al-'Askariyun* (Egypt a new society being built by the military) (Beirut:
Dar al-Tali'ah, 1964).

5. See Ahmad Hamrush, *Misr wa al-'Askariyun* (Egypt and the Military) (Cairo:
Maktabat Madbuli, 1983), chapter 5; and Robert Springborg, "Patterns of Association
in the Egyptian Political Elite," in George Lenczowski, ed., *Political Elites in the Middle
East* (Washington, D.C.: American Enterprise Institute, 1975), p. 93.

6. Gamal Abdel Nasser, *Egypt's Liberation: The Philosophy of the Revolution*
(Washington, D.C.: Public Affairs Press, 1955), p. 23; P. J. Vatikiotis, *Nasser and His
Generation* (London: Croom Helm, 1978), chapter 5; and Ibrahim Karawan, "Egypt's
Defense Policy: Who Makes What? How? and When?" (paper presented to the Columbia
University Workshop on Defense Policy-making in Less-Industrialized States, New York
City, April 16, 1982).

7. See Morris Janowitz, *Military Institutions and Coercion in the Developing Nations*
(Chicago: University of Chicago Press, 1977).

8. See P. J. Vatikiotis, *Nasser and His Generation,* chapters 3–4.

9. See Joel Migdal, *Strong Societies and Weak States* (Princeton: Princeton University Press, 1988), chapter 5.

10. Tariq al-Bishri, *al-Dimuqratiyah wa Nizam 23 Yulyu* (Democracy and the Regime
of 23rd of July) (Cairo: Dar al-Hillal, 1991), chapter 3.

11. Ali Eddin Hillal, *al-Nizam al-Siyasi al-Masri wa Tahadeyat al-Thamaninat* (The
Egyptian political system and the challenges of the 1980s) (Cairo: Maktabat Nahdat al-
Sharq, 1986), p. 18.

12. Rif'at S. Ahmad, *Thawrat al-Janaral Jamal 'Abd al-Nasir* (The revolution of General Jamal 'Abd al-Nasir) (Cairo: Dar al-Huda, 1993), pp. 619–42.

13. Shimon Shamir, "The Marxists in Egypt: The Licensed Infiltration Doctrine in Practice," in Michael Cofino and Shimon Shamir, eds., *The USSR in the Middle East* (Jerusalem: Israel Universities Press, 1973).

14. See Ahmad Ra'if, *al-Bawabah al-Sawda': Safahat min Tarikh al-Ikhwan al-Muslimin* (The Black Gate: Pages from the history of the Muslim Brethren) (Cairo: al-Zahra', 1986); and Ahmad Abdel Majid, *al-Ikhwan wa 'Abdel Nasir: al Qisah al-Kamilah li Tanzim 1965* (The Brethren and Abdel Nasir: The complete story of the 1965 organization) (Cairo: al-Zahra', 1991).

15. Rif'at Sayyid Ahmad, *Revolution,* p. 778.

16. The best study of that affair is Hamied Ansari, *Egypt: The Stalled Society* (Binghamton: State University of New York Press, 1986). See also Ahmad Hamrush, *Qissat Thawrat 23 Yulyu* (The story of the revolution of 23rd of July), vol. 2 (Cairo: Madbuli, 1984), pp. 260–67.

17. Leonard Binder, "The Failure of the Left in Egypt," *Asian and African Studies* 14, no. 1 (March 1980): 23–24.

18. See in particular Dennis Gordon, "Withdrawal in Disgrace: Decline of the Argentine Military," in Constantine Danopoulos, ed., *The Decline of Military Regimes* (Boulder: Westview Press, 1988), pp. 199–224.

19. See, by the leader of the Sinai front Abdel-Muhsin Kamil Mortaji, *al-Fariq Murtaji Yarwi al-Haqa'q* (Major General Murtaji reveals the facts) (Beirut: al-Watan al-'Arabi, 197?), pp. 39–43, 79–85, 109–110, 203–8.

20. For a Nasserist version see *al-Ahram,* 11 September 1967.

21. Fouad Ajami, *The Arab Predicament* (Cambridge: Cambridge University Press, 1981), p. 88; Anwar Abdel Malik, *al-Jaysh wa al-Harakah al-Wataniyah* (The Army and the Nationalist Movement) (Beirut: Dar Ibn Khaldun, n. d.), p. 115; Ahmed Abdalla, *The Student Movement and National Politics in Egypt* (London: Zed Press, 1985), pp. 149–75; and Kirk Beattie, "Egypt: Thirty-Five Years of Praetorian Politics," in Constantine P. Danopoulos, ed., *Military Disengagement from Politics* (London: Routledge, 1988), pp. 213–22.

22. Ibrahim Karawan, "Between State Power and Islamist Opposition" (paper presented at the Woodrow Wilson Center for Scholars, Washington, D.C., 25 February 1994), 6–7.

23. Ahmed Abdalla, *The Student Movement and National Politics in Egypt,* p. 13. See also Mark N. Cooper, "The Demilitarization of the Egyptian Cabinet," *International Journal of Middle East Studies* 14, no. 2 (May 1982): 203–225.

24. On the incremental civilianization after 1967 see Gabriel Ben-Dor, "The Civilianization of Military Regimes in the Arab World," in Henry Bienen and David Morell, eds., *Political Participation under Military Regimes* (Beverly Hills: Sage Publications, 1976); and Robert Springborg, *Mubarak's Egypt: Fragmentation of the Political Order* (Boulder: Westview Press, 1989).

25. Ali Dessouki and Adel El-Labban, "Arms Race, Defense Expenditures, and Development," *Journal of South Asian and Middle Eastern Studies* 4 (Spring 1981): 70–75; and Paul Jabber, *Not by War Alone: Security and Arms Control in the Middle East* (Berkeley: University of California Press, 1981), p. 418.

26. Amos Perlmutter, *The Military and Politics in Modern Times* (New Haven, Conn.: Yale University Press, 1977), pp. 11–13.

27. For more see Mohamed Heikal, *The Road to Ramadan* (London: Collins, 1975); and Ibrahim Karawan, "Egypt and the Western Alliance," in Steven Speigel, ed., *The Middle East and the Western Alliance* (London: Allen and Unwin, 1982), and idem, "Sadat and the Egyptian-Israeli Peace Revisited," *International Journal of Middle East Studies* (May 1994).

28. See the memoirs of former war minister Mohamed Fawzi, *Istratijiyat al-Musalhah* (The Strategy of Accommodation) (Cairo: Dar al-Mustaqbal al-'Arabi, 1986), chapters 8 and 11; and the memoirs of another war minister Field Marshal Mohhamed abd al-Ghani al-Jamsi, *Harb October 1973* (The War of October 1973) (Paris: al-Manshurat al-Sharqiyah, 1989), pp. 457–578; and by the former national security advisor Mohamed Hafiz Isma'il, *Amn Misr al-Qawmi* (Egypt's National Security) (Cairo: al-Ahram, 1987).

29. Dekmejian, "Egypt and Turkey," p. 38.

30. See the *Financial Times* of London, 7 June 1982; and *Arab Report and Record* (1–15 February 1976), p. 70.

31. Michael Burrell and Abbas Kleidar, *Egypt the Dilemmas of a Nation* (Beverly Hills: Sage Publications, 1977), p. 46; Hussen Abd al-Raziq, *Misr fi 18 wa 19 Yanayr* (Egypt on the 18th and 19th of January) (Beirut: Dar al-Kalimah, 1984), p. 13; the *Financial Times* of London, 28 January 1977; and the *New York Times,* 19, 20, 22 January 1977.

32. For an authoritative account of that societal uprising and the state responses to it see Ahmad Baha' al-Din, *Muhawarati ma' al-Sadat* (My Conversations with Sadat) (Cairo: Dar al-Hillal, 1987), pp. 123–46.

33. See the article by Hamdi Saleh in the *Los Angeles Times,* 21 March 1986.

34. On these gradual changes and their implications see Mark Cooper, *The Transformation of Egypt* (London: Croom Helm, 1980), pp. 126–30, 178–234.

35. See 'Adil Hussein, *"al-Jaysh wa Mustaqbal al-Dimuqratiyah"* (The Army and the future of democracy), *al-Sha'b,* 7 January 1986.

36. For an example of the position calling for reducing the military budget by one billion pounds, coming from a former military officer with Nasserist convictions, see the statements of Amin Huwaydi, *al-Ahali,* 25 June 1986. On military reactions see General Ahmad Fakhr, *"al-Infaq al-'Askari al-Masri"* (The Egyptian military expenditure), *al-Ahram,* 25 July 1986; and Mohamed 'Ukasha, *"Madha Nurid . . . Quwat Musalahah am Inkishariyah?!"* (What do we want . . . armed forces or mercenaries?!), *al-Ahram al-Iqtisadi,* 14 July 1986.

37. See Adel Hussein, " *'An al-Jaysh Marah Ukhra"* (On the army once again), *al-Sha'b,* 1 July 1986; and Mohamed Hilmi Murad, *"al-Riqabah al-Gha'ibah 'Ala al-Infaq al-'Askari"* (The missing supervision over military expenditure), *al-Sha'b,* 9 September 1986. See also articles by the liberal writers Ibrahim Dessouki Abaza in *al-Wafd,* 7 July 1986; and Wahid Ra'fat, *"al-Infaq al-'Askari"* (Military Expenditure), *al-Wafd,* 7 July 1986. The response of the military was that regional conditions posed challenges to Egypt that require greater attention and domestic support of the military effort. Discussion about the military budget must take into consideration safeguarding national security. See the statements of former Field Marshal Abd al-Halim Abu Ghazallah in *al-Mussawar,* 12 October 1984.

38. Sa'id Isma'il 'Ali, " *'Afwan Siyadat al-Mushir"* (Forgive me, Field Marshal), *al-Ahali,* 24 October 1984; and Mohamed Noor Farahat, *"Hawl Hukm al-Mu'assassat wa Tahakum al-Mu'assassat"* (On the rule of institutions and domination of institutions), *al-Ahali,* 19 December 1984.

39. General Ahmad Fakhr, *"al-Ahdaf al-Istratijiyah li al-'Askariyah al-Misriyah"* (Strategic objectives of the Egyptian military), *al-Jumhuriyah,* 20 January 1985. See also General Ibrahim Shakib, *"Shukran Ayuha al-Sadaha"* (Thank You, Gentlemen). *al-Ahali,* 7 November 1984.

40. See statement of leftist party on this under the title *"al-Dimuqratiyah fi Khatar"* (Endangered democracy), *al-Ahali,* 13 August 1986.

41. See Midhat al-Zahid's critical article in *al-Ahali,* 6 August 1986. One of Abu-Ghazallah's leftist critics referred to him as the "bright star," which was the name given to Egyptian-American joint exercises; see Sa'id Isma'il Ali, *"Hadha al-Najm al-Sati' "* (This bright star), *al-Ahali,* 8 October 1986.

42. Mahmoud Fawzi, *Abu-Ghazallah wa Asrar al-Iqulah* (The secrets of firing Abu-Ghazallah) (Cairo, al-Jidawi Publishing, 1993), pp. 152–60.

43. See lengthy interviews in prison with Colonel al-Zumur in Mahmud Fawzi, *'Abbud al-Zumur . . . Kayf Ightalna al-Sadat?!* (How we assassinated Sadat?!), (Beirut: Hatiah, 1993), pp. 45–46. 124–47. Al-Zumur revealed that Islamist groups value having members with military background because they enhance the performance of major organizational and fighting tasks, as well as systematize and rationalize decision making. See Ibid., 85–86.

44. Interview with Tal'at Qaslm of the Islamic group in *al-Ahali,* 9 February 1994, p. 3; and statements of a leader of "the vanguards of Islamic conquest" in *al-Ahali,* 8 September 1993, p. 4.

45. Caryle Murphy, "Egypt: An Uneasy Portent of Change," *Current History* 93, no. 580 (February 1994): 78–82.

46. *al-Mussawr,* 17 December 1993, pp. 16–19.

47. See *al-Mussawar,* 8 January 1993, pp. 82–83, and 23 July 1993, pp. 22–23.

48. *al-Ahram,* 7 February 1994, p. 3. A month earlier, the Minister of Defense, Field Marshal Hussein Tantawi, has testified before the National Security committee in the Parliament about the need for coordinating the efforts of all ministries, including his own, to counter the escalation of violence. One influential writer stressed that a role for the army against violent Islamist groups would be in accordance with its constitutional responsibilities and that the coordination between the military and security agencies has to become more comprehensive. Ahmad Hamrush, *"Madha Sayaf'al al-Jaysh Amam al-Irhab?"* (What will the army do against terrorism?), *Roz-al-Youssef,* 3 January 1994; and *"al-Jaysh . . . Limadha Yatasada lil Irhab"* (The army . . . Why should it confront terrorism?), *Roz-al-Youssef,* 24 January 1994, p. 28.

REFERENCES

Beattie, Kirk. "Egypt: Thirty-five Years of Praetorian Politics." In Constantine P. Danopoulos, ed., *Military Disengagement from Politics.* London: Routledge, 1988.
———. *Egypt during the Nasser Years.* Boulder, Colo.: Westview Press, 1994.
Beeri, Eliezer. *Army Officers in Arab Society and Politics.* New York: Praeger, 1970.
Dekmejian, R. Hrair. *Egypt under Sasir: A Study of Political Dynamics.* Albany: State University of New York Press, 1971.
Perlmutter, Amos. *Egypt: The Praetorian State.* New Brunswick: Transaction Books, 1974.
Springborg, Robert. *Mubarak's Egypt: Fragmentation of the Political Order.* Boulder, Colo.: Westview Press, 1989.

FRANCE

Michel Louis Martin

In any social system, the inherent structural tension between the managers of armed violence, who as such participate from the very essence of the state, and political authorities responsible for its administration is most of the time accentuated by the contrasting evolution of the respective systems of values from which the society and the military proceed. Rarely synchronous, these norms, as well as the conducts and loyalties they induce, seem from the point of view of the military either in advance of or lagging with respect to those of the parent social system. France does not escape this tendency, when it is not the very illustration of it, where continuously the armed forces have served as refuge to partisans of ideas and beliefs more or less in opposition to civilian authorities and the society. Thus, throughout the Ancien Régime for example, royal troops appeared to welcome members of the nobility often nostalgic for the Middle Ages and the modes of social organization they implied. Without thinking to question the Capetian legitimacy, they more or less consciously felt somewhat at variance with the policies of modern state-building undertaken by the absolute monarchy. By contrast, after the Revolution and during the first half of the nineteenth century, armed forces were viewed under the Empire, and more so under the Restoration and the July Monarchy, as strongly attached to republican principles; the police were concerned at the time with watching officers closely, as many a potential plotter attested to the threat they posed for the established order. Then, by a characteristic turnabout, under the Second Empire and the Third Republic, the military was again perceived as more conservative, as the institutional niche for men out of the aristocracy, or pretending so, who embraced the career of arms as a way of serving their country without compromising themselves with the regime. After World War II and with the progressive advent of a wide-enough consensus in French society around a few political, economic, and social values, the role of the armed forces as a place of opposition in the name of ideas formerly in vogue and now questioned fades away. It nevertheless remains a privileged area where principles such as the defense of the nation or self-sacrifice are preserved.

In such conditions, the conventional images of an army leaning to the right, perfectly loyal throughout one millenary of the Ancien Régime but becoming a threat to the institutions born out of the Revolution, deserve to be nuanced. Moreover, the means by which the military seeks to push its opinions or to protect its professional integrity and its institutional independence are numerous. They call upon the subtle intrigues of a pressure group as well as upon intrusion on the political scene, upon the questioning of the legitimacy of the authorities in power as well as upon treason. Correlatively, techniques of regulation developed by the political authorities in order to subordinate a state apparatus that disposes of quite a threatening arsenal cover a large scope of means of control.

Thus the present study of French civil-military relations will be conducted from a historical perspective going back to and including the Ancien Régime and integrating in a synthetic approach the mercenary and nobility-led regiments of the monarchy, the levies of revolutionary times, the all-volunteer force of the nineteenth century and the mix of conscript and professional soldiers of today. If the French military has never ceased to appear tempted during the last five centuries to interfere with the civil political power—the point to be dealt with in the first part of this chapter—it remains that the successive regimes have continuously exercised over the military a control whose modalities, not the principle, have varied over time.

PATTERNS OF MILITARY-POLITICAL TENSION: OPPOSITION, THREATS, AND INFLUENCE

The old Roman formula *arma togae cedant,* relayed by the modern conception of the rule of law as well as the time-old disdain for the so-called sultanist modes of government by chiefs of war, leads French public opinion, feeling confronted today by the poor image of Third World military dictatorships, to judge any instance of military intrusion on the political arena not only as a catastrophe from the viewpoint of freedom notably but also as a national humiliation reducing France to among the most politically backward societies. Though brought to power by politicians in search of a sword, Napoleon claimed that "never a military government would take on in France unless the nation become sot by fifty years of ignorance." The antimilarist rhetoric that constitutes one of the currents of the nation's ideology contributes largely to such a discourse. Therefore, French mentalities as well as the history of the country tend to overlook the numerous attempts and cases of military interferences with politics. Yet a survey, even cursory, of successive French regimes since the advent of the Capetians persuades one of the recurring character of this type of phenomenon.

Aristocracy and Military Treason during the Ancien Régime

Under the Ancien Régime, the remarkable dynastical continuity that allowed
the Capetians to govern the country without any interruption nor statutory modifications during nearly nine centuries concealed the frequent cases of treason
and rebellion that military leaders were guilty of at the highest level. A number
of elevated functions generally in the hands of the military had to be abolished
or reduced to a purely honorific role, so important was the number of traitors
holding them. At the summit of the state, it was the *connétablie*—the high
command of the armed forces—whose titulary's immovability and prerogatives
had often constituted a danger to the king himself. Among the best-known instances were the case of the connétable de Saint-Pol calling on King Edward
IV of England in Picardie against Louis XI and the case of the connétable Anne
de Montmorency conspiring in the "triumvirat" with François de Guise and
Marshal de Saint-André against the regency of Catherine de Médicis in 1561.
The situation was such that the monarchy was forced either to leave the function
vacant as after the treason of the connétable Charles III de Bourbon, who in
1523 contributed to Charles Quint's victory at Pavie, or to use it to reward a
prestigious military leader at the end of his career, as with the connétable de
Lesdiguières after whom the charge was abolished in 1626. (It was to be briefly
rehabilitated under Napoleon but for purely honorific ends).

The same problem developed within the local administration, but at the
highest level of responsibility with the provincial governments created at the
end of the thirteenth century whose titularies held considerable military and
administrative powers—a function, incidentally, that François I had already
tried to abolish. The time of the Wars of Religion revealed the rather ambiguous attitude of governors who, acting as quasi viceroys, did not cease to in-
trude on the monarchical powers, if not simply oppose the king. Examples
abound. In 1574, it was the rebellion of Marshal François de Montmorency,
lieutenant-general of Ile de France; later it was Henri I de Guise, governor of
Champaign, who attempted to take over the crown from Henri III; then it was
his brother the duke de Mayenne, governor of Brittany, who at Henri III's
death proclaimed cardinal of Bourbon king, then at the cardinal's death took
the title of lieutenant-general of the kingdom. Henri IV, who would be betrayed by, among others, the duke de Gontaut-Biron, governor of Burgundy
and marshal-general of his camps and armies, found a solution by flanking the
governors with more docile lieutenant-governors and king's commissaries.
Later, after other serious crises, such as the treason of César de Bourbon,
governor of Brittany at the beginning of the seventeenth century, that of
Charles de Lorraine, governor of Provence in 1631, and, above all, the notorious revolt of the Languedoc governor, Marshal Henri de Montmorency, who
after having stirred up the province against Louis XIII was beheaded on Richelieu's order, the title became a simple sinecure for officers living at court,

the reality of local powers belonging henceforth to the intendants, created by Henri II and fully empowered by Richelieu.

Military commanders together with members of the royal family also betrayed a monarch who tried to dominate them. The Praguerie revolt in 1440, which was joined by men of war and princes of the blood such as Charles and Louis de Bourbon, the dauphin Louis, the bastard de Bourbon, Georges de la Tremoille, discontented by the Orleans ordnance that gave the king the monopoly of troop levying, is a celebrated precedent. There will be many emulators. François de Guise and Marshal de Saint-André, already cited, were followed later by Prince de Condé, joined for a time by Marshal de Turenne, ordering to fire at the king's troops during the Fronde, then accepting a command in the Spanish army in 1653, and later still in 1719 that of the duke de Richelieu, future marshal, implicated in the Cellamare conspiracy against the regent Philippe d'Orléans. Most owed it to their relations with the king that they were able to come back into favor once their submission was made (some died, the bastard de Bourbon was drowned, Gontaut-Biron beheaded). It is true that in those times when nations were building, the nobility kept a European tradition permitting its members to switch from the service of one prince to another's according to the opportunities of the moment, without dishonor. Moreover, such behavior stemmed as much from political insubordination as from the incurable undiscipline of grandees engaged in various coteries of which they were at the same time the instigators and the victims.

Political Instability and Military Passivity in the Nineteenth Century

With the Revolution and the nineteenth century, civil-military relations took a different turn. First, because of the consolidation of the legal-rational basis of power, the conduct of the military, wishing to satisfy their ambitions or to promote the view of their corps, was losing the character of personal treason they had in the past. The exaltation of patriotic feelings and the nationalist attachment rendered less and less conceivable shifts in loyalty. Instances like that of General Dumouriez, who after intriguing against the government abandoned his troops after the defeat of Neerwinden on 18 March 1793, deserting in the Austrian ranks while handing over the commissaries of the Convention among whom was the minister of war, General de Beurnonville, or that of General Pichegru in 1795, rallying the royalist cause while commanding the army of Rhin and Moselle, have an exceptional, if not an anachronistic ring. The same can be said of the actions of officers such as General Moreau, the brilliant army commander of the Revolution, who conspired against the imperial regime and served the coalition forces as the military advisor of Tsar Alexander I in 1813 (he died from a wound received at Dresde from a French cannon ball) or Prince Murat, the French cavalry leader, committing himself after the battle of Leipzig to provide thirty thousand men to the nations leagued against France, or Marshal Bernadotte in 1814 participating in the invasion of France. They can be explained either, for Moreau, by the unjust persecutions by Napoleon, who had him arrested and exiled, or, for Murat and Bernadotte, by the fact that, being respectively king of Naples and crown-prince of Sweden since 1810, they had in mind above all the preservation of their dynastical interests.

It would no longer be imaginable, except if the notion of conspiring with the enemy were fully accepted, that high-ranking military leaders could pass into the adversary's ranks. If General Lamoricière, Napoléon III's arch enemy, chose to go foreign, it was after having been jailed and proscripted, and it was under the Holy See's colors that he officered; this was no more a treason than General Magnan's service in the Belgian army after being briefly disgraced in 1831. The case of Marshal Bazaine surrendering in October 1870 the town of Metz and his 180,000 men to Prussia, with which he was negotiating, refusing then to rally the government of national defense, is more complex; though he was sentenced to death for treason with the enemy, it is essentially his refusal to obey the new government, of which he rejected the republican options, that appears central.

The Bazaine episode consequently constitutes rather a case study of the emerging model of open military opposition against political authority, whose ultimate object would be its eviction and replacement. Yet paradoxically, it anticipates events to come during the twentieth century rather than represents a type of behavior significant of the time. In effect, at least if the praetorian activism of the Directory, emblematized by Bonaparte's coup, is put aside, the French military in general, contrary to its Spanish counterpart at the same period, never affected political evolutions of the century, which however witnessed a succession of revolutionary regimes, monarchies, empires, and republics. Indeed, there was the "marshals' insurrection" in 1814, many of whom (sixteen over twenty-two) forswore themselves during the Cent-Jours and then again during the Second Restoration, but such conduct was essentially motivated by the distress of warriors aspiring to enjoy at last their riches in peace. Other members of the armed forces found themselves involved in various plots, as General Berton and the four sergeants of La Rochelle in 1822, Bonapartist *demi-soldes* (on half-pay) linked to the Carbonari, those NCOs plotting in 1831 in Luneville, or marshals de Bourmont and de Saint-Priest taking part in the legitimist uprising attempt led by duchess de Berry in 1832; but they were marginal elements cut from the military institution. Others even held statal positions with quasi-dictatorial powers, such as generals Cavaignac in June 1848 or Trochu, head of the government of national defense, in August 1870; but it was upon the request of the constituted authorities. Others did think to intervene on the political scene, such as generals Ducrot or de Rochebouët, in order to counter the republican victory in the elections of October 1877 or the General Boulanger threat in January 1889, but these were only fancies of sorts.

As for the praetorianist interpretation of prince-president Louis-Napoleon's coup d'etat of 2 December 1851, aping supposedly, according to the classic Marxian view, the 18 brumaire operation of his uncle in 1799, it is a caricature of a different reality in which the armed forces intervened only peripherally in the person of some ambitious officers such as Saint-Arnaud, made marshal and minister of war for the circumstances, and his accomplices colonels Fleury and Lespinasse; the mainstream military hierarchy and even the more adventurous *Armée d'Afrique's* officers abstained or declined to be involved when solicited, though favorable to everything that such an operation supposed politically and though Louis-Napoleon was nominally chief of the armed forces as president of the republic. Besides, some were frankly hostile to the coup, as was General Changarnier commanding the Paris armies. Likewise, the military kept its distance with Boulanger, then Déroulède, who vainly attempted to draw it to overthrow the republic in 1899. In this respect General Roget's refusal to walk on the Elysée is symbolic, despite again a strong ideological affinity among officers with those nationalist movements.

Actually, the military was generally obedient. Despite notoriously progressive sensitivities until the 1850s, it participated with equanimity in the reestablishment of the absolute monarchy in Spain in 1823 and in the repression of worker uprisings in 1830 and 1848. Having become more conservative afterward, it nevertheless participated in the expulsions of the congregations and in the inventories and decided on the execution of the anticlerical laws and the separation of the state and the church at the beginning of the twentieth century; the officers most deeply affected in their religious beliefs only consented to resign in order not to cooperate in these actions.

Professional Independence and Institutional Autonomy

This being said, this notion of political passivity often used to characterize the behavior of the military toward the powers throughout the nineteenth century is ambiguous. That the military remained at the periphery of political changes that have affected French society and that it abstained from any intrusion into politics does not imply that it was unable to make its views prevalent. In this regard, the extraordinary institutional independence that it enjoyed and that was perhaps the price for its political neutrality must be underlined. This institutional autonomy can be measured by several facts. Since 1815, until World War I, ministers of war were quasi-continuously officers who, far from acting as instruments of the political control of the armed forces, behaved rather as their apologists. Numerous, moreover, were the officers seated at Parliament and in parliamentary commissions for national defense questions, assuring that military interests would not be encroached upon. The armed forces also, enjoying an important budget as well as opportunities to use secret funds outside any control, remained the master of its own functions, notably nominations and promotions.

Outside the metropolitan territory, in the colonies whose administration was entrusted to the military, it enjoys a considerable freedom of action. When its members, often for reasons of personal ambition, did initiate territorial conquests, as Major Archinard in the former French Sudan, it disposed in general of all powers, not only military but also political, administrative, and judiciary ones; the multiple functions assumed by *commandants de cercle* and other officers attached to the famous *bureaux arabes* or the *affaires indigènes* attested to such polyvalence at the most decentralized levels. Men like Bugeaud, Faidherbe, Gallieni, and Lyautey governed various African regions as genuine viceroys, practically without consultation with Paris; as for the Navy, it literally lorded over Indochina. Considering this situation, speculations about the praetorian inclination of the armed forces, such as Paschal Grousset's elliptical formula, "Colonies are the school of pronunciamentos," were inevitable, even if they did not materialize in actuality.

Finally, the institutional autonomy of the military was enhanced by other sociological factors. The relative social homogeneity of the officer ranks and an acute and shared sense of identity that everything is separated from the civilian world were clearly two of them. In the second half of the century, a new ideal, if not ideology, that themes like the "school of the nation" or the "social role of the officer," dear to Lyautey, were to symbolize furthered the military cohesion. The armed forces progressively became a state within the state, above the institutions, ever prompt, as publicly revealed by the Dreyfus affair, to denounce any political interference in their business or any criticism of their conceptions of justice and honor.

Two World Wars and a Divided Armed Force

This institutional independence admitted by the political power was to show its full amplitude at the beginning of the first world conflict. As soon as August 1914, it seemed natural that the military be entrusted with the whole responsibility for the conduct of war. Its general chief of staff, General Joffre, disposed of quasi-dictatorial competences, exercised without any control. The assembly had adjourned, and ministers of war acted always in such a way as to shelter the command from any criticism. The aims of the war, the definition of strategy, belonging in principle to the government according to the decree of 28 October 1913, were in fact decided by the military, a trend that the politicians' lack of technological and professional expertise could only accentuate. Joffre reigned over thirty-three departments, dictating his will to the powers, be it about the Balkans or the dismissal of General Sarrail. And with General Gallieni as minister of war in October 1915, rumors of a coup were even voiced. It is true that the prospect of a short war could justify such a resignation on the part of the government. It was only after Sarrail's transfer and above all the bloody encounters of Verdun and the Somme in 1916, when the conflict became a war of attrition and the high command discredited itself, that Parliament attempted to take over the mastery of the decision process. Nominated marshal and sent to the United States, Joffre was replaced by General Nivelle. Finally, after several scandals implicating parliamentary members and after the mutinies of 1917, the government, in the person of its leader, Georges Clemenceau, appropriated the full control of military operations and imposed it on everyone, the army commander first of all, as Marshal Foch was to judge of it, as well as to other military chiefs, such as Pétain or Sarrail, who was relieved from his command in the eastern front because of his too-pronounced independence. The Tiger's famous utterance, "War is too serious a business to be trusted to generals," was not simple bantering.

After that, the sphere of autonomy of the military was reduced. Even outside the country, political power supervised all military activities. Marshals Lyautey and Pétain experienced it in Morocco, as did General Mangin, transfered in 1920 for having to check Rhineland irredentism while commanding the French occupation zone, or Sarrail, again recalled by Painlevé in 1925 from his mission as high commissary in Syria after the cannonade of Damas. In any case, between the wars the military accepted the domination of civilians and remained politically passive. If extreme-right movements such as the "plot of the hood" (between 1932 and 1940) or the "crosses of fire" led by a colonel were joined by members of the military institution, participation was only marginal. However, the military continued to have an acute sense of its specificity, all the more as, with the extension of conscription, its vocation as the educator of the nation became pronounced, which led it to the belief that it embodies the nation and charts its destiny. These convictions were to create a system of more politically active attitudes, which were to modify the relations between the armed forces and the state.

With World War II, in effect, the military entered in a decisive fashion the political arena. From a certain viewpoint, it was Paul Reynaud who, by calling in the "government of the debacle" Marshal Pétain as vice-president of the government and General de Gaulle as undersecretary of national defense, helped to the saddle the two protagonists between whom the great debate of the 1940–45 period was articulated. Both arrived in power by questionable paths—Pétain invested by Parliament, meeting in Bordeaux, in the functions of head of the French state and of the constituting power and de Gaulle, having left for London after the armistice and pretending to maintain there France in the allied camp, imposed by the military staff through General Weygand to Reynaud. Paradoxically, both accused each other of treason and usurpation. In France, a sort of military state was organized by Vichy, in which officers held important functions at the administrative central as well as territorial levels, in the metropole as in the colonies.

Finally, with the defeat of Germany and the liberation of the country by Anglo-American troops joined by the Free French forces, history justified de Gaulle. From this period remains the conviction of the military that, during troubled moments such as that of the German occupation, the difficulty is not that of accomplishing one's own duty but that of knowing where such duty is. Disobedience, including disobedience to orders of an authority that has the appearance of legitimacy, might become an obligation it is necessary to satisfy, even at the risk of sanctions. Despite the final victory and the participation of a French representative at the signing of the German capitulation, French armed forces emerged somewhat shaken from this trial, which put into question a number of values traditionally inculcated in them.

Decolonization and Political Failure of the Military

The French military was to be confronted by a somewhat similar predicament during the crisis of decolonization that began in the 1950s, though less brutally than during the preceding decade. If it was from the Algerian war that these problems took their acuity, nevertheless the withdrawal from Indochina, crowned by the pathetic defeat of Dien Bien Phu, during which the army felt forsaken by the nation and betrayed by an indecisive and corrupt political class, had a critical effect. These difficulties and the reactions to them among the military resulted from the tendency of civilian authorities to rely upon the armed forces not only to maintain order in Algeria but also to assume numerous responsibilities in the administration of this territory. Everything then converged to incite the military to play a political role. Concern not to repeat the errors committed in the Far East some years before, infatuation with the theory of psychological warfare and other applications of the maoist techniques of mass control and complacency or tacit acceptance by political authorities as well as the military command of methods of order maintenance and antiterrorist measures at the margin of legality, such as the use of torture, contributed to the feeling that the regime was incapable of facing a situation of such magnitude, concomitantly with the idea that the armed forces constituted the ultimate but legitimate resort for a nation in peril.

It was the military that, with the riots of 13 May 1958 in Algiers and then the threat of an intervention on the metropolitan territory, attended the accession to power of General de Gaulle and by way of consequence provoked the fall of the Fourth Republic. During the whole decisive period that preceded the investiture of de Gaulle by the national assembly, under conditions incidentally reminiscent of the vote in favor of Marshal Pétain in 1940, the general resorted with talent to the possibility of a takeover by Algeria-based troops of the main cities of France. As he did not want to appear the beneficiary of a prætorian coup d'etat, he affected to restrain officers' threats, but he did not completely disavow them in order to preserve this means of pressure on the national representatives.

The constitution voted and the new regime established in October 1958, General de Gaulle took a whole series of measures aimed at deterring the military from continuing to play a political role. Officers had to leave the committees of public safety, and the leading participants in the events of May 13, generals Salan in December 1958 and Massu in January 1960, were called back to France. The military agreed reluctantly to let the executive branch decide the policy to be followed in Algeria, especially as it was evolving more and more clearly toward the acceptance of Algeria's independence. In January 1960, the affair of the "barricades" of Algiers set up by partisans of a French Algeria developed with the approval of the military. In April 1961, a group of high-ranking officers, generals Challe, Jouhaud, Salan, and Zeller, attempted a putsch, which however could not rally more than one regiment and failed after three days. Finally, between the first half of 1961 and that of 1962, numerous officers and NCOs, the "lost soldiers" regrouped within the "secret armed organization" (OAS), became involved in terrorist actions and assassination attempts against the chief of state.

Throughout this period, the fear of a military overthrow recurred, especially among political groups on the left, and explained their quite benevolent attitude toward General de Gaulle, who appeared the surest rampart against prætorian adventurism. With regard to the military, the president sought to deploy a mindful policy, mixing information, minute attention, symbolized by the "visit around the kanteens," and firmness, notably when he appeared in uniform on television at the time of the barricades or when he urged draftees to oppose orders given by putschist officers. These various elements left no doubt of the nature of the regime: even if de Gaulle wore a brigadier title, albeit conferred on him temporarily during the regime's downfall in 1940, even if he affected when it suited him a familiarity with the senior officer corps, at heart he remained a civilian attached to the republican conception of military submission to political power, having no other function than to "serve and obey."

Political Self-Effacement of the Military Today

In some respects, the French military emerged from the Algerian crisis convinced that it has nothing to win by dabbling in political issues without risking, as in 1962, finding itself divided between loyalists and clandestines and humiliated by having to leave a territory it had promised never to abandon. Today, given this heritage, the recollection of which fades away only slowly because of the youth of those involved then, and given also the rather large consensus created around the political institutions of the Fifth Republic, no one imagines any longer that the military could constitute a danger to the nation and its regime. The possibility of an intervention of some units to reestablish order where it appeared the most urgent and indispensable was certainly evoked by some in May 1968, especially after de Gaulle's trip to Baden-Baden. But the project was quickly dropped, as many were convinced that such procedure would only aggravate the situation, either because the conscripts could refuse such orders or because the brutality of the repression would mobilize more opponents. Similarly, in 1981, the victory of the left was greeted by a few resignations, such as that of General de Boissieu, de Gaulle's son-in-law, quitting his position of Grand Chancellor of the Legion of Honor to protest the election of François Mitterrand and not to have to confer on him, as required by protocol, the cordon of grand-maître of the order. There is no doubt indeed that such an action is quite a symbolic form of opposition. On the whole, convictions that the armed forces have about themselves and their place in society today seem free of the former connotations of superiority that characterized them not so long ago.

The civilian domination of the military also extends to the professional sphere. This appears clearly from the various instances of conflicts that occurred in the last two decades, in which the head of state in particular assumed all responsibilities concerning their management. From rescue operations, as in Kolwezi in 1978, or missions of protection of friendly states, as in Chad in 1983–84, to the management of hostage crises as in New Caledonia in 1988, or participation in large-scale coalition warfare as with the Gulf war, the supervision of the presidency was both continuous and minute. Decisions such as the type of weapon or equipment to be used, the targets to be identified, and the volume and the nature of forces to be engaged are seen as political; in the Gulf war, for example, the flying of the less-able *Jaguar* and the explicit exclusion beforehand of the use of chemical and nuclear weapons were actually decided by the president, as they were also meant as an indication to Arab countries, which France otherwise considers partners, of the modulated level of French involvement in the war. The habit for civilian authorities to be always informed, consulted in depth, and obeyed has combined with symmetrical practices on the part of the military, now accustomed to report regularly and to request instructions before any important action. Moreover, today the inclination of the media to interpret in a political sense any military decision reinforces this process, a process, incidentally, facilitated also by the reliability and rapidity of modern communication systems that allow the political authority to follow the unfolding of operations in actual time and space and to be able to intervene every time a new incentive appears necessary.

Furthermore, in his actions, the president functions with his own staff and the military network surrounding the presidency, notably, his own chief of staff, a position which operates as a genuine counter–minister of defense and de facto general chief of staff of the armed forces. In a way, the role of minister of defense consists of the day-to-day administration of the military institution and the defense of its professional interests. The general chief of staff of the armed forces acts as an advisor and elaborates the strategy defined by the president. The once-powerful chiefs of staff of the army, navy, and air force are reduced to a limited operational role, as they do not actually command the services, but represent them. Far away is the time, therefore, when for want of professional and technical expertise, civilians could have only a superficial control of military operations.

What appears now as a given of the French society and political life, that is, the subordination of the military and its self-effacement outside its specific professional domain, constitutes the conclusion of a long evolution, perhaps not completely achieved. It is in any case the result of the unceasing efforts undertaken by the political powers with a view to confining the military in that subordinate role.

POLITICAL CONTROL OF THE MILITARY AND ITS MODALITIES

The transformations of the military institution during quite a long history and the changes in the political system, especially after the eighteenth century, certainly made France a genuine microcosm of all possible sorts of political-military interactions. As a consequence, the country was also the field of experimentation of every existing technique of subordination of the armed forces by civilian power. In this respect, authors conventionally distinguish between objective modes consisting of encouraging the professional autonomy of the military, confined to a narrow domain of competence, and more subjective types requiring the military to bridge their responsibilities as managers of the defense of the nation and their role as citizen; the former implies a strict separation from politics, the latter a shared outlook with civilian authorities. Added to these, frequently in revolutionary situations and in any case of particular suspicions toward the officer corps, is the resort to modes of penetration such as the dispatch into the ranks of the armed forces of representatives as political delegates. Though French military history cannot pretend to exemplify in a fully chronological manner this typology, at least it offers diversified illustrations of the regulation of civil-military relations, testifying at once to the misgivings and to the imagination of the beholders of the constituted powers.

The Royal Family and the System of Offices during the Ancien Régime

Under the Ancien Régime, the methods deployed to insure the subordination of the military to the monarchical administration were adapted to the perils threatening it. As already observed, it was the survival of a patrimonialist conception of the state that induced many high military figures to consider revolting against the king, all the more willingly in that they saw themselves secure from any severe sanctions and hoped to benefit from any change in the power structure, whatever its characteristics. Against such a danger, the royal power resorted to two techniques. On the one hand, the monarch used the classical practice of penetration of the military organization by leaning on personalities close to him, notably his sons, among whom was the dauphin, often with good results, but sometimes not. If the duke de Bourgogne, one of Louis XIV's sons, attached to Marshal de Vendôme, appeared responsible for the ill-fated campaign of Flanders in 1708, the duke de Chartres, his nephew and future regent, fought brilliantly at Neerwinden in 1693. Likewise later, the duke d'Angoulême, son of Charles X, the dukes d'Orléans, d'Aumale, and de Montpensier, sons of Louis-Philippe, not only were competent commanders but had also a positive influence in the armies of the Restoration and the July Monarchy in favoring the career of many good officers. Actually, every monarchy, even nowadays, have favored this method, which presents the advantage of being at the same time educational to the royal scions and productive of solidarity within an influential social group.

On the other hand, in a more original way, the French king introduced into the military the creation of a number of civilian administrative positions, linking the possibility of exercising various key functions to their purchase, which made them an element of the holder's patrimony which could be sold or transmitted, free of charge. As a matter of fact, the most senior ranks were reserved for individuals coming from the nobility and erected in office to the point that numerous colonels considered themselves owners of their regiments. Such a system of recruitment, despite a number of negative effects in the area of military performance, appeared politically efficient, whereas a too-heavy reliance on mercenaries, with an essentially foreign recruitment, could have led to the constitution of a military force entirely devoted to a few ambitious leaders and obeying them blindly, as with the Roman praetorians during the lower empire or the Janissaries of the Sublime Porte. Actually, in the seventeenth as well as the eighteenth centuries, there was no serious fear that the monarchical government would be jeopardized by the military. It is true that the remarkable continuity reached by the Capetians rendered the monarchy unquestioned for a long time.

"Amalgam," Conscription, and Other Processes of Control since the Revolution

Starting with the Revolution and throughout the nineteenth century, the rapid succession of governments and hence of political legitimacies disrupted significantly the civil-military equilibrium achieved under the Ancien Régime. The issue of control of the military was all the more acute for revolutionary leaders as their regime was quite fragile and as the conjunction of an invasion by European coalition forces and domestic uprisings fomented in the south as well as in the west of the country made them particularly vulnerable and dependent on the loyalty of the armed forces. To consolidate the French military instrument, spoilt by politicization and facing, after the first victories of Valmy and Jemmapes (September and November 1792), defeats by the coalition, Lazare Carnot, put in charge of military affairs by the Committee of Public Safety in August 1793, completely reformed its structure. Central to his policy was the "amalgam," already suggested by Dubois-Crancé, fusing according to precise dosages the survivors of military personnel inherited from the period prior to 1789 who had agreed to stay with the volunteers out of the national guard, newly enrolled in the name of the patrie in danger and the defense of the revolution, as well as those who had been requisitioned through increasingly massive levies. To some extent, the resignation and emigration to foreign states of a notable part of the officer corps coming from the nobility and antirevolutionary—five thousand over a total of nine thousand—spared the new regime from having to purge former cadres. They could count upon the service of those who had stayed on, among whom were many members of the nobility (including well-known names such as La Tour d'Auvergne, Dampierre, Rochambeau, and Biron) who, contrary to the commonly accepted idea, did not have the exclusivity of even the higher ranks of the military hierarchy. With "lower" and junior officers, coming from the bourgeoisie and the petty nobility, these men offered quite competent cadres for the line armies of the republic, all the more faithful that they owed it promotions they would not have hoped for in the Ancien Régime.

This system of amalgam was more than a simple technique of mixing personnel recruited at different periods of time who had received different training and claimed different ideals. It also realized the synthesis between the two classic military organizational formats, one essentially founded on enlisted troops, the other opening gradually on the logic of the general mobilization, based at first on volunteers and then on requisitions, partial then massive, as with the proclamation of the levée en masse declared on 16 August 1793, arriving finally on the routinization of this type of recruitment by the institutionalization, with the Jourdan-Delbrel law in 1798, of conscription. It is to be noted that this transformation of the military was realized through techniques already functioning under the Ancien Régime that became more fully institutionalized and were given a new legitimacy in the emerging concept of the nation-state. The system of the levée en masse, for example, was resorted to in times of great peril, as by Philippe le Bel after the defeat of Courtray in 1302 or by Louis XIV after Denain in 1712, to take two illustrations among many. The revolutionaries have added to it the notion of the endangered patrie and of assembling every French citizen for the defense of freedom. Moreover, what was formerly a tumultuous mobilization became regularized in the form of an increasingly organized military service. As for conscription, it derives from the royal militia introduced by Louvois in 1688, whose recruitment was based on a lottery and at that time quite unpopular, as shown by the high rate of default and desertion as well as by a widespread demand for its abolition in the grievances records. In reviving it, however, at the same time they introduced political suffrage, revolutionaries made it an essential element of the transfer of sovereignty to the nation as well as an element of democratic citizenship, so that military service became in the French political representation inseparable from democratic values. At the same time, it contributed to the consolidation of civilian control of the armed forces. Military pretensions at embodying national destiny could thus be sublimated into a less politicized pedagogical role for the benefit of draftees. Moreover, the very presence of citizens called to the colors appeared as securing the loyalty of the armed forces, at the same time limiting any antipopular use of armies and holding in check any prætorian behavior on the part of its members. From Clemenceau to Jaurès and even de Gaulle, the argument is the same, and it was in such terms that the failure of the putsch of Algiers in April 1961 was interpreted.

The revolutionary leaders completed the system by adding for a time the election of officers in order to ensure the promotion of politically reliable men. They also provided for sending commissaries to the armies to be in charge of looking after not only the ideological faithfulness of commanding officers and staff but also the good execution of the assembly's orders. In fact, the political leadership pervaded the whole professional sphere of the military, not only the strategic level but also the tactical and the logistical. They determined the place and the time of battle, decided on offensives and attacks, modified the functions of the various units, passed judgment and reported on officers' technical and operational competences, transfered or dismissed them at will, and eventually had them sentenced in cases of hesitation to engage fire and defeat. Generals de Custine, de Beauharnais, and Hoche were thus the victims of prosecution by civilian leaders disappointed by their service.

Distrust about troops' loyalty was such that the assemblies even sought to organize a specific system of military protection of their deliberations, with a guard placed under their control and in charge to defend them against popular demonstrations as well as against coups d'etat. The practice has shown at the same time the reality of existing threats and the vanity of such precautions, as illustrated during the revolutionary period, by the conditions of the outlawing of the Girondins in May-June 1793 and then in 1799 by the success of the 18 Brumaire coup d'etat. Later, the conditions of the dissolution of the Chamber of Deputies of the Cent-Jours at the beginning of the Second Restoration and then the consolidation of the powers of the future Napoleon III in December 1851 awakened the fears of the representatives of the people, something of which remains in the way the assemblies are organized today.

Colonial Exile, Release from the Ranks, and Selective Promotions

In a customary rather than an institutionalized fashion, regimes of revolutionary succession inaugurated also the habit of disposing of cumbersome military personalities by offering them operational responsibilities overseas. This was one reason for the expedition to Egypt in 1798, which allowed the government to keep at bay first the ambitious General Bonaparte, who had discovered his inclination toward personal politics, notably during the negotiations of the Campo-Formio treaty, and others like Marshal Menou in 1798, who had also been demoted from his post as commanding general of the home army, for his involvement in the royalist uprising of October 1795. Napoleon himself adopted such a tactic more successfully by sending his brother-in-law, General Leclerc, to quell the secession in Saint-Domingue (Haïti) where he died. The emperor also instituted a softer version of exile in administrative positions, for Marshal Jourdan, who became ambassador, and Marshal Pérignon, who was sent as governor to Parme in 1806 and then to occupy Napoli in 1808. The Monarchy of July and the Second Empire later used colonial conquest partly for similar objectives. General Cavaignac was thus sent to Algeria by Louis-Philippe because of his republican opinions. Overseas exile, moreover, served both to send away and to satisfy the most ambitious officers, giving them opportunities for actions and profits, "recycling" to useful ends the tradition of military adventurism typical of those times, as epitomized by Prince Murat at the beginning of the century. Under the republic, the system became so interiorized in the military that numerous officers, notably of traditionalist bent, volunteered to serve overseas often to seek solace for having to serve a republic from which they felt alienated, freeing themselves from dull garrison life by reconstituting feudal modes of power in Africa and Asia, even by consolidating the monarchy they could not preserve in France, as did the future Marshal Lyautey in Morocco, to name one of the most prestigious among them.

Selective promotion and release from the ranks constituted other means of domination of the military. The first method served obviously to promote the most politically faithful men, but benefitted also a number of opponents who could not simply be dismissed and whose loyalty could then be bought off. The meteoric promotions, matched with considerable material liberalities, enjoyed by many a Napoleonic officer are the best illustrations. Accession to marshalship and to imperial nobility, if not to kingship, for example, as aimed to reward loyalism and bravery but also to associate with the political destiny of the regime men often jealous of a brother in arms they had helped to become head of state (as was the case of Marshals Jourdan and Kellerman, accomplices of the 18 brumaire coup) or disappointed by the antirepublican orientation of the regime (as were Marshals Bernadotte and Moreau) or simply too dangerously ambitious (as was Marshal Murat). For similar reasons Louis XVIII, despite the forswearing of many of them during the Cent-Jours, associated them with the monarchy, by allowing them to keep their rank and titles and even nominating them peers of the realm and giving them political responsibilities; some of them would become minister of war, as did Marshals Gouvion Saint-Cyr and Soult. Only the most flagrant treasons were punished, as with Marshal Ney and General de Labédoyère.

Dismissal from the ranks of the armed forces was the most conventional practice. The Empire had its share of disfavors, temporary as with republican Marshal Kellerman and then his colleague Brune, more definitive with proscription, which led its victims to leave the country and serve its enemies, as with General Moreau. The Restoration instituted the procedure of being put on half-pay, which cut its victim's allowance and ended all chances of further promotion as it restrained his freedom. The argument used, of a necessary budgetary compression, appeared all the less convincing because career reconstitutions to the benefit of émigré officers and the installation of new units to form the King House were undertaken, refuting the financial justification. The large number of officers thus placed on half-pay—twenty thousand after Waterloo—which incidentally provided the first artisans of the Napoleonic legend, constituted a pool of malcontents distrusted by the government, which used it through various provocations such as the affair of the four sergeants of La Rochelle, to legitimate the maintenance of police severities. With the July Monarchy, the system began to regulate itself. The rehabilitation of numerous victims of the Restoration allowed redress for some of the most flagrant injustices. Indeed, the obligation to take an oath still implied a quasi-personal loyalty to the reigning government, but the fear of popular uprisings, which displaced the fear of military plots, led to a relaxation of police constraints over the martial institution.

Afterwards, promotions as well as dismissals, in favor or against officers, especially senior officers, continued to be a means for regulating military influences (as well as a source of confrontation between men in power who saw in them the means to reinforce their authority and to serve their ambitions). Thus, under the Third Republic, the republican majority that emerged from the 1877 and 1879 elections imposed on the chief of state, Marshal MacMahon who preferred to resign, the purging of the officer corps from its monarchist and bonapartist elements. Some years later, General Boulanger, minister of war in the Freycinet government, decided to release from their duty scions of reigning families. After the fears born from the Dreyfus affair, the "radicals" sought "to set the officer corps nearer the nation," to quote General André, minister of war in the Waldeck-Rousseau and Combes governments, with the famous card-indexing of officers that the administration was invited to prepare in order to orient promotions not only according to political criteria but also according to religious ones, as clericalism was viewed as a manifestation of conservatism. In a less scandalous manner, these techniques of sacking remain the ultimate weapon of civilian authorities during crises, as after World War II and in the aftermath of the Algerian war, which saw the regiments most involved in the putsch attempt dissolved and during which the government, to avoid too-drastic measures, by using a benevolent approach to plurality of salaries, favored the passing into civilian life of officers and NCOs too marked by the colonial tradition.

The Constitutionalization of Civilian Control and the Political-Juridical *Capitis Diminutio* of the Military

All these technical devices aiming at insuring the subordination of the armed forces would have no significance or legitimacy if they did not proceed from a normative essence, in other words, if law did not justify their utilization. This dimension portrays civil-military relations as being a purely political issue, lends itself to a solely realist approach excluding then, because of their vanity, the function of purely declarative norms. The legal organization of the statal monopoly over armed violence, by institutionalizing the subordination of its instruments to the public powers on the one hand and their political neutralization on the other, constitutes one of the critical contributions of republican regimes.

These regimes have indeed sought to codify, to the highest normative level, the submission of the armed forces and to organize for the benefit of the constituted authorities their control and utilization. Most constitutional laws voted since the Revolution are witness to this trend, and beginning with that of September 1791, which claims, "the public force is essentially obedient; no armed corps may deliberate" (art. 12, title IV); this principle was taken over more or less faithfully in the constitutions of June 1793 (art. 112 and following), August 1795 (title IX), November 1848 (art. 104 and following), and February 1875. With respect to the direction of the military, the constitutions push aside any form of autonomous command by the military—"there is no generalissimo," according to article 110 of the 1793 text—seeking afterwards, with more or less clarity, to dilute it between various civilian authorities, as in the constitution of October 1946 or the present text of October 1958, which makes the president of the republic "chief of the armies" (art. 15) and the prime minister "responsible for national defense" (art. 20). Furthermore, a series of legislative and infralegislative decisions regarding recruitment, the status of cadres, the organization of command, and so on completed the basic principle by embracing all military activities, in time of peace as well as war, within a complex network of juridical constraints.

If some of these rules were aimed at protecting members of the military institution against political arbitraryness, such as the Soult law of May 1834 by which the officer owns his rank, dissociated from his function, the others have as a goal their political neutralization. The Third Republic went quite far in this regard by elaborating a system of statutory limitations, resulting in a genuine political and juridical curtailment of France's servicemen that won the institution the famous nickname, the "great mute." Thus, besides restrictions affecting their status, such as the obligation of residence, the system of furlough, the requirement for preliminary authorization to get married or to belong to an association, and limitations affecting personal liberties such as the forbidding of unionization or to go on strike, the lawmaker reduced the military's political rights by suspending the right to vote in 1872. To these measures more symbolic though no less symptomatic ones were added, such as the reorganization of the official protocol to give precedence to civilians, placing the prefect before the general. Taken in the light of other repressive but still legal nuances, as the suppression of the condition of endowment for the officer's future wife, or more surreptitious pressures, antiintellectual for example—"MacMahon's utterance : "I strike out from the promotion board any officer whose name I saw on a book cover," was meant seriously—these measures participating from the idea of objective control were ambiguous. Indeed, the military, excluded from the political debate and subject to specific contraints affecting even private life, did not seem to be a danger for the governing authorities; but then retired into a narrow organizational self, it was cut from the national evolutions, a tendency paradoxically not without consequences for their professionalism, as shown by the conflicts of 1870 and 1914.

To avoid these problems, while blotting out the ambivalence that such decisions could have in a democratic context, the Fourth and Fifth Republics sought to implement more flexible and adapted means of control, but without abandoning the principle of juridical and political quartering. The right to vote and be eligible were reestablished after 1945, but a number of incompatibilities and ineligibilities were maintained; if elected, for example, a military person must choose between his function or his mandate. The juridical quartering, quite attenuated by comparison with the past, still places members of the military institution in a situation different from that of other public agents. Thus the Regulation for General Discipline of October 1966 and later the military statute of July 1972 and September 1975 brought this statute closer to common law by abolishing, for example, the need for preliminary authorization in order to join an association or to be married. But, in addition to the fact that the very existence of these texts and a code of military justice implies a specificity, they maintained various restrictions including preliminary authorization (to marry a foreign person), interdictions (to belong to a trade union or to go on strike), and limitations of freedom (obligation of residence for reasons of service, obligation of reserve when political or international questions are at issue). Moreover, while the statute of 1972 forbids obeying orders or acts "contrary to laws, customs of warfare and to international agreements or constituting crimes notably against the security and integrity of the state," it decides also that any breach of the duty of obedience or refusal to execute is a disciplinary offence, even in some cases a penal one.

Nuclear Technology and Defense Doctrine as Means of Political Control of the Military

The Algerian issue and more generally the decolonization question being settled, the country engaged in a complete reorganization of her defense posture. This reform upon which General de Gaulle embarked (the key launching text being the January 1959 ordinance on the organization of national defense) had also as its object the solution of political-military tensions, by orienting the armed forces toward a new ambition to give it a new sense of purpose outside the political realm. Moreover, the modernization implied by this reform contributed to bringing the military institution closer to the parent society. It led, for example, to reforms in the curricula of military academies and other institutions of higher learning by giving precedence to technical competence in recruitment and promotion policies, thus creating a greater reciprocal transferability of military and civilian skills. Interestingly, the nuclearization of French defense around which this reform was articulated and the way French military doctrine was defined had also considerable implications for the subordination of the military to political leadership.

Given the cataclysmic nature of atomic weaponry, especially in its particular employment configuration, which calls on massive retaliation, decisions in this area are inevitably more political than military. Moreover, the integrated character of French deterrence renders decisions regarding tactics on not only nuclear but also on conventional responses inseparable from those concerning strategy. Contrary to the American model of graduated response, against a conventional attack, for example, France has evolved a doctrine according to which conventional and tactical force components are not supposed to be used in an independent fashion as, for example, battle instruments, but rather as means for testing the enemy's intentions and as a warning to signify readiness to resort to a strategic strike, against cities, to boot. The renaming of the tactical nuclear stratum as prestrategic is significant in this respect. Therefore, in such a system, because the ultimate use of massive atomic retaliation is always presupposed, the engagement of even the lowest echelon of the defense machinery is inherently political and may belong only to the civilian powers. Deterrence appears then as a kind of dialogue developed between the French leaders and their foreign adversaries. The military is no longer positioned to determine the terms of this relation; its role is circumscribed to putting into work the various elements of defense by conferring on them the greatest readiness.

As a result, a dynamic of civilian intervention in the area of military actions, from confrontations susceptible to involving the nuclear force to lower-intensity operations, was thus put into motion. Concomitant statutory changes regarding, for instance, pay and retirement pensions, promotions, continuing education and facilities for reintegrating into the civilian labor force lessen military differences with society. Building consensus within public opinion around the military institution and nuclear defense appeased all tensions and indeed facilitated the political control of the institution, putting an end, at least for the time being, to a rather complex history of political-military relations. Whether the situation will last is another question, not to be dealt with here, especially with the reconfiguration of the French defense posture rendered necessary by recent world changes and the probable emergence of a new institutional format, away from the conscription-based system.

REFERENCES

The literature covering civil-military relations in France is considerable. The following selection offers only some of the most salient references on the topic under a book form and written from an academic or scientific perspective.

André, Louis. *Michel Le Tellier et l'organisation de l'armée monarchique.* Paris: n.p., 1906.
Bankwitz, Philip C. F. *Maxime Weygand and Civil-Military Relations in Modern France.* Cambridge: Harvard University Press, 1967.

Baxter, Douglas Clark. *Servants of the Swords: French Intendants of the Army, 1630–70.* Urbana: University of Illinois Press, 1976.

Boëne, Bernard, ed. *La spécificité militaire.* Paris: Armand Colin, 1990.

Boëne, Bernard, and Michel Louis Martin, eds. *Conscription et armée de métier.* Paris: La Documentation française, 1992.

Bourget, J. M., *Government et commandement: Leçons de la première guerre mondiale.* Paris: Payot, 1930.

Chaignot, Jean. *Paris et l'armée au XVIIIe siècle: Étude politique et sociale.* Paris: Economica, 1985.

Chalmin, Pierre. *L'officier français de 1815 à 1871.* Paris: Marcel Rivière, 1957.

Charnay, Jean-Paul. *Société militaire et suffrage politique en France depuis 1789.* Paris: SEVPEN, 1964.

Corvisier, André, ed. *Histoire militaire de la France,* 4 vols. Paris: Presses universitaires de France, 1991–1993.

Ducourneau, L. *Le pouvoir législatif et l'armée sous la révolution.* Paris: Lavauzelle, 1913.

Fauvet, Jacques, and Jean Planchais. *La fronde des généraux.* Paris: Fayard, 1961.

Furniss, Edgar. *De Gaulle and the French Army: A Crisis in Civil-Military Relations.* New York: Twentieth Century Fund, 1964.

De Gaulle, Charles. *La France et son armée.* Paris: Plon, 1945.

Girardet, Raoul. *La société militaire dans la France contemporaine, 1815–1939.* Paris: Plon, 1953.

———, ed. *La crise militaire française, 1945–1962: Aspects sociologiques et idéologiques.* Paris: Armand Colin, 1964.

Jaurès, Jean. *L'armée nouvelle.* Paris: L'Humanité, 1910.

Kelly, George A. *Lost Soldiers: The French Army and Empire in Crisis, 1947–1962.* Cambridge: M.I.T. Press, 1965.

King, Jere Clemens. *Generals and Politicians: Conflict between France's High Command, Parliament, and Government, 1914–1918.* Berkeley: University of California Press, 1951.

de La Gorce, Paul-Marie. *La République et son armée.* Paris: Fayard, 1963.

Martin, Michel Louis. *Warriors to Managers: The French Military Establishment since 1945.* Chapel Hill: University of North Carolina Press, 1981.

Meisel, James H. *The Fall of the Republic: Military Revolt in France.* Ann Arbor: University of Michigan Press, 1962.

Nobécourt, Jacques. *Une Histoire politique de l'armée,* 2 vols. Paris: Seuil, 1967.

Paxton, Robert O. *Parades and Politics at Vichy: The French Officer Corps under Marshal Pétain.* Princeton: Princeton University Press, 1966.

Planchais, Jean. *Le malaise de l'armée.* Paris: 1958.

Ralston, David B. *The Army of the Republic: The Place of the Military in the Political Evolution of France, 1871–1914.* Cambridge: M.I.T. Press, 1967.

Robert, L. *L'officier et ses droits politiques.* Paris: Lavauzelle, 1911.

Sénéchal, Michel. *Droits politiques et liberté d'expression des officiers des forces armées.* Paris: Librairie générale de droit et de jurisprudence, 1963.

Sicard, François. *Histoire des institutions militaires de la France,* 4 vols. Paris: 1834.

Terquem, Emile. *Généraux de débacle et de coup d'Etat.* Paris: C. Bellais, 1905.

GERMANY

Wilfried von Bredow

The development of civil-military relations in Germany and its earlier political entities (Prussia, for example) has been studied at length by historians and social scientists. Until 1945, most German authors showed principally a positive bias toward the military and its role in society and the political process. After 1945, German authors mostly joined the ranks of non-German observers of the German military, writing very critical studies about the origins, features, and consequences of German militarism.

In 1945, demilitarized Germany, divided into two states in antagonistic camps, the East-West conflict, was confronted with the need to rearm; both governments, in Bonn and East Berlin, were determined to build up basically new armed forces with fundamentally changed military-political traditions and legitimacies. This was difficult, but probably successful. One astounding empirical illustration for this hypothesis is the comparative ease with which the armed forces in Germany were completely restructured after the unification of Germany in October 1990.

This chapter concentrates on the armed forces in the Federal Republic of Germany, first describing past ordeals that were translated into West Germany's rearmament. The relations between the armed forces and the civil society were shaped to guarantee political control of the armed forces by democratic institutions, a concept described next. A discussion follows of the problems of forceful social integration of the armed forces into the civil society, with, at the end, a discussion of the changing role of Germany in the international system, in light of internal developments in civil-military relations.

CIVIL-MILITARY RELATIONS IN GERMANY UNTIL 1945

In his *Principles of Sociology* (1886) Herbert Spencer distinguishes between a "militant type of society," in which "all men fit for fighting act in concert against other societies,'' and an industrial type of society with norms, laws, and institutions that induce peaceful economic change to the mutual benefit of all members of the society.[1]

These two types of society were sociological constructions or ideal types in the sense that Max Weber coined this term. Spencer had a clear idea about which states fit into the category of a militant type of society: Dahomé, old Sparta, Egypt, the Incas, Russia, and Prussia. Contemporary Prussia had become a very visible and important part of the German Reich of 1871, which had been forged by Bismarck with the help of three wars—against Denmark (1864), against the Hapsburg monarchy (1866), and against the French empire of Napoleon III. Geopolitical constraints, internal pressures from traditional and newly formed social groups, an odd combination of modernism and social historicism, and the strange appeal of regional and global imperialism came together in shaping the priorities of the political leaders of the German Reich. The armed forces had played an important role in the unification process. The officer corps was composed mainly of members of the old aristocracy and of the richer bourgeois middle classes. These men regarded themselves as the most important pillar of the monarchy, a collective consciousness that was dutifully mirrored by the attitudes and statements of the monarchs Wilhelm I and Wilhelm II.

Even when one considers the binary scheme of Spencer somewhat superficial, his basic assumption about the German Reich as a militant society is certainly undeniable. The usual term to characterize the social and political climate of this society and the style of its foreign policy is *militarism*. Although the concept of militarism seems simple, in fact it is very complicated. As recent surveys of more than 150 years of militarism present in various types of society reveal.[2]

The German historian Gerhard Ritter defined the militarism of the German empire as a combination of two elements: (a) the one-sided determination of political decisions by military-technical considerations, replacing a comprehensive examination of what is required by the interest of the state; and (b) the one-sided predominance of militant and martial traits in the nation's political outlook.[3] These two elements were indeed salient, but one must add a third element: (c) the deep penetration of military values and military attitudes into civil society.

These three features of German militarism left their traces on the collective identity of the Germans. Germany did not follow the dominant pattern of the development of civil-military relations during the nineteenth century. This pattern generated what Morris Janowitz called the ''citizen soldier.'' The citizen soldier was a model or an institution that was compatible with the emergent parliamentary democracies. ''In Germany, where the concept of citizenship was weak, the military continued to operate as a detached status group, as a state within a state, even after World War I. The National Socialist regime, with its ruthless and distorted forms of 'democratization' ended the Prussian military assumptions.''[4]

This perspective on the German military and its impact on the state and society is basically adequate. An enduring problem for historians and sociologists who analyze the course of civil-military relations in Germany after 1871 is the mixture of retrospective, romantic, and reactionary features, on the one hand, and the modernist and mobilizing effects, on the other, that characterized these relations. After Bismarck's resignation as chancellor of the German Reich in 1889, the institutional possibilities for the military leadership to influence the political system (with Wilhelm II then at the top) were fully realized. There was no more balance between the two versions of the "German vision" for the international order. The civil and diplomatic version was increasingly overruled by the military version; and even if the differences in the substance of these two versions were not huge, it became an important signal internationally that Germany's political elite used more and more a military terminology to describe their political goals.

This development within the political system is reflected by a trend affecting the society as a whole. Military norms and values penetrated the society and emerged as a rather dumb nationalism in the schools and universities, in the everyday life of the ordinary citizens, and in Germany's political culture. Their function was to overcome internal cleavages among large groups and classes. At the turn of the century, the typical German officer with a conservative-feudal background and a rather restricted worldview (but with a deep sense of professionalism) and the typical German reserve officer with a deeply felt commitment to imitate his active comrade even under civil circumstances represented the most respected social patterns in Germany.

The decision to go ahead with preparations for the war and, in August 1914, to enter the war was not a purely military one, for the civil elites of the Reich were mostly convinced that this war was necessary or at least inevitable. (This feeling was not restricted to Germany. But the Germans had the poorest civil counterbalance to military perceptions and demands.)

During World War I the political system of Germany was soon overtaken by the military. After 1916, Germany could be described as a military dictatorship. In time of war, this made sense, and the Germans knew too little about a working democracy to question it. Toward the end of the war, the heroic leadership of Hindenburg and the hidden, de facto–emperor Ludendorff lost much of their artificial charisma. When the war was lost, military norms and values and the armed forces seemed to shrink to less importance, but this was only partly true.

The Weimar Republic (1919–33) was a first and abortive attempt to introduce democratic norms and values into the state and society. Many internal and external factors influenced the fall of the republic. One internal factor was the programmatic distance between the armed forces, the Reichswehr, and the democratic institutions. The Treaty of Versailles imposed armed forces on Germany that were handicapped with respect to their posture and to their volume: not more than a hundred thousand soldiers, no modern navy, no tanks, no air force. The officer corps of the Reichswehr, shaped by General von Seeckt, continued to feed its antidemocratic prejudices. The majority believed in the restitution of the monarchy; a small but growing minority envisaged a postdemocratic strong Germany with someone like Adolf Hitler and his party at the head. The number of officers who respected democratic institutions and the legitimacy of the Weimar Republic was always extremely small.

At the end of the Weimar Republic, for one historic second, an alternative to National Socialism seemed possible—a grand coalition of the unions, some conservative groups, the left wing of Hitler's party that he had sacked, and the Reichswehr. General von Schleicher tried to forge this coalition but was unable to convince President Hindenburg and the Social Democrats that his plan was realistic. When Hitler became chancellor on 30 January 1933, the Weimar Republic was dead. His dictatorship led Germany into World War II and the catastrophes that will affect Germany for generations to come. However, not one man ran National Socialist Germany; Hitler had strong backing from most of the people, at least during the successful years of his regime. His foreign and security policies were very popular. He broke the Treaty of Versailles and began to rebuild strong military forces. He introduced general conscription and made a lot of political promises to comfort the military elites. He was eager to gain control over the armed forces and to integrate them as tightly as possible into the National Socialist state, but he was not always successful; and despite a partial identity with expansionist goals, the officer corps and the new National Socialist elites had a rather cool relationship. Officers of the Wehrmacht organized and executed the unsuccessful attempt to kill Hitler on 20 July 1944 and to get rid of National Socialism. Germany had to lose the war by an unconditional surrender, but the moral impetus of the officers' attempt became important for Germany after 1945.

ARMED FORCES AND DEMOCRATIC SOCIETY

National Socialist Germany lost World War II and surrendered to the Allied powers of the anti-Hitler coalition. This coalition was forged by common opposition to National Socialism and fascism, but it was also characterized by a deep and mutual mistrust between the western Allies and the Soviet Union. After the end of the war, programs for a common construction of a new and peaceful world order soon collapsed. The East-West conflict began to restructure world politics.

For a period, the common interest in overcoming the last remains of the National Socialist threat continued to exist among the Allied powers. But their plans for domestication and reeducation of the Germans changed as the Cold War became more and more important. In 1945, Germany was divided into four zones of occupation. Four years later, the three Western zones merged into a new state, the Federal Republic of Germany, and the Soviet zone became the German Democratic Republic. Thereafter the Germans were allies rather than losers. The two states were integrated into the antagonistic blocs of the East-West conflict; they became the European symbol and most exposed territory of this dangerous conflict. This development satisfied many who were afraid of a renewed Germany. As long as the East-West conflict dominated international and especially European affairs, Germany remained divided.

The military dimension of the Cold War in Europe demanded the rearmament of the German states. We shall concentrate here on the Federal Republic of Germany. The perceived threat in western capitals of the enormous military apparatus of the Red Army intensified during the Korean war in 1950–51. Yet how could one allow Germany to rearm, only a few years after the end of World War II? The Allied powers had done everything to destroy what they saw as Prussian and German militarism. The memory of German war crimes committed not only by the SS but also by the Wehrmacht was still fresh in countries like the Netherlands or France, not to mention East European countries and the Soviet Union.

Much has been written about the prehistory and history of West German rearmament.[5] The international situation demanded a rapid process of rearmament, which was difficult to organize; but the lessons of the past demanded a completely new approach for the buildup of new German armed forces. They should be efficient in combatting the Soviet threat, but at the same time they should not become the vehicle of any neonational movement. Allies relied on the professionalism of the soldiers of the Reichswehr and Wehrmacht, who at the same time needed to develop a true devotion to the new democratic structures of the Federal Republic. This was the great and probably unique challenge for the politicians and soldiers who started to build up the Bundeswehr: To form a powerful instrument for the democratic government of the Federal Republic and make sure that this instrument and its leaders would never turn its arms against the democratic structures of society or stand by to let democracy be destroyed by its enemies.

The Problems of Integration

Fears of a revival of traditional Prussian/German militarism (or what was considered to be militarism) spread not only among the victims of National Socialist expansion but also among West German citizens. Despite the imminent threat of communism and the Red Army, it was necessary to find and define not only an organizational but also a legitimate framework for the new armed forces to diminish these fears. The military strategic framework for the Bundeswehr was at first conceived as a multilateral organization, the European Defense Community (EDC). Within the EDC, the German armed forces (as those of other member states) would not function as national forces but would be integrated into a structure of inter/multi/supranational control and command. By the same token, the EDC would promote the idea of the United States of (Western) Europe. This plan did not come into being, and probably was never meant to. When it fell apart, the new armed forces of the Federal Republic were integrated into NATO and the West European Union (WEU) with some special clauses. More or less all troops were assigned to NATO, leaving practically no discretion for a purely national military policy. West Germans accepted this arrangement of 1954–55 gracefully, and they even developed a special orientation toward the alliance, a special NATO-mindedness.

But this was only one prerequisite for the new armed forces as an instrument for the democratic political system, compatible with its norms and values. Perhaps even more important was the demand for a new legitimacy of the armed forces in the democratic society. The term *integration* has played a key role in the public debate in the Federal Republic from the early 1950s to the present. Fortunately, the Federal Republic existed for a time before the question of rearmament arose so that the Parliament, government, experts, and public opinion could initiate and sustain a public debate about the place of the Bundeswehr in society, about the political control of its leadership, and about the mechanisms necessary to guarantee its compatibility with democracy. The concept of integration dealt with the integration of the organization into the constitution (Grundgesetz), integration of the soldiers into the civil society, integration of as much civil spirit and behavior as possible into the everyday life of the armed forces. The concept was hotly debated, especially among officers of the Bundeswehr. There was a lot of opposition, but eventually in formal and informal ways the integration of Bundeswehr into society became part of a new, if somewhat fragile, tradition of the Federal Republic as a democracy.

Conscription and Legal Integration

In a recent account of the internal development of the Bundeswehr, Bernhard Fleckenstein comes to the following conclusion: "In contrast to the armed forces of other countries, whose military history developed without interruptions, the Bundeswehr is a new creation. It was the declared will of the lawmakers to integrate the new German armed forces as much as possible into the industrially developed and democratically constituted society of the Federal Republic, to prevent military life from developing again independently of its society, and to prevent the new military from becoming again a 'state within a state.' "[6] The *institutional* integration took place in the years when the Bundeswehr was founded. Then, the most important regulations regarding the construction and maintenance of the armed forces, their structures, their position within the political system, and their relationship with civilian society were formulated and put into various legal frameworks. The constitution (Grundgesetz) set forth restrictions for the use of the Bundeswehr (no aggression against another state, no mission outside the NATO territory with the potential exception of participation in measures of collective security, and no use of the military within the territory of the Federal Republic against organized strikes). The constitution also contains articles regulating general conscription and conscientious objection.[7]

Over the years, some regulations changed in relation to new political and social developments in the Federal Republic, but the general idea behind this legal construction, which is continued in a series of laws, is still the same: as much integration of the armed forces into civilian society as possible and as much civil control as possible in order to keep the armed forces compatible with the norms, values, and attitudes of a democratic society.

One of the most intriguing elements of this integrational concept is the combination of conscription and conscientious objection. Conscription when introduced in 1955 was regarded as the best possible instrument to link civilian society and the military. The citizen soldier had eventually arrived in Germany. Yet, those whose conscience forced them to object to conscription should not be punished but should find an alternative to show their willingness to serve. Both, conscription and conscientious objection became part of the emerging political culture of the Federal Republic. Thus, conscription has lost much of its appeal among young Germans; and its alternative, civic service, has become a nearly indispensable part of the health- and care-system of the Federal Republic. After the unification of Germany, public pressure against conscription has continued to grow; it is a strange irony that one of the main reasons to try to "save" conscription is the anticipated difficulty in finding a cost-effective substitute for the civic service.[8]

Innere Fuehrung

Integrating the armed forces into civilian society demanded a high degree of institutionalized public control over the armed forces. Probably even more important was the necessity to convince the military personnel of their obligation to accept the norms and values of democracy and civilian society and to combine these norms and values with their professional standards. The credible buildup of fundamentally new armed forces (even with a high percentage of officers and NCOs from the Reichwehr and Wehrmacht) depended on the "success" of a new philosophy for the internal organization, the principles of education and command, the relationship between superiors and subordinates and between military obedience and civil freedom, and the role of politics in the armed forces.

This new philosophy, *Innere Fuehrung,* is hard to translate into English: "inner guidance" is the literal translation, but that does not seem to make much sense. The model soldier of the Innere Fuehrung is the *Staatsbuerger in Uniform* (citizen in uniform).

This new philosophy or ideology was formulated mainly by Wolf Graf von Baudissin, a former officer of the Wehrmacht who participated in the planning phase of the Bundeswehr and was responsible for creating the institutional preconditions for the political *conditio sine qua non* of the new armed forces, for their structural sociopolitical compatibility with the new democracy.

Baudissin regarded his task as a challenge to find a concept that could reconcile the demands of modern democratic political culture with the demands of the military profession in the age of nuclear warfare.

He developed his concept in the 1950s without the help of military sociological research or counselling. For the first years of sweeping reform, its general reception among the officers was not enthusiastic; a strong parliamentary ma-

jority and comparatively strong public support made Innere Fuehrung a corner-
stone of the new image and self-perception of the armed forces.

Internal debates in the Bundeswehr and the public debates about the Bundeswehr have continued to raise the question whether Baudissin's concept is adequately put into practice, has lost substance, or has even failed. Extreme
responses are wrong, but it is difficult to define exactly the degree of realization.

A definition from the early 1960s, still used today, describes Innere Fuehrung
as ''the duty of every military superior to educate soldiers who are capable and
determined to defend freedom and the rights of the German people in a hot and
cold war against every aggressor. Innere Fuehrung is based on the values of the
constitution, acknowledges the political situation, transfers trustworthy military
virtues and experiences of the past into our modern time and takes into consideration the consequences of modern military technology.''[9]

Again, this seems rather vague. For a German ear, however, quite a lot of
neuralgic points emerge in this definition, for example, the difficulty of making
a distinction between ''positive'' and ''negative'' elements of the traditions of
German military history; the hope (partly wishful thinking) that young conscripts
will come as politically educated and highly motivated citizens; the confrontation with communism; the suppressed fear of a military conflict in Europe with
Germans on both sides shooting at each other; and the deep conviction (a con-
vert's conviction) of the superiority of Western democracy.

Had it been possible, as many military counsellors in the 1950s and many
officers of the Bundeswehr thought, to draw a clear line between military efficiency (armament, tactical and strategic principles, and training) and ''internal''
structures of the military organization, which were to guarantee civil control and
the obedience of the armed forces to the constitution and the leaders of the
political system? Such a distinction, so went the argument, would have made
clear that the fatal distance of the Reichswehr toward the Weimar Republic and
the even more fatal affinity of the Wehrmacht for National Socialism were not
to be repeated.

The decisive counterargument of Baudissin and his followers was that in
modern wars as well as in the prewar situation, where ideologies and value
systems influence the soldier's motivation, this line between the military and
organizational aspects of the armed forces has vanished. In order to be combat-
effective, the modern soldier must be deeply convinced of the superiority of the
social and political system he stands and fights for. This requirement was even
more important in a country with divided loyalties where the German soldiers
in the East and the West are integrated into hostile alliances and could become
enemies in combat. The key element of the concept of Innere Fuehrung was the
model of a soldier who was fully aware of the ideological aspects of the East-
West conflict as a conflict between democracies and totalitarianism, understanding the need to defend a democracy.

The democratic citizen in uniform became the ideal modern German soldier.
A set of parliamentary laws and internal regulations are based on the assumption

that the citizen in uniform is a necessary and realistic model of modern military man. In June 1954, Baudissin gave a short outline of his ideas before a committee of the Bundestag. He said "Negatively speaking, we do not think of making the soldier less military and more civilian. . . . Instead, we think of two different aspects. First the mental position of the soldier. He must be part of the political and mental life of the community, because otherwise he might just not know against what he is supposed to fight, but this is not enough. . . . Only the integration of the soldier into civil life provides him with the experience of those values he stands for. Only the chance to participate in social and political actions makes him feel responsible. . . . Furthermore, the new concept implies a special relationship with the armed forces. Among citizens who serve together in the armed forces a relation like that between a superior and a dependent subordinate is anachronistic. They are all partners, in different functions, but with the same human dignity and out of the same responsibility."[10]

The implementation of Innere Fuehrung was a painful process. Apart from personal problems between various groups and schools within the officer corps of the Bundeswehr, these difficulties resulted mainly from:

1. The self-perception and traditional professionalism of the majority of the officer corps stood against the interpretation of the Reichswehr/Wehrmacht as "non-pattern" for the Bundeswehr.

2. The intensity and plausibility of the Soviet threat seemed to make it necessary to rely on anti-Bolshevik military expertise from all sources, even from those that were not compatible with democratic values.

3. Baudissin's concept always had an aura of a "vision," and many pragmatic officers and especially the NCOs had difficulties in finding a way to educate and train the recruits according to "high-minded principles." Most paid lip service to the principles and acted on the basis of a muddling-through scheme.

4. Other officers concerned with the technical aspects of their work rejected the ideological superstructure.

5. The positive echo of the concept in the two main parties of the Bundestag, CDU/CSU and SPD, and with the general public aroused some military mistrust.

6. West German's NATO allies demonstrated a benign noninterest in Innere Fuehrung. They had been expected to watch closely the experience with the new and in some ways avant-gardistic concept, but they refrained from doing so.

NEW DISTANCES AND CHANGING POLITICAL PRIORITIES

The Bundeswehr founded in 1955 was immediately integrated while NATO's strategic doctrines changed over the decades; the Federal Republic was evidently interested in proving to be a reliable ally. The military rationale of the Bundeswehr—to make deterrence more credible, to defend the territory of the Federal Republic, to push an invader from the East back beyond the border—was never popular among the Germans. Deterrence was a risk whose success or failure could not be predicted, for it was the potential aggressor who decided about the one or the other. If deterrence failed, the consequences would be disastrous for Germany.

Yet the officer corps of the Bundeswehr with very few exceptions accepted the NATO strategy for Central Europe. Among the early exceptions was Colonel Bogislav von Bonin, who developed alternative strategic plans for the defense of the Federal Republic. He had been a member of the Amt Blank, the precursor of the Ministry of Defense, but because of his dissent he was fired by Theodor Blank even before the first soldiers of the Bundeswehr were recruited.[11]

However, the name of Bonin survived as a kind of hidden myth of the military culture; every critic of the official military strategy of the Bundeswehr came to mention him during the late 1970s and early 1980s in the context of NATO's double-track decision.[12]

The Bundeswehr and its officer corps did not really take much part in the political debate about political and military priorities until recently. An early attempt by some generals at the end of the 1950s publicly to support the political position of Defense Minister Franz-Josef Strauss in matters of nuclear strategy generated a public storm of political indignation. Another attempt by conservative generals in 1969–70 to gain political support against the reforms of the Bundeswehr planned and executed by Defense Minister Helmut Schmidt resulted in their dismissal. Basically the armed forces did not want to play a political role in the Federal Republic; it is hardly conceivable how they could have played an active political role, given the many institutional restrictions.

The Bundeswehr and the second generation of its leaders have basically no more difficulty in understanding the armed forces according to the ideas of Innere Fuehrung. After the end of the Cold War and Germany's unification, a growing majority seems to regard the armed forces as too expensive. The size of the armed forces will be drastically reduced. Conscription is less popular than ever. And 1950s arguments about the necessary political and social control of the armed forces by means of conscription are no longer understood.[13]

Perhaps this reflects the positive experience with the Bundeswehr in democratic Germany. The coalition government of CDU/CSU and FDP is determined to stick to the system of conscription, but this attitude may change. If the Bundeswehr were to become an all-voluntary force like the armed forces in the United States and Great Britain, it would probably continue to be a loyal and democratically oriented organization. There are no signs of a growing distance between the Bundeswehr and civil society. There are, however, signs of a growing distance between this civil society and its armed forces. It will be interesting to study the middle- and long-term effects on the armed forces.

NOTES

1. Herbert Spencer: *The Principles of Sociology,* vol. II (London and New York: 1886), pp. 568–642.

2. See, e.g., Volker R. Berghahn, *Militarism: The History of an International Debate 1861–1979* (New York: St. Martin's Press, 1982); Wilfried von Bredow, *Moderner Militarismus: Analyse und Kritik* (Stuttgart: Kohlhammer, 1983).

3. Gerhard Ritter's concept of militarism is the fundament of his famous book in four volumes: *Staatskunst und Krieghandwerk* (Munich: Oldenbourg, 1954–1959).

4. Morris Janowitz: *The Last Half-Century: Societal Change and Politics in America* (Chicago, Ill. University of Chicago Press, 1978), p. 183.

5. It would be an endless task to list all these books and articles here. One bibliographical hint may be helpful for those interested in the transatlantic aspect of West Germany's rearmament: Robert McGeehan, *The German Rearmament Question: American Diplomacy and European Defense after World War II* (Urbana: University of Illinois Press, 1971).

6. Bernhard Fleckenstein, "Federal Republic of Germany," in Charles C. Moskos and Frank R. Wood, eds., *The Military: More Than Just A Job?* (Washington, D.C.: Pergamon-Brassey's, 1988), p. 188.

7. It seems paradoxical, but is a kind of symbolic hint of the "conversion" of German society to a decidedly civil mind that the right to conscientious objection was put into the constitution in 1949, when no German armed forces existed.

8. See Juergen Kuhlmann, "National Service Options in Germany." Paper presented at the International Conference National Service: A Global Perspective, Racine, Wisconsin, June 1992.

9. The author of this definition is the former Inspector General, Ulrich de Maizière.

10. Wolf Graf von Baudissin: *Soldat fuer den Frieden: Entwuerfe fuer eine zeitgemaesse Bundeswehr* (Soldiers for peace: Designing German armed forces for our times) (Munich: Piper, 1969), p. 206.

11. A collection of articles of Bonin is Heinz Brill, ed., *Bogislaw von Bonin im Spannungsfeld zwischen Wiederbewaffnung–Westintegration–Wiedervereinigung,* vol. 2 (Bogislaw von Bonin and the conflicting goals of reunification, integration into the West, and rearmament) (Baden-Baden: Nomos, 1989).

12. See Wilfried von Bredow and Rudolf H. Brocke *Krise und Protest: Urspruenge und Elemente der Friedensbewegungen in Westeuropa* (Crisis and protest: Origins and elements of West European peace movements) (Opladen: Westdeutscher Verlag, 1987).

13. A recent example is Wolfram Wette, "Kein Kind der Demokratie," *Die Zeit,* 19 February 1993.

REFERENCES

Bredow, Wilfried von. *Moderner Militarismus: Analyse und Kritik.* Stuttgart: Kohlhammer, 1983.

Bredow, Wilfried von, and Rudolf H. Brocke. *Krise und Protest: Urspruenge und Element der Friedensbewegungen in Westeuropa.* Opladen: Westdeutscher Verlag, 1987.

Fleckenstein, Bernhard. "Federal Republic of Germany." In Charles C. Moskos and Frank R. Wood, *The Military: More Than Just a Job?* Washington: Pergamon-Brassey's, 1988.

Ritter, Gerhard. *Staatskunst und Krieghandwerk,* 4 vols. Munich: Oldenbourg, 1954–1959.

GREECE

Kostas Messas

Today, the Greek military is seen to reflect developments that make it look more like the militaries of Greece's allies in West Europe. It appears that the Greek military has broken its historical pattern of intimate participation in the country's political life and has returned to its primary institutional mission, namely, the defense of Greece's independence, constitutional establishment, and territorial integrity against external enemies.[1]

In the past, the Greek military was a major actor in the country's politics. Conventional explanations attribute the military's political role to the quick and changeable character of Greek history, with particular emphasis on the war of independence against the Ottoman Empire, the enduring conflict over whether to have a monarchy or a republic, the impact of foreign interference, and the gains and losses associated with the extravagant and impractical aspirations of the Greek irredentists for territorial expansion. Unconventional explanations associate the politicization of the Greek armed forces with developments in the class system in Greece. Their basic argument states that rival social groups, in their efforts to win the competition for control of political power, have sought and secured the support of the armed forces. In effect, the military intervened in Greek politics to help certain groups in the society acquire and maintain political power. This chapter refers to both sets of explanations.

FACTORS DETERMINING THE MILITARY'S POLITICAL ROLE

War of Independence

The War of Independence of 1821–29 was fought primarily by Greek irregular forces, the forerunner of the regular military. They were controlled and armed by various leaders who represented powerful families. Following independence, many of the irregulars refused to disarm, as was requested by the republic's government, and chose life in the mountains. Their hit-and-run tactics, which had proved quite successful during the war of independence, were used as a means of harassing bandits of rival groups and, frequently, representatives of the national government. Their presence, as well as their fearsome tactics, became a source of political division in the formative days of the young republic. Inevitably, the society was split into those who showed greater loyalty to the bandits and those who showed greater loyalty to the representatives of the national government.

After the war, the leaders, with the support of their respective irregular forces, formed rival political factions that suffered from anarchy, pettiness, corruption, and self-serving ambitions. Because of their interests in personal gains, they put forth very little effort in restoring the economy or providing relief to those who bore the brunt of the devastation of the war. Moreover, because they lacked political consciousness, they failed to take political initiatives. The political void they helped create inevitably invited foreign intervention in Greek affairs. In time, most of the bandits disarmed or joined the regular military, in response to royal pleas.

Choice between a Monarchy or a Republic

Greece achieved its independence formally in 1831 with the qualified consent of the Great Powers: Britain, France, and Russia. Subsequently, they decided that Greece would be a hereditary monarchy and chose Prince Otto, the second son of King Ludwig I of Bavaria, to become Greece's first king. Monarchy, as a political choice, was suitable to the interests of the Great Powers but foreign to the habits, conventions, and temperament of the Greeks. It inevitably became the source of an enduring societal split, the society's division into republican and royalist groups. The armed forces were destined to play a significant role in the ongoing dispute between the two factions.

In time, the armed forces became the preserve of the crown. However, the military shared the popular agitation for constitutional government and seriously challenged King Otto's absolute rule on 14–15 September 1843 and on 22 October 1862. The two coups were politically significant: the first forced King Otto to agree to constitutional monarchy and parliamentary government and the second forced him to abdicate, resulting in the fall of the Bavarian dynasty.[2]

The revolts provided the armed forces with a foretaste of affecting political change in the society. Because the outcome of the revolts was generally accepted as being essential to Greece's development toward parliamentary rule, the armed forces began to perceive themselves as the embodiment of populist sentiments in the country.[3]

The agitation for parliamentary rule continued under King George I (formerly, Prince William of Denmark) and his prime ministers, especially Charilaos Trikoupis. Trikoupis reformed the electoral law, implemented an extensive domestic development program, and improved the preparedness of the armed forces. Despite economic pressures, revenues were made available to increase the overall size of the military forces and to strengthen the navy. Subsequent governments added to his reforms by improving the military's effectiveness through procurement of better equipment and improvements in training. Following the disastrous defeat of 1897 by Turkey, even the military authorities appeared committed to better organizing and training of the armed forces.

The military revolt of 1909 contributed significantly to the schism between royalists and republicans. It came after the king rejected appeals made by the military and Cretans alike to take steps to unify the island of Crete with Greece. The king was unwilling to risk military action against the Turks. This made him increasingly unpopular and eventually led to the revolution by the Military League, a group of antiroyalist officers. Following the revolt, the Military League assumed power temporarily and dictated government policy.

Moreover, the Military League brought to power Eleftherios Venizelos, an antiroyalist and an enthusiastic modernizer. Venizelos took measures to revise the constitution and make parliamentary government effective, formed the Liberal Party, won the election of 1910, and enjoyed firm control of the government. He even worked with King George I at reorganizing the police, the judicial system, and the country's finances.

Venizelos undertook a military reform program that included improvements in the technical quality and effectiveness of the army and the navy. Most important, he sought to expand civilian control over the military. In order to show his determination, he transferred many officers to posts that would render them apolitical (usually in the provinces) and sent to jail the most stubborn of them. Those moves made Venizelos increasingly unpopular in the palace, contributing significantly to the split between royalist and republican officers and, through them, between royalist and antiroyalist armed forces.

The situation became increasingly more difficult with the outbreak of World War I. Venizelos wanted Greece to intervene in the war by fighting on the side of the Allies. King Constantine I, the new king, strongly pro-German, was keen on keeping Greece neutral. The dispute set off a chain of events that created discord and bitterness in the nation and in the armed forces. Military officers were confronted with the choice between loyalty to Venizelos and loyalty to the king. Many officers on both sides were purged. Inevitably, the antiroyalist sentiments among factions of the armed forces were extended to include the throne as an institution.[4] A military revolt in 1916 ousted the king and replaced him with his younger son, Alexander. Likewise, anti-Venizelist sentiments in the military were extended to include all republican groups.

Eventually, Greek troops assisted the French, the British, and the Serbs in a general offensive in Macedonia in September 1917. Six weeks later the war was over, the Allies had won, and Venizelos was fully justified. As a result of the peace settlements, certain territories were irrevocably restored to Greece. Venizelos also agreed to undertake a military operation in Smyrna and parts of

Anatolia for the alleged purpose of protecting the Christian populations there.[5] On 25 October 1920, King Alexander died; on 20 November 1920, Venizelos and his Liberal Party were defeated at the elections; on 19 December 1920, King Constantine I was returned to the throne.

The expedition in Asia Minor ended in a disastrous military defeat for Greece. The military, blaming the royalist government for the defeat, replaced it with a revolutionary committee on 25 September 1922, ousted King Constantine I (for the last time) in favor of his son, who became George II, and executed six royalist ministers. The revolutionary committee dictated policy from 1922 to 1924. For the first time, Greece's head of state was an active military officer, General Stylianos Gonatas.

In 1924 King George II was deposed by army officers in favor of a republic, which was confirmed in a plebiscite the following year. An unsuccessful counterrevolution by royalist troops, including Ioannis Metaxas, aimed at restoring the monarchy took place in October 1924. After four years of unstable government, punctuated by the military dictatorship of Lieutenant Theodoros Pangalos between 1925 and 1926, the party leaders summoned Venizelos to assume the premiership and introduce effective government.

Venizelos experienced limited success. He was no longer able to hold his Liberal Party together. In order to prevent the opposition from coming to power, he was alleged to have made use of political allies in the armed forces. A series of abortive military coups and assassination attempts accompanied his political decline. He was defeated in the elections of 1931. Subsequently, having been implicated in an abortive naval coup aimed at forcing out the conservative Populist government, he fled into exile and was condemned to death in absentia. Voters in a 1935 plebiscite called overwhelmingly (97%) for the return of George II, in the hope of reversing the trend of unstable governments and frequent military interventions that had started in 1922.

Parliamentary elections the next year (1936), however, produced a deadlock between royalist and republican parties in Parliament, with the communist bloc holding the balance. In order to diffuse the bloc's influence, King George II called on General Ioannis Metaxas, who was popular among royalist army officers, to form a government as prime minister. By 1936 Metaxas dropped all pretense of constitutional government and initiated a dictatorship.

The dictatorship of Metaxas added anticommunism to the split between royalists and antiroyalists. Because communists were known for their strong opposition to the monarchy, being a royalist also came to mean being an anticommunist. The palace itself had become the focal point of anticommunist and nationalist activity. Royalist factions of the military were, inevitably, imbued with sentiments of anticommunism and nationalism. Officers with known, or suspected, communist (and therefore antiroyalist and antinationalist) sentiments were distanced from the military. Steadfast opposition to communism in the military and the society was continued by a series of right-wing governments. In time, the military reflected a strong conservative and royalist outlook for politics and society. The palace had won the struggle over control of the armed forces.

Such was the situation when Georgios Papandreou, of the Center Union, which had won parliamentary majority in 1964, became prime minister. He planned to reorganize the armed forces and bring them under civilian control by transferring or retiring several older, royalist officers and replacing them with younger, liberal men willing to embrace civilian supremacy over the military. Predictably, relations between Papandreou and conservative groups in the society, including the palace, were seriously strained. The armed forces in particular were disturbed by Papandreou's liberal outlook and worried that he would reduce defense expenditures. The situation grew worse when, in May of 1965, a secret, left-wing officers' group, known as Aspida, was uncovered. It was subsequently alleged, though never proved, that the prime minister's son, Andreas, was linked to the Aspida group.

Strong ideological differences, combined with military grievances over organizational interests, prompted a group of mostly colonels and lieutenant colonels to assume direct control of the government through a bloodless coup on 21 April 1967. In their apologia for supplanting the constitutional government, they referred to the threat that Papandreou, and particularly his son, posed to the integrity of the armed forces and national security. They also referred to an imminent threat of communist subversion. A countercoup by the palace in December 1967 failed, forcing the king and his family to leave Greece. On 25 November 1973, General Ioannidis overthrew the military regime of Colonel Papadopoulos. The military government was brought down on 15 July 1974, when Ioannidis supported an ill-conceived coup against President Makarios of Cyprus. A few days later, Karamanlis returned from self-exile in Paris and was sworn in as prime minister. The troublesome issue of whether to have monarchy or a republic was settled by a referendum on 8 December 1974. The outcome was very clear. Nearly 70 % voted for a republic.[6]

Foreign Interference

Foreign interference in Greek politics has at times reached institutional dimensions. Conventional explanations have attributed this phenomenon to foreign interest in the strategic advantages of Greece's geographic location. Accordingly, Greece's geography appealed to every power that was interested in dominating political developments in the Eastern Mediterranean region and in Southeast Europe.

Nonconventional explanations have attributed the phenomenon to Greece's dominant social groups, their origins, and their economic basis. The supporting argument is that Greece's urban classes have either invited foreign intervention or cooperated with foreign forces in their arduous road to formation and development, dating from the middle of the eighteenth century to the present. Either individually or collectively, the two conditions gave foreign interference in Greek affairs enduring qualities.

Although the initiative for the War of Independence came from the Greeks, the first independent and sovereign Greek state came into existence with the qualified recognition of Britain, France, and Russia. They decided which lands would be included in the new Greek state and that Greece would be a monarchy.

Foreign interference in Greece was in fact institutionalized through the enduring mechanism of monarchy, which in turn required the support of a small, privileged, and politicized segment of the Greek population and the support of the armed forces. The foreign powers desired compliant monarchs, who in turn required the presence of social groups and armed forces whose outlook was more royalist than nationalist. The compliance of the monarchs, taken for granted, was at times secured through warnings, intimidation, or the replacement of one monarch with another. Attempting to secure and maintain a royalist outlook in the society, however, led to a devastating schism between royalists and antiroyalists. Foreign interference begot monarchy in Greece, monarchy begot a series of restrictive regimes, including palace cabinets, which led to internal strife and political instability, which in turn led to more restrictive governments. Such has been the legacy of foreign interference in Greece.

For the society at large, foreign tutelage, through its various mechanisms, deprived Greece of the opportunity to develop appropriate political institutions and the Greeks of the opportunity to develop a proper attitude toward authority. Dislike for monarchy was inevitably expanded to include most forms of government authority. Moreover, a series of restrictive governments provided the Greeks with only limited means of political participation and solidarity, leading to an overall low level of political culture that made them dependent on foreign powers for solidarity. Because the Greeks participated in politics mostly in the form of protests, they did not develop an adequate appreciation for the politics of consensus and their importance for political stability. Finally, foreign tutelage prevented the development of clear definitions of national needs and goals.

With regard to the armed forces, foreign interference prevented the military from developing a united national outlook. The armed forces were divided between those who showed primary loyalty to the king and those who showed primary loyalty to civilian political figures. The military revolts of 1843 and 1862 were in response to a struggle for power among the three powers and, through them, among the "Russian," "French," and "British" groups in the society. The situation developed because King Otto appeared to have aligned his political outlook with Russia and France, leaving Britain out. The outcome of the revolts reduced Russian and French influence and gave the British an advantage over the others, as well as creating a strong possibility that the next king would have a more pro-British outlook.[7]

The military's task of embodying Greek irredentism was also made difficult by foreign interference. At times the Great Powers were unanimous in their disapproval. At other times, the French and the Russians supported Greece's national question. The British, out of desire for the preservation of the status quo, emphasized nearly always the necessity of Greece's peaceful relations with Turkey. In another instance, in 1853, an operation to free Thessalia and Macedonia from Ottoman rule was interrupted by both British and French troops.

With regard to the island of Crete, the French, who at first supported unification with Greece, later withdrew their support because King George had become engaged to the czar's niece, Grand Duchess Olga. The French feared increased Russian influence in Greek affairs. On the question of Crete, the British favored autonomy rather than unification.

In time, Britain became Greece's international protector, a special relationship that lasted until 1947. Upon Britain's withdrawal from Greece, the United States emerged as Greece's new patron through the Truman Doctrine. Despite American contribution to the outcome of the Civil War, there was mounting resentment among many Greek groups, including communists, socialists, and moderate Greeks, all of whom desired a more independent Greece.

Membership in NATO provided the United States with an institutionalized framework for influence in Greece. For the Greeks, membership in NATO (1952) provided a source of protection against possible communist threats from Greece's belligerent communist neighbors. Although not always recognized, the Cold War did start in Greece. Membership in NATO was a foregone conclusion and a national imperative. In time, membership reduced Greece's military reliance on the United States by opening to Greece the arsenals of other members, including Great Britain, the Federal Republic of Germany, France, and Norway.

For the military, membership in NATO had its privileges: it confirmed Greece's pro-Western orientation; it implied that the size of the army would be maintained; it also implied that improvements to the army's efficiency and quality of equipment would continue; finally, it provided the military with the opportunity of rubbing elbows with its counterparts from Western Europe. Overall, membership in NATO appeared to address both Greece's interests for security and aspects of the military's corporate interests.

Significant strains in Greek-American relations were caused in 1952, when the United States lobbied for the introduction of a plurality electoral system; in 1967, when the United States reaction to the military regime in Greece was not as disapproving of the regime as the Greeks would have hoped; and in 1974, when the United States did not prevent the Turkish invasion of Cyprus, following the unsuccessful coup against President Makarios of Cyprus by members of the Greek military regime.

With regard to the 1967 military regime, America's stand toward it was characterized by inconsistency: There was public condemnation of the regime by the United States; tangible measures included the ban placed on shipments of heavy arms to the regime from May 1967 to September 1968; but shipments of light arms continued. The United States resumed shipments of heavy weapons in October of 1968 and opposed efforts by the Council of Europe, the European Economic Community, and NATO to impose sanctions against the military regime, apparently out of concern for its military interests in Greece and in the Southeast Mediterranean. The Soviet invasion of Czechoslovakia in 1968 provided the United States with an excuse of geopolitical significance.

Greek Irredentism for Territorial Expansion

The original size of the Greek state was based on a small portion of Greek lands and less than a million Greek people. Areas such as Thessalia, Epirus, and the island of Crete and a population of more than two million Greeks remained under Ottoman rule. Liberation of those lands and people became a national yearning. The Greeks called it "Megali Idea," meaning the "Great Idea." Generations of leaders were judged on whether they shared that yearning or not. The military, royal and antiroyal factions alike, coveted the opportunity to embody Greek irredentism.

It was clear that the notion of the Great Idea was nurtured with very few reality checks. Its success depended on the unrealistic expectation of overpowering the forces of the Ottoman Empire and finding ways to circumvent the objectives of the Great Powers. The Ottoman Empire was a formidable opponent and enjoyed considerable British and French support. The Greek state, on the other hand, suffered from a serious lack of resources. Moreover, years of foreign interference had disrupted the task of developing a coherent policy toward its unliberated lands and people. Inevitably, the passion for irredentism resulted in both territorial gains and losses for Greece.

It was said that the coup of 22 October 1862 against King Otto was staged in part because he was not willing to promote liberation of occupied lands. In March of the same year, Britain transferred the Ionian Islands to Greece, aiming, among other things, to halt Otto's personal decline with the Greek people. In 1881, the annexation of Thessalia took place. In 1897, the military suffered a humiliating defeat in its attempt to unite Crete with Greece. King Constantine I's rejection of pleas made by Greeks and Cretans alike to engage actively in affecting Crete's unification with Greece also prompted the 1909 revolt by the Military League.

Greece made considerable territorial gains as a result of the Balkan Wars. Crete, Epirus, Southeast Macedonia, and Western Thrace were united with Greece. Greek participation on the side of the Allies during World War I resulted in additional territorial gains, as Eastern Thrace became part of Greece. The territorial gains gave the Greek people and the armed forces a renewed sense of confidence and self-respect. In terms of strategy, Greece did not act alone; instead, it pursued its goal by joining other nations in a multinational operation.[8] Everything was contingent on victory. When the Balkan Wars and World War I were over, the multinational operation was successful and Greece was vindicated. Acting alone would have been extravagant, leading to sure defeat.

Greece acted alone in the 1921–22 war with Turkey and suffered both a disastrous military defeat and a major territorial loss. The Treaty of Lausanne of 1923 forced Greece to cede Anatolia irrevocably to Turkey. In addition, Greece was challenged to deal with the problem of settling the 1.3 million Greek refugees who poured into Greece. For the time being, the magnitude of the defeat imbued Greek irredentism with a sense of reality. With the annexation of the Dodecanese in 1948, which had been under Italian occupation since May of 1912, Greece reached its present borders.

The Great Idea was revived on 15 July 1974, when the military government of Greece supported a coup against President Archbishop Makarios III of Cyprus, in order to unite Cyprus with Greece. The coup, like the military expedition in Asia Minor in 1922, was an act of political excess, with disastrous consequences. A major international crisis broke out in the region, accentuated by a Turkish invasion of Cyprus. In the wake of these events, the Greek military regime invited a group of prominent politicians to form a civilian government on 23 July 1974. In effect, revival of the Great Idea contributed to the regime's downfall.

Recruitment Patterns and Social Background of the Officer Corps

Conscription in the military has been universal in Greece. Traditionally, the socioeconomic and regional backgrounds of the recruits determined whether they received army, air force, or navy duty. Recruits assigned to army or air force duty have come primarily from the rural areas, the countryside, and the small towns and mostly from low-income families. Recruits receiving navy duty have represented primarily the urban areas, coastal areas, and the islands and have come mostly from middle- or upper-income families. Officer candidates for army, air force, and navy commissions have reflected similar socioeconomic and regional backgrounds.

In terms of strength, the army has been the leader in the number of conscripts, followed by the air force and the navy. Regarding the duration of the service, army recruits have usually served the shortest term of service, followed by the air force and the navy.[9]

In addition to determining one's duty or commission in the military, socioeconomic and regional factors appear to have shaped one's reasons for entering military service as a profession. It has been demonstrated that army and air force candidate officers were drawn to the military profession primarily by the opportunities for career and social mobility and that navy candidate officers were mostly interested in following family tradition and in maintaining their particular social standing.

With regard to their political ideology, the army and the air force can best be described as having been historically conservative, anticommunist, nationalist, and populist. The army's sentiments of anticommunism and nationalism were particularly strengthened during the Civil War, because the majority of military operations against the communists were carried out by army units. Concerns for

socioeconomic improvement, combined with a conservative and populist outlook, have made army and air force officers more prone to intervention in politics. Their sentiments of anticommunism and nationalism have also made them
susceptible to rumors of communist threats and willing participants in the steadfast opposition to communism during the 1950s and 1960s, culminating in the
military regime of 1967–74. The navy, on the other hand, can best be described
as having been historically more liberal in its outlook.

Most of the military coups in Greece have been army operations, with some
involvement by the air force and reluctant participation by the navy, usually
after the event. Direct military opposition to the colonels' regime of 1967–74
came primarily from the navy, either in cooperation with other military units,
as in the royal countercoup on 13 December 1967, or by acting entirely on their
own, as in the naval mutiny on 22–23 May 1973. A countercoup by army units
on 25 November 1973 merely replaced one president, Colonel Papadopoulos,
with another, General Phaedon Ghizikis.

Relatively speaking, military officers, whether in the army, air force, or navy,
have shared a strong corporate identity and have been highly preoccupied with
the preservation of their corporate interests. Grievances over their welfare have
accompanied nearly all of the military's apologias for intervening in politics.

HOW ARMED FORCES EXERT AND MAINTAIN POLITICAL INFLUENCE

The military's long repertory of participating in Greece's political affairs has
been achieved through a variety of means and processes, including the following:

a. The military has intervened in politics in cooperation with civilian political
figures. Republican factions of the military, in cooperation with republican civilian politicians, opposed the royalist government in power in 1843, 1862,
1909, and 1922; in effect, the coups were an effort to replace a royalist government with a republican one. Royalist factions of the armed forces cooperated
with royalist civilian political figures in 1936 and on 13 December 1967, acting
on the king's behalf.

b. The military has sought to achieve a particular political outcome by assuming direct control of the government, relying on sheer physical coercion.
Supporting examples include the colonel's regime of 1967–74. Use of physical
coercion and the regime's overall restrictive nature made the 1967 coup a symbol of oppression.

c. The military has engaged in patronage, either by serving as a patron or
making use of the influence of patrons, both domestic and foreign. The military
has relied on influential patrons out of concern for its corporate interests, ranging
from military assignments to military and economic assistance. Likewise, domestic and foreign groups have relied on the military's support for the preservation of their own interests, ranging from keeping a government position to

geopolitical considerations. Overall, the manipulation game appears to have been won by those relying on the military. The armed forces intervened in politics mostly in coordination with civilian political figures either to oppose the government in power (1843, 1862, 1909, and 1922) or to prevent a particular group from coming to power (1936 and 1967).

d. The military has made use of its elite status, based on qualitative criteria of organization, hierarchy, discipline, and corporate ethos, which are perceived as being inadequate among their civilian counterparts. Quite frequently, in their explanations for participating in the politics of the country, the military has made allusions to weak political institutions, political deadlock, party rivalry, and failure in leadership.

e. The military has ascribed messianic qualities to its political role. Participation in the country's politics, it was argued, increased the military's effectiveness in achieving national security, in maintaining political stability, and, most important, in "saving the nation" from certain internal and external threats. The military was generally recognized as a progressive political and social force in the aftermath of the 1843, 1862, and 1909 coups.

f. The military has relied almost exclusively on the relative strength and willing spirit of the army. The coups of 1843, 1861, 1909, 1922, 1936, and April of 1967 were primarily army operations. Exceptions include the royal counter-coup of December 1967, which was an operation involving primarily the air force and the navy, and the naval mutiny of 1973, exclusively a naval operation.

g. The military made use of conspiratorial groups, both on the political left and the political right. Right-wing groups included the Military League (known for its sentiments against King George I), Chi, Pericles, Holy Band of Greek Officers (known for their anticommunist sentiments), and the National Association of Greek Officers (known for its pro–military regime sentiments and activities). The military revolt of 1909 was carried out by officers of the Military League. Left-wing groups included Aspida (known for its antimonarchist sentiments). The exposure of the Aspida group among the officers in the summer of 1965 was in part instrumental in the coup by conservative officers in April 1967.

h. Coup makers also attempted to give their regime an ideological and political content. They did so by restricting important provisions of the constitution, particularly those referring to individual freedoms and civil liberties, and by amending the constitution to strengthen the powers of the executive office as well as the powers of the leaders of the armed forces. The colonels' regime of 1967, for example, adopted a new constitution that went into effect on 15 November 1968. It was subsequently amended on 29 July 1973, by a referendum; and Greece was transformed from "crowned parliamentary democracy" into a "presidential parliamentary republic" with Colonel Papadopoulos as president.[10] An all-civilian cabinet was also formed in 1973.

Overall, the military's participation in politics was accomplished through cooperation with civilian officials, reliance on sheer physical coercion, use of domestic and foreign patronage, reliance on the military's perceived superiority, developing a messianic character for its mission, reliance on the numerical strength and political outlook of the army, the use of conspiratorial groups, and through efforts to give the regime ideological and political content.

EVALUATION OF THE POLITICAL ROLE OF THE MILITARY

Until the revolt of 1909, the military's involvement in politics was corrective and altruistic in nature. The armed forces were primarily interested in challenging royal absolutism and royal unwillingness to fulfill the objectives of Greek irredentism, correct for the failure in leadership, reduce political corruption, and eliminate foreign interference in Greek affairs.

The general perception of the military as being a progressive political and social force after the coups of 1843 and 1862 against King Otto was well earned. The public sentiment in Greece at the time supported constitutional government, and the military succeeded in translating that sentiment into action. Likewise, the revolt of 1909 by the Military League was an embodiment of the nation's dream to liberate lands and Greeks still under Turkish rule. Moreover, leaders like Charilaos Trikoupis and Eleftherios Venizelos, both of whom contributed significantly to the country's political and economic modernization, enjoyed considerable support from particular factions of the military.

Subsequent coups, such as those in 1922, 1924, and 1936, diminished the military's altruistic image. Their purpose was either to support the government in power or to promote the opposition, which at that time contributed to the historic split between royalists and antiroyalists and did very little in promoting peaceful development of democratic institutions in the society. Revolutions and counterrevolutions, the basic pattern of military intervention in politics in the 1920s and 1930s, deprived the country of the opportunity to develop lasting political solutions. The military itself was deeply divided as a result of the purges that followed each revolution and counterrevolution.

Parliamentary development was seriously hindered under the dictatorship of General Ioannis Metaxas, between 1936 and 1941. Metaxas became prime minister by default and not by constitutional procedures. Faced with a deadlock in parliamentary elections, King George II ignored the option of a compromise between two of the parties and avoided constitutional procedures that would have enabled the participation of the strong communist block. Ritual anticommunism made the communists more radical in their outlook and stronger in their determination to gain control of the government, as the Civil War of 1944–49 demonstrated.

The military coup of 1967 ended over fifteen years of stable democratic politics in Greece. In their attempt to effect changes in the society, the makers of the coup and their supporters relied on habitual repression, torture, and imprisonment without due process. The military had become a symbol of oppression and the majority of the Greeks opposed the regime. The regime created both a national and an international crisis in July 1974 when the colonels provoked a Turkish invasion of Cyprus by staging a military coup against President Makarios. Unable to repel the invading forces, they withdrew in embarassment.

FUTURE DEVELOPMENTS

A variety of measures, taken immediately after and since the withdrawal of the military regime from politics in 1974, have succeeded in bringing about the democratization of the Greek military. Immediately after the regime's collapse, the government of Konstantinos Karamanlis, the new prime minister, sought and received guarantees from the military that it would stay in the barracks and would not interfere with his government's policies. In return, the government assured the officer corps that their corporate interests would be respected, they would not be criticized, and they would not suffer reprisals.[11] By giving those guarantees, the government succeeded in presenting itself as a viable political alternative, agreeable to the military. Moreover, guarantees aimed at showing respect for the military's corporate interests removed one of the most important reasons for the military's involvement in politics.

Subsequent political developments attested to Greece's rapid transition to democracy: Karamanlis formed a new party, the New Democracy Party, and won the elections of 1974 and 1977; in 1981, following a smooth transition, the Socialists came to power and ruled Greece until 1988, ending thirty-five years of pro-Western, conservative rule. The Conservatives were returned to power in 1990 and were again succeeded by the Socialists in 1993.

The democratization effort benefited further from Greece's pro-Western orientation in general and from membership in the European Community (EC) in particular. The requirements for membership in the EC included commitments to "western" standards of democracy. Having assessed the importance of membership in the EC for Greece, the country's leadership and various interest groups, the military included, appeared to be happy to oblige.

With democratization of the military completed, the future of civil-military relations in Greece will be determined primarily by Greece's membership in the EC and in Europe's main security structures and by the security arrangements that will emerge in Europe to deal with the new security concerns.

Greece is a member of all of Europe's main security structures, including NATO, the Western European Union (WEU), and the Conference on Security and Cooperation in Europe (CSCE). As a NATO member, Greece can assist the alliance in the formulation of a mandate for risky areas such as the Balkans. As a WEU member, Greece can assist in the development of a European defense system by Europeans and an infrastructure that will be able to handle security concerns, such as those rising from the conflict in former Yugoslavia. As a CSCE member, Greece can contribute to the organization's efforts to develop peacekeeping and crisis-management capabilities. Given Greece's location in the

Balkans, it is anticipated that all three security structures will consider Greece's views on Balkan issues and may even assist Greece to emerge as the dominant nation in the Balkans, calling for the maintenance of a sizable, well-trained, and well-equipped military. Greece's potential for a growing influence in the region increased when NATO decided to create Headquarters of Land Units in Larissa, in Central Greece, and to place the Headquarters of the soon-to-be-created NATO Multinational Division of South Europe in the Greek region of Macedonia.

NOTES

1. Recent changes in the leadership of the armed forces in Greece took place quietly, without the usual fuss surrounding them, prompting many observers to characterize them as "European" in style. See, for example, *TO BHMA*, 28 February 1993, p. 10.

2. In addition to his absolute style of rule, King Otto was unpopular because of his unwillingness to make a clear commitment that his successors would embrace the Greek Orthodox faith. Without that commitment, there appeared no separation between the crowns of Bavaria and Greece.

3. An unsuccessful military revolt aimed at King Otto also took place in Nauplion in February 1862. Nauplion and other areas in the Peloponnese region of Greece were under Russian influence. The Russians desired an Orthodox king and did not accept Catholic Otto wholeheartedly. The revolt did not succeed, primarily because it took place away from Athens, but it demonstrated that the republican vs. monarchist split had indeed a foreign dimension. Another mutiny took place in June 1863, after King Otto's abdication. Military units loyal and disloyal to the government, as well as some irregular forces, were involved in the fierce shooting.

4. The king dissolved Parliament in 1915, bringing about a new constitutional and political crisis and leading to his forced resignation; King Constantine was replaced by his son Alexander. Venizelos established a provisional government in Thessaloniki, giving Greece two separate governments; Venizelos dissolved the provisional government, came to Athens, and assumed the premiership on June 26.

5. He even agreed to send troops to fight against the Bolsheviks in the Ukraine.

6. Over the years, the former king expressed interest in returning to Greece as a citizen. It may happen, and he and his family may enjoy some support among the Greeks. Monarchy as an institution, however, never succeeded in bonding with the people.

7. However, in order to help Otto, Britain offered Greece the Ionian islands in March 1862.

8. In the First Balkan War (1912), Greece, Serbia, Bulgaria, and Montenegro forced Turkey out of its European possessions, except Constantinople. In the Second Balkan War (1913), Greece, Serbia, Rumania, and Turkey forced Bulgaria to cede a large part of Macedonia.

9. According to *The Military Balance 1992*, the army had 113,000 conscripts; the air force, 26,800; and the navy, 19,500 conscripts. With regard to the terms of service, army recruits served for up to nineteen months, air force recruits for up to twenty-one months, and navy recruits for up to twenty-three months.

10. The figures of the referendum, reported on 13 August 1973, were 77.2% for ab-

olition and 21% for the retention of the monarchy. All appeals challenging the figures were rejected by the Supreme Court.

11. The government, however, succeeded in subjecting to reprisals the leaders of the 1967 coup, who were arrested and tried for treason; the military police, which was stripped of its sweeping powers and confined to its strict duties as a military police force; and a number of generals and junior officers, who were retired from active duty.

REFERENCES

Clogg, Richard. *Parties and Elections in Greece: The Search for Legitimacy.* Durham, N.C.: Duke University Press, 1987.

Clogg, Richard, and George Yannopoulos, eds. *Greece under Military Rule.* London: Martin Secker and Warburg Limited, 1972.

Close, David H., ed. *The Greek Civil War, 1943–1950.* New York: Routledge, 1993.

Couloumbis, Theodore A., John A. Petropulos, and Harry J. Psomiades. *Foreign Interference in Greek Politics: An Historical Perspective.* New York: Pella Publishing Company, 1976.

Meynaud, J. *Les Forces Politiques en Grèce.* Lausanne, France: Ètude de Science Politique, 1965.

Petropulos, John Anthony. *Politics and Statecraft in the Kingdom of Greece 1833–1843.* Princeton: Princeton University Press, 1968.

Sarafis, Marion, and Martin Eve, eds. *Background to Contemporary Greece.* London: Merlin Press, 1990.

Svoronos, Nikos G. *Histoire de la Grèce Moderne.* Paris: Presses Universitaire de France, 1972.

Vlavianos, Haris. *Greece, 1941–49: From Resistance to Civil War.* New York: St. Martin's Press, 1992.

INDIA

Veena Gill

Democratic institutions and processes have been under considerable strain in the last two decades in India. Tendencies towards the use of force rather than negotiation and compromise in solving conflicts of a socioeconomic and political nature have altered the political landscape. In the light of new political situations with the complete breakdown of civil administration in several states of India and the increasing role of the army in aid of civil authority, it is pertinent to ask if existing civil-military relations are likely to remain unchanged in the near future. The frequent resort by politicians to the army to resolve law-and-order crises, its day-to-day close cooperation with civilians, as in Kashmir, the consequent increased political socialization among officers and the rank and file raises doubts about the future of the "nonpolitical" profile of the Indian army.

In 1947, British colonial rule was terminated; the country was partitioned, and the new state of Pakistan came into existence. In 1971 yet another new state was carved out of Pakistan, Bangladesh. The domestic role of the Indian army has diverged radically from its Pakistan and Bangladesh counterparts, which have been embroiled in politics almost since the inception of those states.

Studies in recent years have focused upon the nature of the military establishment itself in order to answer the question of why the Indian armed forces have exercised restraint in the political arena.[1] An explanation of military nonintervention is expressed in terms of its professionalism and organization. The ethnic composition, socioeconomic background, recruitment, and training of officers and soldiers is seen as not being conducive to military intervention.

It is not sufficient to link the military's political or nonpolitical behavior simply to the level of political institutionalization of a society[2] or to the nature of its military organization.[3] The point of departure in this study therefore is the weight given to the political attitudes and beliefs, the "political perspectives of the military."[4] Decisions to involve militaries politically are made most often by its senior leadership. No analysis of civil-military relations can be made without analyzing their attitudes towards their own appropriate role in society and politics.

In the attempt to analyze the factors responsible for the low levels of "politicization" and political involvement of the Indian army, I will focus on several aspects. The first is the nature of the role played by the (British) Indian Army, given the colonial context, that differentiated it from other professional armies.[5] It will be argued that the colonial patterns of role, organization, and recruitment that were in part continued by the political elite in the postcolonial state profoundly affected the army's perception of its own appropriate role and status within the society. The second section of the chapter will analyze the processes and concrete measures taken to make the Indian army into a modern professional fighting machine effectively under civilian control. The third section will present an overview of the civil-military perspectives of the senior army leadership since Indian independence and the nature of the army's interaction with society. Variables such as ethnicity, social-class background, military organization, budgetary control, and the training and tenure especially of officers, will be analyzed as contributing to the appropriate role and status of the military in Indian society.

In recent years, senior army officers and politicians have been anxious about the likely consequences of a marked increase in the "aid to civil" and counterinsurgency roles of the Indian army.[6] Fearing a growing politicization of the military establishment on the one hand and the growing alienation of the civil population in affected areas to the misuse of armed force on the other, many doubt the continued nonpartisan role of the army in Indian politics. On their part the civilian leadership has been impinging upon the autonomy of the military establishment, especially in the area of promotions to senior leadership positions. Bureaucratic competence in defense and security matters has also expanded, while the participation of the service chiefs at the highest levels of defense decision-making is both reduced and more diffuse. The final section of the chapter will address the issue of changing civil-military relations in India.

COLONIALISM AND THE (BRITISH) INDIAN ARMY: PROFESSIONALISM IN AN ALTERED CONTEXT

The "Old" Indian Army was raised and sustained by the British Indian covering a time span of several centuries as an instrument of colonial rule. This army was as renowned for its traditions of valor, loyalty, and courage as for its professional "ethos," discipline, and efficiency,[7] aspects that were amply demonstrated in its participation in the two world wars. Its heir, the modern Indian army, is the world's largest volunteer army and has a reputation as a highly professional apolitical organization.

One way of approaching a study of the motivational complexes or the ori-

entation of the military toward intervention is to relate it to the level of professionalism. The classic statement is made by Samuel Huntington, who writes:

The one prime essential for any system of civilian control is the minimizing of military
power. Objective civilian control achieves this reduction by professionalizing the military, by rendering them politically sterile and neutral. This produces the lowest possible
level of military power with respect to all civilian groups. . . . A highly professional
officer corps stands ready to carry out the wishes of any civilian group which secures
legitimate authority within the state.[8]

To Huntington, military professionalism involves a balance among expertise,
responsibility, and corporateness. This is seen as being antithetical to political
involvement. In his view professionalism implies the development of institutional autonomy and corporateness in which the military is clearly demarcated,
differentiated from the major complex political roles, and willing to act only
within its own sphere of competence and expertise. The development of a professional ethic would mean that the military sees its own task as insuring national security. According to Huntington's logic, both the organizational and
attitudinal drives of professionalism lead the military to develop its own internalized loyalty to the subservience to civilian authority.[9]

How does this theory relate to the Indian experience? It is argued that the
nature of the predecessor organization, the British Indian Army upon which the
postcolonial armies of India and Pakistan are based, was certainly not informed
by principles of professionalism as we understand it from the writings of
Huntington. A fundamental difference between professional armies elsewhere
and those nurtured under colonial rule as in British India is the redefinition of
the basic principles of the organization, recruitment, and the most important
mission itself, which have had a major bearing on the subsequent development
of civil-military relations in such states.

The British Indian Army from its very inception was trained to be the "cus-
todian of law and order" and a major pillar of support of colonial interests. The
principles of its organization in fact were based upon political rather than professional considerations, aimed at securing British interests in India.[10] This is
evident from the earliest policy of recruitment of combatant troops by the British
East India Company, which was organized not on a secular but on a religious
linguistic and regional basis.[11]

The mutiny of 1857 led to an alteration of the principle of organization of
the Indian regiments. It was recommended by the Imperial Government "that
the native army should be composed of different nationalities and castes, and
as a general rule, mixed promiscuously through each regiment."[12] The principal
strategy of maintaining control over their Indian empire was the British policy
of playing the sentiments of one religious group against each other, the infamous
policy of "divide and rule." The utilization of this strategy is evidenced by a
(British) Indian Army policy statement suggesting the deployment of the mili-

tary, "Keep your Sikh regiments in the Punjab, and they will be ready to act against the Hindoos, keep your Hindoos out of the Punjab and they will be ready to act against the Sikhs."[13]

In the main, the essential role of the army was political, the maintenance of law and order. It would be naive to assume that, given the political environment, the soldiers were socialized professionally and not politically. One of the striking features of the British Indian Army was the fact that the officer corps was largely the preserve of British nationals, the local Indian component being restricted to the recruitment of soldiers.

When in 1918 the imperial government agreed to extend the King's Commission to Indians, it was obvious, as has been argued elsewhere,[14] that the essential motive behind this concession was political rather than in the cause of efficiency. For the recruitment of Indian officers, given a tough competitive examination and elaborate oral interview, guaranteed that only a small section of the privileged elites—the landed aristocracy and "gentry"—could acquire the commission. In the course of their recruitment and organization policy, the British, especially after the Mutiny of 1857, formulated and codified in principle the concept of the "martial" races.[15] The occupational distinctions determined by the Hindu caste system reinforced the myth that some people will make soldiers and some will not.

The difference in the attitude of the British military elite toward professional standards in the Indian Army are borne out in a statement by Lord Roberts, commander in chief of the Bengal Army, who wrote,[16] "In the British Army the superiority of one regiment over another is mainly a matter of training; the same courage and military instinct are inherent in English, Scots and Irish alike, but no comparison can be made between the martial value of the regiment recruited amongst the Gurkhas of Nepal and the warlike races of northern India and of one recruited among the effeminate races of the South."

As a consequence of this policy, combatant troops were primarily recruited from the so-called martial races, the Gurkhas of Nepal, Sikhs, Dogras, Rajputs, Jats, and select Muslims from Punjab, Panthans and Baluchis. There was a further regional concentration within these populations, which is indicated by the fact that in 1939, 48% of the total combatant troops in the Indian army were supplied by the Punjab.[17] Although under the compulsions of World War II, the British were forced to recruit Indians as officers in large numbers. In contrast to the Indian officers of the pre–World War II era, who were sons of princes, landlords, and Viceroy's Commissioned officers, these men came from middle-class and low-middle-class backgrounds.

The overbearing influence that this concept of the superiority of the martial races had on the subsequent organizations of the armies of independent India is clear. The Sikhs, for instance, today constitute barely 2% of India's population but contribute about 11% of the manpower of the armed forces. Sikhs constitute in fact as much as 20% of the officer cadre. These racial issues eroded the Indian army in 1945. Discontent spilled over from the army ranks to those of the navy, where it found expression in mutinies in 1946. There is certainly a measure of truth in the assertion that has been made that the British withdrawal no later than June 1947 from India was influenced by the fact that the government in England feared "the Army might not hold together much past that date."[18]

At the time of independence, the Indian army had an organization whose rank and file were recruited from a narrow social-cultural base, the so-called martial races. This officer class had little command experience; only four of the officers held the rank of brigadier at the time of independence; its leadership was elitist, recruited as it was from upper-class military families, landlords, and princes. However, at the time of World War II the social base of recruitment through emergency commissions was dramatically altered and a more nationally representative officer cadre came into being, mostly from middle-class and lower-middle-class backgrounds. This was an army that in its historical past had a more internal than external security role. Its officers had experienced racism at close hold, had their first independent major command operation of a civil nature in the administration of communally disrupted provinces following the carnage of Hindu-Muslim rioting, and were definitely not untouched by the processes of politicization of Indian society. The army was professional in a colonial way, but it was politically socialized by the historical circumstances of the time.

On the basis of this brief review, an assumption that guides this analysis is that the Indian army is an integral part of the domestic political process. It is irrelevant for our understanding of civil-military relations in the subcontinent to speak of military rule versus democracy. The term "military intervention" is a misnomer, given that the historical involvement by the military can be better understood as varying from degrees of minimal participation to overt control. Drawing boundaries between civil society and the armed forces is not an easy task. Militaries reflect characteristics and problems of the societies of which they are a part. This becomes comprehensible when viewed from the perspective that professional soldiers are not socialized into their profession in the absence of other intervening socialization agents in the society. To what extent their professional training makes them distinct from the societies of which they are a part and thus is inimical to intervention is an empirical question.

The extent to which a country's army is involved in politics is subject to a constellation of factors both internal to its organization and outside it. As we shall see in the later sections of this chapter, despite an underlying continuity the roles, values, and organization of the Indian military institution have undergone change, as has Indian society. There can be no doubt that the enlarged participation in internal security matters in the light of the changing political environment has resulted in an enormous "role expansion" of the Indian military. The changing ethos and values of the Indian officers and soldiers as reflected by their attitudes and behaviors in the last decade or so makes them less immune to ideas of overt political involvement. It would be reasonable to assert that there can be no guarantee that a professional army in a developing country such as India will not engage in politics in the face of total collapse of civilian ability or legitimacy to govern. The army has refrained from an active political role so far not merely because it is professional, but because of other underlying factors. The high degree of political institutionalization and the will of its political elites to sustain and work a parliamentary democracy, a political culture that would not easily consider overt military intervention as legitimate, and the sheer size, diversity, and complexity of Indian society deter military intervention. In this context professionalism may be seen as an important but not sufficient condition for keeping the military out of the political arena.

FROM INDEPENDENCE TO THE PRESENT

The post-independence period is divided into two phases, the first extending to the early 1970s. It is argued that the low political participation of the military in India in this period has to a large extent been conditioned by concrete measures by its civilian elite to depoliticize, reorganize, and redefine the role of the military. Civilian budgetary and financial control of the military and its subordination to civilian authority in the defense decision-making process are key to characterizing civil-military relations. This period may be described as one of increased civilian involvement in "military spheres" of competence. In the conduct of politics, able Indian civilian leadership, committed to democratic practice in the first two decades following independence laid the foundations for a stable policy. Respect for democratic rules by politicians and parties enabled pluralist political institutions to take shape and root. Political means above others were chosen to articulate, negotiate, mediate, and resolve different social interests. The foundations for stable democratic political processes and civilian subordination of the military were thus laid in this period.

The period from Indira Gandhi's second tenure (1980–84) as prime minister to the present has witnessed a dramatic increase of the army's internal security role. Communal and political strife has radically altered India's secular democratic image. As one state administration after the other collapsed in Assam, Punjab, and Kashir (not to mention a perpetual state of insurgent political tension in the northeastern states of Nagaland, Tripura, and Arunachal Pradesh), a marked civilian-role expansion of the military has taken place, affecting the existing civil-military balance. Indian society is considerably "militarized" (in the sense that force rather than negotiation by democratic means has become the medium for the resolution of social conflict) at the same time as the military has become increasingly politicized by participating in the civilian administration of riot-affected areas and in the restoration of law and order. This growing politicization is the consequence of the changing recruitment patterns especially their officer corps, which is both socially and economically more representative of Indian society, being recruited from diverse caste and communal low-income groups. The military is unhappy over the downgrading by civilian elites of its status in terms of salary and rank vis-à-vis other state organs such as the bureaucracy and paramilitary forces. Frustration grows with incompetent politicians who have encroached on the military's institutional autonomy and corporateness and greatly expanded its unpopular role of policing social discontent and disorder. What consequences can these developments have on the future of civil-military relations? Can they result in overt military control of the Indian state, or is civilian control still so pervasive that it rules out categorically the likelihood of such an event? Some possible scenarios will be discussed in the last section of the chapter.

SECURING CIVILIAN CONTROL: PROFESSIONALIZING THE MILITARY

In the period following independence, the historical circumstances of self-government of the nascent Indian state extended further the sphere of functions of the military, the army being pushed to serve national goals, which included not merely defense against external aggression but also aid to internal civil power.

In the light of the historical circumstances leading to partition of the Indian states (the emergence of an independent Muslim state; the army's defense of both Hindu and Muslim population during the sixteen months of communal rioting from August 1946 to November 1947; and the first war with Pakistan over the disputed state of Kashmir as early as May 1948, not even a year after independence) the Indian army assumed a special role as both administrator and sole defender of the territorial integrity of the Indian state. Although fearing the consequences of an expanded internal role for the military, a number of paramilitary forces were created in the 1950s and the 1960s to serve as a buffer between the army and domestic civil disorder.

The task of reorganization was complex, given the total disarray of the army organization at the time of the division of forces between India and Pakistan. Two thirds of the undivided British Indian army remained with India and one third with Pakistan. As regiments were organized on a mixed basis, partition along communal lines cut across the very basis of the army organization. Most soldiers and officers came from riot-devastated areas, and they and their families had been directly affected by the travails of partition. Added to this was the even more serious problem of the command and leadership of the army. British officers with a few years of service and little expertise were promoted to higher ranks. Battalion commanders with six years of service and brigade commanders with ten years became common.

Commenting on the grave danger of the process of partitioning the army, Lieutenant General Sinha writes, "It is indeed very incredible that the soldier's sense of discipline prevailed and the army was partitioned without a single incident in record time."[19]

As Indian politicians were aware of the consequences such actions could have on the future of civil-military relations in the country, from the very outset a policy of effecting civilian control of the military was made. In this context they followed the precedents set by the British in India.

The British legacy of civil-military relations is well illustrated by the Kitchener-Curzon dispute, which finally ended in the resignation of Curzon as viceroy of British India. In 1895, the three separate army units of Bombay, Calcutta, and Madras were merged into a composite organization under the dual control of two authorities: the commander-in-chief, a senior general responsible for its military preparedness, and a less senior officer, known as the military member, representing the government of India, responsible for its administration. Commander-in-Chief Kitchener wanted to abolish this dual control. Curzon opposed abolition, and the ensuing controversy ended in Curzon's resignation. The position of military member was abolished, and in its place the position of Secretary, Army Department under the commander-in-chief was created. The consequence of this event was a temporary dilution of civilian control of the military. In 1921, however, a civil servant was appointed as Secretary, Army Department, with direct access to the viceroy.[20] Further consolidation took place when in 1936 the Army Department, and the Army Secretary became the Defense Secretary with a civil administrative staff, although the commander-in-chief held the position of defense minister. After independence in 1947, the whole department came under the authority of a civilian defense minister. Thus civilian control over defense decision-making was formally institutionalized. The system at present remains largely unchanged. Although much to the chagrin of the military, it is mostly bureaucrats and not popular representatives who have control over financial and military aspects of defense policy.

The objective of bringing the military under firm civilian control involved internal organizational change, affecting its recruitment patterns, role, command, hierarchy, and status. The first measure involved the appointment of a civilian defense minister. In 1947 Sardar Baldev Singh assumed this portfolio. The second devolved authority vested in a commander-in-chief of the integrated defense force to three independent heads for the three armed services, the army, navy, and air force. There can be no doubt that this was done to weaken institutionally centralized command and control of the military establishment, and it definitely detracted from cohesion and corporate feeling among the three sections of the armed forces. At the same time, this action reduced the authority of the commander-in-chief of the army—the numerically dominant wing of the military— by making his position equal to that of the chiefs of the navy and the air force. Viewing the concentration of authority in a chief-of-defense-services staff as a possible threat to India's democratic institutions, an integrated and unified defense organization under a single command was separated by the political leadership. In fact, in the army, power is further delegated to five regional commanders. It would therefore need immense unity of purpose and dedication to effect a coup d'etat originating in the army.

As for recruitment policy, from the very onset the civilian leadership determined not to recruit officers believed to have been politicized during the Indian national movement. Therefore ex-personnel of the Indian National Army (under the commands of General Mohan Singh and later Subhash Chandra Bhose) were given pensions and provided with other rehabilitation benefits but were not taken into the Indian army. This was done in order to ensure that the discipline of the Indian Army was not impaired and its apolitical outlook was not affected.[21]

Since 1963, following the recommendation of the military affairs committee of the cabinet to prevent any one state from dominating recruitment, concentrated effort began to make the army more representative and to recruit from those states that had not traditionally provided many soldiers, such as Tamil Nadu, Bihar, Gujarat, and Andhra Pradesh, although in 1974 the Punjab was still providing over 15% of the army.

The government has also implemented the policy of integrating ethnic groups into mixed units and expanding existing ones. In the Indian army, no single ethnic group dominates either the officer corps or the ranks of the army. In addition the Indian army has a system of castes or class recruitment. Most of the ethnic groups in the country are divided into various subcastes, which are reflected in the army. Because of caste differences it is not possible to recruit them into one regiment, which makes it impossible for the ethnic groups in the army to act as one united body, as illustrated by the mutinies in 1984 by the Sikh battalions, in which only high-caste Jat soldiers of the Sikh infantry regiment participated and not their lower-caste Mazbhi comrades of the Sikh light infantry.[22]

The typical present Indian officer has a lower-middle-class background. The officer corps is a heterogeneous body, broadly representative of Indian society. This largely urbanized and heterogeneous officer corps is not conducive to the formation of an ethnic clique that might attempt to dominate the Indian officer corps and deters political ambitions.

Civilianized institutional control of the military is formalized in the 1950 constitution, which states that the president is the supreme commander of the armed forces, while in effect executive control is exercised by the prime minister and cabinet. The constitution also reserves the defense of India exclusively to the Union government. The defense ministry under a civilian minister has the responsibility of administering and coordinating the three armed services. Defense decision-making takes place in a committee of the cabinet, where civilian ministers of defense and foreign affairs and the prime minister preside. Service chiefs and the defense secretary are invited to give their opinion and advice. It is the civilian leadership that prepares the operational directive, while the planning of actual military operations is left to the chiefs of staff.

Budgetary considerations relating to the procurement of hardware and stores as well as decisions relating to matters internal to the military such as promotions and service conditions are the prerogative of the Defense Minister's Committee and his Production and Supply Committee.

Within the military establishment itself the various service committees including the Chiefs of Staff Committee have no mandatory authority. They par-

ticipate in the defense decision-making process in an advisory capacity. Their
recommendations as and when they are made are processed in the usual way
by defense ministry civil officials. Civilian control is thus affected by political,
financial, and bureaucratic subordination of the military. The pervasiveness of
civilian control mechanisms and the encroachment on military institutional autonomy has been considerably disliked by the military leadership and is a potential source of corporate discontent that can alter the existing civil-military
balance.[23] Voicing this discontent, Lieutenant General Sinha writes, "Subordination has to be to the civil power represented by the elected representatives of
the people and not to any civil department or civil service."[24]

The alteration of precedence finally symbolizes the civilian subordination of
the military by lowering the image and status of the military vis-à-vis the bureaucracy. A secretary in the government of India ranked lower than a lieutenant
general in 1947. Later, a secretary was made to rank with a full general. The
chief secretary of a state formerly ranked with a brigadier; after independence,
a chief secretary was made to rank with a major general and later with a lieutenant general. In addition, in concrete terms, low salaries as compared to the
private and public sectors and discontinuation or drastic reduction of perquisites
such as leave and travel concessions, started in the post-independence period,
have continued. All these developments have considerably altered the morale
and ethos of the military, generating a sense of deprivation among serving officers and deterring potential applicants. At present the military profession is
among the least preferred of professions for educated young men in India. A
growing professional concern thus is the general mediocrity of talent of the
present officer cadre in India.[25]

CIVILIAN INROADS INTO THE MILITARY SPHERE: COMPROMISING PROFESSIONALISM

Civilian leadership in India has been adept at securing control of the military,
leading in practice to the compromise of military institutional autonomy. Time
and again politicians have meddled in matters internal to the military such as
promotions, appointments, and transfers.

Early attempts at building a base of political support in the military establishment was attempted by Defense Minister KPS Menon. A number of senior
officers, among others Major General Kaul, came under the defense minister's
influence in the hope of being promoted to higher ranks. In fact Major General
Kaul was appointed chief of general staff by the defense minister without consulting the chief of the army, General Thapar. Menon's blatant interference in
military matters damaged army morale, discipline, and professional ethic.

The army chief in 1957, General Thimmayya, resigned on account of minister
Menon's interference in army promotions and his distortion of service views on
defense policy to Prime Minister Nehru. He was later persuaded by Nehru to
take back his resignation.[26] "Firm professional advice was given," recalls Gen-

eral P. P. Kumaramangalam, ''and ignored by a menace of a defense minister. . . . I think the politician has learnt the lesson of pre 1961 and 1962 and will be reluctant to interfere with the army.''[27]

The involvement of the civilian leadership in the actual operations of the 1962 Chinese war was the climax of civil intrusion into the decision-making autonomy of the military. As General Chibber details, the Chief of the Army Staff insisted on written orders for a course of action that his military judgment told him was unsound. The written order that precipitated the war was signed and issued by a joint secretary, Mr. Sarin, as the prime minister, the defense minister, and the finance minister were out of the country. It read, in its entirety, as follows: ''The decision throughout has been as discussed at previous meetings that the army should prepare and throw out the Chinese as soon as possible.''[28]

The 1962 India-China war was a watershed for civil-military relations. The civilian leadership realized in the light of Indian military losses that wars require close coordination by statesmen and military leaders and respect for professional views. Subsequent changes therefore included an increased participation of military professionals in defense decision-making and respect for the institutional autonomy of the military. The government financially committed itself to five-year plans of improvement of defense preparedness. A Defense Planning Committee was created, comprising of the cabinet secretary, the three service chiefs, and the defense, foreign, home and finance secretaries.

In the India-Pakistan war of 1971, the military once again had to face political pressure from the prime minister to begin operations in Bangladesh early and against its professional judgment. They were, however, able to resist civilian interference in the actual conduct of operations this time.[29]

The first generation of Indian political leaders was particularly wary about the military's strength vis-à-vis nascent democratic political institutions. Events in neighboring Pakistan, where the military assumed political control in the coup of 1958, certainly influenced the skeptical attitudes of Indian politicians toward the military. The government's intelligence bureau kept a close watch on the activities of senior officers and tapped their telephone lines. Few senior generals escaped a maligning of their character by aspersions cast on their potential political ambitions. In 1962 the home minister expressed his reluctance, on this count, to the appointment of General Chaudhury as army chief, although later that appointment took place.

An illustration of civilian mistrust and fear of overt military intervention was the reaction of the government to the presence of several thousand extra troops in Delhi on 27 May 1964, when Nehru died. The army chief, General Chaudhury, was asked to render an explanation to the defense minister. An irate general pointed out that from his experience of Gandhi's funeral he had good reason to believe that extra troops might be needed to police the cortege to the cremation grounds.[30]

Despite the encroachment by the civilians into ''military spheres of competence,'' Indian generals did not stage a coup or resist civilian authority by non-compliance with civil order. Why? One answer among other factors probably lies in the political perspectives of the military leadership. Political ambition or the lack of it, more often than not, is a better explanatory factor for why militaries do or do not stage coups, rather than the nature and organization of armies. A majority of the senior service officers held the belief that politics and fighting wars do not mix together. Interviews as well as reference to their published memoirs and articles from various military journals document this belief.[31] General Bewoor, army chief from 1973 to 1975, corroborates this when he says, "There is little chance today that the Armed Forces can effect a political change by getting themselves into power. I feel that the Armed Forces under their top echelons will not even find unanimity carrying out a coup contrary to the constitution."[32] General Cariappa, who took over as the first Indian commander-in-chief, "bluntly demanded that officers simply minded their own business and let their seniors and the politicians handle the problems." In an interview with the author, retired Lieutenant General Arora, the victorious commander of the Indian forces in Bangladesh in 1971, said that while he was army commander in West Bengal he was approached by the political leadership to take over the civil administration of two districts, in view of the Naxalite insurgency problem. The general politely refused, suggesting that the government attempt to resolve the problem politically by appointing a good governor in the state.[33] One of the most articulate of the senior generals of the Indian army, Lieutenant General S. K. Sinha, has this to say about civil-military relations:

National interests demand close understanding and rapport between the statesman and the soldier. . . . The soldier must accept the supremacy of the statesman in power and the latter while exercising the supremacy should not expect subservience or blind obedience from the soldier. . . . The top soldier must have the right of direct access to the Head of the Government and the liberty to express any contrary views on military issues in the prescribed manner. Expression of such dissent cannot be considered as an act of discipline. . . . What precisely is meant by remaining apolitical? This should not be construed to mean lack of political awareness or foregoing the right of a citizen to cast a vote at elections. On the contrary, a truly apolitical army should have political awareness and its soldiers interested in exercising their democratic right. However his political awareness should convince him that the army's direct participation in controlling affairs or wielding political power is always counter-productive. Such a realization is the best guarantee for preserving the apolitical outlook of an army.[34]

Creating conditions conducive to the inculcation of such views, the Indian military isolates its officers and soldiers by locating them in cantonments. In their national training and education centers they are taught and encouraged to stay aloof from politicians and civilians.

An appraisal of the military's professional training program for its officers shows that it is only in the thirteenth year after his commission that an officer attends the staff college course where his first preliminary initiation into formal education about politics takes place. He is introduced to the defense policymaking processes and related civil-military matters at the National Defense College only in about the twenty-third year of his service—that is, for those who are promoted to senior positions (brigadier and higher)—at a twelve-month course in defense problems at the national level. Thus it is at Staff College in Wellington and National Defense College in Delhi that officers receive training in national strategy. At senior levels as area, corps, and regional commanders, they often interact in the course of their duties with police officers of equal rank; with civil secretaries in the railways, industry, and labor; and of course with state and chief ministers.

THE MILITARIZATION OF INDIAN SOCIETY AND THE POLITICIZATION OF ITS MILITARY

The decades of the 1970s and 1980s have seen democracy come under considerable strain. The state has been unable to resolve peacefully its socioeconomic and ethnopolitical crises in the light of weak political institutions, evident in the condition of the political parties, the executive, and the judiciary. As a result of this political inertia, violence has become the normal channel for expressing frustration and dissatisfaction over contentious issues. The state has directed its attention toward restoring and maintaining civil order rather than to resolving the fundamental socioeconomic and political issues at stake.[35] The deteriorating political culture in India, characterized by political opportunism and corruption, has drastically reduced the effectiveness of the state police and to a considerable extent that of the paramilitary forces; consequently, the military has been called in to aid the civil power much more frequently, and at times unnecessarily, leading to its politicization. The term *politicization* as it is used here means the socialization of the military with political values, traditionally outside its functional sphere of competence. In this process the military acquires an "enlarged sphere of political reference," owing to the nature of its interaction with the polity and its internal organization, which reflects the social structure of the society of which it is a part.[36]

The socioeconomic and communal crises of the last few decades have an overriding political dimension: the phasing out of a dominant one-party system by an unstable multiparty system. Regional challenges to the once-dominant Congress party, which have crystallized around single-issue political themes such as language, caste, or religious discrimination and a demand for greater autonomy, have mostly emerged as violent outbursts of protest against the government at the center. Choosing to interpret these political demands as illegitimate and in fact subversive, the central government for politically expedient reasons created special paramilitary task forces. These organizations date back to the tenure of Indira Gandhi as prime minister, especially from her second term in office and onwards. Lieutenant General Sinha documents that the Indian military engaged in 476 actions of aid to the civil power between 1961 and 1970, by contract for army assistance to civil authorities.[37] In Punjab, with the appointment of Lieutenant General R. S. Dayal (Chief of Staff, Western Command, as home advisor to the governor of Punjab) the military assumed for the first time de facto control of a state government.

Legislation legitimizing the role in aid to civil power of the armed forces and paramilitary forces, which has led to the direct political involvement of the military in more than one state, reflects the growing militarization of Indian society. The period of Emergency (1975–77) under Indira Gandhi marked the apogee of militarization of Indian society when the use of force to resolve social conflict was institutionalized in the MISA Act, which is the legal basis for the Emergency. Since then the political trend to use the armed forces in aid of civil authority has continued. The Armed Forces Special Powers Act (1956), subsequently amended, gives freedom of action without civilian control to the army and paramilitary commanders in declared "disturbed areas." The National Security Act (1980), which authorizes security forces to arrest and detain suspects for up to six months without a warrant, gives a relatively free hand to the security forces. The Essential Services Maintenance Act allows army troops to replace striking workers in "vital" industries such as oil production and rail transport and confers extensive police magisterial powers upon the armed forces, as does the Terrorist and Disruptive Activities Prevention Act (1987). Interesting data presented by Cohen on unrest within the various police, paramilitary, and military forces in the period 1978–84 reflects their growing politicization and disregard for civilian authority.[38]

In 1984 an uncoordinated mutiny by over fifteen hundred Sikh soldiers took place in army barracks in Bihar, Maharashtra, Tripura, Rajasthan, and Jammu. The mutiny was a reaction to the Government's military action "Operation Bluestar," in the context of the ongoing Hindu-Sikh communal conflict in the country, on the premises of the Golden Temple, the holiest of Sikh shrines, in Amritsar city. While the mutinies did not spread and were quickly put down, they reflect the extent of political socialization among the Sikhs in the rank and file of the army. As the Sikhs constitute around 15% of the army, this is not a trivial matter for the future of civil-military relations.

Another conflict, which has the potential for creating widespread disaffection among the Gorkha ethnic group in the army, which numbers around seventy thousand, is the demand for an autonomous Gorkhaland, comprising about 2,550 square miles in eastern India. The movement crystallized under the leadership of Subhash Ghising, a former noncommissioned officer of the Indian army, of the Gorkha National Liberation Front (GNLF). In late 1988 an agreement was signed between the GNLF, the government of West Bengal, and the Union government that led to the formation of an elected Darjeeling Gorkha Hill Council to provide for local self-government in their defined area. However, other Gorkha groups have rejected the agreement and continued to seek more concessions.

Proliferating literature on the subject by senior military officers points out that army actions in aid of civil authority such as "Operation Bluestar," Woodrose, PAWAN, and Bajrang-Rhino and military operations in Kashmir, the Naga-Mizo hills, and Bodo areas of Assam are "avoidable tragedies." Many officers are of the view that the army has been called out much too often and at times before actual necessity. The frequent use of the army has reduced both its impact and its credibility and has correspondingly increased the level of force used. Its excessively frequent and avoidable involvement in maintaining law and order has also alienated it from the people, the army being accused of behaving as an occupation force in affected states, perpetrating excesses on its own people and violating human rights.[39]

The controversy within the military is over whether the internal political role of the military should be further institutionalized or whether there should be a reduction of its aid-to-civil-power role. Reflecting the former opinion, retired General Sardeshpande writes that, in view of the growing significance of the army's internal role:

The Army must understand politics, be seen to do so, as a necessary part of its formal professional education, at least the higher echelons. Secondly it must discipline and motivate itself to higher planes of consciousness and identify national security dangers resulting from politics or from policies of the Government. Thirdly the army must be provided with sufficient institutionalized power and constitutional avenues to enable it to be heard by the Parliament and the People on professional issues. . . . The Army has to suitably organize or modify its establishment, equipment and approach and evolve befitting strategies, operational doctrines and motivational methods to effectively tackle internal security problems with "minimum force." . . . Wishing away these realities and reluctance to purposefully tackle them are both misleading and detrimental to the Army's role fulfillment.[40]

Proponents of the opposite view argue that the army's occupation with internal security problems adversely affects its operational readiness and that its prolonged use in an internal security role demotivates it.

PROFESSIONALISM AND POLITICIZATION: THE CHANGING ETHOS OF THE INDIAN MILITARY

The future professional integrity of the Indian armed forces, especially the army, is a growing concern among liberal-minded citizens. There are also misgivings over the increasing internal role of the military and its likely consequences for civil-military relations. Today soldiers and officers of the Indian military are much more informed about politics than before. They are affected by it in their homes, among their family and social circle, and amid their economic environs. They are also recruited from a much wider social base than before and are much more representative of regional and cultural diversity. There is a growing disillusionment within the senior military leadership with the abuse of power by politicians and with the general political apathy about resolving socioeconomic and political conflicts. In an interesting book on India's internal security problems, retired Lieutenant General Nayer points out army reluctance to resolve the Punjab crisis militarily. He documents the civilian authorities' complete bypass of professional advice and misgivings on the nature of military action taken in Punjab.

The status and honor associated with being an officer of the Indian military seem to be wearing off, as among the educated elite officership is among the least preferred of occupations. This is not surprising, as a majority of officers retire at the age of fifty and at the rank of colonel; only about 10% go up to higher ranks. The small chances for promotion and the young age of retirement produce dissatisfaction and disillusionment with the profession. The situation for the rank and file is worse, as avenues for occupation are few, and they are completely dependent on rehabilitation or resettlement schemes.

Mediocrity of talent, weak leadership, and corruption, although avenues for the same are limited, seem to comprise the present malaise within the officer corps. Cohen rightly points out the distinction in the Indian military between officers who are interested in primarily professional careers and those who seek positions that they can use for private gain.[41]

In his book on the Indian army, Kadian refers to a letter received by serving officers in 1986 from General Sunderji, chief of the army staff, in which he referred to the low morale and loss of self-esteem of the officer corps. He attributed these to the emergence of an opportunist, money-minded, corrupt class of senior officers.[42] Trends toward corruption and civilian interference in military appointments, promotions, and placements suggest that subjective rather than objective civilian control better characterizes civil-military relations in India. Lured by prospects of promotion to top ranks, many officers have become easy targets for politicization by leading politicians. In recent years military professionalism has been tainted by espionage involving senior officers, such as the Samba scandal, in which a number of officers were implicated in the alleged sale of state secrets to Pakistan, and the Larkins affair, involving some very senior officers who were supplying secret information to Western powers.

The growing number of servicemen seeking redress in civil courts for professional grievances such as verdicts of courts martial or promotions and seniority and retirement benefits has extended the civilian sphere of competence in military matters while also opening the military establishment to public scrutiny on issues concerning its institutional autonomy and corporateness. Recent examples of senior officers seeking recourse in civil courts are the cases of Major General Shabeg Singh and Lieutenant General Airy. The former was dismissed from service without a court martial a day before he was due to retire and therefore lost part of his pension. He had to seek redress in civil courts and later joined camp with Sikh militants in Punjab. The latter in his petition before the Delhi High Court has protested against his appointment as Director General Assam Rifles, being denied command of a corps, and has accused the army chief of staff of being partisan in his policy of placements and senior appointments. What is interesting about these civilian petitions is that they were made by serving military officers who desired a public scrutiny of military policy. This new trend signifies a marked difference in the professional attitudes and ethos among senior military leaders. In the decades of the 1970s and the 1980s, senior lieutenant generals Bhagat retired and Sinha resigned without protest in apparent cases of politically directed supersession for promotion to army chief.

Senior military leaders are only partly insulated from outside civilian influence by any higher authority in that no annual confidential reports are written on them. More indirect ways of affecting control over the senior leadership has been the rewarding of defense service chiefs by post-retirement benefits such as lucrative or prestigious placements in public sector undertakings, as ambassadors and governors of states. Over the years there can be no denying the flagrant violation of professional autonomy by civilian inroads into the promotions of senior military officers.

The most recent illustration of the army's political views is the controversial press interview given by the army chief, General Rodrigues, where in the context of national security among other things he stated that "good governance" is the concern of the army as well. Without any political ambitions in the general's statements, it is clear that in matters of internal security the army sees its contribution as essential in nation-building, or as in the words of the general, "Putting things together so that there is an environment here where democracy can function, where the administration is effective."[43] Following this interview, for the first time in the history of civil-military relations a demand was made by the opposition in Parliament for the dismissal of the army chief. In consequence the government has banned press interviews by service chiefs. Civilian control is thus further tightened over the military.

Two issues that merit a discussion in the context of the future of civil-military relations in India are discussions over a joint defense staff chief and the continuation of the policy of military cantonments—segregated areas on the outskirts of towns where the military are stationed. There is a move for replacing the old practice with the new concept of insular "military stations," without the elected civilian, politicobureaucratic participation of the cantonment administrations, although critics see this as conducive to ideas of Bonapartism within the military. Politicians have been wary about centralizing too much authority in one military office, being concerned about the emergence of a powerful military commander, while the services argue for a more efficient integrated defense command structure. The success of the combined efforts of the Indian defense services in putting down the attempted coup in the Maldives in 1991 seems to have produced a stalemate on the issue.

CONCLUSIONS

Over the last two decades, as the environment and the content of Indian politics has changed, so have the military's attitudes about its role, image, and status in society. The increased participation of the military in internal security matters has expanded its role in domestic politics. At the same time, its extended "aid to civil" operations have made it more vulnerable to public criticism. Close day-to-day participation with civilians in affected areas has led to its political socialization and allowed it to assess at close hand the role of politicians in these crises. A close reading of the published literature by retired senior military officers involved in these various operations suggests the military's frustration with being called in much too frequently and often with good cause by an incapable political leadership to resolve by force what are essentially political crises. In divergence from current political opinion, some of these senior officers suggest political rather than military solutions in the various conflict-ravaged areas, while others argue for new operational doctrines and a greater institutionalization of the military's role in internal security.

There is no doubt that the overriding importance of the military's internal security role in recent years has affected the professional attitudes of its soldiers and officers, although generally the norm of civilian supremacy still prevails. Politicization of the military has slowly but certainly begun to affect the nature of its professionalism. What consequences this is likely to have on the future of civil-military relations depends basically upon how adept politicians are in handling the diverse socio-ethno-political crises by democratic means rather than by the use of armed force and upon the political perspectives of the senior military leadership and their continued belief and acceptance of civilian supremacy. Changes in civil-military relations will as in the past continue to be incremental rather than abrupt and dramatic. With the breakdown of the Soviet Union, uncertainty about future procurement of military hardware has been a hard blow for the Indian military. Undoubtedly the military will give priority to its professional tasks over its other political concerns such as its internal security role, just as, in the changing strategic and political environment, effecting continued civilian control over the military will certainly be on the priority list for India's civilian leadership.

NOTES

1. Interview with Lt. Gen. Jagijit Singh Arora. Also, see Rajesh Kadian's civil-comments concerning the changing ethos of the Indian army; see his *India and Its Army* (New Delhi: Vision Books, 1990).

2. S. P. Huntington, *Political Order in Changing Societies* (New Haven: Yale University Press, 1968); and S. E. Finer, *The Man on Horseback* (London: Pall Mall Press, 1962).

3. S. P. Huntington, *The Soldier and the State* (Cambridge: Harvard University Press, 1957); and Morris Janowitz, *The Military in the Political Development of New Nations* (Chicago: University of Chicago Press, 1964).

4. This perspective has been used by the author in the study of the Pakistan military; see Veena Gill, "Military Rule in Pakistan: A Choice Theoretic Analysis" (paper presented at the 14th IPSA Congress, Washington, D.C., 28 August–1 September 1988).

5. Two excellent studies on the history of the British Indian army are T. A. Heathcote, *The Indian Army* (London: David and Charles, 1974); and Philip Mason, *A Matter of Honour* (London: David and Charles, 1974).

6. Author's interview with Lt. Gen. J. S. Arora, New Delhi, 12 August 1991. For different viewpoints on this theme see Lt. Gen. P. N. Kathpalia (Ret.), ''The use of the Indian Armed Forces in Aid of Civil Authority,'' in *Indian Defence Review* (January 1993), pp. 19–24. Also see in the same issue, Lt. Gen. V. K. Nayar, retired, ''Internal Security: Some Issues and Aspects,'' pp. 25–33; and Ambassador J. F. Ribeiro, ''The Army and the Police,'' pp. 11–12.

7. For an excellent account of the history of the British Indian Army, see Mason, *Matter of Honour.*

8. Huntington, *Soldier and the State.*

9. Ibid., pp. 8–11.

10. See B. Hashmi, ''Dragon Seed: Military in the State,'' p. 149, in Hasan Gardezi and Jamil Rashid, eds., *Pakistan: The Roots of Dictatorship* (Delhi: Oxford University Press, 1962).

11. Mason, *Matter of Honour,* pp. 21–25.

12. C. H. Philip, *The Evolution of India and Pakistan* (Delhi: Oxford University Press, 1962), p. 506.

13. Ibid., p. 508.

14. See B. Hashmi, ''Dragon Seed,'' pp. 150–53.

15. Mason, *Matter of Honour,* chapter 16.

16. Ibid., p. 347.

17. Gwynne Dyer, ''Pakistan,'' in John Keegan, ed., *World Armies* (London: Macmillan, 1979), p. 530.

18. Ibid., p. 529.

19. Sinha, *Of Matters Military* (New Delhi: Vision Books, 1987), p. 95.

20. See Heathcote, *Indian Army,* pp. 21–22.

21. Sinha, *Of Matters Military,* p. 26.

22. B. P. Barua, *Politics and Constitution-Making in India and Pakistan* (New Delhi: Deep and Deep, 1984), p. 132.

23. Sinha, *Of Matters Military,* pp. 43–45; and Lt. Gen. V. K. Nayar, retired, *Threat from Within: Indian's Internal Security Environment* (New Delhi: Lancer, 1992), pp. 6–20.

24. Sinha, *Of Matters Military,* p. 30.

25. See M. L. Chibber, *Military Leadership* (New Delhi: Lancer International, 1986), chapters 3–4, for an interesting survey of the new officer class in India. Also see Kadian, *India and Its Army,* chapter 5.

26. For an interesting discussion on civil-military relations in this period, see Chibber, *Military Leadership,* p. 108.

27. Cited in Chibber, *Military Leadership,* p. 108.

28. Ibid., pp. 109–110; and Naville Maxwell, *India-China War* (Bombay: Jaico, 1970), p. 315.

29. Interview with Lt. Gen. J. S. Arora, retired, New Delhi, 12 August 1991.

30. Chibber, *Military Leadership,* p. 1113.

31. The author conducted interviews with some of the senior retired generals, during two trips to India, in July/August 1991 and March/April 1993. Journals carrying military

viewpoints on this and other aspects of civil-military relations are the *United Services Institution of India Journal* and *Indian Defence Review.*

32. In Chibber, *Military Leadership,* p. 114.

33. Interview with author.

34. Sinha, *Of Matters Military,* pp. 24–27.

35. See P. R. Chari, "Civilian Control over the Military in India," *Indian Defence Review* (October 1991), p. 14.

36. For an excellent discussion of the concept see R. D. McKinlay, "Professionalisation, Politicisation and Civil Military Relations," in M. R. Van Gils, *The Perceived Role of the Military* (Rotterdam: 1971).

37. Maj. Gen. Sinha, "In Aid of the Civil Power," *United Services Institution of India Journal* (June 1974), pp. 115–23; and S. P. Cohen, "The Military and Indian Democracy," p. 124.

38. S. P. Cohen, "The Military and Indian Democracy," in Atul Kohli, ed., *India's Democracy* (Princeton, N.J.: Princeton University Press, 1988), pp. 124–28.

39. For an interesting discussion with arguments for and against the military's internal security role, see articles by retired senior armed forces officers in *Indian Defence Review,* various issues, 1990–1993.

40. Lt. Gen. S. C. Sardeshpande, retired, "The Army and the Change: Criticism and Rebuttal," *Indian Defence Review* (January 1992), pp. 91–93. Also see his "Internal Violence and the Military," *Indian Defence Review* (July 1992), pp. 26–31.

41. Stephen P. Cohen, *The Indian Army* (Berkeley: University of California Press, 1971), pp. 182–87.

42. Kadian, *India and Its Army,* p. 113.

43. Cited in Lt. Gen. S. K. Sinha, retired, "Preserving the Army's Ethos," *Indian Defence Review* (July 1992), pp. 56–57.

REFERENCES

Chari, P. R. "Civil-Military Relations in India," *Armed Forces and Society* 4, no. 1 (Fall 1977).

Chibber, M. L. *Military Leadership to Prevent Military Coups.* New Delhi: Lancer International, 1986.

Cohen, Stephen P. *The Indian Army: Its Contribution to the Development of a Nation.* Berkeley: University of California Press, 1971.

Kadian, Rajesh. *India and Its Army.* New Delhi: Vision Books, 1990.

Kohli, Atul, ed. "The Military and Indian Democracy." *India's Democracy: An Analysis of Changing State-Society Relations.* Princeton: Princeton University Press, 1988.

Praval, K. C. *Indian Army after Independence,* ed. New Delhi: Lancer International, 1990.

Sinha, S. K. *Of Matters Military.* New Delhi: Vision Books, 1987.

INDONESIA

Ulf Sundhaussen

Indonesia, a typical Third World country with a colonial past, is economically underdeveloped, deeply divided along ethnic, religious, and cultural lines, and therefore still uncertain about political structures and goals. To explore the role of the military in Indonesia this chapter provides a historical overview and investigates the reasons for, and modes of, military intervention, the military's achievements and failures while in political control, and the prospects of its retreat to the barracks.

HISTORICAL OVERVIEW

Final Stages of Colonialism, 1910–45

Opposition to Dutch colonial overlordship in this century came in three distinct waves: It began in the 1910s with native Moslem traders and manufacturers protesting against economic advantages granted to immigrant Chinese entrepreneurs, a movement that soon came to articulate political demands, including that for national independence. But before Moslem political aspiration could come near fruition, Communists had infiltrated the *Syarikat Islam,* taking over whole branches, and by 1926–27 had launched their first "revolution." The third wave, ideologically determined by secular nationalism, was led by Sukarno, Hatta and Sutan Syahrir. The colonial authorities had no difficulties in containing all three waves, especially as they occurred separately.

The breakthrough for Indonesian nationalists came when in 1942 the Netherlands East Indies were overrun by the Japanese, who enlisted native support for their war effort by delegating administrative responsibilities to indigenous elites, recruiting local youths into auxiliary military organizations and allowing Sukarno and Hatta to prepare for national independence.

An event of lasting effect was when Sukarno, the undisputed leader of the independence movement, in early 1945 formulated the *Pancasila,* or Five Pillars, as the state ideology for the republic to come. These consisted of nationalism, international cooperation, popular sovereignty, social justice, and belief in one god.[1] The most important aspect of the *Pancasila* was that it blocked the demands of Moslem politicians that Indonesia should become a Moslem republic.

Wartime Republic, 1945–49

On 17 August 1945 Sukarno and Hatta proclaimed the independent Republic of Indonesia, and assumed the offices of president and vice president respectively. Skilled in the art of political negotiation, they were inclined to pursue the goal of national independence by negotiating with the returning Dutch colonial administration. But younger nationalists indoctrinated by the Japanese with anti-Western sentiments were determined to oppose the reimposition of colonial rule by more militant means. With the government reluctant to create a national army, many youths gathered in a variety of militias, while the small number of Indonesians who had received military training in the Dutch colonial army (KNIL) and the much larger group of youths who had been recruited during the Japanese into the Army of the Defenders of the Fatherland (PETA) came to form the nucleus of a national army. In the absence of government legislation on defense, they elected in November 1945 a former PETA officer, Sudirman, as commander in chief and the pro-nationalist Sultan of Jogyakarta as minister of defense.

In the meantime, a multitude of nationalist, religious, and leftist parties had been formed. And in the absence of clear-cut political rules, Sutan Syahrir, the leader of the Indonesian Socialist Party (PSI), a social-democratic gathering of intellectuals, in a parliamentary coup seized power and disregarding the presidential constitution created a parliamentary system of government. He strongly resented having a minister placed by the military into his cabinet, and in an acrimonious debate with the leaders of the emergent national army he denounced PETA officers as Japanese-oriented fascists and former KNIL officers as mercenaries beholden to the Dutch. He also attempted to create a system of political commissars overseeing military commanders along the lines of the Red Army and strengthened the militias vis-à-vis the national army.[2]

Syahrir also favored a negotiated recognition of Indonesia's independence. But in June 1947 the Dutch launched what they euphemistically called a "police action," reducing the area under Republican control to Central Java and the Interior of Sumatra before United Nations intervention saved the republic from total defeat. The Republican army (TNI), undertrained and kept in competition with the militias for funds and equipment, was no match for the well-equipped Dutch troops.

On the political front the republic was also in disarray. In the span of one-and-a-half years, Syahrir had twice been forced by parliamentary majorities to resign; and when he interned the opposition, leaders had been kidnapped by a dissident army division. His successor, Amir Syarifuddin, was also forced to resign.

In this parliamentary melee Vice President Hatta set up a so-called business cabinet, which was to introduce a degree of efficiency into the ramshackle civil administration and rationalize the bloated defense apparatus. The latter task fell to Colonel A. H. Nasution, a young Dutch-trained officer, who set out to reduce the size of the defense forces and reorganize them into battle-worthy combat units. But before these reforms could take root, the Communists in September 1948 rose in revolt, forcing the political and military leaders to concentrate on putting down the insurrection. The army was never to forgive the Communist Party (PKI) for this "stab in the back" at a time when the republic was threatened by another onslaught. Indeed, these internal upheavals provided the Dutch with the pretext for launching another "police action" in December 1948. The renewed Dutch attack was not unexpected. Nasution had devised a guerrilla strategy that would save the TNI from annihilation, and President Sukarno had announced earlier on that "I myself will lead the guerrilla war."[3] But now Sukarno reneged on his promise and allowed himself and the cabinet to be captured, while General Sudirman, terminally ill with tuberculosis, had himself carried in a sedan chair into the hills to lead his troops. Within months the Dutch armed forces had secured all cities and the major lines of communication between them, but the Republican forces largely controlled the countryside in Java and Sumatra, operating from liberated areas run by a military government.[4] Thus a situation had arisen that the Netherlands could not resolve by military means, and in late 1949 negotiations between the two sides led to the creation of a federalist Republic of the United States of Indonesia.

Era of Parliamentary Democracy, 1950–59

With the untimely death of the charismatic General Sudirman, the key leadership positions in the military fell to ex-KNIL officers: Simatupang became chief of staff of the armed forces and Nasution became chief of staff of the army; other Dutch-trained officers came to head the embryonic navy and air force. These military chiefs adopted three essential policies: They undertook to support a democratic system of government, an endeavor they recognized could succeed only if civilian leaders were equally committed to this goal[5]; second, they made a commitment to turn the ramshackle, oversized guerrilla army into a leaner, more professional military establishment[6]; and third, the military supported the abolition of the federal order established in negotiations, using military means where this was required. Federalism was seen by the wartime Republicans as a "time bomb" planted mischieviously by the Dutch. Under the premiership of Vice President Hatta, himself a Sumatran, and with the active support of Simatupang and Nasution, both Bataks from North Sumatra, the federalist system of government had been liquidated by the middle of 1950.

With the federalist order destroyed, Hatta resumed the position of vice president, leaving it to parliamentary forces to assemble coalition cabinets. The first successor government, formed by Natsir, a Masyumi politician, lasted just over six months before it had lost its parliamentary backing. Another Masyumi politician, Sukiman, formed a coalition that was forced from office after ten months; it was followed in March 1952 by a coalition headed by the PNI politician Wilopo. His enemies, both inside and outside his own party, chose defense policy as the lever to unseat his government, criticizing, week after week, Nasution's attempts to professionalize the army.

After having offered his resignation, only to have it turned down, Nasution and a number of headquarters officers on 17 October 1952 petitioned President Sukarno to dissolve the unelected parliament and replace it with a more legitimate assembly based on general elections. But Sukarno rejected the demand and instigated mutinies against the army headquarters in three of the seven army divisions, which forced Wilopo to dismiss Nasution and his closest associates. In the literature the "17 October Affair" is often described as a coup attempt; however, although there were troops in the square in front of the presidential palace and a few temporary arrests were made by the military, the officers did not question the position of Sukarno as head of state, and they had approached him with the explicit blessing of both the prime minister and the minister of defense. In essence they had done no more than to cast doubt on the conduct of a parliament that single-mindedly indulged in toppling cabinets instead of providing much-needed legislation.

The sacking of Nasution did not save the Wilopo cabinet. When it fell in July 1953 the causes of its collapse had nothing to do with defense. Wilopo was replaced by another PNI politician, Ali Sastroamidjojo, who excluded the Masyumi from the government coalition and relied on the parliamentary support of the PKI. Its defense policy was to control the army by playing off the pro- and anti-17 October officers against each other and abolishing the post of armed forces chief of staff, thus severing any organizational links among the three military services. This policy was so successful that the degree of disunity it created threatened to tear the army apart. Therefore, in early 1955, a Unity Congress was held at which both factions resolved to bury their differences and designed professional standards for the promotions of senior officers.

Yet, when the army commander resigned shortly after that congress, Ali decided to ignore these standards by appointing a relatively junior officer politically close to the PNI, to head the army. The acting army commander, Zulkifli Lubis, with the backing of the whole senior officer corps, refused to acknowledge this appointment. Thereupon coalition partners, disenchanted for some time with Ali's high-handedness, quit the government, thereby forcing Ali in July 1955 to tender his resignation.

The main task of the new cabinet formed by Masyumi politician Burhanuddin Harahap was to hold general elections, which after the "17 October Affair" had become unavoidable and for which preparations had been under way for some time. In these first national elections four parties emerged as the winners:

The PNI obtained 22.3% of the popular vote, followed by the Masyumi (20.9%); the Nahdatul Ulama (NU), a conservative breakaway from the Masyumi (18.4%); and the PKI (16.4%). The formerly influential PSI of Sutan Syahrir secured only 2% and five seats in parliament. Another twenty-three parties gained representation in parliament.[7] These results did not release the country from the need to form inherently unstable coalition governments. Moreover, the ethnic Javanese, constituting about half of the population, had overwhelmingly voted for the PNI, the NU, and the PKI, while the Masyumi had emerged as the principal representation for the Sudanese in West Java and the smaller ethnic minorities outside Java. Later in 1955 a constituent assembly was elected, charged with drawing up a new constitution, without substantial changes in the pattern of popular support.

With a consistently defiant Lubis still commanding the army, the other major issue for the Burhanuddin cabinet was to repair civil-military relations. The best man to restore discipline and civilian supremacy over the military was found to be Nasution, who after his sacking in early 1953 had taken to writing books on military issues and during the election campaign had formed his own party (IP-KI), which gained four seats in parliament. He had campaigned on the basis of returning to the values on which the revolution against the Dutch had been fought and had come out in support of ethnic minorities' rights. Renouncing the ''17 October Affair'' and pledging to uphold the principle of civilian supremacy, he also insisted on a clear delineation of civilian and military prerogatives, legislation to support yet another attempt at professionalizing the army, and defense expenditures of no less than one third of the national budget.[8]

Although the Burhanuddin-led coalition had in the elections gathered enough parliamentary seats to stay in office, the NU withdrew its support in March 1956, leading to the formation of another cabinet under Ali Sastroamidjojo, based on the PNI, the Masyumi, and the NU. Although Nasution pledged to work with Ali, many officers considered Ali's additional assumption of the defense portfolio as adding insult to injury. Coupled with Nasution's attempt to reform the army and, particularly, to remove entrenched regional commanders from their position as virtual warlords, this led to heightened restiveness in the army. An abortive attempt by Zulkifli Lubis to launch a coup in West Java was followed by unrest in all provinces outside Java, where military and civilian leaders combined to voice their dissatisfaction with increasing corruption and governmental heavy-handedness. When Vice-President Hatta, long regarded as representing the interests of the Outer Islands in Jakarta, resigned from his office in late 1956, regional disenchantment reached crisis proportion. Thereupon, coalition partners in the usual fashion began to withdraw their support from the government until Ali was forced to resign in March 1957.

Despite the urgent need to tackle the regional crisis, parliamentarians were reluctant to form a new coalition. In this situation President Sukarno appointed a veteran nonparty Sundanese politician, Djuanda, to form a ''business cabinet'' that was to govern regardless of parliamentary support and through martial law, which Ali had declared as his very last act in office. Though the parliament continued to sit, it desisted from taking any political initiatives.

But Djuanda failed to design solutions acceptable to both the regionalists and the political elites in Jakarta. In early 1958 the regional dissidents, reinforced by Masyumi and PSI politicians from Jakarta, demanded that a new government be formed by Hatta and the Sultan of Jogjakarta. When Djuanda refused to resign, a "revolutionary government" was formed in February 1958 in Sumatra and Sulawesi. But troops loyal to the central government had no difficulties in squashing the three army regiments that had declared themselves in support of this countergovernment.

With the regional rebellion "solved," the focus shifted to reforming the system of government. Sukarno had for some time criticized Western-style democracy in which "50% plus one are always right" as too divisive for a country as diverse as Indonesia, as its sixteen cabinets in twelve years had amply demonstrated. Instead, he proposed a more authoritative system of government, a "guided democracy" in which decisions were arrived at by *musyawarah,* the traditional, village-style form of deliberation, carried on until *mufakat,* consensus articulated by an "elder," is reached.[9] But this would require a constitutional framework that the sitting Constituent Assembly, deadlocked in ideological debate between Moslems and more secular Pancasilaists, appeared unlikely to deliver. Immediately after the fall of the second Ali cabinet, the PNI had suggested the reintroduction of the 1945 constitution,[10] which, being presidential rather than parliamentary, could accommodate Sukarno's ideas. Other nationalist parties committed themselves to the reintroduction of this constitution, and in August 1958 Nasution added his voice as well. Sukarno agreed to the reintroduction of this constitution only when it had become clear that no alternative seemed to be available. After the Constituent Assembly had voted three times in favor of a return to the 1945 constitution without, however, reaching the two-thirds majority required for binding constitutional recommendations, President Sukarno on 5 July 1959 reproclaimed the 1945 constitution and discharged the constituent assembly.

Era of Guided Democracy, 1959–66

Sukarno had charted the course of Guided Democracy: the ineffectual western-style democracy was to be replaced by a homegrown version with which ordinary Indonesians could identify and that avoided the pitfalls of cabinet instability; the aims of the "revolution" were finally to be tackled; and internal divisions in society were to be overcome by integrative policies.

Parliamentarians had demonstrated little initiative while the power of their institution eroded, but early in 1960 they defiantly rejected the budget. Sukarno dissolved the parliament and replaced it with an appointed one in which party politicians were matched by representatives from "functional groups," which included workers and peasants, youth and women's groups, veterans and artisans and, significantly, the military (29 out of 283 seats).[11] Also, a (Provisional) People's Consultative Congress, or MPR(S), was appointed that, under the 1945 Constitution, constituted the highest political authority, laid down the broad guidelines of state policy, and elected the president. It consisted of all parliamentarians and an equal number of additional members representing parties, functional groups, and the regions. A new law on the "simplification" of the party system saw the banning of all but ten parties.

Sukarno was the "Guiding Elder" in Guided Democracy: All major policies emanated from the president, who was "elected" as president-for-life by a hand-picked MPR(S). Djuanda remained as "Chief Minister," to relieve Sukarno of the day-to-day administrative chores. The cabinet never became a center of power in its own right, partly because Sukarno inflated its membership to over a hundred ministers, few of whom had clearly defined tasks; partly because other "commands" under the immediate direction of Sukarno were allocated powers exceeding those of the cabinet; and, when Djuanda died in November 1963, no relatively independent-minded civilian politician remained in the cabinet.

The army under Nasution, who also served as minister of defense, was the junior partner in government. The military sat in parliament and the MPR(S); it occupied a number of nonmilitary portfolios in the cabinet; and under its Civic Mission program had penetrated the civil bureaucracy, the diplomatic service, and the management of national enterprises. Most important, through its "territorial" structure, a network of military liaison offices reaching down to the village level, it oversaw the implementation of policies emanating from Jakarta.

Parties and parliament barely had a life of their own. Only the PKI, which initially had been a defender of the parliamentary system because its steadily increasing popularity promised the achievement of power by electoral means, contested the power of the military and from 1963 threatened to outflank the army.

Guided Democracy legitimized itself through the charismatic qualities of Sukarno, the symbolic references to its Indigenousness and the glory of past empires, and the promise to bring about the prosperity and social justice enshrined in the *Pancasila*. But on the domestic front, apart from legislation on land reform, nothing revolutionary eventuated; and even land reform is meaningless if, as in the case of Indonesia, there is no class of large landowners. Instead, Sukarno internationalized his "revolution." All of Indonesia's rapidly declining resources were mobilized for fighting NEKOLIM, the neocolonialists, colonialists, and imperialists. Sukarno in 1961–62 launched a "confrontation," a sort of halfhearted, nondeclared war, to "recover" West New Guinea, the last remnant of the Netherlands East Indies still in Dutch hands, succeeding after some embarrassing military failures only when the United States intervened diplomatically on Indonesia's behalf. When Britain, withdrawing from "East of Suez," attempted to forge its five possessions in Southeast Asia into a new federation, Sukarno in 1963 launched another *konfrontasi* "to smash Malaysia." When the new federation won a seat in the UN Security Council, Indonesia became the first and only nation ever to withdraw from the UN. While the military exploits of the Indonesian military bordered on the absurd, the anti-Malaysia campaign drained the national coffers of its last financial reserves.

Sukarno is often credited as being the Great Unifier of Indonesia, but his policies during Guided Democracy make this assessment questionable. The banning of the Masyumi deprived the ethnic minorities of their principal political representation; and the banning of the PSI and the subsequent internment without trial of Sutan Syahrir alienated most of the politically conscious intellectuals. Sukarno's NASAKOM, the unity of nationalist, religious, and communist forces, remained a hollow slogan; and steadily accelerating polarization between these forces led in the final months of 1965 to a holocaust. On 1 October the army commander and five of his closest associates were kidnapped and killed; Nasution barely managed to escape the same fate, but his five-year-old daughter was killed in the attempt to apprehend him.[12] But when the commander of the Army Strategic Reserve Command (KOSTRAD), Major General Soeharto, crushed the movement behind these kidnappings and when the army demanded that those responsible be brought to justice, Sukarno stalled because the PKI, by now Sukarno's closest ally, was seen to be the mastermind behind what came to be labelled a coup attempt.[13] With legal means barred by Sukarno, the army together with Moslems and other anticommunist forces embarked on a spree of killing communists. The exact number of people killed in the following months will never be known, but the most authoritative study suggests that between a quarter of a million and half a million people vanished.[14]

Although Sukarno had lost his closest ally, his own position as head of state and government leader was not disputed yet. While the killing was still under way, Sukarno made one of his rare attempts to address the disastrous state of the economy, raising prices of basic commodities beyond what people could afford to pay. A cabinet reshuffle in February was an equally severe miscalculation. Nasution, who had lost the command of the army in 1962, now was relieved of his post as minister of defense, a position given to Soeharto. Most damaging was the creation of a new portfolio of internal security, which was filled by a known gang leader with explicit instructions to crush anticommunist students who roamed the streets of Jakarta with their demands for formally banning the PKI, lowering prices, and purging the cabinet of leftists. When on 11 March 1966 unidentified troops assembled in the square in front of the palace, Sukarno fled the capital and signed a presidential order charging Soeharto with restoring law and peace.

While Soeharto assembled a new cabinet largely in favor of a new political and economic order, Sukarno maintained that he was still the head of the government and against drastic changes. Both Sukarno and Soeharto thereupon agreed that the MPR(S) would have to be called into session to clarify the broad guidelines of state policy. Congress, purged of communist deputies, in its June 1966 session elected Nasution as its chairman; revoked Sukarno's presidency-for-life; ordered the holding of general elections, the cessation of the *konfrontasi* against Malaysia, and the implementation of a sound economic policy; asked Sukarno to account for his role in the events of 1 October 1965; and stipulated that Soeharto and Sukarno jointly form a cabinet to implement these decisions.

But in his National Independence Day speech on 17 August 1966 Sukarno rejected these policies and, thereby, provided the advocates of a New Order with the means as well as the necessity to impeach him. A reconvened MPR(S) in March 1967 deprived him of his office and appointed General Soeharto as acting president.

REASONS FOR AND MODES OF MILITARY INTERVENTION

The main issue in Indonesia's civil-military relations is not so much, "Why did the military intervene in politics?" but, "Why did it take so long, more than two decades, before the officers took over the government?" To answer the latter question adequately a systematic inquiry is necessary.

According to Finer's theory of civil-military relations,[15] military intervention in politics succeeds only if there is a disposition within the military to intervene, as well as the opportunity to do so. One without the other will lead to failure. *Disposition* is largely, but not exclusively, defined in terms of interests. Here we can distinguish between six major kinds of interest: individual, class, regional, religious, corporate, and national. Turning to Nasution, who for most of the first two decades of Indonesia's independence dominated the army, it can be ascertained that four of the above six categories of interests hardly impacted his politics; although a devout Moslem, he was a firm supporter of the *Pancasila;* as a Batak from North Sumatra, he nevertheless supported a unitary state; although clearly a member of the elite, he did not discernably display any class loyalty; and there are no indications that he pursued personal interests: In fact, he twice offered his resignation and twice accepted his sacking gracefully.[16]

But Nasution and his fellow officers certainly pursued corporate interests, from when they first perceived the need to elect an army commander and minister of defense in November 1945 and continued their efforts to shield the force against undue interference by party politicians, to various attempts to professionalize their service. Moreover, they demanded funding adequate for the tasks assigned to them. They certainly acted on behalf of the national interest, as they saw it. In 1945–47 they wanted to strengthen the defense establishment when most politicians wanted to negotiate with the Dutch, and they still opposed negotiations when the Dutch in 1949 were ready to negotiate. While most officers were hostile neither to democracy nor the principle of civilian supremacy they came to despise political parties and the parliament for pursuing personal and sectional interests at the expense of the wider national interest.

Of special importance is the interest army officers took in economic matters. In much of the literature on Indonesia military officers are depicted as corruptly exploiting the country for their personal gain, and there is no problem in finding evidence to sustain such an allegation, particularly during the last twenty-five years. But state salaries were pitiful and declining, so that even senior officers could not sustain their families on their official salaries. Moreover, in the semi-feudal patron-client relationships that characterize Indonesian society, officers were obliged to look after the troops under their command. Significantly, the national defense strategy was based on guerrilla warfare because the nation could not afford to build the kind of conventional military needed for the defense of an archipelago. This in itself had enormous ramifications for the political attitudes of the army.[17] Their experiences during the guerrilla war against the Dutch and in antiguerrilla operations against a wide range of regionalist, Islamic-fundamentalist, and far-leftist uprisings had shown that this kind of warfare can only be sustained if it is supported by the local population. Nasution concluded, "The most important thing is to please the people. . . . At bottom, the people struggle for their own interests. For that reason we must make efforts at all times to improve their conditions in questions of economic matters, education, health and the like."[18] The disastrous economic policies not only harmed all state employees directly but also threatened to frustrate the army's efforts to win "the hearts and minds" of the people. Moreover, impoverishment helped the PKI to recruit the masses for its own purposes.

Under these circumstances, enough interests were thus at stake to dispose the military towards intervention. Yet, interests alone, even if they are clearly identified and at times articulated, do not necessarily lead to appropriate action, particularly if it involves effort, sacrifice, and high-level risks. As Finer has observed,[19] to motivate the military into action, interests "have to be catalyzed into an emotion." Such moods, indeed, built up. Increasingly officers proudly came to stress that the army was not the creation of the government but "sprang from the people." Therefore it was not, in the words of the revered late General Sudirman, the "dead tool of the government"[20] but a "shareholder of the revolution." Increasingly, officers pointed out that in 1948 they had kept fighting while the politicians "surrendered" and during 1949 had run a military government that showed more concern for the welfare of the people than any succeeding civilian government.

Yet, no coups were seriously contemplated. Partly this had to do with Nasution's respect for the law. If the political system had to be changed, then first the constitution must change. But, according to Finer, for action there also must be an opportunity to intervene. Though parliamentary democracy had come to be seen a failure, only Sukarno commanded the legitimacy to bring about radical change.

However, the army could play a supportive and more assertive role. Towards the end of 1958 Nasution, in what came to be known as the "Middle Way Concept," argued that the army would neither seize power directly nor emulate the Western model whereby armies are politically passive; rather, the army would seek to be one, but not the dominant one, of the sociopolitical forces that determine the fate of the nation,[21] a "tool of the revolution" striving for the fulfillment of the promises contained in the *pancaslia*.

In the evolving system of Guided Democracy, Nasution and the army occasionally, and usually unsuccessfully, tried to influence the process of policy-making dominated by Sukarno. When Nasution argued that the provision of food and clothing for the people ought to have priority over "regaining West New Guinea," he had clearly overstepped his prerogatives and was relieved by Sukarno from commanding the army. He deployed troops not needed for other duties in civic action programs to win "the hearts and minds" of the rural population and in 1963 allied himself to Djuanda in an attempt to rehabilitate the economy. When the anti-Malaysia confrontation put an end to that, his successor in the army command, General Yani, opposed this new foreign-policy adventure; and the army's representative in the Crush Malaysia Command, Major General Soeharto, in his efforts to slow *konfrontasi* not only undermined efforts to get army units to the front but even conspired with the Malaysians.[22]

By 1965–66 Guided Economy was in total disarray: there had been no budget at all in 1965; there was not enough export earning to service foreign debts; inflation had increased to more than 650% per annum; and whole industries had ground to a halt. State employees, including military personnel, saw their meager incomes further devalued; all state services and the infrastructure were run-down; and Nasution's dictum to "please the people" had become totally out of reach. The embarrassing truth about Jakarta, in Sukarno's increasingly megalomaniac dreams the world center of the anticolonialist/antiimperialist struggle, was that it was excessively dirty, most of the time without running water or electricity, with huge potholes in its unlit streets and tens of thousands of impoverished people camping along its filthy, clogged-up canals. The necessity to address the problem of the economy had dramatically increased, and so had the willingness of particularly the army to take up the issue.

But not only had the disposition to intervene increased, the opportunity to do so had increased as well. After only six years of misrule, all of Sukarno's policies were in tatters. Moreover, the physical elimination of the PKI in late 1965 had demonstrated that Sukarno could be defied: the magic of his charisma had been challenged and found wanting. When the MPR(S) directed him to change his policies and he defied these directions, the army leaders concluded that he could no longer be allowed to determine policy.

THE BALANCE SHEET OF SOEHARTO'S NEW ORDER

Soeharto lacks the charisma and flamboyance of Sukarno, and he has never been under any illusions that mere promises can sustain him in office: his legitimacy stands and falls with his capacity to solve problems. Being not highly educated and proudly a "simple soldier," the problem he had to solve was, in his view, also simple: He had to rehabilitate the economy, which could be achieved only by establishing and enforcing political stability.

Economic Policies

To get economic development under way, Soeharto employed four strategies. To start with, he recruited the best economists to devise and oversee economic policies, filling top positions with the "Berkeley Mafia," mainly United States–trained technocrats. Second, state expenditures were cut, in order to invest every available rupiah into development. This involved heavy cuts in defense spending and the termination of the costly anti-Malaysia confrontation. At the same time, the chaotic tax collection system and fiscal policy were reorganized, resulting within two years in the reduction of the rate of inflation from 650% to 12%. Third, relations with the West were improved to allow for rescheduling foreign debts and obtaining foreign aid. Overseas entrepreneurs who had had their property confiscated during Guided Democracy were invited to take back their businesses, and legislation was passed to make foreign investment more attractive. Finally, in a drive to make Indonesians more entrepreneurial, a campaign for "mental investment," a change in attitudes, was launched.

A number of five-year plans, starting in 1969, have transformed the economy of Indonesia. The ailing infrastructure has been vastly improved; Indonesia has become self-sufficient in rice, its staple food crop; and a process of industrialization has begun. During the 1970s GDP grew at an average annual rate of 7.5%[23] When the worldwide oil bust of the 1980s affected the price of oil, Indonesia's major export earner, manufactured goods took its place, increasing exports between 1980 and 1991 by more than 2300%.[24] The per capita income rose from about $US 30 in 1965 to $US 560 in 1990.

The economic policies of Soeharto's New Order have always been criticized for being too capitalistic and not conducive to social equality. Obviously, some people profited from the regime's development policies more than others. Corruption and nepotism, involving particularly Soeharto's children and relatives, occur on a large scale. Yet there has also been a "trickle-down" effect, with roads, electricity, piped water, schools, and clinics coming to the villages.

New Order Politics

Compared with the first twenty-two years of the history of independent Indonesia, an account of politics in the New Order is a dull affair. Externally, since the termination of the anti-Malaysia campaign Indonesia lives in peace with its neighbors and has played the key role in the formation of the Association of South East Asian Nations. The sole exception to peaceful cooperation was the unnecessarily bloody occupation in 1975 of the former Portuguese colony of East Timor because it threatened, in the view of the Indonesians, to fall into the hands of communists. Internally, cautiously voiced dissent or the occasional demonstration by students or Moslems has not endangered the political survival of Soeharto, nor have uprisings in fundamentalist Aceh or secessionist West New Guinea. Political stability is the declared aim of the regime because this is seen to be the prerequisite for economic development, itself the key to regime legitimacy.

Indonesianists have labored to find the most appropriate label for the regime. Here the nature of the regime is simply defined in terms of power relationships. At the top of the apex is Soeharto, who makes all the important decisions and hires and fires top officeholders at will. The military, from which he is officially retired but which was the vehicle through which he obtained the presidency, is confined to the role of principal pillar of the regime without, however, being allowed any significant input into the process of decision-making. This successful domestication of the armed services was achieved by structural changes at the beginning of his rule, depriving the formerly powerful regional commanders of the control over their combat troops; by changes in the military education system toward professionalism and unreserved recognition of the supremacy of the government over the military; and by a shrewd personnel policy.[25] The military is rewarded for its passive support with social status, political office, and economic rewards.

The party landscape has been further "simplified," based on an instruction by the MPR(S) at its 1966 session. In 1973 four Moslem parties were merged into the Development Unity Party (PPP); and two nationalist parties, the Trotskyists and two Christian parties, formed the Indonesian Democratic Party (PDI) after the 1971 general elections had almost wiped out six of the nine parties. But the most important merger was that of all functional groups into what amounts to the government party, GOLKAR.[26]

In the five general elections held under the New Order, GOLKAR unsurprisingly has done well, gaining between 62% and 73% of the popular vote. Most observers have attributed this success at the ballot box to massive intimidation of the electorate by the army during the election campaigns. Particularly damaging to the PPP and the PDI has been that they were denied a presence in the villages except during election campaigns: the rural population should not be politically stirred up because this might lead to a repetition of the massacres of 1965, which were mainly confined to the villages. But general intimidation has decreased because of the realization that the pragmatic peasants have come to be aware that improvement to their conditions are delivered by the government and GOLKAR, not by either of the parties.

In any case, the government's dominance does not solely depend on GOLKAR's success in elections. To start with, one hundred out of five hundred parliamentarians are appointed military officers, a formula arrived at in 1969 during bargaining over electoral laws between the parties and Soeharto. Moreover, in Soeharto's "Pancasila Democracy" *musyawarah*, deliberation until consensus is reached, has replaced as far as possible any voting. In theory at least this means that any minority can block legislation by refusing to give its consent. The problem in "Pancasila Democracy" is that only middle-of-the-road forces can be allowed to be part of it: participation by "extremists" would lead to permanent deadlock. Consequently, communists, fundamentalist Moslems, and secessionists are denied representation, and liberals wanting to return to the parliamentary system with its provision for voting on issues are regarded with deep suspicion. Nor do the results of general elections affect the elections of the president: The majority of the People's Consultative Congress is appointed so that with the elected GOLKAR parliamentarians Soeharto has controlled some 85% of the MPR, with the other two parties eager to demonstrate support for the president as well.

PROSPECTS FOR A RETURN TO THE BARRACKS

For the last twenty years or so, critics of the Soeharto regime have seized on every minor crisis as evidence that the New Order's collapse is imminent. This prediction is wishful thinking rather than a result of research, as it was seen to be ideologically undesirable to inquire into the ideas and value system of the military and the strength and force of the conviction that officers derived from this in their self-perceived mission to save "their" country.

But the time has now come to question whether the regime in its present form can survive for much longer. At the time of this writing Soeharto has been president for twenty-five years and is thus one of the longest-serving heads of government in the world. Yet, at the age of seventy-two he has been seeking a sixth five-year term in office.

Evidently, after a quarter of a century in office, regime fatigue has set in. Obviously a master politician, Soeharto has made one mistake that has invited criticism even from some of his staunchest supporters: His children have been provided with business opportunities in what is clearly a gross excess of nepotism. His refusals to make amends have clearly affected the legitimacy of the regime.

After such a long period in office any regime is likely to face a legitimacy crisis, and military regimes are particularly vulnerable. If a military regime has solved the problems that justified its assumption of power, it has obviously worked itself out of the job; if it has failed to do so, there is no need for military men to occupy the presidential palace. No matter whether officers perform well or badly, over time the continuation of rule by the military will be questioned.[27]

When so questioned, regime leaders have basically four policy options. They may decide to hang on to power regardless of their waning legitimacy, but the degree of oppression this option requires, as demonstrated by the pariah SLORC regime in Burma, makes it increasingly less feasible. Second, the military may opt to stay in office but broaden the support base of the regime by genuinely sharing power with other social forces. Third, the military may vacate the seat of power but impose a string of conditions on the civilian successor regime; and finally, they may return to the barracks unconditionally. Which option to select depends on a variety of reasons challenging the status quo, such as internal political opposition to the regime or outside interference, as well as the preconditions required for certain options.

In present-day Indonesia, opposition to the regime does not come from established political parties but from particular sections of the professional middle class.[28] It performs an important function in demanding a higher degree of pluralism, but it is not well enough organized to force the regime to quit. Nor is outside intervention likely to go further than to censure the regime for its pitiful human rights record in East Timor and other trouble spots.

But there is an increasingly urgent problem within the armed forces themselves that needs attention. On the one hand, the military is supposed to perform a dual function (*dwi-fungsi*): Apart from providing external defense and internal security, it is also a sociopolitical force in its own right that according to its own view will always have a role to play in deciding the future of the country. On the other hand, the military is trained to be a professional organization that, almost by definition, ought to keep out of politics. *Dwi-fungsi* and professionalism appear to have been coordinated rather well over the last couple of decades, but closer examination reveals that officers fail on both accounts: They are neither very good politicians nor very professional soldiers. Another contradiction has developed between the myth and ethos of the army mission as the puritanical ''savior'' of the country and the commercialism intruding into the officer corps. While Soeharto, the architect of the New Order, may be able to hold together the system he created, his successor, most likely an army general, may not be capable of reconciling these internal contradictions.

Thus sooner or later the military may have to choose between *dwi-fungsi* and professionalism; and if other military regimes facing similar dilemmas are examples to go by, the regime leaders will opt for the coherence of the military establishment at the expense of political omnipotence. Yet, a retreat to the barracks is unlikely, for two reasons. It would be difficult to find many officers who would not be afraid of civilian politicians recreating the shambles of the parliamentary system Indonesia experienced in the 1950s. The second problem is that the most important precondition for handing back power to civilians, namely, the existence of an alternate elite capable of providing stable government, at present does not exist. GOLKAR has not been allowed to have a political life of its own and, as it stands, would be highly unlikely to be able to provide leadership and stable government. Neither the Moslem PPP nor the secular nationalist PDI would tolerate the other in government, nor would they be able to cooperate.

What is most likely is that the regime may recognize that change has become inevitable and opt for broadening its base of power. This would entail allowing GOLKAR to develop as a power in its own right, sharing government responsibility with the military. Such an arrangement, over time, may then develop into a more pluralist, democratic society.

CONCLUSIONS

Civil-military relations in Indonesia started out on a rocky road when Syahrir in November 1945 alienated the officer corps by insulting it; only during the terms of office of the "business cabinets" of Hatta and Djuanda did civilian politicians seriously endeavor to establish a working relationship between the two elites. This enhanced and accentuated the notion that the military had interests separate from those of party politicians. Yet the mood required to catalyze divergent interests into political action was in the first two decades after the proclamation of independence never strong enough for army leaders and their closest associates to contemplate a military takeover.

Instead, Nasution designed the "Middle Way" concept, the forerunner of *dwi-fungsi,* which ruled out coups in return for the military to have a significant, yet not dominant, voice in determining the fate of the nation. In this way the interests of the military were to be reconciled with those of other societal groups and the nation as a whole.

It was only when the economic interests of the military came to coincide with those of practically all other major social groups and demanded urgent attention, that the mood changed, particularly after President Sukarno flatly refused to revamp his disastrous economic policies. Eschewing cruder coup techniques, the military under Soeharto nevertheless came to be convinced that Sukarno had to go.

The military has moved cautiously to expand its role into the political sphere, essentially filling voids left by civilian politicians. While in office the rehabilitation of the economy has been the regime's most important objective. To achieve this goal, political stability has been enforced. But this does not mean that the Soeharto regime has no political goals. In fact, Soeharto has pursued Sukarno's dreams of creating an indigenous form of democracy, with consensus-building at the center. However, these plans may never be realized because it by necessity involves the disfranchisement of all groups with views markedly different from those of the military.

Although the oppressive nature of the Soeharto regime and its political policies have caused dissent, especially among the urban educated middle classes, the major impetus for change lies in the inherent contradictions within the military's value system. However, the notion that the military will always play a political role enshrined in the "Middle Way" and in *dwi-fungsi,* basically rules out a retreat to the barracks; and the nonexistence of an alternate civilian elite makes it impossible, at least in the short run. With good reasons to adjust to new conditions but with preconditions limiting the choice of options, it seems that the only viable course is that of genuinely sharing power with other political forces.

NOTES

1. See George MoTurnan Kahin, *Nationalism and Revolution in Indonesia* (Ithaca: Cornell University Press, 1952), pp. 122–27.

2. See Ulf Sundhaussen, *The Road to Power: Indonesian Military Politics 1945–1967* (Kuala Lumpur: Oxford University Press, 1982), pp. 20–27.

3. See Salim Said, *Genesis of Power: General Sudirman and the Indonesian Military in Politics 1945–49* (North Sydney: Allen and Unwin, 1992), p. 91.

4. See Abdul Haris Nasution, *Fundamentals of Guerilla Warfare* (London: Pall Mall, 1965), pp. 108–178.

5. See T. B. Simatupang, "The Role of the Military in Stabilization of Southeast Asian Nations, with Special Focus on Indonesia" (Unpublished Paper, Jakarta, 1970), p. 1 f.

6. See Abdul Haris Nasution, *Tjatatan2 Sekitar Politik Militer Indonesia* (Jakarta: n.p., 1955), pp. 318–20.

7. See Herbert Feith, *The Decline of Constitutional Democracy in Indonesia* (Ithaca: Cornell University Press, 1962), p. 434 f.

8. See Sundhaussen, *Road to Power,* pp. 91–94.

9. J. D. Legge, *Sukarno: A Political Biography* (Sydney: Allen and Unwin, 1972), p. 283.

10. See Adnan Buyung Nasution, *The Aspiration for Constitutional Government in Indonesia* (Den Haag: Gegevens Koninklijke Bibliotheek, 1992), p 307.

11. See Herbert Feith, "Dynamics of Guided Democracy," in Ruth T. McVey, ed., *Indonesia* (New Haven: HRAF Press, 1963), p. 345.

12. See Harold Crouch, *The Army and Politics in Indonesia* (Ithaca: Cornell University Press, 1978), chapter 4.

13. For the army's indictment of the PKI, see Nugroho Notosusanto and Ismall Saleh, *The Coup Attempt of the 'September 30 Movement' in Indonesia* (Jakarta: n.p., 1967).

14. See Robert Cribb, ed., *The Indonesian Killings 1965–1966* (Clayton: Centre of Southeast Asian Studies, Monash University, 1990), particularly chapter 1.

15. See S. E. Finer, *The Man on Horseback,* 2d rev. ed. (Boulder Colo.: Westview Press, 1988).

16. For a description of this complex personality, see C. L. M. Penders and Ulf Sundhaussen, *Abdul Haris Nasution, A Political Biography* (St. Lucia: University of Queensland Press, 1985).

17. See Ulf Sundhaussen, *Social Policy Aspects in Defense and Security Planning 1947–1977* (Townsville: Southeast Asian Studies, James Cook University, 1980).

18. Nasution, *Guerilla Warfare,* pp. 53 and 273.

19. Ibid., p. 63.

20. See Abdul Haris Nasution, *Tentara Nasional Indonesia,* vol. 2 (Jakarta: n.p., 1968), p. 18.

21. See *Pos Indonesia* (Jakarta daily) of 13 November 1958.

22. See Peter Polomka, "The Indonesian Army and Confrontation," (Master's thesis, Melbourne University, 1969), p. 172.

23. See Richard Robison, *Indonesia: the Rise of Capitalism* (North Sydney: Allen and Unwin, 1986), p. 20.

24. See Hal Hill. "The Economy, 1991/92," in Harold Crouch and Hal Hill, eds.,

Indonesia Assessment 1992 (Canberra: Australian National University, Department of Political and Social Change, 1992), p. 23.

25. See Ulf Sundhaussen and Barry R. Green, "Indonesia: Slow March into an Uncertain Future," in Christopher Clapham and George Philip, eds., *The Political Dilemmas of Military Regimes* (London: Croom Helm, 1985), pp. 99–101.

26. See David Reeve, *GOLKAR of Indonesia* (Singapore: Oxford University Press, 1985), pp. 263–66.

27. See Ulf Sundhaussen, "Military Withdrawal from Government Responsibility," *Armed Forces and Society* 10, no. 4 (1984): 546.

28. For the vitally important distinction between the trading and manufacturing middle classes and the salaried and professional middle classes, see Ulf Sundhaussen, "Democracy and the Middle Classes: Reflections on Political Development," *Australian Journal of Politics and History* 37, no. 1 (1991).

REFERENCES

Crouch, Harold. *The Army and Politics in Indonesia,* rev. ed. Ithaca: Cornell University Press, 1988.

Nasution, Abdul Haris. *Fundamentals of Guerrilla Warfare.* London: Pall Mall Press, 1965.

Penders, C. L. M., and Ulf Sundhaussen. *Abdul Haris Nasution, A Political Biography.* St. Lucia: University of Queensland Press, 1985.

Said, Salim. *Genesis of Power: General Sudirman and the Indonesian Military in Politics 1945–49.* North Sydney: Allen and Unwin, 1992.

Sundhaussen, Ulf. *Social Policy Aspects in Defence and Security Planning in Indonesia 1947–77.* Townsville: Southeast Asian Studies, James Cook University 1980.

———. *The Road to Power: Indonesian Military Politics 1945–67.* Kuala Lumpur: Oxford University Press, 1982.

———. "Military Withdrawal from Government Responsibility," *Armed Forces and Society* 10, no. 4 (1984): 543–62.

Vatikiotis, Michael R. J. *Indonesian Politics under Suharto.* London and New York: Routledge, 1993.

IRAN

Houman Sadri

This chapter focuses on the political role that the military played during three major events in the modern history of Iran: the 1921 coup, which engendered a new order; the 1953 coup, which ended the Musaddiq era; and the 1978–79 revolution, which terminated the Pahlavi regime. This study also includes some observations regarding the impact of the military on Iranian politics, whether by its active or its passive role.

Although the military has been a major part of Iranian society since the establishment of the Persian Empire,[1] it played a relatively lesser role in modern Iran than in neighboring countries.[2] In general, the Iranian military had a mainly instrumental, rather than intrinsic political value. The impact of the military on politics depended on a number of variables, including the structural characteristics of the political system, the historical role of the military, the institutional patterns of the military, and the main domestic and international conditions.

THE 1921 COUP AND ITS AFTERMATH

In the final days of the Qajars, the predominant domestic characteristic of Iranian politics was the decentralized, fragile, unstable, and ineffective nature of the government. Without a permanent national army, Tehran was often incapable of responding to foreign and domestic military challenges, protecting its borders, or even effectively maintaining order. In fact, the lack of adequate military means to carry out policy goals paralyzed Tehran's neutrality policy during World War I when the British, Russian, and Ottoman armies clashed within Iran's borders, causing suffering for Iranians.[3]

Iranian political and military leaders were then faced with an environment conditioned by the traditional rivalry between the British and the Russians in its new context of capitalist-socialist antagonism.[4] Soviet Russia enjoyed an influence in the northern provinces, and Britain in the southern. To protect their interests, these European powers established their own militia in Iran.

Preceding the coup, the Iranian military was weak and divided. The Qajar armed forces consisted of four separate foreign-commanded military units. At times, Tehran also called on some provincial and tribal militia units, but the loyalty of these forces was questionable. The most organized government unit was the eight-thousand-man Persian Cossack Brigade, which was established and commanded by Russian officers until the Russian Revolution.[5] The British then commanded and financed this division until the coup.

Another force was the eighty-four-hundred-man Gendarmerie, the rural security units, created in 1911 and led by Swedish officers. The next largest was the six-thousand-man South Persian Rifles that was established and commanded by the British after 1916, allegedly to fight against German agents in southern Iran. Finally, there was the Nizam, the two-thousand-man palace guard, whose number gradually declined because of rivalry within the court.[6] Moreover, it had symbolic rather than real military value.

In this chaotic environment, the question may be raised, Who engineered the coup? Some have portrayed a supernationalistic picture of Reza Khan and credited only him with the idea of the coup.[7] This portrayal is based on Reza Khan's claim that he had engineered the coup by himself.[8] Moreover, he presented four basic reasons for the coup: foreign intervention in domestic affairs, the 1920–21 Gilan Crisis,[9] ineffective national leaders, and the debasing of the military establishment.

Although Reza Khan led the coup forces, the idea of the coup was not uniquely his. According to several scholars, other officers in the Cossack Division (e.g., Fazlullah Khan), as well as some politicians (e.g., Sayyid Hasan Mudarris), had spoken about a military attempt to end the ineffective government of Sipahdar.[10] Moreover, Reza Khan was not alone in the coup initiative, but was accompanied by Sayyid Zia al-Din.[11] In fact, Zia was quoted as claiming that he was the actual engineer of the coup and that he had had to push the overcautious colonel forward.[12]

Despite the individual claims of Reza Khan and Zia, it is the case that they were jointly responsible for the coup and each represented a different political faction. Zia was a civilian, a member of the intelligentsia, and a nationalist politician with a vision. His leadership gave not only a sense of direction to the coup, but also legitimacy. On the other hand, Reza Khan was a nationalist officer who contributed to the success of the coup with his military skill and dedicated soldiers.

In terms of performance, the coup can be characterized as a small and quick operation that did not face much resistance and was basically bloodless. It was carried out by about two thousand soldiers. The troops entered the capital at night, and by dawn they had captured the main government buildings. Within days, a number of former government officials were arrested and martial law was declared for Tehran and its vicinity. Moreover, the government security forces offered little or no resistance.

The easy success of the coup has led some sources to hypothesize that the coup plotters were working with the British, who had more influence in Iran than other foreign powers after the Russian Revolution. Historical records do indicate that British officials, like the coup leaders, favored a stronger national government in Iran[13] and that the British might have even encouraged Reza Khan to march on Tehran[14]; but there is no concrete evidence suggesting that they gave anything more than moral support to the coup leaders.[15]

Several reasons led to the success of the coup. The political chaos that prevailed among the government forces left them unable to match the well-organized and combat-ready units of the coup forces.[16] Moreover, the coup plotters had the blessing of the major domestic and foreign forces.

A major characteristic of the 1921 coup was that, despite Reza Khan's dominant military role, it took him almost five years to take full control of domestic and foreign affairs.[17] To solidify his power base, Reza Khan organized a new army with an indigenous officer corps taken mainly from the Cossacks and dismissed the foreign officers previously appointed to significant command and field positions.[18]

Reza Khan favored the military personnel who strongly supported him. He sent his officers, who mostly had modest origins, to reputable European military academies for training and allocated one third to one half of the total annual national expenditure to the army. His power increased exponentially when he expanded Iran's heterogeneous military force into a forty-thousand-man-strong army. In 1925, the parliament passed the universal military conscription law that provided the military with the necessary human resources for further growth.

During Reza Khan's era, the main role of the military in politics was twofold: nation-building and modernization. The first task included the unification of the country and centralization of power in a strong national government. The second was a part of the general economic development policy.

In his nation-building effort, although Reza Khan's forces did not meet much resistance during the coup, the now-initiated new order met a measure of opposition from various quarters, namely, the provincial leaders, some tribes, and the older Gendarmerie officers. In this respect, the military contributed significantly as an instrument of policy in the effort by bringing the tribes under control,[19] crushing the rebellion of a few Gendarmerie officers,[20] and spreading the authority of the central government over the semiautonomous provinces. The most significant victory of the army was against Sheik Khaz'al, who had traditionally enjoyed British protection and autonomy in Khuzistan, the domain of the Anglo-Persian Oil Company in which the British government had the controlling interest. Following the unconditional surrender of Sheik Khaz'al, the public image of the whole military establishment reached a new height because of the political, as well as the military, value of this campaign.

In addition to the nation-building task, the military had a socioeconomic mission that also contributed to its political role following the 1921 coup. First, as in many developing countries, military service became a catalyst for social mobility. Not only were the lower ranks filled with peasants from all over the country, but even the officer corps was partly made up of members from relatively underprivileged social classes—the farmers and the lower civil servants. In a way, the emergent modern army destroyed some age-old class distinctions. The emphasis on peasantry in military recruitment may well explain why most of the army supported Reza Khan's land reforms, directed as they were against the large landowners, a well-entrenched class.[21]

Second, the military had been an important source of employment since 1921, competing with the private sector. In fact, only the oil boom of the mid-1970s changed the comparative advantage of the labor market in favor of the private sector.

Third, the military contributed to the modernization process by improving the country's communication and transportation systems by establishing telecommunication lines and building roads and railways. Such a development of the infrastructure, which is also a fairly common task of the military in contemporary developing countries, caused a centralization of authority in Iran on an unprecedented scale.

Fourth, the army was also a significant factor in allowing the organization of the nation's financial affairs, a task undertaken by Dr. A. C. Millspaugh.[22] The extension of central authority over the provinces allowed the central government to monitor the financial health of national and local agencies, regardless of their public or private nature. It was the government's inability to perform ordinary tasks like auditing, collecting taxes, and executing economic plans that led to the failure of Morgan Shuster's mission, the nation's financial disarray, and consequently the political paralysis of the state.[23]

Finally, the rise of the national army, coinciding with the abolition of the foreign militia, allowed Tehran to better secure the country's natural resources and industries, particularly oil. Although oil was a major source of national income, the government's policies and activities had been restricted by the British and Sheik Khaz'al. The former had the controlling interest in the Anglo-Persian Oil Company, and the latter was physically in charge of the oil fields, roads, ports, and administration of the province. The army, taking charge of these facilities, solidly improved Tehran's bargaining position vis-à-vis London in future oil negotiations.[24]

THE POLITICAL ENVIRONMENT OF THE 1950s

To understand the role of the military in the 1953 coup, one must first examine the political environment of the post–Reza Shah era. By 1941, the army had 125,000 troops, but it was no match for either the British or the Soviet forces, which easily invaded neutral Iran in 1941 to establish supply routes for the Red Army. The poor performance of the military in 1941 significantly undermined its public image,[25] which remained poor until the 1946 Azarbaijan crisis. Although the crisis was diffused by politicians (with some international backing), the image of the military was improved by its performance against the separatists in Azarbaijan and Kurdistan.

Despite success in saving Iran's territorial integrity, the main mission of the military continued to be the protection of the monarchy against internal challenges. This was understood by many, including U.S. ambassador John Wiley, who stated, "Iran needs an army capable primarily of maintaining order within the country, an army capable of putting down any insurrection—no matter where or by whom inspired or abetted."[26]

This role of the army did not necessarily mean political suppression. In fact, there was a relatively open political environment during the 1941–53 period. Nationalism was at its peak during the nationalization of the oil industry. In this environment, the main political forces were a coalition of nationalists headed by Musaddiq and royalists led by the Shah.

The short-lived civilian governments led the Shah to appoint General Ali Razmara as the prime minister on 26 June 1950. The general was a strong military figure who had played a significant part in the 1946 Azarbaijan campaign, but his personality and policies soon alienated the nationalists. On 7 March 1951, he was assassinated after a parliamentary speech claiming that Iran could not manage the oil without foreigners. His failure put the ball back in the court of the civilians.[27]

The 20 July 1952 Uprising

After he became premier, Musaddiq came into a conflict with the Shah that centered around the control of the military. In his bid for leadership of the military, Musaddiq argued that according to the constitution the military was at the service of the state (not the Shah),[28] but the Shah referred to the tradition established by his father, who continued to micromanage the military after his coronation.[29]

In July 1952, when the Shah refused Musaddiq's request to choose the war minister, Mussadiq unexpectedly resigned[30] and the royalists selected Qavam, without a quorum, in parliament.[31] Major cities witnessed pro-Musaddiq demonstrations whose turbulence soon escaped the control of the police and brought in the army. In addition to bringing order, one source suggested that Qavam had bigger political plans for the army—to arrest leading political figures, like Ayatollah Kashani.[32] The largest clash between the army and the people occurred near the parliament. The casualties were estimated at about a few hundred[33] but could have been greater if all the troops,[34] for example, some royalist officers,[35] had been willing to shoot.

Despite controlling the military, the Shah reluctantly conceded to popular demand and brought back Musaddiq as both the prime minister and the minister of war. An important result of the uprising was the establishment of civilian

control over the military, which Musaddiq purged by the forced and early retirement of many royalist officers.[36]

The support of the army and the popular mandate were necessary, but not
sufficient, conditions for success during Musaddiq's second term, when he faced
the consequences of his earlier policies. His broad-based anti-Shah coalition
weakened as conflict increased from within. A conflict between Musaddiq and
Kashani started over certain military personnel. Kashani demanded the punishment of the officers who killed protestors and rejected some of Musaddiq's
military appointments.[37]

The premier believed that the army should not be offensive in nature. In this
regard the premier's conception of the role of the military differed significantly
from the Shah's. Accordingly, Musaddig changed the name of the department
from the Ministry of War to the Ministry of National Defence.[38] Also, sure that
the Shah's plan for military growth was to solidify his political power,[39] Musaddiq trimmed the military. Moreover, he did not micromanage the military.

In short, the 1952 uprising succeeded mostly because the military was reluctant to support the unpopular Qavam against the popular Musaddiq. Most soldiers refused to shoot, and some even joined the demonstrators. Many officers
were also doubtful of the legitimacy of a government whose existence was
legally questionable and whose position went against the nationalistic tide.
Moreover, the protestors, who were supported by Ayatollah Kashani, enjoyed
the moral edge against the army.[40]

The Ayatollah neutralized the army by organizing demonstrations so large
that they convinced one expert that Musaddiq's movement was less organized
in comparison.[41] Musaddiq, however, symbolized Iranian nationalism and had a
popular mandate to complete his oil policy, but his political power was mainly
based on the elite, both military and civilian. The Ayatollah, on the other hand,
had great influence among the masses whose support was lacking during the
1953 coup.

The 1953 Coup Attempts

Contrary to the general belief, the downfall of Musaddiq was not accomplished by a typical coup and, according to one expert, had very little military
involvement.[42] On 16 August 1953, the first coup attempt failed, leading to the
Shah's flight. To understand the role of the military, one must review the se-
quence of events.

On 15 August, the Shah issued two commands—one to dismiss Musaddiq,
the other to replace him with General Zahedi. Colonel Nassiri (commander of
the Imperial Guard) was in charge of carrying out the orders. A coup using
three army units[43] was planned for 16 August if Musaddiq did not resign. The
plan failed when Musaddiq unexpectedly arrested Nassiri and the coup units
disobeyed Zahedi, which caused him to go into hiding.[44]

There were three major reasons for the failure of this attempt. First, the plotters had underestimated the loyalty of Musaddiq's top military commanders.[45] Second, the government was not surprised by the coup, while the plotters were surprised by the arrest of Nassiri. Finally, the Shah's decision to stay outside Tehran during this operation demoralized the coup units.

Three days later, while the Tudeh[46] was openly advocating the abolition of the monarchy, another attempt was made. This time anti-Musaddiq demonstrations were organized in Tehran. A mob basically carried out the attack on Musaddiq's residence.[47] By 3:30 P.M. the radio station was captured and Zahedi's radio message announced that he headed a new government. The next day, Musaddiq's arrest confirmed the success of the coup.

The coup leaders were politically naive, underestimated Musaddiq, and put him on military trial to cause him political embarrassment. But, being an effective lawyer, the deposed prime minister used the trial to his advantage. In fact, the prospects for political damage to Zahedi's government led U.S. ambassador Loy Henderson to suggest speeding up the process.[48]

The coup witnessed an interaction of military and civilian politics. While the former changed the latter, it was also obvious that the army underwent a change, mainly as the result of a purge. It was at this point that the Tudeh supporters were the weeded out of the army.[49] Approximately six hundred officers were arrested, sixty of whom were executed while the others were given sentences of up to life imprisonment with hard labor.[50]

In explaining the coup, one must focus on its foreign connections,[51] which were instrumental in compensating for the absence of the Shah during the coup. This fact was highlighted by the Shah's acknowledgment of the assistance of Kermit Roosevelt in regaining the throne.[52] Coup operators, like generals Fazlullah Zahedi and Hassan Akhavi,[53] cooperated closely with foreign agents.[54] These rightist officers had previously tolerated Musaddiq's policies, while he enjoyed popular support. When his support declined, however, they were not going to permit the rise of the Tudeh to power.[55] The Tudeh was the only remaining major force in the formerly broad-based coalition of the prime minister.

The reason for the success of the August 19th coup has never been completely clarified. Some claim that Musaddiq was warned about the possibility of a coup and that he ignored it.[56] Others imply that his inadequate policies created an environment for the coup.[57] Still others argue that Musaddiq took many measures to neutralize a possible coup attempt, but he was defeated by treachery.[58] Some even maintain that Musaddiq was concerned about the rise of the Tudeh, whose power he could not check, and thus agreed to plans for a change of regime.[59]

These reasons suggest a variety of political roles for the military from subordinate to Musaddiq's leadership to insubordinate and cunning in undermining his government. Between these two extremes were the roles of the military as indifferent toward civilian rule and as an anticommunist institution. It would be inaccurate to infer that the military constituted a monolithic establishment. It was, on the contrary, a microcosm of Iran. In this respect, the 1953 coup became the classic example of foreign intervention turning the tide in favor of right-wing forces. Thus, both the timing of events and international factors worked against Musaddiq.[60]

THE MILITARY AND THE 1979 REVOLUTION

On 11 February 1979, the Supreme Council of the Armed Forces declared its neutrality in the struggle between the government and the people. For all practical purposes, this action ended the role of the military as the protector of the monarchy, which led to a complete overhaul of the Iranian political establishment.

While much has been written about the role of the Iranian military during the final days of the Pahlavis,[61] there is no consensus, particularly among policymakers, about the cause of its behavior. The works of most former American and Iranian policymakers appear to agree on two points: They exonerate themselves of policy errors and blame others for showing a lack of leadership and/or making inadequate policies.[62]

For many, the failure of the Iranian military to support the monarchy was unexpected for two reasons. First, the 1970s buildup had created a sizeable and well-equipped military machine, which had increased the expectations regarding its performance.[63] Second, the role of the military in the 1953 coup was perceived as setting a precedent for returning the Shah.[64] This perception of the military, however, was misleading. Contrary to general belief, the military did not have many options in the latter days of the 1978–79 crisis. Its declaration of neutrality was the result not of its maturity in staying away from politics, but rather of its paralysis in decision making and dealing with the crisis.[65]

The military failed to function at all levels. At the rank-and-file level, most soldiers were demoralized, an increasing number were deserting,[66] and many had joined the revolutionary forces.[67] Many officers also became convinced that loyalty to the Shah would not guarantee their safety. After all, Azhari's military cabinet, with the approval of the Shah, issued orders to arrest and punish a number of former government officials, including some high-ranking officers.[68] Furthermore, military commanders failed to function as an effective group of leaders. In the absence of the Shah, no influential officer was respected enough by the military establishment to take leadership and make difficult decisions. The published records of the meetings of military commanders indicate that the command structure had collapsed, although Qarabaghi was formally in charge.[69] Some commanders took individual actions, for example, generals Amir Hussain Rabi'i and Javad Mulavi secretly declared allegiance to the revolution.[70] But cracks in the command structure were evident when generals Ghulam Ali Oveissi and Ghulam Reza Azhari left Iran long before the Shah.[71]

The underlying causes of their failure can be traced to the immediate aftermath of the 1953 coup. After his return, the Shah was determined to create a political environment which would not provide an opportunity to another like Musaddiq. This meant that Iranian politics was so restricted that the parliament became a rubber stamp. Moreover, the Shah seemed less accommodating than his father to the religious leaders.[72]

In dealing with opponents, the Shah used the military as his policy instrument, which consequently contributed significantly to the establishment of the state security apparatus. In 1957, SAVAK[73] was initially formed to round up members of the outlawed Tudeh party; but its task expanded to include gathering intelligence and neutralizing all potential opponents of the Shah. SAVAK had close ties to the military, although it was officially designated as a civilian agency attached to the office of the prime minister. Its directors were among the most trusted military officers of the Shah, but this did not mean that they were immune from his suspicion. SAVAK's first director, General Teymur Bakhtiar, was dismissed in 1961 (for allegedly organizing a coup) and assassinated in 1970 (probably on the Shah's orders).[74] There were reports that other directors, including generals Hassan Pakravan and Nimatullah Nassiri, were closely watched.

The military also contributed to the law enforcement agencies—the National Police and the Gendarmerie—that were subordinate to the Ministry of the Interior. The commanders of these agencies were, as a rule, recruited from the military officer corps, and they had the potential to be politically powerful. That potential was never actualized, however, if only because their forces were not capable of handling large demonstrations, as were the well-equipped and trained army troops. Additionally, the appointments of the officers to civilian positions were often temporary.

The Shah also made sure that the military did not become a powerhouse in itself. He would not allow even his trusted military officers to establish themselves within their agencies.[75] Though they were rarely charged with harboring political plots against the Shah,[76] those officers who were perceived as politically dangerous were transferred or even dismissed, based on accusations of financial misconduct (the exceptions being generals Teymur Bakhtiar and Valiullah Qarani[77]). Moreover, the Shah created rivalries among his top commanders and balanced the power of one against the other. The heads of SAVAK and military intelligence were in a fierce competition that gained a new dimension when the Special Intelligence Bureau was established by General Fardust.[78] The heads of the agencies reported directly to the Shah, received orders from him, and were allowed to communicate with one another only through his personal staff.[79] This applied to all senior officers in major command positions. Additionally, the Shah did not tolerate the independent initiatives of his top commanders. For instance, the increasing independence and prestige of Zahedi was so troublesome for the monarch that Zahedi was dismissed as premier approximately one year after the 1953 coup and was appointed to a ceremonial position as the Grand Ambassador, residing in Geneva.

CONCLUSION

Compared to Iran's long history, its military under the Pahlavis was young and the record of its performance was mixed. Although it succeeded in expanding the authority of the central government, maintaining order, and serving as an agent of modernization, it was no match for European forces in 1941.

During this era, the most important role of the military was to protect the monarchy, which it did, especially between the 1952 and 1979 uprisings. In these uprisings, the military was intact and there was no chance of a civil war, but prominent religious leaders—ayatollahs Kashani and Khomeini—were able to organize large masses to neutralize the army. For the military, these crises had different consequences. While many royalists remained in military and civilian positions after the 1952 uprising, after the revolution they were either driven out of Iran, executed, or imprisoned. This meant that no residual royalist forces remained to reestablish the monarchy with foreign assistance, as had been done after the 1953 coup.

As an institution, the military proved weak because it had an instrumental, not an intrinsic political role. Its weakness was the result of several problems. One was the lack of leadership evident during the revolution. The Shah expanded the size of the military, but he did not allow even his most trusted officers to develop a sense of leadership. After his departure in 1979, there was no experienced leader to take charge. In contrast, during the 1953 Coup, the Shah's absence was compensated for by foreign intervention.

Related to the leadership problem was the lack of institutional independence for the military. Most military decisions including promotions above the rank of colonel required the Shah's approval. He did not tolerate independent thinking or initiative by his officers.[80] For example, upon his return in 1953, the Shah reprimanded Zahedi for promoting Nassiri to general without his approval.

Another problem was the lack of a high-ranking officer accepted by the military establishment. The British knew this and insisted on returning the Shah; otherwise, the Americans were ready to replace Musaddiq with an officer, like Zahedi, when the Shah did not show much interest in returning to Iran during the initial stage of negotiations.[81]

The Shah succeeded not only in depoliticizing the military[82] but also in controlling it by balancing military personalities against one another and through material benefits. In comparison to bureaucrats, military officers enjoyed high salaries and regular raises even during the economic difficulties of 1964.[83] The Shah, however, rarely allowed his senior officers to socialize together. The lack of a sense of solidarity among his top commanders came back to haunt the Shah during his final days.

In short, the political role of the Iranian military was limited, and its support of the government was less than expected during major uprisings. Judging the military according to its impressive size and equipment was misleading; the key to understanding its performance was the human factor. For example, the rank and file were easily influenced by religious leaders, and the top commanders had less-sufficient political experience than their counterparts in neighboring states.

The Pahlavis did not want any political challenge in the domestic arena. Their trademark was to maintain a strong military that had more symbolic than real value and basically served as their police force. By royal command, the military would enter or leave the political scene, but never for an extended period such as had been seen in Pakistan and Iraq. In comparison, the military was apolitical, and Iranian officers knew little about policymaking.

Although an analysis of the military in the postrevolution era is beyond the scope of this chapter, it is important to add that, consistent with its role in the Pahlavi era, the military remained under the Islamic Republic as an instrument of policy, not as an initiator of it. In fact, the regular armed forces had a lesser political role in revolutionary Iran, especially compared to the Revolutionary Guard units.[84]

NOTES

1. For an analysis of the significant role of the military in ancient Persia, see R. Chirshman, *Iran: From the Earliest Times to the Islamic Conquest* (Harmondsworth: Penguin, 1978), esp. pp. 309–314.

2. For example, military leaders have played a more significant role in the politics of Iraq, Pakistan, or Turkey.

3. Hushang Mahdavi, *Tarkih-i Ravabit-i Khariji-i Iran* (Diplomatic history of Iran) (Tehran: Amir Kabin, 1350 [1971]), pp. 327–41.

4. R. K. Ramazani, *The Foreign Policy of Iran* (Charlottesville: University Press of Virginia, 1966), p. 172.

5. For a historical record of the Cossacks, see Firuz Kazemzadeh, "The Persian Cossack Brigade," *American Slavic and East European Review* (1956), pp. 351–63.

6. Helen Metz, ed., *Iran: A Country Study* (Washington, D.C.: Government Printing Office, 1989), pp. 238–39.

7. This type of assessment of Reza Khan's record is especially visible among royalists. For example, see Ibrahim Safahi, *Reza Shah-i Kabir Dar A'yinh-i Khatirat'* (The great Reza Shah in the mirror of memories) (Los Angeles: 1365 [1986]).

8. Hussain Makki, *Tarikh-i Bist Salih-i Iran* (The twenty-year history of Iran), vol. 2, (Tehran: 1323 [1944/45]), pp. 24–27.

9. For information on the Gilan Crisis, see Ramazani, *Foreign Policy of Iran,* pp. 152–55 and 190–92.

10. For example, see Malik al-Shuara Bahar, *Tarikh-i Ahzab-i Siyasi* (The history of political parties) (Tehran: 1323 [1944/45]), pp. 61–66. Also, see J. M. Balfour, *Recent Happenings in Persia* (London: Zeno, 1992), pp. 218–19.

11. Sayyid Zia al-Din (or Zia for short) was a politically active journalist who left his editorial post at *Ra'ad* newspaper just before the coup.

12. Bahar, *Tarikh-i Ahzab-i Siyasi,* pp. 112–15.

13. Ramzani, *Foreign Policy of Iran,* p. 172.

14. Fred Halliday, *Iran: Dictatorship and Development* (Harmondsworth: UK, Penguin Books, 1979), p. 66.

15. For example, see Balfour, *Recent Happenings,* p. 219.

16. Forced by the lack of ammunition and other supplies, Reza Khan's troops had just returned from combat duty during the Gilan Crisis. Mahdavi, *Tarikh-i Ravabit,* pp. 352–53.

17. Ramzani, *Foreign Policy of Iran,* p. 177.

18. Except for the Swedish officers in the Gendarmerie. See Metz, ed., *Iran: A Country Study,* p. 239.

19. The most serious tribal rebellion occurred in 1922, when the Kurds were fighting for autonomy. They were heavily armed, had established a fort near the Turkish border, and were responsible for the death of about five thousand soldiers. By August, the army resolved the issue by force. See Fathullah Nuri Isfandiyari, *Rastakhiz-i Iran* (The rise of Iran) (Tehran, 1335 [1956/57]), especially p. 111.

20. For example, the remnants of the old Gendarmerie in Khorasan rebelled against the national government, jailed the governor, and even spoke about establishing an autonomous republic. The new Cossacks Division also crushed this rebellion. Bahar, *Tarikh-i Ahzab-i Siyasi,* pp. 140–62.

21. Halliday, *Iran: Dictatorship and Development,* pp. 73–74.

22. A. C. Millspaugh, *The American Task in Persia* (New York: Century, 1925), pp. 44–48. See also pp. 20–21.

23. Regarding the mission and difficulties of Shuster, see W. Morgan Shuster, *The Strangling of Persia* (New York: Century, 1921).

24. For example, Lenczowski argued that Tehran succeeded in securing a more favorable oil agreement in 1933. See George Lenczowski, *The Middle East in World Affairs,* 3d ed. (Ithaca: Cornell University Press, 1962), p. 188.

25. For a description of the political image of the military in this period, see Ahmad Kasravi, *Afsaran-i Ma* (Our officers), 3d ed. (Tehran: Roshdiyeh, 1358 [1979/80]).

26. *Department of State Bulletin,* 26 June 1950, p. 1048.

27. According to one expert, "Clearly he [Razmara] had been the wrong man at the wrong time for the wrong job." James Bill, *The Eagle and the Lion* (New Haven: Yale University Press, 1988), p. 52.

28. Surprisingly, Reza Khan made a similar argument while he was the Minister of War. Farhad Diba, *Mohammad Massadegh: A Political Biography* (London: Croom Helm, 1986), p. 154.

29. The British also noticed that the Shah wanted the army to be attached to himself rather than to the government. Sir Reader Bullard's report to the Foreign Office in FO371/35117, E2530, 29 April 1943.

30. Some criticized this action as a sign of political opportunism. Considering the importance of the military for the Shah, Kashani argued that Musaddiq should have negotiated with the Shah instead of resigning, because his action put the national movement in jeopardy. Sayyid Mahmoud Kashani, *Qiyam-i Milat-i Musalman-i Iran* (The revolt of the Muslim nation of Iran), (Tehran: Khushih, 1359 [1980]), pp. 12–14.

31. As the vote for Qavam was taken without a quorum, some concluded that the vote was illegal. Diba, *Mossadegh,* p. 153.

32. For the details, see Kashani, *Qiyam,* pp. 38–45.

33. For example, see Charles Lewis Taylor and David A. Jodice, *World Handbook of*

Political and Social Indicators, vol. 2, 3d ed. (New Haven: Yale University Press, 1983), p. 134.

34. Some army units had broken ranks and joined the demonstrators. See Diba, *Mossadegh,* pp. 155–56.

35. For the officers' names, see Kashani, *Qiyam,* p. 67.

36. Farhad Kazemi, "The Military and Politics in Iran," in Elie Kedourie and Sylvia Haim, eds., *Towards a Modern Iran* (London: Frank Cass, 1980), p. 223.

37. The controversy was over generals Vosoq and Daftari, appointed respectively as the Deputy Defence Minister and the Commander of the Customs Guard. Kashani, *Qiyam,* pp. 113 and 120.

38. Diba, *Mossadegh,* p. 160.

39. Some U.S. officials agreed with this view of the premier. See the opinion of General Lenmnitzer, director of the Office of Military Assistance, in the National Archives, Washington, D.C., S/ISA, Office of International Security/Department of State Files, Lot 52–56: Mutual Defense Assistance Program—Iran, February 16, 1950. Also, see the remarks by Ambassador Wiley in *Foreign Relations of the United States 1949,* Department of State (Washington, D.C.: Government Printing Office, 1950).

40. The text of his declaration is in Kashani, *Qiyam,* pp. 31–32.

41. Hassan Ayat, *Nihzat-i Mili-i Iran* (National Movement of Iran) (Qom, Iran: Intisharat-i Islami, 1362 [1983]), p. 31.

42. Kashani, *Qiyam,* p. 82.

43. One unit was to surround Musaddiq's residence and arrest him, another was to capture the radio station, and the third was to await further instructions. Hussain Fardust, *Zuhur Va Suqut-i Saltanat-i Pahlavi* (The rise and fall of Pahlavi rule), vol. 1 (Tehran: Intisharat-i Ittila'at, 1370 [1991]), p. 177.

44. Fardust quoted the three commanders of the coup units as saying that they did not dare follow Zahedi's instructions when they heard that the Shah had left Tehran. Ibid.

45. They were generals Riyahi (Defense Minister), Sepa Por (Air Force Commander), and Amini (Gendarmerie Commander), whose loyalty became clear when they each participated in disarming one of the three rebel army units. Ibid.

46. For information about the Tudeh party, see Sepehr Zabih, *The Communist Movement in Iran* (Berkeley: University of California Press, 1966).

47. The Rashidian family was one of the mob organizers. About this family, see Bill, *Eagle and the Lion,* pp. 91 and 95.

48. Department of State, No. 1091, Henderson to Secretary of State, November 12, 1953.

49. The majority of the Tudeh officers were from the rank of colonel and below. For information about the Tudeh military network, see Kazemi, "Military and Politics in Iran," pp. 224–33.

50. According to Ayat, the military network of the Tudeh party grew to about one thousand because of Musaddiq's indifferent attitude and lack of leadership. Ayat, *Nihzat,* p. 45.

51. For the views of an involved foreign agent, see Kermit Roosevelt, *Countercoup: The Struggle for the Control of Iran* (New York: McGraw-Hill, 1979).

52. William Shawcross, *The Shah's Last Ride* (New York: Simon and Schuster, 1988), p. 70.

53. Fardust claimed that the master mind of the coup was General Akhavi, who was

one of the main members of the anticommunist officer faction organized during General Arfa's era as the Chief of Army Staff. Fardust, *Zuhur,* pp. 180–81.

54. For a detailed analysis of U.S. involvement, see Mark J. Gasiorowski, "The 1953 Coup d'Etat in Iran," *International Journal of Middle East Studies* 19, no. 3 (August 1987): 261–86.

55. Ayat stated that the activities of the Tudeh convinced many, especially foreigners, that the threat of a procommunist takeover of Iran was high. Ayat, *Nihzat,* pp. 60–62.

56. For example, see Ayat, *Nihzat,* p. 45. On 18 August 1953, Ayatollah Kashani wrote to Dr. Musaddiq warning him about a coup attempt. The texts of this letter and Musaddiq's response can be found in Ayat, pp. 84–85.

57. Sepehr Zabih, *The Mossadegh Era* (Chicago: Lake View Press, 1982), esp. pp. 143–47.

58. Diba, *Mossadegh,* p. 184.

59. Fardust, *Zuhur,* p. 179.

60. Reorganizing his top military commanders on the morning of the coup must not have provided Musaddiq's new commander, General Daftari, enough time to respond to the second attempt. The reorganization involved appointing Daftar as police chief, military commander of Tehran (replacing Khalili), and supreme commander of the army (replacing Riahi). Diba, *Mossadegh,* p. 184.

61. These works include the books written by Shahpour Bakhtiar, Mehdi Bazargan, Zbigniew Brzezinski, Jimmy Carter, General Robert Huyser, Muhammad Reza Pahlavi, General Abbas Qarabaghi, Gary Sick, William Sullivan, and Ibrahim Yazdi.

62. In this regard, the best examples are the contradicting works by generals Robert Huyser and Abbas Qarabaghi. They are, respectively, *Mission to Tehran* (New York: Harper and Row, 1986); and *Asrar-i Mamuriyat-i General Huyser Dar Buhran-i Iran* (The secrets of General Huyser's mission during the Iran crisis), (Los Angeles: Maverick, 1989).

63. On the Iranian arms buildup, see Morris Mehrdad Mottale, *The Arms Buildup in the Persian Gulf* (Lanham: University Press of America, 1986), pp. 58–82.

64. Yazdi was one of the observers who referred to this assumption. See Ibrahim Yazdi, *Akharin Talash-Ha Dar Akharin Ruz-Ha* (The last attempts in the last days) (Tehran: Intisharat-i Ghalam, 1363 [1984/85]), pp. 109–110.

65. Reportedly, the army was unreliable in defending the government buildings and military bases against the protestors. See Abbas Qarabaghi, *Hagayg-i Darbarih-i Buhran-i Iran* (Facts about Iran's crisis) (Paris: Suhiyl, 1363 [1984]), pp. 450–57.

66. According to Zabih, the revolutionary forces had begun a psychological war against the armed forces, particularly those in charge of enforcing martial law. Soldiers were often approached individually by a fellow provincialist who would ask why they were shooting their poor Muslim brothers and provide them with civilian clothes and travel money to return to their own city or province. See Sepehr Zabih, *The Iranian Military in Revolution and War* (London: Routledge, 1988), p. 33.

67. In the military the support for Khomeini came from some unlikely groups, including the air force technicians, who enjoyed a high standard of living among military personnel.

68. Zabih, *Iranian Military in Revolution and War,* p. 1.

69. Iranian Government, *Misl-i Barf Ab Khavahim Shud: Muzakirat-i Shura-i Farmandihan-i Artish* (We will melt like snow: The negotiations of the Council of the Military Commanders), 2d printing (Tehran: Nasr-i Ni, 1366 [1978–87]).

70. "Asrar-i Tuti'y Kudtay Sepahbud Rahimi Fash Shud" (Secrets of General Rahimi's coup was disclosed), *Ittla'at,* 2/12/1357 [21 February 1979]; "Rabi'i Asrar-i Kuditay Nezami Ra Fash Kard" (Rabi'i disclosed the secrets of a military coup), *Ittla'at,* 1/23/1358 [12 April 1979].

71. According to General Huyser, he was dispatched to keep the military intact and to encourage the military to switch their loyalty to Bakhtiar. For the story of his task, see Robert Huyser, *Mission in Tehran.*

72. Reza Khan had made a major concession to the religious leaders concerned about Ataturk's secular reforms by shelving the idea of establishing a republic. Mahdavi, *Tarikh-i Ravabit,* pp. 363–64.

73. This was the acronym for Sazman-i Ittili'at va Amniyat-i Kishvar, which is best translated as the Intelligence and Security Organization of the Country.

74. About the life and role of General Bakhtiar, see Iisa Payman, *Asrar-i Qatl-i va Jindigani-i Shigiftangiz-i Sipahbud Teymur Bahktiar* (The secrets of murder and the astonishing life of General Teymur Bakhtiar), 2d printing (Paris: Jen, 1370 [1991]). This book is written from a pro-Bakhtiar perspective, but a critical book review is included.

75. Halliday, *Iran: Dictatorship and Development,* p. 68.

76. Kazami, "Military and Politics in Iran," p. 236.

77. For a brief review of Qarani's case, see Bill, *Eagle and the Lion,* pp. 127–28.

78. For a review of some differences between Fardust and Nassiri, see Iranian Government, *Faraz-Hai Az Tarikh-i Ingilab* (The high points of the history of the revolution) (Tehran: Ministry of Information 1368 [1989]), pp. 58–62.

79. Qarabaghi, *Hagayg,* pp. 103–4.

80. Nikola Schahgaldian, *The Iranian Military under the Islamic Republic* (Santa Monica: Rand Corporation, 1987), p. 14.

81. Fardust, *Zuhur,* pp. 179–80.

82. Halliday, *Iran: Dictatorship and Development,* p. 67.

83. Marvin Zonis, *The Political Elite of Iran* (Princeton: Princeton University Press, 1971), p. 112.

84. For an examination of the post-revolution Iranian military, see Schahgaldian, *Iranian Military under the Islamic Republic;* and Zabih, *Iranian Military in War and Revolution.* For a study of the Revolutionary Guard, see Kenneth Katzman, *The Warriors of Islam* (Boulder, Colo.: Westview Press, 1993).

REFERENCES

English

Arfa, Hassan. *Under Five Shahs.* London: John Murray, 1986.

Canby, Steven L. "The Iranian Military: Political Symbolism versus Military Usefulness." In Hossein Amirsadeghi, ed., *The Security of the Persian Gulf,* pp. 100–130. New York: St. Martin's Press, 1981.

Cottrell, Alvin J. "Iran's Armed Forces under the Pahlavi Dynasty." In George Lenczowski, ed., *Iran under the Pahlavis,* pp. 389–431. Stanford: Hoover Institution Press, 1978.

Gasiorowski, Mark J. "The 1953 Coup d'Etat in Iran." *International Journal of Middle East Studies* 19, no. 3 (August 1987): 261–86.

Hickman, William F. *Ravaged and Reborn: The Iranian Army.* Washington, D.C.: Brookings Institution, 1982.

Huyser, Robert E. *Mission to Tehran.* New York: Harper and Row, 1986.

Kazemi, Farhad. "The Military and Politics in Iran: The Uneasy Symbiosis." In Elie Kedourie and Sylvia Haim, eds., *Towards a Modern Iran: Studies in Thought, Politics, and Society.* London: Frank Cass, 1980.

Moran, Theodore H. "Iranian Defense Expenditures and the Social Crisis." *International Security* 3, no. 3 (Winter 1978/79): 178–92.

Smith, J. M. "Where Was the Shah's Army?" Master's thesis, Army Command and General Staff College, Ft. Leavenworth, Kansas, 1980.

Persian

Ayat, Hussan. *Nihzat-i Mili-i Iran* [National Movement of Iran], 2d printing. Qom, Iran: Intisharat-i Islami, 1362 [1983/84].

Fardust, Hussain. *Zuhur Va Suqut-i Saltanat-i Pahlavi* [The rise and fall of Pahlavi rule], vol. 1. Tehran: Intisharat-i Ittila'at, 1370 [1991].

Isfihani, Muhammad. *Mugayisi-i Artish-i Islam ba Artish-i Taghutut* [Comparison of the Islamic army with the Shah's army]. Tehran, 1982.

Kashani, Sayyid Mahmoud. *Qiyam Milat-i Musalman-i Iran* [The revolt of the Muslim nation of Iran]. Tehran: Khushih, 1359 [1980].

Kasravi, Ahmad. *Afsaran-i Ma* [Our officers], 3d ed. Tehran: Rushdiyeh, 1358 [1979/80].

Qarabaghi, Abbas. *Asrar-i Mamuriyat-i Jeneral Huyser Dar Buhran-i Iran* [The secrets of General Huyser's mission during the Iran crisis]. Los Angeles: Maverick, 1989.

———. *Hagayg-i Darbarih-i Buhran-i Iran* [Facts about Iran's crisis]. Paris: Suhiyl Publications, 1984.

ISRAEL

Moshe Lissak and Daniel Maman

Israel was born forty-five years ago and is still in the midst of violent clashes with Palestinians inside the West Bank and the Gaza Strip and various groups of fundamentalists in Lebanon. Earlier in the history of the region, violent clashes between the Jewish community in Palestine and the local Arab population were a frequent phenomenon. Thus, quite early in the development of the Jewish community in Palestine, the political leadership had to be concerned with the proper relationship between civilians and the cadre of men of arms that emerged in the 1920s and 1930s. Later, after the establishment of the state, the role and status of the growing defense establishment became a central issue in political life, especially in the wake of wars.

Over the years, the relationship between the civilian sectors and the defense establishment acquired a special configuration, some of whose attributes are common to other democratic countries and some of which are particular to the Israeli case.

The question of survival and the sense of living under constant siege could have led to the emergence of a military elite with its own distinct culture stressing symbols of power, heroism, sacrifice, order, and jingoistic nationalism—and with far-reaching political ambitions. This obvious path of development was not taken, but the adverse conditions under which the Israeli Defense Force (IDF) emerged left their marks on it.

One can notice these marks in many spheres, including education, the media, and economics. In this paper we would like to confine the discussion mainly to the political field. The main thesis is that, despite the extensive and repeated intervention by the IDF command in defense-related foreign-policy matters, the Israeli political system is characterized by a multiparty democracy and an active and critical public opinion. Nevertheless, key positions in the system are held by former senior officers, among them former chiefs of staff and members of

the general staff. A partnership has been established between military and political elites, leading to unique patterns of military-civilian networks.

Concern about politicization of the military and consequently the militarization of the civil sector had been rooted in the history of the Jewish community
in Palestine. More specifically, there was a widespread concern that the preindependence political-military organizations would continue to exist after the declaration of independence.

An awareness of the danger of politicization of the military has been reflected
in the Israel Defense Forces Ordinance, one of the first laws passed by the
provisional government. This law specifies that in the oath of allegiance to the
IDF the loyalty of the recruit will be affirmed to the state of Israel, its laws,
and its legitimate authorities.[1] The stress on the "legitimate authorities" was
intended to block partisan political interference in the army stemming from the
strong loyalties to parties and movements that military men still carried with
them from the time of the preindependence period; virtually all areas of public
life, and especially the area of security, were highly politicized. Attempts to
remove partisan influences from the IDF brought about two major political crises
during the first few months of the state's existence: the sinking of the arms ship
Altalena and the disbanding of the *Palmach.* Just after the establishment of the
state, following months of difficult negotiations, an agreement was reached for
integrating the forces of the IZL (Irgun Zvai Leumi), the right-wing dissident
underground group, into the IDF. However, IZL members were allowed to preserve the framework of their underground units in the IDF instead of being
required to join as individuals. Thus, when the arms ship *Altalena,* which had
been organized by agents of the IZL in Europe and dispatched from France,
arrived in Israel, the IZL leaders demanded that some of the arms be allocated
to IZL battalions in the IDF, with the rest to be divided up as the IDF saw fit.
The rejection of this demand, which was incompatible with the concept of a
unified depoliticized military, led to an armed clash between the IZL and units
of the IDF loyal to the government. David Ben-Gurion, the prime minister and
the minister of defense, ordered an IDF artillery unit to open fire on the ship,
which caused it to burn and sink. This demonstration of fierce determination to
prevent, at all costs, any expression of political autonomy within the IDF secured
the integrity of the IDF as a unified army. The *Altalena* affair reflected the
concern of Ben-Gurion and his government with politicization of the IDF caused
by incorporating formerly independent bodies into its ranks. This was perceived
as particularly threatening where the bodies concerned—the IZL and the LHI—
had a long tradition of rejecting the authority of the democratic elected leadership of the Jewish community in the preindependence period (the so-called
Yishuv).

The second crisis involving partisan influences in the IDF differed considerably from the *Altalena* affair and focused on Ben-Gurion's decision to disband
the *Palmach,* a prestigious military unit that had been an integral part of the
Hagana, the organization from which the IDF itself sprang. In that respect, the

Palmach had been subject to the authority of the elected leadership and continued to accept without question the authority of the Israeli government and the IDF command. Nevertheless, the *Palmach* enjoyed organizational autonomy within the IDF that was manifested in a separate command and staff structure that handled training, supply, and manpower.[2] Moreover, many *Palmach* members were close to the kibbutz movements, especially to the *Kibbutz Hameuhad* organization (the unified kibbutz movement), which was led by a left-wing faction of the labor movement known as *Ahdut Ha'avoda* (the Unity of Labor). These informal ties were especially evident in the *Palmach* command, which was comprised mainly of kibbutz members identified with *Ahdut Ha'avoda.* The latter had once been a faction in Ben-Gurion's party *Mapai,* but later broke away and merged with another left-wing group, *Hashomer Hatzair* (the Young Guard), to form a new party, *Mapam* (United Workers Party). The *Palmach* thus appeared to be providing *Mapam-Mapai*'s (Israeli Workers Party) main rival in the labor movement with a channel of influence of the younger generation.

Politically, then, the *Palmach* was a thorn in the side of Ben-Gurion and his party. In addition, the ideological arguments advanced by those who sought to retain the *Palmach*'s partial autonomy clashed with Ben-Gurion's concepts of statehood (*mamlachtiut*) that adamantly upheld the need for a depoliticized military. While Ben-Gurion justified the disbanding of the *Palmach* separate command in terms of the need to depoliticize the army, his left-wing opponents sought to prevent or at least to delay this step by pointing to the unique character of the *Palmach* as a volunteer force inspired by Labor Zionist values.[3] The decision to disband the *Palmach* was, at least on the ideological plane, a crucial step towards a unitary army cleansed of particularistic political attachments. The controversy surrounding Ben-Gurion's action was conducted within the bounds of democratic rules of the game, and the *Palmach* accepted the inevitable once the decision of the cabinet had been ratified by the Provisional Council of State.

Another expression of politics in the military was the participation during the 1950s of officers on active duty in party activities. An extreme manifestation of this was the appearance of several senior officers as candidates in the elections to the first Knesset in 1949.[4] This was seen to be justified because the elections were held before the major demobilization took place, and the senior officers who stood as candidates were regarded as serving only for the duration of the war and not as military professionals. This phenomenon did not, however, recur and was indeed prohibited by the Basic Law, Knesset. Nevertheless, General Staff rules still permit officers to be inactive members of political parties.

Most parties, especially the Labor Movement parties and kibbutz movements, actively seek to cultivate ties with their members serving as career officers. The settlement movements have set up special officers to handle this task, and the parties periodically organize what are described as "informational" meetings for their members in the officers corps.[5] These considerations were seen as unavoidable, given the close involvement of the IDF in shaping foreign and defense policy. In this context, party ties could still play a role in promotions, shared by senior officers and decision-makers, that predisposed them to similar views on matters of national security.

PATTERNS OF RECRUITMENT OF OFFICERS TO THE POLITICAL ELITE

Another manifestation of close ties between senior officers and the political establishment was the "recruitment" of senior officers for top party and government positions upon their leaving the military. This began in the 1950s with men such as Moshe Dayan, Yigal Allon, and Moshe Carmel and, after a hiatus, resumed following the Six-Day War, which brought considerable public acclaim to a number of generals. After 1967, the parties began to compete with each other in attracting senior officers to their ranks. Even parties that had not done this in the past began to assign top political positions for senior officers to take over as soon as they had dropped their uniforms. Perhaps the most blatant case in the years following the Six-Day War was the appointment of Ezer Weizman, a former air force commander and IDF chief of operations, to a ministerial post by Herut within twenty-four hours after he had officially left the army.

The tendency for parties at both ends of the political spectrum to put up former senior officers as candidates for the Knesset indicates that even parties outside the mainstream saw this as a means of acquiring wider legitimacy and attracting voters, the halo provided by the IDF being used to symbolize their commitment to the security of Israel. The presence of reserve officers at practically all points of the political map indicates that the officers corps does not form a "caste" with a uniform political and ideological outlook. While the political deployment of reserve officers has not been an exact reflection of civilian political preferences, they have also not been bunched at either end of the spectrum. Most of them have gravitated to the two large parties, with an edge to Labor.[6] Only the religious parties lack reserve officers among their leaders.

The political activity of some of the senior officers recruited to leadership positions created problems of a constitutional nature. Some of these ex-commanders continued to hold senior reserve positions that could be activated in wartime. In the Yom Kippur War, for example, Ariel Sharon commanded a division that played a crucial part in the fighting along the Suez Canal, while Haim Bar-Lev, a former chief of staff and then minister of trade and industry, was called on, while the war was still in progress, to take command of the fighting on the Egyptian front. Bar-Lev's position as a leader of the ruling Labor-Alignment bloc and Sharon's position as a leader of the opposition Likud bloc generated mutual suspicion and distrust, which were aggravated by Sharon's tendency to take independent initiatives on the battlefield and by his outspoken comments on the war, made mainly to foreign journalists, while the fighting was still going on. In his characteristically belligerent style, Sharon accused his superiors of showing political and personal bias in their decisions during the fighting, in particular those that affected the tasks assigned to his forces. For his part, Sharon was accused of insubordination, making unwarranted charges of politicization against his superiors, and maintaining personal contact during the fighting with the leader of the opposition, Menachem Begin.[7] Suspicions that each side was using its military exploits to reach political gains led eventually to a decision not to give wartime reserve appointments to senior officers-turned-politicians.[8]

The involvement of the military in political decision-making and the connection between political parties and military men comprise the two main institutional aspects of the permeable boundaries between the military and civilian spheres.[9] Sometimes these tendencies interact with each other, with interesting results. The political roles attained by former senior officers meant that they could influence political decisions by means of the doctrines and expertise acquired by them in the IDF. However, their political roles could also enable the political system to reduce its dependence on the professional expertise provided by the chief of staff and his aids.

The legitimation of military involvement in political decision-making and the civilian influences on the military establishment have also had an impact on the relations between the military and civilian elites. Students of the relations between these elites have referred to them as a "partnership."[10] This term, however, can have different meanings. Some of its possible meanings do not apply to Israel in particular, but rather to trends in civil-military relations in democratic countries since World War II. Students of civil-military relations maintain that the conduct of modern warfare and the role of the military in peacetime both require close formal and informal contacts between the military elite and groups and individuals in the political elite that lead to a "convergence" between the two elites.[11]

MILITARY-CIVILIAN NETWORKS

Israel stands out among Western countries in the scope and intensity of the "partnership" between the political and the military elites mainly because of the circumstances that have made Israel into a "nation in arms." This confers a more central social status and a greater involvement in political affairs on the Israeli military than on their Western counterparts. At the same time, Israeli civilian leaders are more involved in national security affairs through their service in the military reserves and through their contacts with the military elite in shared social networks. These networks are not limited to the formal contacts between military men on active duty and senior politicians and administrators that take place by virtue of their official posts. The networks also include contacts between officers and reservists in their units as well as informal contacts with neighbors and common circles of friends. The practice of officers leaving military service at a relatively young age (forty-five to fifty) to start a second career is also an important factor working against any tendencies of the military to self-segregation. The expectation that they will retire from the service and start a second career leads many military men to cultivate social ties outside the army. One result of these contacts and expectations is that in the final phase of their military careers, when they have reached top positions in the military, officers begin to adopt civilian perspectives on many matters, at least to some extent. Officers who leave the regular army at a relatively young age continue to maintain social contacts with their comrades still on active duty and to take up new positions as commanders in the reserves. These crisscrossing social networks operate to close gaps and to increase the resemblance between civilian and military elites. They also facilitate the exchange of information and help cultivate mutual understanding by generating common conceptions and terminology.

In order to understand the phenomenon of networks between military and civilian elites in more depth, one should distinguish schematically between two officer prototypes throughout the forty years of the IDF's existence: the "ideological officer" and the "professional officer."

Ideological officers are characterized by cohesive intimate friendship networks, with close linkages among the officers themselves. A significant proportion of the network components comprises former senior officers. Acquaintanceships with components of the friendship network are forged before military service (during childhood and adolescence in the British Mandate–pre-state period) and during active duty (especially at the beginning of the officers' IDF military careers in the 1950s). Similarly, there is an essential homogeneity in the occupational profile of network components: Most are salaried, working at high-level white-collar jobs in the public and Labor Federation sectors and holding senior positions in civilian networks, especially in management and economics.

In contrast, professional officers are characterized by a lower level of social cohesion and a wider variety of social networks. Most network components lack any prominent military background and display an overtly civilian orientation; a majority work at lower-level positions in civilian networks, particularly in economics and management. The most significant observation of all is the markedly weaker system of linkages within the group's intimate social networks.

The decline in internal cohesion among the military elite reflects a change in the characteristics of the upper military echelons due to the change in sources of recruitment. Nevertheless, we assume that certain other factors may also affect cohesion patterns, as reviewed briefly below: First, one should consider the changes in the army's dimensions. The IDF has grown dramatically from a militia-like organization (comprising several paramilitary bodies) to a giant bureaucratic system accounting for hundreds of thousands of soldiers (in compulsory, permanent, and reserve service). This change in size and scope (which intensified after the Yom Kippur War) necessarily affects internal cohesion patterns within the military network. In the *Palmach*, for example, everyone knew everyone else, whereas in the IDF, the system of interpersonal acquaintanceships is very limited. In other words, in the prestate underground organizations and in the IDF at its inception, the system of informal relations (interpersonal acquaintanceship and mutual trust) played a prominent role among participants, whereas in the bureaucratic IDF, relations are largely formal and hierarchically based.

Another factor to be considered is the absence of wartime success. War generally constitutes a mechanism for social cohesion and serves as a common experience for fighters. However, recent military setbacks (the early days of the Yom Kippur War, the Litani Campaign, and the Lebanon War) have served as a disintegrative factor regarding internal cohesion. Understating the situation somewhat, we claim that the mutual accusations among the upper echelons, the development of "personality cults" surrounding generals, and debates concerning the merits of various military doctrines obviously did not contribute to social cohesion within the military elite, nor did they foster good relations with other elites in the civilian sector.

The changes in patterns of cohesion among the social networks of the military elite may have direct implications regarding the officers' integration in civilian elites after discharge. We cannot explain the phenomenon without considering changes in the elite market and in sources of recruitment to the military network itself.[12] Between 1974 and 1984 (the conclusion of the research period), the elite market (in which candidates for the various elites positions are both horizontally and vertically mobile) was relatively closed because of structural changes and stagnation in economic-social activity. The civilian elites then had various sources of recruitment: internal recruitment from within each elite and external recruitment from other elites (if we consider the political sphere as an example, internal recruitment addresses candidates from the lower echelons of the political elite, whereas external recruitment draws applicants from other elites: economic, administrative, and so on). Until the mid-1970s, retiring senior officers served as the primary source for external recruitment to the various civilian elites. Since then, it has become only one of many sources.

Social networks have many social functions, including support, mutual assistance, and social advancement. The actors in these networks can rely on one another for exchange of information, advice, material favors, and the like. In Israel, retiring senior officers who desire a second career must maintain a system of contacts and acquaintanceships with functionaries of civilian authorities to exchange the prestige and power they acquired during their military service for positions and functions in the civilian system. In other words, the structure and makeup of intimate social networks play a considerable role in transmitting information on supply and demand concerning elite positions.

Past integration of ideological officers into senior positions in civilian elites, although partly a function of elite market structure and changes in sources of recruitment to the military elite, may also have been facilitated by the cohesion of the officers' intimate social network (augmented by acquaintanceship networks). This internal cohesion enabled the officers to request assistance in as-suming senior civilian positions—especially in politics—on their discharge from the IDF. Furthermore, up to the mid-1970s, the retired officers already in the higher echelons of these elites were able to assist their newly discharged col-leagues, either directly (by accepting them to the same elite) or indirectly (by providing information on vacant elite positions, serving as mediators, and forg-ing linkages with other elites). Our research findings, for example, point to a higher assistance level among ideological officers than among professional ones regarding both mutual assistance and aid to other military persons seeking to join civilian systems after discharge from the IDF.[13] The ideological generals stand out especially for this type of activity.[14]

We believe that the weakening of internal cohesion in the upper echelons is connected with a certain decline in the status of the IDF and the military elite in Israeli society, which may have implications regarding patterns of civilian supervision of the military system and elite.

POLITICAL AND SOCIAL IMPLICATIONS

Since the Yom Kippur War, Israeli society has obviously experienced various social processes that entailed a reduction in the prestige and status of the IDF and its senior officers. For example, consider the intensity of public criticism of the military establishment. Until the Yom Kippur War, there was only minor criticism at most. Survey findings indeed indicated that the public essentially trusted the IDF and the defense system more than any other social institutions in Israeli society.[15] At present, however, we are witnessing various manifesta-tions of overt mistrust, such as criticism of the IDF and its conduct in the mass media, an increase in the number of conscientious objectors on grounds of re-ligion and—even more significant—ideology and conscience (e.g., refusal to serve in Lebanon during the Lebanon War and its aftermath, or in the Admin-istered Territories during the *Intifada*). Furthermore, the military elite is no longer the main source of recruitment to civilian elites. As indicated above, since the 1970s, the upper army echelons have constituted only one of the many sources of recruitment to civilian elites and have thus lost the central role they once played.

Another possible result of the decline in internal cohesion among Israel's senior officers is a change in the patterns of civilian supervision of the military system and elites. Schematically, we may identify two supervision patterns: for-mal and informal (or, following Huntington 1957, *objective* and *subjective*). This is obviously a dichotomous differentiation; intermediate types are also active, and the social system is not based on any one exclusive pattern. Formal super-vision clearly separates the military system from the civilian one, and the bound-aries between the systems are impenetrable.[16] In the informal supervision model, the boundaries are permeable, and supervision is based on the common origin and high social cohesion among members of the different elites.

Until the mid-1970s, civilian supervision of the military was primarily infor-mal. Up to the early 1960s, the supervision pattern was primarily personal. In other words, when David Ben-Gurion was prime minister and defense minister, supervision was based on his own charismatic personality. From the twilight of Ben-Gurion's administration until the mid-1970s, supervision was primarily in-formal, effected through social networks of elites. Reciprocal relations among elites, especially between the political elite and those close to decision-making foci, were based on partnership, although the political elite undoubtedly main-tained a dominant position compared to the military, administrative, and eco-nomic elites. The elite market was characterized by similar recruitment patterns and close contacts among elites, including common intimate networks, values, and social images. Under such conditions, the reciprocal supervision between one elite and another, based on common values and experiences, was still low-key, as there was a de facto partnership between the military and political elites (although de jure the former was subject to the latter).

Expansion of military elite recruitment based (as the process affecting other elites) to social strata other than prestate elites (e.g., immigrants who arrived subsequently), along with the weakening of interpersonal linkages within the military elite and between one elite and another, entailed a high likelihood of change in the patterns of civilian supervision of the military elite. The emergence of the professional officer as the dominant prototype intensified the need for a shift from informal supervision—primarily constituting reciprocal supervision among elites via common social networks—to formal supervision. This pattern also guided the enactment of an Army Basic Law in 1976, in the wake of the Yom Kippur War, defining the division of authority among the government, the prime minister, the defense minister, and the chief of staff. The legislative gap that prevailed until the enactment of this law attests to the informal supervision patterns obtaining until then. The law thus constitutes a symptom of the change in supervision patterns. The emergence of a different pattern of integration be-tween the military and civilian systems may indeed constitute a possible out-come of the shift in orientation of the upper echelons from ideological to professional, the expansion of military elite recruitment bases, the dispersed social networks whose components mostly lack outstanding military back-grounds, and the weak reciprocal linkages among the upper echelons themselves. This integration pattern, in turn, may also entail intensification of civilian su-pervision. In the Israeli case, at least, these developments go hand in hand with a weakening of the military elite and an increasing difficulty in exchanging the resources acquired during one's military service for civilian power and prestige.

In summary, there is an internal contradiction in the "nation in arms" model. Israeli society, which suits this model theoretically, expects the military elite not to close itself off and to be part of civilian society, including mixed social networks. However, because of the decline in internal cohesion engendered by this demand, as well as the changes in the elite market and expansion of re-cruitment bases, the present military elite, which comprises "professional" officers, finds it difficult to preserve its status in the elite market and the social prestige it was accorded previously. As indicated, this situation is manifested to some extent in public distrust of the military system and elite, as well as in the difficulties senior officers encounter when attempting to join civilian elites after discharge from the IDF. Hence the military elite, and especially its professional officers, is an elite in transition. Senior officers fulfill elite functions only when on active military duty. Once they are discharged, they essentially lose the power and prestige entailed by their military status.

CONCLUSIONS

Although Israel has been immersed in a prolonged violent conflict, it does not behave like a society under siege. Its democratic government and routine civilian life are a far cry from the type of "siege mentality" bred by living under a constant state of emergency. Israel has not turned into a garrison state, a modern Sparta ruled by specialists in violence whose entire way of life is subordinated to meeting the challenge of an external threat. Thus, the dilemma facing Israel is how to maintain the democratic rules of the game, especially civilian control of the military, in a society that lives in constant awareness of a threat to its existence.

It can be argued that the partial involvement of the military in areas of national security officially under civilian control has, paradoxically, made it possible for Israel to preserve its democratic regime and its civilian way of life. The tendency of the civilian and military spheres to develop a resemblance to one another—through the practical militarization of civilian activities and the limited "civilianization" of the military—has prevented the military from becoming a separate caste that feels itself alienated from and in conflict with the values represented by the civilian elites. As a result, Israel's susceptibility to a military coup and to the ascendancy of the specialists in violence over the civilian sector has been low. However, the very characteristics that have made a military coup a remote possibility in Israel have made its political decision-making instruments open to manipulation by the defense establishment or portions of it. The ill-defined mechanisms of control, the contradictions between the drive to impose political controls on military activities and the army's professional stress on operative flexibility, the longstanding practice of involving senior officers in policymaking—all these have created possibilities for military leaders and the defense establishment to exercise unwarranted influence on decisions taken by the political echelon. The results of such manipulation, as the War in Lebanon shows, can not only undermine proper governmental process but can also erode the national consensus, at least in those cases where military escalation is the product of manipulation.

Another threat to the rules of the game that have enabled Israel to maintain its democratic regime during a prolonged external conflict is rooted in the rising cost, in both human and material terms, of the national security effort in the years following the Yom Kippur War. The rules of the game were developed in the 1950s and 1960s, when the collective security effort did not impose especially heavy burdens in casualties, morale, and material resources. Both the Sinai Campaign and the Six-Day War claimed relatively few casualties, did not exact inordinate costs, and were short. In the 1970s and 1980s, however, the cost of national security greatly increased, during both wartime and the periods in between, in terms of material resources, casualties, and prolonged emergence mobilization. Thus, the longer periods of reserve duty imposed following the wars of the 1970s and 1980s have been one factor in motivating young people to go abroad for extended periods of time and even to leave Israel altogether. The rising cost of national security has also increased the influence of the military-industrial complex on policymaking, thus imposing other constraints, not directly related to security, on the political leadership.

A third factor that threatens the rules of the game is the weakening of the national consensus concerning the nature of the Arab-Israeli conflict and its possible solutions. The fundamental ideological disputes over Israel's central national goals assumed significance in the wake of the Six-Day War. This has led to a political polarization that could seriously impair the effective functioning of Israel's democracy, making it more difficult to mobilize the resources necessary to maintain current levels of security and to ensure public ease in abiding unconditionally by authoritative policy decisions in matters of national security.

NOTES

1. See *Official Gazette 1948*, Appendix A, p. 9 (Hebrew).

2. See Meir Pail, *The Emergence of Zahal* (Tel Aviv: Zmora; Bitan-Moden, 1970), ch. 11 (Hebrew).

3. See Anita Shapira, *The Army Controversy, 1948: Ben-Gurion's Struggle for Control* (Tel-Aviv: Hakibbutz Hameuchad, 1985), pp. 50–57 (Hebrew); Yoav Gelber, *The Dissolution of the Palmach* (Tel Aviv: Schoken, 1986), pp. 225–26 (Hebrew).

4. See Yoram Peri, *Between Battles and Ballots: Israeli Military in Politics* (Cambridge: Cambridge University Press, 1983), p. 60.

5. Ibid., pp. 64–67.

6. Yoram Peri and Moshe Lissak, "Retired Officers in Israel and the Emergence of a New Elite," in Gwyn Haries-Jenkins and Jacques van Doorn, eds., *The Military and the Problem of Legitimacy,* pp. 188–190 (Beverly Hills and London: Sage Publications, 1976).

7. See interview with Sharon, *New York Times,* 1 November 1973; see also H. Bartov, *Dado: 48 Years Plus 20 Days,* vol. 2 (Tel Aviv: Maariv, 1973), p. 313 (Hebrew).

8. See editorial on Sharon's position in the IDF reserves in *Haaretz,* 17 December 1974 (Hebrew).

9. A. R. Luckham, "A Comparative Typology of Civil-Military Relations," *Government and Opposition* 13 (Winter 1971): 5–25.

10. See Yoram Peri, "Political Military Partnership in Israel," *International Political Science Review* 2, no. 3 (1981): 303–315.

11. See Sam C. Sarkesian, "Military Professionalism and Civil-Military Relations in the West," *International Political Science Review* 2, no. 3 (1981): 283–98; Morris Janowitz, "Armed Forces in Western Europe: Uniformity and Diversity," *Archives Europeenes de sociologie* 6 (1965): 225–37; Charles C. Moskos, "Armed Forces and American Society: Convergence on Divergence?" in C. C. Moskos, ed., *Public Opinion and the Military Establishment* (Beverly Hills and London: Sage Publications, 1971), pp. 271–94.

12. Daniel Mamn, *The Second Career of Top Military Officers and the Civilian Elites in Israel: 1974–1984* (Jerusalem: Academon, 1988) (Hebrew).

13. Among senior officers, 56% claimed that their current civilian workplace has employees who served them and under their command in the IDF, while 62% of them claimed some responsibility for these employees' presence (42% stated that they introduced most such employees, and 22% said they brought in some of them). As indicated, the ideological officers brought in more former military people than the professional officers (70% versus 56%).

14. Of the generals who began their military service in the pre-State period, 78% brought in former military personnel to their place of work, as compared with 64% of brigadiers who began service at that time and 50% of brigadiers who commenced service only after the establishment of the state.

15. Efraim Yuchtman, "Whom Do You Trust? The Israeli Public and Its Institutions," *Israeli Democracy* (Fall 1989), pp. 1–7.

16. A. R. Luckham, "Comparative Typology."

REFERENCES

Horowitz, Dan. "Is Israel a Garrison State?" *Jerusalem Quarterly* 4 (Summer 1977): 58–77.

————. "The Israeli Defense Forces: A Civilianized Military in a Partially Militarized Society." In Roman Kolkowicz and Andrzej Korbonski, eds., *Soldiers, Peasants and Bureaucrats.* London: Allen and Unwin, 1982.

Kimmerling, Baruch. "Determination of the Boundaries and Frameworks of Conscription: Two Dimensions of Civil-Military Relations in Israel." *Studies in Comparative International Development* 14, no. 1 (1979): 22–41.

Lissak, Moshe. "Boundaries and Institutional Linkages between Elites: Some Illustrations from Civil-Military Relations in Israel." In G. Moore, ed., *Research in Politics and Society, A Research Annual* 1 (1985): 129–48.

Luttwak, Edward, and Dan Horowitz. *The Israeli Army.* London: Allen Lane, 1975.

Maman, Daniel, and Moshe Lissak. "The Impact of Social Networks on the Occupational Patterns of Retired Officers: The Case of Israel." In Jurgen Kuhlmann, ed., *Military Related Social Research: Forum International* 9 (1990): 279–308.

Peri, Yoram. *Between Battles and Ballots: Israeli Military in Politics.* Cambridge: Cambridge University Press, 1982.

Perlmutter, Amos. *Military and Politics in Israel: National Building and Role Expansion.* London: Frank Cass, 1969.

JAPAN

Andrew K. Hanami

Two opposing images seem to capture the imagination of those who describe the military in contemporary Japanese society: the pacifist nation that has grown to global economic preeminence and the vision of a growing or resurgent militarism. For four decades Japan has not had a high-profile military, yet the feeling has persisted that beneath Japan's pacifist shell lay the substance of a military figure in waiting. In reality the Japanese military is catching up in the 1980s and 1990s with the West, just as Japan's economy was catching up in the 1950s and 1960s. How large the Japanese military will grow is in part a function of the pressures, constraints, and opportunities that it faces. There are, however, structural limits beyond which it cannot grow. Both past traditions and contemporary forces have seemed to alternately enlarge and contract the military.

HISTORICAL BACKGROUND

The rise of the military class in Japan took place a millennium after the establishment of the imperial system. The Fujiwara family, a culture-oriented, nonmilitary clan governed the country for five centuries on behalf of the emperor, emphasizing scholarship, religion, and the arts. With the ascendance of powerful Shinto and Buddhist religious sects, large private armies were raised to protect and promote the interests of the religious groups. Emperors had great difficulty controlling them, and they frequently massed outside the Kyoto palace walls and attempted to intimidate the emperor.

By the twelfth century the most powerful of the private armies came to be headed by a new leader known as the shogun, or "generalissimo." The militarily dominant shogun set up his headquarters in Tokyo and thereafter ruled in the name of the emperor, drawing from the throne's legitimacy and thus eliminating the need to depose him. This arrangement preserved the imperial system.

One unexpected consequence was that in a sense a twin-headed political system came into existence, which served Japan well. The shogun could absorb the vagaries and criticisms of day-to-day government and be replaced, while the imperial system remained to provide for cultural cohesion and national stability. The official ideology or "religion" adopted by the shogun was Confucianism, since Shintoism was already identified with the emperor and Buddhism was the province of many rival lords. What Confucianism introduced at the center of Japanese power that was new was a model of a hybrid governor, both warrior and scholar. This tradition was to have significant relevance for modern Japan.

With the arrival of a quarter of the American navy headed by Commodore Matthew Perry in the nineteenth century, the shogun system collapsed in part because it was blamed for its inability to protect the country. Thus the emperor was "restored," reintroducing Japan's traditional conservative leadership at a moment in history when modernization was dawning worldwide. The young emperor Meiji rapidly set the nation on a course toward a Western-style society, using the slogan, "rich country, strong army" (fukoku kyohei). Having observed with great alarm the military defeat of China, the Japanese leadership resolved rapidly to create an economy and a military class equivalent to the West in order to hold back Western powers from taking over Japan.

The Meiji restoration, combined with the events of Western imperialism, set the stage for regional and global competition for resources in Manchuria believed necessary for Japan's development. Together with the worldwide depression of the 1930s, the conditions were ripe for the entry of the military in national government. The global depression created severe starvation in the countryside from which lower levels of the military were drawn. The military blamed corrupt civilian politicians and big business, who they felt were step-children of Western capitalism gone awry, for much of the dislocations. Military figures seized control of Japanese foreign policy by forcibly taking Manchuria and assassinating civilian leaders who opposed them. In other words, Japanese militarism, extremism, and ultranationalism were conditioned by economics in the drive for economic security and the perception that Russia would soon annex a helpless China unless Japan acted first. The creation of a military state in the 1930s was a result of a search for economic security that was identified in the Meiji era with the political security of the state. The ensuing defeat in World War II shattered the Japanese military state and created a civilian cabinet-style government led by a prime minister, reducing the emperor to a symbol of the state.[1]

MACARTHUR'S POSTWAR ARCHITECTURE

Under Douglas MacArthur's leadership, the new nation and its constitution reflected a curious mixture of American idealism intent on becoming Japanese tradition. The nation officially renounced war as a means of conducting foreign policy, which led to the establishment of the three nonnuclear principles, and abolished the military and the defense industries. The American occupation prompted the development of a democratic society designed to emphasize civilian rule in Japan by creating political parties, extending the vote, and stressing access to education. Some critics have said MacArthur was trying to make Japan into what America sought to be but never quite attained.

Political events soon overtook MacArthur's vision. The Korean war broke out in 1950, and American foreign policy rapidly converted Japan into a pillar of America's global defense network. American forces required a wide range of military supplies and equipment from Japan for the entrenched Korean war, reopening military factories that had only recently been shut down. In the Cold War era the United States also suddenly saw the need for Japan to possess military forces of its own upon which the United States could rely in its strategy of encirclement of worldwide communism. At a stroke, two pillars of American occupation policy were dismantled and reversed. In this rapidly changing context, Japan's Self-Defense Forces (SDF) were brought into existence.

However, by the 1950s certain Japanese habits and expectations had set in that were not favorable to the reestablishment of a military force. It took a war to fully end the military; it might take another war to fully recreate it. Armies are created not by peace or by politicians but by threats. The Japanese Defense Agency (JDA), the key civil-military body created to manage the new military, was established by administrative fiat. The JDA was therefore born in institutional weakness and suffered from a paucity of legitimacy since it was not the result of national debate nor a parliamentary act.

RECRUITMENT, TRAINING, AND MORALE

Not surprisingly, a military career has consistently ranked as among the least desirable professions among Japanese youth. In fact, the armed forces cannot even fill the personnel levels established as necessary by the government, meeting 87% of the national target. Volunteers ages eighteen to twenty-five sign up for either two- or three-year contracts through one of the fifty SDF offices, and recruitment has become more difficult each year. Trainees are given a balance of practical skills in the martial arts, weapons, and skiing, along with the special skills relating to their basic unit in infantry, armored, naval, and like forces. In Japan, subjective subjects of character building and moral education are also emphasized.[2]

The National Defense Institute, established thirty-five years ago at Yokosuka, where the American Seventh Fleet also makes its home, combines the training of the three services under one roof. The institute recruits largely rural youth whose best avenue for success may be through this military academy. While these academy students arrive with good high school backgrounds, they do not necessarily represent many of the best students in Japan, who instead choose to attend prestigious universities in Tokyo, Kyoto, and elsewhere.[3] Foreign visitors report that the quality of the curriculum seems to be high. Morale is also robust, inspired in part by intense competition among recruits, a dedicated faculty and staff, and frequent reference to the tradition of past military excellance prominently displayed in military museums.[4]

ASYMMETRICAL CIVIL-MILITARY RELATIONS

As a consequence of the postwar legacy, civil-military relations have heavily emphasized civilian control of the military. This skewed relationship, structured by social engineering first by the Americans and subsequently sustained by Japanese authorities, has irritated and dissatisfied the professional military. Japan may be the extreme example of the imbalance of civil-military relations in which the military are "soldiers without a state."

Because the Japanese schools have uniformly socialized school children from an early age to abhor the evils of militarism, a ubiquitous pacifist culture has taken root. The vast majority of young people today relegate the military to a low level. In this national environment unreceptive to the SDF, the military has resorted to volunteering their forces, primarily for disaster relief, in order to win wider acceptance among the population. From the 1950s to the 1970s, the people basically believed the SDF were mainly useful for emergency rescues in national calamities.

However, Japan's opposition parties, like the Socialist, Komeito, and Communist parties, have steadfastly opposed the legitimacy if not the existence and military function of the SDF from the start, calling them unconstitutional (though most now accept the military as a necessary evil). The only assertive political support for the SDF rests with the majority Liberal Democratic Party (LDP), which indirectly created them. American policymakers have been careful not to nudge the conservative LDP from power, as it serves American interests in the region and acts as a bulwark against criticism of the SDF and the attendant instability the absence of the Japanese democratic government could cause. Though there have been close elections, the coalition-oriented LDP has shown a capacity to retain working majorities in the Lower House of the Diet. What is less recognized outside Japan is that the opposition parties are neither prepared for governing nor expect to govern any time soon, which has only encouraged their extreme positions against the LDP.

STRUCTURE OF THE JDA

It should not be surprising that the formal JDA structure reflects the imbalance in civil-military relations. The director-general of the JDA is always a civilian not of cabinet rank, by custom a younger civil servant appointed by the prime minister as his first major post in an upward-spiral rotation of high government posts. Director-generals have occupied their JDA posts for just an average of ten months before moving on.[5] Routine rotation is the norm in Japanese politics, partly because the prime minister must reward many key followers in his faction with such appointments. But the JDA turnover frequency has been somewhat more rapid than for most. One consequence is that the director-general cannot accumulate very much expertise on the subject, although that is a characteristic widespread throughout all ministerial posts. But the short tenure may unduly impact the organization because it sits at the choke point between the civilian and military worlds.

The director-general appoints all of the highest-ranking officers who are to work with him, presumably to further augment direct civilian control. The core of the JDA administrative command structure is basically double-layered, with an "inner" and an "outer" circle. The inner circle that surrounds the director-general, enabling direct access, is more important and is made up of high-ranking civilian bureaucrats. The outer circle is reserved for the uniformed officers.

The prime minister holds the ultimate authority over the JDA, but he is not the commander in chief.[6] Between 1889 and 1946 the emperor retained "supreme command" of the military, possessing the right to make treaties and to declare war. Today's constitution is vague on whether the prime minister can invoke defense forces, favoring the cabinet with "control and supervision" functions. In this sense, Japan lacks a single unified, identifiable commander in chief, as it is a consensus-run government. The prime minister has the ultimate responsibility to "move troops" through the director-general of the JDA, who in turn "gives orders" to the field commanders of the various services. The prime minister also needs the approval of the cabinet and Diet, as well as consultation with others, a very slow process.[7]

The consensus of the inner bureau generally directs the decision of the military and thus in a way serves as an institutionalized commander in chief. A simplified chart may look like Figure 1.

Uniformed personnel cannot testify in person to the parliament. Their views must be represented through spokesmen from the inner bureau. Military men often feel that their views, for example, on the extent of the military threat to Japan, are not properly conveyed to the Diet. Thus direct military input is kept out of higher-level policy consideration, thereby subordinating the military and shutting them out of the policy process. The military commanders have no direct access even to the prime minister, who is insulated by two civilians, the director-general and the head of the Bureau of Defense Policy.[8]

Drawing up the defense budget, a most important process, further reflects the inner dynamics of the civil-military structure. At its point of origin, military specialists draw up yearly requests for each of the three services, based on their analysis of domestic needs and trends in the West. JDA civilian bureaucrats then study and evaluate all requests. After informal discussions lasting between six and nine months between bureau chiefs and military staffs, a consensus is formed. The proposal is then sent on to the Ministry of Finance (MOF) and the Ministry of International Trade and Industry (MITI) simultaneously. The conservative Finance Ministry, the most powerful in Japan, is known to carefully

Figure 1

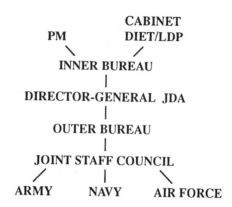

balance each budget increase request against the overall context of other expenditures, while enforcing the defense budget ceiling of 1% of GNP. MITI scrutinizes companies that receive defense contracts and determines the impact on overall industrial development. MITI controls all aircraft and weapons manufacturing throughout the process and can terminate projects not meeting its standards. Next, the National Defense Council examines the budget proposal, regarded as a pro forma stage, before sending it to the prime minister for cabinet ratification. Simultaneously, key political leaders of the LDP Defense Committee have their input and in turn seek Diet approval, and the entire process comes to a conclusion.[9]

THE INFORMAL DEFENSE STRUCTURE

There are five hundred civil servants who comprise the "internal bureau" of the JDA and forty thousand uniformed officers. But informal contacts are more important in Japan than formal ones. The NDC and Joint Staff Council are only ceremonial organizations. What cannot be emphasized enough is that decision making is not majoritarian but consensual. School links, including those established at the National Defense Institute, can often form the point of origin for informal channels.

One Japanese expert describes civil-military relations as "acceptable," though often "tense."[10] Other Japan sources agree, adding that the military officer corps have been holding up under the strain of the lack of autonomy, both internally and from the United States. The officer corps is reported to have felt little sense of self-determination, which has led to a diminished sense of effectiveness.[11] It is widely believed that one objective of American foreign policy in the Pacific, besides the defense of Japan, is keeping Japan's

military down, and hence the presence of troops and 120 U.S. bases and facilities on the archipelago.

In 1969, however, the Nixon Doctrine called for increased self-reliance on
the part of Asian nations for their own defense in the Pacific, causing Japan to
wonder about the quality of U.S. commitment. This event seems to have un-
settled the balance of informal civil-military relations, subtly shifting it in favor
of the military. MOF versus JDA negotiations became "heated," as described
by Japanese sources. By 1985, with a pro-defense prime minister who once
headed the JDA, Yasuhiro Nakasone, at the helm, JDA proposals met with
marked success. JDA's bargaining position was somewhat improved, from one
in which the defense received guidance from MOF with negotiation rights to
one in which the JDA could take greater initiative by defining the security task
for which the government was responsible.[12]

In a more startling illustration, the JDA took the lead in successfully obtaining
the Patriot missile system in the early 1980s. Significant negotiation participation
also came from Japan's major trading companies, who contacted Raytheon,
U.S.A. Subsequent testing of the prototype missile was evaluated by JDA uniformed personnel in conjunction with Mitsubishi Corporation officials. Ministry
officials opposed various aspects of the purchase—its costs, certain capabilities,
and the like—but in the end had fundamentally to acquiesce.[13]

The reason for the modest military ascendance in determining selective aspects is that the technical and complex nature of modern defense is beyond the
training and experience of civilian ministers and policymakers. Thus civilian
ministers must depend on their military subordinates, who often make the critical
evaluations on subjects they know best.[14] In addition, defense companies are
consulted as to the efficacy of prospective military products. After several bids
are offered, the JDA determines which companies are to manufacture a particular
item.[15] Moreover, in matters of United States–Japan defense issues, which usually involve strategic questions and very advanced technological systems, uniformed officers have been reported to have greater importance in decision
making.[16]

NATIONAL SECURITY AND MILITARY CAPABILITY

Throughout most of the postwar era, national security for Japan seems to have
self-consciously steered away from military development and anchored national
security, based on strong domestic economic growth supported by high levels
of trade. The state has guided the growth of self-sustaining strategic industries
in the last few decades, including steel, shipping, automobiles, electronics, and
computers.[17] The old nineteenth-century slogan may be amended to read, "rich
country, strong industry" (fukoku kyosan).

With the surprising rise of Japan's economic position in the world, increased pressures for shouldering greater responsibilities led to the adoption of a policy by 1980 called "comprehensive security," which featured an expanded foreign aid program. By 1987 Japan had overtaken the United States as the world's single largest Official Development Aid (ODA) sponsor, distributed globally, but concentrated in Asia and the Middle East. Japan also created programs to train foreign technicians in infrastructure development and transferred some technologies to assist that effort to encourage sustainable growth in regions of interest to Japanese and American policymakers. The Japanese appear to believe that foreign-assisted self-development is the best measure a nation can take against regime-threatening problems and political instability.

The question is often advanced whether, had Japan not been permitted the benefit of American military protection, Japan's economy would have grown as successfully as it has. Japan's economic expansion, in other words, is attributed to the American defense expense and effort, which should, as critics argue, rightly be at the feet of the Japanese military. The self-imposed 1976 1% ceiling on military spending is widely regarded as simply too low and inappropriate for a modern nation like Japan, though if military pensions were included as NATO countries do, the correct figure would be 1.5%. It is a noteworthy comparison, however, that America's defense expenditure at the early stages of World War II was 1.5%. But the relatively low level of Japan's military costs nonetheless is implied to have led to the eventual relative decline of the United States, erupting into bilateral controversy since at least the mid-1980s as rising trade disequilibrium allegedly impacted the American domestic economic well-being. Recent studies show, however, that even had Japan's defense budget allowed for a NATO-level 3% of GNP spending, the impressive economic growth would not have been significantly affected. During Japan's high-growth period, national capital formation exceeded 30% of GNP, which served as the financial basis of Japan's economic "miracle." Diverting 3% to the military, even if all of it were unproductive as far as the civilian economy was concerned, would have been "negligible."[18] Even through longer periods after the high-growth era, calculations show that between 1970 and 1988 the Japanese GNP would still have achieved 97%–98% of its prevailing growth even with sustained NATO-level defense expenditures.[19]

How have small defense budgets affected military capabilities? As a top-ten military spender for over a decade, some observers believe, Japan's capabilities are approaching world-class military standards. However, a former Soviet diplomat boasted that its forces could successfully penetrate Japanese territory in just tens of minutes. Japanese military officers agreed, although they thought the time might be shorter. Japan's objective is to provide a minimum conventional defense that will serve as a temporary holding force or "tripwire" to signal the arrival of superior American capability.[20] Japan is assigned to provide just local defense or, as one scholar has phrased it, "non-provocative defense,"[21] that is, a defense force without offensive capability, so as not to threaten nervous

Asian neighbors like China, Singapore, and others who recall Japanese occupation during World War II.

Much commentary has surfaced that a stronger Japanese defense is highly desirable because it would act as a general "deterrent," thereby relieving the Americans of some of the military burden in the Pacific. However, military analysts point out that purely defensive forces cannot deter, as they have no ability to inflict commensurate punishment.[22] American forces are necessary for credible deterrence. Henry Kissinger has recently written that the nature of Japan's security threat is more complex and unpredictable than in Europe, where European nations have faced a common adversary throughout the postwar period.[23] Thus a draw-down in Russian forces in its Western frontiers does not necessarily carry the same meaning as it seems to in Russia's Pacific command, which is continuing to modernize its weapons systems and whose Pacific regional command is suggested to be operating somewhat independently of Moscow's official policies. Moreover, Japanese military experts worry about the potential instabilities in the post-Gorbachev era, as well as the multinational nature of possible threats that could implicate Japan. Even if there were a "local" nuclear exchange involving the Korean peninsula, for example, the winds could easily drift over and devastate the Japanese society and economy, creating significant repercussions for the United States and the international economy.[24] The optimal strategy for Japan is to build up forces to the point where they can protect the integrity of Japan's territory out to a radius of one thousand miles. Japan will be charged with providing security for the American Seventh Fleet at the conventional level just as the United States is providing security for Japan at the nuclear level. A military division of labor is thereby attained. In addition, Japanese forces could support the U.S. forces four thousand miles out in joint patrols of vital sea routes to the Middle East as well as relief patrol in the mid-Pacific, at the conventional level.[25]

However, Japan's forces currently do not provide for such minimal missions and, according to a Rand Corporation report, are especially vulnerable to threats or blackmail from states with any significant invasion force.[26] Indeed, Japan has recently become the world's number-three defense spender (thirty billion dollars), just behind the United States and Russia. However, too much should not be made of this fact. When more specific details are examined, it can be seen that Japan's current capabilities are quite modest, for a number of reasons. In terms of sheer numbers, Japan's standing army at approximately 150,000 ranks as only twenty-fifth in the world, behind Ethiopia, Thailand, and Spain. Japan has .2% of its population enlisted in the military. Great Britain has .57%, Germany has .81%, and France and the United States are higher at about 1%.[27]

Training is limited. Military experts have pointed out that only sustained training that is both realistic and dangerous truly prepares troops for effective battle. This is especially important because studies show that normally 10% of a country's troops neutralizes 50% of the enemy. The shortage of ammunition and firing ranges in Japan's populous island restricts extensive live practice. Rocket-fire practice of on-line missile systems intended to defend Hokkaido take place in the United States. Troops are unable to practice integrated maneuvers as a unit for lack of sufficient space. Only segments of larger units can practice maneuvers at any one time, and soldiers are told to imagine there are troops at their side.

While Japan's navy is modernizing, they have had little experience deploying in open seas until recently. It is true that new American weapons systems are coming on line, but it takes more than superior technology to make for an effective naval force. One of Britain's most famous naval figures, Admiral Cunningham, has stated, "I can build a ship in 3 years, but it takes 300 years to build a fighting naval tradition."[28] For most of Japan's history, its navy has remained only a coastal force. Contemporary naval training time is restricted primarily to a few maneuvers in winter because they compete with local fishermen, whose activities take priority. After the 1990 Gulf war, Japan belatedly sent four minesweepers. But American naval officers stated that the Japanese navy would not have been consequential to the efforts of coalition forces.

Japan's air force, perhaps its most modern service, also receives little training. The Gulf war illustrated the principle that technology is no substitute for a pilot's ability to make full use of that technology. Crowded conditions have forced Japanese F-15 training exercises to take place hundreds of miles off the main island. With a fighting radius of just over five hundred miles, Japanese pilots must return after just a few combat simulations. Pilots almost never gain experience in maneuvers at military speeds using maximum thrusters because such sudden accelerations would propel them into the envelope of scheduled commercial air traffic. Moreover, Japanese F-15s are configured for air-to-air interdiction combat over Japan's islands and do not have the capability for the kind of look-down air-to-ground attack used by coalition aircraft in the Gulf war.[29]

Japan's defense budget grew an average of 6.4% during the 1980s, which was commensurate with the nation's economic growth. However, Japan does not squeeze out as much as other states do from their defense dollars. Japan spends 40% of its defense budget on personnel; the United States spends 27%. Licensed-built Japanese F-15s cost 50% more than United States-built F-15s, partly because the Japanese "handcraft" this older, all mechanical American design in order to increase its reliability. Japan's new Type-90 tank, reported to be lighter and less capable than the American equivalent, costs $8.6 million each, with just thirty ordered in 1992. The American M-1 tank costs $4.4 million, partly because the Pentagon buys 225–480 per year, invoking economies of scale.[30]

Japan's military forces are gradually moving toward an increased ability for sustainable defense, monitoring, and patrol missions. Japan has acquired the American global positioning system known as NAVSTAR and has moved down the path of least resistance in terms of military electronics, such as stealth technology, antisubmarine warfare, electronic warfare, and over-the-horizon radar technologies. Acquiring "defense only" weapons appears to be the most pragmatic route. In January 1993 the White House concluded a deal to introduce both the Aegis and AWACs systems into Japan in order to bolster the inadequate naval and air defense systems, at a cost of between $8 and $10 billion. This twin capability acts as an early warning and force-multiplier and should significantly enhance the current force structure and bring into Japan its first credible defense system.[31]

Japan's nuclear options, on the other hand, seem more limited. The prevailing politics are not favorable. However, a modest but sufficient nuclear option in the unforeseen circumstance of American withdrawal could be a small nuclear submarine force capable of carrying deterrent-only weapons. The older American Trident I is an excellent model. Trident I warheads with a single-shot kill-probability (SSKP) of just .05% against hardened targets such as land-based silos do not threaten primary offensive systems; thus, they themselves are not threatening to strategic adversaries. Strategic militaries would not feel inclined to launch their land-based systems prematurely, as the survival of their most prized weapon is assured. Trident II weapons are inappropriate, as their SSKP is 87% against hardened targets, placing Russia's weapons at prompt risk. Such overkill weapons invite anxiety. A hypothetical Japanese submarine force could be held in reserve and undetected beneath the sea and act as a sufficient nuclear deterrent with perhaps as few as a half-dozen submarines. A sea-based force would not deploy nuclear weapons on the Japanese island itself, thus preserving some semblance of not directly nuclearizing the archipelago. It would not disturb society as much or in the same way as land-based weapons have done elsewhere. It would also not be dramatically costly. No additional types of nuclear weapons would be necessary or desirable for strategic defense purposes. Rather, the presence of a sea-based, stealthy, and limited nonoffensive (defined in strategic terms) deterrent nuclear force incapable of detection may be militarily and politically a pragmatic route for a possible Japanese nuclear future. If misused, such forces could be threatening, as is the characteristic of all strategic weapons. But the record of nuclear weapons acquisition has not shown the outbreak of irrationality once forecast in the immediate postwar period. In and of itself, a permanently small submarine force would be a credible second-strike-only, stand-alone and sufficiently deterrent force that could substitute, if necessary, for the stability of the strategic balance currently provided by the American umbrella. Such a scenario would alter the atmospherics of East-West relations. The question is, does either side desire such a development?[32]

POLITICS OF THE U.S. TRADE DEFICIT

With the increasing perception of America's relative decline, calls have been made for Japan to compensate for the U.S. contribution that has benefitted Japan. Jobs, a declining standard of living, and the like have threatened the quality of the bilateral relationship.[33] Because Japan's military forces do not defend its nation, Americans have increasingly felt some need for compensation for their sacrifices on Japan's behalf. No official figures exist to describe the cost for America's defense in the Pacific region (though they do for NATO), but one study estimates the total cost of U.S. forces in the Pacific (including California and Hawaii) is between $36 and $50 billion annually. The Japanese share is reported to be about $8 billion.[34] The trade deficit has become linked to American sponsorship of Japan's national security costs. High on the U.S. list of demands has been restructuring Japan's economy in order to absorb more American imports.

Japanese economists, however, point out that the $45 billion trade deficit can be accounted for in part by the presence in Japan of over twelve hundred highly successful American companies who have chosen to manufacture and sell products in Japan and elsewhere, including back in the United States. Such "re-exports" of American manufacturing are counted as goods from Japan. The "trade deficit" is therefore a cocreation of both Japanese and American companies who are producing in Japan but ship products and components to the United States. Much of this trade is intrafirm transfers. Through the mid-1980s at least, the reciprocal Japanese manufacturing presence in America was only a fraction of the U.S. companies in Japan.

In addition, the flow of invisibles, such as payments for patents and licenses, does not get counted in trade-deficit statistics. Invisible flows have favored the United States. Together with predominantly one-way military sales to Japan from America, invisibles represent an estimated $15–$16 billion not accounted for in the broader United States–Japan economic relationship. If so calculated, the trade deficit could approach zero.[35]

The perception of the trade deficit caused the U.S. government to invoke a structural impediment initiative (SII) in its effort to encourage the expansion of large department stores and supermarkets in Japan that would presumably offer the Japanese consumer a greater choice of American-made goods. Small stores, by contrast, of every description in Japan cater to local tastes by relying on local Japanese producers. But department stores, which gross approximately $75 billion per year, carry a mix of domestic and foreign goods. What American policymakers do not seem to realize is that only about 10% of department store items are foreign, primarily from Europe. American products would capture perhaps one to two billion additional dollars, as Japanese consumers have historically preferred British woolens, French clothing, German cars, and other European products. The SII policy has sought to engineer a $1–$2 billion private corporation profit in exchange for disruptions out of proportion to the gain.

Because Japanese homes are small, space for large quantities of big- and small-ticket items are limited. Even refrigerators are small. Consumers shop every day and could not take advantage of large volumes of groceries at supermarkets, as most housewives must hand-carry what they buy and rely on crowded public transport to get home. There are practically no large supermarkets in Japan, and certainly no malls, and no parking lots for the handful of larger markets that do exist. Just as important, small stores and cafes serve as the backbone of economic and social life in Japan, even in the cities. Because private space in homes is limited, Japanese gather and socialize in cafes and convenience stores. At night the Japanese dine, meet, have coffee, or read magazines at the local small store for hours, usually until at least 10 P.M. and often later. Department stores close at 6 P.M. It is true that Japan's small shops are inefficient, but they serve an effective social and economic function. They absorb social overflow, serving as an extension of the living room, and keep the population employed and off welfare. When SII pressured the Japanese to introduce large department stores and supermarkets, they threatened the cultural structure of a society that has for centuries existed with this kind of neighborhood balance. U.S. authorities may be unwittingly trying to perform social engineering for a culture they do not understand and whose consequences would not be beneficial to anyone. The small shopkeepers are a critical support of the LDP, the party around which much of American foreign policy has rested. SII, at a minimum, is attempting to alter the pattern of wealth and structure in Japan because of its perceived trade deficit, a policy seemingly made necessary because of the cost of American defenses.[36]

In addition, the Japanese are attempting to upgrade their air capability with the joint development and production of the F-16 into an enhanced aircraft called the FS-X (Fighter Support-Experimental). American critics of the project warn of a technology giveaway planting the seed of Japan's impending civilian aircraft industry, further eroding American economic competitiveness. Such critics, however, fail to recognize that the development of a small, single-engine military craft is largely irrelevant to the manufacture of large Boeing 747–type passenger aircraft. The era when older Boeing 707s were converted from military bombers sharing common assemblyline runs is gone in today's increasingly sophisticated aviation industry. Boeing 747s are built for longevity, economy, comfort, and durability because they fly far and wide very frequently, often landing hard on unfamiliar tarmacs. The flight path is always a straight line at modest altitudes, and they are engineered to last for twenty years, placing a premium on fuel efficiency. They are designed to cruise at slow speeds and with high visibility without maneuverability or a capacity to sustain high G's that go beyond the craft's inherent aerodynamic stress and strain configurations. By contrast, the FS-X is a relatively delicate aircraft with a short life span of just five to eight years, with a fighting radius optimized for seek-and-destroy missions with rapid return. Fighters always display great and speedy maneuverability accompanied by an impressive turning radius for attack purposes, maxing out at 8 or 9 G's. They must possess versatile capabilities, not single-purpose capabilities, speeding both at treetop encountering dangerous drag and at extremely high altitudes that deprive engines of oxygen. Such fighters are designed to endure the absolute extremes of heat, cold, and stress over its components, thereby placing a premium on state-of-the-art materials, maximum engineering specifications, and faultless manufacture that optimizes weight-to-engine ratios. Military crafts forego fuel economy in favor of performance and must depend on computerized fly-by-wire navigational systems to point the craft between mountains more efficiently than human pilots could perform at such speeds. High angle-of-attack capabilities in which the fighter moves forward while virtually upright has become standard for defense and offense, using stealthy systems combined with a mix of weapons systems including nuclear-capable ones flying in coordination with complimentary air and naval forces in close quarters in disciplined but often unpredictable ways. In no manner does a lumbering 747 compare with a fighter design. Possession of blueprints from one design cannot be said to automatically transfer over to the other.[37]

MILITARY KEIRETSU?

U.S. political pressures have influenced other dimensions of Japanese society. Partly because of the original American postwar push and subsequent pressures, the Japanese military has formed a triple alliance with powerful LDP politicians and trading houses to form a kind of embedded military-industrial complex inside Japan. The Japanese defense industry exists under the rubric of Japan's major trading houses. Unlike the U.S. military-industrial complex, the Japanese defense industry does not exhibit single large companies that can stand alone based on defense contracts, as with General Dynamics and Lockheed. Rather, Japanese companies are intertwined in families of companies that tend to be functionally interdependent, called "keiretsu" (enterprise groupings). Prime manufacturers will be linked up with subcontractors who normally receive preference in all relevant business dealings over outsiders. Customarily, a major banking institution is associated in such a keiretsu, which provides inexpensive investment capital and generally bolsters the financial stability of the group over the long run.

Prime trading houses like Mitsubishi Heavy Industries (MHI), Kawasaki Heavy Industries (KHI), and Sumitomo make up the first line of Japan's national economy. Defense companies represent the second line. The fact that smaller, more dedicated defense companies represent the second line does not necessarily mean they are secondary. Shared research and development, management, and market expansion, as well as new technologies and financial arrangements, remain the mutual benefits to all group members. Such smaller defense companies depend on defense contracts for a larger proportion of their portfolio, sometimes over 50%, when compared with their larger parent firms. The important characteristics to note, however, are twofold: First, their interests and well-being are protected by the larger trading house, which may represent their ultimate well-being in ways and in places they as smaller firms could not. Second, because defense companies are embedded within the frontline, marquee firms, they can exist below the threshold of public consciousness and thus not call unnecessary attention or controversy to themselves. This gives them the capacity to operate unhindered by public pressures.

Moreover, as they exist beneath the surface of major firms, the second line may be efficiently emphasized or deemphasized, depending on the national and international conditions. That means that the defense industry is never really preeminent, nor is it ever really nonexistent. It is a flexible tier of the national economic structure. In return, it may help lend some flexibility to the parent firms under certain conditions, though it may also weigh them down. What is significant about this embedded relationship is that Japan's defense industry or, to perhaps exaggerate its position, its "military keiretsu" is an integrated part of the primary Japanese civilian industry. The military keiretsu is not a competitor to, apart from, or an irrelevant second to the Japanese economy. The persistence and growth of the military keiretsu is guaranteed. As part of the structure of the overall economy, Japan's defense industry is a permanent but variable feature of one of the world's most dynamic economies.

Since 1954, when the SDF emerged, the arms production tier has become a fixed feature influencing civilian industry. Japan has emphasized self-reliance, building all its own ships, nearly all its own aircraft (90%), ammunition (87%), and firearms (83%). The rate of domestically produced arms increased from 39.6% to 88.6% between 1950 and 1982, keeping pace with the nation's remarkable industrial rate of expansion.[38] Because in part Japan's military has not been permitted to purchase military equipment, other than from the United States, a policy to "buy Japan" has resulted in a situation in which "all manufacturing companies are involved in defense manufacturing." Because of defense industry trickle-down effects, the entire industrial complex of the nation is involved in defense procurements.[39] In an ironic twist, a recent reason for Japan's expansion of domestic arms production is the growing tendency of the United States not to share its latest cutting-edge technology with Japan. An additional pressure for arms growth is that the government needs continually to buy more from the defense firms in order to deflect them from searching for foreign markets. Higher-profile arms exports are not what the government wants.[40]

Only a tenth of Japan's defense procurements have originated from foreign sources since the 1970s. In 1983, twenty companies produced three fourths of Japan's military equipment, though three large firms made up nearly half of the total. In those companies defense production averages approximately 17%–20% of each company's total. If one includes subcontractors, some eight hundred Japanese companies are involved in defense work, compared with twenty-five to thirty thousand defense subcontractors in the United States. In terms of manpower, only 2.7% of the total labor force works directly in defense, but of the forty-nine million workers many more personnel "straddled defense and civilian contracts."[41] Japan has just twenty thousand aerospace workers, less than the number employed by Boeing's commercial aviation division. One hundred defense companies employ fifty-three thousand people. But in 1983, 2,366 Japanese companies registered to do defense contract work. Japanese arms producers lack certain characteristics normally associated with that industry: (1) heavy reliance on arms production for fiscal solvency, (2) prime government R&D

sponsorship, and (3) arms export. Japan's R&D for defense is the most modest among advanced states, at 1.49% compared with 11% or more for the United States and 12% for the United Kingdom.[42]

Arms production in Japan, moreover, appears to be a lucrative business; a survey of sixty-seven companies showed that nearly three quarters expressed the intention to expand their arms division while the remaining ones would continue at current levels. Arms production acts as a "cushion" against possible recessions but is also a source of investment and technology. Arms production earned 50% higher profits than the Japanese automobile industry in recent years. MHI reported military aircraft profits of from 4% to 5%, compared with its typical 1.8% profit margin between 1978 and 1983.[43] More recently, Japan's number-two trading house, Kawasaki Heavy Industries (KHI), and number-three Ishikawajima-Harima Heavy Industries (IHI) received a 10% expansion in certain defense orders and have generally experienced "brisk business" because of their defense divisions in 1989. Since 1991, greater uncertainty has returned, and the big three have stated they will reevaluate their defense emphasis for the next several years, shifting perhaps to communications, robotics, software engineering, and joint jet-engine ventures with General Electric.[44]

One lure of the defense industry is its dual-use nature. Mitsubishi developed an air-to-air missile similar to the Sidewinder, as well as an air-to-surface missile in concert with fifty-three companies, using parts originally developed for civilian applications. Twenty-three percent of the value of Japan's T-74 tank is comprised of electronics.[45] Civilian products may have military applications because the end-user decides how Japanese products can be used. Kawasaki helicopters have been converted by Sweden, Burma, and Saudi Arabia for antisubmarine and related military missions. U.S. smart bombs in Vietnam used Sanyo video cameras as part of their guidance system. Half of Japan's $55 billion electronic industries in 1987 went abroad, surpassing the value of auto exports since 1984. Japan has constructed bases and docking platforms in foreign countries that are used for military purposes, including the installation at Vladivostok that had been announced for civilian purposes. According to one report, Hitachi can, if it chooses, readily use up to half of its twenty-seven factories and six R&D facilities for defense technologies. In 1985, Japan's semiconductor production, valued at $7.7 billion, exported 25%. Kyocera exported its ceramic-coated, highly reliable semiconductors to the United States, which manufactures the nuclear-capable cruise missile Tomahawk, which probably deployed them back to the U.S. Seventh Fleet inside Tokyo Bay.[46]

Primarily through dual-use technologies and because Japan's arms are defined so narrowly, Japan has no figures on arms exports. However, an American study calculated that in 1986 Japan exported $210.8 billion of army-relateable products abroad, a 19% increase from the previous year.[47] Japan's explicit defense industry strategy is a manifestation of the "principle of an integrated civil and military industry." This is possible now that civilian electronics are as rugged and often more reliable than their old military counterparts in the U.S. industry.

Flexible manufacturing allows for low-volume, multiproduct manufacturing that is as efficient as mass production.[48]

Because of Japan's high de facto content of militarily relevant R&D in its civilian production, the United States in turn has come to rely on Japanese innovations for much of its high-tech weapons program. The United States is dependent on Japanese dual-use products for "critical subcomponents," including the silicon field-effect transistors, gallium arsenide chips, and precision optics used extensively in the war with Iraq. The 1983 Memorandum of Understanding with Japan opening the way for Japanese technology to flow into the United States was largely aimed at obtaining products first developed by Japan's civilian industry but which possessed "military applications."[49] The extent of United States–Japan sharing is greater than most Americans realize. Half of NEC is owned by Honeywell, Fujitsu has ties with Siemens, and Mitsubishi with Motorola, Hughes, and IBM. RCA, Ford, G.E., and others more recently, like Texas Instruments and Intel, have a significant presence in Japan.[50] In 1984–85 a team of American military experts from the Defense Department toured eight Japanese companies and subsequently asked to purchase thirty-eight high-technology products. The U.S. government spent $5.6 billion in military orders in Japan in the 1950s and averaged $500 million per year thereafter to the 1980s. Reinhard Drifte summarized that Japan received approximately $10 billion in advanced technology from the United States between 1950 and 1983. In return, the U.S. companies received from 30% to 40% of the cost of building such American weapons systems.[51] Japan, along with Italy, ranked first in the world with regard to worldwide licensed production of major weapons systems between 1960 and 1988. Japan is building close to thirty major weapons systems in this manner and South Korea half that number, with the United Kingdom and Germany following with a third as much. In fact, the United States transfers more major weapons systems to Japan than to any other nation. The Bush administration actively promoted the sale of U.S. arms to American allies, calling it a type of "defense GATT" and proposing that the Export-Import Bank provide funds to Japanese firms to purchase military equipment from U.S. companies.[52] T. J. Pempel has noted that Japan does so because it desires American technology, especially since the rise of American technonationalism, prompting Japan to become more integrated with U.S. industries.[53] But American competitiveness has historically depended primarily on an open economy, even to foreign trade. Changing it now would take away our best attribute.[54] Nonetheless, U.S. arms cooperation with Japan is likely to increase. The Japanese defense industry is still too embedded within its larger civilian industry network to be able to stand on its own. Vertical expansion is not possible. Horizontal extension represents the only other logical route to expansion. Therefore, cooperation with American arms makers represents Japan's best route to acquire technology for possible civilian application, new market entry, and defense products. Moreover, in the emerging context of peace and a downshift in President Clinton's defense force structure, American firms may be pressured to share risks and costs with

Japan as a means of assuring their own financial survival in the post–Cold War era.

Moreover, as the Japanese make use of the enormous inventive civilian capabilities for products that are militarily relevant, U.S. defense companies can tap into them. In this case, Japan's civilian sector can perform some of the R&D that can have a desirable effect in the United States. A symbiosis has emerged between the U.S. and Japanese defense industries. The twin military-industrial complexes have become connected, merging some of their finances, products, engineering, management interoperability, corporate interests, and objectives. What this means, among other consequences, is that to the extent Japan imprints Asia with Japan-compatible civilian industries, the United States gains additional access to dual-use technologies originally out from Japan. While government-to-government technological reciprocity may be more complex and fraught with bottlenecks, firm-to-firm technology sharing may continue independently. Thus a simple two-way flow between the United States and Japan could be enhanced via a thickening network of multiple global sourcing inspired by one or both of the two defense complexes. In Greek mythology the owl of Minerva is supposed to have said, "Wisdom comes only at the end of the day." Only after the day is over, or an era is over, do we understand the true meaning of the events that took place. Such a delayed acknowledgment may not serve global peace and prosperity well. Scholars, policymakers, and ordinary citizens must ponder what will come from the marriage of Japan's military keiretsu with America's military-industrial complex.

NOTES

For their continued guidance and encouragement, I wish to thank Robert Scalapino and Kenneth Waltz both at the University of California and Chalmers Johnson at the University of California at San Diego. At the White House and the Department of Defense, Karl Jackson, Terkel Patterson, and James Auer provided valuable insights and materials without which this chapter would have been diminished. Both Carl and Charles Bernard at CBC Avionics suggested vital technical evaluations, and Richard Slowey and A. R. Mann at General Dynamics provided generously their time and expertise. In Japan, Seizaburo Sato at Tokyo University and Katsuhisa Yamada, president of Kawasaki Heavy Industries and former director-general at JDA, provided much assistance, as did Tohru Nagamori at NKK, Risaburo Nezu at MITI, and Shiro Nagato and Yoshifumi Fujita at the Defense Agency. The students and faculty at the International Relations Department at San Francisco State, along with my research assistant Kazumi Nei, contributed to the insights of this chapter. All errors of interpretation are mine.

1. See Mikiso Hane, *Modern Japan* (Boulder, Colo.: Westview Press, 1984); also John Fairbank, Edwin Reischauer and Albert Craig, *East Asia* (Dallas: Houghton Mifflin, 1978).

2. Defense Agency, *Defense of Japan* (Tokyo: Japan Times, 1987), pp. 126–31.

3. Masashi Nishihara, personal communication, July 1988, Yokosuka.

4. Edwin Hoyt, *The Militarists* (New York: Donald Fine, 1985), pp. 207–9.

5. Tetsuya Kataoka and Ramon Myers, *Defending an Economic Superpower* (Boulder, Colo.: Westview Press, 1989), p. 75.

6. Ibid., pp. 72–74.

7. Masashi Nishihara, "The Japanese Central Organization of Defense," in Martin Edmonds, ed., *Central Organization of Defense* (Boulder, Colo.: Westview Press, 1985), p. 13.

8. Kataoka and Myers, *Economic Superpower*, p. 74; also see Nishihara, "Japanese Central Organization," p. 142.

9. Ibid., pp. 65–68.

10. Nishihara, "Japanese Central Organization," p. 142.

11. Kataoka and Myers, *Economic Superpower*, pp. 75–79.

12. Eiichi Katahar, *Japan's Changing Political and Security Role* (Singapore: Institute of SE Asian Studies Press, 1991), pp. 7, 11–12; see also John Endicott, "Japanese-American Defense Policies for a Post-Reagan Era," in Ronald Morse, ed., *U.S.–Japan Relations* (Lanham, Md.: University Press of America, 1989).

13. Michael Chinworth, "Industry and Government in Japanese Defense Procurement: The Case of the Patriot Missile System," *Comparative Strategy* 9 (1990): 196, 204–5, 211.

14. Katsuya Hirose, *Kanryo to Gunjin (Bureaucrats and Soldiers)* (Tokyo: Iwanami Shoten, 1989), pp. 118, 120, 212, 215.

15. Kataoka and Myers, *Economic Superpowers*, p. 68.

16. Nishihara, "Japanese Central Organization," p. 142.

17. See Chalmers Johnson, *MITI and the Japanese Miracle* (Stanford, Calif.: Stanford University Press, 1982); for a contemporary definition, see Chalmers Johnson, "Japan in Search of a 'Normal' Role," *Daedalus* (Fall 1992); also see Richard Rosecrance, *The Rise of the Trading State.*

18. Ibid., p. 15.

19. Kar-yiu Wong, "National Defense and Foreign Trade," in John Makin and Donald Hellmann, eds., *Sharing World Leadership?* (Washington, D.C.: American Enterprise Institute for Public Policy Research, 1989), p. 110.

20. Kenneth Waltz, "A Strategy for the Rapid Deployment of Force," in Robert Art and Kenneth Waltz, eds., *The Use of Force* (Lanham, Md.: University Press of America, 1988), pp. 566–69.

21. J. Javed Maswood, *Japanese Defence* (Singapore: Institute of SE Asian Studies Press, 1990), p. 27.

22. Waltz, "Rapid Deployment," pp. 566–572.

23. Henry Kissinger, "East Asia, the Pacific and the West: Strategic Trends and Implications," *Adelphi Paper 21* (London: International Institute for Strategic Studies, 1987), pp. 3–4.

24. Len Humphreys, personal communication, Stockton, Calif., 1988; see also Masashi Nishihara, "The Soviet Threat," in Eric Grove, ed., *Global Security* (London: Brassey's, 1991), see esp. pp. 58–59.

25. Kataoka and Myers, *Economic Superpowers*, p. 108.

26. Norman Levin, *Japan Changing Defense Posture* (Santa Monica, Calif.: Rand Corporation, 1988), p. 15.

27. Richard Halloran, *Chrysanthemum and the Sword Revisited* (Honolulu: East-West Center, 1992), pp. 7–9.

28. See Colin Gray, *Seapower and Strategy* (New York: Ramapo Press, 1986).

29. Defense Agency, *Defense of Japan,* 1987.

30. Halloran, *Chrysanthemum,* pp. 6–7.

31. Karl Johnson, personal communication, the White House, January 1993.

32. Seizaburo Sato, personal communication, Tokyo, 1988; see also Kenneth Waltz, "The Spread of Nuclear Weapons: More May Be Better," *Adelphi Paper 171* (London: International Institute for Strategic Studies, 1981).

33. Robert Scalapino, "The United States and Asia," *Foreign Affairs* (Winter 1991/ 2), p. 47.

34. Kataoka and Myers, *Economic Superpowers,* pp. 99–100.

35. See Kenichi Ohmae, *Fact or Friction* (Tokyo: Japan Times Press, 1990).

36. Andrew Hanami, "Japan's Strategy in Europe," unpublished paper, Conference of the European Consortium for Political Research, Heidelberg, Germany, September 1992.

37. Andrew Hanami, *The Military Might of Modern Japan* (Dubuque, Iowa: Kendall/ Hunt, 1995), ch. 2.

38. Reinhard Drifte, *Arms Production in Japan* (Boulder, Colo.: Westview Press, 1986), pp. 11, 13, 21, 34.

39. Malcolm McIntosh, *Japan Re-armed* (London: Frances Pinter, 1986), p. 52.

40. William Keller, *Global Arms Trade* (Washington, D.C.: Office of Technology Assessment, 1991), p. 115.

41. Kataoka and Myers, *Economic Superpowers,* pp. 58–60, 62, 64–65.

42. Drifte, *Arms Production,* p. 3, 26, 29, 62.

43. Ibid., pp. 25–26; see also Reinhard Drifte, *Japan's Rise to International Responsibilities* (London: Athlone Press, 1990), pp. 16–17.

44. Keller, *Global Arms Trade,* pp. 112–14.

45. Drifte, *Arms Production,* pp. 67–68; also McIntosh, *Japan Re-armed,* pp. 51–53.

46. Ibid., pp. 40, 74–75.

47. Dong Joon Kwang, "Regional Arms Production Cooperation and Pacific Security," in Dora Alves, *Change, Interdependence and Security in the Pacific Basin* (Washington, D.C.: National Defense University Press, 1991), p. 128.

48. Jacques Gansler, "Collaboration, Internationalization and Security," in Ethan Kapstein, ed., *Global Arms Production* (Lanham, Md.: University Press of America, 1992), pp. 53–54.

49. Jack Numm, "Arms Cooperation in the Pacific Basin," in Kapstein, ed., *Global Arms Production,* p. 153.

50. Helena Tuomi and Raimo Vayrynen, *Transnational Corporation, Armaments and Development* (Hampshire, Great Britain: Gower, 1982), p. 81.

51. Drifte, *Arms Production,* pp. 10, 12, 81–82.

52. William Keller, "Global Defense Business," in Kapstein, ed., *Global Arms Production* pp. 66, 80–82, 89.

53. See T. J. Pempel, "From Trade to Technology: Japan's Reassessment of Military Policies," *Jerusalem Journal of International Relations* 12, no. 4 (1990).

54. Martin Libicki, *What Makes Industries Strategic* (Washington, D.C.: Institute for National Strategic Studies, 1989), pp. 69–70.

REFERENCES

Chinworth, Michael. "Industry and Government in Japanese Defense Procurement: The Case of the Patriot Missile System." *Comparative Strategy* 9 (1990).

Drifte, Reinhard. *Arms Production in Japan.* Boulder, Colo.: Westview Press, 1986.

Hanami, Andrew K. *The Military Might of Modern Japan.* Dubuque, Iowa: Kendall/ Hunt, 1995.

Hirose, Katsuya. *Kanryo to Gunjin (Bureaucrats and Soldiers).* Tokyo: Iwanami Shoten, 1989.

Kapstein, Ethan, ed. *Global Arms Production.* Lanham, Md.: University Press of America, 1992.

Kataoka, Tetsuya, and Ramon Myers. *Defending an Economic Superpower.* Boulder, Colo.: Westview Press, 1989.

McIntosh, Malcolm. *Japan Re-armed.* London: Frances Pinter, 1986.

Nishihara, Masashi. "The Japanese Central Organization of Defense." In Martin Edmonds, ed., *Central Organizations of Defense.* Boulder, Colo.: Westview Press, 1985.

KENYA

Cobie Harris

The military structure of the African sub-Saharan states was designed by the colonial powers for the sole purpose of subjugating and repressing African people in order to protect and advance their own interests. In the white-settler, colonial states of Kenya, Zimbabawe, and South Africa, the analytic separation between the military and civilian spheres was purely artificial. The military was a partisan, rather than an impartial or neutral, actor whose primary function was to protect the white citizenry from external aggression, which in turn helped to support the political hegemony of the white minority.

The paradigm of a colonial military based on the elimination of all non-British opposition to colonial rule left an indelible imprint on the shaping of the post-colonial relations between the civilian population and the military. The major challenge facing newly independent African states was how to transpose a partisan-structured and colonial military into a neutral professional army. In sub-Saharan Africa this problem was particularly critical because the military was the main provider of employment and also one of the few major organizations in society that was organized to defend the soldiers' ideal and material interests. The military's pursuit of its ideal interest, namely, to maintain their esprit de corps and organizational integrity, and its material interest, to garner sufficient resources to pay soldiers and purchase military supplies, has not achieved significant economic development in Africa. The inevitable result has been an intense rivalry between Africa's civil and military authorities over the utilization of their society's wealth.

This chapter focuses on the interaction between civil and military power in Kenya. Specifically, it addresses how the constellation and evolution of power between these two social forces have prevented direct military intervention.

Historically, Kenyan civil-military relations can be divided into two periods: (1) the seventy-year colonial period beginning in 1895 with the conquest and

Table 1
White Settlement in the Kenya Highlands¹

	Year				
	1915	*1920*	*1934*	*1942*	*1953*
Number of settlers	1,000	1,200	2,000	3,000	4,000
Occupied acreage	4.5 m.	3.1 m.	5.1 m.	6.3 m	7.3 m.

subjugation of African people by British imperial forces and ending in 1964 with independence and the period from 1964 to the present.²

The first period in Kenya was defined by the establishment of British totalitarian rule over African civil society. Complete political and economic dominance over the African majority was achieved through repeated military interventions to maintain the total subordination of African interests to British interests. The greatest period of conflict between the colonial armed forces and the indigenous people occurred from the time of the founding of the British Crown Colony through the next ten to fifteen years of occupation. The last great insurrection, when the Kikuyu people fought against British rule in what is known as the "Mau Mau Revolt," occurred from 1952 to 1960. The catalyst for the "Mau" insurrection was the white settlers' alienation of the most fertile land in Kenya from the Kikuyu people (see Table 1). Their consistent practice of expropriating the Kikuyu's best lands led to the marginalization of the Kikuyu people, eventually forcing them off their own farmlands to become either rural and urban squatters or low-paid agricultural workers on white settlers' plantations.

White settlers also attempted to construct political and economic structures in Kenya that resembled a form of apartheid. In fact, the only major difference between Kenya and South Africa was that in Kenya the Asians had acquired more political and economic rights and the white-settler minority was much smaller.

This peculiar constellation of Asians, Africans, and Europeans coupled with an unequal distribution of political and economic power had a direct impact on the evolution of civil-military forces in postcolonial Kenya. The British subjugation of African people in Kenya radically transformed the precolonial societies when they usurped Africa's heretofore independent nationalities and their territories by superior military force. The British then forcibly combined all of the different African nationalities into a nation-state they called Kenya. The very "idea" of Kenya was a colonial creation. More important, it was a notion created and designed against the will of the African people. Kenya was not created to bring liberty and justice to African people or to establish a more perfect union or to develop the resources of Kenya to benefit African people. Instead, Kenya's primary raison d'être was to serve the needs and interests of the British empire.

In the late 1890s, the primary need of the British was to maintain strategic geographic control over all areas in East Africa connected with Egypt, the Nile River, and the Red Sea. The desire to prevent Germany or France from gaining a strategic advantage over Egypt and the Suez Canal compelled Britain to colonize Sudan and assist the Italians in gaining control over Eritrea. Once the Germans, in search of the source of the Nile, occupied Tanganyika, the British felt compelled to occupy what is today called Kenya and Uganda.

After the British decided to occupy Uganda and Kenya, the next issue was how to pay for the troops and personnel needed to suppress the indigenous population and to protect British interests in the region. The British decision to construct a railroad between Kampala and Mombasa represented the beginnings of "Kenya." When the British began to consolidate control over the region, they realized that the Kenyan highland area contained enough arable land to sustain commercial agricultural production. The High Commissioner for Kenya decided that white settlers could most efficiently produce cash crops that could then be shipped to overseas markets and paid for in foreign currency to defray the costs of the colonies. Their strategy was to make the colony pay for itself by giving huge grants of African-owned lands to white settlers, who would then exploit the labor of the very Africans forced off the land. After the British stole the Africans' land and distributed it to European settlers, they employed colonial armed forces to act as instruments for social control and enforce British land policy.

The Africans responded to the forcible expropriation of their lands and liberty in two ways: resistance and accommodation. African patriots like Harry Thuku, who refused to accept the legitimacy of British rule, were arrested. When Thuku and his supporters led nonviolent protests against the colonial policy that forced Africans to wear *kipandes* (I.D. tags) around their necks like dogs, they were killed.[3] On the other hand, some Kikuyus, particularly from the Kiambu region, who had joined missionary schools actually assisted the colonial authorities to maintain control over Kenya. The African collaborators who helped the British capture African revolutionaries were called "home guards."[4]

The British colonial armed forces did not operate on the principles of neutrality, nonintervention in the domestic affairs of a colony, or majority rule. Instead, the Kenya colonial armed forces were created as a coercive instrument to impose and support colonial totalitarianism against the African population. As in all other colonial regimes, the military was neither neutral nor professional, but instead served the interests of the dominant "political class."[5] Thus, the pattern of military intervention and domination of the polity in African states was more consistent than inconsistent with the colonial model, as colonization was responsible for introducing the concept of "professional armed forces," that is, a permanent group of armed forces in the independent society.

Another way in which the introduction of white settlers shaped Kenyan society was the commercialization of agricultural production, which in turn created a demand for other activities to support it. Light industry emerged to supply tools for expanding the agricultural economy. Urbanization and infrastructure development occurred, such as the construction of roads and water and sewage lines. In addition to the economic implications of the introduction of commercialized agriculture, sociocultural effects also occurred such as the formation of an African working class and a small sector of commercialized African farmers.[6]

Demographic changes took place when the British imported Indian laborers to build the roads connecting the urban centers with the "white highlands" and to install a railroad from Mombasa to Kampala. The urban origin of most of these new arrivals to Kenya permanently changed the demographics of the area and facilitated Kenya's transformation from a working-class to a merchant-class economy. However, the immigrant's mobility was limited, as the British allowed only Africans and Europeans to own land in the highland area and denied this right to Asians. The net effect of the commercialization of agriculture in Kenya was the emergence of capitalism, which served as a brake on military intervention in the postcolonial period. In this environment, strong economic interest groups began to assume the role of a countervailing power to the military.

In Kenya, the mandate to govern the African people was based exclusively on British military power, as Kenya was founded as a British colony. Kenya's constitutional structure had a subsequent evolution of democracy and capitalism because government was based on neither the consent of the people nor majority rule. In Kenya democratic political associations such as parties or interest groups were not allowed until independence. For example, to protect the viability of "white-settler" cash-crop production, Europeans forced Africans to work on their plantations in order to pay the imposed hut taxes, which could be paid only in British currency. Railway unions were also not allowed.

Paradoxically, the internal organization of the white-settler community was very democratic, a fact noted by Winston Churchill, who stated that every settler was a politician.[7] This sense of entitlement was derived from the American Revolution, which made it possible for all British citizens living overseas to retain the basic rights of citizenship afforded to them at home. This particular orientation to citizenship, where legislative and executive councils were developed to advise the colonial governors, provided a colonial institutional framework for African self-government. The Africans, however, were not allowed to participate in such "workshops of democracy" because the colonial administration and white settlers believed such protests would have challenged white supremacy.

In fact, the British did not allow African representation on the legislative and executive councils until after World War II.[8] When African representation was finally allowed, the British gave Africans only one seat on the Legislative Council to represent eight to ten million Kenyans, while whites were allowed more than twenty seats to represent less than five hundred thousand Kenya whites.[9]

Given the small percentage of whites and the proximity of India to Kenya, Asians were able to gain representation on the councils before Africans because they lobbied for coequal status with the white settlers. Even Asian immigrants were able to gain more power than Africans did in their own country.

The end of World War II fundamentally changed the relationship between the colonizer and the colonized. A war fought for freedom and justice became the rallying cry for many of the colonized to demand independence from their colonial rulers. The growing momentum for freedom led to the independence of India and to subsequent wars of liberation in Viet Nam, Malaysia, and within a decade in Kenya.

This upsurge in the demand for independence could be attributed to two factors: First, the colonized, who had been recruited to fight for justice in Europe, were not entitled to justice in their own lands. Second, the United Nations issued the Universal Declaration of Human Rights, which categorically stated that all people had the right to self-determination.

Kenya's ongoing struggle for independence was intensified with the increasing impoverishment of the Kikuyu people who were most directly affected by the white settlers' expropriation of Kenya's most fertile lands. Settler expropriation forcibly incorporated the Kikuyu into the commercialized agricultural system and the more general market economy. The Kikuyu tradition of giving land to new families intensified the conflict with white settlers because the presence of white settlers blocked the natural expansion of Kikuyus into the ''white'' highlands. Moreover, the inability of Kikuyus to give land to start new families endangered the cultural and social integrity of the Kikuyu people.

Instead, the Kikuyus were forced to become either squatters on white plantations or plantation workers. Kikuyus also became squatters and workers in the urban sector. The only option for those few remaining Kikuyus who owned plots was to compete with whites by engaging in cash-crop production.

In the 1950s the Kikuyus faced a growing political cleavage between the smallholder farmers who were producing cash crops and establishing a strong economic position and the urban/rural squatters and peasants who were landless and penniless. The division spiraled into the ''Mau Mau'' revolt, which was essentially two-dimensional. On one side, a civil war developed between the Kikuyus who owned land and collaborated with the British and the Kikuyus who were landless and fought the British. On the other side, the Kikuyus joined forces to overthrow the colonial regime. Eventually, Britain declared a state of emergency, ending in the arrest and detention of Jomo Kenyatta, incorrectly considered the leader of the insurrection. The real leader of the Kenya Land and Freedom Army (Mau Mau) was Dedan Kimathi, who was eventually captured and hanged for leading an insurrection against colonial rule.[10]

Although the British repressed the Mau Mau revolt, it demonstrated that without external support the British could not defend themselves against the African majority. The South African system of apartheid was clearly not a viable option for Kenya's small white minority. Postwar Britain had neither the political nor the economic resources to support white minority rule in Kenya. White settlers came to the somber realization that the future of Kenya meant government by the African majority. Moreover, for the first time since the founding of Kenya, the Asian community also had to contend with the African majority.

It was at this historical juncture that the colonial regime and the white-settler community decided that the role of the military, which from its founding had been biased toward the white minority regime and British colonial policy, should be "neutral" and more "professional." They proposed that, rather than perpetuate its role as the maintainer of social order (i.e., to maintain white supremacy or to support black power) the military should be transformed into a neutral nonpoliticized entity. Just when Africans were prepared to assume power, the colonial regime and its most powerful interest group, the white settlers, attempted to delink the state and politics from the military. The following section examines the transformation of the armed forces from an instrument for implementing government policy to a neutral, nonpolitical armed force.

POSTCOLONIAL INDEPENDENCE PERIOD AND THE ARMED FORCES

On the eve of independence, the major social forces that had led Kenya to independence, namely, white settlers, Asian commercial interests, smallholder African commercial farmers, and the political class, were compelled to redefine the relationship between the state and the armed forces, as the African majority was soon going to assume power. Whereas the primary function of the colonial armed forces had been to support white-settler supremacy and British colonialism, Africans knew that these same armed forces could also be used to destroy the economic power of Asians, white settlers, and the rising class of African commercial farmers and businessmen.

A key issue, however, confronting the nationalist leadership and the other major groups in Kenya's transition to independence and democracy was whether or not an African-controlled country would use the military and state power in a positive way to assist Africans to regain the stolen lands acquired by the white settlers. The independent government also debated over whether the civil service and armed forces should be Africanized and foreign ownership of business in Kenya restricted, compelling all private-sector employers to Africanize their employment patterns. Other options under consideration were whether the Kenyan state should be a constitutional state that emphasized protection of individual rights and property and limited government intervention in civil society or become a liberal constitutional state that would preserve the economic and social position of whites and Asians in Kenya.

The manner in which African nationalist leaders proposed to address these major constitutional issues led to a split within the Kenyan nationalist movement. The Kenyan African National Union (KANU), the leading opposition to colonial rule, was divided because of the emergence of a new opposition movement, called the Kenya African Democratic Union (KADU). KADU was organized by a coalition of minority African nationalities who feared domination by the larger nationalities. KADU advocated that the Kenyan constitution provide statutory protection for minority and property rights. These ideas led to a natural alliance between KADU, the smaller African nationalities, and whites and Asians, all deeply concerned about protecting their property rights from the African majority. However, when it came time to vote for the party that would govern independent Kenya, KADU disbanded, and its members joined KANU. From that point to the present, Kenya became a one-party state governed by KANU.

The political cleavages represented by the formation of KADU were coupled with yet another major cleavage, over the question of whether Kenya should become a capitalist or socialist state. The socialist tendency in KANU was advanced by Oginga Odinga, Bildad Kaggia, Achieng Oneko, J. D. Kali, and Gama Pinto, who advocated Africanization, nationalization of foreign interests and banks, and the free transfer of lands from white settlers to landless Africans.[11] The procapitalist position was represented by Jomo Kenyatta, Tom Mboya, and James Gichuru, who supported close cooperation with their former colonizer, Great Britain, the EEC, and the United States. These leaders also favored private property rights for white settlers and Asians. Freedom fighters of the 1950s and those who favored the socialist tendency believed the procapitalist sentiment betrayed the spirit of the fight for independence because it accepted the right of settlers to retain lands stolen from Africans. Bildad Kaggia articulated the vision of the radical movement in the following comment:

Everyone in this country is very well aware of the land hunger that has existed among Africans as a result of the robbery of their land by the British colonial imperialists. The logical method to solve the problem posed by this robbery would have been to nationalize all big estates owned by the Europeans and make them either state farms, so as to alleviate unemployment, or hand to cooperatives formed by landless Africans.[12]

The radicals also felt that the Lancaster House constitutional settlement, which officially handed power to the African majority, included safeguards that protected white and Asian jobs in the civil service and, most important, required that all property owned in Kenya, especially by whites, be purchased. Kaggia caustically commented on KANU's acceptance of the Lancaster House Agreement:

KANU leaders lost the battle against the immigrant races when they accepted those sections in the constitution which safeguarded private property and interests. Many people thought that the constitution was going to be amended soon after Uhuru. But government policies after independence strengthened the entrenched classes instead of weakening them.[13]

Jomo Kenyatta, Kenya's first president, articulated KANU's conservative position regarding the demand for land redistribution and some form of socialism in the following statement: "Those Africans who think that when we have achieved our freedom they can walk into a shop and say, "This is my property," or go onto a farm and say, "This is my farm" are very much mistaken, because this is not our aim."[14]

The intraparty struggle in KANU over whether Kenya should become a socialist or capitalist state forced the radical wing of KANU to form a new party, the Kenyan Peoples Union. Formed in 1966 to articulate and advance the interests of the landless peasants and urban poor, its leadership was detained after Kisumu residents stoned Kenyatta's motorcade. In response, the police massacred forty-three people.[15] By 1969, KPU was banned, signaling the end of organized opposition to one-party domination in Kenya politics. Although heroic individuals like Josiah Mwangi Kariuki, George Anyona, Raila Odinga, and others resisted the one-party state, it was not until 1992 that opposition parties were legalized in Kenya.

After the procapitalist faction of KANU banned the KPU, detained their leaders, and successfully defeated the radical tendency, Jomo Kenyatta, white settlers, Asian commercial businessmen, and a coalition of commercial African farmers assured the triumph of procapitalist forces. During the transition and early days of the Kenyan state, KANU's raison d'être—private property, commercial agriculture, export crops, urbanization, and profit maximization—was created and nurtured by capitalism. Radical populists were considered primitive rebels because of their desire to organize society around a different ethic. Ironically, radical populists lacked the sophisticated organizational means necessary to effectively combat the social forces engendered by the rise of capitalism because they possessed neither an ideology to displace capitalism nor a strategy to overturn the engine of Kenyan economic development and agricultural commercialization. Like the Luddites, who attempted to stop the march of technological civilization by destroying machines, the Kenyan opposition thought they could stop agribusiness by giving land to the tiller.

The political and economic hegemony of the procapitalists had a decisive impact on the structure and function of the military. In the initial formation of colonialism and the capitalist economy, the armed forces were essential in destroying precolonial African socioeconomic organization by coercing Africans to become laborers and producers for the market economy. Before independence, the armed forces were directly involved in the creation and maintenance of Kenya as a colony; Britain used them to exploit the Africans, to expropriate their lands for the white settlers, and to defend the interests of the white settler minority. In this phase, the military was clearly a partisan actor; through military domination, they successfully created and maintained private property and promoted commercialized agriculture. Ironically, the British armed forces' total repression of all African opposition culminating in the defeat of the Kikuyu national liberation army, which had fought to destroy commercialized agriculture, the anchor of capitalism in Kenya, established the principle that armed forces should be apolitical in the postcolonial period. Hence, military power and repression were used to assure that the social forces that supported the maintenance of capitalism, such as white-settler commercial farmers, African commercial farmers, and Asian and European businesses, would triumph over the more populist/socialist tendency in KANU.

Moreover, in postcolonial Kenya the success of commercial African farmers, businessmen, and salaried workers, reinforced by Asian commercial interests and white settlers, helped to establish KANU's position that the Kenyan armed forces should be apolitical and the continued use of British officers until the mid-1970s. A case in point about the dominance of this coalition was an agreement between the association's members to purchase land in the white highlands from the white settlers, resettle landless Africans, and integrate the civil service.

Beginning in 1960, the great settlement schemes initiated and implemented by the British government to curb the social basis for the MAU MAU insurrection were continued by the independent Kenyan government as a means to ensure continuity between the colonial and postcolonial system. The goals of resettlement were to transform landless African squatters into property owners by buying white-settler lands and creating an African petite-bourgeoisie class (or yeoman class) based on commercialized agriculture that would serve as a stabilizing force in the rural area. By 1970, half a million people had resettled on the major lands, at a cost of about £27 million. A third of the money was borrowed from foreign sources to buy African lands.[16] The income generated by resettlement, which allowed the African farmer to engage in commercialized agriculture, increased by over 400%. Gavin Kitching writes, "In the period between 1958 to 1968 the gross farm revenue of African smallholders in Kenya grew from a little under KL8 million to over KL34 million, an increase of over 425% in a decade."[17]

Two new social classes emerged as a result of these economic developments. The "yeoman" class dramatically increased, coupled with the already established white-settler class. Together they forged a natural alliance with procapitalist Jomo Kenyatta's faction of KANU. These social forces depoliticized the postcolonial armed forces because intervention would have undermined the operation of the market and restricted property ownership.

The other major social force that militated against politicizing the armed forces was the rising urban Kenyan bourgeoisie. Originally, the economic basis for this class comprised mainly cash crops like tea and coffee, rather than light-industry production or commercial business. However, the advent of independence solidified this class of Kenyan entrepreneurs by providing preferential access to such areas of the economy as trade and by the regulation of licensing.[18]

For example, the Trade Licensing Act of 1967 excluded noncitizens from trading in rural and nonurban areas and specified a list of goods that were to be restricted to citizen traders. Initially, the list of goods included such items as maize, rice, and sugar, but it was later expanded to include goods like cement and textiles.[19] In addition, Kenyan businessmen created the Kenyan National Corporation to handle import-export trade in order to penetrate the wholesale and retail market that before independence had been controlled exclusively by noncitizens. To further consolidate their position in the wholesale and retail sector, they successfully lobbied in 1975 to amend the trade and licensing agreement so that all goods manufactured in Kenya by foreign firms had to be distributed through Kenyan National Trade Corporation-appointed citizen agents. Independence enabled this class of African commercial interests to rise through the creation of large-scale credit institutions, such as the Agricultural Finance Corporation and the Industrial and Commercial Development Corporation.

The combination of major resettlements of landless Africans, who became engaged in commercialized agricultural (especially coffee production), and of restrictive trade licensing on noncitizen businesses, which compelled noncitizens to include Kenyan citizens in their commercial transactions, became the anchor for post-independence stability. Smallholder African commercial farmers, white settlers, Asian and African businessmen, and upper-level civil servants were indispensable segments that formed a post-independence corporatist alliance in Kenya. Orchestrated by Kenyatta and the leadership of KANU, this coalition was opposed to a return to the precolonial model of a politicized military. Their prerequisite for effective military rule was the destruction of all autonomous and competing intermediary associations. Hence, liberty expressed through private markets was the primary interest of this post-independence coalition.

The agenda expressed by the more radical wing of KANU composed of populists/socialists for greater social equality that is, the transfer of "land to the tiller," has not been achieved in any society without bloodshed or violence. Therefore socialists in nonindustrial countries have been inclined to use coercion instead of persuasion as an instrument for social engineering when the citizenry is neither self-conscious nor strong enough to implement their own political strategy. That is why the resettlement schemes and the establishment of an African business class were indispensable features of the pro-capitalist faction of KANU's program, buttressed by an apolitical military in independent Kenya.

Recruitment

Historically, one way the British maintained control over their colonial empire was to recruit army personnel from all parts of the empire. They were especially careful not to recruit troops from their home areas because of the increased chance for mutiny. In addition they also purposely excluded the armed forces of the Kikuyu, Kenya's largest ethnic group, because they feared such a military composition could attack the settlers and regain the stolen lands. Hence, the British colonial administration's mercenary military was ethnically unbalanced. The net impact of these political cleavages on colonial army recruitment patterns was indicated by the colonial regime's almost exclusive reliance on the Akamba and Kalenjin peoples for staffing their army, as these groups were viewed as the most apolitical segments of African society. Another glaring example of the colonial imprint on Kenya's postcolonial army was the placement of British advisors in each major branch of the Kenyan armed forces. The last official British advisor to Kenya left in 1975, only eleven years after independence.[20]

However, immediately after independence Kenyatta increased Kikuyu representation in the armed forces. By 1967, Kikuyus represented nearly 23% of the officer corps compared to 28% Akamba.[21] Kenyatta's regime attempted to compensate for the ethnic imbalance in the armed forces by creating a praetorian guard called the General Services Unit (GSU) that numbered two thousand and was comprised mostly of Kikuyus. Kenyatta used the GSU as a political instrument to quell peasant, student, and urban revolts and to repress selective political assassinations. For example, Ben Gethi, leader of the GSU was implicated in the murder of populist politician J. M. Kairuki.[22] Until Moi assumed power, Kikuyus were appointed to head the police and the elite special branch of investigation. The government's decentralized control over the means of violence, divided among the armed forces, the GSU, and the police forces, helped to counteract the tendency for the military, the praetorian guard, or the police forces to mount a coup. In spite of this structure, an attempted coup did occur in 1971. The thirteen plotters were allowed to plead to a lesser charge of sedition rather than treason, while their leader, General Ndolo, was forced to retire. This feeble coup was more a reaction to the rise of the Kikuyu hegemony in the armed forces than a serious attempt to seize power. Kenyatta's casual response to the coup was indicated by the light sentences given to the participants.

After Kenyatta's death in 1978, his strategic plan of controlling the military by balancing ethnic groups and dividing power between the armed forces and the paramilitary forces began to unravel. Simultaneously, Kenya experienced the shock of the world depression in the early 1980s, which made it difficult for the government to co-opt university graduates or buy land for the peasants. The only branch that managed to absorb university graduates was the air force.

From 1975 to 1982 the armed forces experienced a 67% increase in personnel, jumping from 9,600 in 1975 to 16,000 in 1982.[23] This dramatic increase in the armed forces could be viewed as a form of disguised welfare payments, as jobs increasingly became scarce in the private sector.

These new multiethnic army recruits posed a considerable threat to Moi, a president who lacked both charisma and an ethnic group large enough to become the dominant group in the armed forces. Thus, as Moi's popular support began to decline, so to did his support within the military. The principle catalysts for Moi's loss of popularity were a deeping economic crisis, a corrupt administration and the alienation felt by Kenya's major ethnic groups, the Luos, Kikuyus, and Luhyas. Within these groups, sentiments grew around the old KADU idea that a coalition of smaller nationalities would be sufficient enough to govern Kenya.

Confronting the challenge to provide jobs in a declining economy, Moi's regime began to use the armed forces as a form of social welfare and employment. For Nairobi University graduates, the air force became one of the most viable forms of employment. In 1980, the University of Nairobi graduated 6,355, an increase of 39% from 1974. Kenyatta University graduated 2278, and Kenyan Polytechnic 2461.[24] Sixty percent of the graduates were qualified in science and technical fields skills more suitable for the air force than the army.

One of the adverse effects of infusing the armed forces with university graduates was that they were more educated and independent than their rural peasant army counterparts. More important, the university graduates were socialized in opposition politics. In fact, when Charles Njonjo was the attorney general for Kenya, he accused university professors of teaching foreign ideologies and Marxism and eventually fired or arrested professors like Ngugi Wa Thiongo, Micere Mugo, Al Amin Mazuri, Maina Wa Kinyatta, and Anyang Nyongo. What these professors presented to their classes were alternative, critical views about Kenyan development and the widespread inequality that had accompanied that path. Unlike any other place in Kenya, students at the university were able to hear critical ideas and engage in open debates about their validity. For a brief span, from 1975 to 1980, the University of Nairobi and Kenyatta College operated as an oasis of liberty and critical thinking in a society controlled by a paternalistic, one-party regime.

In 1981, Kenya became a de jure one-party state. As Moi's regime became more paranoid and repressive towards its population, people who advocated the creation of a multiparty state, like Anyona, Muliro, and Oginga Odinga, were expelled from KANU.[25] This insecurity coupled with the instability created by a worldwide depression and falling prices for Kenya's primary products (coffee and tea) created a volatile situation for Kenya's masses.

In this context, the Kenyan Air Force attempted an early morning coup seizing the national bank, the Voice of Kenya (VOK) radio, and the two major airports.[26] Rebels woke up students in their dorms asking for their support. Shortly afterward, student leaders broadcasted their support for the coup over the VOK, located adjacent to Nairobi University, while other students demonstrated on the streets.

The coup was disorganized, however, and was quickly quelled by the army and the GSU. Of the 556 tried and courtmartialed, 66% were newly recruited senior privates and corporals.[27] Most of those convicted were between the ages of 25 and 35 and had a university education.[28] The failed coup attempt compelled Moi to reorganize his regime based on the premise that the dominant and majority ethnic groups in society were opposed to his presidency. The coup also highlighted the fragility of Moi's rule, as demonstrations by poor people and students clearly indicated a strong vote against his presidency. Hence, Moi was forced to recruit and staff his armed forces with more marginal groups within the society such as the Somali and the Kalenjin, who he assumed would remain personally loyal to him. However, Moi's transparent attempt to stack the armed forces with minority nationalities only further alienated the majority groups such as the Kikuyu, Luo, and Luhya.

CONCLUSION

To understand civil-military relations in Kenya, one must divide history into three periods. First, the colonial period introduced the concept of permanently quartered troops and the idea that the armed forces could be used by society's dominant classes to maintain political and economic control.

The second period began with the Kenyan Land and Freedom Army (Mau Mau) and ended in 1968 with the formation of the GSU. The most important aspect of civil-military relations in this period was the realization among the British Foreign office and white settlers that apartheid was not sustainable in Kenya and that Kenya was, indeed, a black man's country. Characterized by the inclusion of African Kenyans into the armed forces, this period also represented the consolidation of an alliance among white settlers, Asian businessmen, and African smallholder commercial farmers, whose land was located mainly in the central province. The ideology of postcolonial capitalism was predicated on maintaining a separation between the state and civil society, nonintervention in market activities, and military intervention if the capitalist rules of the game were challenged (e.g., when radicals like Odinga rejected the legitimacy of capitalist economic principles or when squatters seized land).

The third period began with the development of the GSU, the only branch of the armed forces created by Africans. Kenyatta's creation of the GSU was designed to neutralize the armed forces through the separation of powers and spheres covered by each unit. The GSU was explicitly involved in political repression, while the other branches of the armed forces were not directly involved in suppressing minor cases of political instability.

There were also three significant aspects of civil-military relations in Africa. In precolonial Africa, a standing professional armed force did not exist. Later, in the colonial period, the military was treated as a professional force totally dependent on the colonizer's political agenda. After independence, the character and recruitment patterns of the military were based exclusively on the personality of the autocrat. In addition, Kenya's postcolonial military lacked institutional autonomy; the president could order capricious changes of commanding officers and enlisted personnel. More important, the inability of Kenya's armed forces to create an institutional anchor was due to its lack of legitimacy. This fact about the armed forces stems from the fact that the Kenyan army was essentially a colonial creation, the indigenous people having been in charge only for a single generation. Ultimately, no military can survive independent of a country's specific culture and history.

The other major social force that shaped the structure and function of the armed forces was the breakdown in the elite's consensus on governmental policy and its effectiveness. In Kenya, this breakdown was represented by the university professors' critiques of the present government and their presentation of alternative ways to govern. In addition, short-term economic opportunity and well-being resulting from the success of the Kenyan economy effectively preempted economic hardship as a cause for their discontent. However, Kenya's deep economic recessions in the early 1980s and the present have fueled discontent among the people and the armed forces propelling the failed coup in 1982.

A potential trouble spot in Kenya's future of civil-military relations in Kenya is the cost and size of the military compared to other governmental expenditures, especially during the post–Cold War period. Another potential danger involves one-party rule. As Kenya opens its doors to multiparty competition, the development of a coalition government may become a necessity. This move could, in turn, destabilize governmental relations, leading the executive branch of the government to resort to military force and coercion in the absence of a clear political mandate and consensus.

NOTES

1. Colin Leys, *Underdevelopment in Kenya* (Berkeley: University of California Press, 1975), p. 29.

2. See Cobie Harris, "The Persistence and Fragility of Civilian Rule in Kenya," in Constantine Danopoulos, ed., *Civilian Rule in the Developing World* (Boulder, Colo.: Westview Press, 1992).

3. See George Bennett, "Settlers and Politics in Kenya," in Vincent Harlow and E. M. Chilver, eds., *History of East Africa*, vol. 2 (Oxford: Oxford University Press, 1965).

4. Carl G. Rosberg, Jr., and John Nottingham, *The Myth of the "Mau Mau": Nationalism in Kenya* (New York: Praeger, 1966), pp. 120–96.

5. This concept is derived from Richard Sklar's seminal work on class and politics in Nigeria. See Richard Sklar, "Contradictions in the Nigerian Political System," in R. Sklar and C. S. Whitaker, eds., *African Politics and Problems in Development* (Boulder, Colo.: Lynne Reinner, 1991), pp. 77–89.

6. For a detailed and systematic analysis of the impact of the commercialization of agriculture on Kenyan society, see Gavin Kitching, *Class and Economic Change in Kenya* (New Haven: Yale University Press, 1965).

7. Winston Churchill, *My African Journey* (London: Hodder-Stoughton, 1908), p. 36.

8. See Lord Hailey, *Native Administration in the British African Territories. Part I. East Africa: Uganda, Kenya, Tanganyika* (London: H.M.S.O., 1950), p. 101.

9. Donald Rothchild, *Racial Bargaining in Independent Kenya* (Oxford: Oxford University Press, 1973), pp. 62–103. For the most detailed and comprehensive study of British colonial legislative policy, see Martin Wight, *The Development of the Colonial Legislative Council*, vols. 1–4 (London: Faber and Faber, 1945).

10. Oginga Odinga, *Not Yet Ohuru* (London: Hill and Wang, 1967), pp. 285–305.

11. Leys, *Underdevelopment in Kenya*, pp. 125–30.

12. Bilad Kaggia, quoted in William Ochieng, "Independent Kenya 1963–1986," in W. R. Ochieng, ed., *A Modern History of Kenya* (Nairobi: Evans Brothers Limited, 1989), p. 207.

13. Bilad Kaggia, quoted in Paul Ogulla's unpublished manuscript, "A History of the Kenya's People Union," 1980.

14. Jomo Kenyatta, *Harambee! The Prime Minister of Kenya's Speeches, 1963–1964* (London: Oxford University Press, 1964).

15. See John Harbeson, *Nation Building in Kenya* (Evanston, Ill.: Northwestern University Press, 1977), pp. 75–134.

16. Gary Wasserman, *Politics of Decolonization: Kenya Europeans and the Land Issue* (Cambridge: Cambridge University Press, 1976), pp. 98–99.

17. Kitching, *Class and Economic Change,* p. 335.

18. Nicola Swainson, "State and Economy in Post-Colonial Kenya 1963–1978," *Canadian Journal of African Studies* 12, no. 2 (1978): 357–81.

19. Nicola Swainson, *The Development of Corporate Capitalism in Kenya* (London: Hienemann Educational Books, 1980), pp. 35–50.

20. *United States Army Area Handbook Kenya 1984* (Washington, D.C.: U.S. Government Printing Office, 1984).

21. J. M. Lee, *African Armies and Civil Order* (London: Chatto and Windus, 1969), p. 110.

22. See C. Legum and J. Drysdale, *Africa Contemporary Record Annual Survey and Documents 1969–70* (Exter: England-African Research, 1970), p. B123.

23. *United States Army Area Handbook Kenya 1984.*

24. Kate Currie and Larry Kay, "The Pambana Coup of August 1: Kenya's Abortive Coup," *Political Quarterly* 57, no. 1 (1986): 47–60.

25. Anyang' Nyongo, "Struggles for Political Power and Class Contradictions in Kenya," *Journal of African Marxists* 4 (1986): 15–16.

26. Currie and Kay, "Pambana Coup," p. 52.

27. *Weekly Review,* 31 December 1982, Nairobi, Kenya.

28. Kate Currie and Larry Kay, "The Pambana Coup," p. 54.

REFERENCES

Currie, Kate, and Larry Kay. "The Pambana Coup of August 1: Kenya's Abortive Coup," *Political Quarterly* 57, no. 1 (1986): 47–60.

Harris, Cobie. "The Persistence and Fragility of Civilian Rule in Kenya." In Constantine Danopoulos, ed. *Civilian Rule in the Developing World.* Boulder, Colo.: Westview Press, 1992.

Lee, J. M. *African Armies and Civil Order.* London: Chatto and Windus, 1969.

Leys, Colin. *Underdevelopment in Kenya.* Berkeley: University of California Press, 1975.

Rothchild, Donald. *Racial Bargaining in Independent Kenya.* Oxford: Oxford University Press, 1973.

MEXICO

Roderic Camp

An analysis of the political role of the military in Mexico is valuable for what it reveals about the military's withdrawal from politics and about the maintenance of civilian supremacy over the military. The qualities that characterize the military's role in Mexican society have evolved from its historical experience, from institutional patterns ingrained within the military, from structural characteristics of the political system, and from linkages between the military and civilian leadership.

Civil-military relations are necessarily founded on the historical context. Two essential variables emerge from the historical experience of a society as it relates to the military's self-image and role. First, military officers are a product of that larger society, and the values and attitudes that govern society are embedded in their formation, too. Likewise, the civilian population's view of the military and its peripheral roles stems in part from perceptions of its historic role. Second, the historic role of the military and its involvement in internal political affairs determined civil-military patterns, creating structural relationships affecting institutional behavior.

When Mexico became independent from Spain in the 1820s, independence brought with it a political vacuum. Various groups who had received privileges under the Spanish crown in New Spain sought to maintain their favored status. Among these groups, the military played a prominent role. Mexico's political development floundered throughout the nineteenth century because of a lack of consensus about what type of political model was most appropriate to Mexico; what role various interests, such as the Catholic Church or military, should play in their society; what strategies should be fostered to promote economic development; and which social groups should govern.

The descendants of the colonial militia, the basis of the army in early nineteenth-century Mexico, quickly exercised political power, either directly or in association with civilian leaders. Mexico's political weakness prompted external

Table 1
Military Officeholders by Administration

Years	Percentage	Years	Percentage
1885–1888	55	1924–1928	34
1888–1892	51	1928–1930	29
1892–1896	44	1930–1932	32
1896–1900	34	1932–1934	33
1900–1904	30	1935	24
1905–1910	26	1935–1940	27
1911	25	1940–1946	19
1911	22	1946–1952	8
1911–1913	24	1952–1958	14
1913–1914	50	1958–1964	15
1914–1915	64	1964–1970	7
1914–1920	46	1970–1976	10
1920	35	1976–1982	6
1920–1924	40	1982–1988	5

intervention, both from the United States in 1846–47 and from France in 1862–67. No unified military institution existed during this era, as Mexicans were engaged in a series of civil wars involving military factions on both sides.

After 1867, when the Liberal political faction defeated the Conservatives and their European allies, Mexico began to create the foundations for an established, professional military. Although most officers were products of local national guard units and of battlefield training during the Liberal-Conservative conflicts, Mexico's military college began graduating a future cadre of officers. The civilian Liberal leadership lasted only from 1867 to 1876, after which a leading Liberal general, Porfírio Díaz, led a successful rebellion, taking the reins of power personally until 1880. Following a brief interlude by a fellow general as president, Díaz governed Mexico from 1884 until 1911.

Díaz's reign was critical to the political-military relationship in Mexico in the twentieth century. He institutionalized the military's direct influence in government, contributing to their political role in practice and theory. Nevertheless, although Díaz appointed large numbers of his former subordinates and military comrades in arms during his initial administrations (more than half in 1884), their numbers declined over time, to only 25% in his last administration (see Table 1).[1] Though Díaz, as a military man, remained in power immediately before the Mexican revolution of 1910, civilians controlled most important offices. Díaz established a pattern repeated after 1920.

The single most important historical event affecting the outcome of the military's political role in Mexico was the 1910 revolution. The Mexican Revolution was the singular event of the twentieth century, extending on and off for the entire decade, during which time nearly a tenth of Mexico's population died.[2] The revolution was significant to the military's political role for three reasons. First, it forced a confrontation between popular guerrilla armies recruited from the masses and an institutionalized, government force, the Federal Army. Second, a nonprofessional army, made up largely of civilians promoted on the battlefield, emerged victorious, over both the old Federal Army and their dissenting peers after 1914. Third, the effects of the violence were so extensive that they produced a generational impact on all who fought or grew up during the second decade of the twentieth century.

The consequences of these historic events are significant. One of the most distinctive characteristics of Mexico's modern armed forces, especially its leadership, is that it was and perceived itself to be a product of the people. In some respects, it might be considered a "civilian" army. Its generals governed Mexico from 1920 until 1946, when Miguel Alemán, a young lawyer and son of a revolutionary general, became the first elected civilian president.[3] As a revolutionary generation came to power through violence and as civilian and military leadership were blended together in their seizure of political control, once again little distinction existed between civilian and military responsibilities in the political sphere. This new military leadership from popular origins dominated political life, eliminating altogether the establishment military, the Federal Army. This gave Mexico's political-military leadership an opportunity to create a new military institution and to redefine its political role.

A second consequence of these historic events unfolded when the postrevolutionary military leaders, particularly presidents Alvaro Obregón (1920–24) and Plutarco Elías Calles (1924–28), decided to reestablish and professionalize the army's institutional structures. During their terms in office, they reconstituted the former Colegio Militar, hired new military instructors, obtained expertise from abroad, and required many remaining career officers who had no formal training to obtain new technical skills. President Calles, who continued to dominate the political scene from 1928 until 1934, clearly wanted the military removed from direct political participation, implementing legislation and military statutes supportive of this goal. It is important to emphasize, however, that Calles, himself an influential revolutionary general, initiated these reforms. In short, military political leadership, relying on the strength of their revolutionary credentials, opted to remove their peers from the political scene. They were not forced to abandon politics because of popular, civilian pressures.

General Lázaro Cárdenas, who became president in 1934, continued to reduce the number of generals in his administration, while appearing to reverse President Calles's strategy. Pursuing a corporatist political formula, he hoped to strengthen the government's party, the Mexican Revolutionary Party (PRM), a forerunner of the Institutional Revolutionary Party (PRI), by dividing it into four sectors and allocating one to the military. He posed this rationale for his decision: "We are not involving the army in politics, it is already involved. In fact, it has dominated the situation, and we are reducing its influence to one out of four votes."[4] His successor, General Manuel Avila Camacho, immediately rescinded this statute, leaving the party with three major sectors, labor, agrarian, and popular, which characterize its present structure.[5] Instead of incorporating the military within the party, civilian leaders continued to recruit prominent military figures to selected posts, especially as governors and, for a long period, as presidents of the official party.

Finally, the Revolution also influenced the formation of a postrevolutionary generation, represented by the age cohort of President Miguel Alemán (born between 1900 and 1920), who dominated Mexican political life from 1946 through the 1960s. These individuals, most of whom were college-educated civilians, were deeply committed to the peaceful resolution of political disputes, to conciliation rather than confrontation, and to the return and permanence of civilian rule.[6] Alemán himself reflected the latter belief in the low percentage of military appointees in his administration, accounting for only 8% of his collaborators, half the rate of his predecessor's and the lowest figure until 1964.[7]

Certain sectors of the military were unwilling to give up power to a younger generation of civilian leaders. An older group of veterans from the Revolution joined the efforts of general Miguel Henríquez Guzmán to win back control of the presidency, and the political system. Henríquez Guzmán formed a party and hotly contested the 1952 presidential election.[8] The government candidate, Adolfo Ruiz Cortines, defeated his movement, the last significant effort by military officers to obtain political influence directly.

Theorists of civil-military relations generally and of civil-military relations in the Third World have identified a number of propositions explaining the military's political role.[9] Some of these same explanations apply to Mexico, but others peculiar to Mexico offer greater explanatory power. Since 1946, firmly but gradually, the military's political influence in terms of overt control has declined. Its indirect influence, although declining at a slower pace, followed a downward trajectory at least until the late 1960s. Since 1968, its indirect political influence has increased, while remaining firmly subordinate to civilian control.

Indirectly, the military's political influence can be measured by the role it has been asked to play in civic action functions, as a significant actor in combating drug trafficking during the 1970s, 1980s, and 1990s, as an alternative source of intelligence, as a force for stability on the provincial level and, most important, as the civilian leadership's enforcement arm of last resort.[10]

Most of these indirect tasks have increased in prominence since 1968, a benchmark in military-civilian relations and in the Mexican political model's legitimacy. In 1968, Mexico's political leadership failed to resolve a dispute with student activists, ordering or allowing the army to confront a demonstration in Tlatelolco Plaza in Mexico City. The ensuing encounter between the army and students led to violence, resulting in the deaths of hundreds of students, innocent bystanders, and journalists, and placed into question the political leadership's legitimacy and that of the current political and economic model. The military, given the scope of the bloodshed, lost considerable prestige in the eyes of the civilian population.[11]

Mexico's political system never fully recovered from the events set in motion by this repression. Succeeding presidents, especially Luis Echeverría (1970–1976) and José López Portillo (1976–82), relied more heavily on the military for legitimacy and support, increasing benefits to the armed forces and the number of promotions at higher ranks.[12] Under Miguel de la Madrid, the size of the armed forces also increased. After President Carlos Salinas came to power in the highly disputed 1988 elections, he used the military on numerous occasions to bolster his authority and to implement controversial executive policies, including occupying a government-owned enterprise, seizing a drug dealer, and arresting a union leader.

With the decline of military officers in civilian political posts, the military explored other means of maintaining their influence. Basically, civilian and military leadership reached an informal accord involving the following principles. First, civilian leadership will not intervene in internal military affairs, giving it considerable autonomy. This autonomy applies to military expenditures, once budget allocations have been made to the armed forces; to internal military policies, such as the ability of officers to moonlight at other jobs; and, perhaps most important, to designating their leaders through promotions.

By and large, civilian politicians respected military autonomy in these areas, developing practices both actors accepted. In other Latin American countries, civilians politicized the promotion process, threatening the military's internal stability. In Mexico, the military essentially makes its own promotion decisions, although from colonel on up they must be ratified by the president and the senate.

A second principle of this arrangement is that civilian leadership publicly praises the armed forces as an honored and prestigious institution in Mexican life. It constantly invokes favorable comments, identifying the military as a loyal, stalwart partner of the state.

A third principle is that the military will carry out a host of professionally unrelated activities, most of which are designed to sustain civilian leadership, and impose its electoral results on the populace. Among these activities the military functions as guardian of the ballots on election day, even in cases of widespread fraud. The army is often sent in to impose order when civil conflicts arise over electoral fraud. In the extreme, the military is used to suppress dissidence—student, labor, or otherwise. However, since 1968 the military has not been favorably predisposed to repeat that performance. It does not wish to be seen as a savior of the state if killing fellow citizens in large numbers is the price it must pay.

In return for civilian acceptance of these unwritten agreements between the military and political leaders, the military never demanded sharp increases in budgetary funds, it accepted a numerically small force and technologically unsophisticated weaponry, and it willingly carried out civilian-mandated internal police functions rather than focusing on self-defense.

The military's leverage in exerting greater influence over the political leadership is limited by structural features of the Mexican political system. Basically, Mexico witnessed an interlocking leadership from 1920 to the present. The dominance of a single leadership group and the formation of an official party limited the military's political potential. The military has more negotiating power in political systems where viable political alternatives exist. After 1929, with the last of the major military rebellions defeated, General Calles organized a single national party. Mexico quickly evolved into a dominant single-party system, which essentially left the military with two choices. It could either overthrow the civilian leadership class, identifying with dissident civilian elites, or it could overthrow civilian leadership altogether, replacing it with military officers.

Mexican military officers did not have the training, skills, or inclination to function alone as political leaders. The political elite created such a strong sense of discipline and such complete and comprehensive control over the state apparatus that dissident civilians never sought allies among military officers. In other Latin American countries, where opposing parties were the norm, the military could threaten to ally with one group versus another, giving it greater political capital with which to negotiate.

The qualities of the political system itself are not the only features that enhance or impede the military's actual or potential political influence. In most of the literature on the military in Latin America, little effort is made to ascertain citizen attitudes toward military political influence. In Mexico, more than three fifths of all Mexicans believe that the military should never participate in politics. Yet, nearly two fifths of all Mexicans believed that the military should participate in politics all or some of the time.[13] Societal acceptance at some level opens the door for higher levels of military political participation. Those Mexicans who support this role also tend to be the same Mexicans who support the present political system. Interestingly, Mexicans are much stronger in their beliefs about the church staying out of politics than are the military, largely because few constitutional restrictions existed against military compared to church participation until 1992.

Citizen attitudes toward military political involvement can be reinforced by political leadership. Strong objections to military political activities would not prevent the military from ultimately intervening in politics, but they act as a significant deterrent. Not only do the majority of Mexican citizens reject such functions on the part of the military but, as military officers themselves are products of a culture in which the majority reject such involvement, they also are socialized to accept similar principles.

Structural components of the Mexican system not only prevent the military from using strategies to increase their influence similar to those found in other countries but also enhance civilian politicians' ability to maintain successfully its superiority. The political elite established a strong, continuous party organization, complimented by a growing, powerful bureaucracy. Because the military lacked realistic political alternatives, it became a staunch institutional ally of the Mexican state.

The Mexican military has been able to increase its political influence indirectly in recent years. Interestingly, its ability to do so is due less to its exerting influence over the civilian leadership than to that leadership's political condition. Since the end of Luis Echeverría's term (1970–76), the Mexican political system's legitimacy increasingly came under severe pressure. Combined with serious economic crises, each successive president initially revived, then reduced the strength of the presidency and the political model.

This crisis in legitimacy culminated in the 1988 presidential elections. Carlos Salinas de Gortari's designation as the official party candidate prompted several political consequences. For the first time in decades, government leadership faced a strong dissident faction. This group, led by Cuauhtémoc Cárdenas, son of General Lázaro Cárdenas and a youthful supporter of General Miguel Henríquez Guzmán, were forced to abandon the government party and organized an opposition political alliance.[14] Contrary to many political analysts' expectations, Cárdenas attracted considerable support from frustrated members of PRI and from the electorate generally. Eventually on the ballot of four parties, he obtained 32% of the national vote amid widespread charges of fraud.

Many observers believe that Cárdenas, not Salinas, actually won the election and that the government imposed a Salinas victory on the electorate. There is no disagreement among outside observers that widespread fraud occurred, only on the extent to which it affected the outcome. As a consequence of opposition electoral strength in 1988, Mexico briefly stepped into an era of intense political competition. The military institutionally supported the results of the 1988 presidential election, fulfilling its expected role. In private, however, numerous officers and enlisted men voted for Cárdenas.[15]

In 1989, Cárdenas established a new political organization, the Democratic Revolutionary Party (PRD). This party's creation intensified electoral combat in Mexico. In terms of military political influence, it generated two significant consequences. Since 1989, the government has relied repeatedly on the army to maintain order. In 1992, in Cárdenas's home state of Michoacán, the military intervened to prevent PRD activists from disrupting PRI's alleged gubernatorial victory. Each time the military is asked to play this role, it earns political credits that it can call in at a later date.

The other consequence of the PRD's emergence as a viable political alternative, especially at the local and regional level, is that the military increasingly is offered a political alternative to PRI. Elections since 1988, especially the 1991 congressional elections, suggest that PRD lost much of its earlier support and that the strength of National Action Party (PAN), the other major opposition party, remained relatively stable. Their national political fortunes, however, are limited. This means that the military has limited options, if it or a faction within army ranks would decide to associate itself with another political party. Any increase in party system competitiveness enhances the possibilities for generating greater dissent within the military.

The military itself, however, displays limited potential in this regard. One of the most extraordinary features of the Mexican military is its social isolation, secrecy, and level of internal discipline. Mexican military officers increasingly have isolated themselves as a leadership group from all other influential elites, including intellectuals, entrepreneurs, clergy, and politicians. While this reserve has advantages in keeping the military aloof from diverse sources of opposition political influence outside the institution it also makes it extremely difficult to generate close linkages between the military and establishment political leaders.

A consequence of this isolation is that military officers essentially determine their own leadership, even at the very top. Although military zone commanders and defense and naval secretariat leadership are theoretically determined by presidential selection and appointment, recent presidents have had to rely on the recommendations of incumbent military leadership, given their lack of familiarity with and friendships among the officer corps.

A consequence of the high level of discipline maintained within the military is the degree to which officers of all ranks subordinate themselves to the hierarchical command structure. Decision-making within the Mexican armed forces is extremely narrow, focused at the level of the secretaries of national defense and navy. Individual commanders have relatively little autonomy. Any military officer publicly expressing a political view is summarily removed from command. This internal discipline has the advantage of achieving subordination to military authority and indirectly to the commander-in-chief, the Mexican president. On the other hand, the institutional secrecy surrounding Mexico's armed forces makes it difficult to ascertain officers' precise attitudes concerning political or other issues.

In the 1980s, the armed forces began to pursue an educational pattern found elsewhere in the region. The officer corps initially received professional military education at the Heroic Military College. During the 1930s, the defense ministry established a Higher War College and later a naval equivalent. Those academies eventually produced the vast majority of generals, and their graduates dominated influential military posts. In 1982, President José López Portillo established a third tier in the military educational system, the National Defense College. The National Defense College is patterned after similar institutions in South America. It educates the cream of the officer corps, generally fewer than twenty individuals. Its students are made up of colonels and generals, all of whom are slated for higher command. Its curriculum is unique for two reasons. First, it is the only military academy relying on civilian instructors; in fact, prominent civilians provide most of the instruction. Second, it is the only military academy that allows any civilian students to attend, typically from the treasury or the foreign relations secretariat. Third, its curriculum focuses on national security concerns, teaching its graduates political, economic, and social interpretations of contemporary Mexico.[16]

This type of training, at least in the Latin American context, increases the military's desire to become politically involved, because it contributes to the officer corps' own image that they better understand nonmilitary social problems and receive appropriate skills to cope with those issues.

While acquiring this new professional preparation, the Mexican military has increased its visibility and its potential political influence in the realm of national security. President Salinas expanded technical, subcabinet groups. In addition to four in existence under his predecessor, the president added a national security subgroup composed of the secretariats of national defense, navy, government, and foreign relations and the attorney general. Prior to 1988, according to Olga Pellicer, a Mexican expert on national security issues, "one outstanding feature of the national security issue in Mexico is the slight participation of the military sector both in the definition of the concept of national security itself and in the decision as to the most appropriate means of confronting the dangers that threaten it."[17]

In the 1980s, the military began to take a greater interest in foreign policy, particularly involving Central America and Mexico's southern neighbor, Guatemala. On the issue of refugees, the army once again became the enforcement agent, this time for decisions made by the foreign relations and government secretariats.[18] Military leadership expressed a strong desire to eliminate those situations where it is called upon to enforce a policy or resolve a political dispute without prior involvement in the policy formulation stage. It found itself in this situation during the 1968 student movement.

The military's desire to be included more fully in the decision-making process—and several sources suggest it is playing a stronger role in the national security subcabinet—arose at a time when national security concepts were changing. Internal security has been given much more importance as a component of national security since 1986, conceptually shifting the army's focus away from an external to an internal enemy. Although in practice the army never functioned as an external defense force, its theoretical and actual operations now coincide.

The demise of the Cold War seems to have had little effect on the military's perception of internal enemies. But the internationalization of economic and political liberalization does have implications for military political influence. As the free trade agreement among Mexico, Canada, and the United States has been approved by Congress, an economic basis for liberal political influences is in place. Although considerable debate exists as to whether or not economic competition and capitalism have political consequences, the direct association with the United States can only, over the long run, increase pressures on Mexico to democratize.[19] The Zedillo administration has taken several steps aimed at democratizing the Mexican political system.

The democratization of the Mexican political process, especially in the electoral arena, will force the military to make more-astute political choices. Its ability to sustain state-supported fraud is limited. Although it chooses to obey constitutional requirements and has little desire to exert direct political control, it will not continue to guarantee outrageous electoral results. It desires to reinforce and enhance its own institutional legitimacy. At this point in time, the majority of Mexicans rank it somewhere in the middle among political and social institutions, more favorably than politicians but much less favorably than the Catholic church.

CONCLUSIONS

Mexico's military has a unique position among Third World countries generally. It established itself as an institution subordinate to civilian control. This relationship, which has evolved over many decades, can be attributed to a number of features found in Mexico. Mexico's armed forces were the product of a revolution, led by military leaders recruited from the masses. As these individuals, who led Mexico's political system after 1920, carried no loyalty to a military institution, they made the necessary decisions to professionalize the military, simultaneously removing them from direct political involvement. They enhanced the success of such ordinary professional training in the art of warfare, giving a special focus on internal military discipline, subordination to authority, and subordination to civilian leadership. These beliefs were rigidly enforced and ingrained in generation after generation of officers.

Mexico limited the political participation of the military to supporting establishment political leadership, creating a strong federal bureaucracy and a political party organization, mainly as a legitimizing agent for its candidates, to compete in the electoral arena. These institutions grew much stronger than the military, whose budget allocations since 1920 were consistently reduced in percentage terms, although increasing slightly in real pesos. Mexico never provided the military with viable political options through successful opposition parties, at least until 1988. Thus, whatever political ambitions the armed forces shared, they were directed toward government, not in opposition to it.

These characteristics of the Mexican political system and Mexican citizens' gradual rejection of direct military political influence limited the armed forces' ability to influence decision-making. In fact, the little evidence available suggests the military exercised only a limited role in the decision-making process, typically responding to requests from the executive branch. Beginning in the 1980s, as the legitimacy of the executive branch declined and as political leadership resorted increasingly to fraud to maintain control, the military's access to decision-making increased.

Recent events in southern Mexico in early 1994, involving an attack by a well-organized guerrilla group calling itself the Zapatista Army of National Liberation (EZLN), bear out this interpretation. The Chiapan situation demonstrates that whether the military is used as a primary tool to resolve the crisis or is held in abeyance in favor of political negotiation, its voice will have greater presence in the future. Civilian political leadership is indebted to the military because it has subjected its strategy to that of civilian leaders; because civilian leaders did not respond appropriately to early-warning signals from the military; and because the military forces, not civilian authorities, were the victims of the initial guerrilla attack. Differences in opinion between the civilian and military leadership and within the political leadership itself as to what strategy the government should pursue readily became apparent. The longer Mexico's leadership delays in attacking serious economic and social problems, the more likely it is that the military will be called on to resolve violent disputes.

NOTES

1. Roderic Ai Camp, *Generals in the Palacio: The Military in Modern Mexico* (New York: Oxford University Press, 1992), p. 69.

2. For background, see Edwin Lieuwen, *Mexican Militarism* (Albuquerque: University of New Mexico Press, 1968).

3. Emilio Portes Gil, appointed by Congress as the provisional president of Mexico in 1928, was not a revolutionary general, but a lawyer. He replaced general Alvaro Obregón, the president-elect, who was assassinated before taking office.

4. José Luis Piñeyro, *Ejército y sociedad en México: Pasado y presente* (Puebla: Universidad Autónomo de Puebla, 1985), p. 56.

5. Jorge Alberto Loyoza, *El Ejército mexicano (1911–1965)* (Mexico: El Colegio de México, 1970), p. 4.

6. Roderic Ai Camp, *The Making of a Government: Political Leaders in Modern Mexico* (Tucson: University of Arizona Press, 1984), p. 40.

7. Camp, *Generals in the Palacio,* p. 67.

8. Phyllis Greene Walker, "The Modern Mexican Military: Political Influence and Institution Interests in the 1980s," (Master's thesis, American University, 1987), 40.

9. For example, see Calude E. Welch, Jr., *No Farewell to Arms? Military Disengagement from Politics in Africa and Latin America* (Boulder, Colo.: Westview Press, 1987), p. 17.

10. For a discussion of these "residual" roles, see David Ronfeldt, ed., *The Modern Mexican Military: A Reassessment* (La Jolla: Center for United States–Mexican Studies, University of California, San Diego, 1984), pp. 1–31.

11. George Philip, *The Presidency in Mexican Politics* (New York: St. Martin's Press, 1992), pp. 19–63, discusses its implications in considerable detail.

12. For empirical evidence, see my "Generals and Politicians in Mexico: A Preliminary Comparison," in Ronfeldt, ed., *Modern Mexican Military,* p. 136ff.

13. See, for example, Enrique Alducin Abitia, *Los valores de los mexicanos: México entre la tradición y la modernidad* (Mexico: Fondo Cultural Banamex, 1986), p. 176.

14. Peter H. Smith, "The 1988 Presidential Succession in Historical Perspective," in Wayne A. Cornelius et al., eds., *Mexico's Alternative Political Futures* (La Jolla: Center for U.S.–Mexican Studies, UCSD, 1989), pp. 391–416.

15. Oscar Hinojosa, "Su voto demonstró que los militares no son homogeneamente governistas," *Proceso,* 8 August 1988, p. 19.

16. For some background, see Alden Cunningham, "Mexico's National Security in the 1980–1990s," in Ronfeldt, ed., *Modern Mexican Military,* p. 167.

17. Olga Pellicer de Brody, "National Security Concerns in Mexico: Traditional No-

tions and New Preoccupations," in Clark W. Reynolds and Carlos Tello, eds., *U.S.–Mexico Relations: Economic and Social Aspects* (Stanford, Calif.: Stanford University Press, 1983), p. 187.

18. For background on this see, Edward J. Williams, "The Evolution of the Mexican Military and Its Implications for Civil-Military Relations," in Roderic Ai Camp, ed., *Mexico's Political Stability: The Next Five Years* (Boulder, Colo.: Westview Press, 1986), p. 152.

19. For the most complete survey of these issues, see Riordan Roett, ed., *Political and Economic Liberalization in Mexico: At a Critical Juncture?* (Boulder, Colo.: Lynne Rienner, 1993).

REFERENCES

Ackroyd, William S. "Descendants of the Revolution: Civil-Military Relations in Mexico." Ph.D. diss., University of Arizona, 1988.

Camp, Roderic Ai. *Generals in the Palacio: The Military in Modern Mexico.* New York: Oxford University Press, 1992.

Colson, Harold. *National Security Affairs and Civil-Military Relations in Contemporary Mexico: A Bibliography.* Monticello: Vance Bibliographies, 1989.

Lieuwen, Edwin. *Mexican Militarism.* Albuquerque: University of New Mexico Press, 1968.

Piñeyro, José Luis. "The Modernization of the Mexican Armed Forces." In Augusto Varas, ed., *Democracy under Siege: New Military Power in Latin America.* Westport, Conn.: Greenwood Press, 1989.

Ronfeldt, David, ed. *The Modern Mexican Military: A Reassessment.* La Jolla: Center for United States–Mexican Studies, University of California, San Diego, 1984.

Schloming, Gordon C. "Civil-Military Relations in Mexico, 1910–1940: A Case Study." Ph.D. diss., Columbia University, 1974.

Wager, Steven. "The Mexican Army, 1940–1982: The Country Comes First." Ph.D. diss., Stanford University, 1992.

NETHERLANDS

Jan R. Schoeman

THE SETTING[1]

On 18 January 1951 the Dutch prime minister, Willem Drees, gave the following statement in the House of Commons (Tweede Kamer): "In the Netherlands the armed forces are no independent power, that is allowed to act as a pressure group. The decisions are taken by the government and the parliament."[2] These words are an adequate description of the relation between the armed forces and politics ever since the Netherlands became a constitutional democracy after the Napoleonic era, but at the time they meant the escalation of a conflict between the Dutch government and the top of the Royal Netherlands Army, especially the chief of the general staff, General H. J. Kruls.

This conflict had its origins basically in the early 1950s, when Kruls tried to influence the political debate about the strength of the army and the way it should be equipped. The general wanted to enlarge and reinforce the army more quickly than did the politicians, because he perceived the Soviet military threat to Western Europe as much more serious than the Dutch political elite did. The conflict was reinforced because Kruls proved stubborn and self-willed, not afraid to express private opinions that often differed sharply from the official point of view on the question of the number of troops that the Netherlands should put at the disposal of NATO. Due to economic and financial reasons, the government decided that that number should be limited to three army divisions; but on different occasions, both in public and during NATO meetings, Kruls spoke about four, five, and even six divisions.

When NATO commander-in-chief General Dwight D. Eisenhower in January 1951 expressed severe criticism of how the buildup of the Dutch armed forces took place and about the integration of these forces into the military structure of NATO, Kruls publicly agreed with him.[3] By doing so he embarrassed the

Dutch government highly, and in the eyes of the government the position of Kruls became untenable. The general was fired on 23 January 1951.

AN ASSUMPTION

Although the clash between General Kruls and Prime Minister Drees is by no means the only example of conflict between politicians and the military in recent Dutch history, one still might call the forced dismissal of a general a remarkable event: Other disturbances were mostly dealt with in another way. Generally speaking, the relationship between politicians and high-ranking military personnel in the Netherlands was quite harmonious. Can the same be said of the Dutch pattern of civil-military relations in a broader sense? Can these relations also be qualified as fairly harmonious and stable? At first sight, indications for both an affirmative and a negative answer to this question can be found during the last century.[4]

On the one hand, every now and then debates arose about certain specific and concrete aspects of the armed forces and defense policy, both in parliament and in society. Impressive masses of people were mobilized, for instance, in the protest movement against nuclear armament in the 1970s and the early 1980s. Other well-known examples are the political debates around the plans considering the renewal of the Dutch fleet in the 1920s and over the abolition of military conscription and the transition to an all-volunteer force in the beginning of the 1990s.

On the other hand, although during the interbellum the antimilitaristic movement was represented in parliament, neither there nor in society during the last century was the necessity for some sort of military force seriously questioned. This broad consensus suggests a solid relationship between the armed forces and the politicians as representatives of civil society. The goal of this chapter is to examine whether the assumption that the Dutch armed forces are well integrated both in a political and in a social sense is correct and to consider which underlying reasons of a political, social, economic, and military-strategical nature influenced or even caused the situation as it exists today. Extra attention will be paid to situations in which the military tried to influence the political process and to the ways in which the services had to adapt their organization and their personnel management in order to achieve (especially non-military) political goals. Considering the complexity of this subject, most emphasis will be laid on developments that took place during approximately the last half century, starting with the preamble to World War II.

THE MYTH OF 1940

The German invasion of the Netherlands on 10 May 1940 was the first violation of Dutch territorial integrity since 1815. In the five-day war that followed, the Dutch armed forces were no serious match for German troops; after the bombardment of the city of Rotterdam, the Netherlands had no option other than to surrender.[5]

To save face after this unexpectedly quick defeat (both during and after the war), the military and military historians[6] created the myth of a Dutch army that, despite numerous heroic acts of individual soldiers, never had a chance because of the overwhelming superiority of the Germans both in numbers and in equipment. According to these historians, the Dutch government had proven itself to be shortsighted during the interbellum because the need to reinforce the armed forces was recognized too late and because, when it was, too little effort and money were spent to build up an adequate defense organization. The state of mind of Dutch society as a whole was characterized as antimilitaristic; further, these historians cited a lack of appreciation for military tradition, the absence of a separate military caste (in particular, officers), and the low social status of the professional soldier in the Netherlands. In their opinion the war of May 1940 had been lost during the 1920s and 1930s, and the armed forces were not to blame for the defeat.

During the 1980s historians presented a more realistic description of what really happened during the interbellum and in May 1940.[7] They reevaluated Dutch defense politics of the 1930s,[8] showing that although Dutch spending on the national defense was not so high as in France, the United Kingdom, and certainly Germany, it was on a similar or even higher level than in other small European countries like Belgium, Norway, or Denmark. The prewar military buildup was not so late as has been suggested, but was quite reasonable both quantitatively and qualitatively, the best possible under the circumstances. Although the Germans had air superiority, in numbers the invading German troops were inferior to the Dutch army. The Dutch were not trained in offensive actions and therefore were unable to regain the initiative. Dutch morale, finally, was influenced in a negative way because too often important things like logistics and communications failed.

For the most part, these facts were unknown at that time. Both the military and the public were all too eager to believe a myth that would explain and even justify the military defeat. This myth for over forty years repressed the fact that a Dutch army twice as strong and much better equipped might have held out a few days longer, but in the end in no way could have prevented the German military victory in 1940 and the horrors of the occupation that followed.[9]

THE GOLDEN YEARS

After 1945 the influence of the myth of 1940 remained perceptible and was used by the military during defense debates in the late 1940s and in the 1950s,[10] in which the military's role was significant. During this period, two important events took place. (1) In 1949, after a four-year struggle, Dutch colonial rule ended in the East Indies (Indonesia). The decision to give up Indonesia was finally made because of growing international pressure, especially from the

United States, and because the deployment of such a large number of troops[11] far from home nearly bankrupted the Netherlands. (2) The Netherlands joined the Western Union in 1948 and, a year later, the North Atlantic Treaty Organization, realizing that the Netherlands, like other small countries, could no longer guarantee its safety and territorial integrity independently.

This feeling, combined with the popularity that the national and the allied forces gained during World War II, together with the widespread fear of a Soviet military invasion in Western Europe, created a situation in which defense policy formed a major issue in Dutch politics and in which society was prepared to invest a lot of manpower and huge amounts of money in rebuilding the armed forces. In 1954, for instance, 22.5% of the Dutch national budget was spent on defense.[12] As a result, within a few years and with considerable help from the United States,[13] an entire new army, navy, and air force were created. The 1950s in many ways proved to be "golden years" for the Dutch armed forces.[14]

Although the Soviet dictator Joseph Stalin in the mass media was portrayed and looked upon by the population as an "Adolph Hitler," the fear of a possible Soviet occupation never became the number-one problem in Dutch society. Public opinion polls during the 1950s indicate that financial and economic problems like the shortages in houses and jobs or the amount of pensions and taxes were taken much more seriously by the population.[15] In comparison with the prewar years' somewhat more positive circumstances, it is worthwhile looking at the way the new armed forces were given shape and in what way and for what reasons political decisions were influenced by the military during this process.

The Blue-Water Navy

Take the case of rebuilding the Royal Netherlands Navy. During World War II, the Dutch fleet was nearly completely annihilated. The few remaining units played no significant role in the course of the war and were placed under allied command. Within the navy this led to a "never again" feeling of frustration and led the Admiralty in 1944/1945 to work out ambitious plans for a postwar navy consisting of more than fifty thousand men and three carrier-battle groups.[16] But by the time these plans could be realized around 1950 (after the end of the war in Indonesia, due to the experienced Soviet threat and the Dutch partnership in international alliances, especially the Western Union), defense priorities had changed. For instance, the chairman of the commanders-in-chief committee of the Western Union, Field Marshal B. L. Montgomery, argued that the formation of the Dutch army and air force should have priority over the reconstruction of the fleet,[17] as the only ships needed were a number of minesweepers. The Dutch government accepted his point of view and raised the army and air force budgets, keeping the navy budget on a level that downsized shipbuilding plans.

The Dutch tried to reinforce governmental control over the three services, appointing in the spring of 1949, apart from the Minister of War and Navy, two state secretaries, one for the army and the air force and the other one for the navy. J. W. Honig described their duties: "Besides keeping a strict eye on expenditures, they were to tender independent advice to their Minister and improve interservice coordination—a field the Cabinet thought substantial savings could be made. Finding suitable candidates, however, proved a problem. The required specialist knowledge made officers the natural choice, but were they completely reliable politically?"[18] Rear Admiral H. C. W. Moorman was sworn in on 1 May 1949 as State Secretary of the Navy.

Meanwhile the Admiralty objected to a role of merely coastal defense duties in the North Sea and refused to give up the plans for a blue-water navy. Within NATO the navy saw new missions in safeguarding Atlantic sea lines of communication, which became more important because of the involvement of Canada and the United States in the defense of Europe. This was against the will of the United States and the United Kingdom, who were perfectly capable of securing these sea lines themselves and wanted a more substantial Dutch land and air contribution to NATO. Moorman was in favor of an ocean-going navy, but realized that under these conditions the "three-carrier" fleetplan never could be realized. He tried to convince the Admiralty to adopt a more realistic shipbuilding plan that nevertheless would lead to a full-fledged navy. As a result, in the spring of 1950, the Dutch government had to answer the question of whether the adjusted August 1949 fleetplan of the Admiralty[19] would lead to a fleet that the Netherlands needed as a member of NATO. The strategic rationale for such a fleet had to be weighed against national economic advantage, such as employment in the Dutch shipbuilding industry.

By allocating a 1951 navy budget of 250 million guilders (instead of the 325 million the plan required), the government turned the fleetplan down. The navy nevertheless adopted it as a blueprint for the future fleet; although the finance minister remarked that the navy had to operate within the determined budget, no further action was taken.[20] The blueprint was included in the Defence White Paper of June 1950. According to Honig, the procedure continued as follows: "During the Cabinet discussion of the White Paper on the day before its presentation to Parliament, Prime Minister Drees concluded that the section on the navy 'totally failed to take account of what had been agreed upon by the cabinet.' Rather ruefully, no doubt, he remarked that by that time a 'complete redraft' had become impossible."[21]

The discussion of this white paper in the House of Commons proved that many politicians credited more importance to the symbols of the rich Dutch naval tradition, represented by a blue-water navy, than the Cabinet did. They also were more susceptible to the fact that building the proposed ships would stimulate an important part of Dutch industry; therefore, many parties favored the expansion of the fleet rather than its downsizing. They saw their opinions reinforced by developments in the international political situation, culminating in the Korean War. International tensions also played a role in redefining the NATO and the U.S. points of view toward the Dutch navy. Because of these tensions and under the pressure that the United States might reduce its economic and military aid, the Dutch government announced a temporary increase of the annual defense budget from 850 million to 1500 million guilders in the period 1951–54.[22]

Thereafter a fixed distribution of the financial means was introduced between the army, the air force, and the navy, namely, 2:1:1, reinforcing the army and the air force substantially, which was precisely what the Western Union and NATO (and within NATO the United States) desired. The most important government motive behind this increase was keeping the allies satisfied, their interest in the way this extra money was spent limited. Prime Minister Drees saw the defense budget mainly as "some sort of insurance premium to keep the Americans in Western Europe for our protection. For the rest it was really a waste of money."[23] This view was shared by most ministers, who credited more importance to the social-economic development of the country. The navy benefitted from this indifferent attitude. Although the United States still regarded tasks in the North Sea as more important than those on the Atlantic, their most important objection against a Dutch blue-water navy was taken away.

Thus the navy officially was allowed to execute its shipbuilding plans, and around 1957 the Netherlands possessed a modern ocean-going fleet much like that of the August 1949 fleetplan. Clearly, many national and international developments played a role during the planning and construction of this postwar Dutch fleet; not the least of them was Admiralty influence.

ALL QUIET ON THE DEFENSE FRONT

By the end of the 1950s the buildup of the Dutch armed forces was complete, and the organization was well integrated into the NATO structure. The services themselves had influenced this buildup and were in fact too voluminous for the financial situation in the Netherlands. These "oversized" forces were possible only through American military aid; the moment it stopped in the early 1960s, problems arose.

After defining Dutch military tasks within NATO in the early 1950s, the alliance acted as a brake on the national discussions concerning the redistribution of member tasks. The Dutch defense organization during these years limited political control over its services. "Each of the services had its own State Secretary and they were the ones to decide what would happen with the money that was available thanks to the fixed budgets. These State Secretaries acted more as a part of their service than as politicians who were supposed to lead that particular service."[24] This attitude enabled the armed forces to safeguard and in some cases to enlarge their operations. The comfortable and independent position for the services was further consolidated because Dutch Cabinets, during the 1960s especially, were neither energetic nor powerful in matters of national defense.

Nuclear armament was introduced in the Netherlands as a consequence of the

Dutch participation in NATO, but nuclear pacifism was still an isolated phenomenon both in parliament and in society in the late 1950s and early 1960s and did not affect the societal appraisal of the armed forces. Opinion polls[25] during the 1960s show that the major part of Dutch society endorsed the statement of the necessity of the armed forces. In 1963, for instance, 59% of public opinion qualified the armed forces as "necessary," 34% called them "a necessary evil." Only 3% thought armed forces were "hardly necessary," while another 3% called them "superfluous." It is remarkable that in the quarter of a century until the fall of the Berlin Wall in 1989 the combined results of the answers "necessary" and "necessary evil" were always 77% or more.

Conscripts . . .

Partly this stability was due to the degree of social integration of the armed forces. During these years the armed forces lost some of their military characteristics and (partly) became organized like other modern large-scale organizations, in terms of personnel management. This process was influenced by technological developments and the increasing bureaucracy within the forces, the emancipation of women and ethnic minorities, and the democratization within Dutch society. This led, for instance, to the founding of the VVDM, the first trade union of conscripts in the world, on 4 August, 1966. During its first years VVDM was moderate, but in the early 1970s it became a left-wing, politically oriented organization, skillful in manipulating public opinion.[26] In its first ten years VVDM improved the life and working conditions of conscripts dramatically (better payment for conscripts, abolition of the military salute, the right to wear civil clothing after working hours, and freedom of hair length, for example).

This success was due partly to the Labor party (PVDA) and its minister of defense, H. Vredeling, who took office in 1973. PVDA priorities were cuts in the defense budget, the redistribution of military tasks among NATO allies, a reorganization of the Department of Defense to improve political control over the services, shortening of the period of conscription, and continuation of the process of democratization of the armed forces (usually called "societalization"). These last two themes made the minister and the VVDM natural allies.

. . . and Generals

However, the plans of the PVDA and Vredeling led the Minister on a collision course with the professional military and their trade unions. In the early 1970s these trade unions were concerned with protecting the material interests of their members and were active in the field of defense policy. They brought their points of view, especially concerning discipline, material, and equipment, to the attention of Dutch society as a whole. In 1974, when the decision to replace the obsolescent Neptune maritime patrol aircraft was postponed by Vredeling, the unions of naval personnel protested fiercely and successfully against this post-ponement; the order for new aircraft was announced in the Defense White Paper published later that year.[27]

Commotion at the top of the army led to a clash between Minister Vredeling and a number of army generals. A good number of high-ranking army officers wanted a modernization of discipline and more responsibilities for the lower ranks. A second category feared that these adjustments would lead to less discipline and to a decrease in combat readiness and fighting strength. Because material obtained from the Americans in the 1960s had to be replaced and the social-democratic government might be unwilling to provide the necessary financial means, a member of this second category, the chairman of the Joined Chiefs of Staff, Lieutenant General W. van Rijn, resigned on 26 June 1973. Although he publicly declared that this had nothing to do with the coming to power of the Labor government, clearly he thought government would be unable to solve the problems of social unrest within the army and shortages in modern equipment favorably; and he feared for the future of the army under Vredling.[28]

Within a year, and before any major decisions in the field of Defense policy were taken, four other generals, including the chief of the general staff, followed his example. State Secretary of Defense A. Stemerdink remarked, "We could survive the quitting of that many Generals because this exodus occurred before the real political choices had been made." To avoid a second crisis in command, the politicians had to operate carefully, especially concerning the army. "The newly appointed Chief of the General Staff obtained power from that position and used it effectively."[29] Far-reaching reforms and budget cuts were not possible; as a result, in a reorganization of the armed forces a lot of wishes of the top military, especially concerning material, were realized. Although part of the modernization was financed out of personnel reductions,[30] the spending power of defense improved greatly during the Vredeling years,[31] and the existing tasks and structure of the Dutch armed forces were preserved, while operational strength was significantly improved.

Vredeling turned out to be more successful in the restructuring of the Department of Defense itself. In 1976 he completed the process that started in the early 1970s in order to reinforce political control over the armed forces: this led, for example, to the abolition of the state secretaries for the separate services and the appointment of two functional state secretaries, one for personnel and one for material. The responsibilities of the central organization of the Department of Defense were enhanced at the cost of the competence of the separate services.

One might say that during the Vredeling years the armed forces were given a size and structure that would last until the beginning of the 1990s. The period after the resignation of the five generals can also be qualified as a status quo in which the relationship between the armed forces and the Cabinet (in particular the minister of defense) was generally stable. That does not automatically imply that the same can be said of civil-military relations in a more general sense: for various causes, the character and therefore also the degree of the social integration of the armed forces changed in the years from 1975 until the present, and on a number of occasions these changes proved to be fundamental.

BETWEEN TURMOIL AND A NEW STABILITY

One of the most remarkable events during these years was the deployment of Dutch military units against young South Moluccan terrorists[32] in the northern part of the Netherlands in 1977: in that year the occupation of a school, including the taking hostage of children and the hijacking of a train, was ended, thanks to an operation in which the three services worked closely together with the police and the ministries of Internal Affairs and Justice.[33] The Dutch population and the president of the South Moluccan community in the Netherlands, J. H. Manusama,[34] considered the actions justified.

Apart from this incident, public attention concerning national defense was focused primarily on conscription and nuclear armament. The NATO decision of December 1979 to modernize the intermediate-range nuclear forces divided Dutch society seriously for several years. Despite the emotional debates during these years, public opinion toward modernization remained more or less stable: roughly a quarter of the population was in favor, while approximately 60% were against the proposed installation of forty-eight Tomahawk and cruise missiles in the Netherlands.[35] Before the missiles could be mounted, the matter was resolved with the signing of the INF treaty by presidents Reagan and Gorbachev on 8 December 1987.

Although the possible installation of these weapons was a widely discussed NATO initiative, during these years the Dutch membership in NATO was never seriously questioned: Not once during the 1980s did more than 15% of the population think that the Netherlands should abandon NATO.[36] That attitude of the population toward NATO can be compared with the attitude concerning the armed forces in a more general sense: Both organizations were considered useful by a large majority in the Netherlands. Whenever discussion arose around NATO or the armed forces, most of the time it had little to do with the question of necessity, but more often with the way these organizations were given shape in a financial, material, or personnel sense.

Traditionally public discussions dealt with conscription: the period of conscription, the legal rights of conscripts, or their maximum payment. In 1977 a report was published by the so-called committee Mommersteeg in which an answer was formulated to the more fundamental question of whether the Netherlands should stick to conscription or consider transition to an-all volunteer force (AVF).[37] Although for several reasons most members of this committee favored the transition to an AVF, their advice was not to do so because they feared that, considering the image of the armed forces, an AVF would be unable to attract enough young people for a (short) military career. Second, they feared that an AVF would become much too expensive for the Netherlands. Thus conscription was preserved, although clearly both the public and the political support for conscription were not solid, as was usually believed. When, for instance, in 1974 Dutch society was asked whether they favored a professional army or an army based on conscription, 71% preferred the first.[38]

New Faces

An important new development was the introduction of women and ethnic minorities into the armed forces as part of the Dutch governmental policy reinforcing the emancipation of these groups. Women had been present in the services since the end of World War II, especially in logistical and medical functions. In the 1980s, however, as a part of the policy of equal treatment of men and women and as an attempt to improve the reflection of the composition of society into the composition of the armed forces, women were also allowed to exercise combat functions.[39] Plans were made to recruit the necessary number of women to realize the political goal that 8% of the personnel of the services in 1996 should be female and to facilitate their integration.[40] Still, integration proceeds slowly. Partly the forces are (rightly) looked upon as dominated by a macho culture, which not every male soldier is willing to change. The defense organization proves slow in creating facilities, for instance, the possibility of child care or part-time jobs, that may attract women and keep them in the services for a longer spell of time. It is highly unlikely that the above-mentioned political goal will be realized.[41]

More or less the same can be said of the integration of ethnic minorities. Although the armed forces can play a significant role in the social and economic life of ethnic minorities in Dutch society, practical problems like language difficulties intervene. To date, integration is not the success politicians hoped for.

PRIORITIES IN THE 1990S

On 12 January 1993 the Dutch Minister of Defense, A. L. ter Beek, presented a Defense White Paper, the so-called Priority Note,[42] outlining his vision about new missions and the size and structure of the Dutch armed forces in the near future. Two events made this white paper necessary: (1) the changing international security situation after the reunification of Germany and the collapse of the Warsaw Pact and the Soviet Union and (2) increasing UN demands for troops for peacekeeping operations in Cambodia, Angola, and the former Yugoslavia. These events made it clear that, as in other NATO countries, the Dutch armed forces no longer needed to prepare for a full-scale war, but instead were confronted with new main tasks like peacekeeping and peace enforcing. The Dutch armed forces were neither ready nor able to perform these new missions as needed. One reason was that since 1987 the Dutch political situation forbade the nonvoluntary deployment of conscripts outside NATO territory. It became very uncertain whether the army, in which conscripts are still by far the largest group, would be able to provide larger (battalion-size) combat units for UN peacekeeping operations in former Yugoslavia. The most important outcomes of this priority note were as follows. (1) The current substantial reductions both in personnel and in material were announced; compared to the situation in 1989, the armed forces will be downsized by more than 40%. (2) The main mission of the Dutch armed forces, apart from the protection of its own territory, will be the fulfillment of peacekeeping and peace enforcing operations in an international context (United Nations, NATO). (3) The pressure to reduce conscription will grow further, because of the reduced size of the armed forces. That, together with the fact that conscripts can only be deployed on a voluntary base outside NATO territory, led to the conclusion that conscription should be abolished in 1998 at the latest, when the Netherlands should have an AVF.

The Transition

In the discussions about the abolition of conscription and the transition to an AVF, some of the same arguments as in 1977 were heard: Will it be possible to attract enough volunteers, and can society bear the cost of professional armed forces? In contrast with 1977, this last question can be answered affirmatively thanks to the reduced size of the forces. Whether it will be possible to attract enough volunteers is more difficult to assess, especially because until 1998 an unknown number of professional soldiers undoubtedly can be qualified as "draft-motivated volunteers." One thing is certain: In order to find these volunteers, an important but difficult "new mission" of especially the army will be to present itself successfully as a good employer to society.

During these discussions more attention was paid to practical questions than to the more fundamental arguments about an AVF. The previously often-heard statement that a professional army might become "a state within a state" or the opinion that such an organization might endanger democracy by coups d'etat, were heard hardly at all, because of the long and deeply rooted tradition of civil supremacy over the armed forces and because the military do not form a caste separated from the rest of society. Also, by offering the professional soldiers short, two-and-a-half-year contracts, the interaction between the armed forces and society may differ from the period of conscription, but it certainly will not end.

Meanwhile, public opinion had made it very clear that the Netherlands should head for an AVF. In the winter of 1992 the question was asked, "Do you think conscription should be preserved, or do you think an AVF should be introduced?" Of the respondents, 70% felt an AVF should be introduced, while 18% wanted to preserve conscription. "No opinion" was answered by a mere 12%. This broad consensus about the abolition of conscription goes with a strong sympathetic feeling towards the forthcoming AVF: "In general, how would you consider an AVF?" "Positive" was answered by 60% of the respondents, "neither positive nor negative" by 24%, "negative" by 8%, and "no opinion" by another 8%.[43]

Reactions

The priority note was greeted warmly by the majority of parliament and public. Although within the armed forces the trade unions of military personnel demanded no forced dismissals, the need to restructure and the measures themselves were hardly disputed. The only friction occurred when a number of generals actively took part in the public discussion around the restructuring. Although they did not dispute its necessity, in newspaper articles they showed doubts about the pace at which the minister wanted to transform the armed forces.

Other reactions followed. Because defense expenditures have always been unevenly distributed across the various regions, the downsizing of the armed forces had severe economic consequences for those parts of the Netherlands in which the defense organization used to be a "big spender." For example, the naval base at Den Helder has depended on defense for a third of its income.[44] The downsizing of the navy will undoubtedly lead to higher unemployment rates there. But there is another consequence that can be described as some sort of social drain. The mayor of Harderwijk, a city in which the army, according to the priority note, will close down its four barracks, described these consequences: "A good part of the active and retired military personnel plays an important role in social and cultural activities. They are very good in organizing things and they retire at an early age, and because of that they are of great value to our community life. Besides that: as a consequence of the financial cuts also a lot of younger people will have to find a job some place else, and they will leave Harderwijk as well."[45]

CONCLUSIONS AND PREDICTIONS

The military has more than once played an active role in national defense policy, mostly pressing for more material support. The military has stuck to the democratic rules of engagement: In case of conflict between politicians and high-ranking military personnel, the military, either forced or voluntarily, left the defense organization without trying to seize power or even disputing the legitimacy of political supremacy. The relationship between politics and the armed forces over the years has been generally harmonious. There is every reason to think that in the near future, for instance, as a consequence of the transition to an AVF or the drastic reductions in defense, this deeply rooted and stable situation is likely to remain the same.

In those cases when the services had to adapt their organization and their personnel management in order to achieve nonmilitary political goals, especially in the fields of emancipation and employment, in general the attitude of the armed forces was much more defensive. The same can be said of those situations in which the services had to adapt their structure and/or culture as a consequence of societal developments. That might say something about a rather conservative state of mind typical of those who are attracted to the military profession. Unfortunately, in the Netherlands no research on this subject was done, and therefore one can only speculate about this theme. The introduction of the AVF both implies a certain risk and at the same time offers new opportunities. The risk is that this new professional organization might lean more heavily on typical military traditions and the characteristic military culture. That might endanger the social integration of the armed forces, because important groups in society, like women and ethnic minorities, are not likely to consider a military career. On the other hand, because of, for example, a decreasing birthrate in the Netherlands, the services are in no position to neglect these groups and probably will need them desperately to fill the ranks. In that way, the forthcoming AVF might become a better representation of Dutch society than were the old conscription-based armed forces.

Such a representation will surely help to preserve the stable civil-military relationship characteristic of the Netherlands in the beginning of the 1990s. That stability is reflected in the latest opinion poll,[46] in which a remarkable 74% of the population endorsed the necessity of the armed forces. Remarkable, because a direct and serious military threat to the Netherlands no longer exists. This high figure can be explained by looking at the broad political and societal appraisal of the new missions of the armed forces, namely, peacekeeping and peace enforcing in a United Nations context. Dutch participation in these operations is endorsed by all political parties and by 72% of the population, while merely 8% disagree. Of course, these figures should be looked upon with care because they can easily be influenced, for instance, when it becomes clear that these peacekeeping operations are not so successful as expected and hoped for. On the other hand, seldom has there been a moment in Dutch history in which the consensus about the necessity and the form of the armed forces and about the missions that they should fulfill was as broad as nowadays. Nothing lasts forever, but this consensus offers a good indication of the present degree of the social and political integration of the Dutch armed forces. Furthermore, it shows that the basic elements to preserve this situation into the twenty-first century are there. It is now up to the politicians and the military to determine how best to proceed.

NOTES

1. See, for instance, J. W. L. Brouwer, "Politiek-militaire verhoudingen aan het begin van de Koude Oorlog: Rond het ontslag ban generaal H. J. Kruls, januari 1951," in J. Hoffenaar and G. Teitler, *De Koude Oorlog* (The Hague: SDU, 1992).

2. Quoted in J. Hoffenaar, and G. Teiter, eds., *De Koude Oorlong: Maatschappij en krijgsmacht in de jaren '50* (The cold war: Armed forces and society in the 1950s) (The Hague: SDU, 1992), p. 69. See also *Handelingen Tweede Kamer 1950–1951* (Proceedings of the House of Commons of the States General 1950–1951), p. 1141.

3. J. Hoffenaar and B. Schoenmaker eds., *Met de blrik naar het Oosten* (The Hague: SDU, 1993), p. 81.

4. An excellent description of the civil-military relations in the Netherlands during the last two centuries is given by J. C. H. Blom, ''A necessary evil: The armed forces and society in the Netherlands,'' in G. J. A. Raven and N. A. M. Rodger, eds., *Navies and Armies* (Edinburgh: John Donald, 1990).

5. See H. Amersfoort and P. H. Kamphuis, eds., *Mei 1940* (The Hague: SDU, 1990).

6. For instance, army major E. H. Brongers, who published a number of books about the fighting in May 1940. These books became popular during the 1960s and 1970s.

7. See, for instance, G. Teitler, ed., *Tussen crisis en oorlog* (Dieren: De Bataafsche Leeuw, 1984); and Amersfoort and Kamphuis, *Mei 1940.*

8. See J. C. H. Blom, ''Durch kamen sie doch,'' in Teitler, *Tussen crisis und oorlog.*

9. See Amersfoort and Kamphuis, *Mei 1940,* esp. chapter 11.

10. Hoffenaar and Teitler, eds., *De Koude Oorlog,* p. 215.

11. In the period 1945–49 more than 150,000 Dutch soldiers, mainly conscripts, were sent to Indonesia.

12. As a comparison, in 1970 it was 13.4% of the national budget, and in 1980 9.9%.

13. Megens makes clear that in the years 1951–1961 about 26% of the Dutch defense budget was financed out of American aid. C. M. Megens, *American Aid to NATO Allies in the 1950s: The Dutch Case* (Groningen: Thesis, 1994).

14. See Hoffenaar and Teitler, *De Koude Oorlog,* p. 214 ff.

15. Ibid., p. 222.

16. J. J. A. Wijn, ed., *Tussen vloot en politiek* (Dieren: De Bataafsche Leeuw, 1986), p. 148.

17. J. W. Honig, *Defense Policy in the North Atlantic Alliance* (Westport, Conn.: Praeger, 1993), p. 14.

18. Ibid., p. 16.

19. As a result of the work of Moorman, by that time the plans had been downsized to a Dutch fleet consisting of one carrier, two cruisers, twelve destroyers, eight submarines, and forty-eight minesweepers.

20. Honig, *Defense Policy,* p. 19.

21. Ibid., p. 20.

22. Although this increase was intended only for the years 1951–54, it was never cancelled.

23. Honig, *Defense Policy,* p. 35.

24. A. Stemerdink, *Dagboeken* (Amsterdam: Vitgeverij Balans, 1986), p. 138.

25. For instance, the ones that ever since 1963 are regularly held by the Dutch Foundation on Armed Forces and Society.

26. Hoffenaar and Teitler, *De Koude Oorlog,* p. 279.

27. Ministry of Defense, *Om de veiligheid van het bestaan* (Our very existence at stake) (The Hague: SDU, 1974), p. 61.

28. See, for instance, Honig, *Defense Policy,* p. 171; and Hoffenaar and Teitler, *De Koude Oorlog,* p. 289.

29. Semerdink, *Dagboeken,* p. 81.

30. A reduction of 15% from roughly 147,000 in 1972 to 125,000 in 1977 was planned. The factual situation in 1977 was a personnel strength of approximately 130,500, a reduction of 11% compared with 1972.

31. Honig, *Defense Policy,* p. 177.

32. In 1949, the year in which Dutch colonial rule over the East Indies ended, a great number of South Moluccans came to the Netherlands. They feared for their future in an independent Indonesia, because for centuries they had cooperated closely with the Dutch colonial regime. Both economically and socially they never integrated very well into Dutch society, and especially among the young Moluccans this led to feelings of frustration and bitterness, which resulted in several terrorist actions in the 1970s.

33. During the action, six of the terrorists and two hostages were killed.

34. *Keesings Historisch Archief,* 24 June 1977, p. 296.

35. Ph. Everts, *Watdenken de mensen in het land?* (Nijmegen: Studiecentrum voor Vredesvraagstukken, 1992), p. 83.

36. Ibid., p. 53.

37. *Verplicht of vrijwillig dienen? Een onderzok naar de wendselikheid en mogelijkheid van een vrijwilligerskirijgsmacht* (The Hague: Staatsuitgeverij, 1977).

38. Everts, *Wat denken demensen,* p. 44.

39. With the exception of functions aboard submarines and in the Royal Marine Corps.

40. For instance, by the Social Council for the Armed Forces, a civil advisory board to the Minister of Defense.

41. For several years already, the proportion of women is approximately 5%.

42. Minister of Defense, *Prioriteitennota. Een andere wereld, een andere Defensie* (another world, another Defense organization) (The Hague: SDU, 1993).

43. These percentages were measured during opinion polls held by the Dutch Foundation on Armed Forces and Society.

44. "The northern part of Noord-Holland is a special case, due to the presence of a naval base in Den Helder. This region depends on Defense for a third of its income, a dependence which is, however, more the result of direct employment (defense payrolls) than indirect employment resulting from defense orders." In A.J. Hofman, *Het regionaal-economisch effect van Defensie-uitgaven* (The regional-economic impact of Defense-expenditures). Emmen, CDP-publishers, 1991, p. 343.

45. From an interview published in the Dutch magazine *Maatschappij & Krijgsmacht* (Society & The Armed Forces). 15, 3 (June 1993), p. 5.

46. Held in August 1995 by the Dutch Foundation on Armed Forces and Society. The question asked was: Do you think the armed forces are . . .

necessary	(45 %)
a necessary evil	(29 %)
hardly necessary	(12 %)
superfluous	(4 %)
don't know	(10 %)

"Necessary" and "necessary evil" combined gives a remarkable 74%.

REFERENCES

Amersfoort, H., and P. H. Kamphuis, eds. *Mei 1940. De strijd op Nederlands grondgebied* (May 1940. The fighting on Dutch territory). The Hague: SDU, 1990.

Everts, Ph. *Wat denken de mensen in het land?* (What do the people think?). Nijmegen: Studiecentrum voor Vredesvraagstukken, 1992.

Hoffenaar, J., and B. Schoenmaker. *Met de blik naar het Oosten. De Koninklijke land-*

macht 1945–1990 (Looking eastward. The Royal Netherlands Army 1945–1990). The Hague: SDU, 1994.

Hoffenaar, J., and G. Teiter, eds. *De Koude Oorlog: Maatschappij en krijgsmacht in de jaren '50* (The cold war. Armed forces and society in the 1950s). The Hague: SDU, 1992.

Honig, J. W. *Defense Policy in the North Atlantic Alliance: The Case of the Netherlands.* Westport, Conn.: Praeger, 1993.

Megens, C. M. *American Aid to NATO Allies in the 1950s: The Dutch Case.* Groningen: Thesis, 1994.

Raven, G. J. A., and N. A. M. Rodger, eds. *Navies and Armies. The Anglo-Dutch Relationship in War and Peace 1688–1988.* Edinburgh: John Donald, 1990.

Stemerdink, A. *Dagboeken* (Diaries). Amsterdam: Uitgeverij Balans, 1986.

Teitler, G., ed. *Tussen crisis en oorlog: Maatschappij en krijgsmacht in de jaren '30* (Between Crisis and War. Armed Forces and Society in the 1930s). Dieren: De Bataafsche Leeuw, 1984.

Wijn, J. J. A., ed. *Tussen vloot en politiek: Een eeuw marinestaf 1889–1986.* (Between fleet and parliament. The naval staff 1886–1986). Dieren: De Bataafsche Leeuw, 1986.

NIGERIA

Karl P. Magyar

In his discussion of Africa's civil-military pendulum, Professor Ali Mazrui raises the central issues of contention when examining the sensitive problem of the military's role in African society. He identifies in stark terms the tendency of civilian-led governments to offer greater freedom but to lose control over the economic resources of the state, while military governments impose greater discipline but at the price of political liberties. This characterizes Nigeria's history since independence and also Ghana's, of whose civilian-led Limann administration Mazrui observes, "the people of Ghana seemed to be more angered by the economic sins of the Administration than pleased by the political virtues of an open society."[1]

An examination of Africa's civilian-military interplay cannot avoid these issues. Are civilian regimes generally corrupt and incompetent? Are military regimes more honest and efficient, but also politically more authoritarian? Have one-party states offered the greatest opportunity for socioeconomic advancement? And do the masses of Africans prefer governmental economic integrity and their own advancement to the more abstract symbols of political democracy?

The answers to these questions should inform the debate about the virtues of civilian versus military regimes, and it may also highlight the importance of the analytic perspective. Do Western academic and policy analysts sufficiently appreciate the preferences of those most directly affected by the consequences of policies in Africa? Should the prevailing Western democratic paradigm be justifiably assumed to be the appropriate universal panacea for the Third World's ills? In a brief projection of South Africa's political future under a majority government I raised the question: Will South Africa's blacks ultimately judge their liberation by the attainment of abstract political symbols or by their visible economic advancement?

The implications of these questions for the external community are profound, as their recent energies have been channeled towards encouraging Africans to move toward civilian governments, plural parties, elections, freedom, and human rights—all of them commendable virtues that we in the developed West certainly enjoy. But this disregards the fact that most African states started with democratic institutions at independence, but they were soon discarded. Also, those states or regimes that today may be characterized as democratic have not demonstrated the ability to advance their economic fortunes because of that political form.[2]

Those analysts in the past who would tolerate the nondemocratic excesses of African misrule were labeled "apologists." However, in light of Africans experiencing the fourth decade of economic deterioration, political instability, and ongoing conflicts and wars, as epitomized by Somalia's vortex of anarchy, it may indeed be defensible to argue in favor of a radical reexamination of the assumptions made by traditional analyses. This includes taking a critical view of the aura surrounding the democratic mystique that has to date not demonstrated its capacity to reverse Africa's socioeconomic degenerative direction. That continent has recently been described as marginalized, reflecting its peripheral role in global affairs. It is becoming apparent that much more than mere democratic accouterments will be required to elevate Africa's competitive capacity. The Orient's newly industrializing countries (NICs) certainly do not celebrate their envious economic status today as the product of democratic institutions. However, they also shied away from praetorian concerns as the driving force in their advancement. This too should be instructive to Africans.

With one out of four Africans being Nigerians, that country has featured prominently in the recent history of the continent. Its population of over one hundred million dwarfs that of its neighbors; its oil resource has been a rare African beacon of economic interest to external economic concerns; and its unwavering pro-Western stance during the Cold War days earned that pivotal country a measure of respect not generously bestowed on other African countries. Yet Nigeria is an African country and faces the usual problems of governance and of economic survival. Its experience has included alternations between military and civilian rule, and Nigeria has also experienced the gamut of developmental problems. Finding correlations between regime type and administrative performance is of interest to the analyst but it will be argued in this review that from the vantage point of over three decades of developmental frustrations, the old questions regarding civilian versus military rule may need to be channeled into new inquiries.

AFRICA'S CONTEXT OF POLITICAL DEVELOPMENT

Volumes have been written on Africa's developmental environment as it has evolved since most African states received independence in the 1960s. There were some early negative prognostications, but not many analysts or external statesmen expected the deluge of problems associated with the transformation of colonies into viable, competitive, functioning independent states. In part, this stemmed from two sources. The African colonies had lost considerable importance to the Europeans after World War II as European states turned inward to concentrate on rebuilding their own societies. Preparing the colonies for independence consumed little energy or concern, while the emerging African elite focused on one event: the transfer of power as soon as possible. Little thought was expended on the details of their political and economic developmental future beyond naive expectations that, after a period of readjustment, these countries would embark on the beginning stages of economic growth and modernization process—and they would somehow succeed.

The other reason for the inadequate anticipation of developmental challenges was rooted in the Cold War. Neither the Soviet Union nor the United States had colonies in Africa, and both had traditionally lacked interest in the affairs of the Third World. As global powers, the United States and the Soviet Union monitored developments everywhere on earth, but only certain conflicts received their direct attention. Africa's independence caught both countries without an assessment of that vast continent's strategic role; hence, both the Soviet Union and the United States involved themselves modestly in the early tumultuous postindependence days. Little long-term thinking was in evidence, beyond minor efforts to deny whatever advantages Africa might possess to the other side. This meant lending support to opposing sides in conflicts, thereby supporting the division of the continent into two weak ideological camps. However, this modest level of involvement produced little of lasting consequence. The Soviets invested heavily in certain conflicts—most notably in Ethiopia and Angola—while the United States spent most of its funds on aid projects. But neither side showed evidence of seriously appreciating Africa's developmental dilemma. With the demise of the Cold War, Africa has quickly become marginalized.

Explanations for Africa's failure to develop fall into three categories, although rarely are they presented exclusively. First, Africa's problems are traced to the history of external intervention by, initially, Arabs, and then Europe's colonial powers, who wrecked the delicate social balances that had existed in Africa's long history before external penetration. Since independence, it is maintained, this preponderant external influence has not abated as the continent has become subject to intrusive "neocolonial" forces. The second category concerns explanations that blame much of Africa's problems on natural causes, stemming from Africa's harsh geographic conditions. The usual culprits include droughts, desertification, locusts and other pests, heat, storms, and the periodic bouts of hunger and diseases. The third category concerns the managerial dimension. According to this explanation, Africa's developmental problems may be traced to incompetence, corruption, ethnicity, lack of education, paucity of entrepreneurs, and general ineptitude in the political and administrative management of the state. Most agree on the facts of developmental problems, but it is the explanation of them and the recommended cures that generate the controversies.

The response by Africans to their own plight has been perplexingly sanguine. The dual societies that have emerged support a small, modernized, elite class

that enjoys the Western accouterments of wealth, obtained largely through their
exclusive control over their countries' scarce natural resources and public finances. The masses live in abject poverty in the urban centers or in their traditional rural areas, which may hardly have been touched by the symbols and
facts of independence. Africa has not been nor is it becoming competitive with
the First World's driving force of the global economy. In the 1980s, Africa's
contribution to the global product was just under 2%; in the early 1990s this
dropped to 1.2%. While only reluctantly acknowledging Africa's declining capability, African statesmen have offered no convincing solutions to this diminishing performance, ensuring thereby perpetuation of the socioeconomic
dualities that prevail in their states. Civil unrest, inadequate housing, hunger,
unemployment, military rule, wars, and administrative ineptitude persist, while
structural reforms and superficial political transformations offer but a translucent
veneer of progress.

It is imperative that any detailed examination of Africa's military be considered within this context, as it is a premise of this presentation that it is not
appropriate to consider Africa's situation within the context of universal standards derived from First World developmental models. Most of Africa is presently in the consolidative stage of development, a period marked by great social
upheavals as the state embarks on the arduous nation-building and legitimation
process, which, in the history of most nations, is marked by tumultuous social
relations and civil wars. In this stage, the state's authority and geographic extension have not yet been effectively defined; and with the failure to develop
the economy in the face of rising expectations, fragmentationist tendencies
emerge that challenge the central authority of the state. It is at this juncture that
agitation in the military ranks begins as they sense the weakening of the civilian
authorities—but also their own glorious opportunity.

MILITARY RULE IN AFRICA

Claude E. Welch notes three stages when tracing military intervention in
Africa since independence.[3] The first stage is characterized by "relative passivity
and abstention from political interference," during which time armies remained
under substantial expatriate influence. The second stage saw resentment against
European officers and African political leaders explode into mutinies. The third
stage experienced the coups d'etat, with the occupants of presidential palaces
being removed and replaced by military rulers. Richard Hodder-Williams maintains that at independence the civilian rulers did not see the military as a prestigious institution as in the past they had served colonial regimes, were small,
and were largely comprised of the more " 'backward' peoples" of the country.[4]
Nevertheless, the militaries emerged as strong institutions inversely to the weakening of administrative and political structures.

Why the militaries intervene in politics is a question dealt with extensively
but not definitively in many studies. Equally examined is the issue concerning

going "back to the barracks"—yielding power to civilian regimes again. Reasons for intervening include the perceived need to save the state from chaos, political and economic collapse, corruption and mismanagement, resentment of expatriate officers, lack of pay, "contagion"—meaning that it is the trend in the region—personal ambitions of senior, but recently junior officers, the expectation by senior officers of their impending removal, and the "ease" factor—which alludes to the power of having the guns.[5] Others point to "the persistence and strength of ethnicity" as the important factor.[6] It may be deduced from such a broad range of reasons that motives differ from case to case; that motives have evolved and diversified since the original rash of coups; and with such a variety of explanations, we may reasonably expect military interference in politics for some time to come.

The data regarding such interventions are instructive. One compilation lists four African coups before 1963 but sixty-eight coups from 1963 to 1987, averaging nearly three coups per year, with seven in 1966 alone.[7] If coups, unsuccessful attempts, and plots are tallied, they averaged nearly ten per year.[8] Well over half of Africa's states have experienced at least one successful coup, with several states having experienced five.[9] Because of the frequency of plural coups in so many countries, by now most coups take place against military governments.[10] With some notable exceptions as, for example, the brutal coup in Burundi in 1993, the more recent coups have generally been less disruptive of societies as they concerned mostly change at the top levels of military command only. Such relatively peaceful transitions characterize Nigeria's coups.

In power, there is no evidence that decisively points to the superior performance of military over civilian regimes. In the immediate post-independence days, it was expected by some that the military could ward off ethnic and regional pressures, that the military was the most integrated institution in society, that their hierarchic and disciplined structure would be of great administrative advantage, that they would be efficient, and that they would be pragmatically objective and not subject to ideologically based squabbles. Many expected that the military as governors would be less corrupt, as most announced their intention to reverse prevailing corrupt practices immediately upon their accession to power. In office, various approaches toward addressing their responsibilities were demonstrated. Kwazi Sarfo lists the use of repressive tactics, co-option of groups who may be potential challengers, or the dispensation of inducements that ensured military populism.[11] But he concludes, "The [previously] entertained notion that the military might be more successful than the earlier civilian governments in promoting stability, national integration and economic development is no longer a credible proposition."[12] This assessment is echoed by Opoku Agyeman: "few soldiers are in favour of a major restructuring of society after they take over power." Agyeman quotes Ruth First's old observation that a coup is a method of change that changes little.[13] Rene Lemarchand noted, after examining three cases, "In none is there any evidence that the military is either willing or able to engage in the manifold tasks associated with nation-building.''[14] In a similar vein, W. F. Gutteridge observed that the military is not the fabled melting pot; he concludes that military takeovers suffer from the lack of any "clear-cut political objectives."[15]

If the military's entry into power was surprisingly easy, going back to the barracks—and remaining there—has proven to be a formidable challenge. In some fifteen sub-Saharan African countries, no military government has ever been in place, but little can be learned about the reasons by a comparative examination. In fewer cases yet, soldiers have gone from the statehouse back to the barracks and stayed there, but these are rare exceptions.[16] S. E. Finer offers four conditions for disengaging from power: The leader must want his troops to quit politics; a functioning regime must be established; the new regime must be favorable to the military; and the armed forces must have confidence in their leader.[17] Finer observes that these conditions do not prevail in Africa. On a purely rational basis, we could expect the military to disengage from political power as soon as the precipitating causes have been addressed.

This may lead to a paradoxical situation. If the military government were able to resolve the problems that led to its intervention, then the military would have shown that it is more competent than civilian authorities—which raises the question, Why yield power to yet another civilian regime? More likely, however, the military cannot resolve problems easily, for, as we noted, these problems tend to be multifarious and complex and will certainly not be resolved quickly by a few edicts. In that case, if the military bows out, it will leave an unresolved situation to a new civilian government that presumably is less experienced than was the original group that was ousted. The new civilian government must operate while knowing it is being watched by a military with takeover experience. External critics focus almost exclusively on whether the regime is civilian or military, with the precipitating causes and cures receiving secondary consideration. Of course, the preferred regime type for these critics is civilian.

NIGERIA'S POST-COLONIAL DEVELOPMENTS

Much of the preceding comment about Africa's experience with military rule is directly applicable to Nigeria's own praetorian history. This is largely because analysts have focused their examinations more often on Nigeria than on any other African state; hence, Nigeria's experience forms many of the analytic paradigms. There have been periods of relatively respectable military rule such as those of Lieutenant Colonel Yakubu Gowon, Brigadier Murtala Mohammed, and Lieutenant General Olusegun Obasanjo. But the regime of Major General Ibrahim Babangida could not escape the vortex of controversy that culminated in widespread domestic and foreign condemnation for his refusal to accept the results of what had been taken to be a fair civilian election in 1993. This event has cast a pall on the more respectable episodes of military rule, which previously had been convincingly justified because of the events emerging out of Nigeria's civil war or on grounds of corruption and administrative ineptitude such as were alleged about the civilian government of Shehu Shagari, who served as elected president from 1979 to 1983.[18]

Nigeria, like so many African countries, had no historical representation of its current form. In fact, the region was an area of warring tribes whose economic resources became of interest to British slave traders. The British government brought an uneasy peace and eventually united the greatly disparate peoples into the populous colony of Nigeria, which attained independence in 1960.[19] The history of Nigeria's sociopolitical fragmentation has survived to this day; indeed, it may be judged to be more acute than before independence. The military governments have been locked into the policy of keeping the federation together, but the price of perpetuating the unity of this fragile state has been very high, and there is yet no guarantee that Nigeria's unity will be assured into the distant future. On a skeptical note, should in the future Nigeria undergo a permanent breakup, it will be hard to justify the cost in lives and resources that were previously expended to keep the country together.

The military has played a prominent role in Nigeria's history since before independence. Ikenna Nzimiro notes that, at the outset, the organizing principles of Nigeria's modern military forces were "rank, race and a comparatively privileged position—in terms of pay, lodging and food—for the indigenous soldiers relative to the rest of the African labour force."[20] Before independence the colony's indigenous military forces had been utilized on numerous occasions for internal pacification purposes, twenty-eight battalions of Nigerian soldiers served abroad in World War II, and many officers were trained at elite British military institutions. They had been led at the top levels by British officers, whom the Nigerians would replace after independence. There were only fifty-nine officers before independence, but within six years this number increased to 507. There is reason to believe that, while the politicians had concentrated on gaining independence, ascending to power, and then confronting (with little success) the awesome task of building a nation, the military was quietly building its own power base. Both sides encountered the same frustrations and internal cleavages, the consequences of which would emerge as the political state declined and the military likewise experienced fragmentation. However, the military would inevitably emerge in power, which they have dominated directly for twenty-four out of the thirty-four years of independence. Civilians governed for only the first six years after independence and for the four years of President Shagari's rule.

According to General Obasanjo and Akin Mabogunje, the military became engaged in politics when the civilian regime attempted to Nigerianize the army in 1963. At issue was the struggle "between the President and the Prime Minister over which of them had the power to command the armed forces."[21] Both had taken conflicting advice from different army officers, which again demonstrates the fragmentationist tendencies in that country. However, this fragmentation in both political and military ranks had dire consequences, as it led to a coup, the civil war over Biafra, and the subsequent challenge of managing the vast revenues that flowed into Nigeria from the sale of oil. All this transpired within a few years during Nigeria's first decade of independence, and it set an agenda that has hardly been altered since. Politically, Nigeria remains divided by extreme factionalism; social concerns, ethnicity, and religion remain major determinants in social relations; oil and the economy determine the government's priorities and, ultimately, its composition; and the military strives to supply the elusive unifying element, while its ranks are nervous about their own divisions. There is irony in the expectation that the military is to unite the society, whose divisions the military itself reflects.[22]

A review of Nigeria's post-independence history reveals many typical patterns of political turmoil found in other unstable states in Africa where the initial civilian regime is soon discovered to be weak, inept, and corrupt. The demands for satiation of their rising expectations and the unfulfilled realities leave the masses in a political limbo, caught in a dilemma of having to choose on whom to bestow their loyalties: the modern elite that promises them the accouterments of modern lifestyles or their traditional parochial tribal affiliation, which still offers the sanctity of a familiar communal-based security. However, the modern elite fail to ensure progress and wealth, for all except themselves, while traditional structures offer neither hope nor a plan for rapid advancement to modern society. This results in severe attitudinal dislocations, and it certainly does not facilitate nation-building. The state effectively collapses as a national entity, held together weakly by the myth of nationalism and at the expense of sociopolitical turmoil and, ultimately, of lives.

Nigeria experienced this same pattern of development and responded with the usual widespread African formula, military rule. The first coup, which occurred in 1966, put Major General Ironsi in power, along with his Igbo coterie. A major mistake had been made in that coup as numerous Northern and Yoruba (Westerners) top-level political figures and military officers were executed. As should have been expected, this flagrantly ethnic-based takeover was soon met with another ethnic-inspired countercoup, this time led by Northerners. At issue was who would dominate over whom. When the numerically superior Northerners prevailed, the by now highly suspicious Igbos embarked on a bloody secessionist course. The attempt to create an independent state, Biafra, out of Nigeria's eastern province failed by 1970, but not before it produced the war with the greatest number of casualties of any war from World War II to our own day.

The history of Nigeria since this first spate of military takeovers and the ensuing Biafran war has indeed been tumultuous and disturbing to external observers. Gowon's relatively long period of military rule lasted from 1966 until 1975. He was ousted in a mostly peaceful coup and replaced by Murtala Mohammed, who was assassinated in a failed coup attempt in 1976. As next in line, Olusegun Obasanjo replaced him in power, and he indeed prepared the country for civilian elections. These were held, and Shehu Shagari assumed the civilian presidency in 1979 but was ousted in 1983, soon after his reelection, by yet another military coup, which brought an end to the Second Republic. Mohammed Buhari led the next military government until he was ousted and replaced in 1985 by Ibrahim Babangida, who left office under great pressure in 1993.

Public attitudes toward these military interventions were neither unified nor consistent, reflecting the diverse ethnic composition of the populace but also the frustrations with both the civilian and the military regimes. This was manifested by the surprising degree of tolerance of Buhari's coup after Shagari had just been reelected. In general, the military was seen as capable of stabilizing the social order and suppressing sectional antagonism, but at the cost of declining economic development. Civilian governments were supposed to be able to integrate the society socially and to build the economy, but in their weakness they were incapable of overcoming regionalist pressures and were unable to solve the serious problems of administrative ineptitude and associated corruption that stymied economic development. Having to choose between these options aroused no great public passions.

Another factor contributing to the frequently ambivalent public attitude was the curiously absent ideological context for debating the country's direction. The socialism/capitalism debate, common in other parts of the Third World, was almost entirely absent in Nigeria, which had no trouble accepting the broad elements of the prevailing Western liberal-democratic structural paradigm. There is little doubt about Nigeria's steadfastly Western identification, nor about its preference for ideological pragmatism.[23] This pragmatism characterizes the attitudes of the military and most civilian politicians, as well as the population. Religious considerations play a very prominent role, but they are not separable from the ethnic context and regional divisions of the country. Absent are doctrinaire political views, which have been in evidence in some of Africa's early Marxist governments, especially in the ex-Portuguese colonies, where such divisions have led to prolonged civil wars. Nigeria is fortunate in that its huge population does not suffer this source of division. Still, in the face of rising expectations, the population remains frustrated.

A dominant theme in Nigeria's postcolonial history is the pervasive struggle between the broad northern and southern coalitions. Indeed, much of the country's recent history revolves around this theme. During the colonial days, these two regions were administered differently by the British in recognition of their diverse indigenous political histories, but they were united for the purpose of forming one colony.[24] Independence introduced at least an initial expectation of de facto socioeconomic integration, which was manifested notably by Igbo economic penetration of the North, while Northerners capitalized on their numerical superiority to dominate the national administrative apparatus. This economic domination was unacceptable to the North, while the Southerners realized that they had been outflanked politically with the country's major federal political offices coming under the direct influence of the Sardauna of Sokoto and the

North's traditional Muslim establishment, acting through the elected prime minister, a Northerner.

Nigeria's political history since independence revolves around the military's political perception of and intervention in public affairs. By now this may also be characterized as outright domination. Analyzing the reasons for this military intervention can be a lengthy exercise in itself, and there is little evidence to indicate that the reasons differ markedly from those of military interventionists elsewhere in Africa. Given Nigeria's huge population size and historically disparate ethnic composition, it should have been expected that its post-independence political challenges would be particularly formidable. In the newly independent country, the legitimacy of both the political institutions and the persons holding top positions were not readily established, and few had anticipated the rapid decline of authority and the deteriorating economic order. The military's interventions should have come as no surprise, but the rationale for and the length of the interventions became the most interesting considerations. Was the military only to restore order? Introduce a new constitutional system? Install a new set of leaders? Preside over the fuller integration of the country— or perhaps manage its orderly dismemberment? Were there indeed any long-term views, or were the interventions seen as the usual restorative exercises to be followed soon by the promised elections?

Reasons cited for the military's intervention in Nigeria's politics are diverse. The initial civilian government had been ousted when it conceded it could no longer keep order following the Igbo-Hausa confrontations in the North. With the attempt by Biafra to secede and the onset of war, there was little need to justify military rule. The military also found it easy to justify remaining in power after the war, as the society had been severely disrupted and had to be rebuilt again. Gowon had ruled for nine years; when he was ousted, he was accused of being insensitive to the demands of the people, disregarding the traditional chiefs, inaccessibility, indecision, lack of governmental discipline, and improper administration of the armed forces. His successor, Murtala Mohammed, explained that Nigeria was plunging into chaos and it was time to remove Gowon.[25] Other analysts add Gowon's failure to create new states, the problems associated with the 1973 census, and the cancellation of a plan to reinstitute a civilian government.[26] Shagari's civilian government was ousted for reasons that included the failure to stem widespread corruption, which had greatly disenchanted the masses, although paradoxically they had voted Shagari back into power. More revealing was the failed coup against Babangida in 1990. Stated reasons included resentment against Babangida's grandiose personal ambitions, a cabinet reshuffle and personal control of the defense ministry, the new security apparatus, and implied resentment against official domination by Northerners. The perpetrators of that coup were Christian Southerners who allegedly threatened to expel several Muslim-dominated northern states.[27] As indicated, the reasons for the coups are indeed diverse, and they reflect the gamut of problems encountered by the entire society. Once in power, the new regimes attempt to address these problems, but failure soon reintroduces the same conditions, which leads to yet another coup.

THE MILITARY'S POLITICAL CHALLENGES

The problems faced by the military in power have not differed significantly from those faced by civilians when in office. Some specific problems emerged with the passage of time, as in the case of the troublesome management of oil, which had not been a major concern for the first civilian government. For the most part, the challenges that confronted the First and Second civilian-run Republics were the perennial ones faced by the military as well. In both civilian and military periods, the primary concern was with nation-building, which involved the introduction of new constitutional structures, political institutions, regional and local authorities, federal-state relations, the creation of new states, and the attempt to undertake a noncontroversial census. However, while the state was thus being redefined, the country also had to be administered. Various regions experienced social turmoil along ethnic and religious lines; problems with the protection of human rights became manifest; Nigeria's regional foreign policy encountered controversy; the economy experienced severe reversals; and of course the military had to be handled gingerly. The public appears to have been tolerant of both types of regimes, but frustrated in that neither produced the promised results.

The first post-independence civilian regime had assumed authority in 1960 and proceeded on the usual path of consolidation characteristic of all new states. As noted, within the African context, there was quite a bit of naiveté about the assumptions regarding the degree of state integration and about the respect for authority that the elected officials were to have enjoyed. The realities soon set in, and a major problem emerged in the form of subnational identification and wide disrespect for national institutions. The major political parties only polarized the ethnic groups. Early election procedures and results were hotly contested; census results were challenged; minority ethnic groups demanded their own states; and the general election of 1964 and the election in the Western Region in 1965 were disputed.[28] The military was initially reluctant to intervene in the turmoil in the Western Region, although it was evident that the police could not keep order. Then five majors, led by Major K. C. Nzeogwu, staged the first coup in January 1966. According to Nzeogwu, "We wanted to get rid of rotten and corrupt ministers, political parties, trade unions and the whole clumsy apparatus of the federal system. We wanted to gun down all the bigwigs in our way."[29] These rebellious majors failed to impose themselves as the rulers, despite their assassinations of numerous top political officeholders; and the army's commanding officer, Major General Ironsi, took over as the first military ruler. This coup demonstrated at once the emergence of the military in politics, the divisions in their ranks, and the inadequacies of civilian institutions.

Ironsi moved quickly to restore law and order, helped perhaps by a public disillusioned by the incompetence of civilian authorities. Sensing correctly the problems associated with ethnic polarization, which had been encouraged by the existence of the four regions of the federal structure, Ironsi eliminated this regional division and unified all public services. Another decree dissolved numerous political and cultural associations, in an early attempt to come to terms with Nigeria's fragmented nature. Subsequently, Nigeria had to recognize these divisions and expanded the states from four, to twelve, nineteen, and then thirty states. The attempt to unify the administrative units of the country was well intentioned—it would transcend the competitive nature inherent in Nigeria's federal system—but it came too late, as now the unified system was seen as being the vehicle for potential domination by one group, the Northerners, or by the southern Igbos. No solution was universally accepted, as approval was measured by the advantage that would accrue, not to the entire nation, but to one's own ethnic group. At the same time, dissension emerged also in the military ranks concerning promotions, rotation of battalions around the country, and the failure to try the perpetrators of the coup in which military officers had been assassinated. It was clear that first the civilian government and now the military had grossly underestimated the extent of political deterioration in the country. This became evident as all remedies, however well intended, would soon encounter substantial opposition from various quarters. Within six months of coming to power, General Ironsi was killed in another coup.

Lieutenant Colonel Gowon, as chief of staff of the army, headed the next military government, but he stepped into a minefield of discontent. He moved quickly to send soldiers back to the regions of their origins in order to diffuse ethnic tensions. But by now Ibos had encountered overt hostilities in the North, and they streamed back to their southeastern region. Lieutenant Colonel Ojukwu, who had been appointed military governor of the Eastern Region by Ironsi, refused to recognize Gowon as the new ruler. After several reconciliation attempts initiated by Gowon, Ojukwu declared the secession of his region—named Biafra.[30] The national army quickly expanded and recruited many who had had substantial experience fighting for the British overseas during World War II. The ensuing Biafran war was won decisively by the national government in 1970.

The close of the war coincided with rapidly expanding profits from the sale of oil. From 1970 to 1971 oil revenues more than tripled, making the militarization of Nigeria more palatable to the public.[31] Now the country had a military with a proven record of success: Nigeria had been kept united by the military where a civilian government surely would have failed, and the size and professionalism of the military made it an attractive alternative to civilian rule. The military expanded its ranks and was outfitted with an expensive array of weaponry far in excess of what would be needed after the war. Most equipment was purchased from Great Britain and the Soviet Union. This capacity was then utilized at the regional level and in international peacekeeping efforts that, in 1990, resulted in Nigeria's massive commitment to the Liberian operation.

The post-Biafran war era introduced a second period in the history of Nigerian politics in that the military had gone beyond its prewar legacy of staying out of politics in line with the professionalism expected of them according to their British colonial training. Nigeria was "Africanizing," and the military now perceived a new role in public affairs for themselves. While some saw a modest role as a watchdog of stability, others perceived their role in a more ambitious light. This latter view was manifested in the subsequent reluctance to return to the barracks when the military ousted President Shagari in 1983 and when Babangida clumsily annulled the election results for civilian president in 1993.

After the Biafran war had ended and before Gowon was ousted in 1975, he had received wide respect for a mature attitude towards the defeated Igbos in the attempt to rebuild the nation. It helped to have the oil, which soon supplied the great bulk of the government's operating revenues. However, that oil also became a curse in that it fueled regional competition for funds as well as large-scale government corruption. Murtala Mohammed led the military regime that ousted Gowon for, as it was explained, Gowon's personal shortcomings. He had been in power nine years and, as Mohammed explained in his speech to the nation, "Nigeria has been left to drift," and the nation was being plunged into chaos. He also noted that the military had become disillusioned.[32] The government needed energizing; and indeed, Mohammed demonstrated great reformist initiative immediately upon assuming power. His rule was soon viewed as sincere; before he was assassinated the following year, he had gained wide popularity.

Gowon's long tenure in office had been shaped by the civil war and the attempt to reintegrate the Ibos into the state. Mohammed's concern was with the problems of developing the entire country; managing the public sector of the economy, which by now had been dominated by vast oil revenues; reducing the size of the military; and restructuring the government as well as its composition. On assuming power, he quickly retired thousands of top military, police, and civilian officials while elevating new officers to top ranks. He also appointed new military governors for the states. Three organs of government were created at the federal level: the Supreme Military Council, the National Council of States, and the Federal Executive Council. Of great interest were official appointments, which included some controversial figures as well as Obasanjo, Buhari, and Babangida—all three of whom would later become head of state, the latter two by staging their own coups. Mohammed also announced his intention to deal with the question of new states, a new federal capital, the census, and other projects the previous government had started.

Guy Arnold makes a valid observation when he notes that Nigeria's states possess all the attributes of nation-states, which makes the relations between the central government and the regions very precarious. One method for dealing with this problem was the weakening of states by expanding their numbers. In line with this strategy, in 1976 the number of states increased to nineteen. It was evident that the nation was still undergoing consolidation by trial and error. Although the domestic climate had changed considerably from the atmosphere of the first period of civilian rule, nation-building in its various forms was still the ultimate driving force. The federal government would exert its dominant influence especially through the politically conditioned allocation of funds derived from oil sales. And to defuse excessive regional influence on the federal government, the country would rapidly advance the building of Abuja, a new capital, situated centrally in a largely neutral area of the country.

Mohammed's ambitious agenda had barely gotten underway when he was killed in an aborted coup. His deputy, Lieutenant General Obasanjo, succeeded him in office peacefully. As a protégé of Mohammed, Obasanjo adopted his reformist program and brought to the post a more intellectual and low-key attitude. Obasanjo's own agenda began to show with his moves to reorganize, reduce, professionalize, and encourage the education of the military's officers. He also attempted to shake up the civil service, but there he met with less success.[33] Obasanjo may have perceived himself to be more accommodating and tolerant, but he railed against Nigeria's notorious bureaucratic inefficiency. The military rulers expected that the bureaucracy would function with military efficiency and discipline, but the succession of military heads of state remained frustrated in that endeavor. But Obasanjo's greatest success was realized in his determination to advance Mohammed's plans for a return to civilian rule, which occurred in 1979. Prior to that, a new constitution had to be written, a Constituent Assembly had to be formed, elections at various levels had to be held, and political parties were reintroduced. However, Obasanjo may have been overly sanguine about the military's return to the barracks. Certainly there were those in the military who did not relish the prospect of remaining there. These latter forces emerged on the last day of 1983 and have not reversed the military's control of Nigeria to this day.

Shagari's four-year civilian interlude served as a watershed in the two categories of justification for military rule. Hitherto, the authority of the military for ruling the nation derived from the inadequacies of the first civilian administration during the fragile post-independence days and from the civil war that followed. After the war, military rule was justified on the ground that the country had to be reintegrated in advance of the reintroduction of a civilian government. It appears that these early military rulers genuinely believed that civilian rule was plausible and preferable and that the military's intervention was but a short-term necessity during the new nation's teething period. And they may have expected that the next civilian government would encounter further operational problems, but on a reduced basis. Shagari's government did indeed experience such problems, but now a new attitude emerged from the military. Subsequent military rulers showed evidence of a less tolerant attitude toward the mundane problems and politics of civilian rule, and they have accepted the moral rationale of their own authority, which had justified the initial interventions of their military predecessors. These new attitudes evince an inherent disrespect for civilian capabilities and assume incompetence and corruption to be the norm of civilian rule. Taking power and retaining it become an imperative when only the military is seen as being capable of advancing the nation in its challenging historical context.

The next military government, headed by Major General Muhammad Buhari, openly demonstrated this attitude. His government's introduction was offered by Brigadier Sunni Abacha, who in turn acceded to leadership of the nation in 1993. Shagari had been generous to the military's budget and had no major differences with the military's established administration. However, the declining economic environment and the rampage of corruption did not enhance his government's reputation. Shehu Othman notes the emergence of another factor that influenced the military's attitude. The peacekeeping operation in Chad in 1980 had not gone well. Nigeria's intervention was influenced excessively by external powers, and the border skirmishes with Cameroon the following year, in which Nigeria's military lost some men, were not avenged. Shagari insisted that Nigeria's leadership role precluded hasty and heavy-handed actions but, notes Othman, "Some military commanders were unimpressed."[34] This dissent may have been the first clear indication of the military's perception of Nigeria's regional responsibilities and grandiose ambitions that a mere civilian administration could not properly undertake. Nigeria's leadership and domination of ECOMOG's (Economic Community of West African States Cease-Fire Monitoring Group) operation in Liberia, starting in 1990, may be the apogee of this contrasting attitude. Othman notes that both generals Buhari and Babangida also had fundamental disagreements with Shagari on the military's mission in Chad.

Buhari's rule marked another episode of domination of the country through the military apparatus by Northerners. He demonstrated the usual intentions and energies of a military government that had taken over in what was perceived to be a crisis, but soon the same problems and obstacles to solutions emerged. Buhari's approach to these perennial problems did not differ significantly from that of his civilian predecessor, but he promised greater discipline and hard work, as befits a proper military man. The blatant corruption evident under Shagari helped garner wide support for Buhari, but little would actually change. Buhari was willing to impose severe austerity measures, and he moved to cut down the costs of the military. But Nigeria's government, military or civilian, had to reconcile developmental ambitions with the realities of the international marketplace, over which, considering that Nigeria had but one vulnerable product to sell, neither form of government could assert itself sufficiently. Also, the corruption that had plagued Shagari's rule did not entirely vanish under the military government. There was little evident progress or change to unequivocally justify Buhari's coup. Opposition to him emerged soon from within the top ranks of his military colleagues.

Larry Diamond notes that when Ibrahim Babangida overthrew Buhari in mid-1985, he assumed the nation's top office as a "liberal democratic reformer."[35] Again the masses cheered, but by 1993 he had lost all public favor and was pressured out of office. He quickly reversed several what had come to be seen as dictatorial policies introduced by Buhari, and he cultivated a moderately populist image. Notably, he eased restrictions on the press and resisted austere conditions for an IMF loan. Babangida, while still under Buhari, had also proposed a massive program for defense industries. We may ask, Would a civilian government have needed military equipment in such quantities? Or, did this portend Babangida's ambitions, which included an active interventionist role in African affairs? It should be recalled that it was during his tenure in office that Nigeria led the massive peacekeeping effort in Liberia.

Babangida's actions during the early days once again reflected energetic reformist intentions, but the accustomed reversals, born of realities, set in. Within a year the usual restrictions on the economy, political opposition, trade unions, and the press were reintroduced. Again, with historical hindsight, what was the point of Babangida's takeover? Northern military officers still dominated (though to a lesser extent), discipline was again demanded, the ideological vacuum remained, development failed to take off, he soon imposed economic policies more austere than those the IMF had proposed, and the masses were hopeful—but they would soon be disappointed again. He intended to build "a new Nigerian political culture," but eventually Babangida had to be pushed off the stage.[36]

Babangida's tenure in office was characterized most poignantly by preparations for the return to civilian rule while he was concurrently entrenching himself as a seemingly permanent fixture. Several observers speculate that this reflected Babangida's attempt to engineer an arrangement whereby he would remain in power, in a civilian capacity. Babangida appeared to have learned the lessons of previous coups, as he exerted his own personal authority over the military establishment by forced retirements, rotations, elevation of trusted colleagues, dismissal of even old-time cronies, and the like. He also resisted pressures to induct officers unnecessarily into political posts, and he cut the budget for military hardware and reduced the salaries of military personnel.

Nevertheless, a countercoup was planned but not executed against Babangida soon after he had entered office. Shehu Othman offers explanations by the would-be perpetrators that concern Babangida's policies with respect to the IMF problem, human rights, and personnel appointments; but Othman also suspects that the dissidents had preferred the discipline of the previous Buhari regime, as well as opportunities for their own personal advancement.[37] This affair may serve as an important indication of the inherent shortcomings of the military's political capacity in that the new set of coup plotters appeared to lack a single focus, yet found the state of affairs so objectionable only four months into the new regime that they felt they had to resort to drastic measures. This is unreasonable, as all new governments, military or civilian, need a period of time to implement and test their programs. The military is ambitious, impatient, and armed. Against this, no civilian regime stands a chance.

Once settled in, and with power having been consolidated, Babangida's regime began to address a variety of problems confronting the state. Nigeria's economy had run into difficult times and required strong measures. In view of frequently violent reactions by the public to the volatile economic conditions, perhaps the military government was better able to deal convincingly with the crises than a civilian government would have been. Austere structural adjustment measures were introduced as oil prices had plunged, industrial production fell sharply, the gross domestic product experienced negative growth for several years, the naira dropped precipitously against the dollar, and the value of wages fell often to a fraction of what it had been a few years before.[38] Imports were restricted or prohibitively expensive, and the cost of food and consumer goods rose rapidly. The public was particularly incensed over the ongoing corruption and the apparent divergence between the privileged few and the masses. The former included many top military personnel, especially at the state government level. Babangida's government responded with the same repressive measures as had previous regimes.[39]

Work on a transition program had also begun. It was to have formed the foundation for elections, first at lesser levels, then culminating with the election of a president in 1992. Political parties had to be reintroduced, which posed an early dilemma. Mindful of Nigeria's early experience with the tendency of political parties to align along ethnic lines, it was decided that a two-party system would better be able to attain true national representation. Accordingly, in 1989 the National Republican Convention (NRC) and the Social Democratic Party (SDP) were formed by the government. The former was to represent a more conservative view, while the latter represented the more liberal forces. This, however, must be understood within the context of the general disdain for ideological polarization in Nigeria, where ethnicity, religion, and immediate pragmatic issues tend to define the political identities of the masses. Again, though criticized for interference in the political process, it was another attempt to innovate institutions to suit Nigeria's unique character. For this experimentation the government must be given credit, as searches for workable structures are a standard feature of all states in their early consolidative phase. Unfortunately, while the establishment of parties is a positive move towards democratization, doing so under conditions imposed by the military taints the process and raises the immediate question of what will happen if political fractioning will occur after a new civilian order is introduced. Does not this political engineering by the military serve as a dangerous precedent for future military intervention?

Nigeria's established problems with electoral processes were evident again in the 1989 local government level elections, which drew a very low response. Then in 1991, widespread fraud was encountered in the primary election for state governors. In nine states the results were rejected and another election was held. Babangida's government faced a dilemma in that he was criticized for not moving fast enough to install a civilian government but also for excessive interference in the process of developing civilian institutions. While ostensibly preparing to leave power, he had actually centralized considerable authority, especially military offices, in the presidency by 1990.[40] It is this constant dilemma that contributed to the ambiguity surrounding his true intention about yielding power.[41] Contributing to this vacillative progress towards civilian rule were the usual economic and social problems, which resulted on several occasions in widespread public violence. In April 1990, another coup against Babangida was attempted, ostensibly sparked by resentment against his seemingly invincible and dictatorial position. Although there were many conspirators, it was a clumsy affair—and unsuccessful—and it revealed a distinct ethnic foundation in that the Southerners and Christians who led the coup had expressed their concern over northern domination. Indeed, five northern states were threatened with expulsion from Nigeria.[42] This closely echoed the disenchantment expressed by the plotters of the first coup attempt against Babangida. Of those executed in that earlier attempt, all but one were from ethnic minorities in Benue state.[43] An early conclusion may be offered: Most military men are not opposed to military rule; their main concern is with the specific composition of the ruler and his team. Again, this should offer little encouragement to those who place their faith in the permanence of civilian rule in the future.

The problems associated with the transition to civilian rule came to a head in 1993. Civilian rule had been scheduled to start again on 27 August of that year. An election for president was held 12 June but the official results were suppressed by the National Electoral Commission. It was evident that there was interference by the top levels. Available information pointed to a clear victory by the SDP's candidate Chief Moshood Abiola over his opponent, the NRC's Bashir Tofa, whose appeal lay in the North.[44] Abiola allegedly won in nineteen of thirty-one states. In late June, the election was declared null and void by Babangida's government. Public outcry in Nigeria, this time joined by wide international criticism, pressured Babangida into promising that a civilian government would take over as scheduled on 27 August; and he called for new elections from which Tofa and Abiola would be barred. Instead, on 26 August, Babangida stepped out of office, having appointed a civilian, Ernest Shonekan, as head of an interim government. This weak attempt at a compromise was not widely accepted.

Shonekan tried to gain acceptance during his eighty-two days in power, but failed. He was ousted in November 1993 by General Sani Abacha, his defense minister. Abacha was no newcomer to palace intrigues, as he had been identified as the real military power behind Buhari's and Babangida's thrones.[45] Journalist Alan Rake speculates that Abacha acted to preempt a radical coup plot by junior officers who aspired to decisively clean house—and to kill him, among many others.[46] By now, this sounds very plausible, but again much may also be surmised from the fact of Abacha's origin, in Kano, in the North. Would the North willingly yield power, considering that they controlled the country's military? Rake also asserts that Abacha forced Babangida to leave office peacefully, as he too was a prime target of the coup plotters. Once Abacha ensconced himself in power, the usual ouster of incompetent and corrupt officials followed. He closed down the National Assembly and Senate, abolished the political parties, and made proposals for a new constitution and promises for elections. As a start, he indicated that elections to a constitutional conference would be held soon.

CONCLUSION

The details of the rationale for Abacha's takeover are not yet available. If in fact his major consideration was fear of a coup by junior officers, then we have to acknowledge that the military has become its own worst enemy. Having created a Frankensteinian monster, they cannot control it. Anyone in power now fears being succeeded by others with retributive intentions. In this scenario, the most logical response is to stay in power—ruthlessly, if need be.

Abacha's justification of the fear of another coup and its potential for retribution is, within the context of Nigeria's tumultuous history, a plausible explanation. However, previous justifications for coups—which concerned chaos, corruption, incompetence, the transition process, law and order, northern domination, economic stagnation, and the like—were also plausible explanations. This highlights an important dimension. As the causes for takeovers are multifarious, we may be advised to study them collectively within a broader sociopolitical context. Addressing them singly, as in the case of corruption, may not resolve the source of inherent instability, which goes considerably beyond only that one precipitating cause. All corruption could cease tomorrow, but that would not necessarily stimulate rapid economic progress or reduce the incidence of military intervention. Larry Diamond states a similar view: "If a democratic regime is to survive in Nigeria, it must prove that it can govern effectively. This will require more than combating corruption, more than conducting credible elections, more than 'reflecting the federal character' in the distribution of power and rewards. . . . All these are essential, but so is effective economic performance."[47]

This chapter began with a review of the African context in which Nigeria's military rule must be viewed. This is important, as the available literature on this topic reflects the values inherent in the standard Western paradigms drawn from politically advanced and economically developed states. These are inappropriate models, as African countries are in their early periods of the consolidative stage, a time usually marked by great social cleavages, competition, disruption, and lack of national integration. Liberal democracy, although the most preferred form for First World states, may not only be inappropriate for many Third World states at this stage; it could also be dangerously dysfunctional. At independence, Nigeria had democracy, in which climate the nation fractioned and allowed the Biafran war to break out.

However, there is a dilemma. Whereas democracy in the First Republic failed and whereas the Second Republic did not distinguish itself, neither did the longer periods of military rule advance the resolution of problems or the stability of the country. We may therefore be led to conclude in line with Professor Mazrui's observation that each of the two forms of government, civilian and military, has distinct advantages. Nigeria's population shows evidence of tolerating both, as they judge not so much the form as the result. In this respect, the challenge may be to combine the advantages of both forms, recognizing that classical democracy may be the ideal to which the nation aspires but that, for now, a uniquely designed governing structure that reflects the full realities of the great socioeconomic constraints may be more appropriate. This could perhaps be construed to be an impossible task, but it needs to be explored. One factor favoring the attempt is the involvement of the international community, both governments and NGOs, which could act in supportive as well as restraining capacities. Civilian regimes may better build long-term legitimacy and develop the vital equilibrating mechanisms necessary for national integration, but the military component can offer security and order and control resistance to austerity measures.

Nigeria's problems, like those of most other African countries, will not be resolved soon—nor without pain—and to date little progress has been made, although the population numbers advance at a high rate and the country finds itself in a very competitive international environment in which Nigeria has but one diminishing product to sell. Of course, drawing up a scheme for joint rule is in itself challenging, but against this we must consider that constitutional engineering for orthodox democratic structures began long before independence but has not succeeded to this day. At some point in the not too distant future, renewed violent competition for the allocation of Nigeria's increasingly scarce oil revenues may be experienced; there is little reason to believe that a civilian government will be able to manage this peacefully. The prevalence of Northerner/Southerner animosity expressed in most coups and by Southerners who disdain their perceived domination by the North, offers little encouragement to believe that the country will soon enjoy mature national political integration.

A more fundamental question may also be asked. Is oil the only "glue" that has kept the country united? This prospect emerged when the non-Ibos found cause to unite against Biafra, where the oil is concentrated. As this commodity diminishes, it may be expected that the government will be severely challenged to retain the loyalty of all regions as well as its own structural cohesiveness. Africa may possibly encounter a wave of breakups, which could fuel the extant centripetal tendencies in Nigeria. Such events in most countries are very violent. The military, if itself united, may be able to arrest such a development, but at what cost and for what reason? In view of the breakups of the Soviet Union and some Eastern European countries, keeping Nigeria—and many other African countries—united may be a bloody exercise in futility. To date Nigeria's military governments have succeeded at keeping the country intact, but the full rationale for doing so has not been convincingly articulated.

The standard bias in the literature argues in favor of civilian rule. This too needs examination. Unfortunately, we cannot simply measure the performance of civilian against military rulers and determine failure or success attributed solely to that criterion. The First Republic experienced perhaps the best-qualified civilian politicians, and certainly their greatest number. The Second Republic yielded mediocrity at best. And we have reason to be cynical regarding Abiola's mostly business qualifications to head this tumultuous nation of one hundred million and to advance it rapidly beyond poverty. Having been prevented from occupying the presidential office in 1993, he sought to enlist the intervention of certain international powers on his behalf.[48] Had that support been extended, it would have hardly attested to his skill in marshaling domestic political resources, which would have reflected internal power equilibration. This would not have been an encouraging start for a third republic.

Viewed within the context of Africa's developmental history, it is not certain that the military's terms in office were necessarily less productive than civilian rule would have been. Perhaps military efficiency may be a myth when attempted in the administration of state affairs, but several Nigerian military regimes entered power with great energies, reformist agendas, and authority that would not likely have been demonstrated by civilians. However, while these military regimes had to be sensitive to political realities, building permanent political institutions, beyond attempts at new constitutions, was not perceived to be their mission; hence, the military's tenure in office has been more in the capacity of caretakers than of nation-builders. The military seems not to have been able to reconcile these two requirements, while civilians realized little success in the latter endeavor. It is suggested, then, that the assumed superiority of civilian governments within Nigeria's present context also needs critical examination. A system in which the military provides the necessary stability while the civilians build the nation may well be the necessary formula for ensuring progress. In short, the military's activities should be deflected from dubious external missions and redesigned to answer the need for a domestic "super police force" that would ensure compliance with policies introduced by a joint civilian-military "transitional" ruling system. Should this arrangement succeed in stabilizing the country—especially its frequent changes of governmental composition—it would channel the military's interventionist energies into the needs of nation-building. Elements in the military have expressed their disdain for any role in politics, as it has prevented the attainment of true professionalization of the military establishment. It must also be considered that Nigeria hardly needs to support a traditional armed force, as the greatest threat perception is not external, but internal, which a police force alone will not be able to answer.[49]

The domination of Nigeria's post-independence history by the military has discouraged the emergence of the great numbers of civilian politicians steeped in experience that the country will require in the future. The soldiers who stepped into power may have been serious; but, judging with hindsight, their political astuteness was also limited. We may conclude that they failed to operationalize a long-term vision, as the country's position is nearly as precarious today as perhaps it was immediately after independence. We noted the prevalence of the same complaints voiced by each new set of coup perpetrators; all, including Shagari's civilian government, faced the same frustrations once in power. Little perceptible progress has been made. If the military is to take a more responsible and institutionalized administrative role rather than to persist in its haphazard interventionist habits, we may be advised to highlight the military's natural advantage and build its political capacity to more mature levels.[50] Having observed the constant intrigues, dissension, and plotting in the ranks, a first step will call for a reorganization of the military's structure to meet the requirements of its new duties. We cannot expect the government to stabilize before the military is itself stabilized. The military reflects the lethal divisions of Nigerian society; and if the military cannot itself overcome its own problems, only the naive will persist in the fantasy of an optimistic future for Nigeria.

NOTES

1. Ali A. Mazrui, *The Africans: A Triple Heritage* (Boston: Little, Brown, and Company, 1986), p. 181–83.

2. Crawford Young, *Ideology and Development in Africa* (New Haven: Yale University Press, 1982), p. 324.

3. Claude E. Welch, Jr. "Soldier and State in Africa," in Marion E. Doro and Newell M. Stultz, eds., *Governing in Black Africa: Perspectives on New States* (Englewood Cliffs, N.J.: Prentice-Hall, 1970), p. 159.

4. Richard Hodder-Williams, *An Introduction to the Politics of Tropical Africa* (London: George Allen and Unwin, 1984), pp. 127–28.

5. Welch, "Soldier and State in Africa," p. 164. Also Constantine P. Danopoulos, "Military Dictatorships in Retreat: Problems and Perspectives," in Constantine P. Danopoulos, ed., *The Decline of Military Regimes: The Civilian Influence* (Boulder, Colo.: Westview Press, 1988), p. 1.

6. R. Paul Shaw and Yuws Wong, *Genetic Seeds of Warfare: Evolution, Nationalism and Patriotism* (Boston: Unwin Hyman, 1989), p. 134.

7. *Africa Insight* 17, no. 4 (1987): 48.

8. Shaw and Wong, *Genetic Seeds,* p. 117.

9. Ieuan LL. Griffiths, *An Atlas of African Affairs* (London: Methuen, 1984), pp. 66–67.

10. Claude E. Welch, Jr., "Military Disengagement from Politics? Incentives and Obstacles in Political Change," in Simon Baynham, ed., *Military Power and Politics in Black Africa* (New York: St. Martin's Press, 1986), p. 67.

11. Kwazi Sarfo, *The Political Structure of African States* (Dubuque: Kendall/Hunt, 1988), p. 70.

12. Ibid., 77.

13. Opulu Agyeman, "Setbacks to Political Institutionalization by Pretorianism in Africa," *Journal of Modern African Studies* 26, no. 3 (1988): 415.

14. Rene Lemarchand, in S. W. Schmidt and G. A. Dorfman, eds., *Soldiers in Politics* (Los Altos: Geron-X, 1974), p. 94.

15. W. F. Gutteridge, *Military Regimes in Africa* (London: Methuen and Co., 1975), p. 186.

16. Karl P. Magyar, "Military Intervention and Withdrawal in Africa: Problems and Perspectives," in Constantine Danopoulos, ed., *From Military to Civilian Rule* (London: Routledge, 1992), pp. 239–240.

17. S. E. Finer, *The Man on Horseback: The Role of the Military in Politics,* 2d ed. (Boulder, Colo.: Westview Press, 1984), p. 286.

18. A highly critical view of Shagari and the military is offered by Horace Campbell, "The Lessons of the Military Coup in Nigeria," *Ufahamu* 13, no. 2–3 (1984).

19. Shaw and Wong, p. 123.

20. Ikenna Nzimiro, "Militarization in Nigeria: Its Economic and Social Consequences," *International Social Science Journal* 35, no. 1 (1983):128.

21. Olusegun Obasanjo and Akin Mabogune, *Elements of Democracy* (Abeokuta, Nigeria: ALF Publications, 1992), p. 182.

22. William D. Graf, *The Nigerian State: Political Economy, State, Class and Political System in the Post-Colonial Era* (London: James Currey, 1988), p. 45.

23. Anthony Kirk-Greene and Douglas Rimmer, *Nigeria since 1970: A Political and Economic Outline* (New York: Africana Publishing, 1981), p. 20.

24. Guy Arnold, *Modern Nigeria* (London: Longman, 1977), p. ix.

25. Kirk-Greene and Rimmer, *Nigeria since 1970,* p. 11.

26. Anthony V. Williams, "Nigeria in West Africa," in David J. Myers, ed., *Regional Hegemony: Threat Perception and Strategic Response* (Boulder, Colo.: Westview Press, 1991), p. 276.

27. Larry Diamond, "Nigeria's Third Quest for Democracy," *Current History* (May 1991), reproduced in Helen E. Purkitt, ed., *World Politics 92/93* (Guilford, Conn.: Dushkin Publishing Groups, 1992), p. 159.

28. Nigerian Army Education Corps and School, *The History of the Nigerian Army* (Abuja, Nigeria: Nigerian Army HQ, 1992), p. 133.

29. Ibid.

30. Ibid., 139–41.

31. Nzimiro, "Militarization in Nigeria," pp. 130–31.

32. Arnold, *Modern Nigeria,* p. 173.

33. Shehu Othman, "Nigeria: Power for Profit—Class, Corporatism, and Factionalism in the Military," in Donal B. Cruise O'Brien, John Dunn, and Richard Rathbone, eds., *Contemporary West African States* (Cambridge: Cambridge University Press, 1989), p. 128.

34. Ibid., p. 133–34.

35. Diamond, "Nigeria's Third Quest," p. 155.

36. Charles Owusu Kwarteng, "Nigeria's Elusive Search for Nationhood," *Africa Insight* 23, no. 1 (1993): 33.

37. Othman, "Nigeria: Power for Profit," pp. 142–44.

38. Diamond, "Nigeria's Third Quest," pp. 156–57.

39. Williams, "Nigeria in West Africa," p. 284.

40. Diamond, "Nigeria's Third Quest," p. 158.

41. Kwarten, "Elusive Search," p. 32.

42. Diamond, "Nigeria's Third Quest," p. 159.

43. Othman, "Nigeria: Power for Profit," p. 141.

44. *New African* (September 1993): 11.

45. Pini Jaason, "Abacha's Democratic Task," *New African* (January 1994): 13.

46. Alan Rake, "Who Trusts Abacha?" *New African* (January 1994): 28.

47. Diamond, "Nigeria's Third Quest," p. 160.

48. Peter da Costa, "The Power Vacuum," *Africa Report* (November/December

1993): 54. Also, Paul Adams, "Legacy of the General," *Africa Report* (September/October 1993): 68.

49. Nigerian Army Education Corps and School, *History,* pp. 226–27.

50. I addressed this suggestion in Magyar, "Military Intervention and Withdrawal in Africa."

REFERENCES

Arnold, Guy. *Modern Nigeria.* London: Longman, 1977.

Diamond, Larry. *Class, Ethnicity and Democracy in Nigeria.* Syracuse: Syracuse University Press, 1988.

———. "Nigeria's Third Quest for Democracy." *Current History* (May 1991).

Falola, Toyin, and Julius Ihonvbere. *The Rise and Fall of Nigeria's Second Republic: 1979–84.* London: Zed Books, 1985.

Graf, William D. *The Nigerian State: Political Economy, State, Class and Political System in the Post-Colonial Era.* London: James Currey, 1988.

Gutteridge, W. F. *Military Regimes in Africa.* London: Methuen and Company, 1975.

Kirk-Greene, Anthony, and Douglas Rimmer. *Nigeria since 1970: A Political and Economic Outline.* New York: Africana Publishing Company, 1981.

Miners, N. J. *The Nigerian Army, 1956–1966.* London: Methuen and Company, 1971.

Nigerian Army Education Corps and School. *The History of the Nigerian Army.* Abuja, Nigeria: Nigerian Army HQ, 1992.

Nzimiro, Ikenna. "Militarization in Nigeria: Its Economic and Social Consequences." *International Social Science Journal* 35, no. 1 (1983).

Obasanjo, Olusegun, and Akin Mabogunje. *Elements of Democracy.* Abeokuta, Nigeria: ALF Publications, 1992.

NORTH KOREA

Dongsung Kong

North Korea is a remarkably closed country, making it extremely difficult to acquire accurate information about it. The difficulty of measuring the influence of the military in North Korean communist politics is further compounded by the difficulty of distinguishing between military and nonmilitary political actors, as many leading political actors have served or serve in the military or in military-related positions. These research difficulties reflect the characteristics of North Korean politics: closed, secretive, authoritarian, and militaristic.

Most observers share the view that the Korean People's Army (KPA) has played a primary role in North Korean politics since its inception. However, the contingent role of the North Korean military has changed over the years, reflecting the shifting concerns of the North Korean political leadership. A historic overview in relation to the political needs of the times could yield contextual insights into understanding the political role of the North Korean military. In the initial stages of regime building, the KPA served Kim Il-sung as a physical safeguard against his fellow communist opponents. Once the regime was stabilized politically, the primary task of the military was shifted toward socializing the people under the direction of the Korean Workers' Party (KWP). Military intervention in policy decisions weakened as the Pyongyang regime became consolidated. Yet, the military leaders have kept their hands in the distribution of political power among government institutions. One should note that the Pyongyang regime's determination to use force as the only means to achieve its ultimate goal—that is, the communization of the entire Korean peninsula—has never weakened. Today, internally and externally, North Korea is at a crossroads. The country's economic deterioration seems to be too deep to be reversed without opening to the West. Internally, top-positioned revolutionaries are in their natural demise. Kim Il-sung, the country's ultimate leader since 1945, died in July 1994. O Chin-u, the leading military person, followed him in February 1995; and the other politically active revolutionaries are in their 70s and 80s.

This chapter will help analyze the political dynamics between the military and other political institutions in militaristic societies like North Korea. The chapter also will provide comparative insights into the developmental process of conflict and coalition politics between military leaders and civilian technocrats as governing becomes more complicated and the domestic economy becomes ever more dependant on the world economy.

HISTORIC PERSPECTIVE: 1945–95

The North Korean military, known as the Korean People's Army (KPA), was officially established on 8 February 1948, followed by the formal establishment of the Democratic People's Republic of Korea (DPRK) in September 1948.[1] But its origins can be traced to various Korean communist groups and guerrilla movements during Japanese colonialism (1910–45). The first Korean communist group, known as the Korean Socialist Party (Han-in Sahoe-Tang) was formed on 26 June 1918 in Khabarovsk, USSR, headed by Yi Tong-hwi.[2] In addition to the Korean Socialist Party, other communist groups emerged, but they were either crushed by the Japanese police or destroyed each other through factional struggles. However, the spirit of anti-Japanese colonialism was kept alive by succeeding resistance organizations. Kim Il-sung, like most anti-Japanese activists (called revolutionaries), commanded battalions against the Japanese occupation forces. He served in the Northeast Anti-Japanese United Army (NEAJUA) as the Sixth Division commander of the First Route Army. Among his campaigns in the NEAJUA, included is the victorious Jin-Chun-Po (called Pochonbo) battle of 4 June 1937. This helped spread his reputation across the country.[3] These experiences became valuable political assets for the political leaders of North Korea, especially for Kim Il-sung, for they helped cloak his regime with political legitimacy and enabled him to maintain control over the country for decades.

With the defeat of Japan in 1945, the Soviets moved into the northern half (above the 38th Parallel) of the Korean peninsula, while the United States occupied the southern half (below the 38th Parallel). The Soviets presented the thirty-three-year-old Kim Il-sung to the North Korean people as a hero and an authentic national leader. They equipped him with real power, even though he held no official government post. Most studies agree that Kim Il-sung was born Kim Song-ju in 1912, emigrated to Manchuria, attended a Chinese middle school, engaged in anti-Japanese guerrilla activities in eastern Manchuria, and developed relationships with the Soviets during his sojourn in the Soviet Union between probably 1941 and 1945. On the other hand, the United States introduced to the South Koreans the seventy-year-old scholar, Dr. Rhee Syngman, as their leader. Dr. Rhee received a Ph.D. in international law from Princeton University at the age of thirty-five and devoted himself to the Korean independence movement while remaining in the United States for the next thirty-five years.[4]

Soviet and U.S. military commanders in Korea respectively helped each regime to create its own governing system, to maintain law and order, and to keep the economy rolling after Japan had departed. Efforts to build a unified state proved politically impossible. The unbudgeable differences on the trusteeship issue between the political leaders of the North and the South confined each superpower to its own zone of occupation. Those political leaders who took positions against Korea's division were removed from the political scene. Kim Gu, Dr. Rhee's rival, was assassinated. Cho Mansik, a Kim Il-sung antagonist, was kept in confinement. Thus, the respective Sovietization and Americanization of the military forces and society were accelerated in each part of Korea. The Korean people, who had never experienced democracy, tolerated the tough dictatorial regimes.

As in other Marxist/Leninist regimes, control of the military was one of the first aims of the revolutionary government. With Soviet support, Kim Il-sung and his small group of guerrilla activists, known as the *Kapsan* faction, were able to control the emerging military. Even though U.S. intelligence[5] estimated quantitatively that 80% of all officers in the KPA (including Choe Yong-gon, chief commander of the military) had served with Chinese forces, the Soviets were able to exercise great influence in major military and political decisions. Scalapino and Lee describe the early North Korean communist regime:

The system, established during the Soviet occupation, of close interaction with and complete loyalty to Soviet authorities on the part of Korean Communist leaders, continued with appropriate adjustments in the post-occupation era. One prominent aspect of Soviet influence in North Korea had been the presence of Russianized Koreans in positions of major influence.[6]

In 1948, Kim Il-sung was elected premier of the Democratic People's Republic of Korea (DPRK). He then appointed one of his loyal Kapsan allies, Choe Yong-gon, as the chief commander of the KPA. In June 1949, Kim Il-sung became the chairman of a unified Korean Workers' Party (Nodong-Tang).[7] These positions enabled him to consolidate his power over the government (DPRK), the KPA, and the party (KWA). Leaders of other factions were shunted aside into either ceremonial or secondary positions.

Kim Il-sung's political dominance in North Korea enabled him to concentrate his country's efforts toward the communization of the entire Korean Peninsula. Military preparedness became his primary concern, while improving the economy was the major preoccupation of the South Korean leaders. When the Japanese departed from the Korean peninsula, North Korea had a better physical base than South Korea. Most of the best developed mines and 80%–90% of Korea's electricity, gas, and heavy industry were located in the North.[8] Taking advantage of the heavy industrial superiority over South Korea, Kim Il-sung kept expanding the military in manpower and equipment. The withdrawal of the U.S. combat forces and Pyongyang's military superiority over South Korea undoubtedly provided Kim Il-sung with a strong incentive to communize the entire Korean peninsula under his rule.

The Korean War broke out on 25 June 1950 and ended without winners on 27 July 1953. In North Korea, however, the war provided the opportunity for anti–Kim Il-sung groups to resurface and to reshape their fading political status. The Chinese link, the *Yenan* faction, claimed the credit for the massive injection of Chinese manpower that had enabled North Korea to counterattack the U.S. superiority in firepower during the war. This led to the strengthening of diplomatic links to the Chinese communists, even though North Korean leaders still maintained a strong Soviet flavor in military tactics and equipment.

After the war one of the major political disputes among political factions centered around the direction of economic development. Even after the war, the North maintained a better physical base than the South. Massive reconstruction aid poured in from the Soviet Union, China, and Eastern Europe following the end of the war. Pyongyang's level of foreign aid was roughly comparable on a per capita basis to that received by Seoul from the United States during 1953–60. Industrial development grew at a rapid rate, hitting a high of 36% annually between 1956 and 1959.[9] Koon-woo Nam aptly summarizes the North Korean economic structure and the factional disputes regarding economic plans after the war:

Some three-fourths of the total capital investment between 1954 and 1956 (the First Three-Year Economic Plan) was allocated to heavy industry. . . . Because of an intensive campaign carried out by the party, the number of farming families joining the collective farms increased steadily. In November 1954, 21.5 percent of all North Korean farming families were members of collective farms . . . and to 65.6 percent in February 1956 . . . the party moved to tighten its control over the state-owned commercial enterprises that accounted for 71.9 percent of the total North Korean commercial activities as of late 1954. . . . The heavy emphasis on basic industry became a cause of an intra-party dispute in 1953. . . . The Yenan and Soviet Koreans opposed the party line set by Kim Il-sung and asked that more emphasis be put on the development of light industry and the agricultural sector. Kim's opponents were emboldened when Khrushchev revealed his startling policy changes at the 20th Congress of the Soviet Communist Party in February, 1956. Khrushchev's enunciation of the principles of collective leadership and peaceful coexistence with western democracies was contrary to the practices of Kim Il-sung, who was very much in the Stalinist manner.[10]

Kim Il-sung's goal was to build a self-sufficient industrial base as quickly as possible so that he would not be subjected to pressures from the Soviet Union and China. After a temporary compromise with the Soviet and Yenan factions, Kim began to demote or purge his opponents, as officially reflected in the Third KWP Congress (April 1956). The Fourth KWP Congress (September 1961) institutionalized his unchallengeable political supremacy. The Kapsan faction's share in the KWP Central Committee grew from 10% in 1948 to 41% in 1961.[11] The eleven-person Politburo in the KWP Central Committee, the highest guiding

Table 1
Military Representation in the KWP Central Committee, 1948–61

| | KWP Congress | | |
Regular Membership	Second *(March 1948)*	Third *(April 1956)*	Fourth *(Sept. 1961)*
Military	9 (13%)	13 (18%)	20 (24%)
Total	67	71	85

Source: Institute for North Korean Studies. 1983. *North Korea: General Summary.*

party organ, was composed exclusively of individuals who had close personal connections with Kim Il-sung.[12] Kim also placed close associates from the Kapsan group in leading government posts.

One way to determine the extent to which the military elites are involved in policymaking is to ascertain the representation of military officers in major policymaking institutions. The KWP Central Committee was dominated by revolutionaries who had had military experience as anti-Japanese guerrilla activists. Most of them commanded military forces during the Korean War. Military officers who acquired membership in the KWP[13] became the major constituent group in the Central Committee, as shown in Table 1. However, one could argue that the gradual increase of military representation between 1948 and 1961 does not necessarily mean enhancement of the military's political status during the period. Of course, one should be aware of the nature of dictatorial politics where major policies are guided and framed by a small group of top leaders. A quantitative analysis of military representation should be supplemented with studies of how close major military leaders (e.g., Choe Yong-gon, chief commander, as number two in the party in the 1960s and 1970s) are to Kim Il-sung in policymaking. Given the fact that both Pyongyang and Seoul[14] placed a high value on military preparedness, it was only natural for military leaders to exercise and maintain strong influence in foreign and domestic policymaking. Indeed, military concerns mainly shaped the political system of North Korea in important respects.

Kim Il-sung resumed the militarization of the North. Approximately a fourth of the GNP was spent to rebuild the military.[15] Many other economic and social activities were directly and indirectly related to military preparedness. The "Four Military Lines" adopted in December 1962 aimed to (1) arm all the people, (2) fortify the entire country, (3) train every soldier to reach the officer level, and (4) modernize military equipment. Almost all able-bodied men and women were drafted into the People's Militia and received training on a regular basis. Kim also began to imbue his people with warlike spirit for economic rebuilding. The Chollima Movement, introduced in 1959, was a good example of Kim's command economy. All these efforts were guided and orchestrated by Juche thought, the leading philosophy in all aspects of life.

Kim Il Sung's paternalistic posture toward the people and his demand for their loyalty echoes Confucian maxims, but the power he wields exceeds by far that of Yi dynasty (1392–1910) kings who were restrained by the aristocratic Confucian bureaucracy. The official ideology, as in Yi times, cannot be questioned, but it has been transformed from Confucianism into a mutation of Marxism-Leninism known as "Kimilsungism."[16]

North Korea's economic growth in the 1960s was erratic. By the late 1960s, the country's economic growth rate began to be outstripped by that of South Korea, even though it was higher than the records posted by most developing countries.[17] In a speech to the fifth convention of the KWP in November 1970, Kim acknowledged that economic development had fallen short of expectations. The major cause of the slowdown in economic growth, as most studies agree, was the overemphasis on military preparedness. The sharp drop in foreign aid, especially in 1963 and 1964, worsened the situation. The very nature of command economies and the country's sluggish bureaucracy perpetuated the economic slowdown.

In 1972, a major constitutional reform took place, replacing the very beginning constitution of 1948. The 1972 constitution can be characterized as a legal foundation to institutionalize Kimilsungism and as an attempt to reinvigorate the country's erratic economy and sluggish bureaucracy. Article four of the 1972 constitution states that the DPRK is guided by the Juche thought of the KWP. Institutionally, a strong presidency and a new amalgamative bureaucracy were created. Kim Il-sung became a superstate institution, holding all the high posts in the party (as general secretary), the state (as president), and even the military (as supreme commander).

Under the 1972 constitution, the formal structure of the North Korean state diverges from both the USSR and PRC models, symbolic of Kim's desire to show his independence. Yet the most important source of power and authority, the Korean Workers' party, is virtually identical in structure and mode of operation to its Soviet and Chinese counterparts.[18]

Under the new constitution, the formal political structure of North Korea resembles those of presidential democracies. Political power appears to be divided between three branches: the legislative, executive, and judicial. But North Korea's presidential system simply reflects the necessity of *separation of functions,* not the principle of *separation of power* or *checks and balances.* The formal structure tells us little about how the regime actually governs unless one grasps the political dynamics behind the formal structure. The Central People's Committee (CPC), the newly created highest leadership organ of sovereignty of the DPRK, was an attempt to reinvigorate the erratic economy and sluggish bureaucracy. Articles 103 and 104 summarize major functions of the CPC.[19]

Article 103: The Central People's Committee exercises the following functions and powers: (1) to shape the internal and external policies of the state; (2) to direct the work of the Administration Council of the local People's Assemblies and People's Committees; (3) to direct the work of judicial and procuratorial organs; (4) to guide the work of national defense and State security; (5) to supervise the execution of the Constitution, the laws and ordinances of the Supreme People's Assembly, the orders of the President of the Democratic People's Republic of Korea and the decrees, decisions and directives of state organs which contravene them; (6) to establish or abolish ministries, executive bodies of the Administration Council; (7) to appoint or remove vice-premiers, ministers and other members of the Administration Council; (8) to appoint or recall ambassadors and ministers; (9) to appoint or remove high-ranking officers and confer military titles of general; (10) to institute decorations, titles of honor, military titles and diplomatic grades and confer decorations and titles of honor; (11) to grant general amnesties; (12) to institute or change the administrative divisions; (13) to declare a state of war and issue mobilization orders in case of emergency.
Article 104: The Central People's Committee adopts decrees and decisions and issues directives.

The CPC is a middle-ground policymaking body between the party and the executive (Administration Council, Chongmu won). The most distinct aspect of the reform can be identified by examining the membership in the party (KWP) and the CPC. The CPC was composed of top party leaders, including most of the members of the KWP Political Committee (nine of the eleven full members). The military elites among the nine include Choe Yong-gon (ranked #2), Choe Hyon (ranked #5), and O Chin-u (ranked #7).[20] The membership overlap among top leaders across the party, government, and military provided a mechanism to oversee the implementation of the bureaucracy (Administration Council) mostly occupied by postrevolutionary technocrats. Eleven of fourteen vice-prime-minister-level positions were occupied by technocrats.[21] The membership overlap, however, impeded the process of rationalizing the bureaucracy by simply creating another bureaucracy within the executive branch. The dual structure of the bureaucracy was incubating a seed of political conflict between partisan politicians and career bureaucrats. Also, the age distribution of the Political Committee membership strongly implies that political power shift from the revolutionaries (mostly born between 1900 and 1922)[22] to the postrevolutionary generation led by Kim Jong-il is near. The membership increase of the postrevolutionary generation in the Political Committee, which constitutes the most powerful leaders in the KWP, from 40% (six of fifteen) in 1970 to almost 80% (twenty-six of thirty-three) in 1985, also indicates that a generational change is approaching.[23] Yet, the supremacy of ideology over efficiency maintained.

The 1972 constitution also created a dual structure in the military, as shown in Figure 1. By creating the Defense Commission under the DPRK, the military

Figure 1
North Korean Military Command Structure, as of 1972

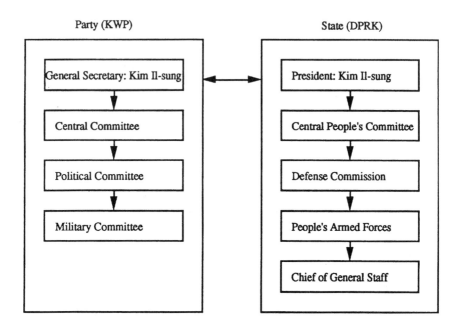

policymaking power was shared by the party (KWP) and the state (DPRK). Kim Il-sung, as chair of the Defense Commission, officially had the military under his direct control. O Chin-u (1916–95), one of the revolutionaries, became the primary implementor of Kim's military directives when he assumed the ministry (1976–95) of the People's Armed Forces.

The Sixth KWP Congress (October 1980) signaled a new political environment. Kim's oldest son, Kim Jong-il, officially emerged right next to his father. A series of actions took place in preparation for a peaceful power succession. First, more military officers were introduced into the Political Committee and the Central Committee of the KWP as shown in Table 2.[24] Second, the formal status of the military was elevated by placing the Ministry of People's Armed Forces, which had been one of the ministries in the Administration Council under the Central People's Committee (CPC), directly under the CPC in April 1982. Third, since 1972 the defense budget has been dramatically reduced. The defense budget had accounted for 30%–35% of the total budget in the 1960s, but dropped to 17% in 1972; and the trend continued throughout the 1970s.[25] Fourth, more new members were introduced into the Central Committee of the KWP, making up approximately 71% of the seats.[26] These new members are very likely in favor of Kim Jong-il.

Table 2
Military Representation in the KWP Political Committee, 1972–93

Regular Membership	KWP Congress		
	Fifth (As of 1973)	Sixth (As of 1983)	As of 1993
Military	4 (36%)	6 (32%)	2 (17%)
Total (candidates excluded)	11	19	12

Despite the reform efforts, the economy of the 1970s and 1980s was still in a slump. Compared to South Korea, the North's economy had worsened substantially. A series of economic reform efforts imitating the free market system turned out to be fruitless. Some technocrats advocated rather fundamental changes towards an open economy. Even such attempts to attract foreign investments by enacting the Joint Venture Law of 1984 were shunted away by most Western countries. A series of military confrontations and threats against South Korea were regularly adopted to repress economic complaints from the people during the 1970s and 1980s.

On 9 April 1992 another constitutional reform took place in the third session of the ninth Supreme People's Assembly (SPA). A series of follow-up actions were taken to reinforce peaceful power succession. First, the status of the military was further elevated by placing the Defense Commission right next to the state presidency. Second, a new chapter dealing with defense matters was inserted (Chapter 4, Articles 58–61). Chapter 4 clarifies Kim's intention to pursue the Four Lines of Military Policy, despite the less-tense atmosphere created by the end of the Cold War. But the word "soldiers" was deleted in defining the source of state sovereignty. Article 7 of the 1972 constitution specified that sovereignty resides in the workers, peasants, soldiers, and working intellectuals.[27] Third, the defense budget dropped further, to 12% of the total budget in 1990. Fourth, the new constitution places high emphasis on the reinforcement of institution and law. All these careful maneuvers seem designed to eliminate the possibility of the military moving against the partisan leader Kim Jong-il as the time for leadership succession approaches.

Following those reforms, Kim Jong-il was officially elected chair of the Defense Commission, the highest position in the military (see Table 3),[28] at the fifth session of the ninth SPA on 9 April 1993. Even though his control over the military is not certain, his elevation to the chairmanship of the Defense Commission had been anticipated when he was elected as first vice-chair in May 1990 and subsequently as Supreme Commander in December 1992 and Marshal in April 1992.

Table 3
Military Elite in North Korea, as of 1993

Membership in the Military Committee of the KWP		Membership in the Defense Commission of the DPRK	
Chair:	Kim Il-sung	Chair:	Kim Jong-il
Member:	O Chin-u	Vice-chair:	O Chin-u
	Lee Ul-sul		Choi Kwang
	Ju Do-il		
	Baek Hak-lim	Member:	Kim Cheol-man
	O Kuk-lyol		Lee Ul-sul
	Lee Doo-ik		Ju Do-il
	Kim Kang-hwan		Jun Byung-ho
	Kim Doo-nam		Kim Bong-lyul
	Jun Mun-sup		Kim Kwang-jin
	Jo Myung-rok		Lee Ha-il
	Lee Bong-won		
	Kim Il-Cheol		
	Choi Sang-ok		
	O Yong-bang		

The sudden death of Kim Il-sung in July 1994, in the middle of a tense confrontation with the United States regarding the inspection of nuclear sites, opened a new era in North Korean politics. It appears that, as planned and prepared, Kim Jong-il has succeeded his father. However, the question is how long he will remain there. As Clough points out, "In the process of succeeding his father Kim Jong-il will face three critical tests: (1) accelerating economic development, (2) perpetuating the myth of the Kim cult, and (3) maintaining support among the military."[29]

In a time of transition the military's support will be crucial, not only for peaceful leadership succession but also for replacing the party leaders, if necessary. The recent comeback of retired revolutionaries can be interpreted as attempts by Kim Il-sung to provide Kim Jong-il with unswerving support in the initial period of his rule. Choi Kwang, a well-known revolutionary and former chair of the joint chiefs of staff, regained the position in 1988. Some other revolutionaries, including Kim Cheol-man (resurged in 1990) and Lee Yong-moo (resurged in 1988), were appointed as leading members of the KWP. Also, Kim Il-sung helped Kim Jong-il staff the leading positions in the military with the latter's allies, including O Kuk-yeol (appointed as chair of the joint chiefs of staff in 1979), Kim Kang-Hwan, Choi Sang-ok, Lee Bong-won, Lee Hong-won, Kim Il-chull, Jo Myung-nok, and O Yong-bang.

However, it is not certain at this point that the military is fully behind Kim Jong-il. After the death of Kim Il-sung, most observers felt that O Chin-u,

Minister of the People's Armed Forces and Vice-chair of the Defense Commission, was the younger Kim's strongest supporter. At the same time, they speculated that O Chin-u, as the leading revolutionary, could also be Kim Jong-il's nemesis. It is well known that O Kuk-yeol, one of Kim Jong-il's closest military allies, was forced to resign from the position of chair of the joint chiefs of staff in 1988. His resignation was caused by the defeat he suffered in his rivalry with O Chin-u. The chairmanship was assumed by Choi Kwang, one of the revolutionaries, who managed to rehabilitate himself from the purge. Choi Kwang had been purged because of a charge that he had implicitly sanctioned anti–Kim Il-sung activities. But O Chin-u's recent death (February 1995) brought the issue to an end. Most likely, the remaining revolutionaries will temporarily fill the gap during the transition period, as planned by Kim Il-sung. No matter who succeeds O Chin-u, the influence of the remaining revolutionaries in the military is waning.

One could speculate that Kim Jong-il's delay in assuming the presidency—rather unusual in an authoritarian state—is a planned effort to extend the myth of his father's cult. However, his long-term survival depends mainly on two internal factors: (1) Kim Jong-il's own health and (2) the state of the economy during the early stages of his leadership. No matter who governs, the political destiny of North Korea depends on how quickly the deteriorating economy recovers. Another ideological and militaristic administration would hardly be able to check the postrevolutionary technocrats, who are growing in power and stature. This is likely to drive the country into an unpredictable political turmoil.

The political environment surrounding North Korea seriously restricted the avenues available to overcome its diplomatic and economic isolation. The end of the Cold War rendered the communization of the entire Korean peninsula almost impossible to achieve. In February 1993, Russia declared the abandonment of its pledge of support to North Korea; the military alliance, which formed part of a 1961 cooperation treaty, came to an end. Moscow also asked North Korea to repay its debt to Russia, which totals about four billion dollars.[30] South Korea's recently established diplomatic relations with Russia and China further complicates Pyongyang's international standing. Furthermore, with the coming of the postrevolutionary generation, there is a strong possibility that the national priority will shift toward economic development and away from nonproductive ideological rhetoric. Kim Jong-il would assume the presidency with the support of his allies and revolutionaries, but in order to retain power he would have to be held to a standard: "what government does" rather than "who governs."

POLITICAL FUNCTIONS OF THE NORTH KOREAN MILITARY

The political role of the North Korean military can be characterized as a mixture of various features common to most communist or military regimes: a close partnership between the party and the military, an extremely centralized governing system staffed by military leaders in the leading posts, and a command economy. Unlike most military regimes, which have a relatively short life span, Kim Il-sung's regime has lasted for almost a half century. East Germany before its subsumption by the Federal Republic was the most similar model to North Korea. However, East Germany was competing with a long-established democratic state (West Germany), while North Korea has been competing with a recently civilianized developing country (South Korea). The uniqueness of North Korean politics can be further characterized by Kim's charismatic, aristocratic, and overbearing personality. The major functions that still deserve our attention can be extracted from the historical context described in the previous parts of this chapter.

First, the North Korean military has provided Kim Il-sung with political legitimacy. Political legitimacy for the Kim Il-sung regime was first earned by the anti-Japanese guerrilla activities. Maintaining this historical legacy, the Korean People's Army (KPA) has expanded its prestige, becoming the primary instrument to complete the regime's ultimate mission: the communization of the entire Korean peninsula. In this context, Kim's military-style governing has been justified, and the sacrifice of the economy for the mission was tolerated by the people. But there are signs that Kim's admonitions have weakened considerably following his death.

Second, the KPA has been a coercive instrument that enforces the directions of the KWP, the primary ideological instrument. Like most communist governments, the symbiotic relationship between the communist party and the military has been essential in North Korea. The military has been controlled by the KWP, in that KWP leaders have taken leading positions on the Military Committee and the Defense Commission. At the same time, the KWP has been intervened by the military in that the top military leaders have been ranked right next to Kim Il-sung in the KWP. Choe Yong-gon was ranked number two in the KWP until the Fifth KWP Congress. O Chin-u was ranked right next to Kim Il-sung and Kim Jong-il. The supremacy of ideology over economy has been maintained, but it has been safeguarded by the military.

Third, the military has worked as an institution of wartime-spirit socialization. The militarization of the whole North Korean society has been systematically strengthened since the inception of the Kim Il-sung regime. The North Korean education system, from kindergarten to college, has strongly stressed military training and spirit. Most North Koreans must serve in the military for several years, and the military population accounts for approximately a third of the total population. One of the main sources of becoming a member of the political elite in North Korea is to get a college education. The college population consists of 70% retired soldiers, 20% industry incumbents, and 10% high school graduates of the privileged class.[31] In addition, the Four Military Lines adopted in 1962, the Chollima Movement introduced by Kim Il-sung in 1959, the Three-Revolution Team Movement directed by Kim Jong-il, and succeeding campaigns clearly demonstrate how the whole society has been militarized. People were pushed to speed competition to set new records in economic production, keeping a wartime spirit with dedication and sacrifice.

Fourth, the military leaders have been actively involved in policymaking, not only for military policies but also for nonmilitary domestic and foreign policies. However, it should be noted that it is extremely difficult to know exactly how policy decisions are made in a secretive country like North Korea. As described previously, the top military leaders have been ranked officially and in reality right next to Kim Il-sung in the KWP hierarchy since 1945. With all available data analysis, it is clear that the military has been more influential in constituent policies that are primarily concerned with the internal distribution of power among government institutions.[32] Even though the military influence in policymaking has been limited by Kim Il-sung, it appears that the military and Kim have built a very close partnership.

Finally, the military has served the Kim Il-sung regime as a safeguard against any anti–Kim Il-sung groups. The armed forces became personalized serving Kim Il-sung, not the state. This implies that the unity within the military is likely to weaken now that Kim Il-sung has passed from the scene. During the leadership transition in such an authoritarian country as North Korea, the military's support will be crucial for the peaceful leadership succession. But the functions of the military described above will gradually diminish during the post–Kim Il-sung era.

NOTES

1. See Gregory F. T. Winn, "North Korea: A Garrison State," in Edward A. Olsen and Steven Jurika, eds., *The Armed Forces in Contemporary Asian Societies* (Boulder, Colo.: Westview Press, 1986), p. 105.

2. See Dae-Sook Suh, *The Korean Communist Movement, 1918–1948* (Princeton: Princeton University Press, 1967), pp. 7–8.

3. See Jae-Hwa Lee, *The Korean Modern History of Independence* (Seoul: Baek San, 1988), p. 324–29. See also Dae-Sook Suh, *Korean Communist,* pp. 281–87.

4. Summarized from Ralph N. Clough, *Embattled Korea: The Rivalry for International Support* (Boulder, Colo.: Westview Press, 1987), pp. 1–2. Almost nothing is reliable about Kim Il-Sung's activities. For detailed reference, see Chong-Sik Lee, "Kim Il-Sung of North Korea," *Asian Survey* 7, no. 6 (June 1967): 374–75.

5. See Bruce Cumings, "Introduction," in Bruce Cumings, ed., *Child of Conflict: The Korean-American Relationship, 1943–1953* (Seattle: University of Washington Press, 1983), p. 39.

6. See Robert A. Scalapino and Chong-Sik Lee, *Communism in Korea, Part I* (Berkeley: University of California Press, 1972), p. 383.

7. The KWP was unified in June 1949. The North Korean Workers' Party (NKWA) was officially formed on 30 August 1946. The NKWA absorbed the South Korean Workers' Party, led by Park Hon-yong, in June 1949.

8. See Joungwan A. Kim, *Divided Korea: The Politics of Development, 1945–1972* (Cambridge: Cambridge University Press, 1975), p. 33.

9. See Joseph Sang-honn Chung, *The North Korean Economy: Structure and Development* (Stanford, Calif.: Hoover Institution Press, 1974), p. 76.

10. See Koon Woo Nam, *The North Korean Communist Leadership, 1945–1965: A Study of Factionalism and Political Consolidation* (University: University of Alabama Press, 1974), pp. 1010–105. In his summary, cited are *Kulloja,* no. 19 (November 1962): 14; *Kin Nichisei Senshu,* vol. 1 (Tokyo 1966): 245–53, and vol. 4, part 2 (Tokyo 1964): 124; and *Pukhan Yoram* (Seoul: Office of Public Information, 1962): 194.

11. See In-duk Kang, *North Korean Politics* (Seoul: Research Center for Far Eastern Studies, 1976), p. 380.

12. See Koon Woo Nam, *The North Korean Communist Leadership, 1945–1965,* 124–32.

13. See Tai-sung An, *North Korea: A Political Handbook* (Wilmington, Del.: Scholarly Resources, 1983), p. 100.

14. In 16 May 1961, a military coup d'etat led by General Park Jung Hee turned South Korea into a military rule. Park's presidency continued until 1979, when he was assassinated by Kim Jae-gyu, one of his loyal allies.

15. See Joo-Hwan Choe, *The North Korean Economy* (Seoul: Daw-wang-sa, 1992), pp. 79–83.

16. See Clough, *Embattled Korea,* p. 30.

17. See Chung, *North Korean Economy: Structure and Development,* pp. 76–93.

18. See Robert Scalapino, Seizaburo Sato, and Jusuf Wanandi, eds., *Asian Political Institutionalization* (Berkeley: Institute of East Asian Studies, University of California Press, 1986), p. 4.

19. See *Korea Today,* no. 196 (1993): 24–30, for an English version. Recited from Chong-Sik Lee, "The 1972 Constitution and Top Communist Leaders," in Dae-Sook Suh and Chae Jim Lee, eds., *Political Leadership in Korea* (Seattle: University of Washington Press, 1976), p. 197.

20. See Chong-Sik Lee, "The 1972 Constitution," pp. 198–201.

21. See Ha-Chung Yeon, *Economic Policy and Implementation: North Korea* (Seoul: Korea Development Institute, 1986), pp. 221–24.

22. See Chong-Sik Lee, "The 1972 Constitution," pp. 198–201.

23. See Planning Board of Unification, *Prospects of North Korea in Preparation for Unification* (Seoul: Planning Board of Unification, 1986), pp. 60–63.

24. Table 2 is a summary of the following studies. For the 1973 data, see Chong-Sik Lee, "The 1972 Constitution." For the 1983 data, see Chin-wee Chung, "The Evolution of Political Institutions in North Korea," in Scalapino, Sato, and Wanandi, eds., *Asian Political Institutionalization.* The 1993 data is mainly based on the study conducted by the Research Institute for National Unification, *The Political Elite in North Korea* (Seoul: RINU, 1992), and updated by the author.

25. See Joo-Hwan Choe, *The North Korean Economy* (Seoul: Daw-wang-saw, 1992), pp. 79–83.

26. See the Research Institute for National Unification, *The Political Elite in North Korea* (Seoul: RINU, 1992), p. 63.

27. See Ho Yeol P. Yoo, "The Features of the Revised Socialist Constitution of North Korea," *RINU Newsletter* 2, no. 1 (March 1992): 16.

28. Table 3 is mainly based on the study conducted by the Research Institute for National Unification, *Political Elite in North Korea* and updated by the author.

29. See Clough, *Embattled Korea,* p. 146.

30. See the *Wall Street Journal* (12 February 1993).

31. See Planning Board of Unification, *Colleges and the College Life in North Korea* (Seoul: Planning Board of Unification, 1985), pp. 25–28.

32. For a detailed explanation of the concept, see Theodore J. Lowi, "The State in Politics: The Relation between Policy and Administration," in Roger G. Noll, ed., *Regulatory Policy and the Social Sciences* (Berkeley: University of California Press, 1985).

REFERENCES

Chung, Chin-Wee. "The Evolution of Political Institutions in North Korea," in Robert Scalapino, Seizaburo Sato, and Jusuf Wanandi, eds., *Asian Political Institutionalization.* Berkeley: Institute of East Asian Studies, University of Southern California Press, 1986.

Clough, Ralph N. *Embattled Korea: The Rivalry for International Support.* Boulder, Colo.: Westview Press, 1987.

Lee, Chong-Sik. "Kim Il-Sung of North Korea," *Asian Survey* 7, no. 6 (June 1967).

———. "The 1972 Constitution and Top Communist Leaders." In Dae-Sook Suh and Chae-Jin Lee, eds., *Political Leadership in Korea.* University: University of Alabama Press, 1974.

Research Institute for National Unification. *The Political Elite in North Korea.* Seoul: RINU, 1992.

Scalapino, Robert A., and Chon-Sik Lee. *Communism in Korea, Parts 1 and 2.* Berkeley: University of California Press, 1972.

Suh, Dae-Sook. *The Korean Communist Movement: 1918–1948.* Princeton: Princeton University Press, 1967.

PERU

George L. Vásquez

Few countries anywhere in the world have experienced as much military intervention in domestic politics as Peru. "From 1821, when Peru became independent, until 1968, the presidency (or its equivalent) has been held by seventy-six individuals; fifty of them were military men who led the country for eighty-six years."[1] More than half of the civilian presidents who led the nation came to power through the use of force and depended upon the military to remain in office. "The first civilian president was elected to the post in 1872, but his followers had to defeat a coup led by four brothers, illiterate colonels, who could not bear the sight of a Peruvian president who was not a military man."[2] The single longest continuous administration in Peruvian history was the leftist military government that governed the faction-ridden nation from 1968 until 1980.

The military, which in the Peruvian context almost always means the army, has not always ruled in its own name. There have been long periods in which the Peruvian oligarchy governed with the tacit consent of the military. The philosophy that excused, if it did not condone, military government said, "Leave it to the soldiers . . . to clean up the mess."[3] No one else wanted to soil their hands and risk their reputations in the quagmire of Peruvian politics. And yet, "Ever since independence the Peruvian army had constituted the only relatively unified and coherent institution in an extremely fragmented and disarticulated polity."[4]

This chapter examines the role of the Peruvian army in the politics of Peru during the twentieth century. It starts with the period of reform during the aftermath of the disastrous war with Chile and continues through Augusto Leguía's civilian dictatorship in 1929. This period witnessed two fundamental changes affecting military/civilian authority, commenced by Nicolás de Piérola and the beginning of the professionalization of the Peruvian army with the arrival of the French military mission in 1896. The next period to be examined is the generation of the last of Peru's military *caudillos* (Sánchez Cerro, Benavides, and Odría), who ruled almost without civilian interruption from 1929 until 1956 with the open support of Peru's oligarchy and who capitalized on the army's hatred and paranoia toward the Aprista party. The third period examined is one of radical intellectual and philosophical change within the armed forces, which prepared it for its new role as an institutional military government. The fourth period is the best known outside Peru, as it coincided with the leftist military regime initiated by General Juan Velasco Alvarado, under whose guidance the first significant land reform in Peruvian history was undertaken. The fifth period examines the anti-sendero campaign launched by the military in December 1982, when it took over from the discredited Peruvian constabulary the primary responsibility for fighting the Maoist-inspired insurrection led by the former philosophy professor Abimael Guzmán. The conclusion summarizes the role of the military in Peruvian politics.

AFTERMATH OF THE WAR OF THE PACIFIC

The defeat experienced at the hands of the Chileans between 1879 and 1884 traumatized the Peruvian nation to such a degree that repercussions can be felt to this day, especially among the military, who still consider the most viable external threat to Peru's security to come from Chile. The Chilean army occupied Lima for over three years, "subjecting the city to a reign of terror."[5] The country was devastated. Worst of all was the feeling that "the war had been lost behind the lines and not on the battlefield."[6] Although the Peruvian navy gave a good account of itself against the more numerous and technically superior vessels of the Chilean navy, the army's performance was anything but credible. But most shameful of all was the unbelievable behavior of Peru's president, General Mariano Prado, who departed for Europe in mid-December 1879, a few months before the actual invasion of Peru by Chilean troops and only weeks after the Battle of Angamos, which gave supremacy of the seas to the Chileans. In an incredible letter to his countrymen, "Prado denied that he was abandoning the ship of state in a gale. His financial expertise and prestige as Peruvian chief executive, wrote the president, would be of great value in securing loans and war material on the continent."[7]

Resistance to the Chilean occupation and to the terms of the Treaty of Ancón (23 October 1883), which ended the war, continued in the mountainous regions of Peru. Two very different but able leaders carried on the struggle: Nicolás de Piérola, a civilian politician who had acted as interim president after General Prado's disgraceful exit, and General Andrés A. Cáceres, a military *caudillo* in the old tradition. Both leaders refused to surrender to the Chileans and launched guerrilla operations relying almost exclusively on Indian recruits—known as *montoneros*—who could not comprehend the fuss being caused by generals "Peru" and "Chile" who were fighting each other! General Cáceres emerged as the leading political figure during the decade that ended in 1895, with the only successful popular rebellion in Peruvian history. The last of the traditional *caudillos,* Cáceres epitomized the general/politician of the nineteenth century in many ways: He disguised his dictatorial rule crudely as an attempt to restore republican institutions, he relied on fraudulent elections to regain power, and he tackled the burgeoning foreign debt by selling out Peruvian railway and mineral rights.[8]

General Cáceres was replaced by a civilian mounted on horseback, Nicolás de Piérola, only the second civilian to lead Peru since independence. Peru's new president believed that the war with Chile "demonstrated that *caudillismo* was a poor substitute for military professionalism."[9] Furthermore, in Piérola's view, "rampant military *caudillismo* and *golpismo* had . . . disrupted the regular, constitutional processes of government for too long."[10] He was determined to bring the military under civilian control by depoliticizing the army while carrying out overdue reforms to modernize the army. It was his intention to turn it into a more technically efficient service arm of the government. Piérola was determined, in short, to end the era of Peru's army being "led by ill-trained military amateurs."[11]

To accomplish these goals, "Piérola first sharply reduced the regular army and its share of the national budget, retiring or dismissing large numbers of officers loyal to the defeated Cáceres."[12] Then he addressed the problem of lack of professionalism among the Peruvian military. Little had changed in the Peruvian army since colonial times.

Piérola's most far-reaching reform was to seek the assistance of a French military mission to revamp the Peruvian army. French influence within the Peruvian army would remain paramount through World War II. Piérola had turned to France for assistance for several reasons. First, the reorganized French army of the 1880s had remained subordinate to civilian authority, and he wanted to inculcate the French army's principle of political obedience into the Peruvian army. Second, the obvious choice, the Prussian army, was already involved in training Chile. Third, he had a natural "affinity for Catholic and Republican France" given his own ultramontane and civilian preferences.[13]

More than anything else, the French military advisers sought to transfer "the patriotic zeal" of their own nineteenth-century empire builders to the officers of the Peruvian army. Indeed, future professional militarism in Peru would be based on the French model, which sought "to apply military solutions to national problems," which evidenced "a distaste for partisan politics," and which believed intrinsically that the army has a social function.[14] It was from its French military advisers that Peruvian army officers first learnt "that they had a social role to perform, that the army was an agent of modernization, and that it was capable of civilizing Peru."[15]

Piérola's military reforms were in full swing by 1898. Chief among these was the reorganization of the Peruvian military academy under the direction of French colonel Clément. The Escuela Militar de Aplicación (later to be renamed Escuela Militar de Chorrillos) graduated its first class in February 1901. A more modern Code of Military Justice modeled, not surprisingly, after French military law and legislation creating guidelines for military recruitment and administration was enacted. The new Law of National Conscription (27 December 1898) made military service compulsory for all Peruvians from the age of nineteen to fifty. Furthermore, Piérola raised salaries and insisted that merit replace lineage "as the means of qualifying for officer status."[16] Advancement through meritocracy, a revolutionary concept not only in Peru but throughout Latin America at the turn of the century,

had the effect of opening up avenues of mobility for the new middle classes who in time would take over the military and further contribute to its changing character. Eventually even exceptional elements from the masses might aspire to a career as an officer. The military became, as the twentieth century developed, a principal vehicle of mobility in a society long calcified along class lines.[17]

Basadre in his *Historia de la República del Perú* praises Piérola's army reforms, which paved the way for the army's depoliticization in two decades prior to World War I. For the first time in Peruvian history, the army acquiesced to the civil authorities and devoted itself exclusively to its professional training. A new type of officer, "molded by vigorous academic study and almost Spartanlike, replaced the officers of yesteryear, sometimes picturesque and ostentatious."[18] However, the aristocracy, with some minor exceptions, shunned careers in the military. So did many other Peruvians who sought to get rich through business "or who were influenced by the European ideas prevailing at the beginning of the twentieth century," which held spending a lifetime in the army in very low esteem.[19] Moreover, Piérola's efforts to instill a more professional attitude within the army "while successful in the short term, were in the long run destined to fail. The historic tendency of the Armed Forces to intervene in politics as guardians of elite interests against threats from below reasserted itself again in 1914, 1919 and 1929, thereafter becoming once again 'endemic.' "[20]

TWENTIETH-CENTURY CAUDILLOS: SÁNCHEZ CERRO, BENAVIDES, ODRÍA

Soldiers of the Lima garrison seized the National Palace on the morning of 4 February 1914, forcing the constitutionally elected populist president Guillermo Billinghurst out of office. The troops led by the most prestigious officer at that time, Colonel Oscar R. Benavides, moved against the civilian leader only after the latter had "dissolved congress, slashed the military budget and threatened to arm his working-class supporters."[21] This *golpe* was the first such military intervention in Peruvian twentieth-century politics. The conspirators "were the technicians, the new professionals, the best in the army."[22]

Ironically, Benavides's *golpe* represented the only occasion in Peruvian history when the army has actually "acted in defense of constitutionalism."[23] The army's intervention, however, was not entirely due to its concern for constitutional irregularities by the demagogue Billinghurst. Not only had Billinghurst evidenced a willingness to accept the Chilean position over the future of the irredentist provinces Tacna and Arica during a delicate phase of the negotiations, he had dared to arouse the mob against the vested interests of Peru's ruling oligarchy by supporting the eight-hour-day demands of greater Lima's growing proletariat.

Colonel Benavides's successful coup "cemented the tacit alliance between the army and the ruling class to maintain the established order."[24] In fact, Benavides's 1914 *golpe* heralded a new era in the military's intervention in Peruvian politics. Beginning in 1914, some type of coup or military uprising would occur on an average of one every two-and-a-half years—in short, of the twenty major coups or military insurrections that took place between 1914 and 1968, nine succeeded in overthrowing the government, resulting in an average of one successful coup every six years.[25]

Much to everyone's amazement, Benavides relinquished power to a civilian, José Pardo, "after twenty months as provisional president and retired to the political sidelines, where he remained for two decades."[26] Benavides's *golpe* had demonstrated that "a more professional army would enter the political arena once its corporate interests were threatened."[27] Furthermore, it offered proof that the "new" *caudillos* of the twentieth century would not act solely on their own behalf when they intervened in politics but as the protectors of the oligarchy whose agricultural, mining, and financial interests needed to be safeguarded against the working class and peasants. As Villanueva concludes, "The Peruvian aristocracy often did not bother to conceal its disdain for the army while relying on it to protect its interests as 'faithful watchdogs' [*perros guardianes*]."[28] Paradoxically, antimilitarism (*civilismo*), which began as a political movement opposing the military, "did not break with it, it only subordinated it to its wishes."[29]

The next major military coup took place in April 1919, when a former finance minister and civilian president, Augusto B. Leguía, "enlisted military support to overthrow Pardo, who had repeated Billinghurst's mistakes by reducing military appropriations in a time of social unrest."[30] Leguía ruled as a dictator for eleven years. For most of this period, Leguía was able to muzzle the Peruvian military. Also, he created a constabulary force (Guardia Civil), which competed head on with the army and which was established to serve as a praetorian guard to safeguard the president against possible coups. Finally, he used political favoritism in senior army appointments. So scandalous, in fact, was the level of corruption regarding army promotions that a common joke of the time insisted that "army officers were like gasoline, they could be bought by the gallon!"[31]

Leguía would eventually be replaced by a young army colonel, Luis M. Sánchez Cerro, who rode the crest of dissatisfaction against the by then unpopular dictator. Without question Sánchez Cerro was the most popular military commander of the twentieth century to occupy Pizarro's Palace. He had a special empathy for the lower classes, whom he manipulated with finesse. He himself was a *cholo* ("civilized Indian," or one of the common people), and so perhaps he could identify with Peru's exploited underclass.

Sánchez Cerro's brief presidency (he would be assassinated) coincided with the emergence of the Aprista party in Peruvian politics. Led by Peru's most enduring politician and ideologue of the twentieth century, Víctor Raúl Haya de la Torre, the Apristas were determined to bring about social revolution through class warfare. At first, they welcomed the emergence of Sánchez Cerro, thinking they could direct his energies. But Sánchez Cerro had his own ideas and was his own man. He founded his own party, Unión Revolucionaria, and began to espouse a radical program that undermined APRA's position. Above all, the upstart colonel decried the "partisan intolerance" of APRA.

The ensuing clash between Sánchez Cerro, the half-breed from Arequipa, and Haya de la Torre, the scion of a well-to-do, landowning creole family from Trujillo, was inevitable. It resulted in the most violent period of Peruvian history in the twentieth century prior to the Shining Path's bloody insurrection of the 1980s and 1990s. The armed struggle began on 7 July 1932, when an Aprista rebel group launched an all-out attack against the garrison in Trujillo, in northern Peru. After fierce resistance, the Apristas, with the help of some turncoat soldiers, succeeded in taking over the garrison. Then word came that government reinforcements in large numbers were on their way to put down the rebellion. The Aprista leaders chose to flee Trujillo, but not before giving orders "for the cold-blooded assassination of some sixty military officers and enlisted men who had been taken prisoner and held as hostages. Not only were the soldiers killed, but the bodies of some were mutilated."[32] The government retaliation was so brutal that the army and APRA have been at each other's throats ever since. Villanueva maintains that "the confrontations between the army and APRA which would last to the present, has been permanent in the political life of our country and can well be considered as a constant struggle for power."[33]

During this struggle, 1931–33, which many Peruvian historians regard as a civil war, the Peruvian oligarchy "regrouped behind the popular *caudillo* Sánchez Cerro."[34] As we shall see, "in alliance with the armed forces, it succeeded in repressing the masses and fashioning a period of 'indirect' rule that endured for another generation and mirrored, in a more subtle way, its hegemony during the 'Aristocratic Republic.'"[35]

The new Peruvian constitution, promulgated in just twelve days before Sánchez Cerro's assassination, "sanctioned the prominent role of the armed forces in national affairs."[36] This was done in article 213, which read, "The purpose of the armed forces is to secure the rights of the Republic, the fulfillment of the constitution and the laws, and preservation of the public order."[37] Missing from the constitution, however, was a provision for a vice-president in case of the president's death or of incapacity that would prevent his performing his duties. Nevertheless, within hours of Sánchez Cerro's death, the Peruvian national assembly unanimously elected General Oscar R. Benavides to complete the late president's term. This choice was in direct violation of the Constitution of 1933, which "barred active members of the armed forces from election to the presidency."[38] This restriction, however, was only a mere technicality to the frightened parliamentarians. Benavides once more appeared to be the man of the hour. He was the commander of the army and thus, de facto, the most powerful figure in Peruvian politics; he had very close ties with leading *civilista* families, most especially the influential Prado brothers; and "he had governed the country creditably during a similar crisis in 1914."[39]

Benavides sought to strengthen his hold on power by gaining favor with the military establishment through increased military spending. He also sought to enhance the professionalization of the armed forces by creating new specialized higher schools for the various sections of the army: infantry, cavalry, artillery, and engineering. Now promotion to the rank of captain and major would require satisfactory completion of their program in one of these advanced training centers. Departing, however, from the traditional nineteenth-century model of the *caudillo,* Benavides was an exponent of the French concept of the army's civilizing mission. This idea had been thoroughly inculcated in the bemedalled field-marshal-to-be by the French military mission and by tours of duty in France.

On 9 December 1939, Benavides brought to an end ten years of direct military rule by transferring presidential power to a civilian aristocrat, Manuel Prado y Ugarteche.

As Sir Robert Marett, a former British ambassador to Peru and author of a perceptive study of Peruvian politics and history, has written: "So long as APRA remained underground, enjoying the loyalty of a large segment of the working population, but an object of fear and suspicion to the Establishment, there could be none of that peace and harmony in the Peruvian family which Benavides had set out so hopefully to achieve."[40]

General Manuel A. Odría's coup against the hapless José Luis Bustamante (in 1948) would prove to be the last instance of an army officer reaching the presidency and ruling the country as a military *caudillo.* He would be the last of the trio of twentieth-century military officers to rule dictatorially in his own name, but with the tacit acquiescence of the armed forces and the active support of the Peruvian oligarchy. Villanueva regards Odría's regime from 1948 to 1956 as the apogee of "the oligarchical-military alliance which lasted for over half a century and was stronger than ever; but the terms of dependency had been inverted. It is not the aristocrats of the 1800s who govern with the support of the military, in 1948 it is the military who are in power and who sign the decrees put in front of them by the dominant class."[41]

Odría quite naturally pursued a repressive policy against the Apristas, forcing their leader to take refuge at the Colombian embassy, where he remained for several years in political asylum while continuing to run the outlawed party. The general was also determined to improve the condition of Peru's working classes and vowed that his government would be "neither of the left nor of the right . . . but thoroughly nationalistic."[42] But his earnest attempts at social reform were overshadowed by the brutality of his regime. His government made a mockery of constitutional and human rights; agro-exporters called the shots throughout the Odría rule.

Odría, even though a military hero in the war against Ecuador in 1941, steadily lost favor in military circles despite blatant attempts to gain the backing of the armed forces. He increased officers' pensions and awarded them a special indemnification equivalent to thirty months' pay when retiring after thirty-five years of service. However, many honest army officers were scandalized by the dictator's ostentatious private life, made possible by gifts from wealthy friends seeking special favors. Mario Vargas Llosa's fictional account of Peru under Odría entitled *Conversations in the Cathedral* depicts this corruption and brutality. But expensive cars and imported whiskey were only superficial concerns. "Odría's loss of support within the military was a measure of the degree to which his *caudillo* style of rule had become a political anachronism in Peru."[43] "A growing body of opinion within the officer corps was opposed to the idea of military leaders behaving as traditional politicians and was attracted to a new view of the military as an institution committed to social engineering."[44] In retrospect, Odría's regime may be viewed as "a bridge between the traditional *caudillismo* of Peru's premodern military and a more unified and professional armed forces."[45]

Sánchez Cerro, Benavides and Odría—the three military presidents from 1930 to 1956—"were strong personalist leaders who used the military as their stepping stone to power rather than embodying the aspirations of the military institution as such."[46] Nevertheless, these regimes were essentially "military oligarchic," that is to say, "the military provided immediate political force, while the oligarchy contributed money, status and economic expertise."[47]

CAEM AND THE 1962 COUP: THE NEW ROLE OF THE MILITARY

The 1950s witnessed a radical change in how the military viewed itself and its role in society. During the nineteenth century, militarism could be equated with *caudillismo:* Each military leader had his cadre of supporters who might or might not have some professional military training, but who were united in their pursuit of political power and wealth. In the period of *civilismo* ushered in by Nicolás de Piérola's reforms, a determined effort was made to transform amateur soldiers into professional servicemen and to subordinate the army to civilian authority. The period of *civilismo* lasted through Leguía's regime (1895 to 1930). In that time, the army's role was of course to defend the nation from external threats but also, as President Prado would maintain during the 1940s, "to keep the right kind of people in power and the wrong kind of people at bay."[48] Such twentieth-century *caudillos* as Benavides and Odría sought power for themselves and, as we have seen, acted in the interests of the exporting/financial oligarchy. Although Benavides did put forward a rudimentary concept of the "civilizing mission" of the army, neither he nor Odría believed that the army's duty was to transform "the vegetating mass of Indians and cholos" into productive members of the Peruvian society.[49]

New ideas after World War II were developed at the Centro de Altos Estudios Militares (CAEM), founded in 1950 under the command of the former APRA sympathizer General José del Cármen Marín.[50] The guiding concept of the new military ideology was "that military preparedness must rest on a solid economic and social foundation and that Peruvian society [especially the backward *sierra*, from which most of the army's conscript manpower was obtained] was in need of restructuring and modernizing."[51] What was novel in Marín's thinking was equating the importance of national defense and social development.

The military deliberately and consciously redefined its mission in the years immediately following the Odría dictatorship in response to the threat of social upheaval, which became increasingly apparent as the 1960s approaches. "Land invasions, guerrilla movements, and acts of political terrorism were seen as the top of an iceberg of inexorably mounting social pressure caused by exploding populations that would, in the long run, overwhelm traditional social structures."[52] The problem facing the army was twofold: First, Peru's level of underdevelopment precluded its waging "total war" successfully. Second, a great number of Peruvians felt totally alienated by the social and economic injustices found throughout the country; this meant that "the population had no 'national identity.'"[53] Peruvian sociologist Julio Cotler commented, "This diagnosis required that the army actively participate in changing the conditions in which the majority of the population lived. Only then would the population identify itself with the nation, grant legitimacy to the state and resist subversion."[54] To accomplish this, the military, under CAEM leadership, "redefined its role in the preservation of order to include a responsibility to serve the interests of all the people, not just the limited interests of the oligarchic elite as in earlier years."[55]

In its first twelve years of existence, CAEM became the most important think tank in Peru for both military officers and civilian bureaucrats. Villanueva wrote in the preface to his monograph on CAEM that "it is very probable that there does not exist a politician, historian, sociologist, or any other intellectual interested in the political development of present-day Peru who has not referred . . . to the role played by . . . CAEM in this process."[56] As far as the military was concerned, "by the early 1960s it had become usual for a colonel to spend a year at CAEM before being promoted to general."[57] Besides advanced courses in military subjects, the officers were exposed to such unorthodox material as geopolitics, national income, and the mechanics of national planning. Appointment to CAEM was made by the commander-in-chief for the three armed services as well as for police officers.

The Peruvian army and consequently the entire military establishment was profoundly influenced by CAEM and its insistence that Peru's security depended on the national well-being (*bien estar nacional*). Under CAEM's guidance, the military "began to accept the doctrine that Peru's development problems could be solved through the application of modern planning and technology."[58] Ironically, the military thinkers adopted a reform program almost indistinguishable from earlier Aprista platforms: "agrarian reform, social planning, economic development, and the nationalization of foreign-held property. It was the program that the military supported both under the junta's rule in 1962–1963 and subsequently under Belaúnde."[59]

CAEM would serve as a catalyst to break the ties the military had had throughout the course of Peru's republican history, since it helped to crystalize a new outlook amongst the officer corps as a whole. This process, although certainly not inevitable, was the long-term result of French influence on the Peruvian army. "Penetration of the interior, colonization, assembly of statistics and data, obligatory military service as an educational experience, *la misión civilizadora*, military-civilian socioeconomic cooperation, and the tying of national development to internal security are all attributable to the French presence."[60] In fact, the influence of French military thought on the Peruvian army cannot be overemphasized. What is also apparent is that by the mid-1950s, "the military's 150-year-old ties with the upper-class oligarchy were weakening, a development that might have come much earlier had it not been for the military's 20-year-feud with APRA, which among Peru's major parties, was the voice of the middle and lower classes."[61]

On 18 July 1962, the Peruvian military staged a successful coup d'état to prevent Haya de la Torre and the Apristas from assuming power. They had had a complicated stratagem by which the Apristas would back Odría's bid for the presidency in exchange for de facto control of the congress. This Machiavellian maneuvering by the Apristas was primarily designed to keep the populist politician-architect Fernando Belaúnde from the presidency; he challenged them with charges of electoral fraud against APRA. The army acted swiftly, announcing a caretaker government in which a military junta acting on behalf of the armed forces would oversee new and honest elections scheduled for 1963. From the very outset, this coup "broke with previous traditions by installing a Junta whose President depended upon the support of the three service ministers, whose positions, in turn, were determined by military seniority. *Authority, therefore, was vested in the military institutions as a whole and not in any single caudillo*"[62] (my italics).

Determined to undermine the appeal that Castro's brand of Cuban socialism was now enjoying throughout the hemisphere, the military junta, acting under the presidency of General Ricardo Pérez Godoy "embarked on a cautious reformist path reflecting the military's growing recognition of the need to address Peru's problems of poverty and underdevelopment."[63] Although this decision to push reform forward predates a well-known CAEM document prepared in 1963, it is interesting to observe how military planners in CAEM viewed Peru at the time of the military government. "The sad and depressing reality," the CAEM document reads, "is that in Peru real power is not held by the executive, legislative, judicial, or electoral branch of government, but by the large landowners, exporters, bankers and North American companies."[64] Peru's leading sociologist, commenting on this document, has stated that "the obvious conclusion was that 'nationalization' and the reorganization of production had become indispensable to enhancing the country's potential and that it was necessary to plan the economy in order to secure national sovereignty."[65]

The military junta's reform program, although modest, was further evidence that the armed forces were determined to distance themselves from previous authoritarian military regimes while achieving autonomy from Peru's oligarchic forces. Of these changes, the limited agrarian reform was perhaps the most significant, as it constituted "the first attempt by any Peruvian government to begin the redistribution of land on a systematic basis."[66] The choice for the first site of junta's land redistribution was further proof of the government's political sensitivity. As Masterson concludes, "It indicates that the armed forces clearly understood that agrarian reform was initially linked to alleviating the conditions promoting rural unrest."[67]

The 1962 coup proved to be a watershed in military-civilian relations in Peru. Prior to 1962, "military regimes, as such, did not exist. Rather, the leader of a successful coup [in some cases, a fairly junior officer] installed himself as President [sometimes with the help of managed elections] and made his own political appointments."[68] After 1962, the military, acting on its own authority and no longer as the pawn of the oligarchy, was convinced that it alone could tackle successfully Peru's growing social and economic unrest. As evident in the 1968 coup, the 1962 junta "applied a policy which sought to subordinate the popular classes to the state apparatus, by adopting nationalist and anti-oligarchic policies."[69] The point to stress is that "in contrast to previous military interventions, the 1962 government did not try to block all reforms, but rather, tried to ensure that such change did not come about by direct action from below, as had occurred a few years earlier in Cuba."[70]

1968: REVOLUTION FROM ABOVE

Barely five years after the Peruvian military returned to their barracks, leaving the government of Peru in the hands of a civilian architect-turned-populist politician, Fernando Belaúnde y Terry, the armed forces staged a coup against the founder of the Acción Popular, Belaúnde's moderate political party, and escorted the president unceremoniously to the airport to begin a long sojourn in exile. On 3 October 1968, the Peruvian military establishment proclaimed the foundation of a "Revolutionary Government of the Armed Forces." The head of this new government, General Juan Velasco Alvarado, declared the wide-ranging objectives of the revolution in various proclamations to the nation. In essence, the military regime intended

to transform Peru's basic economic and social structures; to end external dependence, especially on the United States; to force foreign investors to be more responsive to Peru's needs; to seek a third path to development that was 'neither capitalist nor communist' through such innovative measures as worker-managed enterprises; and even to alter national values in order to create a 'new Peruvian man,' one dedicated to 'solidarity not individualism.'[71]

The military establishment had intervened decisively to set up an institutional regime of the armed forces because a significant number of officers had come to realize that dealing effectively with Peru's internal security threat was beyond the capability "of an inefficient, corrupt, and unjust middle-and-upper-class parliamentary and social system."[72] Moreover, there was growing confidence that the technical and nonmilitary training that Peruvian military officers had received had produced "a cadre of specialists" more capable of carrying out development programs than were the discredited professional politicians. In plain words, the military could be trusted to do a better job than the civilians.

Additionally, there was growing concern within military circles about the extent of Peru's economic dependency on foreign investments and markets, especially those of the United States. "The relative importance of foreign capital in the Peru of 1968" cannot be overstated; "in that year, foreigners controlled some three-quarters of mining capital, two-thirds of the sugar refining industry, half of the commercial banking sector, and roughly a third of the manufacturing sector."[73] That Peru's military chose to act in part to counteract excessive economic dependency on the United States was not in itself unique. "Other Latin American military regimes had adopted similar anti-dependency objectives, most notably Brazil since the early 1970's, but most of these regimes originally came to power in response to perceived internal communist threats."[74] However, in the Peruvian case, there was no communist threat. The guerrillas espousing Castro-type socialism had been summarily defeated in 1965. There was no hint yet of the Shining Path, which came into being during the 1970s. Instead, what prompted the armed forces to intervene was the perceived danger of the growing "linkage between North American imperialism and Peru's ruling oligarchy."[75]

Finally, since "Belaúnde's failure was due to the fact that real power in Peru was held by economic interests rather than elected politicians," then the revolutionary military government would succeed by completely restructuring "the social, political and economic relations in the country."[76] General Velasco and the military officers who had orchestrated the October 3rd coup were convinced that they were ushering in a revolution that would affect all the people of Peru.

Peru's so-called military revolutionary government lasted for twelve years. In doing so it enjoyed the distinction of being the longest uninterrupted regime in modern Peruvian history. Nevertheless, there were two distinct phases during the period: The Velasco years, from 1968 to 1975, were characterized by reformist measures; then there was the counterrevolutionary swing under General Francisco Morales Bermúdez, who replaced Velasco in 1975.

From the military's point of view, the military interlude marked an irreversible watershed in Peruvian history that would have profound effects for the armed forces. First, there was the molding of the "new military officer," which had begun in the early 1960s under CAEM's influence but which became more prevalent in the decade of the 1970s. The "heroic" soldier of yesterday gave way to the "technocratic soldiers" who would administer the transformation of the Peruvian state. Now, the retrained officer could find a line position, not leading troops in counterinsurgency operations but in a government ministry or agency dealing with national economic and social problems; he would be at the head of an army of burgeoning civilian bureaucrats.

Second, not only was the government run by the three branches of the armed forces, but the regime scrupulously respected established military hierarchy. This meant that only generals sat in the cabinet or at the head of government bodies. The days of junior officers such as Sánchez Cerro, who was a colonel at the time he moved against the government, taking control of the nation were over. Also gone was the day of the military *caudillo* who could bully his way to power with a handful of venal troops and an ample abundance of charisma. The military would now act in unison—some would say "institutionally"—or not at all.

Third, the armed forces experienced the largest growth in its 150-year history since independence. Between 1968 and 1981 (the first year of the second Belaúnde administration) the number of troops in uniform increased from approximately 50,000 to 135,000, an increase in excess of 250%. Military expenditures also increased dramatically during the same period, from $143 million to $400 million. To be sure, part of this impressive rise in arms purchases and growth of personnel was an overreaction to the perceived threat from Chile after the Pinochet coup of 1973. Nevertheless, the 6% of GDP that Peru spent annually on military purchases on average in the period between 1975 and 1978 represents "one of the highest figures in Latin America."[77]

Although the armed forces failed to achieve many of their objectives and after 1975 took a course that turned away from Velasco's reformist policies, this "does not alter the fact that the military regime nevertheless intentionally changed the nature of Peruvian political life."[78] Under the military government, Peruvians witnessed the altering of "existing political patterns," the mobilization of the labor sector, the democratization of the university system, and the "emergence of an industrial middle class."[79] In short, "Peru's military rulers contributed importantly to overcoming the previous gap between the country's evolving socio-economic realities and its political institutions and public policies."[80] What is remarkable is the relatively short period of time it took Peru's military leaders to achieve this transformation.

THE MILITARY RETURN TO BARRACKS ONLY TO FIGHT A DIRTY WAR

In February 1977, only eighteen months after Velasco's removal from office marked the end of "military reformism" in Peru, the conservative military government of General Morales Bermúdez announced its intention to return the military to its barracks. This would be accomplished in two phases: First, there would be elections in June 1978 for a Constituent Assembly, which would draft a new constitution. Second, "an elected, civilian government would take office in 1980."[81] The eventual withdrawal from Pizarro's Palace had been prompted by the concatenation of three factors that were undermining the fabric of the military and the nation. First, acute economic deterioration had triggered the worst wave of general strikes the nation had ever known; then, there was bitter factionalism within the armed forces over the president's sensible and long over-due attempt to make peace between the army and APRA; last, an unacceptable level of institutional corruption within the military establishment made a lie of the army's claim to sacrifice and patriotism. It was clear to all sides that "by 1978 Peru's military establishment was psychologically exhausted and ready to return political power to civilians."[82]

The military as "a permanent institution" would still exercise a significant role in Peru's political life, as Morales Bermúdez made clear in a speech prior to the Constituent Assembly elections. In the new civilian regime, the armed forces "without being present directly in the daily political life of the country . . . will be present in POLITICS, with capital letters, which means the life of the fatherland, which means sovereignty and development." However, the new role of the armed forces would be assumed as an institution, not as "individual components or persons of the military."[83]

The new civilian government, headed, ironically, by the politician toppled twelve years earlier when the military revolution was launched, Fernando Belaúnde, had "no wish to upset the military and was scrupulous in respecting military autonomy in such areas as promotions and budgets."[84] Instead, Belaúnde was so deferential in his relations with top military officials of the previous regime when he took office that he kept the command structure of the armed forces unaltered, stating, "There is no reason to enact changes."[85] The obvious kowtowing to the military establishment angered many of Belaúnde's civilian opponents, who suspected some sort of collusion with the outgoing regime. What seemed clear to all was that there appeared to be a tacit under-standing, if not an agreement, between Belaúnde and the military in which "civilians were to stay out of the military's affairs."[86] What resulted was an unusually high degree of institutional autonomy for the armed forces, which has lasted until the present.

The military, however, had left nothing to chance. On 9 July 1980, eleven days before Belaúnde took office, it proclaimed a new Mobilization Law. According to this unique law, the armed forces could be mobilized not only in cases of war but also in cases of "internal subversion" and "disaster," which included such acts "as industrial sabotage, arson, or manifestations which might have a political end."[87]

A second decree eased the military's surrender of power to civilian authority: the 1980 Law of Immunity. This law provided immunity from prosecution in the lower courts for officials of the military government, who could only "be accused of offenses before the Supreme Court. This protection previously applied only to ministers of state."[88]

Not all Peruvians favored the complete autonomy of the armed forces within the Peruvian government. Several measures included in the Constitution of 1978 were in fact designed to discourage future military *golpes* and to strengthen the always tenuous civilian control of the army. One article made null and void "all acts of usurped authority" and went so far as to give Peruvians "a right to insurgency in defense of the constitutional order."[89] A second article, which sought to discredit any future de facto government, stated that the state would only guarantee payment "of the public debt contracted by constitutional government."[90] A third article attempted "to submit the military to civilian control by recognizing that 'the President of the Republic is the Supreme Chief of the Armed Forces and Police Forces.' "[91] An outspoken supporter of these clauses was an Aprista assembly member, Alan García, who in 1985 would head the first APRA administration in Peruvian history.

The major institutional challenge to the military's autonomy in the period after 1980 came in March 1987, when Alan García, by now president, made public his intention to submit a draft law creating "a single Defence Ministry, merging the functions of the three military ministers in charge of each of the three services into a single cabinet post."[92] The uproar among both active and retired officers opposing the measure was severe and even led to "the first overt sign of *golpismo*." This happened when the commander of the air force, who had called for the resignation of García's war minister, reacted to his own dismissal by ordering "Mirage Jets to buzz the presidential palace."[93]

Although García took measures to prevent a coup, including giving instructions for the artillery to shoot down any plane that came close to the Presidential Palace, it was clear that he had gone too far. The issue over the Defense Ministry "rekindled old anti-Aprista animosities, and prompted the question of whether or not the government was seeking to alter the relationship between the civilian authorities and the military, as established in 1980."[94] The upshot of the affair was that Alan García got his single Defense Ministry but "was obliged to appoint the new commander-in-chief of the army, General Enrique López Albújar, as the new minister."[95] It was clear that García's attempt to secure greater control over the military had backfired; indeed, the only change that occurred was in the name of the ministry itself.[96] Everything else had remained as before, in complete consistency with the CAEM-inspired notion of military institutionalism: The minister is not a civilian but the highest-ranking army officer; his immediate deputies are all service officers; and the ministry's principal purpose "is to represent the interests of the military institution and not to exert democratic control over the Armed Forces."[97]

A much more serious threat to the Peruvian armed forces than the creation of a single defense ministry occurred in December 1982. The Belaúnde regime had been struggling for almost three years against the Maoist insurgents known as the Shining Path. Seeking to minimize the role of the military during the early years of his administration and always fearful of a possible coup, Belaúnde had at first ignored the insurgency, referring to the revolutionaries as "carnival guerrillas" and "cattle thieves."[98] Then, when the number of brazen attacks against police and military installations as well as against innocent and unarmed Andean peasants mounted, Belaúnde gave the responsibility of the antiguerrilla campaign to the police and especially to "the Guardia Civil's brutally repressive counter-terrorism force known as the Sinchis."[99]

But Shining Path proved too much for Peru's constabulary and its CIA-trained antiguerrilla specialists. The army's subsequent intervention was a blow to the police's professional reputation. The then minister of war, General Cisneros Vizquerra, sought to exonerate the police force from its failure to deal decisively with the terrorists. As the army commander stated in an interview given to the press shortly after the military had taken operational control of the antiguerrilla campaign, "The police do not know how to handle this problem . . . as they are trained to maintain order, to control a demonstration or a strike. They are prepared to act against a tangible enemy . . . not to confront an enemy they cannot see and whose whereabouts are unknown."[100]

The Peruvian military has been fighting the Shining Path for more than a decade. No engagement by the Peruvian armed forces has lasted longer or taken a heavier toll. Not even the war against Chile can compare with what has become a nightmare for the military establishment. And yet, "the war against this sinister enemy is still not a top priority in the Peruvian military's national defense perspective."[101] It was thanks to the first-rate intelligence operations of DINCOTE, an independent branch of the national police, and not to the army that Abimael Guzmán—the Shining Path's messianic leader—was finally apprehended on 12 September 1992.

The irony of the last ten years of an ostensibly civilian government confronting the intractable guerrilla insurgency is that in fact more of the country is now under outright military jurisdiction than was ever the case in the time of the generals. We will now examine how this startling and as yet unremarked paradox has come to be.

At the same time that the Belaúnde government turned over the battle against the Shining Path to the Armed Forces Joint Command, "the cabinet ratified the decision of the National Defense Council creating the Ayacucho Emergency Zone."[102] In December 1982, four provinces in the Department of Ayacucho—Peru's poorest province and the birthplace of *senderismo*—were placed under a state of emergency. This meant that the military and police could ignore many, if not most, of the constitutional safeguards of the local population.

As the number of provinces placed under the state of emergency increased, the return of the military to political/administrative duties almost nationwide became a fact of life for a majority of Peruvians. There were no more theoretical debates about the involvement, direct or otherwise, of the Peruvian military in the national political scene. As one observer has concluded, "Ironically . . . an ever-expanding portion of Peru came under *de jure* military rule during the very decade that followed the return of the government to civilian and democratic rule.''[103]

When in Lima there was a sudden mushrooming of assassinations against public officials, police, and high-ranking armed forces officers, the military demanded that President Alan García declare the city an emergency zone. The civilian commander-in-chief of the armed forces turned down the request indignantly, claiming that to do so ''would mean the virtual abdication of the democratic government.''[104] However, well before his term of office had expired, President García would be obliged to acquiesce to the earlier demands regarding metropolitan Lima; since late 1988, the capital has in effect been administered by the armed forces and the police, not always acting in tandem.

Many prominent military officers have voiced serious reservations regarding the use of emergency zones, including such different types as the urbane former head of the army and Velasco's Minister of Foreign Affairs, General Edgardo Mercado Jarrín, as well as the blunt, Quechua-speaking *serrano,* the second commander of the Ayacucho Emergency Zone, General Adrián Huamán Centeno. They are concerned not only about the effectiveness of the policy in the war against the Shining Path but also about the negative impact it will have on the armed forces. General Huamán has ridiculed the policy, stating that ''all Peru is an emergency'' and asking rhetorically why the measures should affect only a few areas. He commented that the policy was a clear indication that the Belaúnde government as well as the two subsequent civilian administrations wanted to regard the action against *sendero* solely in military terms when it is not just a military problem:

Here the solution is not military, because if it had been military, I would have resolved it in minutes. If it were a question of destroying Ayacucho, it would not have existed for half an hour. . . . But this is not the answer. What is happening is that we are talking about human beings from the forgotten *pueblos* who have been crying out for 160 years and no one has paid any attention to them. Now we are reaping the result.[105]

CONCLUSION

Since 1821, when Peru declared its independence from Spain, until the present day, there have been seventy-one presidents of Peru. Fifty-one of them have been military officers. On twenty-six occasions an army officer has become president through a coup d'etat. In short, ''in Peru, statistics point out that a military career was the surest way to reach the presidency.''[106] So dominant was the military *caudillo* in the nineteenth century that Peru's first civilian president, Manuel Pardo, was elected to office only after fifty years of military rule.

The Peruvian military has evolved in the twentieth century from a chaotic and unprofessional group of strongmen on horseback to highly trained, dedicated professionals who have not always been in sync with civilian society. As Frederick M. Nunn has written recently, "The Peruvian army had out-paced the civilian institutions by the 1960s."[107]

The future of the Peruvian military and its intervention in politics depends on what happens in the civil war against the Shining Path. "Not since 1879 has the Peruvian military faced as great a challenge as it confronts at the present."[108] Masterson's conclusion is irrefutable: "Peru, now more than ever, needs a stable and progressive armed forces establishment to defeat the Sendero Luminoso insurgency and help rebuild the nation's shattered infrastructure once the war is over."[109] And yet paradoxically, the successful professionalization of the military achieved to date has created a high degree of institutional complacency within the armed forces. Many insist on ignoring the threat posed by the Shining Path; only 15% of the defense budget is allocated to fighting the Sendero insurgents. A few even maintain that there is a limit to what can be expected from military operations, as the struggle against the *senderistas,* like that against the Viet Cong in the 1960s and 1970s, can not be won militarily. Where there is consensus, however, is in the military's determination to preserve "the profession and the institution from excessive individual adventurism."[110] The time of the *caudillos* is gone forever!

NOTES

1. C. Astiz, *Pressure Groups and Power Elites in Peruvian Politics* (Ithaca: Cornell University Press, 1969), p. 131.

2. Ibid.

3. Sir Robert Marett, *Peru* (New York: Praeger, 1969), p. 121.

4. Peter F. Klarén, "The Origins of Modern Peru, 1880–1930," in Leslie Bethell, ed., *The Cambridge History of Latin America,* vol. 5: *c1870 to 1930* (Cambridge: Cambridge University Press, 1986), p. 600.

5. Frederick B. Pike, *The Modern History of Peru* (New York: Praeger, 1967), p. 145.

6. David P. Werlich, *Peru: A Short History* (Carbondale: Southern Illinois University Press, 1978), p. 119.

7. Ibid.

8. Cáceres was the most popular Peruvian war hero to survive the struggle with Chile. Jorge Basadre, Peru's internationally renowned historian of the republican era, praised the general for his military exploits during the War of the Pacific, elevating him to the company of the nation's greatest martyrs, Grau and Bolognesi. Unfortunately for Cáceres' reputation, however, "when Chilean bullets spared his life, he turned automatically into a great national *caudillo.* The nation thought that just as he had led his troops through rough terrain, chasms and cliffs, he could lead it through the prosaic but no less painful path of reconstruction." Basadre, *Historia de la República del Perú,* vol. 6, 5th ed. (Lima: Editorial PeruAmérica, S.A., 1964), p 2736. Cáceres did not live up to these expectations. As Basadre concluded, "even heros cannot craft the reins of government from the bloody wings of liberty. No solid building can be built with bayonets" ("*Con las alas sangrientas de la libertad ni los héroes pueden fabricar riendas. Ningún edificio sólido se construye sobre bayonetas*"). Ibid., 2640.

9. Daniel M. Masterson, *Militarism and Politics in Latin America. Peru from Sánchez Cerro to Sendero Luminoso* (Westport, Conn.: Greenwood Press, 1991), p. 25.

10. Klarén, "Origins of Modern Peru," pp. 600–601.

11. Masterson, *Militarism and Politics,* p. 24.

12. Klarén, "Origins of Modern Peru," p. 601.

13. Ibid., p. 26.

14. Frederick M. Nunn, "Professional Militarism in Twentieth-Century Peru: Historical and Theoretical Background to the Golpe de Estado of 1968," *Hispanic American Historical Review* 59 (August 1979): 406.

15. Ibid., p. 392.

16. Klarén, "Origins of Modern Peru," p. 601. Discrimination against Indian conscripts in the Peruvian army continues to the present day despite the heralded reforms of 1898. Peruvian indigenous conscripts still constitute the overwhelming majority of the rank and file. From time to time, the Peruvian government has made token efforts to make military service more egalitarian, but usually to no avail. One such effort, for instance, occurred under President Augusto Leguía when on 15 June 1920, the government made military instruction compulsory for university students by refusing to allow the University of San Marcos to confer professional degrees on graduates who had not successfully completed their required military courses. These measures were later extended to engineering, agriculture, and normal schools. See Juan Mendoza R., "El ejécito," in José Pareja Paz Soldán, ed., *Visión del Perú en el siglo XX,* vol. 1 (Lima: Ediciones Librería Studium, S.A., 1962), pp. 293–349, for further details.

17. Ibid.

18. Basadre, *Historia,* vol. 10, 4740.

19. Ibid.

20. Klarén, "Origins of Modern Peru," p. 601.

21. Masterson, *Militarism and Politics,* p. 29.

22. Víctor Villanueva, *Ejército peruano: del caudillaje anárquico al militarismo reformista* (Lima: Librería-Editorial Juan Mejía Baca, 1973), p. 156.

23. Ibid., p. 151.

24. Klarén, "Origins of Modern Peru," pp. 626–27.

25. Villanueva, *Ejército peruano,* p. 150.

26. Masterson, *Militarism and Politics,* p. 30.

27. Ibid., p. 29.

28. Villanueva, *Ejército peruano,* p. 135.

29. Ibid., p. 141.

30. Masterson, *Militarism and Politics,* p. 30.

31. Villanueva, *Ejército peruano,* p. 171.

32. Ibid., p. 265.

33. Ibid., p. 212.

34. Klarén, "Origins of Modern Peru," p. 640.

35. Ibid. The "aristocratic republic" was the name given to the civilian period of government ushered in by Nicolás de Piérola in 1895 that continued until Colonel Benavides's *golpe* in 1914. It was characterized by oligarchical rule and total submission of the military to the whims/interests of the Peruvian "aristocracy."

36. Masterson, *Militarism and Politics,* p. 52.

37. Quoted in ibid. Indeed, all subsequent successful military coups—those of 1948,

1962, and 1968—"were all justified under this provision of the 1933 constitution." Ibid., p. 266.

38. Werlich, *Peru,* p. 201.

39. Ibid.

40. Marrett, *Peru,* p. 166.

41. Villanueva, *Ejército peruano,* p. 253.

42. Ibid.

43. Geoffrey Bertram, "Peru, 1930–60," in Leslie Betnell, ed., *The Cambridge History of Latin America,* vol. 8: *Latin America since 1930: Spanish South America* (Cambridge: Cambridge University Press, 1991), p. 439.

44. Ibid.

45. Masterson, *Militarism and Politics,* p. 150.

46. Bertram, "Peru, 1930–60," pp. 407–8.

47. George D. E. Philip, *The Rise and Fall of the Peruvian Military Radicals, 1968–1976,* Monograph No. 9, (London: Athlone Press, Institute of Latin American Studies, University of London, 1978), p. 22.

48. Nunn, "Professional Militarism," p. 405.

49. Ibid.

50. The original name given to the army's new center for advanced studies opened on 14 July 1950, was Centro de Altos Estudios del Ejército (CAEE). It was changed to Centro de Altos Estudios Militares (CAEM) two years later, under General Marín's insistence, as the center's first director envisioned training not only army officers but air force, navy, and police officers as well. Ironically, Odría, who favored the creation of a Peruvian school of military strategy, regarded it as "an opportunity to remove certain officers whom he suspected of Aprista sympathies, but could not dismiss openly." Philip, *Peruvian Military Radicals,* p. 41. For a detailed and provocative analysis of CAEM and its impact on the Peruvian military, see Víctor Villanueva, *El CAEM y la revolución de la fuerza armada* (Lima: Instituto de Estudios Peruanos and Campodónico Ediciones, S.A., 1972).

51. Bertram, "Peru, 1930–60," p. 431.

52. Luigi R. Einaudi and Alfred C. Stepan, *Latin American Institutional Development: Changing Military Perspectives in Peru and Brazil* (Santa Monica, Calif.: Rand Corporation, 1971), p. 21.

53. Julio Cotler, "Peru since 1960," in Leslie Bethell, ed., *The Cambridge History of Latin America,* vol. 8: *Latin America since 1930. Spanish South America* (Cambridge: Cambridge University Press, 1991), p. 457.

54. Ibid.

55. Raymond Estep, *The Role of the Military in Peruvian Politics* (Maxwell Air Force Base, Alabama: Documentary Research Division, Aerospace Studies Institute, Air University Documentary Research Study, 1970), p. 34.

56. Villanueva, El CAEM, p. 17.

57. Philip, *Peruvian Military Radicals,* p. 41.

58. Estep, *Role of the Military,* p. 42.

59. Ibid.

60. Nunn, "Professional Militarism," p. 415.

61. Estep, *Role of the Military,* p. 42.

62. Philip, *Peruvian Military Radicals,* p. 44.

63. Masterson, *Militarism and Politics,* p. 177.

64. Cotler, "Peru since 1960," p. 456.

65. Ibid. Masterson's analysis goes one step further when he remarks that "while not a dominant aspect of the armed forces' professional perspective before 1963, economic nationalism emerged as a key element in the military's ideological between 1963 and 1968" (p. 189). Masterson also points out that although the military junta's creation of a National Institute of Planning "reflected the military government's recognition of the need for long-term economic policy . . . just as with the Velasco government after 1968, CAEM's influence was more ideological than administrative" (p. 185).

66. Masterson, "Militarism and Politics," p. 187.

67. Ibid., pp. 187–88.

68. Philip, *Peruvian Military Radicals,* p. 44.

69. Julio Cotler, "Military Interventions and 'Transfer of Power to Civilians' in Peru," in Guillerno O'Donnell, Philippe C. Schmitter, and Laurence Whitehead, eds., *Transitions from Authoritarian Rule: Latin America* (Baltimore: Johns Hopkins University Press, 1986), p. 148.

70. Ibid., pp. 149–50.

71. Cynthia McClintock and Abraham F. Lowenthal, eds., *The Peruvian Experiment Reconsidered* (Princeton: Princeton University Press, 1983), p. xi. The "Manifesto of the Revolutionary Government of Peru" (dated 3 October 1968) outlined the underlying causes prompting the military to take power. The second paragraph of the "Manifesto" clearly indicated the bold step that the armed forces were taking to secure what they called "the beginning of the definitive emancipation of our fatherland." This passage reads as follows: "Powerful economic forces, both national and foreign, in complicity with contemptible Peruvians motivated by [the desire for] unbridled speculation and profit, have monopolized the economic and political power of the nation. These forces have frustrated the people's desire for basic structural reforms by maintaining the existing unjust social and economic order which allows a privileged few to monopolize the national riches, thereby forcing the great majority to suffer economic deprivation inimical to human dignity." Quoted in Brian Loveman and Thomas M. Davies, Jr., eds., *The Politics of Antipolitics: The Military in Latin America* (Lincoln: University of Nebraska Press, 1989), p. 250.

72. Einaudi and Stepan, *Institutional Development,* p. 125.

73. Philip, *Peruvian Military Radicals,* p. 28.

74. Stephen M. Gorman, "Antipolitics in Peru, 1968–80," in Loveman and Davies, *Politics of Antipolitics,* p. 457.

75. Ibid. Norman Gall, an informed U.S. journalist who has written extensively on Latin America, concluded in an article on the 1968 Peruvian military coup that "the transformation of the Peruvian military from a provincial constabulary to an insurgent force challenging U.S. policy in Latin America probably would have been impossible without an increasingly intimate dialogue with leftist intellectuals, such as took place at the CAEM between high army officers and the leaders of the mini-parties of Peru's 'little left' who today (1971) serve as advisers to the 'Revolutionary Government.' " "Letter from Peru," *Commentary* (June 1964).

76. Philip, *Peruvian Military Radicals,* p. 88; and Gorman, "Antipolitics in Peru," p. 456.

77. Cotler, "Peru since 1960," p. 469. The expenditures on the armed forces have continued to grow during the 1980s, but at a slower rate. Nevertheless, the annual military

expenditures for 1990 amounted to $642 million, an increase of 160% over 1980. See John Keegan, *World Armies* (New York: Facts on File, 1991), for further details.

78. Gorman, "Antipolitics in Peru," p. 456.

79. Masterson, "Militarism and Politics," p. 267. The point referring to the emergence of the Peruvian middle class cannot be overstressed, as it is crucial to the survival of Peru in the long run. Lowenthal underscores this when he states that "the military regime will more likely be remembered in a generation for having expanded Lima's middle class and legitimated its concerns than for profoundly reshaping national ideals." Lowenthal, *The Peruvian Experiment Reconsidered,* p. 418.

80. Lowenthal, pp. 422–23.

81. James D. Rudoph, *Peru: The Evolution of a Crisis* (Westport, Conn.: Praeger, 1992), p. 70.

82. Ibid., p. 13.

83. Ibid.

84. John Crabtree, *Peru under García: An Opportunity Lost* (Pittsburgh: University of Pittsburgh Press, 1992), p. 96.

85. Philip Mauceri, *Militares: Insurgencia y Democratización en el Perú, 1980–1988* (Lima: Instituto de Estudios Peruanos, 1989), p. 13.

86. Ibid., p. 14.

87. Villanueva, "Peru's 'New' Military Professionalism: The Failure of the Technocratic Approach," in Stephen M. Gorman, ed., *Post-Revolutionary Peru: The Politics of Transformation* (Boulder, Colo.: Westview Press, 1982), p. 176.

88. Ibid., pp. 177–78. According to Villanueva, the armed forces relinquished the exercise of formal power only when it returned to its barracks in 1980. "The surrender of the Presidential Palace would have to be purely formal, and nothing more. The army would have to remain present in the councils of political decision-making as counselors, advisors or whatever they wanted to call themselves, but with the ability to oversee laws and programs which touched however remotely on national defense. Furthermore, the armed forces wanted to secure explicit and exclusive authority over all strictly military questions." Ibid., p. 174.

89. Quoted in Mauceri, *Militares,* p. 12.

90. Ibid.

91. Ibid.

92. Ibid.

93. Crabtree, *Peru under García,* p. 111.

94. Ibid., p. 112.

95. Ibid.

96. Ibid.

97. Mauceri, *Militares: Insurgencia y Democratización en el Perú, 1980–1988,* p. 65. A final instance of attempt by civilians to gain the upper hand over the military that has proven successful to a limited extent is the practice of having the Senate ratify promotions to the rank of general or vice-admiral in the three services; ambassadorial appointments are subject to the same ratification procedure. The practical result of this change is that "every December army, navy and air force officers parade through the Senate" lobbying for their promotions. Dirk Kruijt, *Perú: Entre sendero y militares. Seguridad y relaciones cívico-militares. 1950–1990* (Lima: Editor Alfonso Aguilar, 1991), p. 100.

98. *Caretas,* 9 July 1990 (interview with General Adrián Huamán Centeno).

99. Masterson, "Militarism and Politics," p. 279.
100. *QueHacer* 20 (January 1983): 52.
101. Masterson, "Militarism and Politics," p. 283.
102. Crabtree, *Peru under García,* p. 104.
103. Rudolph, *Peru: Evolution,* p. 114.
104. Masterson, "Militarism and Politics," p. 280.
105. Quoted in ibid., p. 283.
106. Kruijt, *Perú,* p. 11.
107. Frederick M. Nunn, *The Time of the Generals: Latin American Professional Militarism in World Perspective* (Lincoln: University of Nebraska Press, 1992), p. 199.
108. Masterson, "Militarism and Politics," p. 288.
109. Ibid.
110. Einaudi and Stepan, *Institutional Development,* p. 59.

REFERENCES

Cotler, Julio. "Military Interventions and 'Transfer of Power to Civilians' in Peru." In Guillerno O'Donnell, Philippe C. Schmitter, and Laurence Whitehead, eds., *Transitions from Authoritarian Rule: Latin America,* 148–72. Baltimore: Johns Hopkins University Press, 1986.

Einaudi, Luigi R., and Alfred C. Stepan. *Latin American Institutional Development: Changing Military Perspectives in Peru and Brazil.* Santa Monica, Calif.: Rand Corporation, 1971.

Fernández Salvatteci, José. *Terrorismo y guerra sucia en el Perú.* Lima: Ediciones Fernández Salvatteci, 1986.

Gorman, Stephen M. "Antipolitics in Peru, 1968–80." In Brian Loveman and Thomas M. Davies, Jr., eds., *The Politics of Antipolitics. The Military in Latin America,* 2d ed., 456–79. Lincoln: University of Nebraska Press, 1989.

Kruijt, Dirk. *Perú entre sendero y militares. Seguridad y relaciones cívico-militares, 1950–1990.* Lima: Editorial Alfonso Aguilar, 1991.

Masterson, Daniel M. *Militarism and Politics in Latin America: Peru from Sánchez Cerro to Sendero Luminoso.* Westport, Conn.: Greenwood Press, 1991.

Nunn, Frederick M. "Professional Militarism in Twentieth-Century Peru: Historical and Theoretical Background to the Golpe de Estado of 1968." *Hispanic American Historical Review* 59, no. 3 (August 1979): 391–417.

Philip, George D. C. *The Rise and Fall of the Peruvian Military Radicals, 1968–1976.* London: Athlone Press, Institute of Latin American Studies, University of London, 1978.

Rodríguez Beruff, Jorge. *Los militares y el poder. Un ensayo sobre la doctrina militar en el Perú, 1948–1968.* Lima: Mosca Azul Editores, 1983.

Villanueva, Víctor. *Ejército peruano: Del caudillaje monárquico al militarismo reformista.* Lima: Librería-Editorial Juan Mejía Baca, 1973.

———. *EL CAEM y la revolución de la Fuerza Armada.* Lima: Instituto de Estudios Peruanos, 1972.

———. "Peru's 'New' Military Professionalism: The Failure of the Technocratic Approach." In Stephen M. Gorman, ed., *Post-Revolutionary Peru: The Politics of Transformation,* 157–78. Boulder, Colo.: Westview Press, 1982.

POLAND

Jerzy J. Wiatr

The collapse of the communist regimes in central Europe and the emergence of new democracies forced the question of relations between the armed forces and the new political institutions in these new countries under a new light. Not only had the armed forces been freed from the tutelage of the communist parties, but they also lost their major adversary of the last decades: the capitalist West. The Cold War is over, and the West is no longer perceived as the enemy. In fact, several of the former communist states have made political gestures indicating their interest in establishing security links with the West, including some form of association with NATO. Domestically, the armed forces have undergone restructuring, downsizing, institutional catharsis, and budgetary belt-tightening. Their loyalty to the new democratic regimes is sometimes questioned, particularly as far as the top ranks are concerned. All these factors combine to create a degree of uncertainty about the future of civil-military relations in the postcommunist world.

From previous experiences we know that the success of new democratic governments to curb the political power of the military is a key condition toward the successful consolidation of democracy.[1] "The problems of force and violence in long-established democracies are difficult," writes Alfred Stepan, "but they are even more challenging in 'newly democratizing' ones."[2] Such difficulties appeared in countries where new democratic regimes succeeded military dictatorships or militarily supported authoritarian regimes. In a different context and under different conditions, postcommunist countries experience difficulties confining the military to security-related and not societal conflict–related responsibilities. This chapter will seek to identify and analyze these difficulties by concentrating on Poland.

While sharing some characteristics common to many, if not all communist states, Poland is unique in a number of ways. Of all communist states, Poland had the strongest democratic opposition (supported by the powerful Roman

Catholic Church) and one of the most outspoken reformist currents within the ruling communist party. In the 1980s, the military became the main pillar of state power, reducing the party to a subordinate position. In 1989, largely under the growing pressure from a dissatisfied public but also because of the reformist policy adopted by the military command, Poland became the first communist country to witness negotiations between the Communist regime and an opposition. These negotiations led to the first contested election in the communist bloc since the 1940s and to the formation of the first opposition-dominated cabinet. Being the pioneer of democratic change in Eastern Europe, Poland experiences strong pains of transition both in the economy and in the political spheres. It would be instructive to examine the changing nature of civil-military relations in Poland during the transition to and the consolidation of democracy.

HISTORICAL BACKGROUND

Since her independence in 1918, Poland experienced conflicts between the civilian democratic institutions and the military, as well as among competing factions within the higher ranks of the armed forces.[3] In May 1926, a coup d'etat led by Marshal Joseph Pilsudski established a moderately authoritarian regime. The regime was backed by the armed forces and was legitimized by the charismatic personality of its leader. After Pilsudski's death in May 1935, tensions between military and civilian wings of the regime surfaced, led by Marshal Edward Smigly-Rydz and President Ignacy Moscicki respectively. A period of weak parliamentary democracy was followed by thirteen years of military domination. These bequeathed a legacy of authoritarianism in Polish political culture, exemplified by the tendency to seek solutions through strong leadership rather than in laws and institutions.

The Nazi invasion, soon followed by a Soviet attack, led to the partition of Poland between Germany and the USSR. The Polish government-in-exile (first in France, and after June 1940 in Britain) and its military forces stationed abroad, along with the domestic resistance movement in the occupied country, as in previous difficult moments, organized an impressive anti-occupation campaign. A military man, General Wladyslaw Sikorski, was put in charge of Polish war efforts, serving simultaneously as prime minister and as commander-in-chief of the armed forces. Poland's contribution to the defeat of Germany, although well recognized, did not translate to political or territorial gains. Because of Soviet military victories and the acceptance of Soviet demands by the United States and the United Kingdom, Poland had to surrender its eastern provinces to the USSR. In return, Warsaw was given some territories in the North and the West that had belonged to Germany. Politically, Poland became part of the Soviet-dominated sphere in Eastern Europe. In 1944, a communist-led government was established in the eastern part of the country. In 1945, following the Yalta conference, the government was somehow expanded to include a number of noncommunist leaders and was recognized as Poland's legitimate government. The Polish armed forces in the western part of the country were demobilized, and the government-in-exile lost diplomatic recognition and disappeared.

During the communist regime, the nation's armed forces underwent deep transformations. In the early years of the regime (1944–48), attempts were made to build the armed forces using as a basis the communist-dominated Polish regiment that had been formed in the USSR and that took part in the war under Soviet command; some elements of the prewar army, underground military organizations, and those military men who had switched their loyalty from the government-in-exile to the new regime were also incorporated into the new army. This policy was abandoned in 1949 and was replaced by an aggressive effort at the Sovietization of the Polish armed forces. The nation's armed forces earned the dubious distinction of being the only army among Soviet bloc states to be led by a Soviet marshal (Polish-born Konstantin Rokossowski), who was installed as minister of defense; a large number of Soviet generals were given command positions in the Polish armed forces.

In 1956, Poland, along with Hungary, underwent the most extensive de-Stalinization process in the entire Soviet bloc. Polish military officers sided with the reformist wing of the party and helped to force the Soviet leaders to abandon their original plans to intervene militarily. Re-Polanization of the armed forces followed; Soviet commanders were replaced with younger Polish officers. In the following decades the military tended to take part in the factional conflict within the ruling party, particularly during the wave of authoritarian (and antisemitic) purges of 1967–68. Eventually, the military, under the new minister of defense, General Wojciech Jaruzelski, obtained a degree of institutional autonomy and what can be described as a veto power over key political decisions.[4]

When mounting economic problems and growing labor unrest brought the communist system to a near collapse in 1980–81, the party turned once more to the military. General Jaruzelski became Poland's prime minister in February 1981 and first secretary of the Polish United Workers Party in October of the same year. With the failure of his effort to find a compromise with the Solidarity Union, and under persistent Soviet pressure, the general and the military high command formed the Military Council of National Salvation (12 December 1981) and declared martial law (13 December 1981). For the first time in the history of European communist regimes, power was now in the hands of the military.

Martial law in Poland was a controversial subject when it was in force and remained so long after it had been lifted. Some saw it as merely an effort to suppress freedom and to impose military rule in order to save the communist regime.[5] Others stress that Poland was under direct danger of Soviet intervention and that declaration of martial law averted such an outcome.[6] Public opinion polls conducted (in the immediate aftermath of the declaration of martial law and ten years later) showed that the public accepted it as justified under the circumstances.[7] Political support for the armed forces and their prestige in the eyes of the public remained high, both during martial law and years after it had been lifted. The fact that martial law in Poland was relatively benign and the liberalization that followed its lifting contributed to the tendency on a large part of Poles to accept, rather than to condemn, this part of their history. On the other hand, the militants of the former opposition overwhelmingly condemned martial law and its originators, as reflected in the decision of the Polish Parliament on 1 February 1992, when martial law was declared retrospectively both illegal and unjustified.[8] The parliamentary decision, however, has not ended the controversy regarding this matter, which is likely to go on for generations.

THE MILITARY AND DEMOCRATIC TRANSFORMATION

Concluding an earlier analysis of the political role of the military in Poland, this author wrote in 1988 that "Future developments will . . . have decisive influence on the nation's eventual perceptions of this political role of its military. Much time will be needed before a definitive answer to this question can be formulated."[9] A year later, the political change in Poland provided the military with a challenge and an opportunity. Having emerged as the most important pillar of state power, the military had the decisive say in the decisions that opened the way to a negotiated regime change in Poland.

In 1986, three years after the lifting of martial law and one year after the arrival of Mikhail Gorbachev on the Soviet political scene, Poland began a prudent process of political liberalization. General amnesty for political offenders allowed the leaders of the still "illegal" Solidarity to resume public activities. The "Consultative Council" created by the chairman of the State Council, General Jaruzelski, consisted of prominent personalities from the opposition, but without the leaders of "Solidarity." Public dialogue became less restricted and reflected the willingness of moderate elements from both sides to find an acceptable compromise.[10] Economic reforms, however, failed to change the centralized character of the economic system and to end the protracted crisis facing the Polish economy. Politically, the regime was increasingly unpopular, as seen from the unsatisfactory results of the referendum on economic and political reforms (29 November 1987) and of the local elections (19 June 1988). Low turnout (67.8% in 1987 and 55.2% in 1988) was connected to public dissatisfaction with the political stagnation of the post–martial law years as well as responsiveness to the call for a boycott made by Solidarity. In the spring and summer of 1988, labor unrest and strikes in many state enterprises provided new proofs that the situation was becoming untenable.

On the other hand, there were new opportunities. Gorbachev's visit to Poland in the summer of 1988 provided the Soviet leader with an opportunity to denounce the "Brezhnev doctrine" of limited sovereignty of Warsaw Pact countries. The danger of Soviet intervention, which had played a decisive role in political calculations in 1981, was no longer hanging over Poland.

In the second half of 1988 tentative steps were taken by the government to explore the possibility of a compromise with the Solidarity leader Lech Walesa.

The talks (mostly kept in secret) were conducted by the minister of internal affairs, General Czeslaw Kiszczak, a professional soldier put in charge of the security apparatus in 1981, who was one of General Jaruzelski's closest collaborators. By the end of the year, the prospectus of a compromise became clear. The relegalization of Solidarity became the key conditions without which no compromise was feasible.

The issue was referred to the plenary session of the Central Committee of the ruling party, held on 17 January 1989. Confronted with the strong opposition to relegalize Solidarity, Jaruzelski, along with the minister of defense, General Siwicki, the minister of internal affairs, General Kiszczak, and Prime Minister Mieczyslaw Rakowski, offered their resignation. It was only under such pressure that the majority of the Central Committee accepted the policy of a negotiated compromise with Solidarity, and thus opened the door to the Round Table talks, which started the following month.[11]

Why was the army high command so strongly committed to democratization in 1989 when only seven years earlier it had crushed the opposition? Part of the answer, perhaps even the crucial part, lies in the changed geopolitical situation, due to the new political thinking emanating from Moscow. What was unthinkable in 1981 became possible in 1988. Other factors played a role as well. Martial law failed to eliminate the opposition, and with the passing of time it became increasingly clear that without some kind of a compromise the political crisis would not end. The economic situation remained very bad, and prospects of improvements failed to materialize. Finally, after several years of governing, the leading generals learned the limits of power and lost a lot of their original simple-minded optimism.

Had they put their own political survival over the interest of the state, they could have prolonged the status quo for a period of time. But they realized that only through democratization could Poland make a serious attempt to solve her problems. In this, the generals were not the initiators, not even within the ruling establishment. One of the peculiarities of the Polish United Workers Party was the perseverance of a reformist faction that, before and after 1981, called for a modus vivendi with ''Solidarity'' and for some kind of power-sharing. But the reformers had no chance until their views were accepted by the military. It was the military command, particularly General Jaruzelski himself, who forced the ruling party on the road to compromise. In this way, the armed forces became the gravediggers of the communist regime, even though at the time the ultimate consequences of this process were not clear to the main actors, including the military itself.

The Round Table talks ended in April 1989 and opened the door to the reemergence of Solidarity as the main legal opposition force. The talks also led to the partly free elections of June 1989,[12] which were won overwhelmingly by Solidarity. The magnitude of the victory surprised even the leaders of Solidarity. The Communist party was deeply demoralized and internally divided. General Jaruzelski was elected president of Poland by the two chambers of Parliament, but only by a one-vote majority and the indirect support offered him by some parliamentarians of the opposition. In August 1989 Solidarity's Tadeusz Mazowiecki became prime minister—an event that was a turning point in the process of doing away with the monopoly of power exercised by communist parties in Eastern Europe.

If there was a time for the military to step in and to turn back the process of democratization, that time was the summer of 1989, following the Communist electoral defeat and the collapse of the coalition between the Polish United Workers Party and its junior partners, the Peasant and the Democratic parties. The latter decided to enter into a new, Solidarity-dominated coalition. There were fears of military intervention, both in Poland and abroad, but nothing happened. The military remained loyal to the civilian institutions, even if the nature of the institutions changed dramatically.

Military support for democratization at this point in time can be explained by several factors working simultaneously. First, the armed forces were much less committed to the party than was officially proclaimed and generally believed. Although the majority of officers were party members, many had joined only because there was no alternative to advance their careers. Most of them considered themselves guardians of the national interest rather than party zealots. Second, the experience of martial law taught the military that seizing power is easier than governing successfully. Officers knew that if they had taken power again, their difficulties would have been even greater. They had no desire to crush the opposition by bloody repression of the type that occurred in Chile following the 1973 coup. Third, the initial steps of democratization looked quite moderate. Two key ministries (defense and internal affairs) remained in the hands of incumbents, and General Jaruzelski as president was still the supreme commander of the armed forces. From the point of view of the military the deal looked good. Finally, the armed forces had come of age under the leadership of Wojciech Jaruzelski, at least since he had become minister of defense in 1968. They were loyal to him, and Jaruzelski stood behind the process of democratization. Without him, or against his wishes, military intervention in politics would have been unthinkable.

Retrospectively, one can say that the way in which Polish armed forces promoted and accepted democratization was nothing special, given the fact that their counterparts in other communist states acted in a similar way. One must, however, take into account two things: First, in Poland the military not only accepted the change of regime (as did their colleagues in Czechoslovakia, Bulgaria, Hungary, the German Democratic Republic, and Albania), but actively promoted it against the opposition of hard-line elements within the ruling party. Second, Poland was the first communist state to set the transition in motion, with no earlier example to follow. For these reasons the role of the Polish military deserves both credit and scholarly interest.

THE DILEMMAS OF CIVIL-MILITARY RELATIONS, 1990–92

Under the new, democratic regime, relations between the military and the civilian authorities underwent thorough profound change. The guiding objective was an unpolitical armed force subordinated to the civilian authorities. Political parties would no longer be allowed to operate within the armed forces, and professional soldiers would no longer be permitted to belong to political parties. In December 1989, the main political administration of the armed forces was abolished. Its replacement, the Educational Department of the Ministry of Defense, is ostensibly nonpolitical and does not have the prerogatives accorded its predecessor.

In April 1990 two civilians, Janusz Onyszkiewicz and Bronislaw Komorowski, both of whom had been previously active in the democratic opposition, were appointed deputy ministers of defense. Their appointments began a process of transformation that led, for the first time in Poland's history, to the emergence of civilian leadership in the ministry of defense. In July 1990, the minister of defense, General Florian Siwicki, was retired. His successor, Admiral Piotr Kolodziejczyk, belonged to the younger and less politically involved generation of professional soldiers (although the admiral had been a member of the Polish United Workers Party and at the time of his appointment served in Parliament). Retirement of senior officers, ostensibly on grounds of age, resulted in the gradual disappearance of commanders directly involved with the politics of the martial law period.

In December 1990, the newly elected president, Lech Walesa, became the supreme commander of the armed forces, replacing in this capacity General Wojciech Jaruzelski. For the military this particular change meant that it was now under the control of a political leader who not only came from outside the armed forces, but only a few years earlier had symbolized the very movement that the army sought to eliminate by imposing martial law. It is important to note that the military accepted this change without the slightest degree of opposition. The new president strongly emphasized his commitment to the policy of nondiscrimination in the armed forces and ruled out politically motivated purges.

During the first year of Walesa's presidency, command of the armed forces remained in the hands of the minister of defense, Admiral Kolodziejczyk. The admiral's reappointment to some post in the new cabinet of Prime Minister Jan Krzysztof Bielecki was credited to the strong support offered him by the president. Under existing law, it was the minister of national defense who commanded the armed forces. There was talk about changing the law and replacing the minister with a civilian politician, but no action was taken at this stage. However, the president took a more active role in military matters, acting through the Bureau of National Security and the Council of National Security, both of which are under his chairmanship.

Matters took a different direction after the parliamentary elections of October 1991. In the highly fragmented parliament, where no party had more than 12.5 percent of seats and only two polled more than 10% of the popular vote, Walesa was unable to build a coalition favorable to him. Eventually he had to accept as head of the cabinet a right-wing lawyer, Jan Olszewski. Prime Minister Olszewski appointed a civilian, Jan Parys, to the defense post. The new minister promptly retired Admiral Kolodziejczyk from active service, without even informing the president in advance of his decision. This was the first sign of the growing conflict between the president and the cabinet over control of the military. Kolodziejczyk was appointed an advisor to the president on military matters, a move clearly indicating the president's displeasure over the way the admiral had been dismissed from active service.

Soon, new areas of conflict emerged. One concerned itself with political purges. Olszewski and, even more so, Minister Parys, while claiming their intention not to engage in purges, in reality began the process of early retirement of senior officers with communist backgrounds and, particularly, those with diplomas from Soviet military colleges. Although these personnel changes were popular among some sectors of the officer corps (for both political and career reasons) and were even promoted by a semi-illegal officer association (Viritim),[13] nevertheless they generated fear and resentment among the great majority of professional soldiers. Moreover, influential circles within the armed forces and civilian politicians alike argued that decommunization of the military command would paralyze the armed forces and would deprive the officer corps of the most qualified specialists.[14] President Walesa supported the moderates, but this did not dissuade the minister of defense from proceeding with the purges.

The other controversial issue concerned the line of command and the prerogatives of Jan Parys, Poland's first-ever civilian defense minister. He inherited the post that in the past had been filled with ministers recruited from among top military officers considered fit to command the armed forces in war. For the first time a sociologist by training with no military background was put at the defense helm. Parys had to command the forces with the help of military specialists. Thus, the chief of general staff became the de facto military commander. It was planned also to give the chief of staff the title of general inspector of the armed forces, as in the prewar Polish Republic, but no action was taken on the issue.

After having lost on the issue of Admiral Kolodziejczyk's role in the armed forces, President Walesa made attempts to place a loyal general, the commander of the Silesia Military district Tadeusz Wilecki, in the now key position of chief of the general staff. When talks took place between senior officials from the presidential office and General Wilecki, Defense Minister Parys denounced them in public, accusing unnamed politicians of conspiring with some generals behind his back. A parliamentary inquiry followed, resulting in a ruling unfavorable for the minister, who was eventually dismissed. Parys's defeat in his quarrel with Walesa predated by just a few weeks the collapse of Olszewski's government.

It fell on 5 June 1992, following a heated controversy with the president and with the majority of Parliament over the politically motivated "lustration" policy aimed at uncovering and purging alleged collaborators in the security police during the communist era. Later, under the new minister of defense, Janusz Onyszkiewicz, General Wilecki was appointed chief of the general staff. Other changes in the nation's military command brought into key positions generals and senior officers loyal to Walesa.

The third issue dealt with defense strategy. Minister Parys favored closer links with NATO and talked publicly about the necessity of Poland's entry into the structure of the Western alliance. He also made it clear that the only potential enemy facing Poland would be the potential reemergence of Soviet power. But President Walesa announced the guidelines of a military doctrine based on the assumption that Poland had no single adversary at this stage and that all of the nation's frontiers should be protected. He also vaguely talked about the need to form a new political and military alliance of Central and Eastern European states, called "NATO-bis." The conflict over security doctrine eventually led Jan Parys to charge several months after his dismissal that Walesa was endangering Poland's national security by steering the country away from the West and closer to cooperation with Russia.[15] By early 1993, this aspect of the controversy had become the most heated element in the rivalry over control of the armed forces among the various political camps.

However, the conflict between President Walesa and Minister Parys did not involve military commanders directly. One can assume that most officers silently sided with the president, who enjoys prestige and popularity among professional soldiers. But in an indirect way, the conflict emphasized the importance of civil-military relations in a new democracy and the need to set them on a strong legal basis.[16]

This was partly done by the new constitutional arrangements that went into effect on 17 October 1992. The "Small Constitution" replaced the 1952 Constitution for the period of time necessary to have a new constitution written and adopted by Parliament. Under the new arrangements, the president of the republic exercises general leadership in the state's external and internal security, assisted by the Council of National Security (article 34). The president is also commander-in-chief of the armed forces, is authorized to appoint and dismiss (in agreement with the minister of national defense) the chief of the general staff, and on the defense minister's recommendation to make other key personnel appointments to the armed forces (article 35). In case of war, the president can appoint and dismiss the chief of the general staff without having consulted the Cabinet or the minister of defense (article 35). The prime minister selects the ministers of foreign affairs, national defense, and internal affairs "after having obtained the opinion of the President" (article 61). Although presidential involvement falls short of an outright veto, it clearly indicates that these three key ministries should be placed in the hands of people acceptable to the president of the republic.

The constitutional changes of 1992 go in the direction postulated by those (including this author)[17] who have argued for a clearer delineation of authority regarding control of the armed forces between the president, the cabinet, and the chief of the general staff. Resulting from compromises within Parliament, the present setup fails to keep the military command structure sufficiently divorced from day-by-day political rivalries. But by increasing the power of the president, the new constitutional arrangement is likely to base democratic control over the armed forces on more stable grounds. The next few years will probably allow the Polish society to make a better judgment concerning the most suitable legal arrangements in the area of civil-military relations and to determine the efficacy of the nation's new constitutional framework.

Developments that took place in 1994 underline the necessity of a more precise definition of constitutional prerogatives in civil-military relations. Following the parliamentary election of September 1993 (won by the parties of the Left) and the formation of the Center-Left Cabinet of Waldemar Pawlak, President Walesa made an attempt to limit the role of Parliament and the cabinet in controlling the armed forces. In November 1994, after a prolonged controversy in which he had been supported by the majority of top military commanders, the president was able to force the removal of the defense minister, retired admiral Piotr Kolodziejczyk. The decision has been strongly criticized by most of the parliamentary parties, and demands have been made for strengthening the parliamentary mechanisms of political control over the military.

ARMED FORCES AND SOCIETY

In an earlier work on the Polish military this author documented the high level of prestige and the popularity of the armed forces among the Polish population, both before and immediately after the declaration of martial law in 1981.[18] For a long time, only the Roman Catholic Church enjoyed stronger support among the Poles. The way the military conducted itself in the first years of the democratic regime boosted the military further in popularity relative to other social institutions.

According to longitudinal studies conducted by the Center of Social Opinion Research (CBOS), in the last few years the relative approval or disapproval rate of various institutions changed in Poland as shown in Table 1.[19]

In differently worded surveys, also conducted by the CBOS, the armed forces scored the highest in positive evaluations of the Poles (66% positive rankings), followed by the Catholic Church (59%) and the police (55%). The armed forces are the only institutions whose role makes consistent gains in public opinions.[20]

The military's stronger public standing compared to other institutions can be understood only against the background of the growing frustration of the Poles with the state's democratic institutions and the Catholic Church. The country's bad economic situation and what the Polish public sees as a relentless and unprincipled power struggle among politicians for power and privilege explain

Table 1
Popular Perceptions of Poland's Government and Social Institutions

Institutions	Approval			Disapproval		
	10/91	5/92	9/94	10/91	5/92	9/94
President	46%	36%	25%	43%	52%	64%
Cabinet	39	32	42	48	53	38
Sejm	34	30	39	54	60	45
Senat	36	29	34	49	53	43
Armed Forces	75	68	74	10	12	9
Catholic Church	64	48	45	25	44	45

the wounds of the newly established democratic political institutions. The Catholic Church's drop in popularity is connected to its fundamentalist policies, particularly to force highly repressive anti-abortion legislation on an unwilling public. When the popularity of other institutions goes down, that of the military remains high.

As long as there is no direct clash between the military and the civilian authorities, the present situation should cause no alarm. But the state of public opinion in Poland will likely work against democratic institutions if they get involved in a conflict with the military. Poles do not favor a military regime. Neither do the military officers. However, dangers to the stability of democratic arrangements usually come more from the failures of democracy than from the manifest will of soldiers for political power. It is, therefore, particularly important for Poland, as well as the other young democracies, to find solid and workable arrangements in the area of civil-military relations. If economic transformation fails and the present civil-military arrangement comes under stress, the military may once again be pushed to assume a more prominent political role. To this author's way of thinking, if such a scenario ever materializes, it will be because of the inability of the civilians to solve Poland's problems, rather than because of the military officers' desire for political power.

NOTES

1. Samuel P. Huntington, *The Third Wave: Democratization in the Late Twentieth Century* (Norman: University of Oklahoma Press, 1991), pp. 231–53.

2. Alfred Stepan, *Rethinking Military Politics: Brazil and the Southern Cone* (Princeton: Princeton University Press, 1988), p. x.

3. For analyses of civil-military relations in Poland before World War II, see in particular Andrzej Korbonski, "Civil-Military Relations in Poland between the Wars, 1918–1939," *Armed Forces and Society* 14, no. 2 (1988): 169–89; Joseph Rothschild, *Pilsudski's Coup d'Etat* (New York: Columbia University Press, 1961); Jerzy J. Wiatr,

"The Military Regime in Poland, 1926–1939, in a Comparative Perspective," in Morris Janowitz and Jacques van Doorn, eds., *On Military Intervention* (Rotterdam: Rotterdam University Press, 1971), pp. 61–91; and Jerzy J. Wiatr, *The Soldier and the Nation: The Role of Military in Polish Politics, 1918–1985* (Boulder, Colo.: Westview Press, 1988).

4. Andrzej Korbonski and Sarah M. Terry, "The Military as a Political Actor in Poland" in Roman Kolkowicz and Andrzej Korbonski, eds., *Soldiers, Peasants and Bureaucrats: Civil-Military Relations in Communist and Modernizing Societies* (London: Allen and Unwin, 1982), pp. 159–80.

5. For details see George C. Malcher, *Poland's Politicized Army: Communists in Uniform* (New York: Praeger, 1984).

6. For details see Adam Bromke, *Eastern Europe in the Aftermath of Solidarity* (New York: Columbia University Press, 1985); and Jerry F. Hough, *The Polish Crisis: American Policy Options* (Washington, D.C.: Brookings Institution, 1982).

7. For earlier data on this issue see my *Soldier and the Nation,* pp. 164–66, for earlier data. A survey conducted by the PENTOR Institute (December 1991) showed that 56% of Poles considered the decision to declare martial law justified, 29% considered it unjustified, and 15% chose the "hard to say" option. This data was reported in the weekly *Prawo i Zycie* (14 December 1991).

8. In a statement made on 1 February 1992 in the Polish Parliament on behalf of the Alliance of the Democratic Left, the author rejected this line of thinking.

9. Wiatr, *Soldier and the Nation,* p. 187.

10. For a good sample of the views expressed at that time, in an anthology of papers contributed by Polish political writers and social scientists, see Lawrence S. Graham and Maria K. Ciechocinski, eds., *The Polish Dilemma: Views from Within* (Boulder, Colo.: Westview Press, 1987).

11. Mieczyslaw F. Rakowski gave his account of this session of the Central Committee in his book *Jak to sie stalo* (Warsaw: BGW 1991), pp. 175–76.

12. The election to the lower chamber (Sejm) was based on a negotiated allocation of seats by the main political forces. Solidarity was allowed to contest only 35% of seats (and won all of them). Elections to the Senate were fully free and were based on a majority system. Solidarity won all senatorial seats but one.

13. The activity of "Viritim" received limited coverage in the Polish press. Cf., in particular, Leszek Bedkowski, "Sprzysiezenie," *Spotkania,* 12 June 1991; and Zbigniew Piatkowski, "Viritim nadzieja czy kompromitacja wojska," *Nowa Europa,* 9 June 1992.

14. Cf. interview with Admiral Piotr Kolodziejczyk, "Droga do cywila" (*Wprost,* 12 January 1992); and Jacek Snopkiewicz, "Duch armii" (*Nowa Europa,* 2 June 1992). The question of "lustration" was hotly debated in the parliamentary Committee on National Defense. Cf. stenographic report of the session of 14 October 1992. While the majority of committee members supported the idea of "lustration," several members (including this author) argued that lustration would not only jeopardize the rights of the military as citizens but also weaken the nation's defense.

15. Cf. stenographic reports of the sessions of the Committee National Defense of the Parliament of 9 April 1992 and 22 May 1992. The controversial statement made by Minister Parys was published in the military daily *Polska Zbrojna* on 7 April 1992.

16. Cf. the interview with Jan Parys in Jacek Kurski and Piotr Semka, eds., *Lewy czerwcowy* (Warsaw: Editions Spotkania, 1993), pp. 93–94. The presidential guidelines of defense policy were published in *Polska Zbrojna,* 13–15 November 1992. Earlier discussions were based on confidential versions.

17. Cf. Jerzy J. Wiatr, "Spor nie tylko o wojsko," *Nowa Europa*, 28 May 1992.
18. Wiatr, *Soldier and the Nation*, pp. 131–42 and 186–87.
19. CBOS mimeographed research reports: "Instytucje spoleczne i politycznc—zmiany w spolecznym odbiorze" (June 1992); "Instytucje publiczne" (September 1993).
20. Andrzej Gestern, "Krzywa falujaca," *Rzeczpospolita*, 7–8 November 1992.

Important personalities

Wojciech Jaruzelski, General Minister of National Defense (1968–83), Prime Minister (1981–85), Chairman of State Council (1985–89), President (1989–90).

Czeslaw Kiszczak, General, Minister of Internal Affairs (1981–90) Janusz Onyszkiewicz, Deputy Minister of National Defense (1990–91), Minister of National Defense since July 1992.

Jan Parys, first civilian of Poland, Head of State and Commander-in-Chief (1918–21), leader of the coup d'etat in 1926, the dominant person in the military regime 1926–35 (several times Prime Minister, Minister of War, and General Inspector of the Armed Forces).

Edward Rydz-Smigly, Marshal of Poland, Pilsudski's successor as General Inspector of the Armed Forces (1935–39), Commander-in-Chief during the campaign of 1939.

Wladyslaw Sikorski, General, Prime Minister (1922–23), Minister of War (1924–25), removed from command positions after the 1926 coup, Prime Minister and Commander-in-Chief in the Polish government-in-exile (1939–43).

Florian Siwicki, General, Minister of National Defense (1983–90).

Marian Spychalski, Marshal of Poland, Minister of National Defense (1956–68).

Lech Walesa, Chairman of Solidarity (1980–90), President of Poland (1990–95).

Tadeusz Wilecki, General, Chief of General Staff (since 1992).

REFERENCES

Korbonski, Andrzej. "Civil-Military Relations in Poland between the Wars, 1918–39." *Armed Forces and Society* 14, no. 2 (1988): 169–89.

———. "The Dilemmas of Civil-Military Relations in Contemporary Poland, 1945–1981." *Armed Forces and Society* 8, no. 1 (1981): 3–20.

Sanford, George. *Military Rule in Poland: The Rebuilding of Communist Power in 1981–1983*. London and Sydney: Croom Helms, 1986.

Walicki, Andrzej. "The Paradoxes of Jaruzelski's Poland." *Archive Européne de Sociologie* 26 (1985): 167–90.

Wiatr, Jerzy J. "The Military Regime in Poland, 1926–1939, in a Comparative Perspective." In Morris Janowitz and Jacques van Doorn, eds., *On Military Intervention*, 61–91. Rotterdam: Rotterdam University Press, 1971.

———. *The Soldier and the Nation: The Role of the Military in Polish Politics, 1918–1985*. Boulder and London: Westview Press, 1988.

REPUBLIC OF SOUTH AFRICA

Margaret C. Lee

By the end of the 1970s, the South African Defense Force (SADF) was playing a very significant role in the maintenance of the white supremacist state. In fact, many have argued that during most of the 1980s the military was in effect running the country. When F. W. de Klerk came to power in 1989, he began to recapture the state from the military. While official governmental structures were returned to civilian control, the military continued to play a major role in the South African political arena. Under the leadership of President Nelson Mandela, a concerted effort is being made to remove the military from any involvement in the politics of South Africa.

This chapter will examine the role of the military in South African politics. A historical overview of the South African military is provided in the first section, which is followed by a section on civil-military relations. The third section looks at the regional and domestic wars South Africa was involved in during the 1980s under the leadership of President P. W. Botha, and the fourth section discusses the military's activities under F. W. de Klerk. The final section examines the military in the post-apartheid era.

HISTORICAL OVERVIEW OF THE SOUTH AFRICAN MILITARY

The Union Defense Force (UDF) was created by the Defense Act of 1912. The UDF was renamed the South African Defense Force (SADF) by the Defense Act of 1957. According to the Act, the SADF was to be used to defend the country against both internal and external threats. In addition, military service was to be performed to defend the country in time of war, to prevent or suppress terrorism and internal disorder, and to preserve life, health, or property and maintenance of essential services.[1]

Prior to May 1994, the SADF had four service arms: the army, the navy, the air force, and the medical service. In addition, there existed the Reconnaissance Regiments (also known as the Special Forces) and the Chaplain General's section. There were six staff divisions, which provided auxiliary services such as personnel, intelligence, operations, planning, logistics, and finance. The SADF consisted of a small Permanent Force, along with national servicemen, members of the Citizen Force, and the Commandos.[2] The Citizen Force and Commandos predated the creation of the UDF, with the former consisting of members of the local rifle associations and British regiments and the latter of members of the storied Boer Commando system.[3] Until 14 September 1993, white males were conscripted to serve twelve months in the National Service, followed by twelve years of part-time service in the Citizen Force. During this time, in any two-year period of call-up, duty was not to exceed sixty days of training. After the twelve years, they were to continue voluntary service in the Citizen Force until age fifty-five, or they could do five years with no commitment in Active Citizen Force Reserve. After this five-year period, they could be allocated to Commandos to age fifty-five, with an annual commitment of twelve days.[4] In 1993, South Africa had an active force of 72,000 and a reserve force of 360,000, including Citizen Force and Commando members.

The policy of white male compulsory conscription was changed on 15 September 1993, when South Africa's Parliament scrapped the policy and replaced it with an all-race volunteer system.[5] This new policy, however, only applied to National Service and therefore did not change the status of Citizen Force and Commando units, which consisted mainly of white males.

Each of the four formerly "nominally" independent states (Bantustans) had its own armed forces. They include Bophuthatswana, Ciskei, Transkei, and Venda.

The Armaments Corporation of South Africa (Armscor) was responsible for the acquisition of weapons and equipment for the SADF and controlled the import and export of armaments. It also marketed surplus SADF equipment.[6] Armscor was under the authority of the minister of defense, although its board of directors reflected the close cooperation that existed between the private sector and the defense establishment. Seven of Armscor's directors were from the private sector.[7]

With the 1994 interim South African constitution, the SADF was changed to the South African National Defense Force (SANDF). The SANDF consist of all members of the SADF, the defense forces of the former "independent" Bantustans, and "any other armed force under the control of a political party or organisation that took part in the first elections for the National Assembly."[8] The latter includes members of the military wing of the African National Congress (ANC), Umkhonto we Sizwe (MK), as well as members of the military wing of the Pan Africanist Congress (PAC) and the Azanian People's Liberation Army (APLA).

The role of the SANDF is to defend the independence of the Republic and the integrity of its territory, to comply with international military obligations of the Republic, and, where necessary, to assist the police to maintain law and order. In addition, the defense force must provide essential services, protect life, health and property, assist state departments for the purposes of socioeconomic upliftment, refrain from party politics, and act in the national interest.[9]

The SANDF has the same four service arms and six staff divisions that existed under the SADF, as well as the Chaplain General's section. The Special Forces, however, was disbanded. Armscor is still under the authority of the ministry of defense. In 1994, the SANDF had a permanent force of 90,000 and a part-time reserve force of 360,000.

CIVIL-MILITARY RELATIONS IN HISTORICAL PERSPECTIVE

Civil-military relations in South Africa have their roots in the "Kommando" system established by the Dutch[10] to fight against the indigenous African population. The "kommando" was basically a "citizen at arms." Although the "liberal" British model[11] of civil-military relations had an influence on the development of the South African military, the "kommando" system was retained.

This section of the article will place in historical perspective civil-military relations in South Africa, beginning in 1659.

The Kommando, Afrikaner Nationalism, and African Resistance (1659–1960)

The kommando was an outgrowth of the principle "established at the Cape in 1659 that all white citizens (or free burgers) would bear arms to assist regular soldiers in its defence and, indeed would bear the brunt of warfare on the border areas of the interior." Kommando units became very significant as Afrikaners fought against the indigenous African population and the British. Kommando members, for the most part, were farmers who were either defending or extending their property. The foundation was thus laid for "the notion of the nation-in-arms, of the sometime-citizen-sometime-soldier engaged in the Afrikaner version of the 'people's war' in defence of community and homeland."[12]

When the Afrikaners gained power in South Africa with the 1948 National Party (NP) victory, Afrikaner nationalism became a rallying cry among the new leaders. The military was identified as a place that needed to be transformed. This included replacing designations, decorations, and ranks that were British with indigenous insignia. Regiments were renamed to deprive them of their traditional identities, and bilingualism was introduced as a requirement for officer status.[13] This latter change discouraged the recruitment of English speakers, who were less inclined during this time to be bilingual. Afrikaners with little or no combat experience were used as replacements in the officer corps.[14]

During the 1950s, the police were left to handle internal threats to the country.

Between 1952 and 1958, police manpower was increased by 50%, and police powers were strengthened with the introduction of a series of repressive laws, beginning with the Suppression of Communism Act.[15]

Following the Sharpeville Massacre of 21 March 1960, in which South African Police (SAP) killed at least sixty nine Africans and wounded at least another 180 during a peaceful anti-pass protest, the government declared a state of emergency and ordered the partial mobilization of the SADF. In addition, all Citizen Force and Reserve troops and Commandos were put on stand-by.[16] This dramatically changed the role of the SADF. The military, however, was well prepared for its new role in protecting the country against internal threats sparked by African resistance. In fact, by 1960, the armed forces had reorganized in preparation for anticipated increased African resistance.

On 8 April 1960, two African liberation groups, the ANC and the PAC, were officially banned. This move by the government closed the door on fifty years of peaceful struggle and marked the beginning of the armed struggle by liberation movements.[17]

The Military's Rise to Power (1961–89)

By 1961, the major concern of the apartheid government was security; namely, how best to maintain the white supremacist state. During the 1960s and 1970s, various elements of the security establishment[18] competed for control and/or influence over national security. Prime Minister Vorster, like his predecessor, continued to mainly rely on the security police to maintain the white supremacist state. For intelligence and security operations, the government relied on the Bureau of State Security (BOSS).

The Vorster government was not successful, however, in handling the major crises that confronted the apartheid regime in the 1970s. They included new forms of black opposition; the beginning of a deep recession; increased international condemnation of the apartheid regime; and the defeat of Portuguese colonialism in Angola and Mozambique. This defeat resulted in the independence of Angola and Mozambique under socialist governments. Vorster also had to deal with the catastrophe of the first South African invasion of Angola in 1975–76 and the humiliating withdrawal of the South African army that followed. In addition, the government's "detente" initiative had failed.[19]

The SADF, under the leadership of Minister of Defense P. W. Botha, was highly critical of the security strategy of the Vorster government, especially the police response to the Soweto Uprising of 1976, where protesting students were shot at indiscriminately. Black resentment and racial polarization were brought to new extremes following this uprising.[20] The changing domestic and regional situation, the military argued, required a new approach to guaranteeing the maintenance of the white supremacist state. South Africa faced a "total onslaught" by revolutionary forces that required a "total (national) strategy" to counter it.

The total onslaught, the military contended, was being mounted by the Soviet

Union, which was planning to overthrow the regime and replace it with a Marxist-oriented form of government. The onslaught, the military determined, was being mounted by the Soviet Union through aid to terrorist organizations. They included the South West African People's Organization (SWAPO) and the ANC. The strategy for overthrowing the government included "instigating social and labor unrest, civilian resistance, terrorist attacks against the infrastructure of the Republic of South Africa and the intimidation of Black leaders and members of the security forces."[21]

The total strategy needed to counter the total onslaught had both a domestic and regional component. The overriding theme and the first objective of the domestic component was "reform." Military leaders urged "that major new steps had to be taken to give blacks a stake in the system and to remove the most blatant forms of white racism."[22] This "reform" was to be made with a view to defusing black resistance. The domestic strategy had as a second objective using the concept of "reform" to solicit other sectors in the society, such as business and the press, to get involved in combating the total onslaught. The third objective was the "development of a much more sophisticated repressive strategy than grand apartheid had been, coopting a class of 'insiders' and using it as a buffer against the frustrations of the vast mass of 'outsiders.' " The last objective was to reorganize and rationalize the state in order to coordinate a state-wide approach to formulating strategy.[23]

The regional component of the total strategy had as its major objective convincing the independent states of Southern Africa that it was in their best interest, both economically and politically, to work cooperatively with the apartheid regime. To this end, South Africa proposed the creation of a regional economic organization, the Constellation of Southern African States (CONSAS), that would serve to enhance the economic viability of the region, under South African domination. As the apartheid regime had built its power base by dominating the region economically during colonial rule, continued regional domination was essential to the maintenance of the apartheid state, albeit now with a new reality—independent black-ruled states.

In addition to CONSAS, the regional component of total strategy included:

- Ensuring that neighboring states would refrain from actively supporting the armed liberation struggles led by SWAPO in Namibia and the ANC in South Africa, and obliging them to act as virtual policing agents for South Africa by prohibiting political activity by South African and Namibian refugees residing in their territory.

- Ensuring that "Soviet-bloc powers" (including Cuba) would gain neither a political nor a military foothold anywhere in the region. Pretoria objected even to any state establishing normal diplomatic relations with the Soviet Union.

- Ensuring that "black states" in the region would not support calls for mandatory sanctions against South Africa and that they would shield South Africa from such sanctions.

- Inducing moderation in the "heady anti-South African rhetoric" of regional states.[24]

The SADF was successful in selling the idea of the need for a "total strategy" against a "total onslaught" to many white South Africans, including the business community. By the end of the 1970s, the official perception was that the SADF had a superior understanding of the threats facing the government and knew best how they should be countered.[25]

The military got its opportunity to implement its ideas following P. W. Botha's ascendancy to power in 1978 as prime minister (and later state president). Botha established the National Security Management System (NSMS), which has been described as a militarized bureaucracy.[26] With himself at the top, Botha was surrounded by military-security chiefs. These "securocrats"

were empowered to intervene in every Government department in the name of national security, which became so broadly defined that it embraced everything from the state of the roads in a township to what was taught in the schools and preached in the churches. Literally everything could be classified as part of the "total onslaught" to weaken South Africa's psychological and physical resolve to fight off the threat of communism, and so the "securocrats" could intervene wherever they pleased, order civil officials around, and take over the functions of government.[27]

The major power within the NSMS was the State Security Council (SSC), which replaced the cabinet as the most significant decision-making body. While it was one of four permanent cabinet subcommittees, it was the only one created by statute, was chaired by the state president, and had a permanent secretariat. The SSC was responsible for shaping "total strategy."[28] The military was able to influence the decision-making process down to the local government level through Joint Management Centers (JMCs) created by the NSMS. There were some 500 JMCs, sub-JMCs, mini-JMCs, and local JMCs. The JMCs were responsible for overseeing the implementation of total strategies at the local level and for supplying intelligence on local conditions and grievances.[29]

Recapturing the State from the Military, 1989–93

When F. W. de Klerk became president in 1989, he took measures to recapture the state from military control. The president's office and the cabinet once again became the locus of state power instead of the SSC. The SSC was renamed the cabinet Committee for Security Affairs and returned to its original status as one of the four standing committees, and its decisions had to be endorsed by the cabinet. A national coordinating mechanism replaced the NSMS, and joint coordinating centers replaced the JMCs. These bodies, according to governmental officials, were to focus on welfare issues, not security.[30]

There were also changes within the intelligence establishment. The central intelligence agency within the state became the National Intelligence Service (NIS), linked to the Department of Foreign Affairs, instead of Military Intelligence and the security police. The NIS took control of the SSC secretariat from the SADF and SAP. De Klerk also did not include SADF and defense ministry officials in his negotiating team. He further reduced the significance of the military by decreasing the defense budget and by decreasing the length of compulsory military service for white youth from twenty-four to twelve months.[31] Many military officials were not pleased with these changes.

THE MILITARY AT WAR, 1980–89

In 1977, the government extended compulsory national military service for white males from one year to two years, and the 1977 Civil Defense Act required local authorities to establish Civil Defense units. Also, older men were activated for local civil defense work, and the 1977 Defense White Paper announced plans to double the "number of cadets, trained during high school for military service, to 200,000."[32] The government was preparing for the "total onslaught."

Estimates of government expenditure on military defense during the 1980s range from 20% of the national budget to 28%. One indication of the increased militarization of South Africa during this period was that between 1977/78 and 1985/86, the military budget almost tripled.[33]

By 1980, the military was actively involved in waging a regional war against its neighbors, and by 1984 the military was waging an internal war.

The Regional War

South Africa's military involvement in the region of Southern Africa was not new. South African military forces during the 1970s were involved in fighting a war in Namibia against the liberation forces (mainly SWAPO), who were fighting for their independence against South Africa's illegal occupation. South African military forces had not only fought alongside white Rhodesian forces in their war against African liberation forces fighting for independence against white-settler rule, but also had funded a large percentage of the war. South African military forces had also been involved in Angola. The military first invaded that country during 1975/76, and throughout the remainder of the decade continued its military attacks against Angola.

South Africa's initial military involvement in the region (Phase I) was to prevent the demise of white regional hegemony. Prior to the 1974 military coup d'etat in Portugal that gave rise to the announcement that Angola and Mozambique would become independent in 1975, the region was dominated by white regimes, with South Africa as the regional economic and political giant. Angola and Mozambique were under Portuguese colonial rule; Rhodesia (Zimbabwe) was under white-settler rule; and Namibia and South Africa were under the control of the apartheid regime. South Africa was determined that the region would not change.

This regional configuration began to change, however, when it was clear that Angola and Mozambique would gain their independence. If majority rule was inevitable in these countries, the apartheid regime reasoned that the new governments must be pro–South Africa. In Phase II of its military involvement in the region, South Africa attempted to ensure that this occurred. In Angola, the apartheid regime supported the United States–backed Union for the Total Independence of Angola (UNITA), and in Zimbabwe the United African National Council (UANC). In Mozambique there was no alternative to the liberation movement that came to power, the Mozambique Liberation Front (FRELIMO).

The South African government failed in its attempt to surround itself with pro–South African governments. Instead, by 1980, the apartheid regime was surrounded by Marxist-oriented governments in Angola, Mozambique, and Zimbabwe. In addition, on the heels of Zimbabwe's independence, the independent nations[34] in the region joined together and formed the Southern African Development Coordination Conference (SADCC) which had as a major objective decreased regional economic dependence on South Africa. By creating SADCC, the regional nations had rejected South Africa's idea of regional economic development via CONSAS. With its regional power further diminished, South Africa entered Phase III of its military's involvement in the region. The apartheid regime declared war against its regional neighbors with a view to (1) forcing the SADCC members to accept South Africa's regional hegemony and (2) preserving the white supremacist state. The South African government implemented a policy of regional "destabilization" that between 1980 and 1989 wreaked havoc on the region. The destabilization strategy included military invasions of countries; support for dissident and surrogate groups; "disinformation" campaigns; the assassination of anti-apartheid leaders; the attempted assassination of two heads of governments; and the destruction of transport, agricultural, and energy structures.

Between 1980 and 1988, it is estimated that 1.5 million people died in Southern Africa as a result of destabilization, half of these children under the age of five. The cost of destabilization to the SADCC members states during this period is estimated at $60 billion.[35]

The two countries most affected by the policy of destabilization were Angola and Mozambique. In Angola, after the failed invasion of 1975/76, the SADF created a line of bases along the Angola-Namibia border and began to rearm and reorganize both UNITA and the National Front for the Liberation of Angola (FNLA). Many of the FNLA soldiers were incorporated into the SADF's 32 Battalion. During April and May 1980, the SADF launched a series of raids on villages; and by the beginning of 1981 there was a state of permanent war in southern Angola, with SADF occupation lasting almost continuously from 1980 to 1988.[36]

The devastation caused by the war to the Angolan economy resulted in the government signing a limited cease-fire with South Africa, the Lusaka Agreement, in February 1984. The agreement stipulated that SADF forces were to withdraw from Angola in phases and that the Angolan government was not to allow SWAPO or Cuban troops to enter the vacated area.[37] The South Africans, nonetheless, did not complete the withdrawal.

By mid-1988, however, the SADF conceded defeat in Angola, and in August a cease-fire agreement was signed. Then, on 22 December 1988, Cuba, South Africa, and Angola signed the Tripartite Agreement, which called for the withdrawal of (1) Cuban troops, which had been in the country since 1975 at the invitation of the Angolan Government to help prevent a South African–UNITA military victory; (2) South African troops; and (3) ANC military bases. In addition, South Africa agreed to the establishment of a timetable for Namibian independence.

In Mozambique, the SADF used a surrogate group, the Mozambique National Resistance (Renamo) to fight its war against the government. Renamo was created as a "pseudo-terrorist" squad in 1974 by the Rhodesian intelligence services.[38] On the eve of Zimbabwe's independence in 1980, Renamo was turned over to the SADF and began waging a war in Mozambique. Under the leadership of the SADF, Renamo was responsible for the deaths of hundreds of thousands of civilians and the destruction of schools, villages, rural shops, and public health installations.

By 1984, the devastation caused by this South African–sponsored war was so great that in March the government signed a nonaggression pact with South Africa, the Nkomati Accord. In the accord, the Mozambican government agreed not to allow ANC military bases to be located in the country and the South African government agreed to discontinue its support for Renamo. While the Mozambican government allowed the ANC to retain only a small diplomatic mission in the country, the SADF continued its support for Renamo throughout Botha's administration. Thus the war continued.

In Angola, the SADF bombed oil installations, and in Mozambique sabotaged railway lines and powerlines. In Mozambique, Botswana, Zambia, Zimbabwe, and Lesotho, SADF forces raided the residences of South African refugees and ANC members (very often killing innocent civilians), as well as "alleged" ANC military bases. ANC leaders and supporters were assassinated throughout the region. The SADF supported dissident groups in Lesotho, Zambia, and Zimbabwe and sabotaged railway lines and military installations in Zimbabwe.[39]

During 1980 in Namibia, the indigenous South West Africa Territory Force (SWATF) was created by the SADF and used to fight against the indigenous population.[40] The war, which lasted over twenty years, resulted in the death of more than twelve thousand, and tens of thousands were forced into exile. The northern part of the country was a war zone under direct South African military occupation. The SADF forces were withdrawn from Namibia during 1989, and the country achieved its independence on 21 March 1990.[41]

By 1989, the Botha government determined that its regional strategy of destabilization had been a success. The SADCC member states had increased, rather than decreased, their economic dependency on the apartheid regime; and the ANC no longer had the ability to launch external military attacks against the government.

The Internal War

Botha's "reforms" failed to stem the rising tide of black resistance. In fact, one of the "reforms," a new constitution that included the establishment of a tricameral parliament that would include "Indians" and "Coloureds," but not blacks, served as a major impetus for the violence that swept the country between 1984 and 1986. The political unrest started on 3 September 1984, the day the new constitution came into force.[42] Over several months, the battles between residents and police became so fierce that the minister of law and order declared: "as far as we're concerned it is war, plain and simple." By the end of 1984, the SADF was sent into the townships to assist the police. Also, during this period all information about Defense Force involvement in joint police-army activities was banned.[43]

With the army and police unable to contain the rebellion, on 21 July 1985 a partial state of emergency was declared on the Witwatersrand, in the Eastern Cape and later in the Western Cape. Far-reaching powers of arrest and detention were given to both SAP and SADF officers. Additional powers were extended to soldiers by mid-December, resulting in the inability of township residents to discern the difference between SAP and SADF forces. The government, in fact, began to refer to them collectively as "security forces."[44]

During the emergency, the security forces harassed and detained community leaders, disrupted political meetings and black funerals, and attempted to break stayaways, consumer boycotts and strikes. They enforced night curfews in townships and manned roadblocks to prevent non-residents from entering them. On a daily basis they patrolled black urban areas, regularly sealing them off to conduct house-to-house searches. They also maintained a provocative presence inside and outside school premises to prevent student mobilisation and organization.[45]

Speaking before Parliament, the minister of defense reported that in 1985, 35, 372 troops were deployed in ninety-six townships. He further noted "that a full list of the occasions on which they were used would 'take months to compile and run to hundreds of pages.' "[46]

African resistance intensified; township residents and the security forces continued to clash; sabotage attacks by MK, the military wing of the ANC, increased; and the international community began imposing economic sanctions against the apartheid regime.

In October 1985, the Eminent Persons Group (EPG) was created and charged by the Commonwealth Heads of Governments with negotiating a settlement to the crisis in South Africa. The EPG met with South African government officials, as well as members of the ANC, including the imprisoned Nelson Mandela. On 15 May 1986, Botha "told Parliament that he was prepared to negotiate with citizens of South Africa, provided that they did not resort to violence as a means of attaining their political goals or call in foreign agencies to support them."[47]

Following discussions with the ANC, the EPG informed Botha that the ANC would "suspend" violence, which Botha had stipulated as a sufficient precondition for negotiations (although later he said the ANC had to "renounce" violence). At this point Botha and the military were confronted with the fact that they had two options. They could release Mandela and begin to negotiate a transfer of power, or they could reestablish control over the country by implementing a "counterrevolutionary" strategy aimed at crushing the resistance.[48]

The government announced its decision to the world on the morning of May 19 when the SADF attacked three alleged ANC targets in Mozambique, Zimbabwe, and Zambia. Although the damage was slight, the attack was of great symbolic importance.[49] This attack killed the EPG initiative and paved the way for the implementation of the "counterrevolutionary" strategy. The strategy, according to Police Chief Major-General Wandrag,

required drastic action to be taken to eliminate the underlying social and economic factors which have caused unhappiness in the population. The only way to render the enemy powerless is to nip revolution in the bud by ensuring there is no fertile soil in which the seeds of revolution can germinate.[50]

As part of the strategy, on 12 June 1986, the government imposed a national state of emergency, and the police and military assured the SSC "that township protest, 'people's power' and popular support for the ANC could be eliminated by applying a sufficient degree of force in a relatively short space of time."[51] The security forces became more aggressive, no longer patrolling the townships in cumbersome vehicles loaded with riot equipment. Instead, they began patrolling in open jeeps with mounted machine guns. Armed commandos on horseback were also deployed.[52] Several thousand people were killed by security forces between 1984 and 1986.

Under the state of emergency, over fifty thousand people were detained without trial; at least 20% of them were children. The children, some as young as seven, told of being brutally beaten and/or electroshocked. In addition, between 1985 and 1989, forty-five political activists were assassinated,[53] many by security SAP and SADF hit squads.

With a view to decreasing the power of the ANC, in 1986 the SADF invested one million dollars in paramilitary training for two hundred members of the Inkatha Freedom Movement, a Zulu-based organization (and later political party) under the leadership of Chief Gatsha Buthelezi. The training took place in Caprivi Stripe in Namibia. It has been alleged that the "men were mobilized into hit squads to be used in the lethal warfare raging in Natal province between Inkatha members and supporters of the United Democratic Front, an African

National Congress ally."[54] By 1987, a civil war was being waged between Zulu supporters of Inkatha and the ANC.

F. W. De KLERK: REINING IN THE MILITARY? 1989–93

By the time de Klerk came to power in September 1989, the draconian strategies pursued by the Botha regime to stem the tide of black resistance had resulted in the imposition of international economic sanctions, greater international isolation, and a rapidly deteriorating economy. Though the security forces had been successful in putting down the unrest that swept the country from 1984 to 1986, it was at great cost, domestically and internationally. Given this reality, de Klerk had two choices. He could continue to hold the situation by force and pay the price of repression, or he could negotiate a future political dispensation with the black majority. De Klerk chose the latter, feeling that the NP would be negotiating from a position of strength.

On 2 February 1990, de Klerk announced to Parliament that he was legalizing the ANC and other heretofore banned political organizations and releasing Nelson Mandela. On February 11, Mandela was released from twenty-seven years of imprisonment.

Although de Klerk had recaptured the state from the military, during the three years of negotiations, one of the greatest constraints to the establishment of a new dispensation in the country were elements within the security forces who continued to be involved in destabilizing the South African townships. These elements became known as the "third force."

In discussing allegations of a "third force" fueling the violence in the townships, Major Nico Basson, a former military intelligence officer, "alleged that the activities of the 'third force' are part of an elaborate plan, code named Operation Agree, drawn up by the SADF and the Department of Foreign Affairs in 1988 to manipulate the 1989 Namibian elections and future Democratic elections in Angola and South Africa."[55]

In addition to "Operation Agree," Major Nico Basson accused the SADF of arming Inkatha members and reported that the assassination of ANC activists (sixty assassinations in 1991 alone) and the random killing of black train commuters (112 killed in attacks on trains on the Reef during the eighteen months ending on 31 January 1992) were part of a government plan of disruption.[56] Between 1990 and 1992, an estimated 119 activists were killed by assassins.[57]

The SADF was also associated with the deployment of members of the 32 Battalion in Natal and the Reef's townships to act against urban unrest. These units proved to be extremely controversial and were accused of fueling the violence. The 32 Battalion were veterans of Operation Zulu, which was South Africa's 1975 invasion of Angola. The troops spoke Portuguese. Although in early 1992 de Klerk announced the disbandment of this highly criticized entity, it was not officially disbanded until April 1993.[58]

During April 1992, further evidence of security-force involvement in the destabilization of the townships was revealed following the arrest of two Directorate of Military Intelligence (DMI)[59] agents in London. They were accused of conspiring with the Royal Ulster Constabulary in an apparent effort to assassinate Dirk Coetzee, a former South African policeman, because he made public past SADF covert operations and had begun cooperating with the ANC.[60]

In November 1992, the Goldstone Commission of Inquiry Regarding Public Violence and Intimidation, which had been appointed by de Klerk, seized documents that revealed that the SADF had employed a double-murderer (Ferdi Bernard) to run a smear campaign against Umkhonto we Sizwe from May to December 1991. Justice Richard Goldstone noted "that Ferdi Bernard's 48 subordinates were to use 'prostitutes, homosexuals, nightclub owners, and criminal elements' to entice Umkhonto members into compromising acts."[61]

Then, in December 1992, de Klerk appointed Lieutenant-General Pierre Steyn, Chief of the South African Air Force, to investigate unauthorized security force actions. After Steyn gave his report, de Klerk dismissed or suspended twenty-three military officers, including two generals and four brigadiers. De Klerk noted that these individuals "might have been motivated by a wish to prevent us from succeeding in our [reform] goals."[62]

Although these individuals were dismissed, no charges of wrongdoing were pressed against them. Also, de Klerk did not dismiss two hardliners who indicated publicly their dislike for the ANC, Kat Liebenberg, then Chief of the SADF and Georg Meiring, then Army Commander and Liebenberg's successor.[63] General van der Westhuizen, head of Military Intelligence, was also retained, although there existed evidence suggesting he was linked to political assassinations.[64]

If de Klerk was really committed to negotiations, why did it take him so long (until late 1992) to begin reforming the security forces? De Klerk, according to Herbert Howe,

had political, corporate, ideological, as well as structural reasons (the localised Commandos) to fear military praetorianism, and these may explain why his security reforms, both in timing and completeness, lagged behind his political initiatives. Yet de Klerk needed a strong security force to ensure that they succeeded, and apropos of de Tocqueville's warning to previously repressive but now-reformist governments, South African officials retained a "security fallback" lest the negotiations failed. If they had, political violence—which had claimed over 15,000 lives since 1986—would have surged even more and required a powerful security response.[65]

In addition, by retaining the hardline officers, de Klerk forced the ANC leadership to sell several compromises to its members and supporters. They were warned not to underestimate "the regime's known counter-revolutionary capabilities," and "Mandela acknowledged the reactionary security threat from South Africa's security forces, and used this to gain acceptance for the transitional power-sharing arrangement as the only method to forestall what he termed the 'already incipient counter-revolutionary movement' with the SADF."[66]

Between February 1990 and April 1994, an estimated twelve thousand people died in political violence.

THE MILITARY IN THE POST-APARTHEID ERA

In commenting on the involvement of both the SAP and the SANDF in the transformation in South Africa, President Mandela stated that, "Whatever mistakes they have made in the past—and whatever certain elements are doing with the security forces—there is no doubt that the overwhelming majority of the security forces are behind the transformation."[67] Given the history of the role of the military in the maintenance of apartheid South Africa, it is indeed amazing that the SANDF has been supportive of the new political dispensation in South Africa. No doubt the decision by the ANC during negotiations to allow all military personnel to retain their jobs has contributed to the stability of the transition, as did the fact that many of the hardliners had been retrenched under de Klerk. Of particular importance for the new government was the fact that General van der Westhuizen took early retirement.

While keeping in place the old guard, Mandela has attempted to give some balance to the SANDF. Siphiwe Nyanda, former MK chief of staff, became the SANDF's first black chief of staff. In addition, seven former MK members were appointed generals and two brigadiers.[68] No doubt with a view to maintaining stability in the military, General Meiring retained his position as chief of the South African defense force.

The greatest problem the military has had to confront to date concerns the integration of MK forces. Specifically, on two occasions within a month (October–November 1994), thousands of MK soldiers went absent without leave from Wallmannsthal, an army base north of Pretoria. A total of twenty-two thousand MK soldiers are to be integrated into the ninety thousand-strong SANDF. Complaints by the soldiers included unequal pay, poor medical facilities, bad food, and racism. In a preliminary report by Parliament's defense committee, conditions at Wallmannsthal were described as appalling, and racial discrimination was determined to be rife.[69] However, at least two thousand soldiers were dismissed by Mandela after they refused to return to the base.[70]

Ironically, members of the ANC could prove to be the greatest challenge to military stability during the post-apartheid era. To prevent this from occurring, major changes no doubt will be required in the near future in order to begin to redress the consequences of apartheid within the ranks of the military.

NOTES

1. "National Security," *Official Yearbook of South Africa 1992*, rev. ed. (Pretoria: South African Communications Service, 1992), p. 47.

2. Ibid.

3. James M. Roherty, *State Security in South Africa: Civil-Military Relations under P. W. Botha* (New York: M. E. Sharpe, 1992), p. 94.

4. *The Military Balance 1992–1993* (London: International Institute for Strategic Studies, 1992), p. 209.

5. "South Africa Scraps Whites-Only Military Conscription," United Press International, Johannesburg, 15 September 1993.

6. Tielman de Waal, "Commercialisation of the Defence Industry: Issues Faced in the Procurement of Arms," *South African Defence Review,* no. 11 (1993).

7. Mark Philipps, "The Nuts and Bolts of Military Power: the Structure of the SADF," in Jacklyn Cock and Laurie Nathan, eds., *Society at War: The Militarisation of South Africa* (New York: St. Martin's Press, 1989), p. 24.

8. Rautenbach, I. M., and E. F. J. Malherbe, *What Does the Constitution Say?* (Auckland Park, South Africa: Faculty of Law, Rand Afrikaans University, 1994), p. 65.

9. Ibid., pp. 65–66.

10. The Dutch arrived at the Cape of Good Hope in South Africa in 1652 and began fighting wars of land dispossession against the indigenous African population. The descendants of the Dutch are the Afrikaners. They are also known as Boers, which means farmers.

11. The "liberal" British model of civil-military relations is "based on separation of political and military functions, the predominance of civil over military authority and the soldier as a servant of the state." See Elling Njal Tjonneland, *Pax Pretoriana: The Fall of Apartheid and the Politics of Regional Destabilisation* (Uppsala: Scandinavian Institute of African Studies, 1989), p. 6.

12. Philip H. Frankel, *Pretoria's Praetorians: Civil-Military Relations in South Africa* (Cambridge: Cambridge University Press, 1984), pp. 19–24.

13. Ibid., p. 19.

14. Kenneth W. Grundy, *The Militarization of South African Politics* (Bloomington: Indiana University Press, 1986), p. 8.

15. Gavin Cawthra, *Brutal Force: The Apartheid War Machine* (London: International Defence and Aid Fund for Southern Africa, 1986), pp. 12–13.

16. Ibid., p. 14.

17. Ibid., p. 15.

18. The security establishment consists of the SADF, the SAP, the bantustan armies and police forces, Armscor, and a range of intelligence, civil defense, and support agencies.

19. Dan O'Meara, "Destabilization in Southern Africa: Total Strategy in Total Disarray," *Monthly Review* 37, no. 11 (April 1986): 52–53.

20. Richard Leonard, *South Africa at War: White Power and the Crisis in Southern Africa* (Westport, Conn.: Lawrence Hill and Co., 1983), p. 14.

21. Ibid., p. 100.

22. Ibid., p. 14.

23. James Selfe, "South Africa's National Management System," in Cock and Nathan, eds., *Society at War: Militarisation of South Africa,* p. 150.

24. O'Meara, *Destabilization,* pp. 55–56.

25. Annette Seegers, "South Africa's National Security Management System, 1972–90," *Journal of Modern African Studies* 29, no. 2 (1991): 254.

26. Selfe, "National Management System," p. 150.

27. Allister Sparks, "Transition in South Africa: Its Prospects and Implications," *PAS* (Winter 1993), p. 4.

28. Selfe, "National Management System," p. 151.

29. Jacklyn Cock, "Introduction," in Cock and Nathan, eds., *Society at War: The Militarisation of South Africa,* p. 8; and Selfe, "National Management System," p. 153.

30. Laurie Nathan and Mark Phillips, " 'Cross-currents': Security Developments under F. W. de Klerk," in Glenn Moss and Ingrid Obery, eds., *South Africa Review: From 'Red Friday' to CODESA* (Johannesburg: Ravan Press, 1992), pp. 114–15.

31. Ibid., p. 115.

32. Leonard, *South Africa at War,* p. 11.

33. Cock, "Introduction," p. 5; and O'Meara, *Destabilization,* p. 56.

34. In April 1980, when SADCC was formed, the member nations included Angola, Botswana, Lesotho, Malawi, Mozambique, Swaziland, Tansania, Zambia, and Zimbabwe. Namibia became a member of the organization following its independence from South Africa in 1990. In 1992, the organization changed its name to the Southern African Development Community (SADC). Additional members include South Africa and Mauritius.

35. *South African Destabilization: The Economic Cost of Frontline Resistance to Apartheid* (New York: United Nations, 1989), p. 4.

36. Jeremy Grest, "The South African Defence Force in Angola," in Cock and Nathan, eds., *Society at War: The Militarisation of South Africa,* pp. 116–24.

37. Ibid., pp. 126–27.

38. Robert Davies, "The SADF's Covert War against Mozambique," in Cock and Nathan, eds., *Society at War: The Militarisation of South Africa,* p. 104.

39. Cawthra, *Brutal Force,* pp. 138–75.

40. Peter Manning and Reginald Green, "Namibia: Preparations for Destabilization," in Phyllis Johnson and David Martin, eds., *Destructive Engagement: Southern Africa at War* (Harare: Zimbabwe Publishing House, 1986), p. 125.

41. Laurie Nathan, "Marching to a Different Drum: A Description and Assessment of the Formation of the Namibian Police and Defence Force", South African Perspectives, A working paper series No. 4, Centre for Southern African Studies, Cape Town, South Africa, February 1990, pp. 4–5.

42. *Illustrated History of South Africa* (Cape Town: Reader's Digest Association South Africa (Pty), 1988), p. 472.

43. Laurie Nathan, "Troops in the Townships, 1984–87," in Cock and Nathan, eds., *Society at War: The Militarisation of South Africa,* pp. 67–68.

44. Ibid., p. 69.

45. Ibid., p. 70.

46. Ibid.

47. Brian Pottinger, *The Imperial Presidency: P. W. Botha, the First 10 Years* (Johannesburg: Southern Book Publishers (Pty), 1988), p. 331.

48. Mark Swilling and Mark Phillips, "State Power in the 1980s: From 'Total Strategy' to 'Counter-Revolutionary,' " in Cock and Nathan, eds., *Society at War: The Militarisation of South Africa,* p. 142.

49. Pottinger, *Imperial Presidency,* p. 332.

50. Swilling and Phillips, "State Power," pp. 144–45.

51. Ibid., pp. 142–43.

52. Nathan, "Troops in the Townships," p. 73.

53. "Amnesty for the South African Government," Southern African Project of the Lawyers' Committee for Civil Rights under Law, 1993, p. 2.

54. Christopher S. Wren, "Zulu Ex-Aide Tells of Arms for Training," *New York Times,* 1 March 1992.

55. Nathan and Phillips, " 'Cross-Currents,' " p. 121.

56. Jacklyn Cock, "The Dynamics of Transforming South Africa's Defense Forces," in Stephen John Stedman, ed., *South Africa: The Political Economy of Transition* (Boulder, Colo.: Lynne Rienner, 1994), p. 144.

57. "Amnesty for the South African Government," p. 2.

58. Herbert Howe, "The South African Defense Force and Political Reform," *Journal of Modern African Studies* 32, no. 1 (1994): 37; "Buffalo Battalion Retreats from Natal Township," in *SouthScan,* 12 June 1992; and "South Africa's Sinister Security Forces Have Their Tentacles Everywhere Despite De Klerk's Efforts to Reduce Their Influence," *New African,* June 1993.

59. The DMI was a covert SADF unit.

60. Howe, pp. "South African Defense Force," pp. 36–37.

61. Ibid.

62. Ibid., p. 40.

63. Ibid.

64. Cock, "Dynamics," p. 143.

65. Ibid., p. 149.

66. Ibid., p. 60.

67. Monitor interview with President Mandela, *Christian Science Monitor,* 12 September 1994.

68. "MK Generals Move in as Kasrils Get Deputy Defence Ministry Job," *SouthScan,* 7 July 1994.

69. Joseph Contreras, "Unrest in Mandela's Ranks," *Newsweek,* 14 November 1994.

70. "Who Exactly Is in Command?" *Economist,* 19 November 1994, p. 48.

REFERENCES

Cawthra, Gavin. *Brutal Force: The Apartheid War Machine.* London: International Defence and Aid Fund for Southern Africa, 1986.

Cock, Jacklyn, and Laurie Nathan, eds. *Society at War: The Militarisation of South Africa.* New York: St. Martin's Press, 1989.

Frankel, Philip H. *Pretoria's Praetorians: Civil-Military Relations in South Africa.* Cambridge: Cambridge University Press, 1984.

Grundy, Kenneth W. *The Militarization of South African Politics.* Bloomington: Indiana University Press, 1986.

Howe, Herbert M. "The South African Defence Force and Political Reform." *Journal of Modern African Studies* 32, no. 1 (1994): 21–51.

Leonard, Richard. *South Africa at War: White Power and the Crisis in Southern Africa.* Westport, Conn.: Lawrence Hill and Company, 1983.

Nathan, Laurie, and Mark Philipps. " 'Cross Currents': Security Developments under F. W. de Klerk." In Glenn Moss and Ingrid Obery, eds., *South Africa Review: from 'Red Friday' to CODESA.* Johannesburg: Ravan Press, 1992.

RUSSIA AND THE FORMER SOVIET UNION

Konstantin E. Sorokin

The place and role of the army in Soviet and, later, Russian society has always been an enigma for Western analysts. In the Soviet era, "official" information was scarce and imprecise, while occasional and unintended leakages were fragmented and not enough to support conclusively any theory. Besides purely propagandistic pamphlets to the effect that "the army and the people are united," no reliable studies by Soviet scientists about the army as a state institution in USSR were available.

In this situation Western experts had to rely heavily on circumstantial evidence, which helped them to come up with some true conclusions about certain aspects of civil-military relations in the top echelons of power. But these were still to be put into a wider context of power distribution in the Soviet hierarchy.

After the collapse of the Soviet Union, there has been much conflicting information about the newly created Russian armed forces' political posture for both Russian and Western researchers. The volume of information is such that it sometimes is difficult to interpret and put into the right context. Still an effort should be made, as in the prevailing volatile situation in that country (which may be expected to last for many more years) the armed forces are potentially well placed to have a weighty say in the political process and to define its eventual results.

But first it is reasonable to clarify what in the Soviet and Russian conditions should be called "a political role" for the military. In this chapter the term means the armed forces' autonomous or independent involvement in purely political decisions and/or their capability to sway the political decision-making bodies; adherence to certain ideological and political doctrines rather than to the Constitution and the legal processes; open support for this or that political force or movement; internal division along political lines; and the combination of professional duties and political activities by servicemen.

THE SOVIET ARMED FORCES AND THE COMMUNIST REGIME

As the Russian military used to form the hard core of the Soviet armed forces and is naturally influenced by its past experiences, it is useful to look first at the nature and magnitude of the Soviet army's involvement in politics.

Even Russian analysts are divided over what the true role of the military in the Communist era was. One view claims that in the former Soviet Union "the military were the chief architects of the political course; they even decided who should stay in power, and who and when should be removed from office."[1] Others assert that "in the Soviet period the interrelation between the political authorities and the socialist Army was based on the principle of unreserved subordination of the latter."[2] Supporters of both views believe that they put forward rather convincing arguments to substantiate their cases.[3]

The truth lies somewhere between the two extremes. Several points suggested by the author will give a clearer understanding of the extent of the military's influence under the Communist regime and its position vis-à-vis other institutions of power.

Generally speaking, the army was one of the chief pillars of the Soviet state. It had crucial internal and external security functions, but it was not the dominant institution in the society. The military leadership was an integral part of the Soviet ruling elite, and as such it had its own interests, lobbyists, privileges, and of course sphere of activity, where it took most "technical" decisions at its own discretion.

In the last thirty or forty years, the military participated in the "rules of the game" played by the national elite in several ways. First, it was to maintain stability inside the leadership and in the society. Second, it was able to avoid excesses of the Stalin era by maintaining equilibrium (in terms of power and privileges) between different branches and institutions of the regime. Most important, it balanced power between the supreme bodies: the Communist party apparatus, three "power" ministries (KGB, Ministry of Defense, Ministry of Internal Affairs), the defense industry commission (whose influence was growing in the Brezhnev years), top executive and legislative branches (the government and the Presidium of the Supreme Soviet), and the top judiciary. These rules were enforced by an intricate system of "checks and balances," Soviet style (the army, for instance, was doubly controlled by the KGB and the CPSU Central Committee through the network of security and political bodies in the armed forces, living side by side with the military chain of command), and by solidifying interinstitutional personal connections.

It was mostly the military leadership, and not the army per se, that strived for a better position inside the elite as the result of behind the scenes dealings, at the expense of other institutions. This led to predictable counteractions on the part of other groups. (By stretching a point, this can be characterized as a "political activity of the military'' under the Soviet regime). But neither military leaders nor the armed forces in general could realistically think of imposing themselves on the party/state hierarchy or the society.

An increment in political influence and position for the military and its leadership, and indeed economic and social benefits for the army from the top down, depended to a large degree on the personal qualities of defense ministers. During the greater part of Soviet postwar history, they were mostly strong and authoritative figures capable of protecting the corporate interests of the armed forces within the permitted boundaries (Marshal Dmitrii Ustinov was the last of the kind).

This situation ensured the political loyalty of the military to the regime and prevented the bulk of the armed forces from acquiring any meaningful political experience.

Limitations on how big a political role the army could play in the Soviet Union developed into a tradition. Though substantially weakened by the poor performance of the last two Soviet defense ministers (Marshal Sokolov and Marshal Yazov), this tradition, coupled with the lack of political experience, is still a significant factor affecting the behavior of the Russian military.

"POLITICIZATION" OF THE ARMY

The decline in the Soviet military's fortune began after the insipid Marshal Sokolov was appointed defense minister and continued under Marshal Yazov, who succeeded him at this post. Both were unable to check the negative sides of the demilitarization crusade by Gorbachev, most significantly the progressive worsening of social and economic conditions for the army. (This decline mostly held true for officers of medium rank and below, or the overwhelming part of the army; but though generals were not affected at that time, they were fearful of losing their privileges in the near future.) Yazov also acquiesced to irresponsible and repeated use of the army to quell political and ethnic unrest in non-Russian republics, which was not crowned with any success but caused a storm of angry protests from the democratic part of Soviet society amounting to a virulent anti-army propaganda campaign. Together with apprehension over Gorbachev's allegedly yielding and defeatist foreign and arms control policies, this engendered growing discontent in the military ranks, triggered a process of "politicization" of the whole army (openly revealed by the end of 1990), and gave rise to a political sense of "unity in need" among the military.

1991 COUP ATTEMPT

All these developments led to the army showing an uncharacteristically high political profile during the attempted coup in August 1991. Still, by that time the army had not been consolidated into a cohesive political force and taken out into the streets in support of the conspiracy, let alone being put at the head of the plot.

The collapse of the Soviet Union was yet another shock to the armed forces. The greater part of the army (with the partial exception of non-Russian officers serving outside Russia and the newly appointed and loyal top military leaders) took the transformation of the USSR into the Commonwealth of Independent States (CIS) as a first step in the "vivisection" of the single armed forces into weak and handicapped parts, to be followed by a deep decline in social standards and the quality of life for the military.

To prevent the military from getting out of control, the new Russian leaders launched a campaign to preserve the unity of the Soviet armed forces, hoping to have a restraining effect on the army. They were also mindful, of course, of their own interests, including the possibility of manipulating the behavior of other republics through military structures dominated by Russia. But growing alienation among the newly independent states frustrated the effort.

By spring, tensions in Russia-based troops reached critical proportions. Polls held in early March 1992 brought another gloomy result: 56% of the servicemen strongly disapproved of the new Russian rulers (only 17% supported them), and 43% spoke strongly against Boris Yeltsin's arms control initiatives.[4]

In this situation the leadership in Moscow realized it should adopt a new strategy vis-à-vis the army. The new approach was a dramatic departure from the previous policy and included several major steps and initiatives.

A national armed forces was the result. The first official hints about this decision were dropped by the head of the Russian Federation Committee on Defense Issues, Pavel Grachev, at the meeting of the CIS High Command on March 27.[5] In early April, President Boris Yeltsin appointed a commission charged to establish the national defense ministry and the national army, and on May 7 he signed a decree, "On Creation of the Armed Forces of the Russian Federation." Among other things, these moves were designed to bestow a clear national identity on the military stationed on Russian territory and to send them a clear message that from now on the state would take care of their needs.

To appease the military, General Pavel Grachev was appointed defense minister, while civilian scientist Andrei Kokoshin (also seeking this job) moved no higher than first deputy defense minister. Another "appeasing appointment" was that of General Boris Gromov, who signed the notoriously conservative "Appeal to the Nation" on the eve of the August coup, to a deputy minister post.

The defense budget was also reconsidered with more money channelled to finance "social programs" in the armed forces. Immediately affected were direct payments to officers, which were raised in June and August 1992 by nearly 250%.[6]

Finally, to pour more oil on troubled military waters, Russian leaders also pledged to carry out a long-promised reform of the armed forces and to work for a much stronger, better organized, and better trained and equipped army.

Apparently speaking on behalf of the whole leadership and clearly reiterating promises made by other top-ranking officials, Vice-President Rutskoi addressed the military audience, declaring that "we must create an Army worthy of Great Russia."[7]

All these "carrots" were offered to the military in one package with sticks. Reminding officers of the presidential decree signed on 24 August 1991 banning political parties and movements from the armed forces, Defense Minister Pavel Grachev warned the military about tough penalties for those who would violate its provisions: "Presidential ruling on departization and depoliticization of the Armed Forces will be carried out without question. Those who can not do without politics, are free to go in for it. But before they must leave the Armed Forces."[8] Tough words were matched with actions: Some officers were sacked for political activity, and the All-Army Officers' Meeting was never officially reconvened. Grachev also banned "commercial activities" in the army permitted earlier by Soviet authorities, claiming that such activities are detrimental to the discipline, morale, and readiness of the armed forces and that economic involvement also carried political bias and allegiances.

DISSATISFACTION IN THE ARMY

After the "taming strategy" was enacted in the spring of 1992, the government tried, apparently in good faith, to deliver the promised goods. But by September 1993, when the armed forces' loyalty came to the test, it had been at best only partially successful, having pushed through military reform and enacted a cluster of defense-related laws. The reasons for its inability to cater properly to many other army needs were basically two-fold. On the one hand, the government was hamstrung by an economic crisis that limited its field for maneuver, to the point that it is amazing that the cabinet managed to do anything for the military. On the other, most problems facing the army (and keeping the level of its politicization high) are of a profound and lasting nature and cannot be resolved overnight. Indeed, they are unlikely to diminish before the end of this century.

Though the problems facing the army are numerous, some are of outstanding proportions; potentially, they may lead to a "surge" involvement of the army in the political process, with unpredictable consequences.

One problem is a continuous and growing shortage of financial resources. This problem has three basic elements. Despite repeated indexation of the defense budget, inflation is still moving faster, leading to progressive depreciation of defense appropriations.[9] These financial troubles are multiplied by complaints on the part of the military that their interests are neglected in the course of the ongoing privatization.[10]

Another grave and seemingly intractable issue is providing housing for officers and their families. This problem grows in severity as Russian troops are withdrawn from Eastern Europe and the former Soviet republics. At present around 125 thousand officers in Russia are virtually homeless. Further, seventy-seven thousand officers and warrant officers who were dismissed from the army or volunteered out of its ranks are eligible for housing provided by the state. It is expected that when the withdrawals are over, some four hundred thousand military men will be angrily queuing for state-financed housing.[11]

Next is the staffing problem. Despite earlier predictions that the Ministry of Defense would be hard put to trim the armed forces to 1.5 million servicemen by 1995 as planned, actually the reverse is taking place. In mid-1993 the Russian army was *understaffed* by 910,000 servicemen, and future decreases seem likely to put it well below the target number.

Additionally, the armed forces will be poorly balanced: There will be 630,000 officers on active duty and only 544,000 conscripts.[12] Two major problems combined to cause this bizarre situation. One is the steadily falling birth rate in Russia for years (in 1992 for the first time in decades more people died than were born). The other is the permissive deferment provisions of the current legislation. The official periodical of the defense ministry once complained that potentially 1,800 young men could be recruited every year but that 1,500 of them are exempt from service under the present law.[13]

Worsening shortages of junior servicemen in many cases forces officers to take up the duties of soldiers and warrant-officers, stretching them physically and morally to the limit, which of course adds to tensions in the army.

Lastly, judging from publications and interviews, the military are seriously worried that they will soon be left without modern "professional instruments," that is, up-to-date weapons and equipment. At present, deliveries of modern weapons to the armed forces are running at a very low level. For instance, in 1992 production of the newest fourth-generation combat aircraft ceased altogether.[14] The Air Force commander in chief, Piotr Deinekin, complained that in 1993 again no new MiG-29s and Su-27s would be supplied to the air force.[15] At present, the national arms industry is capable of supplying the armed forces with sophisticated weapons and equipment (many new items were successfully demonstrated abroad), but the army is unable to pay for them. No wonder that for the next few years the defense ministry is developing a multi-option program of weapons purchases tied to various levels of financing.[16]

In the longer-term perspective, however, there are doubts among the military that national defense manufacturers will manage the designing and production of "clever weapons" of the future. Currently, general science allocations have dropped to 2.6% of the federal budget, while 3.7% is regarded as "survival minimum."[17] More narrowly, in 1992 military R&D was drastically scaled back, and not a single military-related R&D program was started that year.[18] The trend continued in 1993. Piotr Deinekin admitted that the air force was looking at opportunities "beyond the state budget" (including domestic and private investors and benefactors) to save the still-running 113 R&D projects and help the service to survive beyond the year 2000.[19]

FOR NOW THE RUSSIAN ARMY IS "CONTROLLABLE"

Logically, the multiple problems facing the armed forces (only four of the most serious were discussed above) could be expected to maintain discontent with political authorities in the army. Indeed, results of the poll conducted in early summer 1993 in five main military districts and in the Baltic fleet indicated a high level of frustration. Only 16.8% of the servicemen questioned replied that they felt socially protected, while over 60% expressed varying degrees of concern about their social and economic status. Most of them blamed the Russian leadership for their troubles.[20] There is every indication that morale in the armed forces will not improve in the foreseeable future.

Nevertheless, an attempt by a group of uniformed "activists" to reconvene the All-Army Officers' Meeting in late February 1993 brought together only 250 officers (instead of the 1500 expected to attend), most of them retired and sacked from the army.[21] There were mounting reports in the mass media that the armed forces were returning to their normal activities. Western observers were increasingly speaking about diminishing prospects for a "military government."[22] In early summer 1993 President Yeltsin declared that the army had passed the peak of its crisis.[23] Similarly, Defense Minister Pavel Grachev repeatedly asserted that the period when the government temporarily lost control of the army was over and that the armed forces were fully controllable[24] (as events indicated, he meant "controllable by the executive branch"). Of course, in Autumn 1993, when Boris Yeltsin dissolved the Russian Parliament, the army remained largely passive, though its leaders provided the president with only limited support.[25]

But if the military are openly dissatisfied with their conditions, what were the reasons for the military keeping a lower political profile since late 1992? And why did the army not use the opportunity provided by the September political crisis to move closer to the leverage of power or at least press forward its economic, social, and political demands?

There are probably several common answers to these questions. The long-standing tradition of noninvolvement in politics had some restraining effect on the military, though its impact should not be overestimated.

More importantly, since the late 1980s the armed forces have been repeatedly taught bitter lessons of being manipulated by contending political forces fighting for their but not the army's interests (the August 1993 coup is a graphic example), and the bulk of the military were fed up with active political involvements.[26]

Next, numerically the army now is not what it used to be even two years ago: As mentioned earlier, it is rapidly shrinking and is severely understaffed. At present it is hard pressed to muster enough troops to police hot spots on the territory of the former USSR. For instance, the military leadership had to rake through garrisons in the entire European part of Russia to piece together the peacekeeping units later introduced into Ossetia and Ingushetia. Obviously, the army has insufficient strength to support its economic and political demands (if any), let alone impose its will on the whole society. General Staff experts believe that to enforce curfew in Moscow alone would take five full-blooded divisions plus some reinforcement units (some 100,000–125,000 servicemen in all). They also estimate that full mobilization of the Moscow military district will generate no more than fifteen to twenty thousand servicemen, including cadets.[27] Reinforcements from other regions could not be realistically counted on, because troops there would be engaged in maintaining local order.

What is probably most important, below the surface the army now is split along multiple lines.

Though political parties are officially banned from the armed forces, servicemen are threatened with tough punitive measures for political activities, and Pavel Grachev claimed there was no political opposition in the army,[28] it is clear that the army is not immune to the political storms raging in the country. There are different and sometimes opposing political preferences within its ranks. The August 1991 coup was the first to graphically demonstrate that the army is not a politically homogeneous entity: Only two services (Air Defense and Land Troops) sided with the conservative plotters; others opted for what was seen as a democratic choice for the country. This split has never been overcome; in fact, now there are even more shades of political attachments. Practically every political party and movement in Russia claims to have its supporters in the armed forces. Even some radical organizations seem to have put down roots there— from the quasi-democratic "Schit" alliance to the neo-Communist All-Russia Officers' Assembly and the ostensibly independent "underground strike committees."[29]

There are traditional and new antagonisms among the five armed services. Being locked in "natural" struggle over a greater share of scanty defense budgets, some of them are also disputing subordination of other services' arms (for instance, the air force has challenged the inclusion of long-range naval aviation in the navy, arguing that in the course of military reform it should be incorporated into the air force's strategic bomber command[30]); and at least two services are fighting against the others for their survival (Air Defense troops and Strategic Rocket Forces).

Following the creation of the Russian armed forces, the military leadership in Moscow was split between the old Soviet army nomenclature centered around the CIS High Command and the new Russian defense ministry led by second- and third-line generals promoted by the democratic rulers. Dissolution of the CIS High Command meant a defeat for the old-guard leaders and their views on Russia's military policy,[31] but below the top level the antagonisms still exist, as many of the old cadres can not be replaced immediately.

Though Grachev's claims that the army is controllable are apparently justified, it is equally true that he and his first civilian deputy Andrei Kokoshin do not enjoy a good reputation in the armed forces, especially among senior officers. There are also antagonisms between senior and middle/junior officers caused by huge differences in economic and social standards for each of the groups. Additionally, media reports suggest alienation and even hostility between officers and conscripts.[32]

Given all these splits, the army apparently has been finding it difficult for some time to keep itself together as a single institution and to demonstrate its unity to the outside world. It is unable to take any impressive and credible political move on its own or to put forward forcefully its political demands (which probably are difficult to formulate for the whole army).

The multiple splits defined the behavior of the defense minister and his top associates during the September 1993 events in Russia. They abstained from immediately expressing support to the president to whom they owe their promotions and nominations and later limited themselves to words, because anything more than that could have led to displaying the internal schisms of the armed forces and a loss of control by the central military authorities over their local subordinates. Indeed, early in the crisis, Pavel Grachev said (as quoted by UPI) that he feared that any attempt by the army to become involved in politics would break the military into rival camps and set the stage for civil war.

This is not to say that the armed forces at present have no leverage whatsoever to affect the behavior of the political leadership in Moscow. At the top level, there are strong personal connections, which have always mattered much in that country. Despite its internal division, the army is still a bulky institution that impresses political authorities with its sheer size and its potential for uncontrollable flare-ups. One may also argue that the armed forces may count on the support of the still-powerful Russian military-industrial complex, which is only partially successful in conversion and is desperately dependent on weapons orders from the military.

There is also a cluster of laws (the "Law on Defense" is probably the most important of them[33]) regulating civil-military relations in the country and providing the armed forces commanders a great degree of autonomy in defense matters. Though these laws also proclaim the principle of civilian control over the army, it remains to be seen whether this part of the legislation will be scrupulously honored.

PROSPECTS FOR THE FUTURE

The future role of the military in turbulent Russian politics cannot be defined with absolute certainty, of course. In this author's opinion, there are basically two alternatives, depending on further developments in Russia.

If there is no immediate and sharp turn to the world, it looks likely that in several years time the army will narrow or overcome at least some of its current internal divisions. The old military nomenclature will be gradually removed. Between 1995 and 2000 the armed forces will eventually be reorganized, and some intraservice rivalries will be eliminated. In the course of the reform the command structure will be changed; there will be three or four major commands on Russian territory (functionally similar to strategic direction commands created in the Soviet Union in the late 1970s). They will presumably be more easily controlled by Moscow than smaller military districts, which sometimes coincide territorially with regions seeking greater autonomy and are infected with "secession disease." Finally, by 1995 the share of professionals in the armed forces rose to nearly 30%, and by the turn of the century to 50%, bringing up the "team spirit" and integrity of the army.

But with its unity likely to be growing in the years to come, the army will also be developing into a more coherent and meaningful political force. This is well understood by the military themselves. *Voennaia Misl,* a monthly theoretical publication of the defense ministry, launched a discussion on the future political role of the army. That the armed forces should and will play such a role is not questioned whatsoever. "Armed Forces form a part of the society, they are an element of the state mechanism, and as such they can not stay out of politics," said an article recommended by the editorial board for "study and discussion" in the training and education system for officers, generals, and admirals.[34] It is the nature and scope of the military's political influence and ways to exercise it that are being debated, mostly behind closed doors.

To sum up, if the situation develops along the lines of relative stability, then the Russian military will take a place in the Russian hierarchy similar to that of their Soviet predecessors in the Soviet hierarchy. Perhaps, even more influential will be the degree of internal unity that the army eventually achieves, how successful new political leaders will be in tackling multiple domestic problems, and how much new Russian leaders will have to rely on the authority and support of the army in their political struggle with the opposition. If the political leadership needs military support, then the armed forces will be much better placed to demand and get more satisfactory solutions to their problems and to affect wider government policies both at home and abroad.

The second alternative will materialize if political, economic, and social conditions in Russia drastically deteriorate. Among other things, this deterioration will most likely result in further real cuts in the defense budget (or even in a de facto suspension of defense allocations) and an accelerating disintegration of the Russian state, with real authority moving from Moscow to the regions. In this situation (especially if it occurs in the next couple of years, before the army has a chance to consolidate its ranks), the armed forces will be hard pressed to stay a single, centrally controlled institution. There will be open splits between central military authorities in Moscow and at least some regional commanders. The latter will be faced with a stark choice between their oath of loyalty (which is not so unshakable, as indicated by recent events, when former Soviet officers took their second oath of allegiance in newly created national armies) and the need to survive for them and their subordinates. If material interests prevail, then local army commanders will start turning to regional authorities for support much more than they do now. On their part, regional leaders are likely to extend a helping hand both for reasons of prestige and with a view to using locally based troops to maintain stability in their region, defend it against attempts by the central authorities to reimpose control on the province, and possibly against similar armed formations in neighboring regions. It is anyone's guess what will happen to nuclear weapons, air defense and space troops, and the navy when they are highly centralized but spread throughout the country. The classic system of local warlords is unlikely to materialize in Russian conditions because the military seem to be averse to the idea of adding the multiple and stark new economic, social, political, legal, and other problems that would emerge in a devastated and decentralized country to their own.

The second option is less probable than the first one. Though Russia is still in the grip of severe crisis, there are signs that the decline is slowing. In some sectors of the economy low-level stability has finally been established. There are no indications that local authorities are more inclined to secede than they were a year or two ago (while the August coup resulted in the breakup of the Soviet Union, the September 1993 crisis did not bring about the dissolution of Russia). President Yeltsin managed to dispose of the powerful opposition to his policy in Parliament together with the Parliament and also gain reelection. A more homogeneous and stable political leadership may be expected as a result of future elections. In such conditions, option one is much more probable, leading to eventual consolidation of the armed forces and their stronger position among state institutions.

NOTES

1. General V. Serebriannikov, "Demilitarizatsiia obschestva" (Demilitarization of society), *Mirovaia economika i mezhdunarodniie otnosheniia*, no. 12 (December 1992): 35.

2. Colonel V. Rodachin, "Armiia i politicheskaiia vlast" (Army and the political power), *Voennaia misl*, no. 5 (May 1993): 13.

3. Two sets of arguments can be mentioned as an example. First, that the military were lavishly represented in the state legislature—the Supreme Soviet, as well as lower-level Soviets. The counterargument here is that all the Soviets were rather rubber-stamping bodies with no real influence on the political process.

Second, the post of defense minister was held exclusively by the military; defense ministers also used to sit in the highest decision-making body of the CPSU, the Polit-bureau. On the other hand, the armed forces were tightly controlled by a number of the Communist/state institutions over which the army had no control, including several KGB agencies (which pervaded the army); and the CPSU Central Committee, the chief political department of the armed forces (GlavPUR), had the status of a Central Committee's department.

4. *Krasnaia zvezda,* 6 March 1992.

5. *Krasnaia zvezda,* 1 April 1992.

6. "Prioritet-sotsialnim problemam" [Priority to social problems], interview with General V. Vorobiev, chief of the Central Finance Department, in *Krasnaia zvedza,* 30 June 1992.

7. *Krasnaia zvedza*, 22 May 1992.

8. *Krasnaia zvedza*, 1 September 1992.

9. *Krasnaia zvedza*, 8 July 1993.

10. *Krasnaia zvedza*, 21 January 1993.

11. *Krasnaia zvedza*, 19 August 1993.

12. Interview with the chairman of the Committee on Defense and Security Matters of the Russian Parliament, Sergei Stepashin, in *Nezavisimaia gazeta*, 2 July 1993.

13. *Krasnaia zvedza*, 10 June 1993.

14. See interview by Russian Air Force Commander in Chief Piotr Deinekin in the *WE* newspaper, (31 May–13 June, 1993), p. 1.

15. *Izvestiia*, 15 June 1993.

16. *Krasnaia zvedza*, 2 July 1993.

17. *Izvestiia*, 23 July 1993.

18. *Krasnaia zvedza*, 19 August 1992.

19. See interview with Piotr Deinekin in *Komsomolskaia pravda*, 17 March 1993.

20. *Krasnaia zvedza*, 30 July 1993.

21. *Nezavisimaia gazeta*, 23 February 1993.

22. See, for instance, John Erickson, "Fallen from Grace: The New Russian Military," *World Policy Journal* 10, no. 2 (Summer 1993): 22.

23. President Yeltsin's address to the meeting of top military commanders in *Krasnaia zvedza*, 8 June 1993.

24. Interview with Pavel Grachev in *Nezavisimaia gazeta*, 8 June 1993; see also Grachev's statement before the meeting of top military commanders, in *Krasnaia zvedza*, 8 June 1993.

25. Initial statements by Defense Minister Pavel Grachev spoke about the army staying neutral in the flare-up of conflict between the two branches of government (*New York Times*, 22 September 1993, p. A1, and 6 October 1993, p. A4). Support from the Defense Ministry and top military commanders came later. The main body of the army was neutral but tense: there were reports that the armed forces were resisting intense psychological pressure to support Parliament and that the army's allegiance was in doubt (*New York Times*, 24 September 1993, p. A7, and 6 October 1993, p. 4). Finally, unlike the situation in August 1991, the army was not massively out in the streets of Moscow and other major cities; and while security and interior forces (the Alpha antiterrorist commando unit and Dzerzhinski division) led to the takeover of the Parliament building, only a few small units from the elite army formations (Kantemir and Taman guard divisions and Tula airborne division) were used, mostly as a backup and fire support force. Apparently, to reward unambiguous loyalty demonstrated by militia and interior troops—as separate from the army—from the very start of the crisis, Boris Yeltsin signed a decree to increase the numerical strength of militia by forty-five thousand men and divert thirty-four thousand conscripts to serve with the militia. He also ruled that every year seventy thousand conscripts should be sent to interior troops, which would also receive higher financing. (*Krasnaia zvedza*, September 1993). This astounding move came at a time when the armed forces were severely understaffed and hard put to perform their duties.

26. General Vladimir Serebriannikov, "Armiia i putch" (The army and the coup), *Mirovaia economika i mezhdunarodniie otnosheniia*, no. 5 (May 1992): 64; Pavel Felgengauer, "Balans sil vokrug Kremlia" (Balance of forces around the Kremlin), *Segodnia*, 16 March 1993.

27. *Segodnia*, 2 March 1993; *Segodnia*, 16 March 1993.

28. *Nezavisimaia gazeta,* 3 March 1993.
29. *Moskoviskie novosti,* 14 March 1993.
30. *Voennaia misl,* special edition (July 1992): 69–72.
31. See *Moskoviskie novosti,* 25 July 1993.
32. *Izvestiia,* 23 March 1993.
33. Published in *Rossiiskaia gazeta,* 9 October 1992.
34. General V. Strekozov, "Konstitutsionnie osnovi Rossiiskoi federatsii: Mesto Vooruzhennikh sil v gosudarstve." (Constitutional framework for the Russian Federation: Armed forces' role in society), *Voennaia misl,* No. 3 (March 1993): 16.

REFERENCES

Barsukov, Igor. "Problemi perekhoda na novuiy sistemu visshego boennogo obrasova-niia" (Problems of introducing a new system of higher education). *Voennaia misl,* no. 7 (1993): 72–75.

Erickson, John. "Fallen from Grace: The New Russian Military." *World Policy Journal* 10, no. 2 (Summer 1993): 19–24.

Lepingwell, John. "Is the Military Disintegrating from Within?" *RFE/RL Research Report* 2, no. 25 (1993): 9–16.

———. "Restructuring the Russian Military." *RFE/RL Research Report* 2, no. 25 (1993): pp. 17–24.

Plotnikov, Jurii. "Gumanizatsia voennogo obrazovaniia: opit i problemi" (Humanitarization of military education: Experience and problems). *Voennaia misl,* no. 7 (1993): 76–80.

Rodachin, Vladislav. "Armiia i politischeskaia vlast" [Army and political power]. *Voennaia misl,* no. 5 (May 1993): 12–19.

Serebriannikov, Vladimir. "Dimilitarizatsiia obschestva" (Demilitarization of Society). *Mirovaia economika i mezhdunarodnie otnosheniia,* no. 12 (1992): 29–40.

———. "Armiia i putch" [The army and the coup]. *Miravaia economika i mezhdunarodnie otnosheniia,* no. 5 (May 1992): 56–71.

Shofield, Carey. *Inside the Soviet Military.* New York: Abbeville Press, 1991.

Strekozov, Vladimir. "Konstitutsionnie osnovi Rossiiskoi Federatsii: Mesto Vooruzhennikh Sil v gosudarstve." (Constitutional framework for the Russia Federation. Armed forces' role in society). *Voennaia misl,* no. 3 (March 1993): 11–19.

Wolf, Charles, and Steven Popper, eds. *Defense and the Soviet Economy: Military Muscle and Economic Weakness.* Santa Monica, Calif.: Rand Corporation, 1992.

UNITED KINGDOM

Diddy R. M. Hitchins and William A. Jacobs

On Guy Fawkes Day, 1688, the Prince of Orange dropped anchor in Torbay and began to disembark a small invasion force of no more than fifteen thousand men. James II, the English king whom the prince had come to depose, moved against the invader with an army almost twice as large. Within days, several hundred of his officers, including John Churchill (later the Duke of Marlborough), defected to the Dutchman, and the royal army rapidly fell apart. James ultimately fled the country to a safe haven in France, and the prince and his wife ascended the English throne as joint sovereigns in what we now recognize as a constitutional monarchy. These events laid a considerable part of the foundations of the modern British political system; they also constitute the last successful invasion of the British Isles and the last direct intervention of the military[1] intended to displace a government in British politics.

The absence of that kind of intervention is the most striking characteristic of civil-military relations in the United Kingdom, so striking that it serves as a prime example of civilian control of the military.[2] The tradition of civil supremacy is so well established that one writer has described the British military in a memorable phrase as "invincibly subordinate."[3] This tradition is all the more remarkable considering the long span of time over which it has been maintained. Almost every institution involved in relations between the armed forces, the government they serve, and the larger society has changed fundamentally—some several times—since the late seventeenth century. So stable has been the system of civil-military relations that, until the revival of mob action and terrorism in Northern Ireland in 1969, the academic literature on the subject was marked by what one writer has called a "deafening silence."[4]

The "Troubles" in Ulster display another important aspect of civil-military relations: the use of armed forces to repress civil disorder, a function known in Britain as Military Aid to the Civil Power (MACP). Magistrates called out the army on numerous occasions in the eighteenth and nineteenth centuries, but since the 1920s the government has employed the forces in this fashion on very few occasions in England, Scotland, and Wales. The British experience in Ireland has been entirely different. The army and special formations (the Black and Tans and the Auxis) fought a counter-guerrilla war there in 1919–21, and since 1969 the British army has been directly involved in the maintenance of order and an active campaign against the Provisional IRA (PIRA). Indeed, the political role of the army in Ireland has been so dissimilar from that in England, Scotland, and Wales in the last half of the twentieth century that one can say an "Irish differential" is a special feature of modern British civil-military relations.[5]

One final dimension of the subject is worthy of mention. In the twentieth century, the forces, chiefly the army, have been used to aid civil ministries in the maintenance of vital services during industrial disputes and to aid the civilian community when catastrophe strikes.[6]

CIVILIAN SUPREMACY AND MILITARY NONINTERVENTION

The foundation of civilian supremacy over the armed forces is parliamentary sovereignty, the doctrine that Parliament is the supreme power in the state.[7] The men who made the misnamed "revolution" of 1688 were determined above all that the army should not be an instrument of royal tyranny. They were equally resolute that the army should not fall into the hands of an alliance of revolutionary politicians and soldiers. They wished, in short, to avoid the twin terrors of James Stuart and Oliver Cromwell.

The revolutionary settlement provided for a sharing of effective power between Parliament and the Crown. Among other things, the monarch retained the right to conduct foreign affairs, to commission officers, and to command the armed forces. However, after the passage of no more than three generations, these powers had declined from the substantial to the nominal. The King's ministers possessed of a majority in Parliament were the effective power in the state. No other institution, certainly not the courts,[8] possessed the power to invalidate an act of Parliament. As a great constitutional authority once put it, "It is a fundamental principle with English lawyers, that Parliament can do everything but make a woman a man and a man a woman."[9]

The most visible change made in the constitution by the Glorious Revolution was the abolition of the Crown's prerogative power to maintain a standing army in peacetime.[10] From the first Mutiny Act of 1689 to the Army Act of 1955 the very existence of armed forces in the United Kingdom depended on an annual parliamentary statute. Since 1955, Parliament authorizes the forces for a maximum life of five years, subject to an annual confirmation by resolution of an Order in Council.[11]

Beyond placing the armed forces on a statutory rather than prerogative foundation, the revolutionary settlement gave Parliament control over the financial resources of the state. This had the double effect of greatly increasing the money available to fight wars approved by the interests represented in Parliament while virtually eliminating the ability of the Crown to maintain armed men on its own income.[12]

One sometimes hears that the revolutionary settlement was hostile to a standing army. The truth of the matter is that the revolution was hostile to a large standing army maintained in Britain in peacetime. Because Britain is composed of islands, no enemy could threaten significant destruction, certainly not invasion and occupation of territory, at the outset of war before the development of the long-range bomber in the twentieth century. This allowed governments to bring armies into being to fight foreign wars, then to disband them or, rather, to reduce them to small establishments, many of which were based overseas. As Michael Howard puts it, "The vital issue of who was to control the armed forces could be solved in England by a decision to have virtually no armed forces at all— certainly none that might be used by the Crown to secure its authority."[13] In this connection, it is well to remember that the government of the 1770s sought to suppress rebellion in North America, the richest and most important part of its empire, by hiring German mercenaries.

In the twentieth century several attempts were made to change this system, only a few of which have succeeded and endured. Twice in this century, Britain has fought prolonged, total war. Once, its very existence as an independent state was at stake. This required the raising of mass armies by conscription, an expedient which was continued in peacetime after World War II as a way of meeting the many commitments of Britain's far-flung empire. In 1957, Britain abandoned the national-service armed forces, thereby reverting to the model of small volunteer professional forces.

The return to the older system did not bring with it a reversion to earlier levels of expenditure. Britain managed to maintain great power status in the nineteenth century by spending no more than 2%–3% of the national income on its army and navy.[14] In the last quarter of the twentieth century, despite having fallen to the status of a "middle power," the British government was obliged by a combination of high unit costs, the maintenance of a nuclear weapons force, and conventional commitments to the Cold War NATO alliance to lay out the better part of 5% of GNP.[15]

The British armed forces receive their orders from the duly constituted civil government of the day—the ministers of the Crown, drawn from Parliament (chiefly the Commons), formed into a cabinet, and advised by a permanent civil service. The government's source of power is a working majority in the House of Commons. The prime minister, the cabinet, the cabinet committees, and the senior civil servants, with their staffs, are the real power in the modern state, not Parliament as a whole. They receive input from the military leadership at the highest levels of the Ministry of Defence through a system of integrated committees containing both civil servants and serving officers.[16]

From the perspective of efficiency, this is a vast improvement over what one authority has described as the "Gothic eccentricity" of the administration of military affairs in the eighteenth and early nineteenth centuries.[17] While the navy was administered by a relatively rational and centralized system from the Restoration forward, the army was controlled by a hodgepodge of departments and agencies. After Waterloo, no fewer than thirteen ill-coordinated departments administered the affairs of the army.[18]

From the aftermath of the Crimean War to the present day, British governments have sought to change the organization and administration of the armed forces to make them more efficient and more effective in battle.[19] They have also aimed to integrate more closely the leadership of the army and the civil government to assure better strategic decision-making and to provide for secure political direction. In the nineteenth and early twentieth centuries, governments focused on the internal organization of the separate services, chiefly the army. Before World War I and then again during the interwar period, governments emphasized the development of coordination between the cabinet and the heads of the services. However successful these measures were at the top, the experience of World War II showed that the services had much to learn about fighting together.[20]

A single Ministry of Defence was created shortly after the war, and successive governments have struggled to enlarge its powers at the expense of the separate service ministries. This has been done in the name of economy and of fighting effectiveness. The fiscal pressures on the military establishment have been relentless. The mediocre performance of the British economy and the never-ending upward movement in unit costs have forced governments to shrink the forces, even while maintaining the highest level of military expenditure (as a percentage of GDP) in the NATO alliance after that of the United States. Some of the most notable public controversies and parliamentary debates have occurred over proposals to reduce or strike regiments from the army order of battle and to cut down the size of the fleet.[21]

Under the system as it exists at the beginning of the 1990s, the prime minister, the cabinet, the Cabinet Committee on Defence and Overseas Policy, the minister of defence, the chief of the defence staff, the Chiefs of Staff Committee, and the Treasury negotiate, compromise among themselves, and finally determine defense policy. The prime minister does not have the power to make decisions unilaterally; he or she must consult with the cabinet and the party leadership. The unity of the executive and a parliamentary majority gives the government the ability to restrain public discussion of policy until it is ready to be presented to Parliament for passage. Contentious issues can often be settled behind the scenes, because of the combination of a compliant establishment press, a draconian official secrets law, the discipline of the civil service, and the relative weakness of the military service lobbies.[22] Unlike the scene in Washington, where the armed forces are organized as lobbies with virtually independent access to members of Congress (the U.S. Marine Corps is particularly notable in this respect), lobbying by the service chiefs is regarded as a "breach of constitutional usage."[23] The military lobbies do have considerable negative power; that is, they can mobilize parliamentary and public opinion to delay or to prevent some policies, particularly those having to do with the organization and traditions of the services. No government, for example, could expect to eliminate the separate services in favor of a completely integrated force on the Canadian model.[24] This negative power assures that governments have to consult the senior military leadership, even if they do not take their advice in the end.

To have positive influence, the military must present their views to the inner circle of decision-makers through the established service channels within the Ministry of Defence. The politicians set the agenda for discussion of policy; they ask the service leaders for comments and observations on proposals, ideas, and scenarios. The government wishes to maintain efficient military forces with high morale, albeit at the lowest possible cost, and it generally does not ignore the professional interests of the military, if the money can be found.[25]

Apart from debating the defense budget, the impact of Parliament as a whole on defense policy is slight. Given the fact that defense has consistently absorbed 5% of the national income, one might have expected a fairly high level of parliamentary interest. This has not been the case, except in times of major reorganizations, problems caused by the running sore in Northern Ireland, the actual hostilities of the Falklands and the Gulf Wars, and the occasional scandal like the Westland Affair. On the whole, Parliament does not exercise close scrutiny over defense policy, certainly not to the standard of inquisitiveness one finds on Capitol Hill in Washington. This allows the government remarkable freedom and autonomy in major policy decisions.[26]

Parliament also reflects the public's view of defense. It has not been a major election issue in recent years. Public attitudes of indifference, apathy, or pro-tracted acquiescence accompany Parliament's willingness to follow the lead pro-vided by the cabinet. The civilian executive possesses the initiative and sounds out what the public will support. Those few interest groups that wish to influence defense policy—the service and veterans' organizations, manufacturing inter-ests, and members of the attentive public—understand that the most effective contacts are to be found in the civil service and elite decision-makers in the government of the day, not in Parliament. Parliamentary opinion is important in the sense that the government of the day depends on it (especially if it has only a small majority), but Parliament's formal attention to questions of defense is modest at best.[27] The relative passivity of Parliament in defense matters, with some exceptions like regimental reductions, is typical, not unique. Not even the new system of select committees, whose terms of reference are closely aligned with the departments they are to watch, has done much to change this. As a recent authority puts it, "The problem is that select committees at present can hold government accountable only if government wishes to be held account-able."[28]

Apart from parliamentary sovereignty, there is one important legal principle underlying civilian supremacy. British law has never recognized what we might call a separate military caste. The soldier, upon entering the Crown's service, becomes subject to military law; but in so doing he does not lose his standing as a citizen. He is a citizen in uniform possessed of lethal weapons and subject to a special law code, but no part of his duties as a citizen under common law and statute is abandoned.[29]

However important the law and formal institutional arrangements are to the maintenance of civilian authority over the armed forces, they are not the whole cause of this eminently desirable result. As Finer has argued, we should be surprised that armed men do not interfere or intervene in politics more often than they do.[30] With some exceptions, the British armed forces have been relatively immune from the temptation to intervene.

Some part of this indisposition is owing to the special relationship between the Crown and the armed forces. The lengthy discussion of parliamentary sovereignty should not obscure the important truth that, however diminished the real powers of the Crown, the armed forces still identify themselves with the monarch. All soldiers take an oath of allegiance to the Crown, and all officers receive their commissions from the monarch. They see themselves as the Queen's men and women, and both the monarch and the armed forces go to great lengths to assure that these links are maintained and nurtured by elaborate ceremony. This has allowed the military to think of itself as representing or serving the nation rather than the party that dominates the government of the day. To those knowledgeable of the history of France or Germany, this notion is not without its dangers. After all, it is precisely those circumstances where soldiers combine an alienation from contemporary political life with the belief that they alone are above the tawdry business of material calculation and private interest that encourage direct military intervention in politics.[31] In Britain, it has probably served as something of a safety valve, allowing soldiers to obey the government of the day while thinking themselves to be, in some idealistic sense, independent from it.[32]

A considerable portion of the long-standing indisposition to intervene was historically rooted in the unity of interest between those who sat in Parliament and occupied seats in the cabinet and those who ran the army. For the men who made the Glorious Revolution, it was not enough merely to assure that Parliament was sovereign. After all, it was the assertion of parliamentary sovereignty that had brought the New Model Army into being, and that army had spawned revolutionary Leveller officers like Colonel Rainborough and led to government at the gentle hands of Oliver Cromwell and the Major-Generals. The men of 1688 sought to make triply sure of their object. Not only would Parliament be supreme in the state, but the "natural rulers" of society, men of property, would rule both Parliament and the army.[33]

Apart from parliamentary sovereignty and "gothically eccentric" administration, the device chosen for this purpose was the purchase system. Under it, officers in the infantry and cavalry had to buy their commissions and their promotions. That this led to scandal and inefficiency was tolerable in a country unlikely to be invaded. Indeed there were those who thought it positively virtuous. Lord Palmerston thought it kept the army out of the hands of "unprincipled adventurers."[34] To the contrary, the system was intended to keep the army free from men with certain kinds of principles. As a nineteenth-century authority put it, purchase assured that "officers were drawn from that social class more likely to lose than to gain by Military Aggression [meaning intervention]."[35] We need not be impressed by these arguments to recognize that the revolutionary settlement and the purchase system probably helped to prevent the development of a separate military caste in British society. After the disasters of the Crimea,[36] amid a general climate of reform, purchase was finally abolished in the Cardwell Reforms of 1871.[37]

The most dangerous period in the history of the relations between the civilian government and the leadership of the army occurred between 1913 and 1926. A number of regime-changing forces were at work. Before World War I, the franchise had been broadened in 1884 to include all adult males, and powerful extraparliamentary forces in the form of the trade unions began to appear. The Liberal Party, which held power on its own until 1916, abandoned its conservative Whiggish principles under the leadership of men like Lloyd George and moved, among other things, to grant Home Rule to Ireland. Home Rule was not wanted in Northern Ireland; indeed, powerful movements there threatened to resist it by force with the encouragement of the Unionist (Conservative) opposition in Parliament. Elements in the senior army leadership were close to the opposition and were sympathetic to the Ulster resistance; and in the spring of 1914, some officers in Ireland, faced with the hypothetical choice of marching North or resigning their commissions, chose the latter. In the end the government did not use troops against Ulster and suspended Home Rule. Strictly speaking, this affair, known as the Curragh Incident, did not amount to a mutiny as no direct orders were disobeyed and there were other good reasons for suspending Home Rule. It is equally plain that some officers, chief among them Sir Henry Wilson, rejoiced at having coerced the government. The interpretation of this event remains contentious.[38]

This highly unsettling affair was followed by the several crises of World War I. Briefly put, the combination of the overthrow of the Liberal government in the middle of the war by a coalition of Liberals and Conservatives led by Lloyd George, and the lack of success (or simple bloody failure) of the major military operations on the Western Front led to the breakdown of mutual confidence between government and military command. The senior officers did not trust Lloyd George, and he in turn doubted their competence to carry out their own plans. The prime minister even came to believe that a conspiracy was hatched to create a military dictatorship on the Hindenburg-Ludendorff model. This was probably not true, but the fact that the head of government could fear such a thing from his senior officers indicates how badly things had deteriorated.[39]

Relations went from bad to worse at the end of the war. Fears of Bolshevism, the social disruption arising from unemployment, strikes, especially police strikes, and the guerrilla war in Ireland led some to believe that parliamentary government was on the verge of collapse. The chief of the Imperial General Staff, Sir Henry Wilson, was fancied by some as a saving military dictator or at least an aggressive new Conservative dedicated to restoring "real government" in Britain and imperial authority overseas, especially in Ireland. Some evidence of the quality of Wilson's judgment can be found in the rhetorical question posed in his diary, "Is Lloyd George a traitor?"[40] Whatever Wilson's fears and ambitions may have been, they came to an end at the hands of Irish assassins in 1922.[41]

Since the great General Strike of 1926, which was a tame affair by European standards, no similar dangers have arisen. Britain came very close to catastrophic defeat early in World War II, but the much improved machinery of coordination between the civil government and the armed forces and the unusual leadership of Winston Churchill prevented the breakdown of mutual confidence that was so marked a feature of the World War I experience. To be sure there was much pulling and hauling, sometimes pressed almost to the point of resignations, but the system worked.[42] After the war, the Labour government, which embarked on a program of social and economic transformation while abandoning substantial parts of the Empire, experienced no crisis in civil-military relations, partly because it was led by men who had served in Churchill's wartime government. Unlike the French experience, the wholesale loss of empire and the fall into the ranks of the "middle powers" did not produce military intervention.

There were rumors of coup-plotting in the mid-1970s during the second Labour government of Harold Wilson. After he left office, Mr. Wilson voiced suspicions that he had been spied upon by his own security service.[43] These rumors may have been founded on nothing more than clubroom grumbling and journalistic speculation, but the fact that they existed at all demonstrated the extent to which thoughtful persons were worried about the visible decay in British social and economic life, the incessant industrial disorders, and the use of extraparliamentary power by the Miners' Union to bring down the Heath government. As Adam Roberts has written, "The talk of a coup was interesting not because it was even remotely realistic, but only because in a sotto voce way it marked the end of a very long period in which the question had never been raised at all."[44]

Since World War II, the government has sought to broaden the social basis of the officer class with some success. It is true that the close relationships among the top civil servants, especially in the Treasury, the Cabinet Office, and ranking military officers, based on the public-schools network, continues to exist. The most visible survival of the old class-based officer selection system are the Guards regiments of the Household Division.[45] Each service remains a somewhat closed society, especially in the regimental life of the army, but this has been gradually eroded by interservice and allied training and organization. The demands of modern technical education have helped to undermine some of this class identity as well. One major authority doubts that the contemporary armed forces have a class basis that can be activated for political purposes.[46] This reinforces civilian supremacy and reduces the likelihood of intervention.

MILITARY ASSISTANCE TO THE CIVIL POWER

The first duty of the armed forces is to fight the external enemies of the state; the second is to resist the use of force inside the state when called upon by the civilian authorities. Britain has possessed a variety of police forces (mostly unarmed) since the early part of the nineteenth century; while it has occasionally resorted to the use of temporary auxiliary forces to deal with emergencies, it has never created an armed paramilitary police on the model of C.R.S. in France or the Bundesgrenzpolizei in Germany. Therefore, all grave threats to order beyond the capacity of a largely unarmed police force fall to the army. This is a "disagreeable and painful" duty much disliked by contemporary soldiers and governments alike.[47]

The reluctance of the army notwithstanding, some elements of domestic security are an inescapable responsibility of the military forces. Defense of the state includes the maintenance of public order and the suppression of violent unrest, insurrection, or revolution. Fortunately, in England, Scotland, and Wales the government has very rarely ordered operations in aid of the civil power since the 1920s. In these parts of the United Kingdom, the maintenance of order has required little overt force; public life in the twentieth century has been relatively orderly (by comparison with the riotous eighteenth and nineteenth centuries) and the police have been skillfully employed.[48]

If the army is no longer often called out in Britain to suppress mobs, it is important to note the variety of other "interventions" that have become part of "normal" practice in England. The Special Air Service (SAS), who are apparently not disposed to take prisoners, have been used on a number of occasions against terrorists. The army's specialized bomb disposal units are also much occupied. As far as unarmed employment of the forces is concerned, the services have been employed to replace strikers under emergency powers statutes at least thirty times since the end of World War II, twelve of them since 1970. In a further fifteen cases since 1970, troops were "standing by" but were never employed. The incidence of this use of military personnel seems to be rising.[49]

Northern Ireland has been the area of the United Kingdom in which the very legitimacy of the provincial administration and the Westminster government has not been accepted by a significant portion of the population. Since 1969 the UK government has been faced with two problems requiring the use of the army: the maintenance of public order in a region cursed by sectarian hatreds and armed resistance to the gunmen and bombers of the Provisional IRA. The army was first brought in to separate the mobs when the Northern Irish police broke down and were entirely unable to cope with sectarian violence. In a short period of time, the "neutral" position of the army was badly compromised by excesses like Bloody Sunday (1972) and the imposition of internment without trial. Since the mid-1970s, the British government has gradually adopted a policy of "Ulsterisation" under which the army has been gradually withdrawn from policing duties in favor of a reformed and reorganized police force. At the same time, it has settled into a long-term pattern of resistance to the IRA that combines the use of the army and police to gather intelligence and to control the movement of persons while employing more discriminating (and highly controversial) violence in the form of highly specialized ambush units like the SAS. While the size of the army force in Northern Ireland is much smaller than it was in the early 1970s, almost every soldier will do service in the province sometime in his career.[50]

The legal foundations of military aid to the civil power are varied and collectively vague.[51] They begin with the common-law obligation of all subjects (citizens) to maintain the peace. As noted earlier, men and women who enter the armed forces do not thereby shed any of their common-law obligations. Standing by itself, this principle would seem to indicate that soldiers are under a presumptive obligation to use force against force with or without the orders of the civilian authorities.

No one in the British military interprets the law this way for one very good reason: the law also holds everyone responsible for their actions, even when engaged in the civically virtuous business of maintaining the peace. Soldiers are not eager to use lethal weapons when they know they can be tried for manslaughter or murder if the courts determine, after the fact, that they used excessive force.

In short, British soldiers are bound by common law and by their oaths to obey the orders of duly-constituted authority to suppress violent disorder. They can be held accountable if they do not use enough force to restore order; they can be charged if they use too much. Since the early nineteenth century the courts have held that soldiers are "bound to hit the exact line between excess and failure of duty."[52] It is not difficult to see why soldiers have for more than a century demanded much greater clarification and definition of their duties and their discretion in this role.[53] Nor is it hard to understand why few situations are more productive of a want of mutual confidence than aid to the civil power operations. The civil authorities want it done exactly right and quickly, fearing the military as a blunt instrument; the military, on the other hand, often suspect that the vagueness in the law is deliberate. It is there, as Sir Charles Napier once put it, because "it has been convenient for ministers to leave things undefined, so that if circumstances demand it, they may cover themselves by sacrificing the officer."[54]

Something labelled "martial law" was used at various times in the empire in the nineteenth and twentieth centuries and in Ireland during the guerrilla war of 1919–21. The difficulty is that Britain does not have a codified "state of siege" or even a clear set of general legal principles setting out what martial law means. Many authorities have held that the actions of soldiers under a proclamation of martial law may be justiciable. Where martial law has been employed in the past, the government has often accompanied it with acts of indemnity designed to foreclose proceedings against responsible officers.[55]

So unsatisfactory has this situation been that twentieth-century governments have resorted to statute to create something standing between the vagueness of the common law and the undesirable absolutism of a law of siege. Prompted by the requirements of total war, crises in Ireland, and the proper desire to anticipate catastrophe, Parliament has passed Defence of the Realm acts and a variety of Emergency Powers statutes. The operations of the army in Northern Ireland come under the authority of the Northern Ireland (Emergency Provisions) acts of 1973, 1978, and 1987.[56] While these have helped to clarify matters somewhat, many soldiers still think themselves placed in a very difficult position when summoned to aid the civil power.[57]

CONCLUSIONS

When one considers the powerful strains produced by industrialization, urbanization, the business cycle, the dislocations of total war and its aftermath, the democratization of the electoral processes, the growth of mass extraparliamentary forces, political fortunes and misfortunes, the gaining and losing of two empires, the stresses of policing and counterterrorism in Ireland, and the fundamental changes in the armed forces themselves, Britain's long experience of nonintervention and, outside of Ireland, its relatively modest use of the armed forces against popular disorder seem still more remarkable.

Britain seems to have solved what Michael Howard has called a "double problem . . . the subordination of military force to the political government, and of the control of the government in possession of such force by legal restraint and the popular will."[58] This solution is embodied in a combination of parliamentary supremacy (or rather, cabinet supremacy within Parliament), administrative integration (not military unification), and a professional military without a professional military caste. Most importantly, these things have existed for a very long time. They are now woven in the basic fabric of the professional identity of officers, and it is most unlikely that they will come undone.

Still, there are worrisome problems. As Huntington has argued, civil-military relations are, for the most part, derivative. That is, they are a function of the larger political environment. Economic decline, ethnic conflict, the visible decay of public life, the enduring problem of Irish terrorism—all these things could coarsen and poison politics and create opportunities and motives for military intervention.

These things might occur in combination with a reordering of the security priorities of the country so fundamental that it threatens the professional status and existence of the armed forces. In the post-1945 period, Britain lost an empire, but gained an alliance. Moreover, she gained nuclear weapons. The alliance commitments in the Atlantic and on the Elbe River helped to maintain the British armed forces at a fairly high level. If one accepts the principle that alliances are made by their enemies, then it follows that they can be unmade by the disappearance of their adversaries. NATO appears to be a declining asset, and the British army in Germany may not be long for this world. And, the new generation of nuclear weapons platforms (Trident) may simply be too expensive for the United Kingdom. By the turn of the century or sooner, Britain's nuclear force could be obsolete and its conventional forces so reduced in strength and capability that the country could no longer project power. UN roles, such as the guarding of food convoys in Bosnia, will be a poor substitute.

It is likely that the army will be operating in Ireland for some time. One has to worry about the impact on morale and professional values of a service dominated by policing and counterterrorist operations in a political environment where the best one can hope for is to prevent the other side from winning. A long experience of covert operations involving ambush and, some would say, assassination, for which there is little accountability, will do little good for the British army or political life in general.

On balance, the odds are good that Britain will continue the system of civil-military relations that it has enjoyed so long well into the next century. Nothing lasts forever in politics, but the very age of the British system gives to it a legitimacy inferior to none in the developed world. Officers who might seek to supplant or displace the civil government would have to shift the burden of more than three centuries of tradition. Only genuine revolutionaries could do that, and the British army is unlikely to produce another Oliver Cromwell. It would take some great crisis of legitimacy in the regime to produce any great change in the behavior of the military. For some societies, history may weigh, as Marx once wrote, "like a nightmare upon the brain of the living." That may be true of Britain in Ireland but, elsewhere in the country, history is one of the chief supports of a stable regime of civil-military relations and, therefore, of a civilized politics.

NOTES

1. Some clarification of terms is in order here. We use the term "military" in the American sense, that is, we mean by it any one or all of the armed services.

2. S. E. Finer includes Britain among his examples of states with a "mature political culture," in his *The Man on Horseback: The Role of the Military in Politics,* 2d ed. (London: Penguin, 1975), p. 79. In those states, "the intervention of the military would be regarded as a wholly unwarrantable intrusion," and "public sanction" for that kind of behavior "would be unobtainable."

3. J. Sabine, "Civil-Military Relations," in J. Baylis, ed., *British Defence Policy in a Changing World* (London: Croom Helm, 1977), p. 230.

4. Adam Roberts, "The British Armed Forces and Politics: A Historical Perspective," *Armed Forces and Society* 3, no. 4 (August 1977): 531–32.

5. See three works by C. Townshend: *The British Campaign in Ireland 1919–1921: The Development of Political and Military Policies* (London: Oxford University Press, 1976); *Britain's Civil War: Counterinsurgency in the Twentieth Century* (London: Faber

and Faber, 1982); and "Martial Law: Legal and Administrative Problems of Civil Emergency in Britain and the Empire, 1800–1940," *Historical Journal* 25 (1982).

6. M. Midlane, "Military Aid to the Civil Authorities," in John Sweetman, ed., *Sword and Mace: Twentieth Century Civil-Military Relations in Britain* (London: Brassey's Defence Publishers, 1986).

7. In this connection, constitutional scholars, especially the traditional authorities, point out that the term "Parliament" actually means the "King in Parliament." See A. V. Dicey, *Introduction to the Study of the Law of the Constitution,* 9th ed. (London: Macmillan, 1956), p. 39.

8. Only recently has the "constitution" changed to allow a limited species of judicial review. Upon Britain's entry into the European Community, British courts may hold that an act of Parliament is at variance with an article of the Treaty of Rome or a directive of the European Commission. Ian Budge and David McKay, *The Changing British Political System: Into the 1990s,* 2d ed. (London: Longman, 1988), pp. 158–59.

9. Dicey, *Introduction,* p. 43, quoting De Lolme.

10. David Lindsay Keir, *The Constitutional History of Modern Britain,* 8th ed. (New York: Norton, 1966), p. 268.

11. Geoffrey J. Bennett and Christopher L. Ryan, "Armed Forces, Public Disorder, and the Law in the United Kingdom," in Peter J. Rowe and Christopher J. Whelan, eds., *Military Intervention in Democratic Societies* (London: Croom Helm, 1985), pp. 184–86.

12. Keir, *Constitutional History,* pp. 274–77.

13. Michael Howard, ed., *Soldiers and Governments: Nine Studies in Civil-Military Relations* (Westport, Conn.: Greenwood Press, 1978), p. 14.

14. Aaron L. Friedberg, *The Weary Titan: Britain and the Experience of Relative Decline 1895–1905* (Princeton: Princeton University Press, 1988), p. 145.

15. Franklyn A. Johnson, *Defence by Ministry: The British Ministry of Defence, 1944–74* (New York: Holmes and Meier, 1980), p. 36.

16. A good introduction to the system as it exists today is Martin Edmonds, "Central Organizations of Defense in Great Britain," in his *Central Organizations of Defense* (Boulder, Colo.: Westview, 1985).

17. Keir, *Constitutional History,* p. 301.

18. Roberts, "British Armed Forces," p. 538.

19. Ibid., pp. 537–39.

20. A good survey of the history of the development of the machinery at the top is John Sweetman, "A Process of Evolution: Command and Control in Peacetime," in Sweetman, ed., *Sword and Mace.*

21. Apart from the works by Edmonds, Sweetman, and Johnson cited above, see Sir Ewen Broadbent, *The Military and Government: From Macmillan to Heseltine* (New York: St. Martin's, 1988).

22. See the overview in Johnson, *Defence by Ministry,* chapter 1.

23. Finer, *Man on Horseback,* p. 131.

24. Edmonds, "Central Organizations," pp. 102–3.

25. Sabine, "Civil-Military Relations," p. 235.

26. Edmonds, "Central Organizations," pp. 103–4.

27. David Capitanchik, "Public Opinion and Popular Attitudes towards Defence," in Baylis, ed., *British Defence Policy,* 1977.

28. Budge and McKay, *Changing British Political System,* p. 54.

29. Dicey, *Introduction,* pp. 300–2.

30. Finer, *Man on Horseback,* pp. 4–5.

31. Ibid., pp. 22–23.

32. Roberts, "British Armed Forces," pp. 541–42; Sabine, "Civil-Military Relations," p. 245.

33. Christopher Hill, *The Century of Revolution, 1603–1714* (London: Nelson, 1961), chapter 18.

34. Roberts, "British Armed Forces," p. 539.

35. C. M. Clode, *The Military Forces of the Crown,* vol. 2 (London: n.p., 1869), p. 62.

36. There is a vivid portrait of aristocratic officer incompetence in Cecil Woodham-Smith, *The Reason Why* (New York: Time, 1953).

37. Sabine, "Civil-Military Relations," p. 244. Purchase was never applied to the arms requiring technical expertise—the artillery and the engineers—or to the Indian Army, where amateurs were more dangerous.

38. For a variety of views on this affair, consult Sir James Fergusson, *The Curragh Incident* (London: Faber & Faber, 1964); Robert Blake, "Great Britain," in Howard, ed., *Soldiers and Governments,* pp. 36–38; John Sweetman, "Historical Perspective: From Waterloo to the Curragh," in his *Sword and Mace,* pp. 13–17; C. Townshend, *Political Violence in Ireland* (New York: Clarendon, 1983), pp. 268–73; Townshend, "Military Force and Civil Authority in the United Kingdom, 1914–21," *Journal of British Studies* 28; no. 3, (1951): 268–77; and Roberts, "British Armed Forces," 540–41.

39. Blake, "Great Britain," pp. 39–48.

40. Christopher Andrew, *Secret Service: The Making of the British Intelligence Community* (London: Sceptre, 1986), p. 383.

41. See Bernard Ash, *The Lost Dictator* (London: Cassell, 1968).

42. Maxwell P. Schoenfeld, *The War Ministry of Winston Churchill* (Ames: Iowa State University Press, 1972). For an account that emphasizes Churchill's "imperious and delinquent genius," see Alex Danchev, "The Central Direction of War, 1940–41," in Sweetman, *Sword and Mace.*

43. Andrew, *Secret Service,* pp. 699–700.

44. Roberts, "British Armed Forces," pp. 547–48.

45. Anthony Sampson, *The Changing Anatomy of Britain* (New York: Vintage, 1984), pp. 253–54.

46. Johnson, *Defence by Ministry,* pp. 5–6.

47. Keith Jeffrey, "Military Aid to the Civil Power in the United Kingdom: An Historical Perspective," in Rowe and Whelan, *Military Intervention,* p. 53.

48. Ibid., pp. 51–52.

49. Christopher J. Whelan, "Armed Forces, Industrial Disputes and the Law in Great Britain," in Rowe and Whelan, *Military Intervention,* pp. 111–13.

50. For overviews, refer to Paul Arthur and Keith Jeffrey, *Northern Ireland since 1968* (London: Blackwell, 1988), chapter 6; and Anne Mandeville, "The British Army in Northern Ireland, 1969–85: New Professionalism," in Martin Edmonds, ed., *The Defence Equation: British Military Systems, Policy, Planning, and Performance* (Boulder: Westview Press, 1985). See also Townshend, *Political Violence in Ireland,* chapter 8.

51. The best introduction to this subject from the legal angle is Bennett and Ryan "Armed Forces, Public Disorder, and the Law." See also Peter J. Rowe, "Keeping the

Peace: Lethal Weapons, the Soldier, and the Law," in Rowe and Whelan, eds., *Military Intervention.*

52. Townshend, "Martial Law: Legal and Administrative Problems," p. 171.

53. For a contemporary soldier's articulate complaints, see Robin Eveleigh, *Peacekeeping in a Democratic Society* (London: Hurst, 1978).

54. Quoted in Townshend, "Martial Law: Legal and Administrative Problems," n. 108.

55. For a survey of the problems, see ibid., as well as Bennett and Ryan, "Armed Forces, Public Disorder, and the Law."

56. For an overview of security policies in Northern Ireland, consult Paul Arthur and Keith Jeffrey, *Northern Ireland since 1968* (London: Blackwell, 1988), chapter 6.

57. On this see Eveleigh, *Peacekeeping.*

58. Howard, *Soldiers and Governments,* p. 12.

REFERENCES

Bennett, Geoffrey J., and Christopher L. Ryan. "Armed Forces, Public Disorder, and the Law in the United Kingdom." In Peter J. Rowe and Christoper J. Whalen, eds., *Military Intervention in Democratic Societies.* London: Croom Helm, 1985.

Broadbent, Ewen. *The Military and Government: From Macmillan to Heseltine.* London: RUSI and Macmillan, 1988.

Dicey, A. V. *Introduction to the Study of the Law of the Constitution,* 9th ed. London: Macmillan, 1956.

Edmonds, Martin. "Central Organizations of Defense in Great Britain." In Martin Edmonds, ed., *Central Organizations of Defense.* Boulder, Colo.: Westview Press, 1985.

Finer, S. E. *The Man on Horseback: The Role of the Military in Politics.* London: Penguin, 1976.

Howard, Michael, ed. *Soldiers and Governments: Nine Studies in Civil-Military Relations.* Westport, Conn.: Greenwood Press, 1957.

Jeffrey, Keith. "Military Aid to the Civil Power in the United Kingdom: An Historical Perspective." In Peter J. Rowe and Christopher J. Whelan, eds., *Military Intervention in Democratic Societies.* London: Croom Helm, 1985.

Midlane, Matthew. "Military Aid to the Civil Authorities." In John Sweetman, ed., *Sword and Mace: Twentieth Century Civil-Military Relations in Britain.* London: Croom Helm, 1985.

Roberts, Adam. "The British Armed Forces and Politics: A Historical Perspective." *Armed Forces and Society* 3, no. 4 (1977): 531.

Rowe, Peter J. "Keeping the Peace: Lethal Weapons, the Soldier and the Law." In Peter J. Rowe and Christopher J. Whelan, *Military Intervention in Democratic Societies.* London: Croom Helm, 1985.

Sabine, John. "Civil-Military Relations." In John Baylis, ed., *British Defense Policy in a Changing World.* London: Croom Helm, 1977.

Sweetman, John. "A Process of Evolution: Command and Control in Peacetime." In John Sweetman, ed., *Sword and Mace: Twentieth Century Civil-Military Relations in Britain.* London: Brassey's Defence Publishers, 1986.

Townshend, C. "Martial Law: Legal and Administrative Problems of Civil Emergency in Britain and the Empire, 1800–1940." *Historical Journal* 25 (1982).

———. "Military Force and Civil Authority in the UK, 1914–1921." *Journal of British Studies* 28, no. 3 (1989): 262.

UNITED STATES

Stephen J. Cimbala

The issue of military legal and political subordination to duly-constituted civil political authority has long been a decided issue in American politics.[1] Nevertheless, the Cold War presented to U.S. policymakers and military planners some unexpected and unprecedented challenges.[2] The Cold War U.S. military was qualitatively as well as quantitatively different from its predecessor.[3] The following discussion identifies some of the most important attributes of the Cold War U.S. armed forces and their political setting in terms of their implications for civil-military relations.[4] These attributes are bipolarity and U.S.–Soviet hostility; nuclear weapons and mutual deterrence; defense reorganization and developments in command-control technology; the experience of Vietnam and other cases of low-intensity conflict; and, finally, the development of an all-volunteer armed force. Some comments will also anticipate the future international environment and its implications for civil-military relations.

BIPOLARITY AND U.S.–SOVIET CONFLICT

The international system of the Cold War was an unexpected outcome of an unexpected war. The United States had hoped prior to the outbreak of World War II to withdraw to the stance of splendid isolationism that had supposedly characterized its foreign policy prior to World War I. However, this effort at interwar military self-effacement was already compromised by several factors. First, the U.S. imperialist experience in the aftermath of the Spanish-American war gave to Americans a heady sense of world engagement, however selective that engagement might be. Second, European security concerns would not go away from American national interests. To the contrary, during the 1930s the two became inextricably linked. The major significance of Franklin Roosevelt's election to the presidency was not apparent at first blush; touted by his partisans as an economic savior, his actual innovation was to guide brilliantly an isolationist Congress and polity toward European engagement.

A third force driving the United States away from its interwar isolationist reverie was the development of well-armed imperial dictatorships in Germany and Japan with world-class political ambitions. Given the size and competence of its military establishment during the 1930s, the United States could not extend deterrence on behalf of the status quo in Europe and Asia against rising hegemony in Berlin and Tokyo. The League of Nations proved to be feckless. The power vacuum that resulted when Britain and France only belatedly grasped the ring of antifascist resistance had to be filled from outside of Europe. Russia was a possible source of rescue, but Hitler's initial diplomatic moves had neutralized Stalin as an opponent until Germany was ready to deal with Russia. As France crumbled and Britain scrambled to evacuate Dunkirk, American political leaders were forced to confront their responsibility for global political order. The Japanese attack in December 1941 influenced the timing of U.S. national awakening, but the content of that awakening had already been settled.

Forced to rearm on a scale unprecedented before or since, Americans were divided in their assumptions about the probable shape of the postwar world and of U.S. civil-military relations within that world. Some maintained that wars were caused by renegade states and perverse ideologies. Once these states and ideologies had been defeated and discredited, a return to normalcy in U.S. overseas commitments and in the size of the U.S. military establishment could be expected. Others who saw the causes for World War II as more complicated doubted that the United States could extricate itself from postwar responsibility for world peace. President Roosevelt and his advisors, clearly in sympathy with the internationalist viewpoint of postwar global engagement, expected that the United States and other great powers, including the Soviet Union, could cooperate through the United Nations to deter irruptions of world peace.

This expectation was to be disappointed, and bitterly so. There are various explanations for why events turned out so much against the optimism of U.S. wartime leaders. Most important for the discussion here was the immediate postwar distribution of global military power. The bipolar international system that followed the collapse of Axis military power left the United States and the Soviet Union in a position of uniquely global reach. It became the perception of U.S. and Soviet Cold War leaders that world politics was a constant-sum game in which the winnings of one side would have to take place as a consequence of the other's losses.[5] As suspicion hardened into hostility during crises over Greece and Turkey, Iran, Czechoslovakia, and Berlin, President Truman was persuaded that only diplomatic firmness and military preparedness would deter further Soviet adventurism. The Truman doctrine and the Marshall plan declared U.S. universal and regional interests in keeping friendly regimes outside of the Soviet political orbit. But Truman was not prepared to pay the defense costs for these expanded commitments until the outbreak of war in Korea in 1950.

The U.S. postwar military establishment was not returned to a status similar to that awaiting the U.S. armed forces after World War I. Although more than ten million men were demobilized as rapidly as possible, the Truman administration did not foresee the peacetime period ahead as one of pacific deterrence through international organization and U.S. disengagement, as had been the expectation of President Woodrow Wilson following World War I. Instead, the United States committed itself to oversee the postwar reconstruction of Japan and Germany, the former as a political democracy and the latter according to the four-power division of the pie agreed to during wartime conferences. In the event, Germany was permanently divided and rearmed, but not before the United States confronted the need for the rearmament of Europe along with the economic construction of it.

The rearmament of free Europe had to be undertaken with some sensitivity to U.S. and European sensitivities: U.S. body-politic neuroses about overseas commitments in peacetime and European sensitivities about being dominated by American guns and capitalism. The solution for incorporating Western Europe within an American strategic protectorate was NATO, a voluntary alliance of unprecedented scope and inclusiveness in peacetime Europe. NATO grew up along with the maturing of the U.S. nuclear arsenal and the hardening of Cold War lines between the Soviet sphere of interest and the Western one. Eventually the Soviet side copied NATO's approach and organized the Warsaw Pact as a belated answer to NATO's European rearmament, although decisions were not taken by democratic consent within the pact as in NATO.

The extension of U.S. peacetime defense commitments to Western Europe, followed by the stationing of permanent American garrisons there, was a politicomilitary strategy for Cold War competition. But it was also a strategy for freezing the status quo in the center of Europe, thereby reducing the risk of inadvertent war between the United States and the Soviets. NATO was to contain the independent proclivities of the British, French, and Germans to fight with one another, as a by-product of its importance for deterring Soviet attack. Although not fully appreciated even now, NATO's political role was as important as its military one. Most U.S. foreign policy influentials did not anticipate an actual shooting war in Europe during the latter 1940s or early 1950s. As George F. Kennan had anticipated, what was more probable was the slow squeeze of Kremlin pressure against American and allied interests both directly, as in the Berlin crisis of 1948, and through surrogates, as in Korea in 1950.

Prior to the outbreak of the Korean war, the Truman administration had a hard sell for military buildup, including a rapid expansion of the U.S. nuclear arsenal. NSC-68, a high-level policy study calling for major U.S. rearmament in view of an imminent Soviet military threat to Europe and Asia, had been completed shortly before the eruption of North Korea's forces across the 38th parallel in June 1950.[6] U.S. defense spending shot across the previous ceilings imposed by the Truman administration, and the Chinese entry into the war only convinced many Americans that a Sino-Soviet bloc now threatened U.S. global interests. However, Korea was an improbable war, for which American strategic planners had scarcely prepared. Expecting a global war against the Soviet Union begun in Europe, planners had given little consideration to the possibility of U.S. involvement in limited wars supported by the Soviet leadership but fought by other governments and forces.

Korea posed strategic and policymaking dilemmas in Washington. The Truman administration's decision to fight a limited war was controversial on several grounds. Field Commander Douglas MacArthur chafed at political restrictions on military operations. Truman neglected to ask for a formal declaration of war against North Korea or against China after Chinese troops later entered the fighting on the Korean peninsula. The war was fought under the auspices of a United Nations collective security operation. The precedent now set for commitment of U.S. forces to limited war without a Congressional declaration of war would be repeated to disastrous effect in Vietnam.

NUCLEAR WEAPONS AND MUTUAL DETERRENCE

The paradox of nuclear weapons was that they made the United States homeland vulnerable to destruction without invasion for the first time. At the same time, they gave to the United States the retaliatory power to strike back at any aggressor, inflicting unacceptable damage. Therefore, a perceived sense of imminent vulnerability to possibly devastating surprise attack went hand-in-hand with a conviction on the part of leaders that mutual deterrence would guarantee strategic stasis. This vulnerability-invulnerability paradox left some persons confident in U.S. security based on the threat of nuclear retaliation. Other persons were equally confident that nuclear weapons would cancel themselves out and that meaningful military competition between the U.S. and the Soviet Union would occur below the nuclear threshold.[7]

The U.S. nuclear stockpile was relatively small when Truman left office, and control of nuclear weapons in peacetime remained with the Atomic Energy Commission. This situation became unacceptable to the armed forces once the Eisenhower administration had embarked on its preferred strategy of massive retaliation, emphasizing the employment of nuclear weapons instead of conventional forces even in contingencies other than total war. The acquisition of nuclear weapons by U.S. military commanders was a strategic necessity even as it posed problems of civil-military relations and problems for the relationship between the president and Congress.

The Korean war had seen the United States commit combat forces overseas without a congressional declaration of war. The judgment of the Truman administration had been that a formal declaration of war was neither necessary nor desirable. Nuclear weapons posed another kind of challenge to established civil-military relations. The National Security Act of 1947 had established a national military establishment headed by a secretary of defense and responsible for the administration and combat performance of all U.S. arms of service, including the newly independent air force. Amendments to NSC in 1949 strengthened the position of the Secretary of Defense by establishing the Office of the Secretary of Defense (OSD) and removed service secretaries from cabinet rank. Defense reorganization is considered at greater length below, but the preceding points about the initial unification of DOD and the assumptions on which that unification was built are pertinent for the present discussion.

For reasons well understood by the Framers of the U.S. Constitution and accepted by most nineteenth- and twentieth-century presidents, the United States could not have a presidential military force. The armed forces belonged to the people, and to this end were subdivided into active duty forces, reserve forces (trained service reserves and individual ready reserve pools), and unorganized militia (potential draftees). The U.S. Congress had rejected universal military training prior to the Korean war despite President Truman's strong support for UMT. The Constitution lodged the power to declare war in the Congress because the authors of that document distrusted executive power acting without legislative oversight. But the Framers also required a congressional declaration of war for another reason: It would empower the president to conduct a war on behalf of the entire aroused nation in arms. Public opinion was thought to be the bedrock on which effective commitment of U.S. forces had to be based, and congressional assent to war was deemed improbable unless broad public support was available.[8]

Nuclear weapons called into question this carefully circumscribed relationship created by the Constitution between the executive and legislative branches of the U.S. government. They did so in two ways. First, they made necessary the avoidance of total war. As it was easy for the public to perceive that total war was more threatening than limited war, presidents found it harder to make the case for those kinds of wars that the nuclear constraint would permit. Second, nuclear weapons promised unprecedented destructiveness in a short time. Especially once the Soviet Union had acquired a strategic nuclear retaliatory force capable of destroying many targets in the continental United States, the United States had to devise warning and assessment systems and to create a nuclear decision-making process that by implication circumvented the constitutional luxury of a declaration of war. In case of Soviet nuclear attack against targets in the continental United States, with ballistic missiles launched from land or sea, the U.S. effective warning would be measured in minutes rather than hours.

The constitutional bypass created to deal with this situation of unprecedented danger was that the president was recognized as commander in chief and that this status permitted him to retaliate against surprise attack without immediate congressional authorization. The Congress had other ways of reviewing and controlling the development of U.S. nuclear weapons programs and military budgets too. Therefore, the legislative branch was not frozen out of the process of force acquisition and general military-strategic planning. But the arcana of nuclear-weapons target planning and the packaging of strategic and other nuclear options remained largely within the compass of the executive branch during the Cold War years.

By itself this might have been regarded as an unavoidable necessity, but the nuclear-based habit of presidential initiative unencumbered by legislative oversight spilled over into Cold War presidential approaches to other security and defense issues. It was no surprise that maintaining a state of permanent military preparedness raised the status of the Pentagon relative to other cabinet departments, which themselves grew in stature on the coattails of Cold War presidential power. In addition, the play of power within the national security community in response to activist presidents, to the visibility of Cold War crises, and to the possibility of prompt nuclear surprise attack was important in its own right. As discussed in the next section, the implications of instant readiness for deterrence and for total war were far reaching for defense reorganization. This section emphasizes the implications of the strategic paradigm shift from mobilization to deterrence for military strategy.

Nuclear weapons affected the means of defense preparedness and the expectation of surprise attack. But they did not provide usable forces in battle. Therefore, Cold War presidents and their advisors confronted the problem of what to do if deterrence failed. This problem was partly diverted by the expectation of "extended" deterrence: nuclear weapons would deter any Soviet conventional attack against NATO, Europe, or other vital American interests. However, there were several problems with extended deterrence of this sort. First, not all Europeans wanted it; the French, for example, quite vociferously rejected any reliance on American nuclear protection. Second, the absolute character of nuclear weapons did not lend themselves to military separatism: Self-defense by threat of nuclear retaliation was intimately bound up with notions of sovereignty. Third, presidents wanted usable options in time of crisis, which could up the ante by using coercive measures short of war, as President Kennedy showed by his choice of blockade during the Cuban missile crisis of 1962.

Because nuclear weapons implied separate sovereignties, they complicated NATO alliance cohesion unless NATO Europeans were prepared to play only the role of U.S. military satellites. West European economic recovery subsequent to the Marshall Plan and the creation of the European Communities led to assertive self-confidence within NATO deliberative bodies for policy consultation and for military planning. By the 1960s U.S. military strategy had to be marketed aggressively if it were to be adopted consensually by America's NATO European allies. In 1967 NATO settled on a declaratory doctrine, flexible response, which carried it to the end of the Cold War. It was a political success wrapped in a military enigma. Europeans were allowed to believe that flexible response was something other than graduated escalation, whereas American expositors contended that graduated escalation was exactly what flexible response was all about. Although NATO represented singular success in the area of peacetime military planning and coordination, under the stress of actual crisis or war the political diversity of its member states could have prevented consensual response to any Soviet challenge. Fortunately for NATO, such a challenge was not provided by Moscow.

DEFENSE REORGANIZATION

The preceding section noted that nuclear weapons and the possible outbreak of large-scale conventional war in Europe forced U.S. military planners to shift from a mobilization to a deterrence paradigm in force and policy planning. The requirement to be ready for instantaneous response and global military operations meant that both plans and budgets would have to be coordinated across service lines. This caused civilians in the Office of the Secretary of Defense (OSD) to interfere in decisions about military procurement and war planning to an extent without precedent in peacetime American history.

The battles over Planning, Programming and Budgeting Systems (PPBS) during the McNamara years in the Pentagon do not require retelling. The political controversy during those years was not really about budgeting techniques, but about preferred strategy, doctrine, and prerogatives in determining force size. During the latter years of the Eisenhower administration, it was recognized that separate service planning for nuclear retaliation was not acceptable. The Single Integrated Operational Plan (SIOP) was established by McNamara's predecessor as a method for the coordination of navy and air force strategic target planning. It followed that the same model might be extended to general-purpose forces: defining objectives and asking what mixes of forces, regardless of service ownership, would most effectively and efficiently fulfill those objectives.

McNamara and his associates knew that the battle between OSD and the services over conventional forces programs would be more difficult than that over nuclear forces.[9] Nuclear weapons lent themselves to tight presidential control; release would be obtained only in the gravest circumstances. Conventional forces readiness and structure were other matters, and military leaders felt with some justification that they were the experts in residence on war fighting with armies, navies, and air forces apart from nuclear deterrence. Civilians in the McNamara Pentagon doubted openly that there was any such thing as military science or military art and disparaged combat experience as a necessary constituent of fruitful policy analysis. Although the military services outlasted some of McNamara's more ambitious exertions into their domains, his lasting impact on defense decision-making was to exploit the National Security Act of 1947 and the subsequent amendments of 1949, 1953, and 1958 to make the OSD the most powerful of cabinet departments.

Nonetheless, the post-McNamara secretaries of defense would have their hands full. One source of trouble was the already mentioned tradition of decentralized military decision-making within each service. Another was the growth of presidential power and the derivative raising in stature of the president's advisor for national security affairs. The national security advisor became an in-house source on national security issues thus diminishing the role of other players, including the military. The first person to hold formally this title was McGeorge Bundy in the Kennedy administration, and the significance of the national security advisor and his staff grew proportionately as the Cold War demands for U.S. preparedness thrust presidents into the cockpit of military decision-making. Not all of Bundy's successors necessarily enhanced the power and prerogatives of the national security advisor, but one who surely did was Henry Kissinger. As national security advisor to President Nixon, Kissinger became the president's éminence grise for all matters of security and foreign policy, eventually eclipsing Secretary of State William Rogers and finally pre-empting his job.[10]

Kissinger's NSC apparat represented a threat not only to the Department of State, but also to the Pentagon. In defense of the Pentagon it must be said that Kissinger was a formidable and relentless bureaucratic opponent whose grasp of policy and power-mindedness in Washington were uncommon. Kissinger also profited during Nixon's second term from that president's preoccupation with domestic policy, especially with Watergate. But Kissinger's special talents for self-aggrandizement foraged into two areas of great military sensitivity: crisis management and arms control. In addition, the failed U.S. military strategy in Vietnam was, by the time Nixon took office, all too apparent; and the U.S. program of phased withdrawal for American forces from South Vietnam, termed *Vietnamization,* required the orchestration of military and diplomatic instruments to exploit coercive diplomacy in reverse.

Defense secretaries Melvin Laird's and James Schlesinger's Pentagon fought off the NSC about as well as any bureaucrats could have, but the legacy left by Kissinger was an empowered NSC with the prerogative to exert control over the coordination of all matters touching upon foreign and defense policy. Once power had flowed in the direction of NSC, presidents no longer had the choice of reinstituting a weak NSC organization and depending upon cabinet depart-ments to take up the slack. President Ronald Reagan attempted just this solution at the outset of his first term, and it failed. The NSC emerged during the Reagan administration as the locus for highly sensitive covert operations in part because the CIA wanted to avoid congressional investigations related to covert action and in part because the expectation of experienced bureaucrats was that NSC was the place to get things done.

The tendency to empower NSC reappeared during the Bush administration. Brent Scowcroft, formerly NSC advisor in the President Gerald R. Ford admin-istration, accepted the same position under President George Bush. NSC retained its status as a second policy-planning and crisis-management department for national security affairs. Scowcroft served as Bush's most articulate expositor of U.S. security policies, confident that defense management would be carried out according to the president's wishes by long-time Bush political colleague Dick Cheney as secretary of defense. However, one important legacy from the Reagan to the Bush administrations had been Congressional passage of defense reform in the form of the Goldwater-Nichols legislation. This added to the power of the chairman of the Joint Chiefs of Staff (JCS), who became the principal advisor to the president and the secretary of defense on matters of military strategy and force structure. The Joint Staff was also reorganized and made more responsible and responsive to the chairman. In addition, Goldwater-Nichols mandated that future officers aspiring to general or flag rank must have career-defining experiences wearing "purple" in specified joint assignments. Finally, the Goldwater-Nichols legislation mandated that the various commanders in chief of the U.S. military unified and specified commands (LANTCOM, PACOM, CENTCOM, and so forth) be given more weight in the process of developing combat and crisis-management plans.[11]

Throughout the Cold War history of defense reorganization, one could with some justification divide policymakers, military professionals, and scholarly observers into two schools of thought: structural optimists, who believed that defense reorganization was actually related to improved policy outcomes, and bureaucratic pessimists, who rejected the possibility of any direct connection between structural reorganization and better defense policy.[12] In defense of the optimists, one could point to McNamara's introduction of PPBS and its avoidance of waste and duplication in some high-technology, expensive service programs. In defense of the optimists, one could also cite the Goldwater-Nichols legislation and its apparently favorable implications for the conduct of U.S. defense planning and warfighting strategy during the Gulf crisis and war from August 1990 through February 1991. Pessimists could argue, to the contrary, that the reach of McNamara's reforms frequently exceeded their grasp, as in the eventual demise of the TFX (Tactical Fighter, Experimental). Pessimists could also note that "servicism" remained even after the Goldwater-Nichols reforms an unavoidable barrier to jointness in planning and procurement: Command and control systems usable by more than one service provide excellent illustrations of the pervasiveness of single-service opportunism.[13]

PERSONNEL POLICY AND MILITARY DOCTRINE

The U.S. military experience of the Cold War years was marked by unprecedented beginnings and endings with regard to personnel policy and military doctrine, and these beginnings and endings in both areas were related. The early Cold War years saw conscription carried over into the peacetime armed forces in the form of selective service. This went hand in hand with the concept of permanent preparedness for global war. The army was of course more dependent than the navy (including marines) or air force on conscription. Large forces permanently stationed in Europe, Korea, and elsewhere served as trip wires to deter Soviet attack on American allies. U.S. strategy for global war during the Truman administration, given the relative scarcity of nuclear munitions and delivery vehicles compared to forces available to Truman's successors, did not envision an air-atomic offensive against the Soviet Union as capable of fulfilling U.S. wartime objectives by itself. It was assumed in late forties war plans that air-atomic attacks by both sides would be followed by protracted conflict between Soviet and opposed armed forces in Europe and worldwide.

The availability during the Eisenhower administration of larger numbers of nuclear weapons supported the shift to a declaratory strategy for a general war of massive retaliation. While administration officials were eventually forced to retreat from this formulation in cases of less than total war, for global war against the Soviet Union Eisenhower defense planning relied mainly upon promptly delivered and massive air atomic offensives. Special study committees such as the Gaither committee pointed to the need for a larger menu of military responses, and Army officials chafed at the allocation of defense resources within arbitrary ceilings and under planning assumptions favoring air force and navy procurement. NATO's declared objective of ninety-six active-duty and reserve divisions was far beyond any commitment its members were willing or able to provide. Thus, reliance on nuclear weapons for extended deterrence became all the more necessary as a result of allied as well as U.S. domestic budgetary priorities.

The army emerged from the 1950s as the fourth wheel of a defense establishment whose preferred military doctrines favored the more technical and less manpower-intensive arms of service. Under the Kennedy administration things would soon change. Kennedy preferred the strategy that became known as flexible response, calling for improved U.S. conventional forces for crisis response, forward presence and, if necessary, actual war fighting in order to raise the nuclear threshold in Europe. This last rationale was pushed hard within NATO by McNamara, to the detriment of alliance solidarity on doctrine until the French departure from NATO's military command structure in 1966 and the promulgation of flexible response in 1967. Flexible response arguably allowed a greater role for the ground forces in U.S. military doctrine and force planning, but by the time flexible response became official NATO doctrine, the lines between Cold War ''east'' and ''west'' had solidified and neither side seemed interested in even limited probes against the other. The outcome of the imbroglio over the Berlin crisis of 1961 and the Cuban missile crisis of 1962 had been to establish a mini-détente between the superpowers on matters of high politics and security, especially on the likelihood that either side would instigate even a crisis in Europe, let alone a war.

If strategic stasis reigned in Europe, Khrushchev's insistence that wars of national liberation could be unleashed against Third World regimes supportive of U.S. policy called forth from the Kennedy administration a burst of doctrinal innovations. Special operations and low-intensity-conflict studies, as the term was later denoted, led to an emphasis on subconventional warfare, psychological operations, and nation-building as constituent elements of U.S. military strategy.[14] But only a fringe of the armed forces officer corps, such as the Green Berets, committed themselves to careers along these lines. The more traditional arms of service lacked serious interest in special operations and regarded their counterinsurgency brethren with undisguised distaste. As the U.S. commitment to Vietnam escalated well beyond the engagement of special operations forces and intelligence operatives, conventional military mind-sets displaced the political side of the politicomilitary equation on which special operations had been predicated. U.S. conventional forces in Vietnam, on the evidence, fought well against North Vietnamese conventional forces and Viet Cong units when the latter were willing to stand and fight pitched battles.

However, it became apparent by 1968 even to the Department of Defense that the United States could not win the counterinsurgency or propaganda wars at an acceptable cost: Johnson's resignation and Nixon's phased disengagement followed. Many arguments can be started in bars on whether U.S. conventional or unconventional military strategy failed in Vietnam. The present discussion bypasses that temptation and emphasizes the implications of counterinsurgency displacement by conventional strategy for military personnel policy. Having decided that escalation from limited commitment to a major U.S. military campaign in South Vietnam was necessary, President Johnson nonetheless sought to balance the requirement for military escalation against his other priorities in domestic politics, especially his cherished Great Society programs recently passed by Congress. Johnson's "guns and butter" policy filled the armed forces ranks of enlisted personnel by expanded conscription of young persons while forgoing the option to mobilize the organized reserve forces. The result of this approach was to create nationwide dissent against the war, first across U.S. college campuses and then among wider audiences.

The draft more than anything else brought the U.S. military escalation in Vietnam to a stopping point. When the supreme commander of the U.S. forces in Vietnam, General William Westmoreland, asked for several hundred thousand additional troops in 1968, Secretary of Defense Clark Clifford suggested to Johnson that he pull the plug. Johnson did so, announcing his intention not to seek another term of office and thereby conceding the failure of U.S. policy and strategy in Vietnam. However, Johnson left the nation with a major force and policy commitment to a war that would continue without complete U.S. disengagement until 1973, with war continuing between Vietnamese factions until 1975. With military disengagement from Vietnam went another look at U.S. conscription policy, and the Gates Commission recommendation to end conscription was adopted and ordered into effect beginning in 1983. In effect, the United States had come full circle to its pre-twentieth-century peacetime standard of raising armed forces by voluntary enlistment (except for the American Civil War, when both sides drafted).

The onset of the all-volunteer force (AVF) coincided with post-Vietnam doctrinal revisionism. The Nixon administration changed the 1960s strategy of being able to fight two-and-one-half wars simultaneously to one-and-one-half wars, and Nixon emphasized that U.S. support for besieged allies would stop short of involving American ground forces. Voluntary enlistment dictated a strategy of selective rather than ubiquitous military engagement. Selective engagement was also facilitated by the full-blown emergence of U.S.–Soviet détente during the

1970s and Sino-American rapprochement. It was perceived by U.S. foreign and defense policy elites that diplomatic containment of Moscow's ambitions was more cost effective than overpromising of U.S. military involvement in regional conflicts. U.S. and Soviet leaders worked to stabilize the Middle East and to create new expectations about their mutual interests in avoiding nuclear war and inadvertent military escalation. In addition, under the direction of Chief of Staff General Creighton Abrams, army planners during the early 1970s configured the "total force" concept so that future presidents could not avoid substantial reserve call-ups during any national mobilization for war.[15]

The Carter administration ended its term of office on a sour note in U.S.–Soviet relations: the invasion of Afghanistan caused Carter to ask that the Senate suspend consideration of the SALT II treaty he had negotiated. In addition, Carter called for the creation of a Rapid Deployment Force for prompt intervention in the Middle East/Persian Gulf; this force would eventually grow into the Central Command that General Norman Schwartzkopf would take into battle against Iraq in 1991. But Carter's belated acknowledgment of the seriousness of Soviet military potential did not lead to a full-court press with U.S. military forces against perceived Soviet vulnerabilities. Carter maintained the path of selective engagement of U.S. military power previously established under Nixon and Ford. Thus, Carter was disinclined to call for a return to conscription, and Reagan was even less interested in doing so.

Although some describe the Reagan administration as a period of U.S. overcommitment to counterinsurgency or insurgency wars, Reagan's advisors were stronger on anticommunist rhetoric than on bailing out hapless dictators or overthrowing leftist regimes. Reagan preferred to direct U.S. commitments toward counterterrorism and covert action at the low end of the conflict spectrum, and U.S. investment toward conventional high technology supportive of "air-land battle" between the Warsaw Pact and NATO at the higher end of conventional military options. The all volunteer force, so badly underfunded that it could scarcely meet its recruitment goals during the 1970s, fared better in the 1980s after enlisted and officer compensation were raised significantly by Congress. Congress also supported the administration's emphasis on firepower-intensive as opposed to manpower-intensive military strategies, although DOD and the services emphasized the need to make firepower smarter through precision-guided munitions, improved capability for electronic warfare, and eventual applications of sensors and weapons based on other physical principles.

Reagan's high-tech strategic focus extended even into the heavens, where he assumed his proposed Strategic Defense Initiative (SDI) would eventually yield deployments of space-based battle stations and other accouterments of postnuclear deterrence. This vision also seemed to require technology-intensive, not manpower-intensive, forward planning; and the vision of massive manpower wars was pushed even further from planning consciousness. A war that began in Europe might, according to Reagan planning guidance, extend into a world war, but U.S. and allied NATO strategy did not envision a repeat of any conflict as extended in time as World War II. NATO's campaign on the central front in Europe would be based on conventional deep strikes, aided by modernized sensors, battlefield computers, and precision weapons; and it would be designed to disconnect the tail of the Soviet offensive from its teeth in short order. The template for this NATO game plan could be perceived clearly even by lay readers who picked up a copy of Tom Clancy's *Red Storm Rising;* it remains interesting even though experts now suspect that the Red Army was far less capable of carrying out any offensive action in Europe in the 1980s, or earlier, than government and media alarmists supposed.

The modernized U.S. air-land battle template also remains interesting for its subsequent application in the Persian Gulf, against Iraq in 1991.[16] Here U.S. military planners who contemplated how to prevail in a war between NATO and the Warsaw Pact and who were confounded by the commingling of conventional and nuclear forces in Europe found a more amenable theater of operations for the application of U.S. military power. A five-month period of grace for military buildup in Saudi Arabia did no harm to U.S. readiness for war in January 1991; and U.S. air-land battle doctrine played successfully before a packed house.

The results of the Gulf war of 1991 seemed to vindicate not only U.S. conventional military strategy and technology but also the decision in favor of the all-volunteer force taken decades earlier. Columnist Charles Krauthammer, celebrating the "unipolar moment" in which the United States had allegedly found itself by virtue of the collapse of the Soviet Union, noted, "in 1950 the U.S. engaged in a war with North Korea: it lasted three years, cost 54,000 American lives, and ended in a draw. Forty-one years later, the U.S. engaged in a war with Iraq: it lasted six weeks, cost 196 American lives, and ended in a rout. If the Roman Empire had declined at this rate, you would be reading this in Latin."[17]

However, experts recognized the ironic character of the vindication of U.S. strategy, since the air-land battle doctrine had been intended for a force structure that was obviously not going to be preserved intact into the post–Cold War era. The United States might not even be able to repeat Desert Storm by 1997, with forces drawn down considerably from 1990 levels even according to the Bush plan of 1991, which Congress might choose to modify. In addition, the Congress and some politicomilitary strategists in the executive branch were also planning to employ U.S. military capability for nontraditional noncombat missions, including operations designed to preserve sanctuary from attack for besieged ethnic or national populations (such as operation Provide Comfort for the Kurds in Iraq). The Bush strategy for more traditional uses of U.S. military power emphasized the performance of forward-presence and crisis-response missions intended for regional contingency operations outside of Europe, not for global warfare or for large interstate wars in Europe.

PREVENTIVE DIPLOMACY AND MULTILATERAL MILITARY INTERVENTION

The United States had created a conventional force structure of unprecedented size in order to fight the Cold War. That force structure was backed by nuclear deterrence that conveyed the threat of unacceptable retaliatory punishment for any Soviet attack on North America or Europe. U.S. experts now declare that the Cold War has ended and that the United States has won it. It would be more accurate to say that the United States successfully overstated the Soviet threat from the beginning to the end of the Cold War and that this overstated threat never materialized. Whether this was due to successful deterrence or to crisis management or to good fortune, we will never be certain. The point is that, whether success was designed or fortuitous, the sizes and kinds of forces appropriate for the Cold War will be less suitable for the next century. As force sizes and character change, so too will the politicomilitary context within which forces are used for deterrence or compellence.[18]

Recent experience suggests that nuclear deterrence will be less significant in future U.S. policy planning. The improved capabilities of long-range, precision-guided conventional munitions allow policymakers to escape nuclear dependency even for some missions requiring strategic depth. Although the technology spinoffs of SDI are not altogether clear at this writing, the United States and allied experience with SCUD (short-range ballistic missile) attacks and Patriot interceptions in the Gulf war suggest growing military interest in theater missile defenses for U.S. allies. Limited nonnuclear defenses for the U.S. homeland have also been authorized by Congress in the form of support for the Bush GPALS (Global Protection against Limited Strikes) program. There is little apparent congressional interest in overturning nuclear deterrence based on offensive retaliation, even at greatly reduced force levels.[19]

U.S. military interventions of the future will favor the use of tailored forces for rapidly concluded contingency operations, as in the Bush administration Panamanian intervention (Just Cause). Selective unilateral intervention will in all likelihood be combined with increased post–Cold War willingness to support multilateral military interventions or preventive diplomacy, through the United Nations or by means of regional international organizations. One can distinguish in this regard *peacekeeping* and *peace enforcement* operations. Peacekeeping means that the UN or other multinational body authorizes the positioning of neutral forces between combatants, in order to separate their armies and to provide time for negotiations that must precede any conflict resolution. Peace enforcement means that the forces of a multilateral organization impose a solution on reluctant combatants. The United Nations Emergency Force (UNEF) deployed in Egypt from 1956 to 1967 illustrates the UN use of a peacekeeping force; the UN operation in the Congo, involving the forcible reintegration of secessionist Katanga province, is a case study in peace enforcement.

The participation of U.S. forces in peacekeeping and peace enforcement operations is not without difficulties. During the Cold War it was necessary for American and Soviet forces to be excluded from United Nations peacekeeping or peace enforcement operations for obvious reasons: A regional crisis could be turned inadvertently into a superpower conflict. This difficulty no longer obtains. The end of the Cold War opens the door to Security Council peacekeeping or peace enforcement operations backed by both the United States and Russia, among other permanent members. However, the involvement of U.S. forces in multilateral operations will not be noncontroversial on the home front. The commitment of U.S. combat forces under the command of any other government, even under the umbrella of an international organization, creates potential problems of operational integrity and political accountability. These problems did not really arise in Korea or in the Gulf war of 1991 because, although authorized by the UN, they were essentially military campaigns designed and directed by the United States.

The civil war in Yugoslavia leading to the breakup of that country in 1992 provided a case study of the difficulty in obtaining commitments by the great powers to multilateral military intervention. Reports of widespread genocide and the potential for this conflict to escalate beyond the Balkans called for some kind of concerted European or UN action, either to separate the combatants or to impose a cease-fire and return to the status quo ante. However, none of the European security organizations seemed able to take the lead. NATO had been designed for an entirely different mission. The Western European Union (WEU) was enjoying a welcome rebirth, but it had not yet matured as a center of gravity for preventive diplomacy or for multilateral military intervention. The Conference on Security and Cooperation in Europe (CSCE) was the most inclusive body capable of taking a stand, but its very inclusiveness precluded harmonious action of a military sort. Sadly, the recognition dawned in 1992 that only a military organization with the capabilities of NATO or the former Warsaw Pact, without the aura of Cold War illegitimacy either of those organizations would carry, could intervene effectively to put a stop to the slaughter in Croatia and Bosnia.

But even if effective intervention could be obtained, the question remained on whose side intervention should be undertaken. Collective security is the political umbrella under which multilateral military intervention takes place. Collective security presupposes that one can identify an aggressor and a defender, a good guy and a bad guy.[20] In a multinational civil war of the Yugoslav type, the problem of identifying aggressors and defenders would be one that defied consensus or political objectivity. Prominent U.S. politicians and media pundits called for military interventions of various kinds in 1992, and some made compelling cases that the chaos in former Yugoslavia could not be ignored. However strong the imperative, the "how" remained difficult if not impossible to answer. The necessity for multilateral intervention was easier to demonstrate than the feasibility of any military operation involving multinational ground forces under

UN or other auspices. The case of U.S. intervention in Somalia in December 1992 under United Nations auspices was a mirror image of the situation in former Yugoslavia: feasibility was easily demonstrated by deploying a U.S. force of sufficient size to overpower any Somali warlord resistance. On the other hand, the necessity for U.S. intervention, as opposed to that carried out by African states under UN sponsorship, was more controversial in the U.S. news media and in Congress.

The questions about operational feasibility of post–Cold War contingency operations, for U.S. or for multinational military forces, are the same. What is the political objective? What are the military objectives that follow from this political objective? Are these military objectives attainable with the forces that the U.S. or the UN are willing to commit? Similar questions, in case of U.S. commitment of troops to unilateral or multistate operations, must be answered with regard to American domestic politics and its unavoidable connection with foreign policy. The Cold War experience, with a much more evident global military threat facing each administration from Truman through Reagan, was marked by great contention between Congress and the executive branch over the prerogatives held by each in security policy. In addition, the acceptability of unilateral or multilateral interventions to the U.S. public would be relevant to the Congress and, for this reason and others, to the administration.

It is instructive to recall how thin was the margin by which Congress in January 1991 voted to authorize President Bush to use force in order to expel Iraq from Kuwait. Bush wisely avoided the trap into which President Johnson had fallen in Vietnam: marching into battle without getting Congress explicitly committed to the nation's war aims. However, in insisting on getting the explicit endorsement of Congress for Desert Storm, Bush risked a negative vote and a greater domestic obstacle course against the effective use of force. The vote in Congress was close despite the following aspects of the situation, all presumably permissive of intervention: Saddam Hussein acted the role of a textbook villain; the threat to oil supplies provided an obvious and tangible interest; the United States acted with the support, not only of its former Cold War allies, but also with a majority of Middle East and Southwest Asia Arab governments; and the Soviet Union endorsed the use of force if necessary in the UN Security Council.

One might argue, therefore, that the UN support for Desert Storm represents a "best case" of international consensus behind U.S. war aims.[21] Nonetheless, public opinion polls during the U.S. Gulf military buildup and prior to the outbreak of war suggested that the American people were anxious about the feasibility of going to war and divided about the desirability of doing so. Congress reflected this ambivalence in public perceptions of the desirability and feasibility of using force: Congressional and public opinion, fortified by some expert testimony on Capitol Hill, contained strong support for continued economic sanctions as an alternative to war. In the aftermath of the rapid and decisive coalition victory over Iraq, of course, public ambivalence turned into overwhelming approval. But a less successful military campaign would, on the evidence of Korea and Vietnam, have produced a more divided and contentious public policy debate.

In any event, the kinds of forces required for future multilateral or unilateral U.S. military intervention will be, compared to their Cold War predecessors, more mobile, technically advanced, and elitist. As the armed forces are drawn down in size and as decades of voluntary service make the armed forces less familiar to average Americans, the degree of dissociation between the armed forces and the larger society may increase. Objective civilian control of the U.S. armed forces may become more necessary as the assumption of a military embedded in societal values is less sustainable. Careerist and vocational motives for recruitment and retention can be expected to assume even greater importance for the military services in the 1990s and thereafter than they did from 1973 through the 1980s. The AVF of the twenty-first century will therefore constitute a paradox for presidents. It will be easier to set in motion small interventionary or protective reaction strikes, such as those against terrorism. But it will be as difficult as it was during the preceding four decades, if not more so, to make any sustained commitment of large numbers of U.S. forces to unilateral or multilateral military interventions. U.S. long-range conventional maritime and air power will become the makeweights of the U.S. strategic deterrent, with smaller, residual nuclear forces kept in the background. Europe will either pacify itself or fail to, but in either case eventual U.S. disengagement of all but token U.S. combat forces from Western Europe seems unavoidable. U.S. forces remaining in Europe could be incorporated into multistate military frameworks such as WEU or a WEU-deputized remnant of NATO.

CONCLUSIONS

The Cold War enlarged the size of the peacetime U.S. armed forces and imposed unprecedented requirements for the support of U.S. coercive diplomacy, crisis management, and nuclear deterrence. It also led to a reorganized military establishment through which policy makers sought to impose increasingly greater degrees of centralized control. Although more centralized control over military administration and logistics was generally regarded as contributory to improved strategy, centralized control over operations was less favorably received by professional officers. Micromanagement of operations was resisted by field commanders, and the Goldwater-Nichols reforms sought to empower the commander in chief of U.S. forces in their respective areas of responsibility.

The future holds both good and bad news for military traditionalists. Carryover of the Vietnam syndrome from the Cold War makes it likely that presidents will not get into war without congressional backing and allied support and that, once committed to war, U.S. military commanders will be given large amounts of discretion in deciding how to fight. On the other hand, the most frequent uses of U.S. military power will be to support deterrent or coercive diplomatic policy objectives. In deterrence and in coercive diplomacy, the credibility and coherence of policy weighs as heavily as does the power of American military forces.[22] Especially in nuclear crisis management, presidents will want to maintain strict control over military operations in order to avoid inadvertent escalation.[23]

NOTES

The author is grateful to Professor Sam C. Sarkesian for helpful comments on an earlier draft of this study. He bears no responsibility for its contents.

1. Seminal studies of U.S. civil-military relations include Samuel P. Huntington, *The Soldier and the State* (Cambridge: Belknap Press, Harvard University Press, 1957); Huntington, *The Common Defense* (New York: Columbia University Press, 1961); Morris Janowitz, *The Professional Soldier: A Social and Political Portrait* (New York: Free Press, 1961); and Russell F. Weigley, *Towards an American Army: Military Thought from Washington to Marshall* (New York: Columbia University Press, 1962).

2. On U.S. security requirements and responses for the pre–Cold War or "geopolitical era," see Robert J. Art, "A Defensible Defense: America's Grand Strategy after the Cold War," *International Security,* no. 4 (Spring 1991): 5–53.

3. For example, Cold War conditions posed new problems of interservice command and control. This is well treated in historical perspective by C. Kenneth Allard, *Command, Control and the Common Defense* (New Haven: Yale University Press, 1990).

4. An expert analysis of U.S. military professionalism in the Cold War years is provided in Sam C. Sarkesian, *Beyond the Battlefield: The New Military Profession* (New York: Pergamon Press, 1981).

5. These developments can be traced in John Lewis Gaddis, *The United States and the Origins of the Cold War, 1941–1947* (New York: Columbia University Press, 1972), esp. pp. 282–352; and Adam Ulam, *The Rivals: America and Russia since World War II* (New York: Viking Press, 1971).

6. John Lewis Gaddis, *The Long Peace: Inquiries into the History of the Cold War* (New York: Oxford University Press, 1987), p. 114.

7. Robert Jervis, *The Meaning of the Nuclear Revolution* (Ithaca: Cornell University Press, 1989); and Lawrence Freedman, *The Evolution of Nuclear Strategy* (New York: St. Martin's Press, 1981).

8. This case is argued in Harry T. Summers, *On Strategy: A Critical Analysis of the Vietnam War* (New York: Dell Publishers, 1982), chapter 1.

9. For an account from the perspective of McNamara's staff, see Alain C. Enthoven and K. Wayne Smith, *How Much Is Enough? Shaping the Defense Program, 1961–1969* (New York: Harper and Row, 1971), esp. pp. 117–64. See also William W. Kaufmann, *The McNamara Strategy* (New York: Harper and Row, 1964).

10. Evolution of the NSC is discussed in John Prados, *The Keepers of the Keys: A History of the National Security Council from Truman to Bush* (New York: William Morrow and Co., 1991).

11. For assessments of Goldwater-Nichols, see Robert J. Art, *Strategy and Management in the Post–Cold War Pentagon* (Carlisle, Penn.: U.S. Army War College, Strategic Studies Institute, 1992), and Rep. Les Aspin, Chairman, and Rep. William Dickenson, U.S. Congress, House Committee on Armed Services, *Defense for a New Era: Lessons of the Persian Gulf War* (Washington, D.C.: U.S. Government Printing Office, 1992).

12. For a sampling of expert assessments, see Robert J. Art, Vincent Davis, and Samuel P. Huntington, eds., *Reorganizing America's Defenses: Leadership in War and Peace* (New York: Pergamon Brassey's, 1985).

13. Art, *Strategy and Management in the Post–Cold War Pentagon,* pp. 26–27.

14. A critique of U.S. experience in D. Michael Shafer, *Deadly Paradigms: The Failure of U.S. Counterinsurgency Policy* (Princeton: Princeton University Press, 1988). See also Douglas Blaufarb, *The Counterinsurgency Era: U.S. Doctrine and Performance, 1950 to the Present* (New York: Free Press, 1977). For evaluations of American experiences with covert action, see John Prados, *President's Secret Wars: CIA and Pentagon Covert Operations since World War II* (New York: William Morrow, 1986); and Roy Godson, ed., *Intelligence Requirements for the 1980s,* vol. 4, *Covert Action* (Washington, D.C.: National Strategy Information Center, 1983). An assessment of the impact of low-intensity conflict on American military professionalism appears in Sarkesian, *Beyond the Battlefield,* part 2, chapter 4–7.

15. Harry G. Summers, Jr., *On Strategy II: A Critical Analysis of the Gulf War* (New York: Dell Publishing Co., 1992), pp. 72–73.

16. Ibid., pp. 139–50.

17. Charles Krauthammer, "The Unipolar Moment," chapter 8, in Graham Allison and Gregory F. Treverton, eds., *Rethinking America's Security* (New York: W. W. Norton, 1992), p. 298.

18. For prescriptions about future U.S. grand strategy based on careful appreciation of Cold War experience, see Paul Kennedy, "American Grand Strategy, Today and Tomorrow: Learning from the European Experience," chapter 10, in Kennedy, ed., *Grand Strategies in War and Peace* (New Haven: Yale University Press, 1991), pp. 167–84.

19. Diverse expert assessments are provided in *Strategic Defense Initiative: What Are the Costs, What Are the Threats?,* Hearings before the Legislation and National Security Subcommittee of the Committee on Government Operations, U.S. House of Representatives, 102nd Congress, 1st Session, 16 May and 1 October 1991.

20. Comparison of the theoretical principle of collective security with the actual practice of it appears in Inis L. Claude, Jr., "Collective Security after the Cold War," chapter 1, in Gary L. Guertner, ed., *Collective Security in Europe and Asia* (Carlisle, Penn.: U.S. Army War College, Strategic Studies Institute, March 1992), pp. 7–28. Claude notes that excessive optimism about the probable success of collective security frequently follows in the aftermath of successful coalition wars (see esp. pp. 14–15).

21. What the Gulf war of 1991 portends for the future is explored in Aspin and Dickenson, House Armed Services Committee, *Defense for a New Era;* and Norman Friedman, *Desert Victory: The War for Kuwait* (Annapolis: U.S. Naval Institute, 1991), pp. 236–60.

22. See Alexander L. George, ed., *Avoiding War: Problems of Crisis Management* (Boulder, Colo.: Westview Press, 1991), for pertinent theory and case studies; and George, David K. Hall, and William E. Simons, *The Limits of Coercive Diplomacy: Laos, Cuba, Vietnam* (Boston: Little, Brown, 1971).

23. Richard Ned Lebow, *Nuclear Crisis Management: A Dangerous Illusion* (Ithaca: Cornell University Press, 1987).

REFERENCES

Allard, C. Kenneth. *Command, Control and Common Defense.* New Haven: Yale University Press, 1990.

Art, Robert J., Vincent Davis, and Samuel Huntington, eds. *Reorganizing America's Defenses: Leadership in War and Peace.* New York: Pergamon Brassey's, 1985.

Freedman, Lawrence. *The Evolution of Nuclear Strategy.* New York: St. Martin's Press, 1981.

Gaddis, John Lewis. *Strategies of Containment: A Critical Appraisal of Postwar American National Security Policy.* New York: Oxford University Press, 1982.

Huntington, Samuel. *The Soldier and the State.* Cambridge: Belknap Press/Harvard University Press, 1957.

Janowitz, Morris. *The Professional Soldier: A Social and Political Portrait.* New York: Free Press, 1961.

Jervis, Robert. *The Meaning of the Nuclear Revolution.* Ithaca: Cornell University Press, 1989.

Prados, John. *The Keepers of the Keys: A History of the National Security Council from Truman to Bush.* New York: William Morrow and Co., 1991.

Sarkesian, Sam C. *Beyond the Battlefield: The New Military Profession.* New York: Pergamon Press, 1981.

ZAIRE

Frederic Belle Torimoro

In the wake of the growing democratization movements, Africa's political leaders are compelled to take stock of their right to rule. They are increasingly faced with the serious challenge of staying in power by either accepting or rejecting the resurgence of social and political values strongly linked to the idea of rule by the many. Under these circumstances, Africans presently at the helm of government "must secure some degree of internal support in order to survive, let alone achieve political stability."[1] Their behavior toward any kind of political change or commitment to control its pace and direction brings a special attention to the role of the military. Understanding the full range of the attitude and contribution of the military toward politics in Africa clearly lends support to any meaningful discussion on civil-military relations.

Zaire is now one of several African states pressured to rearrange its political fabric. With a population of over thirty-six million people who speak about seven hundred different languages and are from approximately 250 distinct ethnic groups, the political leadership must confront demands emanating from various sectors. It appears that for General Sese Seko Mobutu political survivability is marked by his ability to organize and control rising expectations as well as to achieve military compliance with personal authority. The pursuit of politics, democratic or otherwise, therefore harbors elements that may be perceived by Mobutu as threatening to his political well-being or to the interests of the military.

This chapter examines the political role of the Zairian military. In doing so, it attempts to appreciate the extent to which the political history of Zaire has been visibly influenced by the military. The cycle of political development and decay is therefore evaluated in terms of the character of civil-military relations. A useful analysis of Zaire's political landscape must take into account the disposition of the military. In other words, is it possible simply to see the military as the central instrument of state coercion? Is it equipped to champion the public outcry for democratic reforms? Does the level of professionalism in the Zairian military have any significant impact on the pattern of political change and control in the society? It is necessary to investigate the record of statesmanship from the pre-1965 era to the present to appraise how well the political leaders have managed the military and then, on the basis of those findings, to speculate about the future.

A BRIEF HISTORICAL BACKGROUND

The historical context of civil-military relations in Zaire, like many other African countries, draws special attention to the capacity of the civilian leadership to provide a viable formula for long-standing legitimation of political authority. It reveals the consequences of military involvement in politics often marked by indistinguishable boundaries between civilian and military institutions. The emphasis is usually on theoretical arguments that define the conditions under which the military is inspired and capable of determining its response to civilian initiatives. In the case of Zaire the focus is on civilian control strategies and the military's willingness to capitulate.

The Pre-1965 Era: The Military as an Instrument of Colonial Coercion

The colonial influence in what became known as the Congo Independent State is salient to any analysis of civil-military relations. The state was created in 1879 by King Leopold II of Belgium following H. M. Stanley's exploration of the Congo River Basin. King Leopold was lured to colonization as a means to augment his personal wealth. Put differently, the king's economic campaign in the newly acquired territory was intended to expand his corporate empire. According to Leopold:

> The Congo has been, and could have been, nothing but a personal undertaking. There is no more legitimate or respectable right than that of an author over his own work, the fruit of his labour. . . . My rights over the Congo are to be shared with none; they are the fruit of my own struggles and expenditure.[2]

King Leopold worked on the assumption that the indigenous population in the Congo Independent State was essentially enslaved to him. Using the colony as his personal property, Leopold pursued his economic interests by establishing a claim over what were referred to as "vacant lands." The lands were in turn leased, as were mineral exploration rights, to companies such as Lever Brothers and the Union Minière. However, what is most pertinent here is that Leopold's economic campaigns were enhanced by the military. He used armed militias to exploit violently the local people, who were expected to supply plenty of ivory, wild rubber, and a wide variety of other goods.

The *Force Publique* was formally established as a result of a decree from King Leopold on 5 August 1888. This was a notable policy action in that it initiated a mixture of civilian and military leadership in the Congo Independent State. What followed was the appointment of military officers to serve as administrators of territorial districts. They were held accountable to the commander in chief of the *Force Publique,* who also assumed the office of governor-general. By 1897, the *Force Publique* had grown to roughly fourteen thousand members (including two thousand non-Congolese soldiers).[3] Unlike the French and British, who maintained strong ties with their colonial armies (imparting similar military values and ethics to their African officers), the Belgians instituted a distinct organizational demarcation. There was no strong desire to tie the colonial army to their counterparts in Belgium. This separation was fueled by racial discrimination and by the animosity that thrived between Belgian officers in the colony and those in the metropolis.

The social composition of the *Force Publique* was influenced by the voluntary recruitment practice that persisted until 1891. This practice was nevertheless accompanied by conscription. The Congolese selected by the local administrative chiefs appointed by the Belgians were frequently social outcasts and those captured during tribal wars. The pattern of recruitment that emerged also favored ethnic groups such as the Bangala, Azande, and Batetela, as they were considered to be true warriors in the state. The *Force Publique* was therefore an organization dominated by a few select ethnic groups. Several groups in the Congo were underrepresented, and the recruitment practice produced a climate for mutiny. The 1896 mutiny by Batetela soldiers, for example, was enough evidence to support a recruitment pattern that reflected a cross-section of the Congolese society.

Of related importance is the internal organization of the *Force Publique.* For the most part, the Congolese soldiers were intentionally isolated from their own ethnic groups and from the rest of the civil society. The Belgian officers presumed that the fermentation of an esprit de corps, founded on an allegiance to King Leopold, could be facilitated by such isolation. To maintain this posture, it was necessary to extend psychological assurance to the soldiers. They were usually praised for their bravery during the war against slavery. This intangible element was also supplemented with an equally strong tangible effect. As Jean-Claude Williame points out:

White officers also took special care to emphasize the heroic deeds of the *Force Publique* during the antislavery campaigns. Finally, autonomous technical schools, specialized newspapers, journals, and radio broadcasts, veterans' associations, and the use of a common vernacular, the lingala, were all institutional devices that enhanced the troops' pride in belonging to a military elite.[4]

The longevity of this elitist climate was secured through a series of material and fringe benefits spread to the soldiers and their families. It was immediately apparent that those who served in the *Force Publique* were the most fortunate group of Africans in the Congo.

The character of civil-military relations in the colony may also be explained in terms of the *Force Publique*'s role. It was established to perform the traditional mission of defending the colony from external attack, maintaining internal order, and carrying out the laws of the state. Nonetheless, the focus of its function was on sustaining the compliance of the ordinary people with the demands of the Belgian crown. The *Force Publique* embarked on police operations calculated to crush any resistance, especially from Afro-Arab traders in the eastern Congo, to Belgian control of the territory. They were frequently used to brutalize insurgents from different ethnic groups and local leaders whose political aspirations ran contrary to the wishes of the colonial government.

Positively, the *Force Publique* was used by the colonial government for "pacification" crusades, labor recruitment, and tax collection.[5] The takeover of Congo by the Belgian government in 1908 therefore did not shift the focus from maintaining internal order. The soldiers were used repeatedly to put down popular rebellions of various sorts. The *Force Publique,* for example, was used to halt the disturbances in parts of the Equateur and Kasai provinces in the period between 1918 and 1921. It was also employed to break up labor strikes in Elizabethville and Matadi. As a whole, the colonial government's use of the military for its pacification campaign against disaffected ethnic groups resulted in major civilian casualties.[6]

By 1926 the colonial government had passed an ordinance that provided for the reorganization of the *Force Publique*. It was structurally altered with the creation of the *troupes campées* (responsible for preventing external aggression) and the *troupes en service territoriale*. The latter, subsequently called *gendarmes* by 1959, was placed under civilian bureaucrats and mandated to perform constabulary duties. Interestingly enough, this was a responsibility also exercised by the *troupes campées,* as they were often invited by the civilian leaders to maintain internal security. This overlapping of functions obviously made it difficult for the ordinary citizens to see the two organizational units as separate entities. Both were perceived by the civilian population as instruments of coercion utilized by the colonial government to advance its political objectives. In addition, the absence of discipline indicated that these soldiers and *gendarmes* could freely operate within the domain of civilians. The *troupes campées* became more interested in making life a tremendous burden for the civilian population than in protecting the sovereignty and territorial integrity of the colonial state.

Pre-1965 Era: The Fragmentation of Coercion

The independence movement was a real test of tolerance between the civilian and military institutions in Congo. The anxiety of the soldiers in the *Force Publique* heightened as they speculated on their status in a post-independence Congo. When the Democratic Republic of the Congo achieved political freedom on 30 June 1960, under the leadership of President Joseph Kasavubu and Prime Minister Patrice Lumumba, the soldiers looked ahead to increased material benefits and promotions. However, the failure of the new group of Congolese *évolués* (elites) to respond to these expectations resulted in a feeling of animosity by the military toward the civilian leadership. Perhaps the most immediate outcome was military mutinies that incited widespread public disorder. There were attacks on the residence of Lumumba, Kasavubu, and a good number of the parliamentarians.

The mutinies in the First Republic had far reaching consequences. The *Force Publique*, which was now called the *Armée Nationale Congolaise* (ANC), was marked with ethnic differentiations. Several of the civilian politicians viewed the orientation of the disenchanted soldiers as a means to promote their political agenda. In the 1960 elections:

the military became involved in tribal politics by attending political rallies and by selling party membership, especially in the [*Mouvement National Congolais*] MNC-Lumumba, which was very active among the Batetela and related groups in the army. Also, the 1960 mutinies allowed several political leaders to establish close relations with tribal leaders in the *Force Publique*.[7]

These civilian-military alliances brought the latter much closer to the political arena. The politicization and tribalization of the ANC was subsequently distinguished by the breaking away of South Kasai, South Katanga, and Orientale provinces.

Each of the political leaders involved in the secessionist movements found it expedient to build a partnership with factions in the military whose ethnic loyalties were similar. Accordingly, the durability of the secessionist regimes of Albert Kalonji in the South Kasai, Moise Tshombe in the South Katanga, and Lumumba-led Stanleyville nationalists was heavily dependent on military support. Their effort to reshape the landscape of Congolese politics meant they had to sustain something close to a symbiotic relationship with ethnically based factions in the ANC. Arguably, the soldiers were invited, even if reluctantly, to share the political ambitions of these civilian leaders. Perhaps the most striking aspect of this national crisis is that a willingness to use the military to pursue political ends became a common practice in post-1960 Congo.

THE MILITARY AND POST-INDEPENDENCE POLITICS: THE MAINTENANCE OF PERSONAL HEGEMONY

One of the most common explanations of coups d'etat is connected to the extent of the military mission of protecting the national honor of the state. Egil Fossum identifies a connection between political disorder and the likelihood of military involvement. Fossum contends that political chaos may "serve as a pretext to intervene"[8] or, as Claude Welch and Arthur Smith point out, the military officers define their mission "as safeguarding the entire state from the machination of political leaders."[9] The military may find it indispensable to weaken the idea of civilian control if the officers are convinced that their actions would save the state from the blunders of politicians. In effect, Samuel Finer notes that "where public attachment to civilian institutions is weak or non-existent, military intervention in politics will find wide scope—both in manner and in substance."[10] Various conditions of social disequilibrium that involve the prevalence of social divisions or a lack of consensus among ethnically based political groups in the society may provide the impetus for military intervention. This view is weighted by the absence of civilian institutions with the capacity to prevent the violent clash of primordial sentiments.

Indisputably, the institutional weakness of the First Republic was readily assisted by ethnic rebellions that characterized Congolese politics between 1960 and 1965. The conversion of ethnic associations into political parties suggested that each of the political rivals could hardly build a broad coalition. Kasavubu ascended to the presidency through his affiliation with the *Alliance des Bakongo* (ABAKO). A similar ethnic linkage was apparent in Tshombe's Katangese-dominated *Convention Nationale Congolaise* (CONACO). It was Lumumba's *Mouvement National Congolais* (MNC-L) that was in some ways seen as a "catchall" political organization. Of course, the true drama of power politics materialized with President Kasavubu's removal of the idealistic Lumumba from the position of prime minister. Lumumba was eventually imprisoned and killed in 1961, while a United Nations peacekeeping force was still in the country.

On independence day Prime Minister Lumumba had sought to rally the Congolese toward a collective endeavor at nation-building. It was Lumumba who said, "Together, my brothers, we are going to begin a new struggle, a sublime struggle which is going to lead our country to peace, prosperity, and grandeur. . . . we are going to make the Congo the center of radiance for the whole of Africa."[11]

The idea of making Congo the "hub" of all Africa was no doubt handicapped by the persistent rift between Kasavubu and Tshombe. As both leaders sought to capture the presidency and expand their political holdings, the First Republic was simultaneously experiencing a collapse of central authority. Their struggle for power was defined by shifting alliances, regional fragmentation, and ethnic rebellions. By mid-1965 Congo had been ushered into a climate of political disorder that threatened to tear the nation apart. The political conflict had reached an impasse that made the need for military intervention urgent.

The Coup of 1965: A Promise of Stability and Authenticity

As already indicated, the mode of civil-military relations in the Congo allowed the military to operate as a loyal instrument of the state. The military acknowledged civilian supremacy and simply executed the policy decisions decreed by its political masters. For the most part, the military officers saw as their primary responsibility the internal pacification of the colony. Claude Welch has argued that "in states in which political rivalry could not be contained within the framework of a single party, the likelihood of coups d'état increased. . . . on other occasions, splits among top political leaders furnished the pretext for military incursions into politics."[12]

The 25 November 1965 coup was therefore an opportunity for the military to arrest the political schism in the Congo. In doing so it seriously challenged civilian domination of the country's political destiny. The coup came to represent "the collective decision of the military high command to put an end to a deteriorating state of affairs created by the inability of the politicians to govern effectively."[13] Whether as public "servants" or as "masters," the military was now perceived as an impartial organization responding to the growing need to protect the state from ineffective civilian political authority. General Mobutu and members of the high command emerged as leaders committed to restoring political stability and authenticity to Congo.

In the beginning, it appeared that the coup was a corrective measure aimed at restoring internal order and returning the nation to civilian control after five years. General Mobutu appointed Colonel (Leonard) Mulamba Nyunyi, an officer with an unblemished professional reputation for bravery, as prime minister. Colonel Mulamba formed a military-civilian government that included politicians affiliated with the *Front Démocratique Congolaise* (FDC), the Kinshasha-based Binza group (which had provided Mobutu with a political foundation during the chaotic period of 1960 to 1965), and CONACO. The Parliament and most other civilian institutions were not dismantled. This outcome was rather unusual because the politicians were basically blamed for the vulnerability of the First Republic's institutions to what Young and Turner describe as "opportunism and venality."[14] It is also noteworthy that politicians who had no choice but to accept military intrusion were allowed to retain their personal economic interests in a climate that still assured constitutionally derived civil liberties.

As General Mobutu set out to consolidate his power, the relationship between civilian and military institutions was noticeably altered. He stamped out or co-opted likely political opponents. The existing constitutional devices that sanctioned the governmental structure were replaced with autocratic leadership. The Mobutu government chose to rule by fiat. An immediate target of this rule by decree was the growing number of political parties. The government abrogated all political parties and social organizations for five years. The ban on political parties was conceived by Mobutu as a means to lessen political disorder in the Congo. All political parties that endured before the coup were identified as instruments of political decay. The practice of using decrees to change the constitutional framework of the Congo was also evident by the reduction in the number of provinces from twenty-one to six, as well as the selection of provincial governors with weak ethnic ties to their administrative regions.[15] Equally important, the police force was nationalized and brought under the military's administrative control. This policy was another attempt by Mobutu to "central-ize power by depriving the provinces of their own military forces."[16]

The emphasis on rule by fiat initiated the idea that Mobutu was no longer fervent about developing institutions to allow increased popular participation. The draconian measures of the government were again intended to promote a centralized administrative structure. The unification scheme reflected Mobutu's interest in creating political institutions with weak regional and ethnic ties. Be-tween March and October of 1966, the powers of the legislature were eroded, the proposed presidential elections were repudiated, and Mulamba was removed as prime minister. What had emerged by 1967 was a unitary government re-moved from popular support and increasingly susceptible to public resentment.

Nevertheless, the so-called Pentecost Plot revealed Mobutu's resolve to crush any potential political opposition. In Mobutu's communiqué on 30 May 1966, he announced the following:

Tonight, a plot against me and the new regime has been hatched by some irresponsible politicians. They have been arrested and will be indicted for high treasons. This plot has been thwarted thanks to the vigilance and loyalty of the National Congolese Army.[17]

The four civilians (former Prime Minister Evariste Kimba, former Defense Min-ister Jérôme Anany, former Finance Minister Emmanuel Bamba, and former Minister of Mines and Energy Alexandre Mahamba) were used to demonstrate how Mobutu planned to manage any threatening conspiracy against his govern-ment. General Mobutu sought to create a climate of fear, or what he called the "conditions of regime discipline."[18]

Perhaps the strongest indication of Mobutu's gravitation toward personal rule was the creation of the *Mouvement Populaire de la Revolution* (MPR). Aristide Zolberg has remarked that the supremacy of one-partyism is rooted in its adept-ness to accommodate an ideology.[19] In this case, the official ideology of the MPR was fundamentally Mobutuism (*Mobutiste*). The MPR provided Mobutu with an opportunity to present himself to the people of Zaire[20] as their sole legitimate representative. The personalization of power through the MPR was enhanced by arresting all forms of opposition. The military was readily used to break up trade union strikes and student demonstrations. In particular, university students were required to secure membership with the youth branch of the party (*Jeunesse du Mouvement Populaire de la Révolution*).

The "cult of Mobutuism" thrived as the MPR's raison d'être was interrelated with the "omnipotence" of Mobutu. Following the 1970 MPR Congress, the party as the central political organ of the state came to depict the "will" and the "political policy" of Mobutu. The Congress agreed that:

only one man, previously noted for his outstanding services to his country, can assure the well-being of each one of us and create the conditions propitious for the people's moral and spiritual growth, and offer them a common ideal, the feelings of a joint destiny and the knowledge of belonging to one country.[21]

The relationship between the party and the state evolved into one that recognized President Mobutu as the supreme leader of Zaire. Mobutu's ability to build a personal hegemony was also distinguished by the party's control over the military. The 1972 MPR congress allowed for the formation of party cells in the *Forces Armées Zairoises* (FAZ). By the time Mobutuism was instituted as the official ideology in 1974, the political status of the Zairian leader had significantly risen to new heights. There were songs of adulation and references to him as the "Messiah," "Founding President," and "Grand Patron," to name just a few.

A corresponding result of Mobutuism was the push for Zairian "authenticity." As Eric Nordlinger suggests, military leaders "may adopt and support traditional practices that were originally unrelated to the military."[22] In other words, it is assumed that they may seek to legitimize their governmental power on a traditional basis. President Mobutu's "authenticity movement" was intended to inspire a commitment to indigenous values. Zairians were forced to identify with symbols, names, and various signs that underscored their pride in what is homegrown. They were, for example, compelled to replace their Christian names with indigenous ones. Mobutu dropped his European names, Joseph-Desiré, and adopted Sese Seko (the all-powerful). The nationality law also pushed Zairians to accept a national dress code that made it illegal to wear neckties. Women were obliged to wear the *wrapper (le pagne),* while men were required to wear Mobutu's "abacost" suit. The authenticity program, or cultural revolution, came to have far-reaching effects in the political and economic arena.

The program of Zairization that accompanied the authenticity movement resulted in the seizure of some foreign businesses. The Union Minière and several foreign-owned agribusinesses were placed under government control. This radicalization of the cultural revolution was another effort by Mobutu to legitimize his rulership. It has been suggested that the nationalization program was also undertaken "to appease certain elements in the huge standing army" and the civil service.[23] Apparently, Mobutu was aware of the need to indulge military officers even though the military was not his primary source of support.

In essence, the FAZ and the *Gendarmerie Nationale* (GDN) (the latter was a consolidation of rural gendarmes and the municipal national police) were used to respond to political disorder. As Schatzberg points out, both units "seem to receive most of their 'combat' experience against essentially unarmed peasants, students, or schoolteachers."[24] The fact that the GDN was institutionally a separate element of the FAZ was somewhat blurred by the latter's involvement in maintaining internal stability. As instruments of state oppression that directly served Mobutu, they were given the opportunity to terrorize and exploit ordinary citizens and businessmen. Their political influence was therefore measured in terms of Mobutu's determination to make Zairians appreciate the impact of leadership based on coercion. The military and gendarmes were used to inspire fear and to serve as the overseers of public order. They were repeatedly employed to ensure public "surrender" and discipline in the process of Mobutuism.

The Economic Consequences of Personal Hegemony

The personalistic character of leadership in Zaire is germane to any appraisal of the national economic malaise. The Mobutu years not only draw attention to policy miscalculations but also to the behavior of the military. To begin with, the economic ills of Zaire were exacerbated by the dynamics of government expenditures. Although most of the government outlays were earmarked for state payrolls, it was also estimated that revenue accounting for about 20% of operating budget costs and approximately 30% of capital expenditures were placed in off-budget accounts (comptes hors budget) controlled by the presidency.[25] This practice by the Mobutu government gave way to widespread corruption. It allowed Mobutu to amass a wealth estimated at five billion dollars and assisted in expanding the scope of what has often been described as kleptocracy in Zaire. The existence of revenue outside budgetary control made it easier for ordinary Zairians to be exploited and strengthened the patrimonial system. Put differently, these undisclosed funds were used to maintain the loyalty of Zairians to Mobutu.

The patrimonial nature of the government was also obvious in the transfer of industries from foreign hands to local control. The rights to these properties were given to Zairian elites who had proven their loyalty to Mobutu. The radicalization of the Zairian revolution thus served to sponsor a system in which allies of the government were rewarded for their acceptance of Mobutu as the "political messiah."[26] A backlash effect of this policy was the removal of effective management and entrepreneurship from the Zairian economy. It also created higher inflation rates of 60% to 80% a year and extensive food shortages.[27] Even the decision to reverse the disastrous effect of this policy by altering the 40% (foreign) to 60% (local) equity share of foreign-owned business was unsuccessful.

The malaise of the economy was equally aggravated by the plan to expand the copper industry. The revenue generated from copper grew rapidly from 1965 to 1974 even though the production level was at 50%. The government therefore sought to boost production with the assistance of loans from Western industrialized states. However, the plan was handicapped by the drastic drop in the price of copper in 1974. This drop in price of Zaire's main export and the world oil crisis resulted in a growth in the national debt to three billion dollars by 1975 and in an unfavorable balance of payments.[28] The military budget's share of central government expenditures declined from 10.4% in 1974 to 5.2% in 1984. There were nevertheless considerable increases in 1975 and from 1977 to 1979 after a plunge in 1976.[29] What the government allocated to the fifty-two-thousand strong military (including the gendarmerie) in 1987 was $46.56 million, which accounted for 4.9% of government spending.[30]

Evidence suggests that several of Mobutu's military officers received favors as a result of his policies. However, the Zairization scheme was not universally supported by the military. There were various coup attempts, especially one in 1975, which associated army discontent with the radicalization policy. The failure of the coup nevertheless gave Mobutu another chance to modify the behavior of the military officers. Several members of the officer corps were purged, and others were routinely transferred from their command posts. Such behavior modification was in part justified by Mobutu's claim that the abortive coup received external support. Accordingly, Zairian officers were prohibited by decree from marrying noncitizens. The officers who already had foreign spouses were forced to make a choice between their careers and their wives. The ultimate restriction on the personal disposition of the soldiers was decreed by Mobutu who ordered that officers should be "single, or married legitimately, and monogamously, to a Zairian citizen."[31] Undoubtedly, Mobutu's willingness to use the military to quell internal political problems was matched by a strong determination to control its threat to his regime.

MILITARIZATION OF EXTERNAL RELATIONS

The idea that African militaries are significant actors in the dynamics of foreign policy objectives of individual states is something that is seldom the focus of most civil-military relations research. Of particular interest is the extent to which they influence the foreign policy processes and outcomes.[32] Zaire is one of several African countries that has regularly attracted foreign actors. These are actors whose roles have swayed the direction and results of its foreign policy pursuits. Zaire's ideological affiliation has been shaped by the economic and military activities of the French, Belgians, and Americans in the region as well as by the former Soviet Union and Cuba. Put differently, there is an urgency to examine the extent to which the Cold War stirred the Zairian government.

The climate in which Zairian politics operates is one that exposes political discontent and the readiness of the government to respond harshly. It is generally assumed that the role of the FAZ is to protect the territorial integrity of the state against external aggression. Yet the Shaba incident in 1977 and 1978 brought to light the incapability of the FAZ to defend Zaire's sovereignty and honor. The two events were preceded by Mobutu's decision to oust some of the politically disaffected from his government. The purge of the powerful Binza group was not only indicative of the "Zairian sickness" (*mal Zairois*) but also a sign of Mobutu's inclination to consolidate his power. He dismissed Justin Bomboko (foreign minister since the Lumumba days), Victor Nendaka, who had served as chief of the secret police (*Sureté*), Albert Ndele (governor of the National Bank), and Joseph Nsinga (a minister of state). The removal of the popular Bomboko and Nendaka was notable, as both had been considered firm pillars in Zairian power politics.

The aftereffect of their elimination was the growth of political opposition.

Several of these dissident organizations were compelled to operate from outside of Zaire. One such group was the National Front for the Liberation of the Congo (FNLC). The FNLC identified as its primary goal the overthrow of Mobutu's regime and its replacement with a democratic system. It was basically a political-military organization that included former Katangan gendarmes of Tshombe's secession. Under General Mbumbu, FNLC forces easily uprooted Zairian army units from Kasaji, Mutshatsha, and subsequently the copper-rich town of Kolwezi. The capture of Kolwezi was vital, as it made the Lubumbashi-Kamina rail connection accessible to the FNLC.

The military victories of the FNLC in the Shaba I invasion laid bare the lack of discipline and organization in the Zairian military and prompted Mobutu to appeal to the international community for assistance. The United States responded by increasing its military assistance to Zaire. The Carter administration recognized a necessity to help Mobutu, although it was determined not to involve American troops. The restraint of the Carter administration was also matched by the decision of the Congress to reduce its "military sales credit to Zaire from $30 million to $15 million." As Ogunbadejo speculates, the restraint may "be attributed to the U.S. determination, at the time, to rid itself of unreasonable fears of communist threats and instead, to embark on a more realistic and progressive foreign policy."[33] In contrast, West Germany, France, and Belgium were alarmed by what was increasingly perceived as Soviet expansionism in Africa. It was a plausible stance because the USSR was actively involved in neighboring Angola. The French were the most active allies and furnished military transport planes used to deploy Moroccan soldiers to Kolowezi. Apparently, Mobutu's anti-Israel policy (including the break in diplomatic relations following the Arab-Israeli war of 1973) also brought him support from Arab states such as Egypt, Saudi Arabia, and Sudan. Throughout the conflict Egyptian pilots were utilized to fly the Mirage aircrafts supplied by the French.

The multinational military campaign was successful in its effort to repel the rebel invasion. It also brought to question the capacity of the Zairian military to carry out the traditional role of defending the nation from external threats. Similarly, the May 1978 invasion reaffirmed the fragility of Mobutu's power and the internationalization of a solution. The Shaba II invasion inspired a Belgium-French military operation bolstered logistically by the use of American C-141 transport planes. Mobutu relied initially on a thousand Belgian and French paratroopers. They were eventually replaced by a Pan-African force represented from Morocco (1,500), Senegal (600), Central African Empire (390), Côte D'Ivoire (110), and about a hundred soldiers from Togo and Gabon. Evidently, the response of the West was incited by Cuban-Soviet aggressive campaigns in Africa. As President Jimmy Carter declared, "We and our African friends want to see a continent that is free of the domination of outside powers; the persistent and increasing involvement of the Soviets and Cuba in Africa deny this vision."[34] The vigor of Cold War politics made it easier for Mobutu to secure external support in order to protect the sovereignty of Zaire.

THE CHALLENGES OF DEMOCRATIZATION

Political activism in many African countries reflects an increasing demand for democracy. The democratization movements recognize the need to place restraints on the relationship between state power and ordinary citizens. Various political organizations are repeatedly calling for an end to political monopoly and the creation of legitimate authority with the capacity to advance the political and economic development of the individual states. The emphasis is on the shift from what Richard Joseph has called "prebendalism"[35] or what Max Weber termed "patrimonialism"[36] to a responsive system. Africans are demanding broad and effective political institutions that can be readily held accountable and seen as legitimate. Whether the impetus for these movements in Africa comes from the former Eastern European experiences or the collapse of the Soviet Union, they have nevertheless unmasked the weakness of authoritarian regimes.

Equally important, the culmination of the Cold War has brought to an end the proxy wars between the United States and the USSR in Africa. Authoritarian regimes are now forced to adopt democratic reforms or to develop a new international statecraft salient to receiving economic and military assistance. In fact, the latter is increasingly made difficult by the decision of the major industrialized states to tie democratic reforms to foreign aid.[37] France under François Mitterand is now pushing for a correction of what has been described as "*déficit démocratique*" in several francophone countries.

The 1980s and 1990s: Regime Security or National Security?

In separate studies on African militaries, Claude Welch and J. M. Lee stress the frailty of these institutions as viable agents of political change. Welch argues that African armies lack legitimacy because of their dependence upon coercion and the absence of bargaining skills.[38] Much the same, Lee is not convinced that African militaries necessarily yearn to affect political or social change in their societies.[39] It has already been established that Mobutu's stay in power is directly associated with heavy reliance on coercion to achieve compliance or to punish. Any transition from the personalistic character of Zairian politics to a democratic type of regime must therefore accede to the influence of the military.

Mobutu has consistently resisted or handicapped the implementation of any of the three phases (preparatory, decision, consolidation) that Georg Sørensen has identified as necessary in the "transition from a non-democratic to a democratic form of regime."[40] Acts of violence by the FAZ and GDN against Zairians had become a permanent fixture in the society. The GDN, for example, was used in June 1983 to terrorize the population. The gendarmes were allowed to organize an extensive *ratissage* (cleanup) of Kinshasha. Military operations were also completed by the FAZ in 1985 in such towns as Moba and Kalemie, whose inhabitants were alleged to have harbored political insurgents. Several of these military attacks were frequently marked by "arbitrary arrest, torture, and extra-judicial execution."[41] As guardians of President Mobutu's institutional devices and implementors of public order, the FAZ and GDN have been used by the government to educate the population on the seriousness of forceful authority. They have come "to represent the power of the state and to occupy available political space."[42]

The continuity of state-sponsored violence against the population also has become the hallmark of Mobutu's ambition to create a false favorable impression of his authoritarian leadership. Political maneuverability and oppression were used to drown the voices of political liberalization in Zaire. Faced with growing national and international pressure for democracy, however, Mobutu pledged to implement wide-ranging changes, which included the abrogation of one-partyism and the "limited introduction of liberal democracy."[43] He also promised to depoliticize the military and make it operate under the rule of law. Unfortunately, the difficulty of eliminating the cancer of violence was demonstrated by the attack launched by Mobutu's security forces against members of the *Union pour la Democracie et le Progrés Sociale* (UDPS). The residence of the UDPS leader, Tshisekedi wa Mulumba, was violently attacked on 30 April 1990 in order to break up a political gathering.

A few days later Mobutu imposed a ban on all opposition parties and formed a transitional government led by Lunda Bululu as prime minister. The MPR-dominated regime was rejected by the principal opposition parties, including the UDPS, the *Partie Démocratique et Social Chrétien* (PDSC), the *Partie Lu-mumbiste Unifié* (PALU), and the *Union des Federalistes et Républicains In-dépendants* (UFERI). Perhaps the most severe abuse of police power at this time was the 11 May 1990 attack against students at the University of Lumumbashi. Troops of the Special Presidential Division stormed the campus and bayoneted to death over three hundred students.[44] The Lumumbashi massacre attracted worldwide attention and pressure for an independent inquiry. The reluctance of Mobutu's regime to thoroughly investigate the incident aroused more political opposition. The outcome was the collapse of the Bululu government in March 1991, along with heightened pressure for democratization.

The Political Lexicon of Change

In Zaire and in several francophone African states, national conferences have become the political lexicon of reform. The absence of broadly based civil or grassroot institutions with independent strength has led to a mushrooming of national conventions, which provide a means for organized groups to challenge the legitimacy of authoritarian regimes and to demand political accountability and the rule of law. It is obvious that change can be a burden for those who advocate it and for those who may be apprehensive about its character and direction. The call for a national conference in Zaire was designed to lessen Mobutu's grip on the reins of power. Accordingly, Mobutu made an effort to break the waves of opposition by selecting another transitional government and initiating his own call for a national conference in April 1991. Mulumba Lukoji was appointed to serve as prime minister and to organize the national conference. This conference was supposed to map out the road to multipartyism.

The reaction of the opposition parties was one of distrust and skepticism. They challenged the ability of a Mulumba-led national conference to be impartial. The preparatory phase between 13 May 1991 and 19 June 1991 immediately revealed that Mobutu was determined to control the composition of the conference and its agenda. It is estimated that 75% of the members to the conference were loyal supporters of Mobutu. Furthermore, 110 of the 159 political parties that attended the preparatory meeting were under the influence of the MPR.[45] As the leader of the PDSC observed, Mobutu was eager to turn the national conference into "a simple congress of the former state party [MPR]."[46] The opposition parties withdrew from the conference in protest.

The national conference raised the political stakes for both sides. On the one hand, the organized opposition was concerned about the legitimacy of the conference and its capacity to champion genuine political reforms. On the other hand, President Mobutu was not anxious to see his powers eroded and to have his actions subject to the scrutiny of a national referendum. Even when the conference eventually reconvened in August, it was still inundated with serious problems. Mobutu still exercised monopoly over the rules of engagement and impeded any meaningful political dialogue. The collapse of the conference in September 1991 was soon followed by fighting between mutinous soldiers and forces loyal to the government.

President Mobutu's ability to frustrate the process of democratization has enlarged the internal opposition to his regime. The relationship between the oppressor and the oppressed has been adversely affected by the lack of tolerance, willingness, and good faith. To be exact, the frequent cancellation and resumption of a prodemocracy conference has been an attempt to keep the opposition not only unbalanced but also unprepared in its challenge to Mobutu's leadership. As the voices of the opposition grow louder, the government has intensified its response. Soldiers loyal to the government have been used to intimidate and mistreat the protesters. For instance, the antigovernment protest on 16 February 1992 was viciously repressed by Zairian troops. It is estimated that thirteen people were killed as protesters peacefully demonstrated after a Roman Catholic church service in Kinshasha. Their call on Mobutu to reconvene a national democracy conference was met with the show of force. In the words of Kitenge Yezu, Minister of Information, the action against the demonstration was to reinforce the government's "firm determination to see the authority of the state respected."[47]

Equally significant, the battle for change and the fight to preserve the personal hegemony of Mobutu have sharpened the rift in the FAZ. Disgruntled soldiers have mutinied in order to express displeasure about their low salaries and to show their support of the prodemocracy movement. The abortive 23 January

1992 coup to remove President Mobutu from power echoed the call for the prodemocracy conference suspended by Prime Minister Nguza-i-Bond. More recently, the refusal of the regular army troops to accept the government's new five-million Zaire currency resulted in a power struggle between loyalist forces and those supportive of the democracy movement. This split in the FAZ challenges Mobutu's control of the military and also measures his determination to hold on to power.

CONCLUSION

It is not far-fetched to assert that the political atmosphere in Africa today is one that challenges the cultivation or maintenance of autocratic leadership. When Mobutu assumed power in 1965 a noticeable trademark was the centralization of power. He created a system of governance that perpetuated corruption, patrimonialism, economic miscalculations, and intolerance for any form of organized opposition. Any structural rearrangements would suggest that Mobutu must adopt new and more effective ways to respond to the interests and demands of the central and peripheral (provincial) sectors of the polity. He must now test his ability to manipulate the national conferences that are seen as the first step toward liberalizing Zaire. So far, Mobutu's success in frustrating the prodemocracy movement is partly attributed to the fragile alliances of the opposition parties. His frequent use of the policy of "divide and conquer," exemplified by the appointment of prime ministers from the opposition, seems to delay a total collapse of the society. After twenty-seven years in power it is not unreasonable to assume that Mobutu has mastered the art of refusing to cede the institutions that form the basis of his authority.

As Jackson and Rosberg indicate, the military "served as a springboard to prominence and power" for Mobutu.[48] However, Mobutu was careful not to create a regime that depended solely on the military. The military's political influence has been scripted and directed by Mobutu. That is why the current schism in the FAZ is of special importance. The rebellions imply that the soldiers may at some point cease to accept his leadership. The soldiers loyal to Mobutu appear to reaffirm the claim that the military remains the most visible obstacle to the democracy movement in Zaire, though this view is undermined by the fact that some regular soldiers are sympathetic to the democratization process. At this juncture, it is uncertain that a successful coup would yield a willingness on the part of a "factionalized" military elite to accept civilian leadership.

Finally, the end of the Cold War poses a new and serious challenge to Mobutu. During the Cold War era, the Western states and the Soviet bloc fueled proxy wars that kept many authoritarian regimes in power. The battles between the superpowers meant a constant flow of arms to be used to prop up the instruments of state coercion. In addition, the Shaba invasions underscored the saliency of perception and misperception in international relations. The number of international players in the conflict was no doubt based on perceived or anticipated posturing by the United States and the former Soviet Union. Mobutu's comprehensive knowledge of the political alignments in the international system enabled him to build external support. He must now deal with the reality that the elimination of the Cold War seems to have "devalued the global 'worth' of Africa."[49] The emergence of a unipolar system suggests that African leaders like Mobutu must demonstrate a political acumen that enhances their ability to deal with the "conscience" of the western industrialized states now placing enough pressure on them to embark on democracy and improved governance. In short, the analytical importance of the democratization movement in Zaire is now centered on the interplay between internal and international pressures for change.

NOTES

1. Jean-Claude Williame, "Congo-Kinshasa: General Mobutu and Two Political Generations," in Claude E. Welch, Jr., *Soldier and State in Africa: A Comparative Analysis of Military Intervention and Political Change* (Evanston: Northwestern University Press, 1970), p. 148.

2. Cited in Ruth Slade, *King Leopold's Congo: Aspects of the Development of Race Relations in the Congo Independent State* (Westport, Conn.: Greenwood Press, 1974), 175.

3. Michael G. Schatzberg, *The Dialectics of Oppression in Zaire* (Bloomington: Indiana University Press, 1988), p. 54. Also see Jean-Claude Williame, *Patrimonialism and Political Change in the Congo* (Stanford: Stanford University Press, 1972), p. 59.

4. Williame, *Patrimonialism and Political Change in the Congo,* p. 60.

5. L. H. Gann and Peter Duignan, *The Rulers of Belgian Africa: 1884–1914* (Princeton: Princeton University Press, 1979), pp. 65–66.

6. Williame, *Patrimonialism and Political Change in the Congo,* p. 61.

7. Ibid., 65.

8. Egil Fossum, "Factors Influencing the Occurrence of Military Coups d'Etat in Latin America," *Journal of Peace Research* 3 (1987): 236.

9. Claude E. Welch, Jr., and Arthur K. Smith, *Military Role and Rule: Perspectives on Civil-Military Relations* (North Scituate, Mass.: Duxbury Press, 1974), 12.

10. Samuel E. Finer, *The Man on Horseback: The Role of the Military in Politics* (New York: Praeger, 1962), p. 21.

11. Alan P. Merriam, *Congo: Background of Conflict* (Evanston, Ill.: Northwestern University Press, 1970), p. 23.

12. Claude E. Welch, Jr., "The Roots and Implication of Military Intervention," in Welch, ed., *Soldier and State in Africa: A Comparative Analysis of Military Intervention and Political Change* (Evanston, Ill.: Northwestern University Press, 1970), p. 23.

13. Nzongola-Ntalaja, "The Continuing Struggle for National Liberation in Zaire," *Journal of Modern African Studies* 17 (1979): 600–601.

14. Crawford Young and Thomas Turner, *The Rise and Decline of the Zairian State* (Madison: University of Wisconsin Press, 1985), p. 52.

15. Victor A. Olurunsola with Dan Muhzewi, "Security and Stability Implications of

Ethnicity and Religious Factors," in Bruce E. Arlinghaus, ed., *African Security Issues: Sovereignty, Stability, and Solidarity* (Boulder, Colo.: Westview Press, 1984), pp. 152–53.

16. Schatzberg, *Dialectics of Oppression in Zaire*, p. 55.

17. Williame, "Congo-Kinshasha: General Mobutu and Two Political Generations," p. 148.

18. Young and Turner, *Rise and Decline of the Zairian State*, p. 57.

19. Aristide R. Zolberg, *Creating Political Order: The Party-States of West Africa* (Chicago: Rand McNally, 1966). For another example of this aspect of personalism in African politics, see Frédéric Belle Torimiro, "Personal Rule and the Search for Political Pluralism in Cameroon," in Constantine Danopoulos, ed., *Civilian Rule in the Developing World: Democracy on the March?* (Boulder, Colo.: Westview Press, 1992).

20. The name was officially changed in 1971, even though the word was initially used in 1967 with reference to the national currency.

21. Robert H. Jackson and Carl G. Rosberg, *Personal Rule in Black Africa: Prince, Autocrat, Prophet, Tyrant* (Berkeley: University of California Press, 1982), p. 173.

22. Eric A. Nordlinger, *Soldiers in Politics: Military Coups and Governments* (Englewood Cliffs, N.J.: Prentice-Hall, 1977), pp. 129–30.

23. Oye Ogunbadejo, "Conflict in Africa: A Case Study of the Shaba Crisis, 1977," *World Affairs* 141 (Winter 1979): 224.

24. Schatzberg, *Dialectics of Oppression in Zaire*, p. 55.

25. Crawford Young, "Zaire: The Unending Crisis," *Foreign Affairs* 57 (Fall 1978): 172.

26. For additional discussion on the effect of authenticity on the Zairian economy, see Tukumbi Lumumba-Kasongo, "Zaire's Ties to Belgium: Persistence and Future Prospects in Political Economy," *Africa Today* 39 (1992).

27. Young and Turner, *Rise and Decline of the Zairian State*, p. 71.

28. Ibid.

29. *World Military Expenditures and Arms Transfers 1986* (Washington, D.C.: U.S. Arms Control and Disarmament Agency, 1986), p. 99.

30. *The Military Balance 1988–89* (London: International Institute for Strategic Studies, 1989), pp. 144, 226.

31. Oye Ogunbadejo, "Conflict in Africa," p. 224.

32. See Henry S. Bienen, *Armed Forces, Conflict, and Change in Africa* (Boulder, Colo.: Westview Press, 1989).

33. See Ogunbadejo, "Conflict in Africa," p. 226.

34. Colin Legum, "The African Crisis," *Foreign Affairs* 57 (Fall 1978): 637.

35. Richard A. Joseph, "Class, State and Prebendal Politics in Nigeria," *Journal of Commonwealth and Comparative Politics,* 21 (September 1983): 21–38.

36. See Reinhard Bendix, *Max Weber: An Intellectual Portrait* (Garden City, N.J.: Doubleday, 1962).

37. Kaye Whiteman, "The Gallic Paradox," *Africa Report* 36 (January–February 1991): 18–20.

38. Claude E. Welch, Jr., "The African Military and Political Development," in Henry Bienen, ed., *The Military and Modernization* (New York: Aldine-Atherton, 1971).

39. J. M. Lee, *African Armies and Civil Order* (New York: Praeger, 1969).

40. George Sørensen, "Kant and Processes of Democratization: Consequences for Neorealist Thought," *Journal of Peace Research* 29 (November 1992): 402.

41. Schatzberg, *Dialectics of Oppression in Zaire,* p. 58.

42. Ibid., p. 68.

43. Makau Wa Mutua, "Decline of the Despot?" *Africa Report* 36 (November–December 1991): 14.

44. Ibid., p. 15.

45. Ibid., p. 16.

46. Ibid.

47. *New York Times* (17 February 1992), 3.

48. Jackson and Rosberg, *Personal Rule in Black Africa,* p. 67.

49. Samuel Decalo, "Democracy in Africa: Toward the Twenty-First Century," in Tatu Vanhanen, ed., *Strategies of Democratization* (Washington, D.C.: Crane Russak, 1992), p. 133.

REFERENCES

Gann, L. H., and Peter Duignan. *The Rulers of Belgian Africa: 1884–1914.* Princeton, NJ: Princeton University Press, 1979.

Ntalaja-Nzongola. "The Continuing Struggle for National Liberation in Zaire." *Journal of Modern African Studies* 17, no. 4 (1979): 595–614.

Schatzberg, Michael. *The Dialectics of Oppression in Zaire.* Bloomington, Ind.: Indiana University Press, 1988.

Williame, Jean Claude. "Congo-Kinshasha: General Mobutu and Two Political Generations." In Claude E. Welch, Jr., ed., *Soldier and State in Africa: A Comparative Analysis of Military Intervention and Political Change.* Evanston, Ill.: Northwestern University Press, 1970.

————. *Patrimonialism and Political Change in the Congo.* Stanford: Stanford University Press, 1972.

Young, Crawford. "Zaire: The Unending Crisis." *Foreign Affairs* 57, no. 1 (Fall 1978): 169–85.

Young, Crawford, and Thomas Turner. *The Rise and Decline of the Zairian State.* Madison: University of Wisconsin Press, 1985.

INDEX

Abacha, Brigadier Sunni
  acceded to leadership (1993), 313
Abacha, General Sani, 316
  closure of National Assembly and Senate, 316
  rationale for his takeover, 317
abertura, 26
Abiola, Chief Moshood, 316
Abiola, General Sani, 319
Abrams, General Creighton, Chief of
    Staff
  "total force" concept, 431
Abu-Ghazallah, 116
  removal, 117
Abuja, 312
Acción Popular, 348
Active Citizen Force Reserve, 375
Administered Territories, 230
administration
  Sarney, 28
Administration Council, 329, 330
administrative integration, 414
Admiralty
  Dutch, 286, 287
  influence, 288
affaires indigènes, 128
Afghanistan
  Soviet invasion, 431
Africa, 308, 318, 445

Cuban-Soviet aggressive campaigns,
    451
  global 'worth,' 456
African, 256, 309
African civil society, 257
African Kenyans
  inclusion into armed forces, 268
African majority, 257
African militaries, 450
African National Congress (ANC), 375,
    377, 378, 383–84, 387
  elimination of support, 384
  military bases, 382
African people, 258
  response to Britain's occupation, 258
African resistance, 377, 378, 383
  intensification, 383
African working class
  creation, 259
Africanization, 262
Africanized
  armed forces, 261
  civil service, 261
  employment patterns, 261
"Africanizing," 311
Africans, 257, 440
Afrikaner
  nationalism, 376
  'people's war,' 376

CONTRIBUTORS

Douglas Bland
Adjunct Professor of Politics and Security, Queens University at Kingston

Roderic Camp
Professor and Chair of Political Science, Tulane University

Stephen J. Cimbala
Professor of Political Science, Pennsylvania State University

Sharyl Cross
Assistant Professor of Political Science, San José State University

Constantine Danopoulos
Professor of Political Science, San José State University

Rut Clara Diamint
Professor of Political Science, the University of Buenos Aires

Veena Gill
Research Fellow and Professor of Comparative Politics, the Centre for Social Research, the University of Bergin

Andrew K. Hanami
Associate Professor of Political Science, San Francisco State University

Cobie Harris
Associate Professor of Political Science and Chair of African American Studies, San José State University

Diddy R. M. Hitchins
Professor of Political Science, the University of Alaska at Anchorage

William A. Jacobs
Professor of History and Political Science, the University of Alaska at Anchorage

Ibrahim A. Karawan
member of the Directing Staff, the International Institute for Strategic Studies, London, UK

Dongsung Kong
Assistant Professor of Political Science, San José State University

Zhiyong Lan
Assistant Professor of Public Affairs, Arizona State University at Tempe

Margaret C. Lee
Associate Professor of Political Science, Spelman College

Moshe Lissak
Professor of Sociology, the Hebrew University in Israel

Karl P. Magyar
Professor of National Security, the Air Command and Staff College, Maxwell Air Force Base, Alabama

Daniel Maman
Lecturer in Sociology, the Hebrew University in Israel

Michel Louis Martin
Professor of Political Science and Director of the Centre d'analyse géopolitique et internationale, the Université des Antilles, French Guyana

Kostas Messas
Adjunct Professor of Political Science, the Metropolitan State College of Denver, Colorado

Houman Sadri
Assistant Professor of Political Science, the University of Central Florida

Jan R. Schoeman
Research Fellow, the Dutch Foundation on the Armed Forces and Society at The Hague

Henning Sørensen
Director, the Institute for Sociological Research, Lyngby, Copenhagen

Konstantin E. Sorokin
head of the section of Intelligence, Security, and Arms Control, the Institute of Europe in Moscow

Ulf Sundhaussen
Associate Professor of Political Science, Queensland University, Queensland, Australia

Frederic Belle Torimoro
Associate Professor of Political Science, Ferrum College

George L. Vásquez
Associate Professor of History, San José State University

Wilfried von Bredow
Professor of Political Science, Philipps University at Marburg, Germany

Cynthia Watson
Professor of National Security, National War College, Washington, D.C.

Jerzy J. Wiatr
Minister of Education and Professor of Sociology, the University of Warsaw, Poland

Daniel Zirker
Associate Professor of Political Science, the University of Idaho

ISBN 0-313-28837-2

90000>

EAN

9 780313 288371

HARDCOVER BAR CODE